HENRY JAMES

HENRY JAMES

COLLECTED TRAVEL WRITINGS: THE CONTINENT

A Little Tour in France
Italian Hours
Other Travels

THE LIBRARY OF AMERICA

The paper used in this publication meets the
minimum requirements for the American National Standard for
Information Sciences—Permanence of Paper for Printed
Library Materials, ANSI Z39.48—1984.

Distributed to the trade in the United States
and Canada by the Viking Press.

Library of Congress Catalog Number: 93-9193
For cataloging information, see end of Index
ISBN 0—940450—77—1

First Printing
The Library of America—65

Manufactured in the United States of America

RICHARD HOWARD
WROTE THE NOTES FOR THIS VOLUME

Grateful acknowledgment is made to the National Endowment for the Humanities, the Ford Foundation, and the Andrew W. Mellon Foundation for their generous support of this series.

Contents

Each section has its own table of contents.

Nîmes: the Garden

A LITTLE
TOUR IN FRANCE

WITH NINETY-FOUR ILLUSTRATIONS BY

JOSEPH PENNELL

Aigues-Mortes

Preface

The notes presented in this volume were gathered, as will easily be perceived, a number of years ago and on an expectation not at that time answered by the event, and were then published in the United States. The expectation had been that they should accompany a series of drawings, and they themselves were altogether governed by the pictorial spirit. They made, and they make in appearing now, after a considerable interval and for the first time, in England, no pretension to any other; they are impressions, immediate, easy, and consciously limited; if the written word may ever play the part of brush or pencil, they are sketches on "drawing-paper" and nothing more. From the moment the principle of selection and expression, with a tourist, is not the delight of the eyes and the play of fancy, it should be an energy in every way much larger; there is no happy mean, in other words, I hold, between the sense and the quest of the picture, and the surrender to it, and the sense and the quest of the constitution, the inner springs of the subject —springs and connections social, economic, historic.

One must really choose, in other words, between the benefits of the perception of surface—a perception, when fine, perhaps none of the most frequent—and those of the perception of very complex

3

underlying matters. If these latter had had, for me, to be taken into account, my pages would not have been collected. At the time of their original appearance the series of illustrations to which it had been their policy to cling for countenance and company failed them, after all, at the last moment, through a circumstance not now on record; and they had suddenly to begin to live their little life without assistance. That they have seemed able in any degree still to prolong even so modest a career might perhaps have served as a reason for leaving them undisturbed. In fact, however, I have too much appreciated—for any renewal of inconsistency—the opportunity of granting them at last, in an association with Mr. Pennell's admirable drawings, the benefit they have always lacked. The little book thus goes forth finally as the picture-book it was designed to be. Text and illustrations are, altogether and alike, things of the play of eye and hand and fancy—views, head-pieces, tail-pieces; through the artist's work, doubtless, in a much higher degree than the author's.

But these are words enough on a minor point. Many things come back to me on reading my pages over—such a world of reflection and emotion as I can neither leave unmentioned nor yet, in this place, weigh them down with the full expression of. Difficult indeed would be any full expression for one who, deeply devoted always to the revelations of France, finds himself, late in life, making of the sentiment no more substantial, no more direct record than this mere revival of an accident. Not one of these small chapters but suggests to me a regret that I might not, first or last, have gone farther, penetrated deeper, spoken oftener—closed, in short, more intimately with the great general subject; and I mean, of course, not in such a form as the present, but in many another, possible and impossible. It all comes back, doubtless, this vision of missed occasions and delays overdone, to the general truth that the observer, the enjoyer, may, before he knows it, be practically too far in for all that free testimony and pleasant, easy talk that are incidental to the earlier or more detached stages of a relation. There are relations that soon get beyond all merely showy appearances of value for us. Their value becomes thus private and practical, and is represented by the process—the quieter, mostly, the better—of absorption and assimilation of what the relation has done for us. For persons thus indebted to the genius of France—however, in its innumerable ways, manifested—the profit to be gained, the lesson to be learnt, is almost of itself occupation enough. They feel that they bear witness by the intelligent use and application of their advantage, and the consciousness of the artist is therefore readily a consciousness of pious service. He may repeatedly have dreamt of some such happy combination of mood and moment as shall launch him in a profession of faith, a demonstration *of the interesting business; he may have had inner glimpses of an explicit statement, and vaguely have sketched it to himself as one of the most candid and charming ever drawn up; but time, meanwhile, has passed, interruptions have done their dismal work, the indirect tribute, too, has perhaps, behind the altar, grown and grown; and the reflection has at all events established itself that honour is more rendered by seeing and doing one's work in the light than by brandishing the torch on the house-tops. Curiosity and admiration have operated continually, but with as little waste as they could. The drawback is only that in this case, to be handsomely consequent, one would perhaps rather not have appeared to celebrate any rites. The moral of all of which is that those here embodied must pass, at the best, but for what they are worth.*

H. J.

August 9, 1900.

Saint-Bénazet: the Broken Bridge

Contents

Avignon from Villeneuve

List of Illustrations

Nantes

Introductory

THOUGH the good city of Paris appears to be less in fashion than in other days with those representatives of our race—not always, perhaps, acknowledged as the soundest and stiffest—curious of foreign opportunity and addicted to foreign sojourns, it probably none the less remains true that such frequentations of France as may be said still to flourish among us have as much as ever the wondrous capital, and the wondrous capital alone, for their object. The taste for Paris, at all events, is—or perhaps I should say was, alluding as I do, I fear, to a vanished order—a taste by itself; singularly little bound up, of necessity, with such an interest in the country at large as would be implied by an equal devotion, in other countries, to other capitals. Putting aside the economic inducement, which may always operate, and limiting the matter to the question of free choice, it is sufficiently striking that the free chooser would have to be very fond of England to quarter himself in London, very fond of Germany to quarter himself in Berlin, very fond of America to quarter himself in New York. It had, on the other hand, been a common reflection for the author of these light pages that the fondness for France (throughout the company of strangers more or less qualified) was oddly apt to feed only on such grounds for it as made shift to spread their surface between the Arc de Triomphe and the Gymnase Theatre: as if there were no good things in the *doux pays* that could not be harvested in that field. It matters little how the assumption began to strike him as stupid, especially since he himself had doubtless equally shared in the guilt of it. The light pages in question are but the simple record of a small personal effort to shake it off. He took, it must be confessed, no extraordinary measures; he merely started, one rainy morning in mid-September, for the charming little city of Tours, where he felt that he might as immediately as anywhere else see it demonstrated that, though France might be Paris, Paris was by no means France. The beauty of the demonstration—quite as prompt as he could have desired—drew him considerably farther, and his modest but eminently successful adventure begot, as aids to amused remembrance, a few informal notes.

Tours

Chapter I

I AM ashamed to begin with saying that Touraine is the garden of France; that remark has long ago lost its bloom. The town of Tours, however, has something sweet and bright, which suggests that it is surrounded by a land of fruits. It is a very agreeable little city; few towns of its size are more ripe, more complete, or, I should suppose, in better humour with themselves and less disposed to envy the responsibilities of bigger places. It is truly the capital of its smiling province; a region of easy abundance, of good living, of genial, comfortable, optimistic, rather indolent opinions. Balzac says in one of his tales that the real Tourangeau will not make an effort, or displace himself even, to go in search of a pleasure; and it is not difficult to understand the sources of this amiable cynicism. He must have a vague conviction that he can only lose by almost any change. Fortune has been kind to him: he lives in a temperate, reasonable, sociable climate, on the banks of a river which, it is true, sometimes floods the country around it, but of which the ravages appear to be so

19

easily repaired that its aggressions may perhaps be regarded (in a region where so many good things are certain) merely as an occasion for healthy suspense. He is surrounded by fine old traditions, religious, social, architectural, culinary; and he may have the satisfaction of feeling that he is French to the core. No part of his admirable country is more characteristically national. Normandy is Normandy, Burgundy is Burgundy, Provence is Provence; but Touraine is essentially France. It is the land of Rabelais, of Descartes, of Balzac, of good books and good company, as well as good dinners and good houses. George Sand has somewhere a charming passage about the mildness, the convenient quality, of the physical conditions of central France—"son climat souple et chaud, ses pluies abondantes et courtes." In the autumn of 1882 the rains perhaps were less short than abundant; but when the days were fine it was impossible that anything in the way of weather could be more charming. The vineyards and orchards looked rich in the fresh, gay light; cultivation was everywhere, but everywhere it seemed to be easy. There was no visible poverty; thrift and success presented themselves as matters of good taste. The white caps of the women glittered in the sunshine, and their well-made sabots clicked cheerfully on the hard, clean roads. Touraine is a land of old châteaux,—a gallery of architectural specimens and of large hereditary properties. The peasantry have less of the luxury of ownership than in most other parts of France; though they have enough of it to give them quite their share of that shrewdly conservative look which, in the little chaffering *place* of the market-town, the stranger observes so often in the wrinkled brown masks that surmount the agricultural blouse. This is, moreover, the heart of the old French monarchy; and as that monarchy was splendid and picturesque, a reflection of the splendour still glitters in the current of the Loire. Some of the most striking events of French history have occurred on the banks of that river, and the soil it waters bloomed for a while with the flowering of the Renaissance. The Loire gives a great "style" to a landscape of which the features are not, as the phrase is, prominent, and carries the eye to distances even more poetic than the green horizons of Touraine. It is a very fitful stream, and is sometimes observed to run thin and ex-

pose all the crudities of its channel—a great defect certainly
in a river which is so much depended upon to give an air to
the places it waters. But I speak of it as I saw it last; full,
tranquil, powerful, bending in large slow curves and sending
back half the light of the sky. Nothing can be finer than the
view of its course which you get from the battlements and
terraces of Amboise. As I looked down on it from that elevation one lovely Sunday morning, through a mild glitter of
autumn sunshine, it seemed the very model of a generous,
beneficent stream. The most charming part of Tours is naturally the shaded quay that overlooks it, and looks across too at
the friendly faubourg of Saint Symphorien and at the terraced
heights which rise above this. Indeed, throughout Touraine it
is half the charm of the Loire that you can travel beside it.
The great dyke which protects it, or protects the country from
it, from Blois to Angers, is an admirable road; and on the
other side as well the highway constantly keeps it company. A
wide river, as you follow a wide road, is excellent company; it
brightens and shortens the way.

The inns at Tours are in another quarter, and one of them,
which is midway between the town and the station, is very
good. It is worth mentioning for the fact that every one be-
longing to it is extraordinarily polite—so unnaturally polite
as at first to excite your suspicion that the hotel has some
hidden vice, so that the waiters and chambermaids are trying
to pacify you in advance. There was one waiter in especial
who was the most accomplished social being I have ever encountered; from morning till night he kept up an inarticulate
murmur of urbanity, like the hum of a spinning-top. I may
add that I discovered no dark secrets at the Hôtel de l'Uni-
vers; for it is not a secret to any traveller to-day that the obligation to partake of a lukewarm dinner in an overheated
room is as imperative as it is detestable. For the rest, at Tours
there is a certain Rue Royale which has pretensions to the
monumental; it was constructed a hundred years ago, and
the houses, all alike, have on a moderate scale a pompous
eighteenth-century look. It connects the Palais de Justice, the
most important secular building in the town, with the long
bridge which spans the Loire—the spacious, solid bridge
pronounced by Balzac, in "Le Curé de Tours," "one of the

finest monuments of French architecture." The Palais de Justice was the seat of the Government of Léon Gambetta in the
autumn of 1870, after the dictator had been obliged to retire
in his balloon from Paris and before the Assembly was constituted at Bordeaux. The Germans occupied Tours during that
terrible winter: it is astonishing, the number of places the
Germans occupied. It is hardly too much to say that, wherever one goes in certain parts of France, one encounters two
great historic facts: one is the Revolution; the other is the
German invasion. The traces of the Revolution remain in a
hundred scars and bruises and mutilations, but the visible
marks of the war of 1870 have passed away. The country is so
rich, so living, that she has been able to dress her wounds, to
hold up her head, to smile again, so that the shadow of that
darkness has ceased to rest upon her. But what you do not see
you still may hear; and one remembers with a certain shudder
that only a few short years ago this province, so intimately
French, was under the heel of a foreign foe. To be intimately
French was apparently not a safeguard; for so successful an
invader it could only be a challenge. Peace and plenty, however, have succeeded that episode; and among the gardens
and vineyards of Touraine it seems only a legend the more in
a country of legends.

It was not, all the same, for the sake of this chequered story
that I mentioned the Palais de Justice and the Rue Royale.
The most interesting fact, to my mind, about the high-street
of Tours was that as you walk toward the bridge on the right
hand *trottoir* you can look up at the house, on the other side
of the way, in which Honoré de Balzac first saw the light.
That violent and complicated genius was a child of the good-
humoured and succulent Touraine. There is something anomalous in this fact, though, if one thinks about it a little, one
may discover certain correspondences between his character
and that of his native province. Strenuous, laborious, constantly infelicitous in spite of his great successes, he suggests
at times a very different set of influences. But he had his jovial, full-feeding side—the side that comes out in the "Contes
Drolatiques," which are the romantic and epicurean chronicle
of the old manors and abbeys of this region. And he was,
moreover, the product of a soil into which a great deal of

Tours—the House of Balzac

history had been trodden. Balzac was genuinely as well as affectedly monarchical, and he was saturated with a sense of the past. Number 39 Rue Royale—of which the basement, like all the basements in the Rue Royale, is occupied by a shop—is not shown to the public; and I know not whether tradition designates the chamber in which the author of "Le Lys dans la Vallée" opened his eyes into a world in which he was to see and to imagine such extraordinary things. If this were the case I would willingly have crossed its threshold; not for the sake of any relic of the great novelist which it may possibly contain, nor even for that of any mystic virtue which may be supposed to reside within its walls, but simply because to look at those four modest walls can hardly fail to give one a strong impression of the force of human endeavour. Balzac, in the maturity of his vision, took in more of human life than any one, since Shakspeare, who has attempted to tell us stories about it; and the very small scene on which his consciousness dawned is one end of the immense scale that he traversed. I confess it shocked me a little to find that he was born in a house "in a row"—a house, moreover, which at the date of his birth must have been only about twenty years old. All that is contradictory. If the tenement selected for this honour could not be ancient and embrowned, it should at least have been detached.

There is a charming description in his little tale of "La Grenadière" of the view of the opposite side of the Loire as you have it from the square at the end of the Rue Royale—a square that has some pretensions to grandeur, overlooked as it is by the Hôtel de Ville and the Musée, a pair of edifices which directly contemplate the river, and ornamented with marble images of François Rabelais and René Descartes. The former, erected a few years since, is a very honourable production; the pedestal of the latter could, as a matter of course, only be inscribed with the *Cogito ergo Sum*. The two statues mark the two opposite poles to which the wondrous French mind has travelled; and if there were an effigy of Balzac at Tours it ought to stand midway between them. Not that he by any means always struck the happy mean between the sensible and the metaphysical; but one may say of him that half of his genius looks in one direction and half in the other. The side that turns toward François Rabelais would be, on the whole, the side that takes the sun. But there is no statue of Balzac at Tours; there is only in one of the chambers of the melancholy museum a rather clever, coarse bust. The description in "La Grenadière" of which I just spoke is too long to quote; neither have I space for any one of the brilliant attempts at landscape-painting which are woven into the shimmering texture of "Le Lys dans la Vallée." The little manor of Clochegourde, the residence of Madame de Mortsauf, the heroine of that extraordinary work, was within a moderate walk of Tours, and the picture in the novel is presumably a copy from an original which it would be possible to-day to discover. I did not, however, even make the attempt. There are so many châteaux in Touraine commemorated in history that it would take one too far to look up those which have been commemorated in fiction. The most I did was to endeavour to identify the former residence of Mademoiselle Gamard, the sinister old maid of "Le Curé de Tours." This terrible woman occupied a small house in the rear of the cathedral, where I spent a whole morning in wondering rather stupidly which house it could be. To reach the cathedral from the little *place* where we stopped just now to look across at the Grenadière, without, it must be confessed, very vividly seeing it, you follow the quay to the right and pass out of sight of the charming *côteau* which, from beyond the river, faces the town—a soft agglomeration of gardens, vineyards, scattered villas, gables and turrets of slate-roofed châteaux, terraces with grey balustrades, moss-grown walls draped in scarlet Virginia-creeper. You turn into the town again beside a great military barrack which is ornamented with a rugged mediæval tower, a relic of the ancient fortifications, known to the Tourangeaux of to-day as the Tour de Guise. The young Prince of Joinville, son of that Duke of Guise who was murdered by the order of Henry III. at Blois, was, after the death of his father, confined here for more than two years, but made his escape one summer evening in 1591, under the nose of his keepers, with a gallant audacity which has attached the memory of the exploit to his sullen-looking prison. Tours has a garrison of five regiments, and the little red-legged soldiers light up the town. You see them stroll upon the clean, uncommercial quay, where there are no signs of navigation, not even by oar, no barrels nor bales, no loading nor unloading, no masts against the sky nor booming of steam in the air. The most active business that goes on there is that patient and fruitless angling in which the French, as the votaries of art for art, excel all other people. The little soldiers, weighed down by the contents of their enormous pockets, pass with respect from one of these masters of the rod to the other, as he sits soaking an indefinite bait in the large, indifferent stream. After you turn your back to the quay you have only to go a little way before you reach the cathedral.

Langeais

Chapter II

IT IS a very beautiful church of the second order of importance, with a charming mouse-coloured complexion and a
pair of fantastic towers. There is a commodious little square
in front of it, from which you may look up at its very ornamental face; but for purposes of frank admiration the sides
and the rear are perhaps not sufficiently detached. The cathedral of Tours, which is dedicated to Saint Gatianus, took a
long time to build. Begun in 1170, it was finished only in the
first half of the sixteenth century; but the ages and the weather
have interfused so well the tone of the different parts that it

27

presents, at first at least, no striking incongruities, and looks
even exceptionally harmonious and complete. There are many
grander cathedrals, but there are probably few more pleasing;
and this effect of delicacy and grace is at its best towards the
close of a quiet afternoon, when the densely decorated towers, rising above the little Place de l'Archevêché, lift their curious lanterns into the slanting light and offer a multitudinous
perch to troops of circling pigeons. The whole front, at such a
time, has an appearance of great richness, although the niches
which surround the three high doors (with recesses deep
enough for several circles of sculpture) and indent the four
great buttresses that ascend beside the huge rose-window,
carry no figures beneath their little chiselled canopies. The
blast of the great Revolution blew down most of the statues
in France, and the wind has never set very strongly towards
putting them up again. The embossed and crocketed cupolas
which crown the towers of Saint Gatien are not very pure in
taste; but, like a good many impurities, they have a certain
character. The interior has a stately slimness with which no
fault is to be found and which in the choir, rich in early glass
and surrounded by a broad passage, becomes very bold and
noble. Its principal treasure perhaps is the charming little
tomb of the two children (who died young) of Charles VIII.
and Anne of Brittany, in white marble embossed with symbolic dolphins and exquisite arabesques. The little boy and
girl lie side by side on a slab of black marble, and a pair of
small kneeling angels, both at their head and at their feet,
watch over them. Nothing could be more elegant than this
monument, which is the work of Michel Colomb, one of the
earlier glories of the French Renaissance; it is really a lesson
in good taste. Originally placed in the great abbey-church of
Saint Martin, which was for so many ages the holy place of
Tours, it happily survived the devastation to which that edifice, already sadly shattered by the wars of religion and successive profanations, finally succumbed in 1797. In 1815 the tomb
found an asylum in a quiet corner of the cathedral.

I ought perhaps to be ashamed to acknowledge that I
found the profane name of Balzac capable of adding an interest even to this venerable sanctuary. Those who have read the
terrible little story of "Le Curé de Tours" will perhaps remember

Tours: the Cathedral

that, as I have already mentioned, the simple and childlike old Abbé Birotteau, victim of the infernal machinations of the Abbé Troubert and Mademoiselle Gamard, had his quarters in the house of that lady (she had a specialty of letting lodgings to priests), which stood on the north side of the cathedral, so close under its walls that the supporting pillar of one of the great flying buttresses was planted in the spinster's garden. If you wander round behind the church in search of this more than historic habitation you will have occasion to see that the side and rear of Saint Gatien make a delectable and curious figure. A narrow lane passes beside the high wall which conceals from sight the palace of the archbishop and beneath the flying buttresses, the far-projecting gargoyles, and the fine south porch of the church. It terminates in a little dead grass-grown square entitled the Place Grégoire de Tours. All this part of the exterior of the cathedral is very brown, ancient, Gothic, grotesque; Balzac calls the whole place "a desert of stone." A battered and gabled wing or out-house (as it appears to be) of the hidden palace, with a queer old stone pulpit jutting out from it, looks down on this melancholy spot, on the other side of which is a seminary for young priests, one of whom issues from a door in a quiet corner, and, holding it open a moment behind him, shows a glimpse of a sunny garden, where you may fancy other black young figures strolling up and down. Mademoiselle Gamard's house, where she took her two abbés to board, and basely conspired with one against the other, is still farther round the cathedral. You cannot quite put your hand upon it to-day, for the dwelling of which you say to yourself that it must have been Mademoiselle Gamard's does not fulfil all the conditions mentioned in Balzac's description. The edifice in question, however, fulfils conditions enough; in particular, its little court offers hospitality to the big buttress of the church. Another buttress, corresponding with this (the two, between them, sustain the gable of the north transept), is planted in the small cloister, of which the door on the farther side of the little soundless Rue de la Psalette, where nothing seems ever to pass, opens opposite to that of Mademoiselle Gamard. There is a very genial old sacristan, who introduced me to this cloister from the church. It is very small and solitary, and much mutilated; but it nestles with a kind of wasted friendliness beneath the big walls of the cathedral. Its lower arcades have been closed, and it has a small plot of garden in the middle, with fruit-trees which I should imagine to be too much overshadowed. In one corner is a remarkably picturesque turret, the cage of a winding staircase which ascends (no great distance) to an upper gallery, where an old priest, the *chanoine-gardien* of the church, was walking to and fro with his breviary. The turret, the gallery, and even the chanoine-gardien, belonged, that sweet September morning, to the class of objects that are dear to painters in water-colours.

Chaumont

Chapter III

I HAVE mentioned the church of Saint Martin, which was for many years the sacred spot, the shrine of pilgrimage, of Tours. Originally the simple burial-place of the great apostle who in the fourth century Christianised Gaul and who, in his day a brilliant missionary and worker of miracles, is chiefly known to modern fame as the worthy that cut his cloak in two at the gate of Amiens to share it with a beggar (tradition fails to say, I believe, what he did with the other half), the abbey of Saint Martin, through the Middle Ages, waxed rich and powerful, till it was known at last as one of the most luxurious religious houses in Christendom, with kings for its titular abbots (who, like Francis I., sometimes turned and despoiled it) and a great treasure of precious things. It passed, however, through many vicissitudes. Pillaged by the Normans in the ninth century and by the Huguenots in the sixteenth, it received its death-blow from the Revolution, which must have brought to bear upon it an energy of destruction proportionate to its mighty bulk. At the end of the last century a huge group of ruins alone remained, and what we see to-day may be called the ruin of a ruin. It is difficult to understand how so vast an edifice can have been so completely obliterated. Its site is given up to several ugly streets, and a pair of tall towers, separated by a space which speaks volumes as to the size of the church and looking across the close-pressed roofs to the happier spires of the cathedral, preserve for the modern world the memory of a great fortune, a great abuse, perhaps, and at all events a great penalty. One may believe that to this day a considerable part of the foundations of the great abbey is buried in the soil of Tours. The two surviving towers, which are dissimilar in shape, are enormous; with those of the cathedral they form the great landmarks of the town. One of them bears the name of the Tour de l'Horloge; the other, the so-called Tour Charlemagne, was erected (two centuries after her death) over the tomb of Luitgarde, wife of the great Emperor, who died at Tours in 800. I do not pretend to understand in what relation these very mighty and effectually detached masses of masonry stood to each other, but in their grey elevation and loneliness they are striking and suggestive to-day; holding their hoary heads far above the modern life of the town and looking sad and conscious, as they had outlived all uses. I know not what is supposed to have become of the bones of the blessed saint during the various scenes of confusion in which they may have got mislaid; but a mystic connection with his wonder-working relics may be perceived in a strange little sanctuary on the left of the street, which opens in front of the Tour Charlemagne—whose immemorial base, by the way, inhabited like a cavern, with a diminutive doorway where, as I passed, an old woman stood cleaning a pot, and a little dark window decorated with homely flowers, would be appreciated by a painter in search of "bits." The present shrine of Saint Martin is enclosed (provisionally, I suppose) in a very modern structure of timber, where in a dusky cellar, to which you descend by a wooden staircase adorned with votive tablets and paper roses, is placed a tabernacle surrounded by twinkling tapers and prostrate worshippers. Even this crepuscular vault, however, fails, I think, to attain solemnity; for the whole place is strangely vulgar and garish. The Catholic Church, as churches go to-day, is certainly the most spectacular; but it must feel that it has a great fund of impressiveness to draw upon when it opens such sordid little shops of sanctity as this. It is impossible not to be struck with the grotesqueness of such an establishment as the last link in the chain of a great ecclesiastical tradition.

In the same street, on the other side, a little below, is something better worth your visit than the shrine of Saint Martin. Knock at a high door in a white wall (there is a cross above it), and a fresh-faced sister of the convent of the Petit Saint Martin will let you into the charming little cloister, or rather fragment of cloister. Only one side of this surpassing structure remains, but the whole place is effective. In front of the beautiful arcade, which is terribly bruised and obliterated, is one of those walks of interlaced *tilleuls* which are so frequent in Touraine, and into which the green light filters so softly through a lattice of clipped twigs. Beyond this is a garden, and beyond the garden are the other buildings of the convent, where the placid sisters keep a school—a test, doubtless, of placidity. The imperfect arcade, which dates from the beginning of the sixteenth century (I know nothing of it but what is related in Mrs. Pattison's "Renaissance in France"), is a truly enchanting piece of work; the cornice and the angles of the arches being covered with the daintiest sculpture of arabesques, flowers, fruit, medallions, cherubs, griffins, all in the finest and most attenuated relief. It is like the chasing of a bracelet in stone. The taste, the fancy, the elegance, the refinement, are of the order that straightens up again our drooping standard of distinction. Such a piece of work is the purest flower of the French Renaissance; there is nothing more delicate in all Touraine.

There is another fine thing at Tours which is not particularly delicate, but which makes a great impression—the very interesting old church of Saint Julian, lurking in a crooked corner at the right of the Rue Royale, near the point at which this indifferent thoroughfare emerges, with its little cry of

Tours: the Towers of St. Martin

admiration, on the bank of the Loire. Saint Julian stands to-
day in a kind of neglected hollow, where it is much shut in by
houses; but in the year 1225, when the edifice was begun, the
site was doubtless, as the architects say, more eligible. At
present indeed, when once you have caught a glimpse of the
stout, serious Romanesque tower—which is not high, but
strong—you feel that the building has something to say and
that you must stop to listen to it. Within, it has a vast and
splendid nave, of immense height, the nave of a cathedral,
with a shallow choir and transepts and some admirable old
glass. I spent half an hour there one morning, listening to
what the church had to say, in perfect solitude. Not a worshipper entered, not even an old man with a broom. I have
always thought there be a sex in fine buildings; and Saint
Julian, with its noble nave, is of the gender of the name of its
patron.

It was that same morning, I think, that I went in search of
the old houses of Tours; for the town contains several goodly
specimens of the domestic architecture of the past. The dwelling to which the average Anglo-Saxon will most promptly
direct his steps, and the only one I have space to mention, is
the so-called Maison de Tristan l'Hermite—a gentleman
whom the readers of "Quentin Durward" will not have forgotten—the hangman-in-ordinary to that great and prompt
chastener Louis XI. Unfortunately the house of Tristan is not
the house of Tristan at all; this illusion has been cruelly dispelled. There are no illusions left at all, in the good city of
Tours, with regard to Louis XI. His terrible castle of Plessis,
the picture of which sends a shiver through the youthful
reader of Scott, has been reduced to suburban insignificance;
and the residence of his *triste compère*, on the front of which a
festooned rope figures as a motive for decoration, is observed
to have been erected in the succeeding century. The Maison
de Tristan may be visited for itself, however, if not for Sir
Walter; it is an exceedingly picturesque old façade, to which
you pick your way through a narrow and tortuous street—a
street terminating, a little beyond it, in the walk beside the
river. An elegant Gothic doorway is let into the rusty-red
brickwork, and strange little beasts crouch at the angles of the
windows, which are surmounted by a tall graduated gable,

pierced with a small orifice, where the large surface of brick, lifted out of the shadow of the street, looks yellow and faded. The whole thing is disfigured and decayed; but it is a capital subject for a sketch in colours. Only I must wish the sketcher better luck—or a better temper—than my own. If he ring the bell to be admitted to see the court, which I believe is more sketchable still, let him have patience to wait till the bell is answered. He can do the outside while they are coming.

The Maison de Tristan, I say, may be visited for itself; but I hardly know for what the remnants of Plessis-les-Tours may be investigated. To reach them you wander through crooked suburban lanes, down the course of the Loire, to a rough, undesirable, incongruous spot, where a small, crude building of red brick is pointed out to you by your cabman (if you happen to drive) as the legendary frame of the grim portrait, and where a strong odour of pigsties and other unclean things so prostrates you for the moment that you have no energy to protest against this obvious fiction. You enter a yard encumbered with rubbish and a defiant dog, and an old woman emerges from a shabby lodge and assures you that you stand deep in historic dust. The red brick building, which looks like a small factory, rises on the ruins of the favourite residence of the dreadful Louis. It is now occupied by a company of night-scavengers, whose huge carts are drawn up in a row before it. I know not whether this be what is called the irony of fate; in any case, the effect of it is to accentuate strongly the fact (and through the most susceptible of our senses) that there is no honour for the authors of great wrongs. The dreadful Louis is reduced simply to an offence to the nostrils. The old woman shows you a few fragments—several dark, damp, much-encumbered vaults, denominated dungeons, and an old tower staircase in good condition. There are the out-lines of the old moat; there is also the outline of the old guard-room, which is now a stable; and there are other silhouettes of the undistinguishable, which I have forgotten. You need all your imagination, and even then you cannot make out that Plessis was a castle of large extent, though the old woman, as your eye wanders over the neighbouring *pota-gers*, discourses much of the gardens and the park. The place looks mean and flat; and as you drive away you scarcely know whether to be glad or sorry that all those bristling horrors have been reduced to the commonplace.

A certain flatness of impression awaits you also, I think, at Marmoutier, which is the other indispensable excursion in the near neighbourhood of Tours. The remains of this famous abbey lie on the other bank of the stream, about a mile and a half from the town. You follow the edge of the big brown river; of a fine afternoon you will be glad to go farther still. The abbey has gone the way of most abbeys; but the place is a restoration as well as a ruin, inasmuch as the Sisters of the Sacred Heart have erected a terribly modern convent here. A large Gothic doorway, in a high fragment of ancient wall, admits you to a garden-like enclosure, of great extent, from which you are further introduced into an extraordinarily tidy little parlour, where two good nuns sit at work. One of these came out with me and showed me over the place—a very definite little woman, with pointed features, an intensely distinct enunciation, and those pretty manners which (for whatever other teachings it may be responsible) the Catholic Church so often instils into its functionaries. I have never seen a woman who had got her lesson better than this little trotting, murmuring, edifying nun. The interest of Marmoutier to-day is not so much an interest of vision, so to speak, as an interest of reflection—that is, if you choose to reflect (for instance) upon the wondrous legend of the seven sleepers (you may see where they lie in a row), who lived together—they were brothers and cousins—in primitive piety, in the sanctuary constructed by the blessed Saint Martin (emulous of his precursor, Saint Gatianus), in the face of the hillside that overhung the Loire, and who, twenty-five years after his death, yielded up their seven souls at the same moment and enjoyed the rare convenience of retaining in their faces, in spite of mortality, every aspect of health. The abbey of Marmoutier, which sprang from the grottos in the cliff to which Saint Gatianus and Saint Martin retired to pray, was therefore the creation of the latter worthy, as the other great abbey, in the town proper, was the monument of his repose. The cliff is still there; and a winding staircase, in the latest taste, enables you conveniently to explore its recesses. These sacred niches are scooped out of the rock, and will give you an impression if you cannot do without one. You will feel them to be sufficiently venerable when you learn that the particular pigeon-hole of Saint Gatianus, the first Christian missionary to Gaul, dates from the third century. They have been dealt with as the Catholic Church deals with most of such places to-day; polished and furbished up, labelled and ticketed—*edited*, with notes, in short, like an old book. The process is a mistake—the early editions had more sanctity. The modern buildings (of the Sacred Heart), on which you look down from these points of vantage, are in the vulgar taste which sets its so mechanical stamp on all new Catholic work; but there was nevertheless a great sweetness in the scene. The afternoon was lovely, and it was flushing to a close. The large garden stretched beneath us, blooming with fruit and wine and succulent promise, and beyond it flowed the shining river. The air was still, the shadows were long, and the place, after all, was full of memories, most of which might pass for virtuous. It certainly was better than Plessis-les-Tours.

Blois

Chapter IV

YOUR BUSINESS at Tours is to make excursions; and if you make them all you will be always under arms. The land is a rich reliquary, and an hour's drive from the town in almost any direction will bring you to the knowledge of some curious fragment of domestic or ecclesiastical architecture, some turreted manor, some lonely tower, some gabled village, some scene of something. Yet even if you do everything—which was not my case—you cannot hope to tell everything, and, fortunately for you, the excursions divide themselves into the greater and the less. You may achieve most of the greater in a week or two; but a summer in Touraine (which, by the way, must be a delectable thing) would hold none too many days for the others. If you come down to Tours from Paris your best economy is to spend a few days at Blois, where a clumsy

Blois

but rather attractive little inn on the edge of the river will offer you a certain amount of that familiar and intermittent hospitality which a few weeks spent in the French provinces teaches you to regard as the highest attainable form of accommodation. Such an economy I was unable to practise. I could only go to Blois (from Tours) to spend the day; but this feat I accomplished twice over. It is a very sympathetic little town, as we say nowadays, and a week there would be sociable even without company. Seated on the north bank of the Loire, it presents a bright, clean face to the sun and has that aspect of cheerful leisure which belongs to all white towns that reflect themselves in shining waters. It is the water-front only of Blois, however, that exhibits this fresh complexion; the interior is of a proper brownness, as old sallow books are bound in vellum. The only disappointment is perforce the discovery that the castle, which is the special object of one's pilgrimage, does not overhang the river, as I had always allowed myself to understand. It overhangs the town, but is scarcely visible from the stream. That peculiar good fortune is reserved for Amboise and Chaumont.

The Château de Blois is one of the most beautiful and elaborate of all the old royal residences of this part of France, and I suppose it should have all the honours of my description. As you cross its threshold you step straight into the sunshine and storm of the French Renaissance. But it is too rich to describe—I can only pick out the high lights. It must be premised that in speaking of it as we see it to-day we speak of a monument unsparingly restored. The work of restoration has been as ingenious as it is profuse, but it rather chills the imagination. This is perhaps almost the first thing you feel as you approach the castle from the streets of the town. These little streets, as they leave the river, have pretensions to romantic steepness; one of them, indeed, which resolves itself into a high staircase with divergent wings (the *escalier monumental*), achieved this result so successfully as to remind me vaguely —I hardly know why—of the great slope of the Capitol, beside the Ara Cœli, at Rome. The view of that part of the castle which figures to-day as the back (it is the only aspect I had seen reproduced) exhibits the marks of restoration with the greatest assurance. The long façade, consisting only of balconied windows deeply recessed, erects itself on the summit of a considerable hill, which gives a fine, plunging movement to its foundations. The deep niches of the windows are all aglow with colour. They have been repainted with red and blue, relieved with gold figures; and each of them looks more like the royal box at a theatre than like the aperture of a palace dark with memories. For all this, however, and in spite of the fact that, as in some others of the châteaux of Touraine (always excepting the colossal Chambord, which is not in Touraine), there is less vastness than one had expected, the least hospitable aspect of Blois is abundantly impressive. Here, as elsewhere, lightness and grace are the keynote; and the recesses of the windows, with their happy proportions, their sculpture and their colour, are the hollow sockets of the human ornament. They need the figure of a Francis I. to complete them, or of a Diane de Poitiers, or even of a Henry III. The stand of this empty gilt cage emerges from a bed of light verdure which has been allowed to mass itself there and which contributes to the springing look of the walls; while on the right it joins the most modern portion of the castle, the building erected, on foundations of enormous height and solidity, in 1635, by Gaston d'Orléans. This fine frigid mansion—the proper view of it is from the court within—is one of the masterpieces of François Mansard, whom a kind providence did not allow to make over the whole palace in the superior manner of his superior age. That had been a part of Gaston's plan—he was a blunderer born, and this precious project was worthy of him. This execution of it would surely have been one of the great misdeeds of history. Partially performed, the misdeed is not altogether to be regretted; for as one stands in the court of the castle and lets one's eye wander from the splendid wing of Francis I.—which is the last word of free and joyous invention—to the ruled lines and blank spaces of the ponderous pavilion of Mansard, one makes one's reflections upon the advantage, in even the least personal of the arts, of having something to say, and upon the stupidity of a taste which had ended by becoming an aggregation of negatives. Gaston's wing, taken by itself, has much of the *bel air* which was to belong to the architecture of Louis XIV.; but, taken in contrast to its flowering, laughing, living neighbour, it marks the difference between inspiration and calculation. We scarcely grudge it its place, however, for it adds a price to the rest of the pile.

We have entered the court, by the way, by jumping over the walls. The more orthodox method is to follow a modern terrace which leads to the left, from the side of the edifice that I began by speaking of, and passes round, ascending, to a little square on a considerably higher level, a square not, like the rather prosaic space on which the back (as I have called it) looks out, a thoroughfare. This small empty *place*, oblong in form, at once bright and quiet, and which ought to be grass-grown, offers an excellent setting to the entrance-front of the palace—the wing of Louis XII. The restoration here has been lavish; but it was perhaps but an inevitable reaction against the injuries, still more lavish, by which the unfortunate building had long been overwhelmed. It had fallen into a state of ruinous neglect, relieved only by the misuse proceeding from successive generations of soldiers, for whom its charming chambers served as barrack-room. Whitewashed, mutilated, dishonoured, the castle of Blois may be said to have escaped simply with its life. This is the history of Amboise as well, and is to a certain extent the history of Chambord. Delightful, at any rate, was the refreshed façade of Louis XII. as I stood and looked at it one bright September morning. In that soft, clear, merry light of Touraine, everything shows, everything speaks. Charming are the taste, the happy proportions, the colour of this beautiful front, to which the new feeling for a purely domestic architecture—an architecture of security and tranquillity, in which art could indulge itself—gave an air of youth and gladness. It is true that for a long time to come the castle of Blois was neither very safe nor very quiet; but its dangers came from within, from the evil passions of its inhabitants, and not from siege or invasion. The front of Louis XII. is of red brick, crossed here and there with purple; and the purple slate of the high roof, relieved with chimneys beautifully treated and with the embroidered caps of pinnacles and arches, with the porcupine of Louis, the ermine and the festooned rope which formed the devices of Anne of Brittany— the tone of this decorative roof carries out the mild glow of the wall. The wide, fair windows open as if they had ex-

Blois: the Chateau

panded to let in the rosy dawn of the Renaissance. Charming, for that matter, are the windows of all the châteaux of Touraine, with their squareness corrected (as it is not in the Tudor architecture) by the curve of the upper corners, which gives this line the look, above the expressive aperture, of a pencilled eyebrow. The low door of this front is crowned by a high, deep niche, in which, under a splendid canopy, stiffly astride of a stiffly-draped charger, sits in profile an image of the good King Louis. Good as he had been—the father of his people, as he was called (I believe he remitted various taxes)—he was not good enough to pass muster at the Revolution; and the effigy I have just described is no more than a reproduction of the primitive statue demolished at that period.

Pass beneath it into the court, and the sixteenth century closes round you. It is a pardonable flight of fancy to say that the expressive faces of an age in which human passions lay very near the surface seem to peep out at you from the windows, from the balconies, from the thick foliage of the sculpture. The portion of the wing of Louis XII. that fronts toward the court is supported on a deep arcade. On your right is the wing erected by Francis I., the reverse of the mass of building which you see on approaching the castle. This exquisite, this extravagant, this transcendent piece of architecture is the most joyous utterance of the French Renaissance. It is covered with an embroidery of sculpture in which every detail is worthy of the hand of a goldsmith. In the middle of it, or rather a little to the left, rises the famous winding staircase (plausibly, but I believe not religiously, restored), which even the ages which most misused it must vaguely have admired. It forms a kind of chiselled cylinder, with wide interstices, so that the stairs are open to the air. Every inch of this structure, of its balconies, its pillars, its great central columns, is wrought over with lovely images, strange and ingenious devices, prime among which is the great heraldic salamander of Francis I. The salamander is everywhere at Blois—over the chimneys, over the doors, on the walls. This whole quarter of the castle bears the stamp of that eminently pictorial prince. The running cornice along the top of the front is like an unfolded, an elongated bracelet. The windows of the attic are like shrines for saints. The gargoyles, the medallions, the statuettes, the festoons are like the elaboration of some precious cabinet rather than the details of a building exposed to the weather and to the ages. In the interior there is a profusion of restoration, and it is all restoration in colour. This has been, evidently, a work of great energy and cost, but it will easily strike you as overdone. The universal freshness is a discord, a false note; it seems to light up the dusky past with an unnatural glare. Begun in the reign of Louis Philippe, this terrible process—the more terrible always the better case you conceive made out for it—has been carried so far that there is now scarcely a square inch of the interior that preserves the colour of the past. It is true that the place had been so coated over with modern abuse that something was needed to keep it alive; it is only perhaps a pity the clever doctors, not content with saving its life, should have undertaken to restore its bloom. The love of consistency, in such a business, is a dangerous lure. All the old apartments have been rechristened, as it were; the geography of the castle has been re-established. The guard-rooms, the bed-rooms, the closets, the oratories have recovered their identity. Every spot connected with the murder of the Duke of Guise is pointed out by a small, shrill boy, who takes you from room to room and who has learned his lesson in perfection. The place is full of Catherine de' Medici, of Henry III., of memories, of ghosts, of echoes, of possible evocations and revivals. It is covered with crimson and gold. The fireplaces and the ceilings are magnificent; they look like expensive "sets" at the grand opera.

I should have mentioned that below, in the court, the front of the wing of Gaston d'Orléans faces you as you enter, so that the place is a course of French history. Inferior in beauty and grace to the other portions of the castle, the wing is yet a nobler monument than the memory of Gaston deserves. The second of the sons of Henry IV.—who was no more fortunate as a father than as a husband—younger brother of Louis XIII. and father of the great Mademoiselle, the most celebrated, most ambitious, most self-complacent and most unsuccessful *fille à marier* in French history, passed in enforced retirement at the castle of Blois the close of a life of clumsy intrigues against Cardinal Richelieu, in which his rashness was only equalled by his pusillanimity and his ill-luck by his inaccessibility to correction, and which, after so many follies and shames, was properly summed up in the project—begun, but not completed—of demolishing the beautiful habitation of his exile in order to erect a better one. With Gaston d'Orléans, however, who lived there without dignity, the history of the Château de Blois declines. Its interesting period is that of the wars of religion. It was the chief residence of Henry III., and the scene of the principal events of his depraved and dramatic rule. It has been restored more than enough, as I have said, by architects and decorators; the visitor, as he moves through its empty rooms, which are at once brilliant and ill-lighted (they have not been refurnished), undertakes a little restoration of his own. His imagination helps itself from the things that remain; he tries to see the life of the sixteenth century in its form and dress—its turbulence, its passions, its loves and hates, its treacheries, falsities, sincerities, faith, its latitude of personal development, its presentation of the whole nature, its nobleness of costume, charm of speech, splendour of taste, unequalled picturesqueness. The picture is full of movement, of contrasted light and darkness, full altogether of abominations. Mixed up with them all is the great theological motive, so that the drama wants little to make it complete. What episode was ever more perfect—looked at as a dramatic occurrence—than the murder of the Duke of Guise? The insolent prosperity of the victim; the weakness, the vices, the terrors, of the author of the deed; the perfect execution of the plot; the accumulation of horror in what followed it—render it, as a crime, one of the classic things.

But we must not take the Château de Blois too hard: I went there, after all, by way of entertainment. If among these sinister memories your visit should threaten to prove a tragedy, there is an excellent way of removing the impression. You may treat yourself at Blois to a very cheerful afterpiece. There is a charming industry practised there, and practised in charming conditions. Follow the bright little quay down the river till you get quite out of the town and reach the point where the road beside the Loire becomes sinuous and attractive, turns the corner of diminutive headlands and makes you wonder what is beyond. Let not your curiosity induce you, however, to pass by a modest white villa which overlooks the

stream, enclosed in a fresh little court; for here dwells an artist
—an artist in faience. There is no sort of sign, and the place
looks peculiarly private. But if you ring at the gate you will
not be turned away. You will, on the contrary, be ushered
upstairs into a parlour—there is nothing resembling a
shop—encumbered with specimens of remarkably handsome
pottery. The ware is of the best, a careful reproduction of old
forms, colours, devices; and the master of the establishment is
one of those completely artistic types that are often found in
France. His reception is as friendly as his work is ingenious;
and I think it is not too much to say that you like the work
better because he has produced it. His vases, cups and jars,
lamps, platters, *plaques*, with their brilliant glaze, their innumerable figures, their family likeness and wide variations, are
scattered through his occupied rooms; they serve at once as
his stock-in-trade and as household ornament. As we all
know, this is an age of prose, of machinery, of wholesale production, of coarse and hasty processes. But one brings away
from the establishment of the very intelligent M. Ulysse the
sense of a less eager activity and a greater search for perfection. He has but a few workmen and he gives them plenty of
time. The place makes a little vignette, leaves an impression—
the quiet white house in its garden on the road by the wide,
clear river, without the smoke, the bustle, the ugliness, of so
much of our modern industry. It struck me as an effort Mr.
Ruskin might have inspired and Mr. William Morris—
though that be much to say—have forgiven.

Chambord

Chapter V

T HE SECOND TIME I went to Blois I took a carriage for Chambord, and came back by the Château de Cheverny and the forest of Russy—a charming little expedition, to which the beauty of the afternoon (the finest in a rainy season that was spotted with bright days) contributed not a little. To go to Chambord you cross the Loire, leave it on one side and strike away through a country in which salient features become less and less numerous and which at last has no other quality than a look of intense and peculiar rurality—the characteristic, even when it be not the charm, of so much of the landscape of France. This is not the appearance of wildness, for it goes with great cultivation; it is simply the presence of the delving, drudging, economising peasant. But it is a deep, unrelieved rusticity. It is a peasant's landscape; not, as in England, a landlord's. On the way to Chambord you enter the flat and sandy Sologne. The wide horizon opens out like a great *potager*, without interruptions, without an eminence, with here and there a long, low stretch of wood. There is an absence of hedges, fences, signs of property; everything is absorbed in the general flatness—the patches of vineyard, the scattered cottages, the villages, the children (planted and staring and almost always pretty), the women in the fields, the white caps, the faded blouses, the big sabots. At the end of an hour's drive (they assure you at Blois that even with two horses you will spend double that time), I passed through a sort of gap in a wall which does duty as the gateway of the domain of a proscribed pretender. I followed a straight avenue through a disfeatured park—the park of Chambord has twenty-one miles of circumference; a very sandy, scrubby, melancholy plantation, in which the timber must have been cut many times over and is to-day a mere tangle of brushwood. Here, as in so many spots in France, the traveller perceives that he is in a land of revolutions. Nevertheless its great extent and the long perspective of its avenues give this frugal shrubbery a certain state; just as its shabbiness places it in agreement with one of the strongest impressions awaiting you. You pursue one of these long perspectives a proportionate time, and at last you see the chimneys and pinnacles of Chambord rise apparently out of the ground. The filling-in of the wide moats that formerly surrounded it has, in vulgar parlance, let it down and given it a monstrous over-crowned air that is at the same time a magnificent Orientalism. The towers, the turrets, the cupolas, the gables, the lanterns, the chimneys look more like the spires of a city than the salient points of a single building. You emerge from the avenue and find yourself at the foot of an enormous fantastic mass. Chambord has a strange mixture of society and solitude. A little village clusters within view of its liberal windows, and a couple of inns near by offer entertainment to pilgrims. These things of course are incidents of the political proscription which hangs its thick veil over the place. Chambord is truly royal—royal in its great scale, its grand air, its indifference to common considerations. If a cat may look at a king, a tavern may look at a palace. I enjoyed my visit to this extraordinary structure as much as if I had been a legitimist; and indeed there is something interesting in any monument of a great system, any bold presentation of a tradition.

You leave your vehicle at one of the inns, which are very decent and tidy and in which every one is very civil, as if in this latter respect the neighbourhood of a Court veritably set the fashion, and you proceed across the grass and the gravel to a small door, a door infinitely subordinate and conferring no title of any kind on those who enter it. Here you ring a bell, which a highly respectable person answers (a person perceptibly affiliated, again, to the old régime), after which she ushers you over a vestibule into an inner court. Perhaps the strongest impression I got at Chambord came to me as I stood in this court. The woman who admitted me did not come with me; I was to find my guide somewhere else. The specialty of Chambord is its prodigious round towers. There are, I believe, no less than eight of them, placed at each angle of the inner and outer square of buildings; for the castle is in the form of a larger structure which encloses a smaller one. One of these towers stood before me in the court; it seemed to fling its shadow over the place; while above, as I looked up, the pinnacles and gables, the enormous chimneys, soared into the bright blue air. The place was empty and silent; shadows of gargoyles, of extraordinary projections, were thrown across the clear grey surfaces. One felt that the whole thing was monstrous. A cicerone appeared, a languid young man in a rather shabby livery, and led me about with a mixture of the impatient and the desultory, of condescension and humility. I do not profess to understand the plan of Chambord, and I may add that I do not even desire to do so; for it is much more entertaining to think of it, as you can so easily, as an irresponsible, insoluble labyrinth. Within it is a wilderness of empty chambers, a royal and romantic barrack. The exiled prince to whom it gives its title has not the means to keep up four hundred rooms; he contents himself with preserving the huge outside. The repairs of the prodigious roof alone must absorb a large part of his revenue. The great feature of the interior is the celebrated double staircase, rising straight through the building, with two courses of steps, so that people may ascend and descend without meeting. This staircase is a truly majestic piece of humour; it gives you the note, as it were, of Chambord. It opens on each landing to a vast guard-room, in four arms, radiations of the winding shaft. My guide made me climb to the great open-work lantern which, springing from the roof at the termination of the rotund staircase

Chambord

(surmounted here by a smaller one), forms the pinnacle of the bristling crown of the pile. This lantern is tipped with a huge *fleur-de-lis* in stone—the only one, I believe, that the Revolution did not succeed in pulling down. Here, from narrow windows, you look over the wide, flat country and the tangled, melancholy park, with the rotation of its straight avenues. Then you walk about the roof in a complication of galleries, terraces, balconies, through the multitude of chimneys and gables. This roof, which is in itself a sort of castle in the air, has an extravagant, fabulous quality, and with its profuse ornamentation—the salamander of Francis I. is a constant motive—its lonely pavements, its sunny niches, the balcony that looks down over the closed and grass-grown main entrance, a strange, half-sad, half-brilliant charm. The stonework is covered with fine mould. There are places that reminded me of some of those quiet mildewed corners of courts and terraces into which the traveller who wanders through the Vatican looks down from neglected windows. They show you two or three furnished rooms, with Bourbon portraits, hideous tapestries from the ladies of France, a collection of the toys of the *enfant du miracle*, all military and of the finest make. "Tout cela fonctionne," the guide said of these miniature weapons; and I wondered, if he should take it into his head to fire off his little cannon, how much harm the Comte de Chambord would do.

From below the castle would look crushed by the redundancy of its upper protuberances if it were not for the enormous girth of its round towers, which appear to give it a robust lateral development. These towers, however, fine as they are in their way, struck me as a little stupid; they are the exaggeration of an exaggeration. In a building erected after the days of defence and proclaiming its peaceful character from its hundred embroideries and cupolas, they seem to indicate a want of invention. I shall risk the accusation of bad taste if I say that, impressive as it is, the Château de Chambord seemed to me to have altogether a touch of that quality of stupidity. The trouble is that it stands for nothing very momentous; it has not happened, in spite of sundry vicissitudes, to have a strongly-marked career. Compared with that of Blois and Amboise its past is rather vacant; and one feels to a certain extent the contrast between its pompous appearance and its spacious but somewhat colourless annals. It had indeed the good fortune to be erected by Francis I., whose name by itself expresses a good deal of history. Why he should have built a palace in those sandy plains will ever remain an unanswered question, for kings have never been obliged to give reasons. In addition to the fact that the country was rich in game and that Francis was a passionate hunter, it is suggested by M. de la Saussaye, the author of the very complete little account of the place which you may buy at the bookseller's at Blois, that he was governed in his choice of the site by the chance that a charming woman had previously lived there. The Comtesse de Thoury had a manor in the neighbourhood, and the Comtesse de Thoury had been the object of a youthful passion on the part of the most susceptible of princes before his accession to the throne. This great pile was reared, therefore, according to M. de la Saussaye, as a *souvenir de premières amours*! It is certainly a very massive memento; and if these tender passages were proportionate to the building that commemorates them, the flame blazed indeed. There has been much discussion as to the architect employed by Francis I., and the honour of having designed this splendid residence has been claimed for several of the Italian artists who early in the sixteenth century came to seek patronage in France. It seems well established to-day, however, that Chambord was the work neither of Primaticcio, of Vignola, nor of Il Rosso, all of whom have left some trace of their sojourn in France; but of an obscure yet very complete genius, Pierre Nepveu, known as Pierre Trinqueau, who is designated in the papers which preserve in some degree the history of the origin of the edifice, as the *maistre de l'œuvre de maçonnerie*. Behind this modest title, apparently, we must recognise one of the most original talents of the French Renaissance; and it is a proof of the vigour of the artistic life of that period that, brilliant production being everywhere abundant, an artist of so high a value should not have been treated by his contemporaries as a celebrity. We make our celebrities to-day at smaller cost.

The immediate successors of Francis I. continued to visit Chambord; but it was neglected by Henry IV. and was never afterwards a favourite residence of any French king. Louis XIV. appeared there on several occasions, and the apparition was characteristically brilliant; but Chambord could not long detain a monarch who had gone to the expense of creating a Versailles ten miles from Paris. With Versailles, Fontainebleau, Saint-Germain and Saint-Cloud within easy reach of their capital, the later French sovereigns had little reason to take the air in the dreariest province of their kingdom. Chambord therefore suffered from royal indifference, though in the last century a use was found for its deserted halls. In 1725 it was occupied by the luckless Stanislaus Leczynski, who spent the greater part of his life in being elected King of Poland and being ousted from his throne, and who, at this time a refugee in France, had found a compensation for some of his misfortunes in marrying his daughter to Louis XV. He lived eight years at Chambord and filled up the moats of the castle. In 1748 it found an illustrious tenant in the person of Maurice de Saxe, the victor of Fontenoy, who, however, two years after he had taken possession of it, terminated a life which would have been longer had he been less determined to make it agreeable. The Revolution, of course, was not kind to Chambord. It despoiled it in so far as possible of every vestige of its royal origin, and swept like a whirlwind through apartments to which upwards of two centuries had contributed a treasure of decoration and furniture. In that wild blast these precious things were destroyed or for ever scattered. In 1791 an odd proposal was made to the French Government by a company of English Quakers, who had conceived the bold idea of establishing in the palace a manufacture of some peaceful commodity not to-day recorded. Napoleon allotted Chambord, as a "dotation," to one of his marshals, Berthier, for whose benefit it was converted, in Napoleonic fashion, into the so-called principality of Wagram. By the Princess of Wagram, the marshal's widow, it was, after the Restoration, sold to the trustees of a national subscription which had been established for the purpose of presenting it to the infant Duke of Bordeaux, then prospective King of France. The presentation was duly made; but the Comte de Chambord, who had changed his title in recognition of the gift, was despoiled of his property by the government of Louis Philippe. He appealed for redress to the tribunals of his country; and the consequence of his appeal was an interminable litigation, by which, however, finally, after the lapse of twenty-five years, he was established in his rights. In 1871 he paid his first visit to the domain which had been offered him half a century before, a term of which he had spent forty years in exile. It was from Chambord that he dated his famous letter of the 5th of July of that year—the letter, directed to his so-called subjects, in which he waves aloft the white flag of the Bourbons. This rare miscalculation—virtually an invitation to the French people to repudiate, as their national ensign, that immortal tricolour, the flag of the Revolution and the Empire, under which they have won the glory which of all glories has hitherto been dearest to them and which is associated with the most romantic, the most heroic, the epic, the consolatory, period of their history—this luckless manifesto, I say, appears to give the measure of the political wisdom of the excellent Henry V. The proposal should have had less simplicity or the people less irony.

On the whole Chambord makes a great impression; and the hour I was there, while the yellow afternoon light slanted upon the September woods, there was a dignity in its desolation. It spoke, with a muffled but audible voice, of the vanished monarchy, which had been so strong, so splendid, but to-day had become a vision almost as fantastic as the cupolas and chimneys that rose before me. I thought, while I lingered there, of all the fine things it takes to make up such a monarchy; and how one of them is a superfluity of mouldering, empty palaces. Chambord is touching—that is the best word for it; and if the hopes of another restoration are in the follies of the Republic, a little reflection on that eloquence of ruin ought to put the Republic on its guard. A sentimental tourist may venture to remark that in presence of all the haunted houses that appeal in this mystical manner to the retrospective imagination it cannot afford to be foolish. I thought of all this as I drove back to Blois by the way of the Château de Cheverny. The road took us out of the park of Chambord, but through a region of flat woodland, where the trees were not mighty, and again into the prosy plain of the Sologne—a thankless soil to sow, I believe, but lately much amended by the magic of cheerful French industry and thrift. The light had already begun to fade, and my drive reminded me of a passage in some rural novel of Madame Sand. I passed a couple of timber and plaster churches, which looked very old, black and crooked, and had lumpish wooden porches and galleries encircling the base. By the time I reached Cheverny the clear twilight had approached. It was late to ask to be allowed to visit an inhabited house; but it was the hour at which I like best to visit almost anything. My coachman drew up before a gateway, in a high wall, which opened upon a short avenue, along which I took my way on foot; the coachmen in those parts being, for reasons best known to themselves, mortally averse to driving up to a house. I answered the challenge of a very tidy little portress who sat, in company with a couple of children, enjoying the evening air in front of her lodge, and who told me to walk a little farther and turn to the right. I obeyed her to the letter, and my turn brought me into sight of a house as charming as an old manor in a fairy tale. I had but a rapid and partial view of Cheverny; but that view was a glimpse of perfection. A light, sweet mansion stood looking over a wide green lawn, over banks of flowers and groups of trees. It had a striking character of elegance, produced partly by a series of Renaissance busts let into circular niches in the façade. The place looked so private, so reserved, that it seemed an act of violence to ring, a stranger and foreigner, at the graceful door. But if I had not rung I should be unable to express—as it is such a pleasure to do—my sense of the exceeding courtesy with which this admirable house is shown. It was near the dinner-hour—the most sacred hour of the day; but I was freely conducted into the inhabited apartments. They are extremely beautiful. What I chiefly remember is the charming staircase of white embroidered stone, and the great *salle des gardes* and *chambre à coucher du roi* on the second floor. Cheverny, built in 1634, is of a much later date than the other royal residences of this part of France; it belongs to the end of the Renaissance and has a touch of the rococo. The guard-room is a superb apartment; and as it contains little save its magnificent ceiling and fireplace and certain dim tapestries on its walls, you the more easily take the measure of its noble proportions. The servant opened the shutters of a single window, and the last rays of the twilight slanted into the rich brown gloom. It was in the same picturesque fashion that I saw the bedroom (adjoining) of Henry IV., where a legendary-looking bed, draped in folds long unaltered, defined itself in the haunted dusk. Cheverny remains to me a very charming, a partly mysterious vision. I drove back to Blois in the dark, some nine miles, through the forest of Russy, which belongs to the State and which, though consisting apparently of small timber, looked under the stars sufficiently vast and primeval. There was a damp autumnal smell and the occasional sound of a stirring thing; and as I moved through the evening air I thought of Francis I. and Henry IV.

Chaumont

Chapter VI

You MAY GO to Amboise either from Blois or from Tours; it is about half-way between these towns. The great point is to go, especially if you have put it off repeatedly; and to go, if possible, on a day when the great view of the Loire, which you enjoy from the battlements and terraces, presents itself under a friendly sky. Three persons, of whom the author of these lines was one, spent the greater part of a perfect Sunday morning in looking at it. It was astonishing, in the course of the rainiest season in the memory of the oldest Tourangeau, how many perfect days we found to our hand. The town of Amboise lies, like Tours, on the left bank of the river—a little white-faced town staring across an admirable bridge and leaning, behind, as it were, against the pedestal of rock on which the dark castle masses itself. The town is so small, the pedestal so big and the castle so high and striking, that the clustered houses at the base of the rock are like the crumbs that have fallen from a well-laden table. You pass among them, however, to ascend by a circuit to the château, which you attack, obliquely, from behind. It is the property of the Comte de

Paris, another pretender to the French throne; having come to him remotely, by inheritance, from his ancestor, the Duc de Penthièvre, who toward the close of the last century bought it from the Crown, which had recovered it after a lapse. Like the castle of Blois, it has been injured and defaced by base uses, but, unlike the castle of Blois, it has not been completely restored. "It is very, very dirty, but very curious"—it is in these terms that I heard it described by an English lady who was generally to be found engaged upon a tattered Tauchnitz in the little *salon de lecture* of the hotel at Tours. The description is not inaccurate; but it should be said that if part of the dirtiness of Amboise is the result of its having served for years as a barrack and as a prison, part of it comes from the presence of restoring stonemasons, who have woven over a considerable portion of it a mask of scaffolding. There is a good deal of neatness as well, and the restoration of some of the parts seems finished. This process, at Amboise, consists for the most part simply of removing the vulgar excrescences of the last two centuries.

The interior is virtually a blank, the old apartments having been chopped up into small modern rooms; it will have to be completely reconstructed. A worthy woman with a military profile and that sharp, positive manner which the goodwives who show you through the châteaux of Touraine are rather apt to have, and in whose high respectability, to say nothing of the frill of her cap and the cut of her thick brown dress, my companions and I thought we discovered the particular note, or *nuance*, of Orleanism—a competent, appreciative, peremptory person, I say—attended us through the particularly delightful hour we spent upon the ramparts of Amboise. Denuded and disfeatured within and bristling without with bricklayers' ladders, the place was yet extraordinarily impressive and interesting. I should mention that we spent a great deal of time in looking at the view. Sweet was the view, and magnificent; we preferred it so much to certain portions of the interior, and to occasional effusions of historical information, that the old lady with the profile sometimes lost patience with us. We laid ourselves open to the charge of preferring it even to the little chapel of Saint Hubert, which stands on the edge of the great terrace and has, over the portal, a wonderful

sculpture of the miraculous hunt of that holy man. In the way
of plastic art this elaborate scene is the gem of Amboise. It
seemed to us that we had never been in a place where there
are so many points of vantage to look down from. In the
matter of position Amboise is certainly supreme in the list of
perched places; and I say this with a proper recollection of the
claims of Chaumont and of Loches—which latter, by the way
(the afterthought is due), is not on the Loire. The platforms,
the bastions, the terraces, the high-niched windows and balconies, the hanging gardens and dizzy crenellations, of this
complicated structure, keep you in perpetual intercourse with
an immense horizon. The great feature of the place is the
obligatory round tower which occupies the northern end of
it, and which has now been completely restored. It is of astounding size, a fortress in itself, and contains, instead of a
staircase, a wonderful inclined plane, so wide and gradual that
a coach and four may be driven to the top. This colossal cylinder has to-day no visible use; but it corresponds, happily
enough, with the great circle of the prospect. The gardens of
Amboise, lifted high aloft, covering the irregular remnants of
the platform on which the castle stands and making up in
picturesqueness what they lack in extent, constitute of course
but a scanty domain. But bathed, as we found them, in the
autumn sunshine and doubly private from their aerial site,
they offered irresistible opportunities for a stroll interrupted,
as one leaned against their low parapets, by long contemplative pauses. I remember in particular a certain terrace planted
with clipped limes upon which we looked down from the
summit of the big tower. It seemed from that point to be
absolutely necessary to one's happiness to go down and spend
the rest of the morning there; it was an ideal place to walk to
and fro and talk. Our venerable conductress, to whom our
relation had gradually become more filial, permitted us to
gratify this innocent wish—to the extent, that is, of taking a
turn or two under the mossy *tilleuls*. At the end of this terrace
is the low door, in a wall, against the top of which, in 1498,
Charles VIII., according to an accepted tradition, knocked his
head to such good purpose that he died. It was within the
walls of Amboise that his widow, Anne of Brittany, already in
mourning for three children, two of whom we have seen

Amboise: the Chateau

commemorated in sepulchral marble at Tours, spent the first violence of that grief which was presently dispelled by a union with her husband's cousin and successor, Louis XII. Amboise was a frequent resort of the French Court during the six-teenth century; it was here that the young Mary Stuart spent sundry hours of her first marriage. The wars of religion have left here the ineffaceable stain which they left wherever they passed. An imaginative visitor at Amboise to-day may fancy that the traces of blood are mixed with the red rust on the crossed iron bars of the grim-looking balcony to which the heads of the Huguenots executed on the discovery of the conspiracy of La Renaudie are rumoured to have been suspended. There was room on the stout balustrade—an admirable piece of work—for a ghastly array. The same ru-mour represents Catherine de' Medici and the young queen as watching from this balcony the *noyades* of the captured Hu-guenots in the Loire. The facts of history are bad enough; the fictions are, if possible, worse; but there is little doubt that the future Queen of Scots learnt the first lessons of life at a horrible school. If in subsequent years she was a prodigy of innocence and virtue, it was not the fault of her whilom mother-in-law, of her uncles of the house of Guise, or of the examples presented to her either at the windows of the castle of Amboise or in its more private recesses.

It was difficult to believe in these dark deeds, however, as we looked through the golden morning at the placidity of the far-shining Loire. The ultimate consequence of this spectacle was a desire to follow the river as far as the castle of Chau-mont. It is true that the cruelties practised of old at Amboise might have seemed less phantasmal to persons destined to suf-fer from a modern form of inhumanity. The mistress of the little inn at the base of the castle-rock—it stands very pleas-antly beside the river, and we had breakfasted there—de-clared to us that the Château de Chaumont, which is often during the autumn closed to visitors, was at that particular moment standing so wide open to receive us that it was our duty to hire one of her carriages and drive thither with speed. This assurance was so satisfactory that we presently found ourselves seated in this wily woman's most commodious vehicle and rolling, neither too fast nor too slow, along the margin of the Loire. The drive of about an hour, beneath constant clumps of chestnuts, was charming enough to have been taken for itself; and indeed when we reached Chaumont we saw that our reward was to be simply the usual reward of virtue, the consciousness of having attempted the right. The Château de Chaumont was inexorably closed; so we learned from a talkative lodge-keeper, who gave what grace she could to her refusal. This good woman's dilemma was almost touching; she wished to reconcile two impossibles. The castle was not to be visited, for the family of its master was staying there; and yet she was loath to turn away a party of which she was good enough to say that it had a *grand genre*; for, as she also remarked, she had her living to earn. She tried to arrange a compromise, one of the elements of which was that we should descend from our carriage and trudge up a hill which would bring us to a designated point where, over the paling of the garden, we might obtain an oblique and surreptitious view of a small portion of the castle walls. This suggestion led us to inquire (of each other) to what degree of baseness it is lawful for an enlightened lover of the picturesque to resort in order not to have a blank page in his collection. One of our trio decided characteristically against any form of derogation; so she sat in the carriage and sketched some object that was public property while her two companions, who were not so proud, trudged up a muddy ascent which formed a kind of back-stairs. It is perhaps no more than they deserved that they were disappointed. Chaumont is feudal, if you please; but the modern spirit is in possession. It forms a vast clean-scraped mass, with big round towers, ungarnished with a leaf of ivy or a patch of moss, surrounded by gardens of moderate extent (save where the muddy lane of which I speak passes near it), and looking rather like an enormously magnified villa. The great merit of Chaumont is its position, which almost exactly resembles that of Amboise; it sweeps the river up and down and seems to look over half the province. This, however, was better appreciated as, after coming down the hill and re-entering the carriage, we drove across the long suspension-bridge which crosses the Loire just beyond the village and over which we made our way to the small station of Onzain, at the farther end, to take the train back to Tours. Look back from the middle of this bridge; the whole picture composes, as the painters say. The towers, the pinnacles, the fair front of the château, perched above its fringe of garden and the rusty roofs of the village and facing the afternoon sky, which is reflected also in the great stream that sweeps below, all this makes a contribution to your happiest memories of Touraine.

Chenonceaux

Chapter VII

WE NEVER went to Chinon; it was a fatality. We planned it a dozen times; but the weather interfered, or the trains didn't suit, or one of the party was fatigued with the adventures of the day before. This excursion was so much postponed that it was finally postponed to everything. Besides, we had to go to Chenonceaux, to Azay-le-Rideau, to Langeais, to Loches. So I have not the memory of Chinon; I have only the regret. But regret, as well as memory, has its visions; especially when, like memory, it is assisted by photographs. The castle of Chinon in this form appears to me as an enormous ruin, a mediæval fortress of the extent almost of a city. It covers a hill above the Vienne, and after being impregnable in its time is indestructible to-day. (I risk this phrase in the face of the prosaic truth. Chinon, in the days when it was a prize, more than once suffered capture, and at present it is crumbling inch by inch. It is apparent, however, I believe, that these inches encroach little upon acres of masonry.) It was in the castle that Jeanne Darc had her first interview with

67

Charles VII., and it is in the town that François Rabelais is supposed to have been born. To the castle, moreover, the lover of the picturesque is earnestly recommended to direct his steps. But one always misses something, and I would rather have missed Chinon than Chenonceaux. Fortunate exceedingly were the few hours we passed on the spot on which we missed nothing.

"In 1747," says Jean-Jacques Rousseau in his "Confessions," "we went to spend the autumn in Touraine, at the Château of Chenonceaux, a royal residence upon the Cher, built by Henry II. for Diana of Poitiers, whose initials are still to be seen there, and now in possession of M. Dupin, the farmer-general. We amused ourselves greatly at this fine place; the living was of the best, and I became as fat as a monk. We made a great deal of music and acted comedies."

This is the only description that Rousseau gives of one of the most romantic houses in France and of an episode that must have counted as one of the most agreeable in his uncomfortable career. The eighteenth century contented itself with general epithets; and when Jean-Jacques has said that Chenonceaux was a "beau lieu," he thinks himself absolved from further characterisation. We later sons of time have, both for our pleasure and our pain, invented the fashion of special terms, and I am afraid that even common decency obliges me to pay some larger tribute than this to the architectural gem of Touraine. Fortunately I can discharge my debt with gratitude. In going from Tours you leave the valley of the Loire and enter that of the Cher, and at the end of about an hour you see the turrets of the castle on your right, among the trees, down in the meadows, beside the quiet little river. The station and the village are about ten minutes' walk from the château, and the village contains a very tidy inn, where, if you are not in too great a hurry to commune with the shades of the royal favourite and the jealous queen, you will perhaps stop and order a dinner to be ready for you in the evening. A straight, tall avenue leads to the grounds of the castle; what I owe to exactitude compels me to add that it is crossed by the railway-line. The place is so arranged, however, that the château need know nothing of passing trains—which pass, indeed, though

Chenonceaux

the grounds are not large, at a very sufficient distance. I may add that the trains throughout this part of France have a noiseless, desultory, dawdling, almost stationary quality, which makes them less of an offence than usual. It was a Sunday afternoon and the light was yellow save under the trees of the avenue, where, in spite of the waning of September, it was duskily green. Three or four peasants, in festal attire, were strolling about. On a bench at the beginning of the avenue sat a man with two women. As I advanced with my companions he rose, after a sudden stare, and approached me with a smile in which (to be Johnsonian for a moment) certitude was mitigated by modesty and eagerness was embellished with respect. He came toward me with a salutation that I had seen before, and I am happy to say that after an instant I ceased to be guilty of the brutality of not knowing where. There was only one place in the world where people smile like that, only one place where the art of salutation has that perfect grace. This excellent creature used to crook his arm, in

Venice, when I stepped into my gondola; and I now laid my hand on that member with the familiarity of glad recognition; for it was only surprise that had kept me even for a moment from accepting the genial Francesco as an ornament of the landscape of Touraine. What on earth—the phrase is the right one—was a Venetian gondolier doing at Chenonceaux? He had been brought from Venice, gondola and all, by the mistress of the charming house, to paddle about on the Cher. Our meeting was affectionate, though there was a kind of violence in seeing him so far from home. He was too well dressed, too well fed; he had grown stout, and his nose had the tinge of good claret. He remarked that the life of the household to which he had the honour to belong was that of a *casa regia*; which must have been a great change for poor Checco, whose habits in Venice were not regal. However, he was the sympathetic Checco still; and for five minutes after I left him I thought less about the little pleasure-house by the Cher than about the palaces of the Adriatic.

But attention was not long in coming round to the charming structure that presently rose before us. The pale yellow front of the château, the small scale of which is at first a surprise, rises beyond a considerable court, at the entrance of which a massive and detached round tower, with a turret on its brow (a relic of the building that preceded the actual villa), appears to keep guard. This court is not enclosed—or is enclosed at least only by the gardens, portions of which are at present in process of radical readjustment. Therefore, though Chenonceaux has no great height, its delicate façade stands up boldly enough. This façade, one of the most finished things in Touraine, consists of two storeys, surmounted by an attic which, as so often in the buildings of the French Renaissance, is the richest part of the house. The high-pitched roof contains three windows of beautiful design, covered with embroidered caps and flowering into crocketed spires. The window above the door is deeply niched; it opens upon a balcony made in the form of a double pulpit—one of the most charming features of the front. Chenonceaux is not large, as I say, but into its delicate compass is packed a great deal of history—history which differs from that of Amboise and Blois in being of the private and sentimental kind. The echoes of the place, faint and far as they are to-day, are not political, but personal. Chenonceaux dates, as a residence, from the year 1515, when the shrewd Thomas Bohier, a public functionary who had grown rich in handling the finances of Normandy and had acquired the estate from a family which, after giving it many feudal lords, had fallen into poverty, erected the present structure on the foundations of an old mill. The design is attributed, with I know not what justice, to Pierre Nepveu, *alias* Trinqueau, the audacious architect of Chambord. On the death of Bohier the house passed to his son, who, however, was forced, under cruel pressure, to surrender it to the Crown in compensation for a so-called deficit in the official accounts of this rash parent and predecessor. Francis I. held the place till his death; but Henry II., on ascending the throne, presented it out of hand to that mature charmer, the admired of two generations, Diana of Poitiers. Diana enjoyed it till the death of her protector; but when this event occurred the widow of the monarch, who had been obliged to submit in silence, for years, to the ascendency of a rival, took the most pardonable of all the revenges with which the name of Catherine de' Medici is associated and turned her out of doors. Diana was not in want of refuges, and Catherine went through the form of giving her Chaumont in exchange; but there was only one Chenonceaux. Catherine devoted herself to making the place more completely unique. The feature that renders it sole of its kind is not appreciated till you wander round to either side of the house. If a certain springing lightness is the characteristic of Chenonceaux, if it bears in every line the aspect of a place of recreation—a place intended for delicate, chosen pleasures—nothing can confirm this expression better than the strange, unexpected movement with which, from behind, it carries itself across the river. The earlier building stands in the water; it had inherited the foundations of the mill destroyed by Thomas Bohier. The first step therefore had been taken upon solid piles of masonry; and the ingenious Catherine—she was a *raffinée*—simply proceeded to take the others. She continued the piles to the opposite bank of the Cher, and over them she threw a long, straight gallery of two tiers. This part of the château, which mainly resembles a house built upon a bridge and occupying its entire length, is of course the great curiosity of Chenonceaux. It forms on each floor a charming corridor, which, within, is illuminated from either side by the flickering riverlight. The architecture of these galleries, seen from without, is less elegant than that of the main building, but the aspect of the whole thing is delightful. I have spoken of Chenonceaux as a "villa," using the word advisedly, for the place is neither a castle nor a palace. It is a very exceptional villa, but it has the villa-quality—the look of being intended for life in common. This look is not at all contradicted by the wing across the Cher, which only suggests indoor perspectives and intimate pleasures—walks in pairs on rainy days; games and dances on autumn nights; together with as much as may be of moonlighted dialogue (or silence) in the course of evenings more genial still, in the well-marked recesses of windows.

It is safe to say that such things took place there in the last century, during the kindly reign of Monsieur and Madame Dupin. This period presents itself as the happiest in the annals of Chenonceaux. I know not what festive train the great Diana may have led, and my imagination, I am afraid, is only feebly kindled by the records of the luxurious pastimes organised on the banks of the Cher by that terrible daughter of the Medici whose appreciation of the good things of life was perfectly consistent with a failure to perceive why others should live to enjoy them. The best society that ever assembled there was collected at Chenonceaux during the middle of the eighteenth century. This was surely, in France at least, the age of good society, the period when the "right people" made every haste to be born in time. Such people must of course have belonged to the fortunate few—not to the miserable many; for if a society be large enough to be good, it must also be small enough. The sixty years that preceded the Revolution were the golden age of fireside talk and of those amenities that proceed from the presence of women in whom the social art is both instinctive and acquired. The women of that period were, above all, good company; the fact is attested in a thousand documents. Chenonceaux offered a perfect setting to free conversation; and infinite joyous discourse must have mingled with the liquid murmur of the Cher. Claude Dupin was not only a great man of business, but a man of honour and a patron of knowledge; and his wife was gracious, clever, and wise. They had acquired this famous property by purchase (from one of the Bourbons, as Chenonceaux, for two centuries after the death of Catherine de' Medici, remained constantly in princely hands), and it was transmitted to their son, Dupin de Francueil, grandfather of Madame George Sand. This lady, in her Correspondence, lately published, describes a visit that she paid more than thirty years ago to those members of her family who were still in possession. The owner of Chenonceaux to-day* is the daughter of an Englishman naturalised in France. But I have wandered far from my story, which is simply a sketch of the surface of the place. Seen obliquely, from either side, in combination with its bridge and gallery, the structure is singular and fantastic, a striking example of a wilful and capricious conception. Unfortunately all caprices are not so graceful and successful, and I grudge the honour of this one to the false and blood-polluted Catherine. (To be exact, I believe the arches of the bridge were laid by the elderly Diana. It was Catherine, however, who completed the monument.) Within, the house has been, as usual, restored. The staircases and ceilings, in all the old royal residences of this part of France, are the parts that have suffered least; many of them have still much of the life of the old time about them. Some of the chambers of Chenonceaux, however, encumbered as they are with modern detail, derive a sufficiently haunted and suggestive look from the deep setting of their beautiful windows, which thickens the shadows and makes dark corners. There is a charming little Gothic chapel, with its apse hanging over the water, fastened to the left flank of the house. Some of the upper balconies, which look along the outer face of the gallery and either up or down the river, are delightful protected nooks. We walked through the lower gallery to the other bank of the Cher; this fine apartment appeared to be for the moment a purgatory of ancient furniture. It terminates rather abruptly; it simply stops, with a blank wall. There ought, of course, to have been a pavilion here, though I prefer very much the old defect to any modern

*1884.

remedy. The wall is not so blank, however, but that it contains a door which opens on a rusty drawbridge. This drawbridge traverses the small gap which divides the end of the gallery from the bank of the stream. The house, therefore, does not literally rest on opposite edges of the Cher, but rests on one and just fails to rest on the other. The pavilion would have made that up; but after a moment we ceased to miss this imaginary feature. We passed the little drawbridge, and wandered awhile beside the river. From this opposite bank the mass of the château looked more charming than ever; and the little peaceful, lazy Cher, where two or three men were fishing in the eventide, flowed under the clear arches and between the solid pedestals of the part that spanned it, with the softest, vaguest light on its bosom. This was the right perspective; we were looking across the river of time. The whole scene was deliciously mild. The moon came up; we passed back through the gallery and strolled about a little longer in the gardens. It was very still. I met my old gondolier in the twilight. He showed me his gondola, but I hated, somehow, to see it there. I don't like, as the French say, to *mêler les genres*. A gondola in a little flat French river? The image was not less irritating, if less injurious, than the spectacle of a steamer in the Grand Canal, which had driven me away from Venice a year and a half before. We took our way back to the Bon Laboureur, and waited in the little inn-parlour for a late train to Tours. We were not impatient, for we had an excellent dinner to occupy us; and even after we had dined we were still content to sit awhile and exchange remarks upon the superior civilisation of France. Where else, at a village inn, should we have fared so well? Where else should we have sat down to our refreshment without condescension? There were a couple of countries in which it would not have been happy for us to arrive hungry, on a Sunday evening, at so modest an hostelry. At the little inn at Chenonceaux the *cuisine* was not only excellent, but the service was graceful. We were waited on by mademoiselle and her mamma; it was so that mademoiselle alluded to the elder lady as she uncorked for us a bottle of Vouvray mousseux. We were very comfortable, very genial; we even went so far as to say to each other that Vouvray mousseux was a delightful wine. From this opinion indeed one of our trio differed; but this member of the party had already exposed herself to the charge of being too fastidious by declining to descend from the carriage at Chaumont and take that back-stairs view of the castle.

Azay-le-Rideau

Chapter VIII

WITHOUT fastidiousness it was fair to declare on the other hand that the little inn at Azay-le-Rideau was very bad. It was terribly dirty and it was in charge of a fat *mégère* whom the appearance of four trustful travellers—we were four, with an illustrious fourth, on that occasion— roused apparently to fury. I attached great importance to this incongruous hostess, for she uttered the only uncivil words I heard spoken (in connection with any business of my own) during a tour of some six weeks in France. Breakfast not at Azay-le-Rideau therefore, too trustful traveller; or if you do so, be either very meek or very bold. Breakfast not, save under stress of circumstance; but let no circumstance whatever prevent your going to see the great house of the place, which is a fair rival to Chenonceaux. The village lies close to the gates, though after you pass these gates you leave it well behind. A little avenue, as at Chenonceaux, leads to the castle, making a pretty vista as you approach the sculptured doorway. Azay is a most perfect and beautiful thing; I should place it third in any list of the great houses of this part of

76

Azay-le-Rideau

France in which these houses should be ranked according to charm. For beauty of detail it comes after Blois and Chenonceaux, but it comes before Amboise and Chambord. On the other hand, of course it is inferior in majesty to either of these vast structures. Like Chenonceaux, it is a watery place, though it is more meagrely moated than the small château on the Cher. It consists of a large square *corps de logis*, with a round tower at each angle, rising out of a somewhat too slumberous pond. The water—the water of the Indre—surrounds it, but it is only on one side that it bathes its feet in the moat. On one of the others stretches a little terrace, treated as a garden, and in front prevails a wide court formed by a wing which, on the right, comes forward. This front, covered with sculptures, is of the richest, stateliest effect. The court is approached by a bridge over the pond, and the house would reflect itself in this wealth of water if the water were a trifle less opaque. But there is a certain stagnation—it affects more senses than one—about the picturesque pools of Azay. On the hither side of the bridge is a garden overshadowed by fine old sycamores—a garden shut in by greenhouses and by a fine last-century gateway flanked with twin lodges. Beyond the château and the standing waters behind it is a so-called *parc*, which, however, it must be confessed, has little of park-like beauty. The old houses—a large number—remain in France; but the old timber does not remain, and the denuded aspect of the few acres that surround the châteaux of Touraine is pitiful to the traveller who has learned to take the measure of such things from the country of "stately homes." The garden-ground of the lordly Chaumont is that of an English suburban villa; and in that and in other places there is little suggestion, in the untended aspect of walk and lawns, of the gardener the British Islands know. The manor as we see it dates from the early part of the sixteenth century; and the industrious Abbé Chevalier, in his very entertaining though slightly rose-coloured book on Touraine,* speaks of it as "perhaps the purest expression of the *belle Renaissance françoise.*" "Its height," he goes on "is divided between two storeys, terminating under the roof in a projecting entablature which

---

*"Promenades pittoresques en Touraine." Tours: 1869.

imitates a row of machicolations. Carven chimneys and tall dormer windows, covered with imagery, rise from the roofs; turrets on brackets, of elegant shape, hang with the greatest lightness from the angles of the building. The soberness of the main lines, the harmony of the empty spaces and those that are filled out, the prominence of the crowning parts, the delicacy of all the details, constitute an enchanting whole." And then the Abbé speaks of the admirable staircase which adorns the north front and which, with its extension inside, constitutes the principal treasure of Azay. The staircase passes beneath one of the richest of porticos— a portico over which a monumental salamander indulges in the most decorative contortions. The sculptured vaults of stone which cover the windings of the staircase within, the fruits, flowers, ciphers, heraldic signs, are of the noblest effect. The interior of the château is rich, comfortable, extremely modern; but it makes no picture that compares with its external face, about which, with its charming proportions, its profuse yet not extravagant sculpture, there is something very tranquil and pure. I took a particular fancy to the roof, high, steep, old, with its slope of bluish slate, and the way the weather-worn chimneys seemed to grow out of it—living things in a deep soil. The single defect of the house is the blankness and bareness of its walls, which have none of that delicate parasitic deposit that agrees so well—to the eye—with the surface of old dwellings. It is true that this bareness results in a kind of silvery whiteness of complexion which carries out the tone of the quiet pools and even that of the scanty and shadeless park.

Langeais

Chapter IX

I HARDLY know what to say about the tone of Langeais, which, though I have left it to the end of my sketch, formed the objective point of the first excursion I made from Tours. Langeais is rather dark and grey; it is perhaps the simplest and most severe of all the castles of the Loire. I don't know why I should have gone to see it before any other, unless it be because I remembered that Duchesse de Langeais who figures in several of Balzac's novels, and found this association very potent. The Duchesse de Langeais is a somewhat transparent fiction; but the castle from which Balzac borrowed the title of his heroine is an extremely solid fact. My doubt just above as to whether I should pronounce it exceptionally grey came from my having seen it under a sky which made most things look dark. I have, however, a very kindly memory of that moist and melancholy afternoon, which was much more autumnal than many of the days that followed it. Langeais lies down the Loire, near the river, on the opposite side from Tours, and to go to it you will spend half an hour in the train. You pass on the way the Château de Luynes, which,

with its round towers catching the afternoon light, looks uncommonly well on a hill at a distance; you pass also the ruins
of the castle of Cinq-Mars, the ancestral dwelling of the
young favourite of Louis XIII., the victim of Richelieu, the
hero of Alfred de Vigny's novel, which is usually recommended to young ladies engaged in the study of French.
Langeais is very imposing and decidedly sombre; it marks the
transition from the architecture of defence to that of elegance.
It rises, massive and perpendicular, out of the centre of the
village to which it gives its name and which it entirely domi-
nates; so that as you stand before it in the crooked and empty
street there is no resource for you but to stare up at its heavy
overhanging cornice and at the huge towers surmounted with
extinguishers of slate. If you follow this street to the end,
however, you encounter in abundance the usual embellishments of a French village: little ponds or tanks, with women
on their knees on the brink, pounding and thumping a lump
of saturated linen; brown old crones, the tone of whose facial
hide makes their nightcaps (worn by day) look dazzling; little
alleys perforating the thickness of a row of cottages and showing you behind, as a glimpse, the vividness of a green garden.
In the rear of the castle rises a hill which must formerly have
been occupied by some of its appurtenances and which indeed
is still partly enclosed within its court. You may walk round
this eminence, which, with the small houses of the village at
its base, shuts in the castle from behind. The enclosure is not
defiantly guarded, however; for a small, rough path, which
you presently reach, leads up to an open gate. This gate admits you to a vague and rather limited *parc*, which covers the
crest of the hill and through which you may walk into the
gardens of the castle. These gardens, of small extent, confront
the dark walls with their brilliant parterres and, covering the
gradual slope of the hill, form, as it were, the fourth side of
the court. This is the stateliest view of the structure, which
looks to you sufficiently grim and grey as, after asking leave of
a neat young woman who sallies out to learn your errand, you
sit there on a garden bench and take the measure of the three
tall towers attached to this inner front and forming severally
the cage of a staircase. The huge bracketed cornice (one of the
features of Langeais), which is merely ornamental, as it is not

machicolated, though it looks so, is continued on the inner face as well. The whole thing has a fine feudal air, though it was erected on the ruins of feudalism.

The main event in the history of the castle is the marriage of Anne of Brittany to her first husband, Charles VIII., which took place in its great hall in 1491. Into this great hall we were introduced by the neat young woman—into this great hall and into sundry other halls, winding staircases, galleries, chambers. The cicerone of Langeais is in too great a hurry; the fact is pointed out in the excellent Guide-Joanne. This ill-dissimulated vice, however, is to be observed, in the country of the Loire, in every one who carries a key. It is true that at Langeais there is no great occasion to indulge in the tourist's weakness of dawdling; for the apartments, though they contain many curious odds and ends of antiquity, are not of first-rate interest. They are cold and musty indeed, with that touching smell of old furniture, as all apartments should be through which the insatiate American wanders in the rear of a bored domestic, pausing to stare at a faded tapestry or to read the name on the frame of some simpering portrait.

To return to Tours my companion and I had counted on a train which (as is not uncommon in France) existed only in the "Indicateur des Chemins de Fer;" and instead of waiting for another we engaged a vehicle to take us home. A sorry *carriole* or *patache* it proved to be, with the accessories of a lumbering white mare and a little wizened, ancient peasant, who had put on, in honour of the occasion, a new blouse of extraordinary stiffness and blueness. We hired the trap of an energetic woman, who put it "to" with her own hands; women in Touraine and the Blésois appearing to have the best of it in the business of letting vehicles, as well as in many other industries. There is, in fact, no branch of human activity in which one is not liable, in France, to find a woman engaged. Women, indeed, are not priests; but priests are, more or less, women. They are not in the army, it may be said; but then they *are* the army. They are very formidable. In France one must count with the women. The drive back from Langeais to Tours was long, slow, cold; we had an occasional spatter of rain. But the road passes most of the way close to the Loire, and there was something in our jog-trot through the darkening land, beside the flowing river, which it was very possible to enjoy.

Loches

Chapter X

THE CONSEQUENCE of my leaving to the last my little mention of Loches is that space and opportunity fail me; and yet a brief and hurried account of that extraordinary spot would after all be in best agreement with my visit. We snatched a fearful joy, my companion and I, the afternoon we took the train for Loches. The weather this time had been terribly against us: again and again a day that promised fair became hopelessly foul after lunch. At last we determined that if we could not make this excursion in the sunshine we would make it with the aid of our umbrellas. We grasped them firmly and started for the station, where we were detained an unconscionable time by the evolutions, outside, of certain trains laden with liberated (and exhilarated) conscripts, who, their term of service ended, were about to be restored to civil life. The trains in Touraine are provoking; they serve as little as possible for excursions. If they convey you one way at the right hour, it is on the condition of bringing you back at the

Loches

wrong; they either allow you far too little time to examine the castle or the ruin, or they leave you planted in front of it for periods that outlast curiosity. They are perverse, capricious, exasperating. It was a question of our having but an hour or two at Loches, and we could ill afford to sacrifice to accidents. One of the accidents, however, was that the rain stopped before we got there, leaving behind it a moist mildness of temperature and a cool and lowering sky which were in perfect agreement with the grey old city. Loches is certainly one of the greatest impressions of the traveller in central France—the largest cluster of curious things that presents itself to his sight. It rises above the valley of the Indre, the charming stream set in meadows and sedges, which wanders through the province of Berry and through many of the novels of Madame George Sand; lifting from the summit of a hill, which it covers to the base, a confusion of terraces, ramparts, towers, and spires. Having but little time, as I say, we scaled the hill amain and wandered briskly through this labyrinth of antiquities. The rain had decidedly stopped and, save that we had our train on our minds, we saw Loches to the best advantage. We enjoyed that sensation with which the conscientious tourist is—or ought to be—well acquainted and for which, at any rate, he has a formula in his rough-and-ready language. We "experienced," as they say (most irregular of verbs), an "agreeable disappointment." We were surprised and delighted; we had for some reason suspected that Loches was scarce good.

I hardly know what is best there: the strange and impressive little collegial church, with its romanesque atrium or narthex, its doorways covered with primitive sculpture of the richest kind, its treasure of a so-called pagan altar embossed with fighting warriors, its three pyramidal domes, so unexpected, so sinister, which I have not met elsewhere in church architecture; or the huge square keep of the eleventh century—the most cliff-like tower I remember, whose immeasurable thickness I did not penetrate; or the subterranean mysteries of two other less striking but not less historic dungeons, into which a terribly imperative little cicerone introduced us, with the aid of downward ladders, ropes, torches, warnings, extended hands, and many fearful anecdotes—all in

Loches: the Church

impervious darkness. These horrible prisons of Loches, at an incredible distance below daylight, enlivened the consciousness of Louis XI. and were for the most part, I believe, constructed by him. One of the towers of the castle is garnished with the hooks or supports of the celebrated iron cage in which he confined the Cardinal La Balue, who survived so much longer than might have been expected this extraordinary mixture of seclusion and exposure. All these things form part of the castle of Loches, whose enormous *enceinte* covers the whole of the top of the hill and abounds in dismantled gateways, in crooked passages, in winding lanes that lead to postern doors, in long façades that look upon terraces interdicted to the visitor, who perceives with irritation that they command magnificent views. These views are the property of the sub-prefect of the department, who resides at the Château de Loches and who has also the enjoyment of a garden—a garden compressed and curtailed, as those of old castles that perch on hill-tops are apt to be—containing a horse-chestnut tree of fabulous size, a tree of a circumference so vast and so perfect that the whole population of Loches might sit in concentric rows beneath its boughs. The gem of the place, however, is neither the big *marronier*, nor the collegial church, nor the mighty dungeon, nor the hideous prisons of Louis XI.; it is simply the tomb of Agnes Sorel, *la belle des belles*, so many years the mistress of Charles VII. She was buried in 1450, in the collegial church, whence, in the beginning of the present century, her remains, with the monument that marks them, were transferred to one of the towers of the castle. She has always, I know not with what justice, enjoyed a fairer fame than most ladies who have occupied her position, and this fairness is expressed in the delicate statue that surmounts her tomb. It represents her lying there in lovely demureness, her hands folded with the best modesty, a little kneeling angel at either side of her head, and her feet, hidden in the folds of her decent robe, resting upon a pair of couchant lambs, innocent reminders of her name. Agnes, however, was not lamb-like, inasmuch as, according to popular tradition at least, she exerted herself sharply in favour of the expulsion of the English from France. It is one of the suggestions of Loches that the young Charles VII., hard put to it as he was for a treasury and a capital—"le roi de Bourges," he was called at Paris—was yet a rather privileged mortal, to stand up as he does before posterity between the noble Joan and the *gentille Agnès*; deriving, however, much more honour from one of these companions than from the other. Almost as delicate a relic of antiquity as this fascinating tomb is the exquisite oratory of Anne of Brittany, among the apartments of the castle the only chamber worthy of note. This small room, hardly larger than a closet, and forming part of the addition made to the edifice by Charles VIII., is embroidered over with the curious and remarkably decorative device of the ermine and festooned cord. The objects in themselves are not especially graceful, but the constant repetition of the figure on the walls and ceiling produces an effect of richness in spite of the modern whitewash with which, if I remember rightly, they have been endued. The little streets of Loches wander crookedly down the hill and are full of charming pictorial "bits:" an old town-gate, passing under a mediæval tower, which is ornamented by Gothic windows and the empty niches of statues; a meagre but delicate *hôtel de ville* of the Renaissance nestling close beside it; a curious *chancellerie* of the middle of the sixteenth century, with mythological figures and a Latin inscription on the front—both of these latter buildings being rather unexpected features of the huddled and precipitous little town. Loches has a suburb on the other side of the Indre, which we had contented ourselves with looking down at from the heights while we wondered whether, even if it had not been getting late and our train were more accommodating, we should care to take our way across the bridge and look up that bust in terra-cotta of Francis I. which is the principal ornament of the Château de Sansac and the faubourg of Beaulieu. I think we decided that we should not, that we had already often measured the longest nose in history.

Bourges

Chapter XI

I KNOW not whether the exact limits of an excursion as distinguished from a journey have ever been fixed; at any rate, it seemed none of my business at Tours to settle the question. Therefore, though the making of excursions had been the purpose of my stay, I thought it vain, while I started for Bourges, to determine to which category that little expedition might belong. It was not till the third day that I returned to Tours; and the distance, traversed for the most part after dark, was even greater than I had supposed. That, however, was partly the fault of a tiresome wait at Vierzon, where I had more than enough time to dine, very badly, at the *buffet* and to observe the proceedings of a family who had entered my railway carriage at Tours and had conversed unreservedly, for my benefit, all the way from that station—a family whom it entertained me to assign to the class of *petite noblesse de province*. Their noble origin was confirmed by the way they all "made *maigre*" in the refreshment-room (it happened to be a Friday), as if it had been possible to do anything else. They ate two or three omelets apiece and ever so many little cakes, while the positive, talkative mother watched her children as the waiter handed about the roast fowl. I was destined to share the secrets of this family to the end; for while I took my place in the empty train that was in waiting to convey us to Bourges the same vigilant woman pushed them all on top of me into my compartment, though the carriages on either side contained no travellers at all. It was better, I found, to have dined (even on omelets and little cakes) at the station at Vierzon than at the hotel at Bourges, which, when I reached it at nine o'clock at night, did not strike me as the prince of hotels. The inns in the smaller provincial towns in France are all, as the term is, commercial, and the *commis-voyageur* is in triumphant possession. I saw a great deal of him for several weeks after this; for he was apparently the only traveller in the southern provinces, and it was my daily fate to sit opposite to him at tables d'hôte and in railway trains. He may be known by two infallible signs—his hands are fat and he tucks his napkin into his shirt-collar. In spite of these idiosyncrasies, he seemed to me a reserved and inoffensive person, with singularly little of the demonstrative good-humour that he has been described as possessing. I saw no one who reminded me of Balzac's "illustre Gaudissart;" and indeed in the course of a month's journey through a large part of France I heard so little desultory conversation that I wondered whether a change had not come over the spirit of the people. They seemed to me as silent as Americans when Americans have not been "introduced," and infinitely less addicted to exchanging remarks in railway trains and at tables d'hôte than the colloquial and cursory English; a fact perhaps not worth mentioning were it not at variance with that reputation which the French have long enjoyed of being a pre-eminently sociable nation. The common report of the character of a people is, however, an indefinable product, and is apt to strike the traveller who observes for himself as very wide of the mark. The English, who have for ages been described (mainly by the French) as the dumb stiff, unapproachable race, present to-day a remarkable appearance of good-humour and garrulity and are distinguished by their facility of intercourse. On the other hand, any one who has seen half-a-dozen Frenchmen

pass a whole day together in a railway-carriage without breaking silence is forced to believe that the traditional reputation
of these gentlemen is simply the survival of some primitive
formula. It was true, doubtless, before the Revolution; but
there have been great changes since then. The question of
which is the better taste, to talk to strangers or to hold your
tongue, is a matter apart; I incline to believe that the French
reserve is the result of a more definite conception of social
behaviour. I allude to it only because it is at variance with the
national fame and at the same time compatible with a very
easy view of life in certain other directions. On some of these
latter points the Boule d'Or at Bourges was full of instruction; boasting as it did of a hall of reception in which, amid
old boots that had been brought to be cleaned, old linen that
was being sorted for the wash, and lamps of evil odour that
were awaiting replenishment, a strange, familiar, promiscuous
household life went forward. Small scullions in white caps
and aprons slept upon greasy benches; the Boots sat staring at
you while you fumbled, helpless, in a row of pigeon-holes, for
your candlestick or your key; and, amid the coming and going of the *commis-voyageurs*, a little sempstress bent over the
under-garments of the hostess—the latter being a heavy,
stern, silent woman, who looked at people very hard.

It was not to be looked at in that manner that one had
come all the way from Tours; so that within ten minutes after
my arrival I sallied out into the darkness to form somehow
and somewhere a happier relation. However late in the
evening I may arrive at a place, I never go to bed without my
impression. The natural place at Bourges to look for it seemed
to be the cathedral; which, moreover, was the only thing that
could account for my presence *dans cette galère*. I turned out
of a small square in front of the hotel and walked up a narrow, sloping street paved with big, rough stones and guiltless
of a footway. It was a splendid starlight night; the stillness of
a sleeping *ville de province* was over everything; I had the
whole place to myself. I turned to my right, at the top of the
street, where presently a short, vague lane brought me into
sight of the cathedral. I approached it obliquely, from behind;
it loomed up in the darkness above me enormous and sublime. It stands on the top of the large but not lofty eminence

over which Bourges is scattered—a very good position as French cathedrals go, for they are not all so nobly situated as Chartres and Laon. On the side on which I approached it (the south) it is tolerably well exposed, though the precinct is shabby; in front, it is rather too much shut in. These defects, however, it makes up for on the north side and behind, where it presents itself in the most admirable manner to the garden of the Archevêché, which has been arranged as a public walk, with the usual formal alleys of the *jardin français*. I must add that I appreciated these points only on the following day. As I stood there in the light of the stars, many of which had an autumnal sharpness, while others were shooting over the heavens, the huge, rugged vessel of the church overhung me in very much the same way as the black hull of a ship at sea would overhang a solitary swimmer. It seemed colossal, stupendous, a dark leviathan.

The next morning, which was lovely, I lost no time in going back to it, and found with satisfaction that the daylight did it no injury. The cathedral of Bourges is indeed magnificently huge, and if it is a good deal wanting in lightness and grace, it is perhaps only the more imposing. I read in the excellent handbook of M. Joanne that it was projected "*dès* 1172," but commenced only in the first years of the thirteenth century. "The nave," the writer adds, "was finished *tant bien que mal, faute de ressources*; the façade is of the thirteenth and fourteenth centuries in its lower part, and of the fourteenth in its upper." The allusion to the nave means the omission of the transepts. The west front consists of two vast but imperfect towers; one of which (the south) is immensely buttressed, so that its outline slopes forward like that of a pyramid. This is the taller of the two. If they had spires these towers would be prodigious; as it is, given the rest of the church, they are wanting in elevation. There are five deeply recessed portals, all in a row, each surmounted with a gable, the gable over the central door being exceptionally high. Above the porches, which give the measure of its width, the front rears itself, piles itself, on a great scale, carried up by galleries, arches, windows, sculptures, and supported by the extraordinarily thick buttresses of which I have spoken and which, though they embellish it with deep shadows thrown sidewise, do not improve its style. The portals, especially the middle one, are extremely interesting; they are covered with curious early sculptures. The middle one, however, I must describe alone. It has no less than six rows of figures—the others have four —some of which, notably the upper one, are still in their places. The arch at the top has three tiers of elaborate imagery. The upper of these is divided by the figure of Christ in judgment, of great size, stiff and terrible, with outstretched arms. On either side of him are ranged three or four angels, with the instruments of the Passion. Beneath him in the second frieze stands the angel of justice with the scales; and on either side of him is the vision of the last judgment. The good prepare, with infinite titillation and complacency, to ascend to the skies; while the bad are dragged, pushed, hurled, stuffed, crammed, into pits and caldrons of fire. There is a charming detail in this section. Beside the angel, on the right, where the wicked are the prey of demons, stands a little female figure, that of a child, who, with hands meekly folded and head gently raised, waits for the stern angel to decide upon her fate. In this fate, however, a dreadful big devil also takes a keen interest: he seems on the point of appropriating the tender creature; he has a face like a goat and an enormous hooked nose. But the angel gently lays a hand upon the shoulder of the little girl—the movement is full of dignity—as if to say: "No; she belongs to the other side." The frieze below represents the general resurrection, with the good and the wicked emerging from their sepulchres. Nothing can be more quaint and charming than the difference shown in their way of responding to the final trump. The good get out of their tombs with a certain modest gaiety, an alacrity tempered by respect; one of them kneels to pray as soon as he has disinterred himself. You may know the wicked, on the other hand, by their extreme shyness; they crawl out slowly and fearfully; they hang back, and seem to say "Oh, dear!" These elaborate sculptures, full of ingenuous intention and of the reality of early faith, are in a remarkable state of preservation; they bear no superficial signs of restoration and appear scarcely to have suffered from the centuries. They are delightfully expressive; the artist had the advantage of knowing exactly the effect he wished to produce.

The interior of the cathedral has a great simplicity and majesty and, above all, a tremendous height. The nave is extraordinary in this respect; it dwarfs everything else I know. I should add, however, that I am in architecture always of the opinion of the last speaker. Any great building seems to me while I look at it the ultimate expression. At any rate, during the hour that I sat gazing along the high vista of Bourges the interior of the great vessel corresponded to my vision of the evening before. There is a tranquil largeness, a kind of infinitude, about such an edifice; it soothes and purifies the spirit, it illuminates the mind. There are two aisles, on either side, in addition to the nave—five in all--and, as I have said, there are no transepts; an omission which lengthens the vista, so that from my place near the door the central jewelled window in the depths of the perpendicular choir seemed a mile or two away. The second or outward of each pair of aisles is too low and the first too high; without this inequality the nave would appear to take an even more prodigious flight. The double aisles pass all the way round the choir, the windows of which are inordinately rich in magnificent old glass. I have seen glass as fine in other churches, but I think I have never seen so much of it at once.

Beside the cathedral, on the north, is a curious structure of the fourteenth or fifteenth century, which looks like an enormous flying buttress, with its support, sustaining the north tower. It makes a massive arch, high in the air, and produces a romantic effect as people pass under it to the open gardens of the Archevêché, which extend to a considerable distance in the rear of the church. The structure supporting the arch has the girth of a largeish house, and contains chambers with whose uses I am unacquainted, but to which the deep pulsations of the cathedral, the vibration of its mighty bells and the roll of its organ-tones must be transmitted even through the great arm of stone.

The archiepiscopal palace, not walled in as at Tours, is visible as a stately habitation of the last century, at the time of my visit under repair after a fire. From this side and from the gardens of the palace the nave of the cathedral is visible in all its great length and height, with its extraordinary multitude of supports. The gardens aforesaid, accessible through tall iron gates, are the promenade—the Tuileries—of the town, and, very pretty in themselves, are immensely set off by the overhanging church. It was warm and sunny; the benches were empty; I sat there a long time in that pleasant state of mind which visits the traveller in foreign towns, when he is not too hurried, while he wonders where he had better go next. The straight, unbroken line of the roof of the cathedral was very noble; but I could see from this point how much finer the effect would have been if the towers, which had dropped almost out of sight, might have been carried still higher. The archiepiscopal gardens look down at one end over a sort of esplanade or suburban avenue lying on a lower level on which they open, and where several detachments of soldiers (Bourges is full of soldiers) had just been drawn up. The civil population was also collecting, and I saw that something was going to happen. I learned that a private of the Chasseurs was to be "broken" for stealing, and every one was eager to behold the ceremony. Sundry other detachments arrived on the ground, besides many of the military who had come as a matter of taste. One of them described to me the process of degradation from the ranks, and I felt for a moment a hideous curiosity to see it, under the influence of which I lingered a little. But only a little; the hateful nature of the spectacle hurried me away at the same that others were hurrying forward. As I turned my back upon it I reflected that human beings are cruel brutes, though I could not flatter myself that the ferocity of the thing was exclusively French. In another country the concourse would have been equally great, and the moral of it all seemed to be that military penalties are as terrible as military honours are gratifying.

Bourges: the Hôtel Lallemont

Chapter XII

THE CATHEDRAL is not the only lion of Bourges; the house of Jacques Cœur awaits you in posture scarcely less leonine. This remarkable man had a very strange history, and he too was "broken" like the wretched soldier whom I did not stay to see. He has been rehabilitated, however, by an age which does not fear the imputation of paradox, and a marble statue of him ornaments the street in front of his house. To interpret him according to this image—a womanish figure in a long robe and a turban, with big bare arms and a dramatic pose—would be to think of him as a kind of truculent sultana. He wore the dress of his period, but his spirit was very modern; he was a Vanderbilt or a Rothschild of the fifteenth century. He supplied the ungrateful Charles VII. with money to pay the troops who, under the heroic Maid, drove the English from French soil. His house, which to-day is used as a Palais de Justice, appears to have been regarded at the time it was built very much as the residence of Mr. Vanderbilt is regarded in New York to-day. It stands on the edge of the hill on which most of the town is planted, so that, behind, it plunges down to a lower level, and, if you approach it on that side, as I did, to come round to the front of it you have to ascend a longish flight of steps. The back, of old, must have formed a portion of the city wall; at any rate it offers to view two big towers which Joanne says were formerly part of the defence of Bourges. From the lower level of which I speak—the square in front of the post-office—the palace of Jacques Cœur looks very big and strong and feudal; from the upper street, in front of it, it looks very handsome and delicate. To this street it presents two tiers and a considerable length of façade; and it has both within and without a great deal of curious and beautiful detail. Above the portal, in the stonework, are two false windows, in which two figures, a man and a woman, apparently household servants, are represented, in sculpture, as looking down into the street. The effect is homely, yet grotesque, and the figures are sufficiently living to make one commiserate them for having been condemned, in so dull a town, to spend several centuries at the window. They appear to be watching for the return of their master, who left his beautiful house one morning and never came back.

The history of Jacques Cœur, which has been written by M. Pierre Clément in a volume crowned by the French Academy, is very wonderful and interesting, but I have no space to go into it here. There is no more curious example, and few more tragical, of a great fortune crumbling from one day to the other, or of the antique superstition that the gods grow jealous of human success. Merchant, millionaire, banker, shipowner, royal favourite and minister of finance, explorer of the East and monopolist of the glittering trade between that quarter of the globe and his own, great capitalist who had anticipated the brilliant operations of the present time, he expiated his prosperity by poverty, imprisonment, and torture. The obscure points in his career have been elucidated by M. Clément, who has drawn, moreover, a very vivid picture of the corrupt and exhausted state of France during the middle of the fifteenth century. He has shown that the spoliation of the great merchant was a deliberately calculated act, and that

Bourges: the House of Jacques Cœur

the king sacrificed him without scruple or shame to the avidity of a singularly villanous set of courtiers. The whole story is
an extraordinary picture of high-handed rapacity—the crud-
est possible assertion of the right of the stronger. The victim
was stripped of his property, but escaped with his life, made
his way out of France and, betaking himself to Italy, offered
his services to the Pope. It is proof of the consideration that
he enjoyed in Europe, and of the variety of his accomplish-
ments, that Calixtus III. should have appointed him to take
command of a fleet which his Holiness was fitting out against
the Turks. Jacques Cœur, however, was not destined to lead it
to victory. He died shortly after the expedition had started, in
the island of Chios, in 1456. The house at Bourges, his native
place, testifies in some degree to his wealth and splendour,
though it has in parts that want of space which is striking in
many of the buildings of the Middle Ages. The court indeed
is on a large scale, ornamented with turrets and arcades, with
several beautiful windows and with sculptures inserted in the
walls, representing the various sources of the great fortune of
the owner. M. Pierre Clément describes this part of the house
as having been of an "incomparable richesse"—an estimate of
its charms which seems slightly exaggerated to-day. There is,
however, something delicate and familiar in the bas-reliefs of
which I have spoken, little scenes of agriculture and industry
which show that the proprietor was not ashamed of calling
attention to his harvests and enterprises. To-day we should
question the taste of such allusions, even in plastic form, in
the house of a "merchant prince" however self-made. Why
should it be, accordingly, that these quaint little panels at
Bourges do not displease us? It is perhaps because things very
ancient never, for some mysterious reason, appear vulgar.
This fifteenth-century millionaire, with his palace, his "swagger" sculptures, may have produced that impression on some
critical spirits of his own day.

The portress who showed me into the building was a dear
little old woman, with the gentlest, sweetest, saddest face—a
little white, aged face, with dark, pretty eyes—and the most
considerate manner. She took me up into an upper hall,
where there were a couple of curious chimney-pieces and a
fine old oaken roof, the latter representing the hollow of a

Bourges: Doorway, House of Jacques Cœur

long boat. There is a certain oddity in a native of
Bourges—an inland town if ever there was one, without even
a river (to call a river) to encourage nautical ambitions—having found his end as admiral of a fleet; but this boat-shaped
roof, which is extremely graceful and is repeated in another
apartment, would suggest that the imagination of Jacques
Cœur was fond of riding the waves. Indeed, as he trafficked
in Oriental products and owned many galleons, it is probable
that he was personally as much at home in certain Mediterranean ports as in the capital of the pastoral Berry. If, when he
looked at the ceilings of his mansion, he saw his boats upside
down, this was only a suggestion of the shortest way of emp-
tying them of their treasures. He is presented in person above
one of the great stone chimney-pieces, in company with his
wife, Macée de Léodepart—I like to write such an extraordinary name. Carved in white stone, the two sit playing at chess
at an open window, through which they appear to give their
attention much more to the passers-by than to the game.
They are also exhibited in other attitudes; though I do not
recognise them in the composition on top of one of the fireplaces which represents the battlements of a castle, with the
defenders (little figures between the crenellations) hurling
down missiles with a great deal of fury and expression. It
would have been hard to believe that the man who surrounded himself with these friendly and humorous devices
had been guilty of such wrong-doing as to call down the
heavy hand of justice.

It is a curious fact, however, that Bourges contains legal
associations of a purer kind than the prosecution of Jacques
Cœur, which, in spite of the rehabilitations of history, can
hardly be said yet to have terminated, inasmuch as the law-
courts of the city are installed in his quondam residence. At a
short distance from it stands the Hôtel Cujas, one of the curiosities of Bourges and the habitation for many years of the
great jurisconsult who revived in the sixteenth century the
study of the Roman law and professed it during the close of
his life in the university of the capital of Berry. The learned
Cujas had, in spite of his sedentary pursuits, led a very wandering life; he died at Bourges in the year 1590. Sedentary
pursuits are perhaps not exactly what I should call them,

having read in the "Biographie Universelle" (sole source of my knowledge of the renowned Cujacius) that his usual manner of study was to spread himself on his belly on the floor. He did not sit down, he lay down; and the "Biographie Universelle" has (for so grave a work) an amusing picture of the short, fat, untidy scholar dragging himself *à plat ventre*, across his room, from one pile of books to the other. The house in which these singular gymnastics took place, and which is now the headquarters of the gendarmerie, is one of the most picturesque at Bourges. Dilapidated and discoloured, it has a charming Renaissance front. A high wall separates it from the street, and on this wall, which is divided by a large open gateway, are perched two overhanging turrets. The open gateway admits you to the court, beyond which the melancholy mansion erects itself, decorated also with turrets, with fine old windows and with a beautiful tone of faded red brick and rusty stone. It is a charming encounter for a provincial by-street; one of those accidents in the hope of which the traveller with a propensity for sketching (whether on a little paper block or on the tablets of his brain) decides to turn a corner at a venture. A brawny gendarme in his shirt-sleeves was polishing his boots in the court; an ancient, knotted vine, forlorn of its clusters, hung itself over a doorway and dropped its shadow on the rough grain of the wall. The place was very sketchable. I am sorry to say, however, that it was almost the only "bit." Various other curious old houses are supposed to exist at Bourges, and I wandered vaguely about in search of them. But I had little success, and I ended by becoming sceptical. Bourges is a *ville de province* in the full force of the term, especially as applied invidiously. The streets, narrow, tortuous, and dirty, have very wide cobble-stones; the houses for the most part are shabby, without local colour. The look of things is neither modern nor antique—a kind of mediocrity of middle age. There is an enormous number of blank walls—walls of gardens, of courts, of private houses—that avert themselves from the street as if in natural chagrin at there being so little to see. Round about is a dull, flat, featureless country, on which the magnificent cathedral looks down. There is a peculiar dulness and ugliness in a French town of this type, which, I must immediately add, is not the most frequent one. In Italy everything has a charm, a colour, a grace; even desolation and ennui. In England a cathedral city may be sleepy, but it is pretty sure to be mellow. In the course of six weeks spent *en province*, however, I saw few places that had not more expression than Bourges.

I went back to the cathedral; that, after all, was a feature. Then I returned to my hotel, where it was time to dine, and sat down, as usual, with the *commis-voyageurs*, who cut their bread on their thumb and partook of every course; and after this repast I repaired for a while to the café, which occupied a part of the basement of the inn and opened into its court. This café was a friendly, homely, sociable spot, where it seemed the habit of the master of the establishment to *tutoyer* his customers and the practice of the customers to *tutoyer* the waiter. Under these circumstances the waiter of course felt justified in sitting down at the same table with a gentleman who had come in and asked him for writing materials. He served this gentleman with a horrible little portfolio covered with shiny black cloth and accompanied with two sheets of thin paper, three wafers, and one of those instruments of torture which pass in France for pens—these being the utensils invariably evoked by such a request; and then, finding himself at leisure, he placed himself opposite and began to write a letter of his own. This trifling incident reminded me afresh that France is a democratic country. I think I received an admonition to the same effect from the free, familiar way in which the game of whist was going on just behind me. It was attended with a great deal of noisy pleasantry, flavoured every now and then with a dash of irritation. There was a young man of whom I made a note; he was such a beautiful specimen of his class. Sometimes he was very facetious, chattering, joking, punning, showing off; then, as the game went on and he lost and had to pay the *consommation*, he dropped his amiability, slanged his partner, declared he wouldn't play any more, and went away in a fury. Nothing could be more perfect or more amusing than the contrast. The manner of the whole affair was such as, I apprehend, one would not have seen among our English-speaking people; both the jauntiness of the first phase and the petulance of the second. To hold the balance straight, however, I may remark that if the men were

Bourges: the Cathedral (West Front)

all fearful "cads," they were, with their cigarettes and their inconsistency, less heavy, less brutal, than our dear English-speaking cad; just as the bright little café where a robust ma-terfamilias, doling out sugar and darning a stocking, sat in her place under the mirror behind the *comptoir*, was a much more civilised spot than a British public-house or a "commercial room," with pipes and whisky, or even than an American saloon.

Le Mans

Chapter XIII

IT IS very certain that when I left Tours for Le Mans it was a journey and not an excursion; for I had no intention of coming back. The question indeed was to get away, no easy matter in France in the early days of October, when the whole *jeunesse* of the country is returning to school. It is accompanied, apparently, with parents and grandparents, and it fills the trains with little pale-faced *lycéens*, who gaze out of the windows with a longing, lingering air not unnatural on the part of small members of a race in which life is intense, who are about to be restored to those big educative barracks that do such violence to our American appreciation of the opportunities of boyhood. The train stopped every five minutes; but fortunately the country was charming—hilly and bosky, eminently good-humoured, and dotted here and there with a smart little château. The old capital of the province of the Maine, which has given its name to a great American State, is a fairly interesting town, but I confess that I found in it less than I expected to admire. My expectations had doubtless been my own fault; there is no particular reason why Le Mans should fascinate. It stands upon a hill, indeed—a much better

hill than the gentle swell of Bourges. This hill, however, is
not steep in all directions; from the railway, as I arrived, it
was not even perceptible. Since I am making comparisons, I
may remark that, on the other hand, the Boule d'Or at Le
Mans is an appreciably better inn than the Boule d'Or at
Bourges. It looks out upon a small market-place which has a
certain amount of character and seems to be slipping down
the slope on which it lies, though it has in the middle an ugly
halle, or circular market-house, to keep it in position. At Le
Mans, as at Bourges, my first business was with the cathedral,
to which I lost no time in directing my steps. It suffered by
juxtaposition to the great church I had seen a few days before; yet it has some noble features. It stands on the edge of
the eminence of the town, which falls straight away on two
sides of it, and makes a striking mass, bristling behind, as you
see it from below, with rather small but singularly numerous
flying buttresses. On my way to it I happened to walk
through the one street which contains a few ancient and curious houses, a very crooked and untidy lane, of really mediæval
aspect, honoured with the denomination of the Grand' Rue.
Here is the house of Queen Berengaria—an absurd name, as
the building is of a date some three hundred years later than
the wife of Richard Cœur de Lion, who has a sepulchral
monument in the south aisle of the cathedral. The structure in
question—very sketchable, if the sketcher could get far
enough away from it—is an elaborate little dusky façade,
overhanging the street, ornamented with panels of stone,
which are covered with delicate Renaissance sculpture. A fat
old woman standing in the door of a small grocer's shop next
to it—a most gracious old woman, with a bristling moustache and a charming manner—told me what the house was,
and also indicated to me a rotten-looking brown wooden
mansion in the same street, nearer the cathedral, as the Maison Scarron. The author of the "Roman Comique" and of a
thousand facetious verses enjoyed for some years, in the early
part of his life, a benefice in the cathedral of Le Mans, which
gave him a right to reside in one of the canonical houses. He
was rather an odd canon, but his history is a combination of
oddities. He wooed the comic muse from the arm-chair of a
cripple, and in the same position—he was unable even to go

down on his knees—prosecuted that other suit which made him the first husband of a lady of whom Louis XIV. was to be the second. There was little of comedy in the future Madame de Maintenon; though, after all, there was doubtless as much as there need have been in the wife of a poor man who was moved to compose for his tomb such an epitaph as this, which I quote from the "Biographie Universelle":

"Celui qui cy maintenant dort,
Fit plus de pitié que d'envie,
Et souffrit mille fois la mort,
Avant que de perdre la vie.
Passant, ne fais icy de bruit,
Et garde bien qu'il ne s'éveille,
Car voicy la première nuit,
Que le pauvre Scarron sommeille."

There is rather a quiet, satisfactory *place* in front of the cathedral, with some good "bits" in it; notably a turret at the angle of one of the towers and a very fine steep-roofed dwelling, behind low walls, which it overlooks, with a tall iron gate. This house has two or three little pointed towers, a big black, precipitous roof, and a general air of having had a history. There are houses which are scenes, and there are houses which are only houses. The trouble with the domestic architecture of the United States is that it is not scenic, thank goodness, and the characteristic of an old structure like the turreted mansion on the hillside of Le Mans is that it is not simply a house. It is a person, as it were, as well. It would be well, indeed, if it might have communicated a little of its personality to the front of the cathedral, which has none of its own. Shabby, rusty, unfinished, this front has a romanesque portal, but nothing in the way of a tower. One sees from without, at a glance, the peculiarity of the church—the disparity between the romanesque nave, which is small and of the twelfth century, and the immense and splendid transepts and choir, of a period a hundred years later. Outside, this end of the church rises far above the nave, which looks merely like a long porch leading to it, with a small and curious romanesque porch in its own south flank. The transepts, shallow but very lofty, display to the spectators in the *place* the reach of their two clere-storey windows, which occupy, above, the whole expanse of the wall. The south transept terminates in a sort of tower, which is the only one of which the cathedral can boast. Within, the effect of the choir is superb; it is a church in itself, with the nave simply for a point of view. As I stood there I read in my Murray that it has the stamp of the date of the perfection of pointed Gothic, and I found nothing to object to the remark. It suffers little by confrontation with Bourges and, taken in itself, seems to me quite as fine. A passage of double aisles surrounds it, with the arches that divide them supported on very thick round columns, not clustered. There are twelve chapels in this passage, and a charming little lady-chapel filled with gorgeous old glass. The sustained height of this almost detached choir is very noble; its lightness and grace, its soaring symmetry, carry the eye up to places in the air from which it is slow to descend. Like Tours, like Chartres, like Bourges (apparently like all the French cathedrals, and unlike several English ones), Le Mans is rich in splendid glass. The beautiful upper windows of the choir make, far aloft, a brave gallery of pictures, blooming with vivid colour. It is the south transept that contains the formless image—a clumsy stone woman lying on her back—which purports to represent Queen Berengaria aforesaid.

The view of the cathedral from the rear is, as usual, very fine. A small garden behind it masks its base; but you descend the hill to a large *place de foire*, adjacent to a fine old public promenade which is known as Les Jacobins, a sort of miniature Tuileries, where I strolled for a while in rectangular alleys destitute of herbage and received a deeper impression of vanished things. The cathedral, on the pedestal of its hill, looks considerably farther than the fair-ground and the Jacobins, between the rather bare poles of whose straightly planted trees you may admire it at a convenient distance. I admired it till I thought I should remember it (better than the event has proved), and then I wandered away and looked at another curious old church, Notre-Dame-de-la-Couture. This sacred edifice made a picture for ten minutes, but the picture has faded now. I reconstruct a yellowish-brown façade and a portal fretted with early sculptures; but the details have gone the

Le Mans: the Cathedral

way of all incomplete sensations. After you have stood awhile, in the choir of the cathedral there is no sensation at Le Mans that goes very far. For some reason not now to be traced I had looked for more than this. I think the reason was to some extent simply in the name of the place; for names, on the whole, whether they be good reasons or not, are very active ones. Le Mans, if I am not mistaken, has a sturdy, feudal sound; suggests something dark and square, a vision of old ramparts and gates. Perhaps I had been unduly impressed by the fact, accidentally revealed to me, that Henry II., first of the English Plantagenets, was born there. Of course it is easy to assure one's self in advance, but does it not often happen that one had rather not be assured? There is a pleasure sometimes in running the risk of disappointment. I took mine, such as it was, quietly enough, while I sat before dinner at the door of one of the cafés in the market-place with a *bitter-et-curaçao* (invaluable pretext at such an hour!) to keep me company. I remember that in this situation there came over me an impression which both included and excluded all possible disappointments. The afternoon was warm and still; the air was admirably soft. The good Manceaux, in little groups and pairs, were seated near me; my ear was soothed by the fine shades of French enunciation, by the detached syllables of that perfect tongue. There was nothing in particular in the prospect to charm; it was an average French view. Yet I felt a charm, a kind of sympathy, a sense of the completeness of French life and of the lightness and brightness of the social air, together with a desire to arrive at friendly judgments, to express a positive interest. I know not why this transcendental mood should have descended upon me then and there; but that idle half-hour in front of the café, in the mild October afternoon suffused with human sounds, is perhaps the most abiding thing I brought away from Le Mans.

Angers: the Castle

Chapter XIV

I AM shocked at finding, just after this noble declaration of principles, that in a little note-book which at that time I carried about with me the celebrated city of Angers is denominated a "sell." I reproduce this vulgar word with the greatest hesitation, and only because it brings me more quickly to my point. This point is that Angers belongs to the disagreeable class of old towns that have been, as the English say, "done up." Not the oldness, but the newness, of the place is what strikes the sentimental tourist to-day, as he wanders with irritation along second-rate boulevards, looking vaguely about him for absent gables. "Black Angers," in short, is a victim of modern improvements and quite unworthy of its admirable name—a name which, like that of Le Mans, had always had, to my eyes, a highly picturesque value. It looks particularly well on the Shakespearean page (in "King John"), where we imagine it uttered (though such would not have been the utterance of the period) with a fine grinding insular accent. Angers figures with importance in early English history: it was the capital city of the Plantagenet race, home of that Geoffrey of Anjou who married, as second husband, the Empress Maud, daughter of Henry I. and competitor of Stephen, and became father of Henry II., first of the Plantagenet kings, born, as we have seen, at Le Mans. These facts create a natural presumption that Angers will look historic; I turned them over in my mind as I travelled in the train from Le Mans, through a country that was really pretty and looked more like the usual English than like the usual French scenery, with its fields cut up by hedges and a considerable rotundity in its trees. On my way from the station to the hotel, however, it became plain that I should lack a good pretext for passing that night at the Cheval Blanc; I foresaw that I should have contented myself before the end of the day. I remained at the White Horse only long enough to discover that it was an exceptionally good provincial inn, one of the best that I encountered during six weeks spent in these establishments.

"Stupidly and vulgarly modernised"—that is another flower from my note-book, and note-books are not obliged to be reasonable. "There are some narrow and tortuous streets, with a few curious old houses," I continue to quote; "there is a castle, of which the exterior is most extraordinary, and there is a cathedral of moderate interest." It is fair to say that the Château d'Angers is by itself worth a pilgrimage; the only drawback is that you have seen it in a quarter of an hour. You cannot do more than look at it, and one good look does your business. It has no beauty, no grace, no detail, nothing that

charms or detains you; it is simply very old and very big—so
big and so old that this simple impression is enough, and it
takes its place in your recollections as a perfect specimen of a
superannuated stronghold. It stands at one end of the town,
surrounded by a huge, deep moat, which originally contained
the waters of the Maine, now divided from it by a quay. The
water-front of Angers is poor—wanting in colour and in
movement; and there is always an effect of perversity in a
town lying near a great river and yet not upon it. The Loire is
a few miles off; but Angers contents itself with a meagre af-
fluent of that stream. The effect was naturally much better
when the vast dark bulk of the castle, with its seventeen prodigious towers, rose out of the protecting flood. These towers
are of tremendous girth and solidity; they are encircled with
great bands, or hoops, of white stone, and are much enlarged
at the base. Between them hang high curtains of infinitely
old-looking masonry, apparently a dense conglomeration of
slate, the material of which the town was originally built
(thanks to rich quarries in the neighbourhood), and to which
it owed its appellation of the Black. There are no windows,
no apertures, and to-day no battlements nor roofs. These accessories were removed by Henry III., so that, in spite of its
grimness and blackness, the place has not even the interest of
looking like a prison; it being, as I suppose, the essence of a
prison not to be open to the sky. The only features of the
enormous structure are the blank, sombre stretches and protrusions of wall, the effect of which, on so large a scale, is
strange and striking. Begun by Philip Augustus and terminated by St. Louis, the Château d'Angers has of course a
great deal of history. The luckless Fouquet, the extravagant
minister of finance of Louis XIV., whose fall from the heights
of grandeur was so sudden and complete, was confined here
in 1661, just after his arrest, which had taken place at Nantes.
Here also Huguenots and Vendeans suffered effective cap-
tivity.

I walked round the parapet which protects the outer edge
of the moat (it is all up-hill, and the moat deepens and deepens), till I came to the entrance which faces the town, and
which is as bare and strong as the rest. The concierge took me
into the court; but there was nothing to see. The place is used

as a magazine of ammunition, and the yard contains a multi-tude of ugly buildings. The only thing to do is to walk round the bastions for the view; but at the moment of my visit the weather was thick, and the bastions began and ended with themselves. So I came out and took another look at the big, black exterior, buttressed with white-ribbed towers, and per-ceived that a desperate sketcher might extract a picture from it, especially if he were to bring in, as they say, the little black bronze statue of the good King René (a weak production of David d'Angers), which, standing within sight, ornaments the melancholy faubourg. He would do much better, however, with the very striking old timbered house (I suppose of the fifteenth century) which is called the Maison d'Adam and is easily the first specimen at Angers of the domestic architecture of the past. This admirable house, in the centre of the town, gabled, elaborately timbered, and much restored, is a really imposing monument. The basement is occupied by a linen-draper, who flourishes under the auspicious sign of the Mère de Famille; and above his shop the tall front rises in five over-hanging storeys. As the house occupies the angle of a little *place*, this front is double, and the black beams and wooden supports, displayed over a large surface and carved and inter-laced, have a high picturesqueness. The Maison d'Adam is quite in the grand style, and I am sorry to say I failed to learn what history attaches to its name. If I spoke just above of the cathedral as "moderate," I suppose I should beg its pardon; for this serious charge was probably prompted by the fact that it consists only of a nave, without side aisles. A little reflection now convinces me that such a form is a distinction; and in-deed I find it mentioned, rather inconsistently, in my note-book, a little further on, as "extremely simple and grand." The nave is spoken of in the same volume as "big, serious, and Gothic," though the choir and transepts are noted as very shallow. But it is not denied that the air of the whole thing is original and striking; and it would therefore appear, after all, that the cathedral of Angers, built during the twelfth and thir-teenth centuries, is a sufficiently honourable church; the more that its high west front, adorned with a very primitive Gothic portal, supports two elegant tapering spires, between which, unfortunately, an ugly modern pavilion has been inserted.

Angers: Old Timbered Houses

I remember nothing else at Angers but the curious old Café Serin, where, after I had had my dinner at the inn, I went and waited for the train which, at nine o'clock in the evening, was to convey me, in a couple of hours, to Nantes—an establishment remarkable for its great size and its air of tarnished splendour, its brown gilding and smoky frescoes, as also for the fact that it was hidden away on the second floor of an unassuming house in an unilluminated street. It hardly seemed a place where you would drop in; but when once you had found it, it presented itself, with the cathedral, the castle, and the Maison d'Adam, as one of the historical monuments of Angers.

Nantes: the Quay

Chapter XV

IF I spent two nights at Nantes, it was for reasons of convenience rather than of sentiment; though indeed I spent them in a big circular room which had a stately, lofty, last-century look—a look that consoled me a little for the whole place being dirty. The high, old-fashioned inn (it had a huge windy *porte-cochère*, and you climbed a vast black stone staircase to get to your room) looked out on a dull square, surrounded with other tall houses and occupied on one side by the theatre, a pompous building decorated with columns and statues of the muses. Nantes belongs to the class of towns which are always spoken of as "fine," and its position near the mouth of the Loire gives it, I believe, much commercial movement. It is a spacious, rather regular city, looking, in the parts that I traversed, neither very fresh nor very venerable. It derives its principal character from the handsome quays on the Loire, which are overhung with tall eighteenth-century houses (very numerous too in the other streets)—houses with big *entresols* marked by arched windows, classic pediments, balcony-rails of fine old iron-work. These features exist in still better form at Bordeaux; but, putting Bordeaux aside, Nantes is quite architectural. The view up and down the quays has the cool, neutral tone of colour that one finds so often in French water-side places—the bright greyness which is the tone of French landscape art. The whole city has rather a grand, or at least an eminently well-established, air. During a day passed in it of course I had time to go to the Musée; the more so that I have a weakness for provincial museums—a sentiment that depends but little on the quality of the collection. The pictures may be bad, but the place is often curious; and indeed from bad pictures, in certain moods of the mind, there is a degree of entertainment to be derived. If they are tolerably old they are often touching; but they must have a relative antiquity, for I confess I can do nothing with works of art of which the badness is of recent origin. The cool, still, empty chambers in which indifferent collections are apt to be preserved, the red brick tiles, the diffused light, the musty odour, the mementos around you of dead fashions, the snuffy custodian in a black skull-cap, who pulls aside a faded curtain to show you the lustreless gem of the museum—these things have a mild historical quality, and the sallow canvases after all illustrate something. Many of those in the museum of Nantes illustrate the taste of a successful warrior, having been bequeathed to the city by Napoleon's marshal Clarke (created Duc de Feltre). In addition to these there is the usual number of specimens of the contemporary French school, culled from the annual Salons and presented to the museum by the State. Wherever the traveller goes, in France, he is reminded of this very honourable practice—the purchase by the Government of a certain number of "pictures of the year," which are presently distributed in the provinces. Governments succeed each other and bid for success by different devices; but the "patronage of art" is a plank, as we should say here, in every platform. The works of art are often ill-selected—there is an official taste which you immediately recognise—but the custom is essentially liberal, and a Government which should neglect it would be felt to be painfully common. The only thing in this particular Musée that I remember is a fine portrait of a woman by Ingres—very flat and Chinese, but with an interest of line and a great deal of style.

There is a castle at Nantes which resembles in some degree that of Angers, but has, without, much less of the impressiveness of great size, and, within, much more interest of detail. The court contains the remains of a very fine piece of late Gothic—a tall elegant building of the sixteenth century. The château is naturally not wanting in history. It was the residence of the old Dukes of Brittany, and was brought, with the rest of the province, by the Duchess Anne, the last representative of that race, as her dowry, to Charles VIII. I read in the excellent handbook of M. Joanne that it has been visited by almost every one of the kings of France, from Louis XI. downward; and also that it has served as a place of sojourn less voluntary on the part of various other distinguished persons, from the horrible Maréchal de Retz, who in the fifteenth century was executed at Nantes for the murder of a couple of hundred young children, sacrificed in abominable rites, to the ardent Duchess of Berry, mother of the Count of Chambord, who was confined there for a few hours in 1832, just after her arrest in a neighbouring house. I looked at the house in question—you may see it from the platform in front of the château—and tried to figure to myself that embarrassing scene. The Duchess, after having unsuccessfully raised the standard of revolt (for the exiled Bourbons) in the legitimist Bretagne, and being "wanted," as the phrase is, by the police of Louis Philippe, had hidden herself in a small but loyal house at Nantes, where, at the end of five months of seclusion, she was betrayed, for gold, to the austere M. Guizot by one of her servants, an Alsatian Jew named Deutz. For many hours before her capture she had been compressed into an interstice behind a fireplace, and by the time she was drawn forth into the light she had been ominously scorched. The man who showed me the castle indicated also another historic spot, a house with little *tourelles* on the Quai de la Fosse, in which Henry IV. is said to have signed the Edict revoked by Louis XIV. I am, however, not in a position to answer for this pedigree.

There is another point in the history of the fine old houses which command the Loire, of which, I suppose, one may be tolerably sure; that is their having, placid as they stand there to-day, looked down on the horrors of the Terror of 1793, the bloody reign of the monster Carrier and his infamous *no-yades*. The most hideous episode of the Revolution was en-acted at Nantes, where hundreds of men and women, tied together in couples, were set afloat upon rafts and sunk to the bottom of the Loire. The tall eighteenth-century house, full of the *air noble*, in France always reminds me of those dreadful years—of the street-scenes of the Revolution. Su-perficially, the association is incongruous, for nothing could be more formal and decorous than the patent expression of these eligible residences. But whenever I have a vision of prisoners bound on tumbrels that jolt slowly to the scaffold, of heads carried on pikes, of groups of heated *citoyennes* shaking their fists at closed coach-windows, I see in the background the well-ordered features of the architecture of the period—the clear grey stone, the high pilasters, the arch-ing lines of the *entresol*, the classic pediment, the slate-covered attic. There is not much architecture at Nantes except the domestic. The cathedral, with a rough west front and stunted towers, makes no impression as you approach it. It is true that it does its best to recover its reputation as soon as you have passed the threshold. Begun in 1434 and finished about the end of the fifteenth century, as I discover in Murray, it has a magnificent nave, not of great length, but of extraordinary height and lightness. On the other hand, it has no choir whatever. There is much entertainment in France in seeing what a cathedral will take upon itself to possess or to lack; for it is only the smaller number that have the full complement of features. Some have a very fine nave and no choir; others a very fine choir and no nave. Some have a rich outside and nothing within; others a very blank face and a very glowing heart. There are a hundred possi-bilities of poverty and wealth, and they make the most un-expected combinations.

The great treasure of Nantes is the two noble sepulchral monuments which occupy either transept, and one of which has (in its nobleness) the rare distinction of being a produc-tion of our own time. On the south side stands the tomb of Francis II., the last of the Dukes of Brittany, and of his sec-ond wife, Margaret of Foix, erected in 1507 by their daughter Anne, whom we have encountered already at the Château de

Nantes, where she was born; at Langeais, where she married her first husband; at Amboise, where she lost him; at Blois, where she married her second, the "good" Louis XII., who divorced an impeccable spouse to make room for her, and where she herself died. Transferred to the cathedral from a demolished convent, this monument, the masterpiece of Michel Colomb, author of the charming tomb of the children of Charles VIII. and the aforesaid Anne, which we admired at Saint Gatien of Tours, is one of the most brilliant works of the French Renaissance. It has a splendid effect and is in perfect preservation. A great table of black marble supports the reclining figures of the duke and duchess, who lie there peacefully and majestically, in their robes and crowns, with their heads each on a cushion, the pair of which are supported from behind by three charming little kneeling angels; at the foot of the quiet couple are a lion and a greyhound, with heraldic devices. At each of the angles of the table is a large figure in white marble of a woman elaborately dressed, with a symbolic meaning, and these figures, with their contemporary faces and clothes, which give them the air of realistic portraits, are truthful and living, if not remarkably beautiful. Round the sides of the tomb are small images of the apostles. There is a kind of masculine completeness in the work, and a certain robustness of taste.

In nothing were the sculptors of the Renaissance more fortunate than in being in advance of us with their tombs: they have left us nothing to say in regard to the great final contrast—the contrast between the immobility of death and the trappings and honours that survive. They expressed in every way in which it was possible to express it the solemnity of their conviction that the marble image was a part of the personal greatness of the defunct, and the protection, the redemption, of his memory. A modern tomb, in comparison, is a sceptical affair; it insists too little on the honours. I say this in the face of the fact that one has only to step across the cathedral of Nantes to stand in the presence of one of the purest and most touching of modern tombs. Catholic Brittany has erected in the opposite transept a monument to one of the most devoted of her sons, General de Lamoricière, the defender of the Pope, the vanquished of Castelfidardo. This noble work, from the hand of Paul Dubois, one of the most interesting of that new generation of sculptors who have revived in France an art of which our over-dressed century had begun to despair, has every merit but the absence of a certain prime feeling. It is the echo of an earlier tune—an echo with a beautiful cadence. Under a Renaissance canopy of white marble elaborately worked with arabesques and cherubs, in a relief so low that it gives the work a certain look of being softened and worn by time, lies the body of the Breton soldier with a crucifix clasped to his breast and a shroud thrown over his body. At each of the angles sits a figure in bronze, the two best of which, representing Charity and Military Courage, had given me extraordinary pleasure when they were exhibited (in the clay) in the Salon of 1876. They are admirably cast and not less admirably conceived: the one a serene, robust young mother, beautiful in line and attitude; the other a lean and vigilant young man, in a helmet that overshadows his serious eyes, resting an outstretched arm, an admirable military member, upon the hilt of a sword. These figures contain abundant assurance that M. Paul Dubois has been attentive to Michael Angelo, whom we have all heard called a splendid example and a bad model. The visor-shadowed face of his warrior is more or less a reminiscence of the figure on the tomb of Lorenzo de' Medici at Florence; but it is doubtless none the worse for that. The interest of the work of Paul Dubois is its peculiar seriousness, a kind of moral good faith which is not the commonest feature of French art, and which, united as it is in this case with exceeding knowledge and a remarkable sense of form, produces an impression of deep refinement. The whole monument is a proof of exquisitely careful study; but I am not sure that this impression on the part of the spectator is the happiest possible. It explains much of the great beauty, and it also explains perhaps a little of the slight pedantry. That word, however, is scarcely in place; I only mean that M. Dubois has made a visible effort, which has visibly triumphed. Simplicity is not always strength, and our complicated modern genius contains treasures of intention. This fathomless modern element is an immense charm on the part of M. Paul Dubois. I am lost in admiration of the deep æsthetic experience, the enlightenment of taste, revealed by such work. After that I only hope that Giuseppe Garibaldi may have somewhere or other some commemoration as distinguished.

La Rochelle: Tour de la Lanterne

Chapter XVI

To go from Nantes to La Rochelle you travel straight southward across the historic *bocage* of La Vendée, the home of royalist bush-fighting. The country, which is exceedingly pretty, bristles with copses, orchards, hedges, and with trees more spreading and sturdy than the traveller is apt to find the feathery foliage of France. It is true that as I proceeded it flattened out a good deal, so that for an hour there was a vast featureless plain, which offered me little entertainment beyond the general impression that I was approaching the Bay of Biscay (from which, in reality, I was yet far distant). As we drew near La Rochelle, however, the prospect brightened considerably, and the railway kept its course beside a charming little canal, or canalised river, bordered with trees and with small, neat, bright-coloured and yet old-fashioned cottages and villas, which stood back, on the farther side, behind small gardens, hedges, painted palings, patches of turf. The whole effect was Dutch and delightful; and in being delightful, though not in being Dutch, it prepared me for the charms of La Rochelle, which from the moment I entered it I perceived to be a fascinating little town, a quite original mixture of brightness and dulness. Part of its brightness comes from its being extraordinarily clean—in which, after all, it *is* Dutch; a virtue not particularly noticeable at Bourges, Le Mans, and Angers. Whenever I go southward, if it be only twenty miles, I begin to look out for the south, prepared as I am to find the careless grace of those latitudes even in things of which it may be said that they may be south of something, but are not southern. To go from Boston to New York (in this state of mind) is almost as soft a sensation as descending the Italian side of the Alps; and to go from New York to Philadelphia is to enter a zone of tropical luxuriance and warmth. Given this absurd disposition, I could not fail to flatter myself, on reaching La Rochelle, that I was already in the Midi, and to perceive in everything, in the language of the country, the *caractère méridional*. Really a great many things had a hint of it. For that matter it seems to me that to arrive in the south at a bound—to wake up there, as it were—would be a very imperfect pleasure. The full pleasure is to approach by stages and gradations; to observe the successive shades of difference by which it ceases to be the north. These shades are exceedingly fine, but your true south-lover has an eye for them all. If he perceives them at New York and Philadelphia—we imagine him boldly as liberated from Boston—how could he fail to perceive them at La Rochelle? The streets of this dear little city are lined with arcades—good, big, straddling arcades of stone, such as befit a land of hot summers and which recalled to me, not to go further, the dusky porticos of Bayonne. It contains, moreover, a great wide *place d'armes* which looked for all the world like the piazza of some dead Italian town, empty, sunny, grass-grown, with a row of yellow houses overhanging it, an unfrequented café with a striped awning, a tall, cold, florid, uninteresting cathedral of the eighteenth century on one side, and on the other a shady walk which forms part of an old rampart. I followed this walk for some time, under the stunted trees, beside the grass-covered bastions; it is very charming, winding and wandering, always with trees. Beneath the rampart is a tidal river, and on the other side, for a long distance, the mossy walls of the immense garden of a seminary. Three

hundred years ago La Rochelle was the great French stronghold of Protestantism, but to-day it appears to be a nursery of
Papists.

The walk upon the rampart led me round to one of the
gates of the town, where I found some small modern fortifications and sundry red-legged soldiers, and, beyond the fortifications, another shady walk—a *mail*, as the French say, as
well as a *champ de manœuvre*—on which latter expanse the
poor little red-legs were doing their exercise. It was all very
quiet and very picturesque, rather in miniature; and at once
very tidy and a little out of repair. This, however, was but a
meagre back-view of La Rochelle, or poor side-view at best.
There are other gates than the small fortified aperture just
mentioned; one of them, an old grey arch beneath a fine
clock-tower, I had passed through on my way from the station. This substantial Tour de l'Horloge separates the town
proper from the port; for beyond the old grey arch the place
presents its bright, expressive little face to the sea. I had a
charming walk about the harbour and along the stone piers
and sea-walls that shut it in. This indeed, to take things in
their order, was after I had had my breakfast (which I took on
arriving) and after I had been to the *hôtel de ville*. The inn had
a long narrow garden behind it, with some very tall trees; and
passing through this garden to a dim and secluded *salle à
manger*, buried in the heavy shade, I had, while I sat at my
repast, a feeling of seclusion which amounted almost to a
sense of incarceration. I lost this sense, however, after I had
paid my bill, and went out to look for traces of the famous
siege, which is the principal title of La Rochelle to renown. I
had come thither partly because I thought it would be interesting to stand for a few moments in so gallant a spot, and
partly because, I confess, I had a curiosity to see what had
been the starting-point of the Huguenot emigrants who
founded the town of New Rochelle in the State of New York,
a place in which I had passed sundry memorable hours. It was
strange to think, as I strolled through the peaceful little port,
that these quiet waters, during the wars of religion, had
swelled with a formidable naval power. The Rochelais had
fleets and admirals, and their stout little Protestant bottoms
carried defiance up and down.

La Rochelle

To say that I found any traces of the siege would be to misrepresent the taste for vivid whitewash by which La Rochelle is distinguished to-day. The only trace is the dent in the marble top of the table on which, in the *hôtel de ville*, Jean Guiton, the mayor of the city, brought down his dagger with an oath when in 1628 the vessels and regiments of Richelieu closed about it on sea and land. This terrible functionary was the soul of the resistance; he held out from February to October in the midst of pestilence and famine. The whole episode has a brilliant place among the sieges of history; it has been related a hundred times, and I may only glance at it and pass. I limit my ambition in these light pages to speaking of those things of which I have personally received an impression, and I have no such impression of the defence of La Rochelle. The *hôtel de ville* is a pretty little building, in the style of the Renaissance of Francis I.; but it has left much of its interest in the hands of the restorers. It has been "done up" without mercy; its natural place would be at Rochelle the New. A sort of battlemented curtain, flanked with turrets, divides it from the street and contains a low door (a low door in a high wall is always felicitous), which admits you to an inner court, where you discover the face of the building. It has statues set into it and is raised upon a very low and very deep arcade. The principal function of the deferential old portress who conducts you over the place is to call your attention to the indented table of Jean Guiton; but she shows you other objects of interest besides. The interior is absolutely new and extremely sumptuous, abounding in tapestries, upholstery, morocco, velvet, satin. This is especially the case with a really beautiful *grande salle*, where, surrounded with the most expensive upholstery, the mayor holds his official receptions. (So at least said my worthy portress.) The mayors of La Rochelle appear to have changed a good deal since the days of the grim Guiton; but these evidences of municipal splendour are interesting for the light they throw on French manners. Imagine the mayor of an English or an American town of twenty thousand inhabitants holding magisterial soirées in the town hall! The said *grande salle*, which is unchanged in form and in its larger features, is, I believe, the room in which the Rochelais debated as to whether they should shut themselves

La Rochelle: the Hôtel de Ville

up, and decided in the affirmative. The table and chair of Jean Guiton have been restored, like everything else, and are very elegant and coquettish pieces of furniture—incongruous relics of a season of starvation and blood. I believe that Protestantism is somewhat shrunken to-day at La Rochelle, and has taken refuge mainly in the *haute société* and in a single place of worship. There was nothing particular to remind me of its supposed austerity as, after leaving the *hôtel de ville*, I walked along the empty porticos and out of the Tour de l'Horloge, which I have already mentioned. If I stopped and looked up at this venerable monument, it was not to ascertain the hour, for I foresaw that I should have more time at La Rochelle than I knew what to do with; but because its high, grey, weather-beaten face was an obvious subject for a sketch.

The little port, which has two basins and is accessible only to vessels of light tonnage, had a certain gaiety and as much local colour as you please. Fisher-folk of picturesque type were strolling about, most of them Bretons; several of the men with handsome, simple faces, not at all brutal, and with a splendid brownness—the golden-brown colour on cheek and beard that you see on an old Venetian sail. It was a squally, showery day, with sudden drizzles of sunshine; rows of rich-toned fishing-smacks were drawn up along the quays. The harbour is effective to the eye by reason of three battered old towers which at different points overhang it and look infinitely weather-washed and sea-silvered. The most striking of these, the Tour de la Lanterne, is a big grey mass of the fifteenth century, flanked with turrets and crowned with a Gothic steeple. I found it was called by the people of the place the Tour des Quatre Sergents, though I know not what connection it has with the touching history of the four young sergeants of the garrison of La Rochelle who were arrested in 1821 as conspirators against the Government of the Bourbons, and executed, amid general indignation, in Paris in the following year. The quaint little walk, with its label of Rue sur les Murs, to which one ascends from beside the Grosse Horloge, leads to this curious Tour de la Lanterne and passes under it. This walk has the top of the old town-wall, towards the sea, for a parapet on one side, and is bordered on the other with decent but irregular little tenements of fishermen, where brown old women, whose caps are as white as if they were painted, seem chiefly in possession. In this direction there is a very pretty stretch of shore, out of the town, through the fortifications (which are Vauban's, by the way); through, also, a diminutive public garden or straggling shrubbery which edges the water and carries its stunted verdure as far as a big Établissement des Bains. It was too late in the year to bathe, and the Établissement had the bankrupt aspect which belongs to such places out of the season; so I turned my back upon it and gained, by a circuit in the course of which there were sundry water-side items to observe, the other side of the cheery little port, where there is a long breakwater and a still longer sea-wall, on which I walked a while, to inhale the strong, salt breath of the Bay of Biscay. La Rochelle serves, in the months of July and August, as a *station de bains* for a modest provincial society; and, putting aside the question of inns, it must be charming on summer afternoons.

Poitiers: the Cathedral

Chapter XVII

IT IS an injustice to Poitiers to approach her by night, as I
did some three hours after leaving La Rochelle; for what
Poitiers has of best, as they would say at Poitiers, is the appearance she presents to the arriving stranger who puts his
head out of the window of the train. I gazed into the gloom
from such an aperture before we got into the station, for I
remembered the impression received on another occasion; but
I saw nothing save the universal night, spotted here and there
with an ugly railway lamp. It was only as I departed, the following day, that I assured myself that Poitiers still makes
something of the figure she ought on the summit of her considerable hill. I have a kindness for any little group of towers,
any cluster of roofs and chimneys, that lift themselves from an
eminence over which a long road ascends in zigzags; such a
picture creates for the moment a presumption that you are in
Italy, and even leads you to believe that if you mount the
winding road you will come to an old town-wall, an expanse
of creviced brownness, and pass under a gateway surmounted

by the arms of a mediæval despot. Why I should find it a pleasure in France to imagine myself in Italy, is more than I can say; the illusion has never lasted long enough to be analysed. From the bottom of its perch Poitiers looks large and high; and indeed, the evening I reached it, the interminable climb of the omnibus of the hotel I had selected, which I found at the station, gave me the measure of its commanding position. This hotel, "magnifique construction ornée de statues," as the Guide-Joanne, usually so reticent, takes the trouble to announce, has an omnibus, and, I suppose, has statues, though I didn't perceive them; but it has very little else save immemorial accumulations of dirt. It is magnificent, if you will, but it is not even relatively proper; and a dirty inn has always seemed to me the dirtiest of human things—it has so many opportunities to betray itself.

Poitiers covers a large space, and is as crooked and straggling as you please; but these advantages are not accompanied with any very salient features or any great wealth of architecture. Although there are few picturesque houses, however, there are two or three curious old churches. Notre Dame la Grande, in the market-place, a small romanesque structure of the twelfth century, has a most interesting and venerable exterior. Composed, like all the churches of Poitiers, of a light brown stone with a yellowish tinge, it is covered with primitive but ingenious sculptures, and is really an impressive monument. Within, it has lately been daubed over with the most hideous decorative painting that was ever inflicted upon passive pillars and indifferent vaults. This battered yet coherent little edifice has the touching look that resides in everything supremely old; it has arrived at the age at which such things cease to feel the years; the waves of time have worn its edges to a kind of patient dulness; there is something mild and smooth, like the stillness, the deafness, of an octogenarian, even in its rudeness of ornament, and it has become insensible to differences of a century or two. The cathedral interested me much less than Our Lady the Great, and I have not the spirit to go into statistics about it. It is not statistical to say that the cathedral stands half-way down the hill of Poitiers, in a quiet and grass-grown *place*, with an approach of crooked lanes and blank garden-walls, and that its most striking dimension is the width of its façade. This width is extraordinary, but it fails, somehow, to give nobleness to the edifice, which looks within (Murray makes the remark) like a large public hall. There are a nave and two aisles, the latter about as high as the nave; and there are some very fearful modern pictures, which you may see much better than you usually see those specimens of the old masters that lurk in glowing side-chapels, there being no fine old glass to diffuse a kindly gloom. The sacristan of the cathedral showed me something much better than all this bright bareness; he led me a short distance out of it to the small Temple de Saint-Jean, which is the most curious object at Poitiers. It is an early Christian chapel, one of the earliest in France; originally, it would seem—that is, in the sixth or seventh century—a baptistery, but converted into a church while the Christian era was still comparatively young. The Temple de Saint-Jean is therefore a monument even more venerable than Notre Dame la Grande, and that numbness of age which I imputed to Notre Dame ought to reside in still larger measure in its crude and colourless little walls. I call them crude, in spite of their having been baked through by the centuries, only because, although certain rude arches and carvings are let into them and they are surmounted at either end with a small gable, they have (so far as I can remember) little fascination of surface. Notre Dame is still expressive, still pretends to be alive; but the temple has delivered its message and is completely at rest. It retains a kind of atrium, on the level of the street, from which you descend to the original floor, now uncovered, but buried for years under a false bottom. A semicircular apse was, apparently at the time of its conversion into a church, thrown out from the east wall. In the middle is the cavity of the old baptismal font. The walls and vaults are covered with traces of extremely archaic frescoes, attributed, I believe, to the twelfth century. These vague, gaunt, staring fragments of figures are, to a certain extent, a reminder of some of the early Christian churches in Rome; they even faintly recalled to me the great mosaics of Ravenna. The Temple de Saint-Jean has neither the antiquity nor the completeness of those extraordinary monuments, nearly the most impressive in Europe; but, as one may say, it is very well for Poitiers.

Not far from it, in a lonely corner which was animated for the moment by the vociferations of several old women who were selling tapers, presumably for the occasion of a particular devotion, is the graceful romanesque church erected in the twelfth century to Saint Radegonde—a lady who found means to be a saint even in the capacity of a Merovingian queen. It bears a general resemblance to Notre Dame la Grande, and, as I remember it, is corrugated in somewhat the same manner with porous-looking carvings; but I confess that what I chiefly recollect is the row of old women sitting in front of it, each with a tray of waxen tapers in her lap, and upbraiding me for my neglect of the opportunity to offer such a tribute to the saint. I know not whether this privilege is occasional or constant; within the church there was no appearance of a festival, and I see that the name-day of Saint Radegonde occurs in August, so that the importunate old women sit there always perhaps and deprive of its propriety the epithet I just applied to this provincial corner. In spite of the old women, however, I suspect that the place is lonely; and indeed it is perhaps the old women who have made the desolation.

The lion of Poitiers in the eyes of the natives is doubtless the Palais de Justice, in the shadow of which the statue-guarded hotel, just mentioned, erects itself; and the gem of the court-house, which has a prosy modern front, with pillars and a high flight of steps, is the curious *salle des pas perdus*, or central hall, out of which the different tribunals open. This is a feature of every French court-house, and seems the result of a conviction that a palace of justice—the French deal in much finer names than we—should be in some degree palatial. The great hall at Poitiers has a long pedigree, as its walls date back to the twelfth century and its open wooden roof, as well as the remarkable trio of chimney-pieces at the right end of the room as you enter, to the fifteenth. The three tall fireplaces, side by side, with a delicate gallery running along the top of them, constitute the originality of this ancient chamber, and make one think of the groups that must formerly have gathered there—of all the wet boot-soles, the trickling doublets, the stiffened fingers, the rheumatic shanks, that must have been presented to such an incomparable focus of heat. To-day,

I am afraid, these mighty hearths are for ever cold; justice is probably administered with the aid of a modern *calorifère*, and the walls of the palace are perforated with regurgitating tubes. Behind and above the gallery that surmounts the three fire-places are high Gothic windows, the tracery of which masks, in some sort, the chimneys; and in each angle of this and of the room to the right and left of the trio of chimneys is an open-work spiral staircase, ascending to—I forget where; perhaps to the roof of the edifice. The whole side of the *salle* is very lordly, and seems to express an unstinted hospitality, to extend the friendliest of all invitations, to bid the whole world come and get warm. It was the invention of John, Duke of Berry and Count of Poitou, about 1395. I give this information on the authority of the Guide-Joanne, from which source I gather much other curious learning; as, for instance, that it was in this building, when it had surely a very different front, that Charles VII. was proclaimed king in 1422; and that here Jeanne Darc was subjected, in 1429, to the in-quisition of sundry doctors and matrons.

The most charming thing at Poitiers is simply the Prome-nade de Blossac—a small public garden at one end of the flat top of the hill. It has a happy look of the last century (having been arranged at that period), and a beautiful sweep of view over the surrounding country, and especially of the course of the little river Clain, which winds about a part of the base of the big mound of Poitiers. The limit of this dear little garden is formed, on the side that turns away from the town, by the rampart erected in the fourteenth century and by its big semi-circular bastions. This rampart, of great length, has a low par-apet; you look over it at the charming little vegetable-gardens with which the base of the hill appears exclusively to be gar-nished. The whole prospect is delightful, especially the details of the part just under the walls, at the end of the walk. Here the river makes a shining twist which a painter might have invented, and the side of the hill is terraced into several hedges—a sort of tangle of small blooming patches and little pavilions with peaked roofs and green shutters. It is idle to attempt to reproduce all this in words; it should be repro-duced only in water-colours. The reader, however, will al-ready have remarked that disparity in these ineffectual pages,

Poitiers: Church of St. Radegonde

which are pervaded by the attempt to sketch without a palette or brushes. He will doubtless also be struck with the grovelling vision which, on such a spot as the ramparts of Poitiers, peoples itself with carrots and cabbages rather than with images of the Black Prince and the captive king. I am not sure that in looking out from the Promenade de Blossac you command the old battle-field; it is enough that it was not far off, and that the great rout of Frenchmen poured into the walls of Poitiers, leaving on the ground a number of the fallen equal to the little army (eight thousand) of the invader. I did think of the battle. I wondered, rather helplessly, where it had taken place; and I came away (as the reader will see from the preceding sentence) without finding out. This indifference, however, was a result rather of a general dread of military topography than of a want of admiration of this particular victory, which I have always supposed to be one of the most brilliant on record. Indeed, I should be almost ashamed, and very much at a loss, to say what light it was that this glorious day seemed to me to have left for ever on the horizon, and why the very name of the place had always caused my blood gently to tingle. It is carrying the feeling of race to quite inscrutable lengths when a vague American permits himself an emotion because more than five centuries ago, on French soil, one rapacious Frenchman got the better of another. Edward was a Frenchman as well as John, and French were the cries that urged each of the hosts to the fight. French is the beautiful motto graven round the image of the Black Prince as he lies for ever at rest in the choir of Canterbury: *à la mort ne pensai-je mye.* Nevertheless, the victory of Poitiers declines to lose itself in these considerations; the sense of it is a part of our heritage, the joy of it a part of our imagination, and it filters down through centuries and migrations till it titillates a New Yorker who forgets in his elation that he happens at that moment to be enjoying the hospitality of France. It was something done, I know not how justly, for England; and what was done in the fourteenth century for England was done also for New York.

Bordeaux

Chapter XVIII

IF IT was really for the sake of the Black Prince that I had
stopped at Poitiers (for my prevision of Notre Dame la
Grande and of the little temple of St. John was of the dimmest), I ought to have stopped at Angoulême for the sake of
David and Eve Séchard, of Lucien de Rubempré and of Madame de Bargeton, who when she wore a *toilette étudiée*
sported a Jewish turban ornamented with an Eastern brooch,
a scarf of gauze, a necklace of cameos, and a robe of "painted
muslin," whatever that may be; treating herself to these luxuries out of an income of twelve thousand francs. The persons
I have mentioned have not that vagueness of identity which is
the misfortune of historical characters; they are real, supremely real, thanks to their affiliation to the great Balzac,
who had invented an artificial reality which was as much better than the vulgar article as mock-turtle soup is than the liquid it emulates. The first time I read "Les Illusions Perdues" I
should have refused to believe that I was capable of passing
the old capital of Anjou without alighting to visit the
Houmeau. But we never know what we are capable of till we

are tested, as I reflected when I found myself looking back at Angoulême from the window of the train just after we had emerged from the long tunnel that passes under the town. This tunnel perforates the hill on which, like Poitiers, Angoulême rears itself, and which gives it an elevation still greater than that of Poitiers. You may have a tolerable look at the cathedral without leaving the railway carriage, for it stands just above the tunnel and is exposed, much foreshortened, to the spectator below. There is evidently a charming walk round the plateau of the town commanding those pretty views of which Balzac gives an account. But the train whirled me away, and these are my only impressions. The truth is that I had no need, just at that moment, of putting myself into communication with Balzac, for opposite to me in the compartment were a couple of figures almost as vivid as the actors in the "Comédie Humaine." One of these was a very genial and dirty old priest, and the other was a reserved and concentrated young monk—the latter (by which I mean a monk of any kind) being a rare sight to-day in France. This young man indeed was mitigatedly monastic. He had a big brown frock and cowl, but he had also a shirt and a pair of shoes; he had, instead of a hempen scourge round his waist, a stout leather thong, and he carried with him a very profane little valise. He also read, from beginning to end, the *Figaro* which the old priest, who had done the same, presented to him; and he looked altogether as if, had he not been a monk, he would have made a distinguished officer of engineers. When he was not reading the *Figaro* he was conning his breviary or answering, with rapid precision and with a deferential but discouraging dryness, the frequent questions of his companion, who was of quite another type. This worthy had a bored, good-natured, unbuttoned, expansive look; was talkative, restless, almost disreputably human. He was surrounded by a great deal of small luggage, and had scattered over the carriage his books, his papers, and fragments of his lunch, and the contents of an extraordinary bag which he kept beside him—a kind of secular reliquary—and which appeared to contain the odds and ends of a lifetime, as he took from it successively a pair of slippers, an old padlock (which evidently did not belong to it), an opera-glass, a collection of almanacs, and a large sea-shell, which he very carefully examined. I think that if he had not been afraid of the young monk, who was so much more serious than he, he would have held the shell to his ear like a child. Indeed, he was a very childish and delightful old priest, and his companion evidently thought him quite frivolous. But I liked him the better of the two. He was not a country curé, but an ecclesiastic of some rank, who had seen a good deal both of the church and of the world; and if I too had not been afraid of his colleague, who read the *Figaro* as seriously as if it had been an encyclical, I should have entered into conversation with him.

All this while I was getting on to Bordeaux, where I permitted myself to spend three days. I am afraid I have next to nothing to show for them, and that there would be little profit in lingering on this episode, which is the less to be justified as I had in former years examined Bordeaux attentively enough. It contains a very good hotel—an hotel not good enough, however, to keep you there for its own sake. For the rest, Bordeaux is a big, rich, handsome, imposing commercial town, with long rows of fine old eighteenth-century houses which overlook the yellow Garonne. I have spoken of the quays of Nantes as fine, but those of Bordeaux have a wider sweep and a still more architectural air. The appearance of such a port as this makes the Anglo-Saxon tourist blush for the sordid water-fronts of Liverpool and New York, which, with their larger activity, have so much more reason to be stately. Bordeaux gives a great impression of prosperous industries, and suggests delightful ideas, images of prune-boxes and bottled claret. As the focus of distribution of the best wine in the world, it is indeed a sacred city—dedicated to the worship of Bacchus in the most discreet form. The country all about it is covered with precious vineyards, sources of fortune to their owners and of satisfaction to distant consumers: and as you look over to the hills beyond the Garonne you see them, in the autumn sunshine, fretted with the rusty richness of this or that immortal *clos*. But the principal picture, within the town, is that of the vast curving quays, bordered with houses that look like the *hôtels* of farmers-general of the last century, and of the wide, tawny river, crowded with shipping and spanned by the largest of bridges.

Some of the types on the water-side are of the sort that arrest a sketcher—figures of stalwart, brown-faced Basques, such as I had seen of old in great numbers at Biarritz, with their loose circular caps, their white sandals, their air of walking for a wager. Never was a tougher, a harder race. They are not mariners nor watermen, but, putting questions of temper aside, they are the best possible dock-porters. "Il s'y fait un commerce terrible," a *douanier* said to me, as he looked up and down the interminable docks; and such a place has indeed much to say of the wealth, the capacity for production, of France—the bright, cheerful, smokeless industry of the wonderful country which produces, above all, the agreeable things of life, and turns even its defeats and revolutions into gold. The whole town has an air of almost depressing opulence, an appearance which culminates in the great *place* which surrounds the Grand-Théâtre—an establishment of the highest style, encircled with columns, arcades, lamps, gilded cafés. One feels it to be a monument to the virtue of the well-selected bottle. If I had not forbidden myself to linger, I should venture to insist on this and, at the risk of being called fantastic, trace an analogy between good claret and the best qualities of the French mind; pretend that there is a taste of sound Bordeaux in all the happiest manifestations of that fine organ, and that, correspondingly, there is a touch of French reason, French completeness, in a glass of Pontet-Canet. The danger of such an excursion would lie mainly in its being so open to the reader to take the ground from under my feet by saying that good claret doesn't exist. To this I should have no reply whatever. I should be unable to tell him where to find it. I certainly didn't find it at Bordeaux, where I drank a most vulgar fluid; and it is of course notorious that a large part of mankind is occupied in vainly looking for it. There was a great pretence of putting it forward at the Exhibition which was going on at Bordeaux at the time of my visit, an "exposition philomathique," lodged in a collection of big temporary buildings in the Allées d'Orléans, and regarded by the Bordelais for the moment as the most brilliant feature of their city. Here were pyramids of bottles, mountains of bottles, to say nothing of cases and cabinets of bottles. The contemplation

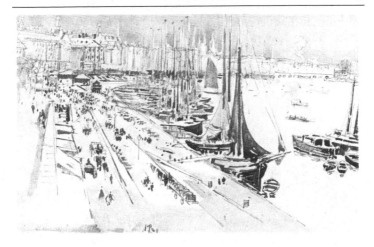

Bordeaux: the Quay

of these glittering tiers was of course not very convincing; and indeed the whole arrangement struck me as a high impertinence. Good wine is not an optical pleasure, it is an inward emotion; and if there was a chamber of degustation on the premises, I failed to discover it. It was not in the search for it, indeed, that I spent half an hour in this bewildering bazaar. Like all "expositions," it seemed to me to be full of ugly things, and gave one a portentous idea of the quantity of rubbish that man carries with him on his course through the ages. Such an amount of luggage for a journey after all so short! There were no individual objects; there was nothing but dozens and hundreds, all machine-made and expressionless, in spite of the repeated grimace, the conscious smartness, of "the last new thing," that was stamped on all of them. The fatal facility of the French *article* becomes at last as irritating as the refrain of a popular song. The poor "Indiens Galibis" struck me as really more interesting—a group of stunted savages who formed one of the attractions of the place and were confined in a pen in the open air, with a rabble of people pushing and squeezing, hanging over the barrier, to look at them. They had no grimace, no pretension to be new, no desire to catch your eye. They looked at their visitors no more than they looked at each other, and seemed ancient, indifferent, terribly bored.

Toulouse: the Cathedral

Chapter XIX

THERE is much entertainment in the journey through the wide, smiling garden of Gascony; I speak of it as I took it in going from Bordeaux to Toulouse. It is the south, quite the south, and had for the present narrator its full measure of the charm he is always determined to find in countries that may even by courtesy be said to appertain to the sun. It was, moreover, the happy and genial view of these mild latitudes, which, goodness knows, often have a dreariness of their own; a land teeming with corn and wine and speaking everywhere (that is everywhere the phylloxera had not laid it waste) of wealth and plenty. The road runs constantly near the Garonne, touching now and then its slow, brown, rather sullen stream, a sullenness that encloses great dangers and disasters. The traces of the horrible floods of 1875 have disappeared, and the land smiles placidly enough while it waits for another immersion. Toulouse, at the period I speak of, was up to its middle (and in places above it) in water, and looks still as if it had been thoroughly soaked—as if it had faded and shrivelled with a long steeping. The fields and copses, of course, are more forgiving. The railway line follows as well the charming Canal du Midi, which is as pretty as a river, barring the straightness, and here and there occupies the foreground, beneath a screen of dense, tall trees, while the Garonne takes a larger and more irregular course a little way beyond it. People who are fond of canals—and, speaking from the pictorial standpoint, I hold the taste to be most legitimate—will delight in this admirable specimen of the class, which has a very interesting history, not to be narrated here. On the other side of the road (the left), all the way, runs a long, low line of hills, or rather one continuous hill, or perpetual cliff, with a straight top, in the shape of a ledge of rock, which might pass for a ruined wall. I am afraid the reader will lose patience with my habit of constantly referring to the landscape of Italy as if that were the measure of the beauty of every other. Yet I am still more afraid that I cannot apologise for it, and must leave it in its culpable nakedness. It is an idle habit; but the reader will long since have discovered that this was an idle journey and that I give my impressions as they came to me. It came to me, then, that in all this view there was something transalpine, with a greater smartness and freshness and much less elegance and languor. This impression was occasionally deepened by the appearance, on the long eminence of which I speak, of a village, a church, a château, that seemed to look down at the plain from over the ruined wall. The perpetual vines, the bright-faced flat-roofed houses, covered with tiles, the softness and sweetness of the light and air, recalled the prosier portions of the Lombard plain. Toulouse itself has a little of this Italian expression, but not enough to give a colour to its dark, dirty, crooked streets, which are irregular without being eccentric, and which, if it were not for the superb church of Saint-Sernin, would be quite destitute of monuments.

I have already alluded to the way in which the names of certain places impose themselves on the mind, and I must add that of Toulouse to the list of expressive appellations. It certainly evokes a vision—suggests something highly *méridional*. But the city, it must be confessed, is less pictorial than the word, in spite of the Place du Capitole, in spite of the quay of the Garonne, in spite of the curious cloister of the old museum. What justifies the images that are latent in the word is not the aspect, but the history, of the town. The hotel to which the well-advised traveller will repair stands in a corner of the Place du Capitole, which is the heart and centre of Toulouse, and which bears a vague and inexpensive resemblance to Piazza Castello at Turin. The Capitol, with a wide modern face, occupies one side, and, like the palace at Turin, looks across at a high arcade, under which the hotels, the principal shops, and the lounging citizens are gathered. The shops, are probably better than the Turinese, but the people are not so good. Stunted, shabby, rather vitiated looking, they have none of the personal richness of the sturdy Piedmontese; and I will take this occasion to remark that in the course of a journey of several weeks in the French provinces I rarely encountered a well-dressed male. Can it be possible that republics are unfavourable to a certain attention to one's boots and one's beard? I risk this somewhat futile inquiry because the proportion of neat coats and trousers seemed to be about the same in France and in my native land. It was notably lower than in England and in Italy, and even warranted the supposition that most good provincials have their chin shaven and their boots blacked but once a week. I hasten to add, lest my observation should appear to be of a sadly superficial character, that the manners and conversation of these gentlemen bore (whenever I had occasion to appreciate them) no relation to the state of their chin and their boots. They were almost always marked by an extreme amenity. At Toulouse there was the strongest temptation to speak to people simply for the entertainment of hearing them reply with that curious, that fascinating accent of the Languedoc, which appears to abound in final consonants and leads the Toulousians to say *bien-g* and *maison-g* like Englishmen learning French. It is as if they talked with their teeth rather than with their tongue. I find in my note-book a phrase in regard to Toulouse which is perhaps a little ill-natured, but which I will transcribe as it stands: "The oddity is that the place should be both animated and dull. A big, brown-skinned population, clattering about in a flat, tortuous town, which produces nothing whatever that I can discover. Except the church of Saint-Sernin and the fine old court of the Hôtel d'Assézat, Toulouse has no architecture; the houses are for the most part of brick, of a greyish-red colour, and have no particular style. The brickwork of the place is in fact very poor—inferior to that of the North Italian towns and quite wanting in the wealth of tone which this homely material takes on in general in the climates of dampness and greenness." And then my note-book goes on to narrate a little visit to the Capitol, which was soon made, as the building was in course of repair and half the rooms were closed.

Toulouse: the Place de Capitol

Chapter XX

THE HISTORY of Toulouse is detestable, saturated with
blood and perfidy; and the ancient custom of the Floral
Games, grafted upon all sorts of internecine traditions, seems,
with its false pastoralism, its mock chivalry, its display of fine
feelings, to set off rather than to mitigate these horrors. The
society was founded in the fourteenth century, and it has held
annual meetings ever since—meetings at which poems in the
fine old *langue d'oc* are declaimed and a blushing laureate is
chosen. This business takes place in the Capitol, before the
chief magistrate of the town, who is known as the *capitoul*,
and of all the pretty women as well—a class very numerous at
Toulouse. It is unusual to present a finer person than that of
the portress who pretended to show me the apartments in
which the Floral Games are held; a big, brown, expansive
woman, still in the prime of life, with a speaking eye, an extraordinary assurance, and a pair of magenta stockings, which
were inserted into the neatest and most polished little black
sabots, and which, as she clattered up the stairs before me,
lavishly displaying them, made her look like the heroine of an

opéra-bouffe. Her talk was all in *n*'s, *g*'s and *d*'s, and in mute *e*'s strongly accented, as *autré*, *théâtré*, *splendidé*—the last being an epithet she applied to everything the Capitol contained, and especially to a horrible picture representing the famous Clémence Isaure, the reputed foundress of the poetical contest, presiding on one of these occasions. I wondered whether Clémence Isaure had been anything like this terrible Toulousaine of to-day, who would have been a capital figure-head for a floral game. The lady in whose honour the picture I have just mentioned was painted is a somewhat mythical personage, and she is not to be found in the "Biographie Universelle." She is, however, a very graceful myth; and if she never existed, her statue at least does—a shapeless effigy transferred to the Capitol from the so-called tomb of Clémence in the old church of La Daurade. The great hall in which the Floral Games are held was encumbered with scaffoldings, and I was unable to admire the long series of busts of the bards who have won prizes and the portraits of all the capitouls of Toulouse. As a compensation I was introduced to a big bookcase filled with the poems that have been crowned since the days of the troubadours (a portentous collection), and the big butcher's knife with which, according to the legend, Henry, Duke of Montmorency, who had conspired against the great cardinal with Gaston of Orleans and Mary de' Medici, was, in 1632, beheaded on this spot by the order of Richelieu. With these objects the interest of the Capitol was exhausted. The building indeed has not the grandeur of its name, which is a sort of promise that the visitor will find some sensible embodiment of the old Roman tradition that once flourished in this part of France. It is inferior in impressiveness to the other three famous Capitols of the modern world—that of Rome (if I may call the present structure modern) and those of Washington and Albany!

The only Roman remains at Toulouse are to be found in the museum—a very interesting establishment, which I was condemned to see as imperfectly as I had seen the Capitol. It was being rearranged; and the gallery of paintings, which is the least interesting feature, was the only part that was not upside-down. The pictures are mainly of the modern French school, and I remember nothing but a powerful though disagreeable specimen of Henner, who paints the human body, and paints it so well, with a brush dipped in blackness; and, placed among the paintings, a bronze replica of the charming young David of Mercié. These things have been set out in the church of an old monastery, long since suppressed, and the rest of the collection occupies the cloisters. These are two in number—a small one, which you enter first from the street, and a very vast and elegant one beyond it, which, with its light gothic arches and slim columns (of the fourteenth century), its broad walk, its little garden with old tombs and statues in the centre, is by far the most picturesque, the most sketchable, spot in Toulouse. It must be doubly so when the Roman busts, inscriptions, slabs, and sarcophagi are ranged along the walls; it must indeed (to compare small things with great, and as the judicious Murray remarks) bear a certain resemblance to the Campo Santo at Pisa. But these things are absent now; the cloister is a litter of confusion, and its treasures have been stowed away confusedly in sundry inaccessible rooms. The custodian attempted to console me by telling me that when they are exhibited again it will be on a scientific basis and with an order and regularity of which they were formerly innocent. But I was not consoled. I wanted simply the spectacle, the picture, and I didn't care in the least for the classification. Old Roman fragments exposed to light in the open air, under a southern sky, in a quadrangle round a garden, have an immortal charm simply in their general effect; and the charm is all the greater when the soil of the very place has yielded them up.

Toulouse: Saint-Sernin

Chapter XXI

M Y REAL CONSOLATION was an hour I spent in Saint-Sernin, one of the noblest churches in southern France, and easily the first among those of Toulouse. This great structure, a masterpiece of twelfth-century romanesque and dedicated to Saint Saturninus—the Toulousains have abbreviated—is, I think, alone worth a journey to Toulouse. What makes it so is the extraordinary seriousness of its interior; no other term occurs to me as expressing so well the character of its clear grey nave. As a general thing, I favour little the fashion of attributing moral qualities to buildings; I shrink from talking about tender cornices and sincere campanili; but one feels that one can scarce get on without imputing some sort of morality to Saint-Sernin. As it stands to-day,

Toulouse: St. Sernin (the Transept)

the church has been completely restored by Viollet-le-Duc. The exterior is of brick, and has little charm save that of a tower of four rows of arches, narrowing together as they ascend. The nave is of great length and height, the barrel-roof of stone, the effect of the round arches and pillars in the triforium especially fine. There are two low aisles on either side. The choir is very deep and narrow; it seems to close together, and looks as if it were meant for intensely earnest rites. The transepts are most noble, especially the arches of the second tier. The whole church is narrow for its length and is singularly complete and homogeneous. As I say all this I feel that I quite fail to give an impression of its manly gravity, its strong proportions, or of the lonesome look of its renovated stones as I sat there while the October twilight gathered. It is a real work of art, a high conception. The crypt, into which I was eventually led captive by an importunate sacristan, is quite another affair, though indeed I suppose it may also be spoken of as a work of art. It is a rich museum of relics, and contains the head of Saint Thomas Aquinas wrapped up in a napkin and exhibited in a glass case. The sacristan took a lamp and guided me about, presenting me to one saintly remnant after another. The impression was grotesque, but some of the objects were contained in curious old cases of beaten silver and brass: these things at least, which looked as if they had been transmitted from the early church, were venerable. There was, however, a kind of wholesale sanctity about the place which overshot the mark; it pretends to be one of the holiest spots in the world. The effect is spoiled by the way the sacristans hang about and offer to take you into it for ten sous—I was accosted by two and escaped from another—and by the familiar manner in which you pop in and out. This episode rather broke the charm of Saint-Sernin, so that I took my departure and went in search of the cathedral. It was scarcely worth finding, and struck me as an odd, dislocated fragment. The front consists only of a portal beside which a tall brick tower of a later period has been erected. The nave was wrapped in dimness, with a few scattered lamps. I could only distinguish an immense vault, like a high cavern, without aisles. Here and there in the gloom was a kneeling figure; the whole place was mysterious and lopsided. The choir was cur-

Toulouse: the Garonne

tained off; it appeared not to correspond with the nave—that is, not to have the same axis. The only other ecclesiastical impression I gathered at Toulouse came to me in the church of La Daurade, of which the front, on the quay by the Garonne, was closed with scaffoldings; so that one entered it from behind, where it is completely masked by houses, through a door which has at first no traceable connection with it. It is a vast, high, modernised, heavily decorated church, dimly lighted at all times, I should suppose, and enriched by the shades of evening at the time I looked into it. I perceived that it consisted mainly of a large square, beneath a dome, in the centre of which a single person—a lady—was praying with the utmost absorption. The manner of access to the church interposed such an obstacle to the outer profanities that I had a sense of intruding and presently withdrew, carrying with me a picture of the vast, still interior, the gilded roof gleaming in the twilight, and the solitary worshipper. What was she praying for, and was she not almost afraid to remain there alone?

For the rest, the picturesque at Toulouse consists principally of the walk beside the Garonne, which is spanned, to the faubourg of Saint-Cyprien, by a stout brick bridge. This hapless suburb, the baseness of whose site is noticeable, lay for days under the water at the time of the last inundations. The Garonne had almost mounted to the roofs of the houses, and the place continues to present a blighted, frightened look. Two or three persons with whom I had some conversation spoke of that time as a memory of horror. I have not done with my Italian comparisons; I shall never have done with them. I am therefore free to say that in the way in which Toulouse looks out on the Garonne there was something that reminded me vaguely of the way in which Pisa looks out on the Arno. The red-faced houses—all of brick—along the quay have a mixture of brightness and shabbiness, as well as the fashion of the open *loggia* in the top-storey. The river, with another bridge or two, might be the Arno, and the buildings on the other side of it—a hospital, a suppressed convent—dip their feet into it with real southern cynicism. I have spoken of the old Hôtel d'Assézat as the best house at Toulouse; with the exception of the cloister of the museum, it is the only "bit" I remember. It has fallen from the state of a noble residence of the sixteenth century to that of a warehouse and a set of offices; but a certain dignity lingers in its melancholy court, which is divided from the street by a gateway that is still imposing and in which a clambering vine and a red Virginia-creeper were suspended to the rusty walls of brick and stone.

The most interesting house at Toulouse is far from being the most striking. At the door of No. 50 Rue des Filatiers, a featureless, solid structure, was found hanging, one autumn evening, the body of the young Marc-Antoine Calas, whose ill-inspired suicide was to be the first act of a tragedy so horrible. The fanaticism aroused in the townsfolk by this incident; the execution by torture of Jean Calas, accused as a Protestant of having hanged his son, who had gone over to the Church of Rome; the ruin of the family; the claustration of the daughters; the flight of the widow to Switzerland; her introduction to Voltaire; the excited zeal of that incomparable partisan and the passionate persistence with which, from year to year, he pursued a reversal of judgment till at last he obtained it and devoted the tribunal of Toulouse to execration

and the name of the victims to lasting wonder and pity—
these things form part of one of the most interesting and
touching episodes of the social history of the eighteenth century. The story has the fatal progression, the dark rigour, of
one of the tragic dramas of the Greeks. Jean Calas, advanced
in life, blameless, bewildered, protesting his innocence, had
been broken on the wheel; and the sight of his decent dwelling, which brought home to me all that had been suffered
there, spoiled for me, for half an hour, the impression of
Toulouse.

Carcassone

Chapter XXII

I SPENT but a few hours at Carcassonne; but those hours
had a rounded felicity, and I cannot do better than transcribe from my note-book the little record made at the moment. Vitiated as it may be by crudity and incoherency, it has
at any rate the freshness of a great emotion. This is the best
quality that a reader may hope to extract from a narrative in
which "useful information" and technical lore even of the
most general sort are completely absent. For Carcassonne is
moving, beyond a doubt; and the traveller who in the course
of a little tour in France may have felt himself urged, in melancholy moments, to say that on the whole the disappointments are as numerous as the satisfactions, must admit that
there can be nothing better than this.

The country after you leave Toulouse continues to be
charming; the more so that it merges its flatness in the distant
Cévennes on one side, and on the other, far away on your
right, in the richer range of the Pyrenees. Olives and cypresses, pergolas and vines, terraces on the roofs of houses,

soft, iridescent mountains, a warm yellow light—what more could the difficult tourist want? He left his luggage at the station, warily determined to look at the inn before committing himself to it. It was so evident (even to a cursory glance) that it might easily have been much better, that he simply took his way to the town, with the whole of a superb afternoon before him. When I say the town, I mean the towns; there being two at Carcassonne, perfectly distinct, and each with excellent claims to the title. They have settled the matter between them, however, and the elder, the shrine of pilgrimage, to which the other is but a stepping-stone, or even, as I may say, a humble door-mat, takes the name of the Cité. You see nothing of the Cité from the station; it is masked by the agglomeration of the *ville-basse*, which is relatively (but only relatively) new. A wonderful avenue of acacias leads to it from the station—leads past it, rather, and conducts you to a little high-backed bridge over the Aude, beyond which, detached and erect, a distinct mediæval silhouette, the Cité presents itself. Like a rival shop on the invidious side of a street, it has "no connection" with the establishment across the way, although the two places are united (if old Carcassonne may be said to be united to anything) by a vague little rustic faubourg. Perched on its solid pedestal, the perfect detachment of the Cité is what first strikes you. To take leave, without delay, of the *ville-basse*, I may say that the splendid acacias I have mentioned flung a summerish dusk over the place, in which a few scattered remains of stout walls and big bastions looked venerable and picturesque. A little boulevard winds round the town, planted with trees and garnished with more benches than I ever saw provided by a soft-hearted municipality. This precinct had a warm, lazy, dusty, southern look, as if the people sat out-of-doors a great deal and wandered about in the stillness of summer nights. The figure of the elder town at these hours must be ghostly enough on its neighbouring hill. Even by day it has the air of a vignette of Gustave Doré, a couplet of Victor Hugo. It is almost too perfect—as if it were an enormous model placed on a big green table at a museum. A steep, paved way, grass-grown like all roads where vehicles never pass, stretches up to it in the sun. It has a double enceinte, complete outer walls and complete inner (these, elaborately fortified, are the more curious); and this congregation of ramparts, towers, bastions, battlements, barbicans, is as fantastic and romantic as you please. The approach I mention here leads to the gate that looks toward Toulouse—the Porte de l'Aude. There is a second, on the other side, called, I believe, the Porte Narbonnaise, a magnificent gate, flanked with towers thick and tall, defended by elaborate outworks; and these two apertures alone admit you to the place—putting aside a small sally-port, protected by a great bastion, on the quarter that looks toward the Pyrenees.

As a votary, always, in the first instance, of a general impression, I walked all round the outer enceinte—a process on the very face of it entertaining. I took to the right of the Porte de l'Aude, without entering it, where the old moat has been filled in. The filling-in of the moat has created a grassy level at the foot of the big grey towers, which, rising at frequent intervals, stretch their stiff curtain of stone from point to point: the curtain drops without a fold upon the quiet grass, which was dotted here and there with a humble native dozing away the golden afternoon. The natives of the elder Carcassonne are all humble; for the core of the Cité has shrunken and decayed, and there is little life among the ruins. A few tenacious labourers who work in the neighbouring fields or in the *ville-basse*, and sundry octogenarians of both sexes, who are dying where they have lived and contribute much to the pictorial effect—these are the principal inhabitants. The process of converting the place from an irresponsible old town into a conscious "specimen" has of course been attended with eliminations; the population has, as a general thing, been restored away. I should lose no time in saying that restoration is the great mark of the Cité. M. Viollet-le-Duc has worked his will upon it, put it into perfect order, revived the fortifications in every detail. I do not pretend to judge the performance, carried out on a scale and in a spirit which really impose themselves on the imagination. Few architects have had such a chance, and M. Viollet-le-Duc must have been the envy of the whole restoring fraternity. The image of a more crumbling Carcassonne rises in the mind, and there is no doubt that forty years ago the place was more affecting. On the other hand, as we see it to-day it is a wonderful evocation; and if there is a great deal of new in the old, there is plenty of old in the new. The repaired crenellations, the inserted patches of the walls of the outer circle, sufficiently express this commixture. My walk brought me into full view of the Pyrenees, which, now that the sun had begun to sink and the shadows to grow long, had a wonderful violet glow. The platform at the base of the walls has a greater width on this side, and it made the scene more complete. Two or three old crones had crawled out of the Porte Narbonnaise to examine the advancing visitor; and a very ancient peasant, lying there with his back against a tower, was tending half a dozen lean sheep. A poor man in a very old blouse, crippled and with crutches lying beside him, had been brought out and placed on a stool, where he enjoyed the afternoon as best he might. He looked so ill and so patient that I spoke to him; found that his legs were paralysed and he was quite helpless. He had formerly been seven years in the army, and had made the campaign of Mexico with Bazaine. Born in the old Cité, he had come back there to end his days. It seemed strange, as he sat there with those romantic walls behind him and the great picture of the Pyrenees in front, to think that he had been across the seas to the far-away new world, had made part of a famous expedition, and was now a cripple at the gate of the mediæval city where he had played as a child. All this struck me as a great deal of history for so modest a figure—a poor little figure that could only just unclose its palm for a small silver coin.

He was not the only acquaintance I made at Carcassonne. I had not pursued my circuit of the walls much farther when I encountered a person of quite another type, of whom I asked some question which had just then presented itself, and who proved to be the very genius of the spot. He was a sociable son of the *ville-basse*, a gentleman, and, as I afterwards learned, an employé at the prefecture—a person, in short, much esteemed at Carcassonne. (I may say all this, as he will never read these pages.) He had been ill for a month, and in the company of his little dog was taking his first airing; in his own phrase, he was *amoureux-fou de la Cité*—he could lose no time in coming back to it. He talked of it indeed as a lover, and, giving me for half an hour the advantage of his company, showed me all the points of the place. (I speak here always of the outer enceinte; you penetrate to the inner— which is the specialty of Carcassonne and the great curiosity—only by application at the lodge of the regular custodian, a remarkable functionary, who, half an hour later, when I had been introduced to him by my friend the amateur, marched me over the fortifications with a tremendous accompaniment of dates and technical terms.) My companion pointed out to me in particular the traces of different periods in the structure of the walls. There is a portentous amount of history embedded in them, beginning with Romans and Visigoths; here and there are marks of old breaches hastily repaired. We passed into the town—into that part of it not included in the citadel. It is the queerest and most fragmentary little place in the world, as everything save the fortifications is being suffered to crumble away in order that the spirit of M. Viollet-le-Duc alone may pervade it and it may subsist simply as a magnificent shell. As the leases of the wretched little houses fall in, the ground is cleared of them; and a mumbling old woman approached me in the course of my circuit, inviting me to condole with her on the disappearance of so many of the hovels which in the last few hundred years (since the collapse of Carcassonne as a stronghold) had attached themselves to the base of the walls, in the space between the two circles. These habitations, constructed of materials taken from the ruins, nestled there snugly enough. This intermediate space had therefore become a kind of street, which has crumbled in turn, as the fortress has grown up again. There are other streets beside, very diminutive and vague, where you pick your way over heaps of rubbish and become conscious of unexpected faces looking at you out of windows as detached as the cherubic heads. The most definite thing in the place was the little café, where the waiters, I think, must be the ghosts of the old Visigoths; the most definite, that is, after the little château and the little cathedral. Everything in the Cité is little; you can walk round the walls in twenty minutes. On the drawbridge of the château, which, with a picturesque old face, flanking towers, and a dry moat, is to-day simply a bare *caserne*, lounged half a dozen soldiers, unusually small.

Nothing could be more odd than to see these objects enclosed in a receptacle which has much of the appearance of an enormous toy. The Cité and its population vaguely reminded me of an immense Noah's ark.

Carcassonne

Chapter XXIII

C ARCASSONNE dates from the Roman occupation of Gaul.
The place commanded one of the great roads into
Spain, and in the fourth century Romans and Franks ousted
each other from such a point of vantage. In the year 436 Theodoric King of the Visigoths superseded both these parties;
and it was during his occupation that the inner enceinte was
raised upon the ruins of the Roman fortifications. Most of the
Visigoth towers that are still erect are seated upon Roman
substructions which appear to have been formed hastily,
probably at the moment of the Frankish invasion. The authors of these solid defences, though occasionally disturbed,
held Carcassonne and the neighbouring country, in which
they had established their kingdom of Septimania, till the year
713, when they were expelled by the Moors of Spain, who
ushered in an unillumined period of four centuries, of which
no traces remain. These facts I derive from a source no more
recondite than a pamphlet by M. Viollet-le-Duc—a very luminous description of the fortifications, which you may buy
from the accomplished custodian. The writer makes a jump to

166

the year 1209, when Carcassonne, then forming part of the realm of the viscounts of Béziers and infected by the Albigensian heresy, was besieged, in the name of the Pope, by the terrible Simon de Montfort and his army of crusaders. Simon was accustomed to success, and the town succumbed in the course of a fortnight. Thirty-one years later, having passed into the hands of the King of France, it was again besieged by the young Raymond de Trincavel, the last of the viscounts of Béziers; and of this siege M. Viollet-le-Duc gives a long and minute account, which the visitor who has a head for such things may follow, with the brochure in hand, on the fortifications themselves. The young Raymond de Trincavel, baffled and repulsed, retired at the end of twenty-four days. Saint Louis and Philip the Bold, in the thirteenth century, multiplied the defences of Carcassonne, which was one of the bulwarks of their kingdom on the Spanish quarter; and from this time forth, being regarded as impregnable, the place had nothing to fear. It was not even attacked; and when in 1355 Edward the Black Prince marched into it, the inhabitants had opened the gates to the conqueror before whom all Languedoc was prostrate. I am not one of those who, as I said just now, have a head for such things, and having extracted these few facts, had made all the use of M. Viollet-le-Duc's pamphlet of which I was capable.

I have mentioned that my obliging friend the *amoureux-fou* handed me over to the doorkeeper of the citadel. I should add that I was at first committed to the wife of this functionary, a stout peasant-woman, who took a key down from a nail, conducted me to a postern door, and ushered me into the presence of her husband. Having just begun his rounds with a party of four persons, he was not many steps in advance. I added myself perforce to this party, which was not brilliantly composed, except that two of its members were gendarmes in full toggery, who announced in the course of our tour that they had been stationed for a year at Carcassonne and had never before had the curiosity to come up to the Cité. There was something brilliant certainly in that. The *gardien* was an extraordinarily typical little Frenchman, who struck me even more forcibly than the wonders of the inner enceinte; and as I am bound to assume, at whatever cost to my literary vanity,

that there is not the slightest danger of his reading these remarks, I may treat him as public property. With his diminutive stature and his perpendicular spirit, his flushed face,
expressive protuberant eyes, high peremptory voice, extreme
volubility, lucidity and neatness of utterance, he reminded me
of the gentry who figure in the revolutions of his native land.
If he was not a fierce little Jacobin, he ought to have been, for
I am sure there were many men of his pattern on the Committee of Public Safety. He knew absolutely what he was
about, understood the place thoroughly, and constantly reminded his audience of what he himself had done in the way
of excavations and reparations. He described himself as the
brother of the architect of the work actually going forward
(that which has been done since the death of M. Viollet-le-
Duc, I suppose he meant), and this fact was more illustrative
than all the others. It reminded me, as one is reminded at
every turn, of the democratic conditions of French life: a man
of the people, with a wife *en bonnet*, extremely intelligent, full
of special knowledge, and yet remaining essentially of the
people and showing his intelligence with a kind of ferocity, of
defiance. Such a personage helps one to understand the red
radicalism of France, the revolutions, the barricades, the sinister passion for theories. (I do not, of course, take upon myself
to say that the individual I describe—who can know nothing
of the liberties I am taking with him—is actually devoted to
these ideals; I only mean that many such devotees must have
his qualities.) In just the *nuance* that I have tried to indicate
here it is a terrible pattern of man. Permeated in a high degree
by civilisation, it is yet untouched by the desire which one
finds in the Englishman, in proportion as he rises in the
world, to approximate to the figure of the gentleman. On the
other hand, a *netteté*, a faculty of exposition, such as the English gentleman is rarely either blessed or cursed with.

This brilliant, this suggestive warden of Carcassonne
marched us about for an hour, haranguing, explaining, illustrating as he went; it was a complete little lecture, such as
might have been delivered at the Lowell Institute, on the
manner in which a first-rate *place forte* used to be attacked and
defended. Our peregrinations made it very clear that Carcas-

Carcassonne

sonne was impregnable; it is impossible to imagine without having seen them such refinements of immurement, such ingenuities of resistance. We passed along the battlements and *chemins de ronde*, ascended and descended towers, crawled under arches, peered out of loopholes, lowered ourselves into dungeons, halted in all sorts of tight places while the purpose of something or other was described to us. It was very curious, very interesting; above all it was very pictorial, and involved perpetual peeps into the little crooked, crumbling, sunny, grassy, empty Cité. In places, as you stand upon it, the great towered and embattled enceinte produces an illusion; it looks as if it were still equipped and defended. One vivid challenge, at any rate, it flings down before you; it calls upon you to make up your mind on the matter of restoration. For myself I have no hesitation; I prefer in every case the ruined, however ruined, to the reconstructed, however splendid. What is left is more precious than what is added; the one is history, the other is fiction; and I like the former the better of the two—it is so much more romantic. One is positive, so far as it goes; the other fills up the void with things more dead than the void itself, inasmuch as they have never had life. After that I am free to say that the restoration of Carcassonne is a splendid achievement. The little custodian dismissed us at last, after having, as usual, inducted us into the inevitable repository of photographs. These photographs are a great nuisance all over the Midi. They are exceedingly bad for the most part; and the worst—those in the form of the hideous little *album-panorama*—are thrust upon you at every turn. They are a kind of tax that you must pay; the best way is to pay to be let off. It was not to be denied that there was a relief in separating from our accomplished guide, whose manner of imparting information reminded me of the energetic process by which I had seen mineral waters bottled. All this while the afternoon had grown more lovely; the sunset had deepened, the horizon of hills grown purple; the mass of the Canigou became more delicate, yet more distinct. The day had so far faded that the interior of the little cathedral was wrapped in twilight, into which the glowing windows projected something of their colour. This church has high beauty and value,

Carcassonne

but I will spare the reader a presentation of details which I myself had no opportunity to master. It consists of a romanesque nave, of the end of the eleventh century, and a Gothic choir and transepts of the beginning of the fourteenth; and, shut up in its citadel like a precious casket in a cabinet, it seems—or seemed at that hour—to have a sort of double sanctity. After leaving it and passing out of the two circles of walls, I treated myself, in the most infatuated manner, to another walk round the Cité. It is certainly this general impression that is most striking—the impression from outside, where the whole place detaches itself at once from the landscape. In the warm southern dusk it looked more than ever like a city in a fairy tale. To make the thing perfect, a white young moon, in its first quarter, came out and hung just over the dark silhouette. It was hard to come away—to incommode one's self for anything so vulgar as a railway train; I would gladly have spent the evening in revolving round the walls of Carcassonne. But I had in a measure engaged to proceed to Narbonne, and there was a certain magic in that name which gave me strength—Narbonne, the richest city in Roman Gaul.

Arles

Chapter XXIV

AT NARBONNE I took up my abode at the house of a *serru-rier mécanicien*, and was very thankful for the accommo-dation. It was my misfortune to arrive at this ancient city late at night, on the eve of market-day; and market-day at Nar-bonne is a very serious affair. The inns, on this occasion, are stuffed with wine-dealers; for the country round about, dedi-cated almost exclusively to Bacchus, has hitherto escaped the phylloxera. This deadly enemy of the grape is encamped over the Midi in a hundred places; blighted vineyards and ruined proprietors being quite the order of the day. The signs of distress are more frequent as you advance into Provence, many of the vines being laid under water in the hope of wash-ing the plague away. There are healthy regions still, however, and the vintners find plenty to do at Narbonne. The traffic in wine appeared to be the sole thought of the Narbonnais; ev-ery one I spoke to had something to say about the harvest of gold that bloomed under its influence. "C'est inouï, monsieur, l'argent qu'il y a dans ce pays. Des gens à qui la vente de leur vin rapporte jusqu'à 500,000 francs par an." That little speech addressed to me by a gentleman at the inn gives the note of these revelations. It must be said that there was little in the appearance either of the town or of its population to suggest the possession of such treasures. Narbonne is a *sale petite ville* in all the force of the term, and my first impression on arriving there was an extreme regret that I had not remained for the night at the lovely Carcassonne. My journey from that delectable spot lasted a couple of hours and was performed in darkness—a darkness not so dense, however, but that I was able to make out, as we passed it, the great figure of Béziers, whose ancient roofs and towers, clustered on a goodly hilltop, looked as fantastic as you please. I know not what appearance Béziers may present by day, but by night it has quite the grand air. On issuing from the station at Narbonne I found that the only vehicle in waiting was a kind of bastard tramcar, a thing shaped as if it had been meant to go upon rails; that is, equipped with small wheels, placed beneath it, and with a platform at either end, but destined to rattle over the stones like the most vulgar of omnibuses. To complete the oddity of this conveyance, it was under the supervision, not of a conductor, but of a conductress. A fair young woman with a pouch suspended from her girdle had command of the platform; and as soon as the car was full she jolted us into the town through clouds of the thickest dust I ever have swallowed. I have had occasion to speak of the activity of women in France—of the way they are always in the ascendant; and here was a signal example of their general utility. The young lady I have mentioned conveyed her whole company to the wretched little Hôtel de France, where it is to be hoped that some of them found a lodging. For myself, I was informed that the place was crowded from cellar to attic, and that its inmates were sleeping three or four in a room. At Carcassonne I should have had a bad bed, but at Narbonne, apparently, I was to have no bed at all. I passed an hour or two of flat suspense while fate settled the question of whether I should go on to Perpignan, return to Béziers, or still discover a modest couch at Narbonne. I shall not have suffered in vain,

Narbonne: the Washing Place

however, if my example serves to deter other travellers from alighting unannounced at that city on a Wednesday evening. The retreat to Béziers, not attempted in time, proved impossible, and I was assured that at Perpignan, which I should not reach till midnight, the affluence of wine-dealers was not less than at Narbonne. I interviewed every hostess in the town, and got no satisfaction but distracted shrugs. Finally, at an advanced hour, one of the servants of the Hôtel de France, where I had attempted to dine, came to me in triumph to proclaim that he had secured for me a charming apartment in a *maison bourgeoise*. I took possession of it gratefully, in spite of its having an entrance like a stable and being pervaded by an odour compared with which that of a stable would have been delicious. As I have mentioned, my landlord was a locksmith, and he had strange machines which rumbled and whirred in the rooms below my own. Nevertheless I slept, and I dreamed of Carcassonne. It was better to do that than to dream of the Hôtel de France.

I was obliged to cultivate relations with the cuisine of this establishment. Nothing could have been more *méridional*; indeed, both the dirty little inn and Narbonne at large seemed to me to have the infirmities of the south without its usual graces. Narrow, noisy, shabby, belittered and encumbered, filled with clatter and chatter, the Hôtel de France would have been described in perfection by Alphonse Daudet. For what struck me above all in it was the note of the Midi as he has represented it—the sound of universal talk. The landlord sat at supper with sundry friends in a kind of glass cage, with a genial indifference to arriving guests; the waiters tumbled over the loose luggage in the hall; the travellers who had been turned away leaned gloomily against door-posts; and the landlady, surrounded by confusion, unconscious of responsibility, and animated only by the spirit of conversation, bandied high-voiced compliments with the *voyageurs de commerce*. At ten o'clock in the morning there was a table d'hôte for breakfast—a wonderful repast, which overflowed into every room and pervaded the whole establishment. I sat down with a hundred hungry marketers, fat, brown, greasy men, with a good deal of the rich soil of Languedoc adhering to their hands and their boots. I mention the latter articles because they almost put them on the table. It was very hot, and there were swarms of flies; the viands had the strongest odour; there was in particular a horrible mixture known as *gras-double*, a light grey, glutinous, nauseating mess, which my companions devoured in large quantities. A man opposite to me had the dirtiest fingers I ever saw; a collection of fingers which in England would have excluded him from a farmers' ordinary. The conversation was mainly bucolic; though a part of it, I remember, at the table at which I sat, consisted of a discussion as to whether or no the maid-servant were *sage*—a discussion which went on under the nose of this young lady, as she carried about the dreadful *gras-double*, and to which she contributed the most convincing blushes. It was thoroughly *méridional*.

In going to Narbonne I had of course counted upon Roman remains; but when I went forth in search of them I perceived that I had hoped too fondly. There is really nothing in the place to speak of; that is, on the day of my visit there was nothing but the market, which was in complete possession. "This intricate, curious, but lifeless town," Murray calls it; yet to me it appeared overflowing with life. Its streets are mere crooked, dirty lanes, bordered with perfectly insignificant houses; but they were filled with the same clatter and chatter that I had found at the hotel. The market was held partly in the little square of the hôtel de ville, a structure which a flattering woodcut in the Guide-Joanne had given me a desire to behold. The reality was not impressive, the old colour of the front having been completely restored away. Such interest as it superficially possesses it derives from a fine mediæval tower which rises beside it with turrets at the angles—always a picturesque thing. The rest of the market was held in another *place*, still shabbier than the first, which lies beyond the canal. The Canal du Midi flows through the town, and, spanned at this point by a small suspension-bridge, presented a certain sketchability. On the farther side were the vendors and chafferers—old women under awnings and big umbrellas, rickety tables piled high with fruit, white caps and brown faces, blouses, sabots, donkeys. Beneath this picture was another—a long row of washerwomen, on their knees on the edge of the canal, pounding and wringing the dirty linen of

Narbonne—no great quantity, to judge by the costume of the people. Innumerable rusty men, scattered all over the place, were buying and selling wine, straddling about in pairs, in groups, with their hands in their pockets, and packed together at the doors of the cafés. They were mostly fat and brown and unshaven; they ground their teeth as they talked; they were very *méridionaux*.

The only two lions at Narbonne are the cathedral and the museum, the latter of which is quartered in the hôtel de ville. The cathedral, closely shut in by houses and with the west front undergoing repairs, is singular in two respects. It consists exclusively of a choir, which is of the end of the thirteenth century and the beginning of the next, and of great magnificence. There is absolutely nothing else. This choir, of extraordinary elevation, forms the whole church. I sat there a good while; there was no other visitor. I had taken a great dislike to poor little Narbonne, which struck me as sordid and overheated, and this place seemed to extend to me, as in the Middle Ages, the privilege of sanctuary. It is a very solemn corner. The other peculiarity of the cathedral is that, externally, it bristles with battlements, having anciently formed part of the defences of the *archevêché*, which is beside it and which connects it with the hôtel de ville. This combination of the church and the fortress is very curious, and during the Middle Ages was not without its value. The palace of the former archbishops of Narbonne (the hôtel de ville of to-day forms part of it) was both an asylum and an arsenal during the hideous wars by which all Languedoc was ravaged in the thirteenth century. The whole mass of buildings is jammed together in a manner that from certain points of view makes it far from apparent which feature is which. The museum occupies several chambers at the top of the hôtel de ville, and is not an imposing collection. It was closed, but I induced the portress to let me in—a silent, cadaverous person, in a black coif, like a *béguine*, who sat knitting in one of the windows while I went the rounds. The number of Roman fragments is small, and their quality is not the finest; I must add that this impression was hastily gathered. There is, indeed, a work of art in one of the rooms which creates a presumption in favour

Narbonne: the Cathedral and Hôtel de Ville

of the place—the portrait (rather a good one) of a citizen of Narbonne, whose name I forget, who is described as having devoted all his time and his intelligence to collecting the objects by which the visitor is surrounded. This excellent man was a connoisseur, and the visitor is doubtless often an ignoramus.

Montpellier: the Aqueduct

Chapter XXV

"Cette, with its glistening houses white,
Curves with the curving beach away
To where the lighthouse beacons bright,
Far in the bay."

T HAT STANZA of Matthew Arnold's, which I happened to
remember, gave a certain importance to the half-hour I
spent in the buffet of the station at Cette while I waited for
the train to Montpellier. I had left Narbonne in the afternoon, and by the time I reached Cette the darkness had descended. I therefore missed the sight of the glistening houses,
and had to console myself with that of the beacon in the bay,
as well as with a *bouillon* of which I partook at the buffet
aforesaid; for, since the morning, I had not ventured to return to the table d'hôte at Narbonne. The Hôtel Nevet at
Montpellier, which I reached an hour later, has an ancient
renown all over the south of France—advertises itself, I believe, as *le plus vaste du midi*. It seemed to me the model of a
good provincial inn; a big rambling, creaking establishment,

with brown, labyrinthine corridors, a queer old open-air vestibule, into which the diligence, in the *bon temps*, used to penetrate, and an hospitality more expressive than that of the new caravansaries. It dates from the days when Montpellier was still accounted a fine winter residence for people with weak lungs; and this rather melancholy tradition, together with the former celebrity of the school of medicine still existing there, but from which the glory has departed, helps to account for its combination of high antiquity and vast proportions. The old hotels were usually more concentrated; but the school of medicine passed for one of the attractions of Montpellier. Long before Mentone was discovered or Colorado invented, British invalids travelled down through France in the postchaise or the public coach, to spend their winters in the wonderful place which boasted both a climate and a faculty. The air is mild, no doubt, but there are refinements of mildness which were not then suspected, and which in a more analytic age have carried the annual wave far beyond Montpellier. The place is charming, all the same; and it served the purpose of John Locke, who made a long stay there, between 1675 and 1679, and became acquainted with a noble fellow-visitor, Lord Pembroke, to whom he dedicated the famous Essay. There are places that please without your being able to say wherefore, and Montpellier is one of the number. It has some charming views, from the great promenade of the Peyrou; but its position is not strikingly fine. Beyond this it contains a good museum and the long façades of its school, but these are its only definite treasures. Its cathedral struck me as quite the weakest I had seen, and I remember no other monument that made up for it. The place has neither the gaiety of a modern nor the solemnity of an ancient town, and it is agreeable as certain women are agreeable who are neither beautiful nor clever. An Italian would remark that it is sympathetic; a German would admit that it is *gemüthlich*. I spent two days there, mostly in the rain, and even under these circumstances I carried away a kindly impression. I think the Hôtel Nevet had something to do with it, and the sentiment of relief with which, in a quiet, even a luxurious, room that looked out on a garden, I reflected that I had washed my hands of Narbonne. The phylloxera has destroyed the vines in the country that surrounds

Montpellier, and at that moment I was capable of rejoicing in the thought that I should not breakfast with vintners.

The gem of the place is the Musée Fabre, one of the best collections of paintings in a provincial city. François Fabre, a native of Montpellier, died there in 1837, after having spent a considerable part of his life in Italy, where he had collected a good many valuable pictures and some very poor ones, the latter class including several from his own hand. He was the hero of a remarkable episode, having succeeded no less a person than Vittorio Alfieri in the affections of no less a person than Louise de Stolberg, Countess of Albany, widow of no less a person than Charles Edward Stuart, the second pretender to the British crown. Surely no woman ever was associated sentimentally with three figures more diverse—a disqualified sovereign, an Italian dramatist, and a bad French painter. The productions of M. Fabre, who followed in the steps of David, bear the stamp of a cold mediocrity; there is not much to be said even for the portrait of the genial countess (her life has been written by M. Saint-Réné-Taillandier, who depicts her as delightful), which hangs in Florence, in the gallery of the Uffizzi, and makes a pendant to a likeness of Alfieri by the same author. Stendhal, in his "Mémoires d'un Touriste," says that this work of art represents her as a cook who has pretty hands. I am delighted to have an opportunity of quoting Stendhal, whose two volumes of the "Mémoires d'un Touriste" every traveller in France should carry in his portmanteau. I have had this opportunity more than once, for I have met him at Tours, at Nantes, at Bourges; and everywhere he is suggestive. But he has the defect that he is never pictorial, that he never by any chance makes an image, and that his style is perversely colourless for a man so fond of contemplation. His taste is often singularly false; it is the taste of the early years of the present century, the period that produced clocks surmounted with sentimental "subjects." Stendhal does not admire these clocks, but he almost does. He admires Domenichino and Guercino, he prizes the Bolognese school of painters because they "spoke to the soul." He is a votary of the new classic, is fond of tall, square, regular buildings, and thinks Nantes, for instance, full of the "air noble." It was a pleasure to me to reflect that five-and-forty years ago he had alighted in that city, at the very inn in which I spent a night and which looks down on the Place Graslin and the theatre. The hotel that was the best in 1837 appears to be the best to-day. On the subject of Touraine Stendhal is extremely refreshing; he finds the scenery meagre and much overrated, and proclaims his opinion with perfect frankness. He does, however, scant justice to the banks of the Loire; his want of appreciation of the picturesque—want of the sketcher's sense—causes him to miss half the charm of a landscape which is nothing if not "quiet," as a painter would say, and of which the felicities reveal themselves only to waiting eyes. He even despises the Indre, the river of Madame Sand. The "Mémoires d'un Touriste" are written in the character of a commercial traveller, and the author has nothing to say about Chenonceaux or Chambord, or indeed about any of the châteaux of that part of France; his system being to talk only of the large towns, where he may be supposed to find a market for his goods. It was his ambition to pass for an ironmonger. But in the large towns he is usually excellent company, though as discursive as Sterne and strangely indifferent, for a man of imagination, to those superficial aspects of things which the poor pages now before the reader are mainly an attempt to render. It is his conviction that Alfieri, at Florence, bored the Countess of Albany terribly; and he adds that the famous Gallophobe died of jealousy of the little painter from Montpellier. The Countess of Albany left her property to Fabre; and I suppose some of the pieces in the museum of his native town used to hang in the sunny saloons of that fine old palace on the Arno which is still pointed out to the stranger in Florence as the residence of Alfieri.

The institution has had other benefactors, notably a certain M. Bruyas, who has enriched it with an extraodinary number of portraits of himself. As these, however, are by different hands, some of them distinguished, we may suppose that it was less the model than the artists to whom M. Bruyas wished to give publicity. Easily first are two large specimens of David Teniers, which are incomparable for brilliancy and a glowing perfection of execution. I have a weakness for this singular genius, who combined the delicate with the grovelling, and I have rarely seen richer examples. Scarcely less valuable is a Gerard Dow which hangs near them, though it must rank lower, as having kept less of its freshness. This Gerard Dow did me good, for a master is a master, whatever he may paint. It represents a woman paring carrots, while a boy before her exhibits a mouse-trap in which he has caught a frightened victim. The goodwife has spread a cloth on the top of a big barrel which serves her as a table, and on this brown, greasy napkin, of which the texture is wonderfully rendered, lie the raw vegetables she is preparing for domestic consumption. Beside the barrel is a large caldron lined with copper, with a rim of brass. The way these things are painted brings tears to the eyes; but they give the measure of the Musée Fabre, where two specimens of Teniers and a Gerard Dow are the jewels. The Italian pictures are of small value; but there is a work by Sir Joshua Reynolds, said to be the only one in France — an infant Samuel in prayer, apparently a repetition of the picture in England which inspired the little plaster image, disseminated in Protestant lands, that we used to admire in our childhood. Sir Joshua, somehow, was an eminently Protestant painter; no one can forget that, who in the National Gallery in London has looked at the picture in which he represents several young ladies as nymphs, voluminously draped, hanging garlands over a statue — a picture suffused indefinably with the Anglican spirit and exasperating to a member of one of the Latin races. It is an odd chance therefore that has led him into that part of France where Protestants have been least *bien vus*. This is the country of the dragonnades of Louis XIV. and of the pastors of the desert. From the garden of the Peyrou, at Montpellier, you may see the hills of the Cévennes, to which they of the religion fled for safety and out of which they were hunted and harried.

I have only to add, in regard to the Musée Fabre, that it contains the portrait of its founder — a little, pursy, fat-faced, elderly man, whose countenance contains few indications of the power that makes distinguished victims. He is, however, just such a personage as the mind's eye sees walking on the terrace of the Peyrou of an October afternoon in the early years of the century; a plump figure in a chocolate-coloured coat and a *culotte* that exhibits a good leg — a culotte provided with a watch-fob from which a heavy seal is suspended. This

Peyrou (to come to it at last) is a wonderful place, especially to be found in a little provincial city. France is certainly the country of towns that aim at completeness; more than in other lands they contain stately features as a matter of course. We should never have ceased to hear about the Peyrou if fortune had placed it at a Shrewsbury or a Buffalo. It is true that the place enjoys a certain celebrity at home, which it amply deserves, moreover; for nothing could be more impressive and monumental. It consists of an "elevated platform," as Murray says—an immense terrace laid out, in the highest part of the town, as a garden, and commanding in all directions a view which in clear weather must be of the finest. I strolled there in the intervals of showers, and saw only the nearer beauties—a great pompous arch of triumph in honour of Louis XIV. (which is not, properly speaking, in the garden, but faces it, straddling across the *place* by which you approach it from the town), an equestrian statue of that monarch set aloft in the middle of the terrace, and a very exalted and complicated fountain, which forms a background to the picture. This fountain gushes from a kind of hydraulic temple, or *château d'eau*, to which you ascend by broad flights of steps, and which is fed by a splendid aqueduct, stretched in the most ornamental and unexpected manner across the neighbouring valley. All this work dates from the middle of the last century. The combination of features—the triumphal arch, or gate; the wide fair terrace, with its beautiful view; the statue of the grand monarch; the big architectural fountain, which would not surprise one at Rome, but does surprise one at Montpellier; and to complete the effect, the extraordinary aqueduct, charmingly fore-shortened—all this is worthy of a capital, of a little court-city. The whole place, with its repeated steps, its balustrades, its massive and plentiful stonework, is full of the air of the last century—*sent bien son dix-huitième siècle*; none the less so, I am afraid, that, as I read in my faithful Murray, after the revocation of the Edict of Nantes the block, the stake, the wheel had been erected here for the benefit of the desperate Camisards.

The Pont du Gard

Chapter XXVI

IT WAS a pleasure to feel one's self in Provence again—the land where the silver-grey earth is impregnated with the light of the sky. To celebrate the event, as soon as I arrived at Nîmes I engaged a calèche to convey me to the Pont du Gard. The day was yet young and was exceptionally fair; it appeared well, for a longish drive, to take advantage, without delay, of such security. After I had left the town I became more intimate with that Provençal charm which I had already enjoyed from the window of the train, and which glowed in the sweet sunshine and the white rocks and lurked in the smoke-puffs of the little olives. The olive-trees in Provence are half the landscape. They are neither so tall, so stout, nor so richly contorted as you have seen them beyond the Alps; but this mild colourless bloom seems the very texture of the country. The road from Nîmes, for a distance of fifteen miles, is superb; broad enough for an army and as white and firm as a dinnertable. It stretches away over undulations which have a kind of rhythmic value, and in the curves it makes through the wide, free country, where there is never a hedge or a wall and the detail is always exquisite, there is something majestic, almost processional. Some twenty minutes before I reached the little inn that marks the termination of the drive my vehicle met with an accident which just missed being serious, and which engaged the attention of a gentleman who, followed by his groom and mounted on a strikingly handsome horse, happened to ride up at the moment. This young man, who, with his good looks and charming manner, might have stepped out of a novel of Octave Feuillet, gave me some very intelligent advice in reference to one of my horses that had been injured, and was so good as to accompany me to the inn, with the resources of which he was acquainted, to see that his recommendations were carried out. The result of our interview was that he invited me to come and look at a small but ancient château in the neighbourhood, which he had the happiness— not the greatest in the world, he intimated—to inhabit, and at which I engaged to present myself after I should have spent an hour at the Pont du Gard. For the moment, when we separated, I gave all my attention to that great structure. You are very near it before you see it; the ravine it spans suddenly opens and exhibits the picture. The scene at this point grows extremely beautiful. The ravine is the valley of the Gardon, which the road from Nîmes has followed some time without taking account of it, but which, exactly at the right distance from the aqueduct, deepens and expands and puts on those characteristics which are best suited to give it effect. The gorge becomes romantic, still and solitary, and, with its white rocks and wild shrubbery, hangs over the clear-coloured river, in whose slow course there is, here and there, a deeper pool. Over the valley, from side to side and ever so high in the air, stretch the three tiers of the tremendous bridge. They are unspeakably imposing, and nothing could well be more Roman. The hugeness, the solidity, the unexpectedness, the monumental rectitude of the whole thing leave you nothing to say—at the time—and make you stand gazing. You simply feel that it is noble and perfect, that it has the quality of greatness. A road, branching from the highway, descends to the level of the river and passes under one of the arches. This road has a wide margin of grass and loose stones, which slopes upward into the bank of the ravine. You may sit here as long

The Pont du Gard

as you please, staring up at the light, strong piers; the spot is sufficiently "wild," though two or three stone benches have been erected on it. I remained there an hour and got a complete impression; the place was perfectly soundless and, for the time at least, lonely; the splendid afternoon had begun to fade, and there was a fascination in the object I had come to see. It came to pass that at the same time I discovered in it a certain stupidity, a vague brutality. That element is rarely absent from great Roman work, which is wanting in the nice adaptation of the means to the end. The means are always exaggerated; the end is so much more than attained. The Roman rigour was apt to overshoot the mark, and I suppose a race which could do nothing small is as defective as a race that can do nothing great. Of this Roman rigour the Pont du Gard is an admirable example. It would be a great injustice, however, not to insist upon its beauty—a kind of manly beauty, that of an object constructed not to please but to serve, and impressive simply from the scale on which it carries out this intention. The number of arches in each tier is different; they are smaller and more numerous as they ascend. The preservation of the thing is extraordinary; nothing has crumbled or collapsed; every feature remains, and the huge blocks of stone, of a brownish-yellow (as if they had been baked by the Provençal sun for eighteen centuries), pile themselves, without mortar or cement, as evenly as the day they were laid together. All this to carry the water of a couple of springs to a little provincial city! The conduit on the top has retained its shape and traces of the cement with which it was lined. When the vague twilight began to gather, the lonely valley seemed to fill itself with the shadow of the Roman name, as if the mighty empire were still as erect as the supports of the aqueduct; and it was open to a solitary tourist, sitting there sentimental, to believe that no people has ever been, or will ever be, as great as that, measured, as we measure the greatness of an individual, by the push they gave to what they undertook. The Pont du Gard is one of the three or four deepest impressions they have left; it speaks of them in a manner with which they might have been satisfied.

I feel as if it were scarcely discreet to indicate the whereabouts of the château of the obliging young man I had met on the way from Nîmes; I must content myself with saying that it nestled in an enchanting valley—*dans le fond*, as they say in France—and that I took my course thither on foot after leaving the Pont du Gard. I find it noted in my journal as "an adorable little corner." The principal feature of the place is a couple of very ancient towers, brownish-yellow in hue, and mantled in scarlet Virginia-creeper. One of these towers, reputed to be of Saracenic origin, is isolated, and is only the more effective; the other is incorporated in the house, which is delightfully fragmentary and irregular. It had got to be late by this time, and the lonely *castel* looked crepuscular and mysterious. An old housekeeper was sent for, who showed me the rambling interior; and then the young man took me into a dim old drawing-room, which had no less than four chimney-pieces, all unlighted, and gave me a refection of fruit and sweet wine. When I praised the wine and asked him what it was, he said simply "C'est du vin de ma mère!" Throughout my little journey I had never yet felt myself so far from Paris; and this was a sensation I enjoyed more than my host, who was an involuntary exile, consoling himself with laying out a *manège* which he showed me as I walked away. His civility was great, and I was greatly touched by it. On my way back to the little inn where I had left my vehicle I passed the Pont du Gard and took another look at it. Its great arches made windows for the evening sky, and the rocky ravine, with its dusky cedars and shining river, was lonelier than before. At the inn I swallowed, or tried to swallow, a glass of horrible wine with my coachman; after which, with my reconstructed team, I drove back to Nîmes in the moonlight. It only added a more solitary whiteness to the constant sheen of the Provençal landscape.

Aigues-Mortes

Chapter XXVII

THE WEATHER the next day was equally fair, so that it seemed an imprudence not to make sure of Aigues-Mortes. Nîmes itself could wait; at a pinch I could attend to Nîmes in the rain. It was my belief that Aigues-Mortes was a little gem, and it is natural to desire that gems should have an opportunity to sparkle. This is an excursion of but a few hours, and there is a little friendly, familiar, dawdling train that will convey you, in time for a noonday breakfast, to the small dead town where the blessed Saint Louis twice embarked for the Crusades. You may get back to Nîmes for dinner; the run—or rather the walk, for the train doesn't run—is of about an hour. I found the little journey charming and looked out of the carriage window, on my right, at the distant Cévennes, covered with tones of amber and blue, and, all around, at vineyards red with the touch of October. The grapes were gone, but the plants had a colour of their own. Within a certain distance of Aigues-Mortes they give place to wide salt-marshes, traversed by two canals; and over this expanse the train rumbles slowly upon a narrow causeway, failing for some time, though you know you are near the object of your curiosity, to bring you to sight of anything but the horizon. Suddenly it appears, the towered and embattled mass, lying so low that the crest of its defences seems to rise straight out of the ground; and it is not till the train stops close before them that you are able to take the full measure of its walls.

Aigues-Mortes stands on the edge of a wide *étang*, or shallow inlet of the sea, the farther side of which is divided by a narrow band of coast from the Gulf of Lyons. Next after Carcassonne, to which it forms an admirable *pendant*, it is the most perfect thing of the kind in France. It has a rival in the person of Avignon, but the ramparts of Avignon are much less effective. Like Carcassonne, it is completely surrounded with its old fortifications; and if they are far simpler in character (there is but one circle), they are quite as well preserved. The moat has been filled up, and the site of the town might be figured by a billiard-table without pockets. On this absolute level, covered with coarse grass, Aigues-Mortes presents quite the appearance of the walled town that a school-boy draws upon his slate or that we see in the background of early Flemish pictures—a simple parallelogram, of a contour almost absurdly bare, broken at intervals by angular towers and square holes. Such, literally speaking, is this delightful little city, which needs to be seen to tell its full story. It is extraordinarily pictorial, and if it is a very small sister of Carcassonne, it has at least the essential features of the family. Indeed, it is even more like an image and less like a reality than Carcassonne; for by position and prospect it seems even more detached from the life of the present day. It is true that Aigues-Mortes does a little business; it sees certain bags of salt piled into barges which stand in a canal beside it, and which carry their cargo into actual places. But nothing could well be more drowsy and desultory than this industry as I saw it practised, with the aid of two or three brown peasants and under the eye of a solitary douanier, who strolled on the little quay beneath the western wall. "C'est bien plaisant, c'est bien paisible," said this worthy man, with whom I had some conversation; and pleasant and peaceful is the place indeed, though the former of these epithets may suggest an element of gaiety in which Aigues-Mortes is deficient. The sand, the salt, the dull sea-view, surround it with a bright, quiet melancholy. There are fifteen towers and nine gates, five of which are on the southern side, overlooking the water. I walked all round the place three times (it doesn't take long), but lingered most under the southern wall, where the afternoon light slept in the dreamiest, sweetest way. I sat down on an old stone and looked away to the desolate salt-marshes and the still, shining surface of the *étang*; and, as I did so, reflected that this was a queer little out-of-the-world corner to have been chosen, in the great dominions of either monarch, for that pompous interview which took place, in 1538, between Francis I. and Charles V. It was also not easy to perceive how Louis IX., when in 1248 and 1270 he started for the Holy Land, set his army afloat in such very undeveloped channels. An hour later I purchased in the town a little pamphlet by M. Marius Topin, who undertakes to explain this latter anomaly and to show that there is water enough in the port, as we may call it by courtesy, to have sustained a fleet of crusaders. I was unable to trace the channel that he points out, but was glad to believe that, as he contends, the sea has not retreated from the town since the thirteenth century. It was comfortable to think that things are not so changed as that. M. Topin indicates that the other French ports of the Mediterranean were not then *disponibles*, and that Aigues-Mortes was the most eligible spot for an embarkation.

Behind the straight walls and the quiet gates the little town has not crumbled like the Cité of Carcassonne. It can hardly be said to be alive; but if it is dead it has been very neatly embalmed. The hand of the restorer rests on it constantly; but this artist has not, as at Carcassonne, had miracles to accomplish. The interior is very still and empty, with small stony, whitewashed streets tenanted by a stray dog, a stray cat, a stray old woman. In the middle is a little *place*, with two or three cafés decorated by wide awnings—a little *place* of which the principal feature is a very bad bronze statue of Saint Louis by Pradier. It is almost as bad as the breakfast I had at the inn that bears the name of that pious monarch. You may walk round the enceinte of Aigues-Mortes both outside and in; but you may not, as at Carcassonne, make a portion of this circuit

Aigues-Mortes

on the *chemin de ronde*, the little projecting footway attached to the inner face of the battlements. This footway, wide enough only for a single pedestrian, is in the best order, and near each of the gates a flight of steps leads up to it; but a locked gate at the top of the steps makes access impossible, or at least unlawful. Aigues-Mortes, however, has its citadel, an immense tower, larger than any of the others, a little detached and standing at the north-west angle of the town. I called upon the *casernier*—the custodian of the walls—and in his absence I was conducted through this big Tour de Constance by his wife, a very mild, meek woman, yellow with the traces of fever and ague—a scourge which, as might be expected in a town whose name denotes "dead waters," enters freely at the nine gates. The Tour de Constance is of extraordinary girth and solidity, divided into three superposed circular chambers, with very fine vaults, which are lighted by embrasures of prodigious depth, converging to windows little larger than loopholes. The place served for years as a prison to many of the Protestants of the south whom the revocation of the Edict of Nantes had exposed to atrocious penalties, and the annals of these dreadful chambers in the first half of the last century were written in tears and blood. Some of the recorded cases of long confinement there make one marvel afresh at what man has inflicted and endured. In a country in which a policy of extermination was to be put into practice this horrible tower was an obvious resource. From the battlements at the top, which is surmounted by an old disused lighthouse, you see the little compact rectangular town, which looks hardly bigger than a garden-patch, mapped out beneath you, and follow the plain configuration of its defences. You take possession of it, and you feel that you will remember it always.

Nîmes: the Maison Carrée

Chapter XXVIII

AFTER THIS I was free to look about me at Nîmes, and I did so with such attention as the place appeared to require. At the risk of seeming too easily and too frequently disappointed, I will say that it required rather less than I had been prepared to give. It is a town of three or four fine features rather than a town with, as I may say, a general figure. In general Nîmes is poor; its only treasures are its Roman remains, which are of the first order. The new French fashions prevail in many of its streets; the old houses are paltry, and the good houses are new; while beside my hotel rose a big spick-and-span church, which had the oddest air of having been intended for Brooklyn or Cleveland. It is true that this church looked out on a square completely French—a square of a fine modern disposition, flanked on one side by a classical *palais de justice* embellished with trees and parapets and occupied in the centre with a group of allegorical statues such as one encounters only in the cities of France, the chief of these being a colossal figure by Pradier representing Nîmes. An English, an American town which should have such a

monument, such a square as this would be a place of great
pretensions; but, like so many little *villes de province* in the
country of which I write, Nîmes is easily ornamental. What
nobler element can there be than the Roman baths at the foot
of Mont Cavalier and the delightful old garden that surrounds
them? All that quarter of Nîmes has every reason to be proud
of itself; it has been revealed to the world at large by copious
photography. A clear, abundant stream gushes from the foot
of a high hill (covered with trees and laid out in paths), and is
distributed into basins which sufficiently refer themselves to
the period that gave them birth—the period that has left its
stamp on that pompous Peyrou which we admired at Montpellier. Here are the same terraces and steps and balustrades,
and a system of waterworks less impressive perhaps, but very
ingenious and charming. The whole place is a mixture of old
Rome and of the French eighteenth century; for the remains
of the antique baths are in a measure incorporated in the
modern fountains. In a corner of this umbrageous precinct
stands a small Roman ruin, which is known as a temple of
Diana, but was more apparently a *nymphæum*, and appears to
have had a graceful connection with the adjacent baths. I
learn from Murray that this little temple, of the period of
Augustus, "was reduced to its present state of ruin in 1577;"
the moment at which the townspeople, threatened with a
siege by the troops of the Crown, partly demolished it lest it
should serve as a cover to the enemy. The remains are very
fragmentary, but they serve to show that the place was lovely.
I spent half an hour in it on a perfect Sunday morning (it is
enclosed by a high *grille*, carefully tended, and has a warden
of its own), and with the help of my imagination tried to
reconstruct a little the aspect of things in the Gallo-Roman
days. I do wrong perhaps to say that I *tried*; from a flight so
deliberate I should have shrunk. But there was a certain contagion of antiquity in the air; and among the ruins of baths
and temples, in the very spot where the aqueduct that crosses
the Gardon in the wondrous manner I had seen discharged
itself, the picture of a splendid paganism seemed vaguely to
glow. Roman baths—Roman baths; those words alone were
a scene. Everything was changed: I was strolling in a *jardin
français*; the bosky slope of the Mont Cavalier (a very modest

Nîmes: the Cathedral

mountain), hanging over the place, is crowned with a shapeless tower, which is as likely to be of mediæval as of antique
origin; and yet, as I leaned on the parapet of one of the fountains, where a flight of curved steps (a hemicycle, as the
French say) descended into a basin full of dark, cool recesses,
where the slabs of the Roman foundations gleam through the
clear green water—as in this attitude I surrendered myself to
contemplation and reverie, it seemed to me that I touched for
a moment the ancient world. Such moments are illuminating,
and the light of this one mingles, in my memory, with the
dusky greenness of the Jardin de la Fontaine.

The fountain proper—the source of all these distributed
waters—is the prettiest thing in the world, a reduced copy of
Vaucluse. It gushes up at the foot of the Mont Cavalier, at a
point where that eminence rises with a certain cliff-like effect,
and, like other springs in the same circumstances, appears to
issue from the rock with a sort of quivering stillness. I
trudged up the Mont Cavalier—it is a matter of five minutes—and having committed this cockneyism, enhanced it
presently by another. I ascended the stupid Tour Magne, the
mysterious structure I mentioned a moment ago. The only
feature of this dateless tube, except the inevitable collection of
photographs to which you are introduced by the doorkeeper,
is the view you enjoy from its summit. This view is of course
remarkably fine, but I am ashamed to say I have not the smallest recollection of it; for while I looked into the brilliant
spaces of the air I seemed still to see only what I saw in the
depths of the Roman baths—the image, disastrously confused and vague, of a vanished world. This world, however,
has left at Nîmes a far more considerable memento than a few
old stones covered with water-moss. The Roman arena is the
rival of those of Verona and of Arles; at a respectful distance it
emulates the Colosseum. It is a small Colosseum, if I may be
allowed the expression, and is in much better preservation
than the great circus at Rome. This is especially true of the
external walls, with their arches, pillars, cornices. I must add
that one should not speak of preservation, in regard to the
arena at Nîmes, without speaking also of repair. After the
great ruin ceased to be despoiled it began to be protected,
and most of its wounds have been dressed with new material.

Nîmes: the Amphitheatre

These matters concern the archæologist; and I felt here, as I felt afterwards at Arles, that one of the profane, in the presence of such a monument, can only admire and hold his tongue. The great impression, on the whole, is an impression of wonder that so much should have survived. What remains at Nîmes, after all dilapidation is estimated, is astounding. I spent an hour in the Arènes on that same sweet Sunday morning, as I came back from the Roman baths, and saw that the corridors, the vaults, the staircases, the external casing, are still virtually there. Many of these parts are wanting in the Colosseum, whose sublimity of size, however, can afford to dispense with detail. The seats at Nîmes, like those at Verona, have been largely renewed; not that this mattered much, as I lounged on the cool surface of one of them and admired the mighty concavity of the place and the elliptical sky-line, broken by uneven blocks and forming the rim of the monstrous cup—a cup that had been filled with horrors. And yet I made my reflections: I said to myself that though a Roman arena is one of the most impressive of the works of man, it has a touch of that same stupidity which I ventured to discover in the Pont du Gard. It is brutal; it is monotonous; it is not at all exquisite. The Arènes at Nîmes were arranged for a bull-fight—a form of recreation that, as I was informed, is much *dans les habitudes Nîmoises*, and very common throughout Provence, where (still according to my information) it is the usual pastime of a Sunday afternoon. At Arles and Nîmes it has a characteristic setting, but in the villages the patrons of the game make a circle of carts and barrels, on which the spectators perch themselves. I was surprised at the prevalence in mild Provence of the Iberian vice, and hardly know whether it makes the custom more respectable that at Nîmes and Arles the thing is shabbily and imperfectly done. The bulls are rarely killed, and indeed often are bulls only in the Irish sense of the term—being domestic and motherly cows. Such an entertainment of course does not supply to the arena that element of the exquisite which I spoke of as wanting. The exquisite at Nîmes is mainly represented by the famous Maison Carrée. The first impression you receive from this delicate little building, as you stand before it, is that you have already seen it many times. Photographs, engravings, models, medals, have placed it definitely in your eye, so that from the sentiment with which you regard it curiosity and surprise are almost completely, and perhaps deplorably, absent. Admiration remains, however—admiration of a familiar and even slightly patronising kind. The Maison Carrée does not overwhelm you; you can conceive it. It is not one of the great sensations of antique art; but it is perfectly felicitous, and, in spite of having been put to all sorts of incongruous uses, marvellously preserved. Its slender columns, its delicate proportions, its charming compactness, seem to bring one nearer to the century that built it than the great superpositions of arenas and bridges, and give it the interest that vibrates from one age to another when the note of taste is struck. If anything were needed to make this little toy-temple a happy production, the service would be rendered by the second-rate boulevard that conducts to it, adorned with inferior cafés and tobacco-shops. Here, in a respectable recess, surrounded by vulgar habitations and with the theatre, of a classic pretension, opposite, stands the small "square house," so called because it is much longer than it is broad. I saw it first in the evening, in the vague moonlight, which made it look as if it were cast in bronze. Stendhal says, justly, that it has the shape of a playing-card, and he expresses his admiration for it by the singular wish that an "exact copy" of it should be erected in Paris. He even goes so far as to say that in the year 1880 this tribute will have been rendered to its charms; nothing would be more simple, to his mind, than to "have" in that city "le Panthéon de Rome, quelques temples de Grèce." Stendhal found it amusing to write in the character of a *commis-voyageur*, and sometimes it occurs to his reader that he really was one.

Tarascon and Beaucaire

Chapter XXIX

O N MY WAY from Nîmes to Arles I spent three hours at Tarascon; chiefly for the love of Alphonse Daudet, who has written nothing more genial than "Les Aventures Prodigieuses de Tartarin," and the story of the "siege" of the bright, dead little town (a mythic siege by the Prussians) in the "Contes du Lundi." In the introduction which, for the new edition of his works, he has lately supplied to "Tartarin," the author of this extravagant but kindly satire gives some account of the displeasure with which he has been visited by the ticklish Tarasconnais. Daudet relates that in his attempt to shed a humorous light upon some of the more vivid phases of the Provençal character he selected Tarascon at a venture; not because the temperament of its natives is more vainglorious than that of their neighbours, or their rebellion against the "despotism of fact" more marked, but simply because he had to name a particular Provençal city. Tartarin is a hunter of lions and charmer of women, a true *"produit du midi,"* as Daudet says, a character of the most extravagant, genial comedy. He is a minimised Don Quixote, with much less dignity but with equal good faith; and the story of his exploits is a little masterpiece of the free fantastic. The Tarasconnais, however, declined to take the joke, and opened the vials of their wrath upon the mocking child of Nîmes, who would have been better employed, they doubtless thought, in showing up the infirmities of his own family. I am bound to add that when I passed through Tarascon they did not appear to be in the least out of humour. Nothing could have been brighter, easier, more suggestive of amiable indifference, than the picture it presented to my mind. It lies quietly beside the Rhone, looking across at Beaucaire, which seems very distant and independent, and tacitly consenting to let the castle of the good King René of Anjou, which projects very boldly into the river, pass for its most interesting feature. The other features are, primarily, a sort of vivid sleepiness in the aspect of the place, as if the September noon (it had lingered on into October) lasted longer there than elsewhere; certain low arcades which make the streets look grey and exhibit empty vistas; and a very curious and beautiful walk beside the Rhone, denominated the Chaussée—a long and narrow causeway, densely shaded by two rows of magnificent old trees planted in its embankment and rendered doubly effective at the moment I passed over it by a little train of collegians who had been taken out for mild exercise by a pair of young priests. Lastly one may say that a striking element of Tarascon, as of any town that lies on the Rhone, is simply the Rhone itself; the big brown flood, of uncertain temper, which has never taken time to forget that it is a child of the mountain and the glacier, and that such an origin carries with it great privileges. Later, at Avignon, I observed it in the exercise of these privileges, chief among which was that of frightening the good people of the old papal city half out of their wits.

The château of King René serves to-day as the prison of a district, and the traveller who wishes to look into it must obtain his permission at the Mairie of Tarascon. If he have had a certain experience of French manners, his application will be accompanied with the forms of a considerable obsequiosity, and in this case his request will be granted as civilly as it has been made. The castle has more of the air of a severely feudal fortress than I should suppose the period of its construction (the first half of the fifteenth century) would have warranted; being tremendously bare and perpendicular, and constructed for comfort only in the sense that it was arranged for defence. It is a square and simple mass, composed of small yellow stones and perched on a pedestal of rock which easily commands the river. The building has the usual circular towers at the corners and a heavy cornice at the top, and immense stretches of sun-scorched wall relieved at wide intervals by small windows, heavily cross-barred. It has, above all, an extreme steepness of aspect; I cannot express it otherwise. The walls are as sheer and inhospitable as precipices. The castle has kept its large moat, which is now a hollow filled with wild plants. To this tall fortress the good René retired in the middle of the fifteenth century, finding it apparently the most substantial thing left him in a dominion which had included Naples and Sicily, Lorraine and Anjou. He had been a much-tried monarch and the sport of a various fortune, fighting half his life for thrones he didn't care for, and exalted only to be quickly cast down. Provence was the country of his affection, and the memory of his troubles did not prevent him from holding a joyous court at Tarascon and at Aix. He finished the castle at Tarascon, which had been begun earlier in the century—finished it, I suppose, for consistency's sake, in the manner in which it had originally been designed rather than in accordance with the artistic tastes that formed the consolation of his old age. He was a painter, a writer, a dramatist, a modern dilettante, addicted to private theatricals. There is something very attractive in the image that he has imprinted on the page of history. He was both clever and kind, and many reverses and much suffering had not embittered him nor quenched his faculty of enjoyment. He was fond of his sweet Provence, and his sweet Provence has been grateful; it has woven a light tissue of legend around the memory of the good King René.

I strolled over his dusky habitation—it must have taken all his good humour to light it up—at the heels of the custodian, who showed me the usual number of castle-properties: a deep, well-like court; a collection of winding staircases and vaulted chambers, the embrasures of whose windows and the recesses of whose doorways reveal a tremendous thickness of

Tarascon

wall. These things constitute the general identity of old castles; and when one has wandered through a good many, with due discretion of step and protrusion of head, one ceases very much to distinguish and remember, and contents one's self with consigning them to the honourable limbo of the romantic. I must add that this reflection did not in the least deter me from crossing the bridge which connects Tarascon with Beaucaire, in order to examine the old fortress whose ruins adorn the latter city. It stands on a foundation of rock much higher than that of Tarascon, and looks over with a melancholy expression at its better-conditioned brother. Its position is magnificent and its outline very gallant. I was well rewarded for my pilgrimage; for if the castle of Beaucaire is only a fragment, the whole place, with its position and its views, is an ineffaceable picture. It was the stronghold of the Montmorencys, and its last tenant was that rash Duke François whom Richelieu, seizing every occasion to trample on a great noble, caused to be beheaded at Toulouse, where we saw, in the Capitol, the butcher's knife with which the cardinal pruned the crown of France of its thorns. The castle, after the death of this victim, was virtually demolished. Its site, which nature to-day has taken again to herself, has an extraordinary charm. The mass of rock that it formerly covered rises high above the town and is as precipitous as the side of the Rhone. A tall, rusty iron gate admits you from a quiet corner of Beaucaire to a wild tangled garden covering the side of the hill—for the whole place forms the public promenade of the townsfolk—a garden without flowers, with little steep, rough paths that wind under a plantation of small, scrubby stone-pines. Above this is the grassy platform of the castle, enclosed on one side only (toward the river) by a large fragment of wall and a very massive dungeon. There are benches placed in the lee of the wall, and others on the edge of the platform, where one may enjoy a view, beyond the river, of certain peeled and scorched undulations. A sweet desolation, an everlasting peace, seemed to hang in the air. A very old man (a fragment, like the castle itself) emerged from some crumbling corner to do me the honours—a very gentle, obsequious, tottering, toothless, grateful old man. He beguiled me into an ascent of the solitary tower, from which you may look down on the big sallow river and glance at diminished Tarascon and the barefaced, bald-headed hills behind it. It may appear that I insist too much upon the nudity of the Provençal horizon—too much considering that I have spoken of the prospect from the heights of Beaucaire as lovely. But it is an exquisite bareness; it seems to exist for the purpose of allowing one to follow the delicate lines of the hills and touch with the eyes, as it were, the smallest inflections of the landscape. It makes the whole thing wonderfully bright and pure.

Beaucaire used to be the scene of a famous fair, the great fair of the south of France. It has gone the way of most fairs, even in France, where these delightful exhibitions hold their own much better than might be supposed. It is still held in the month of July; but the bourgeoises of Tarascon send to the Magasin du Louvre for their smart dresses, and the principal glory of the scene is its long tradition. Even now, however, it ought to be the prettiest of all fairs, for it takes place in a charming wood which lies just beneath the castle, beside the Rhone. The booths, the barracks, the platforms of the mountebanks, the bright-coloured crowd, diffused through this midsummer shade and spotted here and there with the rich Provençal sunshine, must be of the most pictorial effect. It is highly probable too that it offers a large collection of pretty faces; for even in the few hours that I spent at Tarascon I discovered symptoms of the purity of feature for which the women of the *pays d'Arles* are renowned. The Arlesian head-dress was visible in the streets; and this delightful coiffure is so associated with a charming facial oval, a dark mild eye, a straight Greek nose, and a mouth worthy of all the rest, that it conveys a presumption of beauty which gives the wearer time either to escape or to please you. I have read somewhere, however, that Tarascon is supposed to produce handsome men, as Arles is known to deal in handsome women. It may be that I should have found the Tarasconnais very fine fellows if I had encountered enough specimens to justify an induction. But there are very few males in the streets, and the place presented no appearance of activity. Here and there the black coif of an old woman or of a young girl was framed by a low doorway; but for the rest, as I have said, Tarascon was mostly involved in a siesta. There was not a creature in the little church of Saint Martha, which I made a point of visiting before I returned to the station, and which, with its fine romanesque side-portal and its pointed and crocketed gothic spire, is as curious as it need be in view of its tradition. It stands in a quiet corner where the grass grows between the small cobble-stones, and you pass beneath a deep archway to reach it. The tradition relates that Saint Martha tamed with her own hands and attached to her girdle a dreadful dragon who was known as the Tarasque and is reported to have given his name to the city on whose site (amid the rocks which form the base of the château) he had his cavern. The dragon perhaps is the symbol of a ravening paganism dispelled by the eloquence of a sweet evangelist. The bones of the interesting saint, at all events, were found, in the eleventh century, in a cave beneath the spot on which her altar now stands. I know not what had become of the bones of the dragon.

Provençal Landscape

Chapter XXX

THERE are two shabby old inns at Arles which compete closely for your custom. I mean by this that if you elect to go to the Hôtel du Forum, the Hôtel du Nord, which is placed exactly beside it (at a right angle), watches your arrival with ill-concealed disapproval; and if you take the chances of its neighbour, the Hôtel du Forum seems to glare at you invidiously from all its windows and doors. I forget which of these establishments I selected; whichever it was, I wished very much that it had been the other. The two stand together on the Place des Hommes, a little public square of Arles which somehow quite misses its effect. As a city, indeed, Arles quite misses its effect in every way; and if it is a charming place, as I think it is, I can hardly tell the reason why. The straight-nosed Arlésiennes account for it in some degree; and the remainder may be charged to the ruins of the arena and the theatre. Beyond this, I remember with affection the ill-proportioned little Place des Hommes; not at all monumental, and given over to puddles and to shabby cafés. I recall with tenderness the tortuous and featureless streets, which looked like the streets of a village and were paved with villainous little sharp stones, making all exercise penitential. Consecrated by association is even a tiresome walk that I took the evening I arrived, with the purpose of obtaining a view of the Rhone. I had been to Arles before, years ago, and it seemed to me that I remembered finding on the banks of the stream some sort of picture. I think that on the evening on which I speak there was a watery moon, which it seemed to me would light up the past as well as the present. But I found no picture, and I scarcely found the Rhone at all. I lost my way, and there was not a creature in the streets to whom I could appeal. Nothing could be more provincial than the situation of Arles at ten o'clock at night. At last I arrived at a kind of embankment where I could see the great mud-coloured stream slipping along in the soundless darkness. It had come on to rain, I know not what had happened to the moon, and the whole place was anything but gay. It was not what I had looked for; what I had looked for was in the irrecoverable past. I groped my way back to the inn over the infernal *cailloux*, feeling like a discomfited Dogberry. I remember now that this hotel was the one (whichever that may be) which has the fragment of a Gallo-Roman portico inserted into one of its angles. I had chosen it for the sake of this exceptional ornament. It was damp and dark, and the floors felt gritty to the feet; it was an establishment at which the dreadful *gras-double* might have appeared at the table d'hôte, as it had done at Narbonne. Nevertheless I was glad to get back to it; and nevertheless too—and this is the moral of my simple anecdote—my pointless little walk (I don't speak of the pavement) suffuses itself, as I look back upon it, with a romantic tone. And in relation to the inn I suppose I had better mention that I am well aware of the inconsistency of a person who dislikes the modern caravansary and yet grumbles when he finds a hotel of the superannuated sort. One ought to choose, it would seem, and make the best of either alternative. The two old taverns at Arles are quite unimproved; such as they must have been in the infancy of the modern world, when Stendhal passed that way and the lumbering diligence

Arles: St. Trophimus

deposited him in the Place des Hommes, such in every detail they are to-day. *Vieilles auberges de France*, one ought to enjoy their gritty floors and greasy window-panes. Let it be put on record therefore that I have been, I won't say less comfortable, but at least less happy, at better inns.

To be really historic, I should have mentioned that before going to look for the Rhone I had spent part of the evening on the opposite side of the little place, and that I indulged in this recreation for two definite reasons. One of these was that I had an opportunity of gossiping at a café with a conversable young Englishman whom I had met in the afternoon at Tarascon and more remotely, in other years, in London; the other was that there sat enthroned behind the counter a splendid mature Arlésienne, whom my companion and I agreed that it was a rare privilege to contemplate. There is no rule of good manners or morals which makes it improper, at a café, to fix one's eyes upon the *dame de comptoir*; the lady is, in the nature of things, a part of your *consommation*. We were therefore free to admire without restriction the handsomest person I had ever seen give change for a five-franc piece. She was a large quiet woman, who would never see forty again; of an intensely feminine type, yet wonderfully rich and robust, and full of a certain physical nobleness. Though she was not really old, she was antique; and she was very grave, even a little sad. She had the dignity of a Roman empress, and she handled coppers as if they had been stamped with the head of Cæsar. I have seen washerwomen in the Trastevere who were perhaps as handsome as she; but even the head-dress of the Roman contadina contributes less to the dignity of the person born to wear it than the sweet and stately Arlesian cap, which sits at once aloft and on the back of the head; which is accompanied with a wide black bow covering a considerable part of the crown; and which, finally, accommodates itself indescribably well to the manner in which the tresses of the front are pushed behind the ears.

This admirable dispenser of lumps of sugar has distracted me a little, for I am still not sufficiently historical. Before going to the café I had dined, and before dining I had found time to go and look at the arena. Then it was that I discovered that Arles has no general physiognomy and, except the

Arles: Ruins of the Roman Theatre

delightful little church of Saint Trophimus, no architecture, and that the rugosities of its dirty lanes affect the feet like knife-blades. It was not then, on the other hand, that I saw the arena best. The second day of my stay at Arles I devoted to a pilgrimage to the strange old hill town of Les Baux, the mediæval Pompeii, of which I shall give myself the pleasure of speaking. The evening of that day, however (my friend and I returned in time for a late dinner), I wandered among the Roman remains of the place by the light of a magnificent moon and gathered an impression which has lost little of its silvery glow. The moon of the evening before had been aqueous and erratic; but if on the present occasion it was guilty of any irregularity, the worst it did was only to linger beyond its time in the heavens in order to let us look at things comfortably. The effect was admirable; it brought back the impression of the way, in Rome itself, on evenings like that, the moonshine rests upon broken shafts and slabs of antique pavement. As we sat in the theatre looking at the two lone columns that survive—part of the decoration of the back of the stage—and at the fragments of ruin around them, we might have been in the Roman Forum. The arena at Arles, with its great magnitude, is less complete than that of Nîmes; it has suffered even more the assaults of time and the children of time, and it has been less repaired. The seats are almost wholly wanting; but the external walls, minus the topmost tier of arches, are massively, ruggedly complete; and the vaulted corridors seem as solid as the day they were built. The whole thing is superbly vast and as monumental, for a place of light amusement—what is called in America a "variety-show"—as it entered only into the Roman mind to make such establishments. The *podium* is much higher than at Nîmes, and many of the great white slabs that faced it have been recovered and put into their places. The proconsular box has been more or less reconstructed, and the great converging passages of approach to it are still majestically distinct; so that, as I sat there in the moon-charmed stillness, leaning my elbows on the battered parapet of the ring, it was not impossible to listen to the murmurs and shudders, the thick voice of the circus, that died away fifteen hundred years ago.

The theatre has a voice as well, but it lingers on the ear of time with a different music. The Roman theatre at Arles seemed to me one of the most charming and touching ruins I had ever beheld; I took a particular fancy to it. It is less than a skeleton—the arena may be called a skeleton—for it consists only of half a dozen bones. The traces of the row of columns which formed the scene—the permanent back-scene— remain; two marble pillars—I just mentioned them—are up-right, with a fragment of their entablature. Before them is the vacant space which was filled by the stage, with the line of the proscenium distinct, marked by a deep groove impressed upon slabs of stone, which looks as if the bottom of a high screen had been intended to fit into it. The semicircle formed by the seats—half a cup—rises opposite; some of the rows are distinctly marked. The floor, from the bottom of the stage, in the shape of an arc of which the chord is formed by the line of the orchestra, is covered by slabs of coloured mar-ble—red, yellow and green—which, though terribly battered and cracked to-day, give one an idea of the elegance of the interior. Everything shows that it was on a great scale: the large sweep of its enclosing walls, the massive corridors that passed behind the auditorium and of which we can still per-fectly take the measure. The way in which every seat com-manded the stage is a lesson to the architects of our epochs, as also the immense size of the place is a proof of extraordinary power of voice on the part of the Roman actors. It was after we had spent half an hour in the moonshine at the arena that we came on to this more ghostly and more exquisite ruin. The principal entrance was locked, but we effected an easy *escalade*, scaled a low parapet, and descended into the place behind the scenes. It was as light as day, and the solitude was complete. The two slim columns, as we sat on the broken benches, stood there like a pair of silent actors. What I called touching just now was the thought that here the human voice, the utterance of a great language, had been supreme. The air was full of intonations and cadences; not of the echo of smashing blows, of riven armour, of howling victims and roaring beasts. The spot is, in short, one of the sweetest lega-cies of the ancient world; and there seems no profanation in the fact that by day it is open to the good people of Arles, who use it to pass, by no means in great numbers, from one part of the town to the other; treading the old marble floor and brushing, if need be, the empty benches. This familiarity does not kill the place again; it makes it, on the contrary, live a little—makes the present and the past touch each other.

Montmajeur

Chapter XXXI

THE THIRD LION of Arles has nothing to do with the ancient world, but only with the old one. The church of Saint Trophimus, whose wonderful romanesque porch is the principal ornament of the principal *place*—a *place* otherwise distinguished by the presence of a slim and tapering obelisk in the middle, as well as by that of the hôtel de ville and the museum—the interesting church of Saint Trophimus swears a little, as the French say, with the peculiar character of Arles. It is very remarkable, but I would rather it were in another place. Arles is delightfully pagan, and Saint Trophimus, with its apostolic sculptures, is rather a false note. These sculptures are equally remarkable for their primitive vigour and for the perfect preservation in which they have come down to us. The deep recess of a round-arched porch of the twelfth century is covered with quaint figures which have not lost a nose or a finger. An angular Byzantine-looking Christ sits in a

diamond-shaped frame at the summit of the arch, surrounded
by little angels, by great apostles, by winged beasts, by a hundred sacred symbols and grotesque ornaments. It is a dense
embroidery of sculpture, black with time, but as uninjured as
if it had been kept under glass. One good mark for the French
Revolution! Of the interior of the church, which has a nave of
the twelfth century and a choir three hundred years more recent, I chiefly remember the odd feature that the romanesque
aisles are so narrow that you literally—or almost—squeeze
through them. You do so with some eagerness, for your natural purpose is to pass out to the cloister. This cloister, as
distinguished and as perfect as the porch, has a great deal of
charm. Its four sides, which are not of the same period (the
earliest and best are of the twelfth century), have an elaborate
arcade, supported on delicate pairs of columns, the capitals of
which show an extraordinary variety of device and ornament.
At the corners of the quadrangle these columns take the form
of curious human figures. The whole thing is a gem of lightness and preservation and is often cited for its beauty; but—if
it doesn't sound too profane—I prefer, especially at Arles, the
ruins of the Roman theatre. The antique element is too precious to be mingled with anything less rare. This truth was
very present to my mind during a ramble of a couple of hours
that I took just before leaving the place; and the glowing
beauty of the morning gave the last touch to the impression. I
spent half an hour at the Museum; then I took another look
at the Roman theatre; after which I walked a little out of the
town to the Aliscamps, the old Elysian Fields, the meagre
remnant of the old pagan place of sepulture, which was afterwards used by the Christians, but has been for ages deserted
and now consists only of a melancholy avenue of cypresses
lined with a succession of ancient sarcophagi, empty, mossy
and mutilated. An iron-foundry, or some horrible establishment which is conditioned upon tall chimneys and a noise of
hammering and banging, has been established near at hand;
but the cypresses shut it out well enough, and this small patch
of Elysium is a very romantic corner.

The door of the Museum stands ajar, and a vigilant custodian, with the usual batch of photographs on his mind, peeps
out at you disapprovingly while you linger opposite, before

Arles: Door of St. Trophimus

the charming portal of Saint Trophimus, which you may look at for nothing. When you succumb to the silent influence of his eye and go over to visit his collection, you find yourself in a desecrated church, in which a variety of ancient objects disinterred in Arlesian soil have been arranged without any pomp. The best of these, I believe, were found in the ruins of the theatre. Some of the most curious of them are early Christian sarcophagi, exactly on the pagan model, but covered with rude yet vigorously wrought images of the apostles and with illustrations of scriptural history. Beauty of the highest kind, either of conception or of execution, is absent from most of the Roman fragments, which belong to the taste of a late period and a provincial civilisation. But a gulf divides them from the bristling little imagery of the Christian sarcophagi, in which, at the same time, one detects a vague emulation of the rich examples by which their authors were surrounded. There is a certain element of style in all the pagan things; there is not a hint of it in the early Christian relics, among

Arles: the Cloisters

which, according to M. Joanne, of the Guide, are to be found more fine sarcophagi than in any collection but that of St. John Lateran. In two or three of the Roman fragments there is a noticeable distinction; principally in a charming bust of a boy, quite perfect, with those salient eyes that one sees in antique portraits, and to which the absence of vision in the marble mask gives a look, often very touching, as of a baffled effort to see; also in the head of a woman, found in the ruins of the theatre, who, alas! has lost her nose and whose noble, simple contour, barring this deficiency, recalls the great manner of the Venus of Milo. There are various rich architectural fragments which indicate that that edifice was a very splendid affair. This little Museum at Arles, in short, is the most Roman thing I know of out of Rome.

Les Baux

Chapter XXXII

I FIND that I declared one evening, in a little journal I was keeping at that time, that I was weary of writing (I was probably very sleepy), but that it was essential I should make some note of my visit to Les Baux. I must have gone to sleep as soon as I had recorded this necessity, for I search my small diary in vain for any account of that enchanting spot. I have nothing but my memory to consult—a memory which is fairly good in regard to a general impression, but is terribly infirm in the matter of details and items. We knew in advance, my companion and I, that Les Baux was a pearl of picturesqueness; for had we not read as much in the handbook of Murray, who has the testimony of an English nobleman as to its attractions? We also knew that it lay some miles from Arles, on the crest of the Alpilles, the craggy little mountains which, as I stood on the breezy platform of Beaucaire, formed to my eye a charming, if somewhat remote, background to Tarascon; this assurance having been given us by the landlady of the inn at Arles, of whom we hired a rather lumbering conveyance. The weather was not promising, but it proved a good day for the mediæval Pompeii; a grey, melancholy,

moist, but rainless, or almost rainless day, with nothing in the
sky to flout, as the poet says, the dejected and pulverised past.
The drive itself was charming, for there is an inexhaustible
sweetness in the grey-green landscape of Provence. It is never
absolutely flat and yet is never really ambitious, and is full
both of entertainment and repose. It is in constant undula-
tion, and the bareness of the soil lends itself easily to outline
and profile. When I say the bareness I mean the absence of
woods and hedges. It blooms with heath and scented shrubs
and stunted olive, and the white rock shining through the
scattered herbage has a brightness which answers to the
brightness of the sky. Of course it needs the sunshine, for all
southern countries look a little false under the ground-glass of
incipient bad weather. This was the case on the day of my
pilgrimage to Les Baux. Nevertheless I was glad to keep going,
as I was to arrive; and as I went it seemed to me that true
happiness would consist in wandering through such a land on
foot, on September afternoons, when one might stretch one's
self on the warm ground in some shady hollow and listen to
the hum of bees and the whistle of melancholy shepherds; for
in Provence the shepherds whistle to their flocks. I saw two
or three of them, in the course of this drive to Les Baux,
meandering about, looking behind and calling upon the sheep
in this way to follow, which the sheep always did, very
promptly, with ovine unanimity. Nothing is more picturesque
than to see a slow shepherd threading his way down one of
the winding paths on a hillside, with his flock close behind
him, necessarily expanded, yet keeping just at his heels, bending and twisting as it goes and looking rather like the tail of a
dingy comet.

About four miles from Arles, as you drive northward towards the Alpilles, of which Alphonse Daudet has spoken so
often and, as he might say, so intimately, stand on a hill that
overlooks the road the very considerable ruins of the abbey of
Montmajour, one of the innumerable remnants of a feudal
and ecclesiastical (as well as an architectural) past that one
encounters in the south of France; remnants which, it must
be confessed, tend to introduce a certain confusion and satiety
into the passive mind of the tourist. Montmajour, however, is
very impressive and interesting; the only trouble with it is

that, unless you have stopped and returned to Arles, you see it in memory over the head of Les Baux, which is a much more absorbing picture. A part of the mass of buildings (the monastery) dates only from the last century; and the stiff architecture of that period does not lend itself very gracefully to desolation: it looks too much as if it had been burnt down the year before. The monastery was demolished during the Revolution, and it injures a little the effect of the very much more ancient fragments that are connected with it. The whole place is on a great scale; it was a rich and splendid abbey. The church, a vast basilica of the eleventh century and of the noblest proportions, is virtually intact; I mean as regards its essentials, for the details have completely vanished. The huge solid shell is full of expression; it looks as if it had been hollowed out by the sincerity of early faith, and it opens into a cloister as impressive as itself. Wherever one goes, in France, one meets, looking backward a little, the spectre of the great Revolution; and one meets it always in the shape of the destruction of something beautiful and precious. To make us forgive it at all, how much it must also have destroyed that was more hateful than itself! Beneath the church of Montmajour is a most extraordinary crypt, almost as big as the edifice above it and making a complete subterranean temple, surrounded with a circular gallery, or deambulatory, which expands at intervals into five square chapels. There are other things, of which I have but a confused memory: a great fortified keep; a queer little primitive chapel hollowed out of the rock beneath these later structures and recommended to the visitor's attention as the confessional of Saint Trophimus, who shares with so many worthies the glory of being the first apostle of the Gauls. Then there is a strange, small church, of the dimmest antiquity, standing at a distance from the other buildings. I remember that after we had let ourselves down a good many steepish places to visit crypts and confessionals, we walked across a field to this archaic cruciform edifice and went thence to a point farther down the road, where our carriage was awaiting us. The chapel of the Holy Cross, as it is called, is classed among the historic monuments of France; and I read in a queer, rambling, ill-written book which I picked up at Avignon, and in which the author, M. Louis de

Laincel, has buried a great deal of curious information on the subject of Provence under a style inspiring little confidence, that the "délicieuse chapelle de Sainte-Croix" is a "véritable bijou artistique." He speaks of "a piece of lace in stone" which runs from one end of the building to the other, but of which I am obliged to confess that I have no recollection. I retain, however, a sufficiently clear impression of the little superannuated temple, with its four apses and its perceptible odour of antiquity—the odour of the eleventh century.

The ruins of Les Baux remain quite indistinguishable even when you are directly beneath them, at the foot of the charming little Alpilles, which mass themselves with a kind of delicate ruggedness. Rock and ruin have been so welded together by the confusions of time that as you approach it from behind—that is, from the direction of Arles—the place presents simply a general air of cragginess. Nothing can be prettier than the crags of Provence; they are beautifully modelled, as painters say, and they have a delightful silvery colour. The road winds round the foot of the hills on the top of which Les Baux is planted, and passes into another valley, from which the approach to the town is many degrees less precipitous and may be comfortably made in a carriage. Of course the deeply inquiring traveller will alight as promptly as possible, for the pleasure of climbing into this queerest of cities on foot is not the least part of the entertainment of going there. Then you appreciate its extraordinary position, its picturesqueness, its steepness, its desolation and decay. It hangs—that is, what remains of it—to the slanting summit of the mountain. Nothing would be more natural than for the whole place to roll down into the valley. A part of it has done so—for it is not unjust to suppose that in the process of decay the crumbled particles have sought the lower level, while the remainder still clings to its magnificent perch.

If I called Les Baux a city, just above, it was not that I was stretching a point in favour of the small spot which to-day contains but a few dozen inhabitants. The history of the place is as extraordinary as its situation. It was not only a city, but a state; not only a state, but an empire; and on the crest of its little mountain called itself sovereign of a territory, or at least of scattered towns and counties, with which its present aspect is grotesquely out of relation. The lords of Les Baux, in a word, were great feudal proprietors; and there was a time during which the island of Sardinia, to say nothing of places nearer home, such as Arles and Marseilles, paid them homage. The chronicle of this old Provençal house has been written, in a style somewhat unctuous and flowery, by M. Jules Canonge. I purchased the little book—a modest pamphlet—at the establishment of the good sisters, just beside the church, in one of the highest parts of Les Baux. The sisters have a school for the hardy little Baussenques, whom I heard piping their lessons while I waited in the cold *parloir* for one of the ladies to come and speak to me. Nothing could have been more perfect than the manner of this excellent woman when she arrived; yet her small religious house seemed a very out-of-the-way corner of the world. It was spotlessly neat, and the rooms looked as if they had lately been papered and painted: in this respect, at the mediæval Pompeii, they were rather a discord. They were, at any rate, the newest, freshest thing at Les Baux. I remember going round to the church after I had left the good sisters, and to a little quiet terrace which stands in front of it, ornamented with a few small trees and bordered with a wall, breast-high, over which you look down steep hillsides, off into the air and all about the neighbouring country. I remember saying to myself that this little terrace was one of those felicitous nooks which the tourist of taste keeps in his mind as a picture. The church was small and brown and dark, with a certain rustic richness. All this, however, is no general description of Les Baux.

I am unable to give any coherent account of the place, for the simple reason that it is a mere confusion of ruin. It has not been preserved in lava like Pompeii, and its streets and houses, its ramparts and castle, have become fragmentary not through the sudden destruction, but through the gradual withdrawal, of a population. It is not an extinguished, but a deserted city; more deserted far than even Carcassonne and Aigues-Mortes, where I found so much entertainment in the grass-grown element. It is of very small extent, and even in the days of its greatness, when its lords entitled themselves counts of Cephalonia and Neophantis, kings of Arles and Vienne, princes of Achaia and emperors of Constantinople—

even at this flourishing period, when, as M. Jules Canonge remarks, "they were able to depress the balance in which the fate of peoples and kings is weighed," the plucky little city contained at the most no more than thirty-six hundred souls. Yet its lords (who, however, as I have said, were able to present a long list of subject towns, most of them, though a few are renowned, unknown to fame) were seneschals and captains-general of Piedmont and Lombardy, grand admirals of the kingdom of Naples, and its ladies were sought in marriage by half the first princes in Europe. A considerable part of the little narrative of M. Canonge is taken up with the great alliances of the House of Baux, whose fortunes, matrimonial and other, he traces from the eleventh century down to the sixteenth. The empty shells of a considerable number of old houses, many of which must have been superb, the lines of certain steep little streets, the foundations of a castle, and ever so many splendid views, are all that remains to-day of these great titles. To such a list I may add a dozen very polite and sympathetic people who emerged from the interstices of the desultory little town to gaze at the two foreigners who had driven over from Arles and whose horses were being baited at the modest inn. The resources of this establishment we did not venture otherwise to test, in spite of the seductive fact that the sign over the door was in the Provençal tongue. This little group included the baker, a rather melancholy young man, in high boots and a cloak, with whom and his companions we had a good deal of conversation. The Baussenques of to-day struck me as a very mild and agreeable race, with a good deal of the natural amenity which, on occasions like this one, the traveller who is waiting for his horses to be put in or his dinner to be prepared observes in the charming people who lend themselves to conversation in the hill-towns of Tuscany. The spot where our entertainers at Les Baux congregated was naturally the most inhabited portion of the town; as I say, there were at least a dozen human figures within sight. Presently we wandered away from them, scaled the higher places, seated ourselves among the ruins of the castle, and looked down from the cliff overhanging that portion of the road which I have mentioned as approaching Les Baux from behind. I was unable to trace the configuration of the castle as plainly as the writers who have described it in the guide-books, and I am ashamed to say that I did not even perceive the three great figures of stone (the three Marys, as they are called; the two Marys of Scripture, with Martha) which constitute one of the curiosities of the place and of which M. Jules Canonge speaks with almost hyperbolical admiration. A brisk shower, lasting some ten minutes, led us to take refuge in a cavity of mysterious origin, where the melancholy baker presently discovered us, having had the *bonne pensée* of coming up for us with an umbrella which certainly belonged, in former ages, to one of the Stéphanettes or Berangères commemorated by M. Canonge. His oven, I am afraid, was cold so long as our visit lasted. When the rain was over we wandered down to the little disencumbered space before the inn, through a small labyrinth of obliterated things. They took the form of narrow, precipitous streets bordered by empty houses with gaping windows and absent doors, through which we had glimpses of sculptured chimney-pieces and fragments of stately arch and vault. Some of the houses are still inhabited, but most of them are open to the air and weather. Some of them have completely collapsed; others present to the street a front which enables one to judge of the physiognomy of Les Baux in the days of its importance. This importance had pretty well passed away in the early part of the sixteenth century, when the place ceased to be an independent principality. It became—by bequest of one of its lords, Bernardin des Baux, a great captain of his time—part of the appanage of the kings of France, by whom it was placed under the protection of Arles, which had formerly occupied with regard to it a different position. I know not whether the Arlesians neglected their trust, but the extinction of the sturdy little stronghold is too complete not to have begun long ago. Its memories are buried under its ponderous stones. As we drove away from it in the gloaming my friend and I agreed that the two or three hours we had spent there were among the happiest impressions of a pair of tourists very curious of the picturesque. We almost forgot that we were bound to regret that the shortened day left us no time to drive five miles farther, above a pass in the little mountains—it had beckoned to us in the morning, when we came in sight of it, almost irresistibly—to see the Roman arch and mausoleum of Saint Remy. To compass this larger excursion (including the visit to Les Baux) you must start from Arles very early in the morning; but I can imagine no more delightful day.

Avignon

Chapter XXXIII

I HAD BEEN twice at Avignon before, and yet I was not satisfied. I probably am satisfied now; nevertheless I enjoyed
my third visit. I shall not soon forget the first, on which a
particular emotion set an indelible stamp. I was creeping
northward, in 1870, after four months spent, for the first time,
in Italy. It was the middle of January, and I had found myself
unexpectedly forced to return to England for the rest of the
winter. It was an insufferable disappointment; I was wretched
and broken-hearted. Italy appeared to me at that time so
much better than anything else in the world, that to rise from
table in the middle of the feast was a prospect of being hungry for the rest of my days. I had heard a great deal of praise
of the south of France; but the south of France was a poor
consolation. In this state of mind I arrived at Avignon, which
under a bright, hard winter sun was tingling—fairly spin-
ning—with the *mistral*. I find in my journal of the other day
a reference to the acuteness of my reluctance in January 1870.
France, after Italy, appeared in the language of the latter
country *poco simpatica*; and I thought it necessary, for reasons
now inconceivable, to read the *Figaro*, which was filled with

descriptions of the horrible Troppmann, the murderer of the *famille* Kink. Troppmann, Kink, *le crime de Pantin*—the very names that figured in this episode seemed to wave me back. Had I abandoned the sonorous south to associate with vocables so base?

It was very cold the other day at Avignon, for though there was no mistral, it was raining as it rains in Provence, and the dampness had a terrible chill in it. As I sat by my fire late at night—for in genial Avignon, in October, I had to have a fire—it came back to me that eleven years before I had at that same hour sat by a fire in that same room and, writing to a friend to whom I was not afraid to appear extravagant, had made a vow that at some happier period of the future I would avenge myself on the *ci-devant* city of the Popes by taking it in a contrary sense. I suppose that I redeemed my vow on the occasion of my second visit better than on my third; for then I was on my way to Italy, and that vengeance, of course, was complete. The only drawback was that I was in such a hurry to get to Ventimiglia (where the Italian custom-house was to be the sign of my triumph), that I scarcely took time to make it clear to myself at Avignon that this was better than reading the *Figaro*. I hurried on almost too fast to enjoy the consciousness of moving southward. On this last occasion I was unfortunately destitute of that happy faith. Avignon was my southernmost limit, after which I was to turn round and proceed back to England. But in the interval I had been a great deal in Italy, and that made all the difference.

I had plenty of time to think of this, for the rain kept me practically housed for the first twenty-four hours. It had been raining in these regions for a month, and people had begun to look askance at the Rhone, though as yet the volume of the river was not exorbitant. The only excursion possible, while the torrent descended, was a kind of horizontal dive, accompanied with infinite splashing, to the little *musée* of the town, which is within a moderate walk of the hotel. I had a memory of it from my first visit; it had appeared to me more pictorial than its pictures. I found that recollection had flattered it a little, and that it is neither better nor worse than most provincial museums. It has the usual musty chill in the air, the usual grass-grown forecourt, in which a few lumpish Roman fragments are disposed, the usual red tiles on the floor and the usual specimens of the more livid schools on the walls. I rang up the *gardien*, who arrived with a bunch of keys, wiping his mouth; he unlocked doors for me, opened shutters, and while (to my distress, as if the things had been worth lingering over) he shuffled about after me, he announced the names of the pictures before which I stopped in a voice that reverberated through the melancholy halls and seemed to make the authorship shameful when it was obscure and grotesque when it pretended to be great. Then there were intervals of silence, while I stared absent-mindedly, at haphazard, at some indistinguishable canvas and the only sound was the downpour of the rain on the skylights. The museum of Avignon derives a certain dignity from its Roman fragments. The town has no Roman monuments to show; in this respect, beside its brilliant neighbours, Arles and Nîmes, it is a blank. But a great many small objects have been found in its soil—pottery, glass, bronzes, lamps, vessels and ornaments of gold and silver. The glass is especially charming—small vessels of the most delicate shape and substance, many of them perfectly preserved. These diminutive, intimate things bring one near to the old Roman life; they seem like pearls strung upon the slender thread that swings across the gulf of time. A little glass cup that Roman lips have touched says more to us than the great vessel of an arena. There are two small silver *casseroles*, with chiselled handles, in the museum of Avignon, that struck me as among the most charming survivals of antiquity.

I did wrong, just above, to speak of my attack on this establishment as the only recreation I took that first wet day; for I remember a terribly moist visit to the former palace of the Popes, which could have taken place only in the same tempestuous hours. It is true that I scarcely know why I should have gone out to see the Papal palace in the rain, for I had been over it twice before, and even then had not found the interest of the place so complete as it ought to be; the fact nevertheless remains that this last occasion is much associated with an umbrella, which was not superfluous even in some of the chambers and corridors of the gigantic pile. It had already seemed to me the dreariest of all historical buildings, and my final visit confirmed the impression. The place is as intricate as

Avignon: the Church

it is vast, and as desolate as it is dirty. The imagination has, for some reason or other, to make more than the effort usual in such cases to restore and repeople it. The fact indeed is simply that the palace has been so incalculably abused and altered. The alterations have been so numerous that, though I have duly conned the enumerations, supplied in guide-books, of the principal perversions, I do not pretend to carry any of them in my head. The huge bare mass, without ornament, without grace, despoiled of its battlements and defaced with sordid modern windows, covering the Rocher des Doms and looking down over the Rhone and the broken bridge of Saint-Bénazet (which stops in such a sketchable manner in mid-stream), and across at the lonely tower of Philippe le Bel and the ruined wall of Villeneuve, makes at a distance, in spite of its poverty, a great figure, the effect of which is carried out by the tower of the church beside it (crowned though the latter be, in a top-heavy fashion, with an immense modern image of the Virgin) and by the thick, dark foliage of the garden laid out on a still higher portion of the eminence. This garden recalls faintly and a trifle perversely the grounds of the Pincian at Rome. I know not whether it is the shadow of the Papal name, present in both places, combined with a vague analogy between the churches—which, approached in each case by a flight of steps, seemed to defend the precinct—but each time I have seen the Promenade des Doms it has carried my thoughts to the wider and loftier terrace from which you look away at the Tiber and Saint Peter's.

As you stand before the Papal palace, and especially as you enter it, you are struck with its being a very dull monument. History enough was enacted here: the great schism lasted from 1305 to 1370, during which seven Popes, all Frenchmen, carried on the court of Avignon on principles that have not commended themselves to the esteem of posterity. But history has been whitewashed away, and the scandals of that period have mingled with the dust of dilapidations and repairs. The building has for many years been occupied as a barrack for regiments of the line, and the main characteristics of a barrack—an extreme nudity and a very queer smell—prevail throughout its endless compartments. Nothing could have been more cruelly dismal than the appearance it presented at the time of this third visit of mine. A regiment, changing quarters, had departed the day before, and another was expected to arrive (from Algeria) on the morrow. The place had been left in the befouled and belittered condition which marks the passage of the military after they have broken camp, and it would offer but a melancholy welcome to the regiment that was about to take possession. Enormous windows had been left carelessly open all over the building, and the rain and wind were beating into empty rooms and passages, making draughts which purified, perhaps, but which scarcely cheered. For an arrival it was horrible. A handful of soldiers had remained behind. In one of the big vaulted rooms several of them were lying on their wretched beds, in the dim light, in the cold, in the damp, with the bleak bare walls before them and their overcoats, spread over them pulled up to their noses. I pitied them immensely, though they may have felt less wretched than they looked. I thought not of the old profligacies and crimes, not of the funnel-shaped torture-chamber (which, after exciting the shudder of generations, has been ascertained now, I believe, to have been a mediæval bakehouse), not of the tower of the *glacière* and the horrors perpetrated here in the Revolution, but of the military burden of young France. One wonders how young France endures it, and one is forced to believe that the French conscript has, in addition to his notorious good-humour, greater toughness than is commonly supposed by those who consider only the more relaxing influences of French civilisation. I hope he finds occasional compensation for such moments as I saw those damp young peasants passing on the mattresses of their hideous barrack, without anything around to remind them that they were in the most civilised of countries. The only traces of former splendour now visible in the Papal pile are the walls and vaults of two small chapels, painted in fresco, so battered and effaced as to be scarcely distinguishable, by Simone Memmi. It offers of course a peculiarly good field for restoration, and I believe the Government intend to take it in hand. I mention this fact without a sigh, for they cannot well make it less interesting than it is at present.

Villeneuve-lès-Avignon

Chapter XXXIV

F ORTUNATELY it did not rain every day (though I believe it was raining everywhere else in the department); otherwise I should not have been able to go to Villeneuve and to Vaucluse. The afternoon indeed was lovely when I walked over the interminable bridge that spans the two arms of the Rhone, divided here by a considerable island, and directed my course, like a solitary horseman—on foot, to the lonely tower which forms one of the outworks of Villeneuve-lès-Avignon. The picturesque, half-deserted little town lies a couple of miles farther up the river. The immense round towers of its old citadel and the long stretches of ruined wall covering the slope on which it lies are the most striking features of the nearer view, as you look from Avignon across the Rhone. I spent a couple of hours in visiting these objects, and there was a kind of pictorial sweetness in the episode; but I have not many details to relate. The isolated tower I just mentioned has much in common with the detached donjon of Montmajour, which I had looked at in going to Les Baux and to which I paid my respects in speaking of that excursion. Also the work of Philippe le Bel (built in 1307), it is amazingly big and stubborn, and formed the opposite limit of the broken bridge whose first arches (on the side of Avignon) alone remain to give a measure of the occasional volume of the Rhone. Half an hour's walk brought me to Villeneuve, which lies away from the river, looking like a big village half depopulated and occupied for the most part by dogs and cats, old women and small children; these last, in general, remarkably pretty, in the manner of the children of Provence. You pass through the place, which seems in a singular degree vague and unconscious, and come to the rounded hill on which the ruined abbey lifts its yellow walls—the Benedictine abbey of Saint-André, at once a church, a monastery, and a fortress. A large part of the crumbling enceinte disposes itself over the hill; but for the rest, all that has preserved any traceable cohesion is a considerable portion of the citadel. The defence of the place appears to have been entrusted largely to the huge round towers that flank the old gate; one of which, the more complete, the ancient warden (having first inducted me into his own dusky little apartment and presented me with a great bunch of lavender) enabled me to examine in detail. I would almost have dispensed with the privilege, for I think I have already mentioned that an acquaintance with many feudal interiors has wrought a sad confusion in my mind. The image of the outside always remains distinct; I keep it apart from other images of the same sort; it makes a picture sufficiently ineffaceable. But the guard-rooms, winding staircases, loopholes, prisons, repeat themselves and intermingle; they have a wearisome family likeness. There are always black passages and corners, and walls twenty feet thick; and there is always some high place to climb up to for the sake of a "magnificent" view. The views, too, are apt to run together. These dense gate-towers of Philippe le Bel struck me, however, as peculiarly wicked and grim. Their capacity is of the largest, and they contain ever so many devilish little dungeons, lighted by the narrowest slit in the prodigious wall, where it comes over one with a good deal of vividness and still more horror that wretched human beings once lay there rotting in the dark. The dungeons of Villeneuve made a particular impression on me—greater than any except those of Loches, which must surely be the most gruesome in Europe. I hasten to add that every dark hole at Villeneuve is called a dungeon; and I believe it

is well established that in this manner, in almost all old castles and towers, the sensibilities of the modern tourist are
unscrupulously played upon. There were plenty of black
holes in the Middle Ages that were not dungeons, but
household receptacles of various kinds; and many a tear
dropped in pity for the groaning captive has really been addressed to the spirits of the larder and the faggot-nook. For
all this, there are some very bad corners in the towers of Villeneuve, so that I was not wide of the mark when I began to
think again, as I had often thought before, of the stoutness
of the human composition in the Middle Ages and the tranquillity of nerve of people to whom the groaning captive
and the blackness of a "living tomb" were familiar ideas
which did not at all interfere with their happiness or their
sanity. Our modern nerves, our irritable sympathies, our easy
discomforts and fears, make one think (in some relations)
less respectfully of human nature. Unless indeed it be true, as
I have heard it maintained, that in the Middle Ages every
one did go mad—every one *was* mad. The theory that this
was a period of general dementia is not altogether untenable.

Within the old walls of its immense abbey the town of
Villeneuve has built itself a rough faubourg; the fragments
with which the soil was covered having been, I suppose, a
quarry of material. There are no streets; the small, shabby
houses, almost hovels, straggle at random over the uneven
ground. The only important feature is a convent of cloistered
nuns, who have a large garden (always within the walls) behind their house, and whose doleful establishment you look
down into, or down at simply, from the battlements of the
citadel. One or two of the nuns were passing in and out of
the house; they wore grey robes with a bright red cape. I
thought their situation most provincial. I came away and
wandered a little over the base of the hill, outside the walls.
Small white stones cropped through the grass, over which
low olive-trees were scattered. The afternoon had a yellow
brightness. I sat down under one of the little trees, on the
grass—the delicate grey branches were not much above my
head—and rested and looked at Avignon across the Rhone. It
was very soft, very still and pleasant, though I am not sure it
was all I once should have expected of that combination of

elements: an old city wall for a background, a canopy of olives, and for a couch the soil of Provence.

When I came back to Avignon the twilight was already thick, but I walked up to the Rocher des Doms. Here I again had the benefit of that amiable moon which had already lighted up for me so many romantic scenes. She was full, and she rose over the Rhone and made it look in the distance like a silver serpent. I remember saying to myself at this moment that it would be a beautiful evening to walk round the walls of Avignon—the remarkable walls which challenge comparison with those of Carcassonne and Aigues-Mortes, and which it was my duty, as an observer of the picturesque, to examine with some attention. Presenting themselves to that silver sheen, they could not fail to be impressive. So, at least, I said to myself; but unfortunately I did not believe what I said. It is a melancholy fact that the walls of Avignon had never impressed me at all, and I had never taken the trouble to make the circuit. They are continuous and complete, but for some mysterious reason they fail of their effect. This is partly because they are very low, in some places almost absurdly so, being buried in new accumulations of soil and by the filling in of the moat up to their middle. Then they have been too well tended; they not only look at present very new, but look as if they had never been old. The fact that their extent is very much greater makes them more of a curiosity than those of Carcassonne; but this is exactly, at the same time, what is fatal to their pictorial unity. With their thirty-seven towers and seven gates, they lose themselves too much to make a picture that will compare with the admirable little vignette of Carcassonne. I may mention, now that I am speaking of the general mass of Avignon, that nothing is more curious than the way in which, viewed from a distance, it is all reduced to naught by the vast bulk of the palace of the Popes. From across the Rhone, or from the train as you leave the place, this great grey block is all Avignon; it seems to occupy the whole city, extensive, with its shrunken population, as the city is.

Vaucluse

Chapter XXXV

It was the morning after this, I think (a certain Saturday), that when I came out of the Hôtel de l'Europe, which lies in a shallow concavity just within the city gate that opens on the Rhone—came out to look at the sky from the little *place* before the inn and see how the weather promised for the obligatory excursion to Vaucluse—I found the whole town in a terrible taking. I say the whole town advisedly, for every inhabitant appeared to have taken up a position on the bank of the river, or on the uppermost parts of the promenade of the Doms, where a view of its course was to be obtained. It had risen surprisingly in the night, and the good people of Avignon had reason to know what a rise of the Rhone might signify. The town, in its lower portions, is quite at the mercy of the swollen waters; and it was mentioned to me that in 1856 the Hôtel de l'Europe, in its convenient hollow, was flooded up to within a few feet of the ceiling of the dining-room, where the long board which had served for so many a table d'hôte floated disreputably, with its legs in the air. On the present occasion the mountains of the Ardêche, where it had

been raining for a month, had sent down torrents which, all
that fine Friday night, by the light of the innocent-looking
moon, poured themselves into the Rhone and its tributary the
Durance. The river was enormous and continued to rise, and
the sight was beautiful and horrible. The water in many places
was already at the base of the city walls, the quay, with its
parapet just emerging, being already covered. The country,
seen from the Plateau des Doms, resembled a vast lake, with
protrusions of trees, houses, bridges, gates. The people
looked at it in silence, as I had seen people before—on the
occasion of a rise of the Arno, at Pisa—appear to consider
the prospect of an inundation. "Il monte; il monte toujours"—there was not much said but that. It was a general
holiday, and there was an air of wishing to profit, for sociability's sake, by any interruption of the commonplace (the
popular mind likes "a change," and the element of change
mitigates the sense of disaster); but the affair was not otherwise a holiday. Suspense and anxiety were in the air, and it
never is pleasant to be reminded of the helplessness of man.
In the presence of a loosened river, with its ravaging, uncon-
querable volume, this impression is as strong as possible; and
as I looked at the deluge which threatened to make an island
of the Papal palace I perceived that the scourge of water is
greater than the scourge of fire. A blaze may be quenched,
but where could the flame be kindled that would arrest the
quadrupled Rhone? For the population of Avignon a good
deal was at stake, and I am almost ashamed to confess that in
the midst of the public alarm I considered the situation from
the point of view of the little projects of a sentimental tourist.
Would the prospective inundation interfere with my visit to
Vaucluse, or make it imprudent to linger twenty-four hours
longer at Avignon? I must add that the tourist was not perhaps, after all, so sentimental. I have spoken of the pilgrimage
to the shrine of Petrarch as obligatory, and that was, in fact,
the light in which it presented itself to me; all the more that I
had been twice at Avignon without undertaking it. This is
why I was vexed at the Rhone—if vexed I was—for representing as impracticable an excursion which I cared nothing
about. How little I cared was manifest from my inaction on
former occasions. I had a prejudice against Vaucluse, against

Petrarch, even against the incomparable Laura. I was sure that
the place was cockneyfied and threadbare, and I had never
been able to take an interest in the poet and the lady. I was
sure that I had known many women as charming and as
handsome as she, about whom much less noise had been
made; and I was convinced that her singer was factitious and
literary, and that there are half a dozen stanzas in Wordsworth
that speak more to the soul than the whole collection of his
fioriture. This was the crude state of mind in which I determined to go, at any risk, to Vaucluse. Now that I think it
over, I seem to remember that I had hoped, after all, that the
submersion of the roads would forbid it. Since morning the
clouds had gathered again, and by noon they were so heavy
that there was every prospect of a torrent. It appeared absurd
to choose such a time as this to visit a fountain—a fountain
which would be indistinguishable in the general cataract.
Nevertheless I took a vow, that if at noon the rain should not
have begun to descend upon Avignon I would repair to the
head-spring of the Sorgues. When the critical moment arrived
the clouds were hanging over Avignon like distended water-
bags, which only needed a prick to empty themselves. The
prick was not given, however; all nature was too much occupied in following the aberrations of the Rhone to think of
playing tricks elsewhere. Accordingly I started for the station
in a spirit which, for a tourist who sometimes had prided
himself on his unfailing supply of sentiment, was shockingly
perfunctory.

> "For tasks in hours of insight willed
>   May be in hours of gloom fulfilled."

I remembered these lines of Matthew Arnold (written, apparently, in an hour of gloom), and carried out the idea, as I
went, by hoping that with the return of insight I should be
glad to have seen Vaucluse. Light has descended upon me
since then, and I declare that the excursion is in every way to
be recommended. The place makes a great impression, quite
apart from Petrarch and Laura.

There was no rain; there was only, all the afternoon, a mild,
moist wind and a sky magnificently black, which made a *repoussoir* for the paler cliffs of the fountain. The road, by train,

crosses a flat, expressionless country, towards the range of
arid hills which lie to the east of Avignon, and which spring
(says Murray) from the mass of the Mont-Ventoux. At Isle-
sur-Sorgues, at the end of about an hour, the foreground becomes much more animated and the distance much more (or
perhaps I should say much less) actual. I descended from the
train and ascended to the top of an omnibus which was to
convey me into the recesses of the hills. It had not been
among my previsions that I should be indebted to a vehicle of
that kind for an opportunity to commune with the spirit of
Petrarch; and I had to borrow what consolation I could from
the fact that at least I had the omnibus to myself. I was the
only passenger; every one else was at Avignon watching the
Rhone. I lost no time in perceiving that I could not have
come to Vaucluse at a better moment. The Sorgues was almost as full as the Rhone, and of a colour much more romantic. Rushing along its narrowed channel under an avenue of
fine *platanes* (it is confined between solid little embankments
of stone), with the goodwives of the village, on the brink,
washing their linen in its contemptuous flood, it gave promise
of high entertainment farther on.

The drive to Vaucluse is of about three-quarters of an hour;
and though the river, as I say, was promising, the big pale
hills, as the road winds into them, did not look as if their
slopes of stone and shrub were a nestling-place for superior
scenery. It is a part of the merit of Vaucluse indeed that it is as
much as possible a surprise. The place has a right to its name,
for the valley appears impenetrable until you get fairly into it.
One perverse twist follows another until the omnibus suddenly deposits you in front of the "cabinet" of Petrarch. After
that you have only to walk along the left bank of the river.
The cabinet of Petrarch is to-day a hideous little *café*, bedizened, like a signboard, with extracts from the ingenious
"Rime." The poet and his lady are of course the stock-in-trade
of the little village, which has had for several generations
the privilege of attracting young couples engaged in their
wedding-tour and other votaries of the tender passion. The
place has long been familiar, on festal Sundays, to the swains
of Avignon and their attendant nymphs. The little fish of the
Sorgues are much esteemed, and, eaten on the spot, they con-

stitute, for the children of the once Papal city, the classic suburban dinner. Vaucluse has been turned to account, however,
not only by sentiment, but by industry; the banks of the
stream being disfigured by a pair of hideous mills for the
manufacture of paper and of wool. In an enterprising and
economical age the water-power of the Sorgues was too obvious a motive; and I must say that, as the torrent rushed past
them, the wheels of the dirty little factories appeared to turn
merrily enough. The footpath on the left bank, of which I just
spoke, carries one fortunately quite out of sight of them, and
out of sound as well, inasmuch as on the day of my visit the
stream itself, which was in tremendous force, tended more
and more, as one approached the fountain, to fill the valley
with its own echoes. Its colour was magnificent, and the
whole spectacle more like a corner of Switzerland than a nook
in Provence. The protrusions of the mountain shut it in, and
you penetrate to the bottom of the recess which they form.
The Sorgues rushes and rushes; it is almost like Niagara after
the jump of the cataract. There are dreadful little booths beside the path, for the sale of photographs and *immortelles*—I
don't know what one is to do with the immortelles—where
you are offered a brush dipped in tar to write your name
withal on the rocks. Thousands of vulgar persons, of both
sexes, and exclusively, it appeared, of the French nationality,
had availed themselves of this implement, for every square
inch of accessible stone was scored over with some human
appellation. It is not only we in America, therefore, who be-
smirch our scenery; the practice exists, in a more organised
form (like everything else in France), in the country of good
taste. You leave the little booths and stalls behind; but the
bescribbled crag, bristling with human vanity, keeps you company even when you stand face to face with the fountain. This
happens when you find yourself at the foot of the enormous
straight cliff out of which the river gushes. It rears itself to an
extraordinary height—a huge forehead of bare stone—looking as if it were the half of a tremendous mound split open by
volcanic action. The little valley, seeing it there, at a bend,
stops suddenly and receives in its arms the magical spring. I
call it magical on account of the mysterious manner in which
it comes into the world, with the huge shoulder of the

Vaucluse: Ruins of Castle

mountain rising over it as if to protect the secret. From under the mountain it silently rises, without visible movement, filling a small natural basin with the stillest blue water. The contrast between the stillness of this basin and the agitation of the water directly after it has overflowed, constitutes half the charm of Vaucluse. The violence of the stream when once it has been set loose on the rocks is as fascinating and indescribable as that of other cataracts; and the rocks in the bed of the Sorgues have been arranged by a master-hand. The setting of the phenomenon struck me as so simple and so fine—the vast sad cliff, covered with the afternoon light, still and solid for ever, while the liquid element rages and roars at its base— that I had no difficulty in understanding the celebrity of Vaucluse. I understood it, but I will not say that I understood Petrarch. He must have been very self-supporting, and Madonna Laura must indeed have been much to him.

The aridity of the hills that shut in the valley is complete, and the whole impression is best conveyed by that very expressive French epithet *morne*. There are the very fragmentary ruins of a castle (of one of the bishops of Cavaillon) on a high spur of the mountain, above the river; and there is another remnant of a feudal habitation on one of the more accessible ledges. Having half an hour to spare before my omnibus was to leave (I must beg the reader's pardon for this atrociously false note; call the vehicle a *diligence*, and for some undiscoverable reason the offence is minimised), I clambered up to this latter spot and sat among the rocks in the company of a few stunted olives. The Sorgues, beneath me, reaching the plain, flung itself crookedly across the meadows like an unrolled blue ribbon. I tried to think of the *amant de Laure*, for literature's sake; but I had no great success, and the most I could do was to say to myself that I must try again. Several months have elapsed since then, and I am ashamed to confess that the trial has not yet come off. The only very definite conviction I arrived at was that Vaucluse is indeed cockneyfied, but that I should have been a fool, all the same, not to come.

The arch at Orange — a rather pretty village of the Romans.

Orange: the Gateway

Chapter XXXVI

I MOUNTED into my diligence at the door of the Hôtel de Pétrarque et de Laure, and we made our way back to Isle-sur-Sorgues in the fading light. This village, where at six o'clock every one appeared to have gone to bed, was fairly darkened by its high, dense plane-trees, under which the rushing river, on a level with its parapets, looked unnaturally, almost wickedly, blue. It was a glimpse which has left a picture in my mind: the little closed houses, the place empty and soundless in the autumn dusk but for the noise of waters, and in the middle, amid the blackness of the shade, the gleam of the swift, strange tide. At the station every one was talking of the inundation being in many places an accomplished fact, and, in particular, of the condition of the Durance at some point that I have forgotten. At Avignon, an hour later, I found the water in some of the streets. The sky cleared in the evening, the moon lighted up the submerged suburbs, and the population again collected in the high places to enjoy the spectacle. It exhibited a certain sameness, however, and by nine o'clock there was considerable animation in the Place Crillon, where there is nothing to be seen but the front of the theatre and of several cafés—in addition indeed to a statue of this celebrated brave, whose valour redeemed some of the numerous military disasters of the reign of Louis XV. The next morning the lower quarters of the town were in a pitiful state: the situation seemed to me odious. To express my disapproval of it I lost no time in taking the train to Orange, which, with its other attractions, had the merit of not being seated on the Rhone. It was destiny to move northward; but even if I had been at liberty to follow a less unnatural course I should not then have undertaken it, inasmuch as the railway between Avignon and Marseilles was credibly reported to be (in places) under water. This was the case with almost everything but the line itself on the way to Orange. The day proved splendid, and its brilliancy only lighted up the desolation. Farmhouses and cottages were up to their middle in the yellow liquidity; haystacks looked like dull little islands; windows and doors gaped open, without faces; and interruption and flight were represented in the scene. It was brought home to me that the *populations rurales* have many different ways of suffering, and my heart glowed with a grateful sense of cockneyism. It was under the influence of this emotion that I alighted at Orange to visit a collection of eminently civil monuments.

The collection consists of but two objects, but these objects are so fine that I will let the word pass. One of them is a triumphal arch, supposedly of the period of Marcus Aurelius; the other is a fragment, magnificent in its ruin, of a Roman theatre. But for these fine Roman remains and for its name, Orange is a perfectly featureless town, without the Rhone—which, as I have mentioned, is several miles distant—to help it to a physiognomy. It seems one of the oddest things that this obscure French borough—obscure, I mean, in our modern era, for the Gallo-Roman Arausio must have been, judging it by its arches and theatre, a place of some importance—should have given its name to the heirs-apparent of the throne of Holland and been borne by a king of England who had sovereign rights over it. During the Middle Ages it formed part of an independent principality; but in 1531 it fell, by the marriage of one of its princesses, who had inherited it, into the family of Nassau. I read in my indispensable Murray that it was made over to France by the treaty of Utrecht. The arch of triumph, which stands a little way out of the town, is rather a pretty than an imposing vestige of the Romans. If it had greater purity of style one might say of it that it belonged to the same family of monuments as the Maison Carrée at Nîmes. It has three passages—the middle much higher than the others—and a very elevated attic. The vaults of the passages are richly sculptured, and the whole structure is covered with friezes and military trophies. This sculpture is rather mixed; much of it is broken and defaced, and the rest seemed to me ugly, though its workmanship is praised. The arch is at once well preserved and much injured. Its general mass is there, and as Roman monuments go it is remarkably perfect; but it has suffered, in patches, from the extremity of restoration. It is not, on the whole, of absorbing interest. It has a charm, nevertheless, which comes partly from its soft, bright yellow colour, partly from a certain elegance of shape, of expression; and on that well-washed Sunday morning, with its brilliant tone, surrounded by its circle of thin poplars, with the green country lying beyond it and a low blue horizon showing through its empty portals, it made, very sufficiently, a picture that hangs itself to one of the lateral hooks of the memory. I can take down the modest composition and place it before me as I write. I see the shallow, shining puddles in the hard, fair French road; the pale blue sky, diluted by days of rain; the disgarnished autumnal fields; the mild sparkle of the low horizon; the solitary figure in sabots, with a bundle under its arm, advancing along the *chaussée*; and in the middle I see the little ochre-coloured trio of apertures, which, in spite of its antiquity, looks bright and gay, as everything must look in France of a fresh Sunday morning.

It is true that this was not exactly the appearance of the Roman theatre, which lies on the other side of the town; a fact that did not prevent me from making my way to it in less than five minutes, through a succession of little streets concerning which I have no observations to record. None of the

Roman remains in the south of France are more impressive than this stupendous fragment. An enormous mound rises above the place, which was formerly occupied—I quote from Murray—first by a citadel of the Romans, then by a castle of the princes of Nassau, razed by Louis XIV. Facing this hill a mighty wall erects itself, thirty-six metres high and composed of massive blocks of dark brown stone simply laid one on the other; the whole naked, rugged surface of which suggests a natural cliff (say of the Vaucluse order) rather than an effort of human or even of Roman labour. It is the biggest thing at Orange—it is bigger than all Orange put together—and its permanent massiveness makes light of the shrunken city. The face it presents to the town—the top of it garnished with two rows of brackets perforated with holes to receive the staves of the *velarium*—bears the traces of more than one tier of ornamental arches; though how these flat arches were applied, or incrusted, upon the wall, I do not profess to explain. You pass through a diminutive postern—which seems in proportion about as high as the entrance of a rabbit-hutch—into the lodge of the custodian, who introduces you to the interior of the theatre. Here the mass of the hill affronts you, which the ingenious Romans treated simply as the material of their auditorium. They inserted their stone seats, in a semicircle, in the slope of the hill, and planted their colossal wall opposite to it. This wall, from the inside, is, if possible, even more imposing. It formed the back of the stage, the permanent scene, and its enormous face was coated with marble. It contains three doors, the middle one being the highest and having above it, far aloft, a deep niche apparently intended for an imperial statue. A few of the benches remain on the hillside, which, however, is mainly a confusion of fragments. There is part of a corridor built into the hill, high up, and on the crest are the remnants of the demolished castle. The whole place is a kind of wilderness of ruin; there are scarcely any details; the great feature is the overtopping wall. This wall being the back of the scene, the space left between it and the chord of the semicircle (of the auditorium) which formed the proscenium is rather less than one would have supposed. In other words, the stage was very shallow, and appears to have been arranged for a number of performers placed in a line like a company of

Orange: the Theatre

soldiers. There stands the silent skeleton, however, as impressive by what it leaves you to guess and wonder about as by what it tells you. It has not the sweetness, the softness of melancholy, of the theatre at Arles; but it is more extraordinary, and one can imagine only tremendous tragedies being enacted there—

"Presenting Thebes' or Pelops' line."

At either end of the stage, coming forward, is an immense wing—immense in height, I mean, as it reaches to the top of the scenic wall; the other dimensions are not remarkable. The division to the right, as you face the stage, is pointed out as the green-room; its portentous altitude and the open arches at the top give it the air of a well. The compartment on the left is exactly similar, save that it opens into the traces of other chambers, said to be those of a hippodrome adjacent to the theatre. Various fragments are visible which refer themselves plausibly to such an establishment; the greater axis of the hippodrome would appear to have been on a line with the triumphal arch. This is all I saw, and all there was to see, of Orange, which had a very rustic, bucolic aspect, and where I was not even called upon to demand breakfast at the hotel. The entrance of this resort might have been that of a stable of the Roman days.

Valence

Chapter XXXVII

I HAVE been trying to remember whether I fasted all the way to Macon, which I reached at an advanced hour of the evening, and think I must have done so except for the purchase of a box of nougat at Montélimart (the place is famous for the manufacture of this confection, which, at the station, is hawked at the windows of the train) and for a bouillon, very much later, at Lyons. The journey beside the Rhone—past Valence, past Tournon, past Vienne—would have been charming, on that luminous Sunday, but for two disagreeable accidents. The express from Marseilles, which I took at Orange, was full to overflowing; and the only refuge I could find was an inside angle in a carriage laden with Germans who had command of the windows, which they occupied as strongly as they have been known to occupy other strategical positions. I scarcely know, however, why I linger on this particular discomfort, for it was but a single item in a considerable list of grievances—grievances dispersed through six weeks of constant railway-travel in France. I have not touched upon them at an earlier stage of this chronicle, but my reserve is not owing to any sweetness of association. This form of locomotion, in the country of the amenities, is attended with a dozen dis-comforts; almost all the conditions of the business are detest-able. They force the sentimental tourist again and again to ask himself whether, in consideration of such mortal annoyances, the game is worth the candle. Fortunately a railway journey is a good deal like a sea-voyage; its miseries fade from the mind as soon as you arrive. That is why I completed, to my great satisfaction, my little tour in France. Let this small effusion of ill-nature be my first and last tribute to the whole despotic *gare*: the deadly *salle d'attente*, the insufferable delays over one's luggage, the porterless platform, the overcrowded and illiberal train. How many a time did I permit myself the secret reflection that it is in perfidious Albion that they order this matter best! How many a time did the eager British merce-nary, clad in velveteen and clinging to the door of the carriage as it glides into the station, revisit my invidious dreams! The paternal porter and the responsive hansom are among the best gifts of the English genius to the world. I hasten to add, faith-ful to my habit (so insufferable to some of my friends) of ever and again readjusting the balance after I have given it an hon-est tip, that the bouillon at Lyons, which I spoke of above, was, though by no means an ideal bouillon, much better than any I could have obtained at an English railway-station. After I had imbibed it I sat in the train (which waited a long time at Lyons) and, by the light of one of the big lamps on the plat-form, read all sorts of disagreeable things in certain radical newspapers which I had bought at the bookstall. I gathered from these sheets that Lyons was in extreme commotion. The Rhone and the Saone, which form a girdle for the splendid town, were almost in the streets, as I could easily believe from what I had seen of the country after leaving Orange. The Rhone, all the way to Lyons, had been in all sorts of places where it had no business to be, and matters were naturally not improved by its confluence with the charming and copi-ous stream which, at Macon, is said once to have given such a happy opportunity to the egotism of the capital. A visitor from Paris (the anecdote is very old), being asked on the quay of that city whether he didn't admire the Saone, replied good-naturedly that it was very pretty, but that in Paris they spelled it with the *ei*. This moment of general alarm at Lyons had

Lyons

been chosen by certain ingenious persons (I credit them perhaps with too sure a prevision of the rise of the rivers) for practising further upon the apprehensions of the public. A bombshell filled with dynamite had been thrown into a café, and various votaries of the comparatively innocuous *petit verre* had been wounded (I am not sure whether any one had been killed) by the irruption. Of course there had been arrests and incarcerations, and the *Intransigeant* and the *Rappel* were filled with the echoes of the explosion. The tone of these organs is rarely edifying, and it had never been less so than on this occasion. I wondered as I looked through them whether I was losing all my radicalism; and then I wondered whether, after all, I had any to lose. Even in so long a wait as that tiresome delay at Lyons I failed to settle the question, any more than I made up my mind as to the probable future of the militant democracy, or the ultimate form of a civilisation which should have blown up everything else. A few days later the water went down at Lyons; but the democracy has not gone down.

I remember vividly the remainder of that evening which I spent at Macon—remember it with a chattering of the teeth. I know not what had got into the place; the temperature, for the last day of October, was eccentric and incredible. These epithets may also be applied to the hotel itself—an extraordinary structure, all façade, which exposes an uncovered rear to the gaze of nature. There is a demonstrative, voluble landlady, who is of course part of the façade; but everything behind her is a trap for the winds, with chambers, corridors, staircases all exhibited to the sky as if the outer wall of the house had been lifted off. It would have been delightful for Florida, but it didn't do for Burgundy even on the eve of November 1, so that I suffered absurdly from the rigour of a season that had not yet begun. There was something in the air; I felt it the next day, even on the sunny quay of the Saone, where in spite of a fine southerly exposure I extracted little warmth from the reflection that Alphonse de Lamartine had often trodden the flags. Macon struck me, somehow, as suffering from a chronic numbness, and there was nothing exceptionally cheerful in the remarkable extension of the river. It was no longer a river—it had become a lake; and from my window, in the painted face of the inn, I saw that the opposite bank had been moved back, as it were, indefinitely. Unfortunately the various objects with which it was furnished had not been moved as well, the consequence of which was an extraordinary confusion in the relations of things. There were always poplars to be seen, but the poplar had become an aquatic plant. Such phenomena, however, at Macon attract but little attention, as the Saone, at certain seasons of the year, is nothing if not expansive. The people are as used to it as they appeared to be to the bronze statue of Lamartine, which is the principal monument of the *place*, and which, representing the poet in a frogged overcoat and top-boots, improvising in a high wind, struck me as even less casual in its attitude than monumental sculpture usually succeeds in being. It is true that in its present position I thought better of this work of art, which is from the hand of M. Falguière, than when I had seen it through the factitious medium of the Salon of 1876. I walked up the hill where the older part of Macon lies, in search of the natal house of the *amant d'Elvire*, the Petrarch whose Vaucluse was the bosom of the public. The Guide-Joanne quotes from "Les Confidences" a description of the birthplace of the poet, whose treatment of the locality is indeed poetical. It tallies strangely little with the reality, either as regards position or other features; and it may be said to be not an aid, but a direct obstacle, to a discovery of the house. A very humble edifice, in a small back street, is designated by a municipal tablet, set into its face, as the scene of Lamartine's advent into the world. He himself speaks of a vast and lofty structure, at the angle of a *place*, adorned with iron clamps, with a *porte haute et large* and many other peculiarities. The house with the tablet has two meagre storeys above the basement, and (at present, at least) an air of extreme shabbiness; the *place*, moreover, never can have been vast. Lamartine was accused of writing history incorrectly, and apparently he started wrong at first; it had never become clear to him where he was born. Or is the tablet wrong? If the house is small, the tablet is very big.

Macon

Chapter XXXVIII

THE FOREGOING reflections occur, in a cruder form, as it were, in my note-book, where I find this remark appended to them: "Don't take leave of Lamartine on that contemptuous note; it will be easy to think of something more sympathetic!" Those friends of mine, mentioned a little while since, who accuse me of always tipping back the balance, could not desire a paragraph more characteristic; but I wish to give no further evidence of such infirmities, and will therefore hurry away from the subject—hurry away in the train which, very early on a crisp, bright morning, conveyed me, by way of an excursion, to the ancient city of Bourg-en-Bresse. Shining in early light, the Saone was spread, like a smooth white tablecloth, over a considerable part of the flat country that I traversed. There is no provision made in this image for the long, transparent screens of thin-twigged trees which rose at intervals out of the watery plain; but as, in all the conditions, there seemed to be no provision for them in fact, I will let my metaphor go for what it is worth. My journey was (as I remember it) of about an hour and a half; but I passed no object of interest, as the phrase is, whatever. The phrase

260

hardly applies even to Bourg itself, which is simply a town *quelconque*, as M. Zola would say. Small, peaceful, rustic, it stands in the midst of the great dairy-feeding plains of Bresse, of which fat county, sometime property of the house of Savoy, it was the modest capital. The blue masses of the Jura give it a creditable horizon, but the only nearer feature it can point to is its famous sepulchral church. This edifice lies at a fortunate distance from the town, which, though inoffensive, is of too common a stamp to consort with such a treasure. All I ever knew of the church of Brou I had gathered, years ago, from Matthew Arnold's beautiful poem which bears its name. I remember thinking, in those years, that it was impossible verses could be more touching than these; and as I stood before the object of my pilgrimage, in the gay French light (though the place was so dull), I recalled the spot where I had first read them and where I had read them again and yet again, wondering whether it would ever be my fortune to visit the church of Brou. The spot in question was an armchair in a window which looked out on some cows in a field; and whenever I glanced at the cows it came over me—I scarcely know why—that I should probably never behold the structure reared by the Duchess Margaret. Some of our visions never come to pass; but we must be just—others do. "So sleep, for ever sleep, O princely pair!" I remembered that line of Matthew Arnold's, and the stanza about the Duchess Margaret coming to watch the builders on her palfrey white. Then there came to me something in regard to the moon shining on winter nights through the cold clere-storey. The tone of the place at that hour was not at all lunar; it was cold and bright, but with the chill of an autumn morning; yet this, even with the fact of the unexpected remoteness of the church from the Jura added to it, did not prevent me from feeling that I looked at a monument in the production of which—or at least in the effect of which on the tourist-mind of to-day— Matthew Arnold had been much concerned. By a pardonable licence he has placed it a few miles nearer to the forests of the Jura than it stands at present. It is very true that, though the mountains in the sixteenth century can hardly have been in a different position, the plain which separates the church from them may have been bedecked with woods. The visitor to-day cannot help wondering why the beautiful building, with its splendid works of art, is dropped down in that particular spot, which looks so accidental and arbitrary. But there are reasons for most things, and there were reasons why the church of Brou should be at Brou, which is a vague little suburb of a vague little town.

The responsibility rests, at any rate, upon the Duchess Margaret—Margaret of Austria, daughter of the Emperor Maximilian and his wife Mary of Burgundy, daughter of Charles the Bold. This lady has a high name in history, having been regent of the Netherlands in behalf of her nephew, the Emperor Charles V., of whose early education she had had the care. She married in 1501 Philibert the Handsome, Duke of Savoy, to whom the province of Bresse belonged, and who died two years later. She had been betrothed, as a child, to Charles VIII. of France, and was kept for some time at the French court—that of her prospective father-in-law, Louis XI.; but she was eventually repudiated, in order that her *fiancé* might marry Anne of Brittany—an alliance so magnificently political that we almost condone the offence to a sensitive princess. Margaret did not want for husbands, however, inasmuch as before her marriage to Philibert she had been united to John of Castile, son of Ferdinand V., King of Aragon—an episode terminated by the death of the Spanish prince within a year. She was twenty-two years regent of the Netherlands and died, at fifty-one, in 1530. She might have been, had she chosen, the wife of Henry VII. of England. She was one of the signers of the League of Cambray against the Venetian Republic, and was a most politic, accomplished, and judicious princess. She undertook to build the church of Brou as a mausoleum for her second husband and herself, in fulfilment of a vow made by Margaret of Bourbon, mother of Philibert, who died before she could redeem her pledge and who bequeathed the duty to her son. He died shortly afterwards, and his widow assumed the pious task. According to Murray, she entrusted the erection of the church to "Maistre Loys von Berghem," and the sculpture to "Maistre Conrad." The author of a superstitious but carefully prepared little Notice which I bought at Bourg calls the architect and sculptor (at once) Jehan de Paris, au-

Brou: the Church

thor (*sic*) of the tomb of Francis II. of Brittany, to which we
gave some attention at Nantes, and which the writer of my
pamphlet ascribes only subordinately to Michel Colomb.
The church, which is not of great size, is in the last and
most flamboyant phase of gothic and in admirable preservation; the west front, before which a quaint old sun-dial is
laid out on the ground—a circle of numbers marked in
stone, like those on a clock-face, let into the earth—is covered with delicate ornament. The great feature, however (the
nave is perfectly bare and wonderfully new-looking, though
the warden, a stolid yet sharp old peasant in a blouse, who
looked more as if his line were chaffering over turnips than
showing off works of art, told me that it has never been
touched and that its freshness is simply the quality of the
stone)—the great feature is the admirable choir, in the midst
of which the three monuments have bloomed under the
chisel like exotic plants in a conservatory. I saw the place to
small advantage, for the stained glass of the windows, which
are fine, was under repair, and much of it was masked with
planks.

In the centre lies Philibert-le-Bel, a figure of white marble
on a great slab of black, in his robes and his armour, with two
boy-angels holding a tablet at his head, and two more at his
feet. On either side of him is another cherub; one guarding
his helmet, the other his stiff gauntlets. The attitudes of these
charming children, whose faces are all bent upon him in pity,
have the prettiest tenderness and respect. The table on which
he lies is supported by elaborate columns adorned with niches
containing little images and with every other imaginable elegance; and beneath it he is represented in that other form so
common in the tombs of the Renaissance—a man naked and
dying, with none of the state and splendour of the image
above. One of these figures embodies the duke, the other
simply the mortal; and there is something very strange and
striking in the effect of the latter, seen dimly and with difficulty through the intervals of the rich supports of the upper
slab. The monument of Margaret herself is on the left, all in
white marble tormented into a multitude of exquisite patterns, the last extravagance of a gothic which had gone so far

that nothing was left it but to return upon itself. Unlike her husband, who has only the high roof of the church above him, she lies under a canopy supported and covered by a wilderness of embroidery—flowers, devices, initials, arabesques, statuettes. Watched over by cherubs, she is also in her robes and ermine, with a greyhound sleeping at her feet (her husband, at his, has a waking lion); and the artist has not, it is to be presumed, represented her as more beautiful than she was. She looks indeed like the regent of a turbulent realm. Beneath her couch is stretched another figure—a less brilliant Margaret, wrapped in her shroud, with her long hair over her shoulders. Round the tomb is the battered iron railing placed there originally, with the mysterious motto of the duchess worked into the top—*fortune infortune fort une*. The other two monuments are protected by barriers of the same pattern. That of Margaret of Bourbon, Philibert's mother, stands on the right of the choir; and I suppose its greatest distinction is that it should have been erected to a mother-in-law. It is but little less florid and sumptuous than the others; it has, however, no second recumbent figure. On the other hand, the statuettes that surround the base of the tomb are of even more exquisite workmanship: they represent weeping women, in long mantles and hoods, which latter hang forward over the small face of the figure, giving the artist a chance to carve the features within this hollow of drapery—an extraordinary play of skill. There is a high, white marble shrine of the Virgin, as extraordinary as all the rest (a series of compartments representing the various scenes of her life, with the Assumption in the middle); and there is a magnificent series of stalls, which are simply the intricate embroidery of the tombs translated into polished oak. All these things are splendid, ingenious, elaborate, precious; it is goldsmith's work on a monumental scale, and the general effect is none the less beautiful and solemn because it is so rich. But the monuments of the church of Brou are not the noblest that one may see; the great tombs of Verona are finer, and various other early Italian work. These things are not insincere, as Ruskin would say; but they are pretentious, and they are not positively *naïfs*. I should mention that the walls of the choir are embroidered in places with

Margaret's tantalising device, which—partly perhaps because it is tantalising—is so very decorative, as they say in London. I know not whether she was acquainted with this epithet, but she had anticipated one of the fashions most characteristic of our age.

One asks one's self how all this decoration, this luxury of fair and chiselled marble, survived the French Revolution. An hour of liberty in the choir of Brou would have been a carnival for the image-breakers. The well-fed Bressois are surely a good-natured people. I call them well-fed both on general and on particular grounds. Their province has the most savoury aroma, and I found an opportunity to test its reputation. I walked back into the town from the church (there was really nothing to be seen by the way), and as the hour of the midday breakfast had struck, directed my steps to the inn. The table d'hôte was going on, and a gracious, bustling, talkative landlady welcomed me. I had an excellent repast—the best repast possible—which consisted simply of boiled eggs and bread and butter. It was the quality of these simple ingredients that made the occasion memorable. The eggs were so good that I am ashamed to say how many of them I consumed. "La plus belle fille du monde," as the French proverb says, "ne peut donner que ce qu'elle a;" and it might seem that an egg which has succeeded in being fresh has done all that can reasonably be expected of it. But there was a bloom of punctuality, so to speak, about these eggs of Bourg, as if it had been the intention of the very hens themselves that they should be promptly served. "Nous sommes en Bresse, et le beurre n'est pas mauvais," the landlady said with a sort of dry coquetry, as she placed this article before me. It was the poetry of butter, and I ate a pound or two of it; after which I came away with a strange mixture of impressions of late gothic sculpture and thick *tartines*. I came away through the town, where, on a little green promenade, facing the hotel, is a bronze statue of Bichat the physiologist, who was a Bressois. I mention it not on account of its merit (though, as statues go, I don't remember that it is bad), but because I learned from it—my ignorance, doubtless, did me little honour—that Bichat had died at thirty years of age, and this revelation was almost agitating. To have done so much in so short a life was to be truly great. This reflection, which looks deplorably trite as I write it here, had the effect of eloquence as I uttered it for my own benefit on the bare little mall at Bourg.

Macon: the Bridge

Chapter XXXIX

ON MY RETURN to Macon I found myself fairly face to face with the fact that my tour was near its end. Dijon had been marked by fate as its farthest limit, and Dijon was close at hand. After that I was to drop the tourist and re-enter Paris as much as possible like a Parisian. Out of Paris the Parisian never loiters, and therefore it would be impossible for me to stop between Dijon and the capital. But I might be a tourist a few hours longer by stopping somewhere between Macon and Dijon. The question was where I should spend these hours. Where better, I asked myself (for reasons not now

Beaune: the Hospital

entirely clear to me), than at Beaune? On my way to this town
I passed the stretch of the Côte d'Or, which, covered with a
mellow autumn haze, with the sunshine shimmering through,
looked indeed like a golden slope. One regards with a kind of
awe the region in which the famous *crûs* of Burgundy (Vou-
geot, Chambertin, Nuits, Beaune) are, I was going to say,
manufactured. Adieu, paniers; vendanges sont faites! The vintage was over; the shrunken russet fibres alone clung to their
ugly stick. The horizon on the left of the road had a charm,
however; there is something picturesque in the big, comfortable shoulders of the Côte. That delicate critic M. Emile
Montégut, in a charming record of travel through this region
published some years ago, praises Shakespeare for having
talked (in "Lear") of "waterish Burgundy." Vinous Burgundy
would surely be more to the point. I stopped at Beaune in
pursuit of the picturesque, but I might almost have seen the
little I discovered without stopping. It is a drowsy Burgun-
dian town, very old and ripe, with crooked streets, vistas always oblique, and steep, moss covered roofs. The principal
lion is the Hôpital-Saint-Esprit, or the Hôtel-Dieu simply, as
they call it there, founded in 1443 by Nicholas Rollin, Chancellor of Burgundy. It is administered by the sisterhood of the
Holy Ghost, and is one of the most venerable and stately of
hospitals. The face it presents to the street is simple, but striking—a plain, windowless wall, surmounted by a vast slate
roof, of almost mountainous steepness. Astride this roof sits a
tall, slate-covered spire, from which, as I arrived, the prettiest
chimes I ever heard (worse luck to them, as I will presently
explain) were ringing. Over the door is a high, quaint canopy,
without supports, with its vault painted blue and covered
with gilded stars. (This, and indeed the whole building, have
lately been restored, and its antiquity is quite of the spick-
and-span order. But it is very delightful.) The treasure of the
place is a precious picture—a Last Judgment, attributed
equally to John van Eyck and Roger van der Weyden—given
to the hospital in the fifteenth century by Nicholas Rollin
aforesaid.

I learned, however, to my dismay, from a sympathising but
inexorable concierge, that what remained to me of the time I
had to spend at Beaune, between trains—I had rashly wasted

half an hour of it in breakfasting at the station—was the one
hour of the day (that of the dinner of the nuns; the picture is
in their refectory) during which the treasure could not be
shown. The purpose of the musical chimes to which I had so
artlessly listened was to usher in this fruitless interval. The
regulation was absolute, and my disappointment relative, as I
have been happy to reflect since I "looked up" the picture.
Crowe and Cavalcaselle assign it without hesitation to Roger
van der Weyden, and give a weak little drawing of it in their
"Flemish Painters." I learn from them also—what I was ignorant of—that Nicholas Rollin, Chancellor of Burgundy and
founder of the establishment at Beaune, was the original of
the worthy kneeling before the Virgin in the magnificent John
van Eyck of the Salon Carré. All I could see was the court of
the hospital and two or three rooms. The court, with its tall
roofs, its pointed gables and spires, its wooden galleries, its
ancient well, with an elaborate superstructure of wrought
iron, is one of those places into which a sketcher ought to be
let loose. It looked Flemish or English rather than French,
and a splendid tidiness pervaded it. The porter took me into
two rooms on the ground-floor, into which the sketcher
should also be allowed to penetrate, for they made irresistible
pictures. One of them, of great proportions, painted in elaborate "subjects," like a ball-room of the seventeenth century,
was filled with the beds of patients, all draped in curtains of
dark red cloth, the traditional uniform of these eleemosynary
couches. Among them the sisters moved about in their robes
of white flannel with big white linen hoods. The other room
was a strange, immense apartment, lately restored with much
splendour. It was of great length and height, had a painted
and gilded barrel-roof, and one end of it—the one I was introduced to—appeared to serve as a chapel, as two white-
robed sisters were on their knees before an altar. This was
divided by red curtains from the larger part; but the porter
lifted one of the curtains and showed me that the rest of it, a
long, imposing vista, served as a ward lined with little red-
draped beds. "C'est l'heure de la lecture," remarked my guide;
and a group of convalescents—all the patients I saw were
women—were gathered in the centre around a nun, the
points of whose white hood nodded a little above them and

whose gentle voice came to us faintly, with a little echo, down the high perspective. I know not what the good sister was reading—a dull book, I am afraid—but there was so much colour and such a fine, rich air of tradition about the whole place that it seemed to me I would have risked listening to her. I turned away, however, with that sense of defeat which is always irritating to the appreciative tourist, and pottered about Beaune rather vaguely for the rest of my hour: looked at the statue of Gaspard Monge, the mathematician, in the little *place* (there is no *place* in France too little to contain an effigy to a glorious son); at the fine old porch—completely despoiled at the Revolution—of the principal church; and even at the meagre treasures of a courageous but melancholy little museum, which has been arranged—part of it being the gift of a local collector—in a small hôtel de ville. I carried away from Beaune the impression of something mildly autumnal—something rusty yet kindly, like the taste of a sweet russet pear.

Beaune: the Hospital

Chapter XL

IT WAS very well that my little tour was to terminate at Dijon, for I found, rather to my chagrin, that there was not a great deal, from the pictorial point of view, to be done with Dijon. It was no great matter, for I held my proposition to have been by this time abundantly demonstrated—the proposition with which I started: that if Paris is France, France is by no means Paris. If Dijon was a good deal of a disappointment, I felt therefore that I could afford it. It was time for me to reflect, also, that for my disappointments, as a general thing, I had only myself to thank. They had too often been

the consequence of arbitrary preconceptions produced by influences of which I had lost the trace. At any rate, I will say
plumply that the ancient capital of Burgundy is wanting in
character; it is not up to the mark. It is old and narrow and
crooked, and it has been left pretty well to itself: but it is not
high and overhanging; it is not, to the eye, what the Burgun-
dian capital should be. It has some tortuous vistas, some
mossy roofs, some bulging fronts, some grey-faced hotels,
which look as if in former centuries—in the last, for instance,
during the time of that delightful Président de Brosses whose
Letters from Italy throw an interesting sidelight on Dijon—
they had witnessed a considerable amount of good living. But
there is nothing else. I speak as a man who, for some reason
which he doesn't remember now, did not pay a visit to the
celebrated Puits de Moïse, an ancient cistern embellished with
a sculptured figure of the Hebrew lawgiver.

The ancient palace of the dukes of Burgundy, long since
converted into an hôtel de ville, presents to a wide, clean
court, paved with washed-looking stones, and to a small semi-
circular *place*, opposite, which looks as if it had tried to be
symmetrical and had failed, a façade and two wings character-
ized by the stiffness, but not by the grand air, of the early part
of the eighteenth century. It contains, however, a large and
rich museum—a museum really worthy of a capital. The gem
of this collection is the great banqueting hall of the old palace, one of the few features of the place that has not been
essentially altered. Of great height, roofed with the old beams
and cornices, it exhibits, filling one end, a colossal gothic
chimney-piece with a fireplace large enough to roast, not an
ox, but a herd of oxen. In the middle of this striking hall, the
walls of which are covered with objects more or less precious,
have been placed the tombs of Philippe-le-Hardi and Jean-
sans-Peur. These monuments, very splendid in their general
effect, have a limited interest. The limitation comes from the
fact that we see them to-day in a transplanted and mutilated
condition. Placed originally in a church which has disappeared from the face of the earth, demolished and dispersed at
the Revolution, they have been reconstructed and restored
out of fragments recovered and pieced together. The piecing
has been beautifully done; it is covered with gilt and with

Dijon

brilliant paint; the whole result is most artistic. But the spell of the old mortuary figures is broken, and it will never work again. Meanwhile the monuments are immensely decorative.

I think the thing that pleased me best at Dijon was the little old Parc, a charming public garden, about a mile from the town, to which I walked by a long, straight autumnal avenue. It is a *jardin français* of the last century—a dear old place, with little blue-green perspectives and alleys and *rond-points*, in which everything balances. I went there late in the afternoon, without meeting a creature, though I had hoped I should meet the Président de Brosses. At the end of it was a little river that looked like a canal, and on the farther bank was an old-fashioned villa, close to the water, with a little French garden of its own. On the hither side was a bench, on which I seated myself, lingering a good while; for this was just the sort of place I like. It was the farthermost point of my little tour. I thought that over, as I sat there, on the eve of taking the express to Paris; and as the light faded in the Parc the vision of some of the things I had enjoyed became more distinct.

Dijon: the Park

ITALIAN HOURS

ILLUSTRATED BY JOSEPH PENNELL

Preface

The chapters of which this volume is composed have with few exceptions already been collected, and were then associated with others commemorative of other impressions of (no very extensive) excursions and wanderings. The notes on various visits to Italy are here for the first time exclusively placed together, and as they largely refer to quite other days than these—the date affixed to each paper sufficiently indicating this—I have introduced a few passages that speak for a later and in some cases a frequently repeated vision of the places and scenes in question. I have not hesitated to amend my text, expressively, wherever it seemed urgently to ask for this, though I have not pretended to add the element of information or the weight of curious and critical insistence to a brief record of light inquiries and conclusions. The fond appeal of the observer concerned is all to aspects and appearances— above all to the interesting face of things as it mainly *used* to be.

H. J.

1909.

Contents

List of Illustrations

Venice

IT IS a great pleasure to write the word; but I am not sure
there is not a certain impudence in pretending to add
anything to it. Venice has been painted and described many
thousands of times, and of all the cities of the world is the
easiest to visit without going there. Open the first book and
you will find a rhapsody about it; step into the first picture-
dealer's and you will find three or four high-coloured
"views" of it. There is notoriously nothing more to be said
on the subject. Every one has been there, and every one has
brought back a collection of photographs. There is as little
mystery about the Grand Canal as about our local thoroughfare, and the name of St. Mark is as familiar as the postman's
ring. It is not forbidden, however, to speak of familiar
things, and I hold that for the true Venice-lover Venice is always in order. There is nothing new to be said about her
certainly, but the old is better than any novelty. It would be
a sad day indeed when there should be something new to
say. I write these lines with the full consciousness of having
no information whatever to offer. I do not pretend to en-
lighten the reader; I pretend only to give a fillip to his memory; and I hold any writer sufficiently justified who is himself in love with his theme.

I

Mr. Ruskin has given it up, that is very true; but only after
extracting half a lifetime of pleasure and an immeasurable
quantity of fame from it. We all may do the same, after it has
served our turn, which it probably will not cease to do for
many a year to come. Meantime it is Mr. Ruskin who beyond
any one helps us to enjoy. He has indeed lately produced
several aids to depression in the shape of certain little
humorous—ill-humorous—pamphlets (the series of *St.
Mark's Rest*) which embody his latest reflections on the subject
of our city and describe the latest atrocities perpetrated there.
These latter are numerous and deeply to be deplored; but to

admit that they have spoiled Venice would be to admit that
Venice may be spoiled—an admission pregnant, as it seems to
us, with disloyalty. Fortunately one reacts against the Ruskinian contagion, and one hour of the lagoon is worth a hundred
pages of demoralised prose. This queer late-coming prose of
Mr. Ruskin (including the revised and condensed issue of the
Stones of Venice, only one little volume of which has been published, or perhaps ever will be) is all to be read, though much
of it appears addressed to children of tender age. It is pitched
in the nursery-key, and might be supposed to emanate from
an angry governess. It is, however, all suggestive, and much
of it is delightfully just. There is an inconceivable want of
form in it, though the author has spent his life in laying down
the principles of form and scolding people for departing from
them; but it throbs and flashes with the love of his subject—a
love disconcerted and abjured, but which has still much of the
force of inspiration. Among the many strange things that
have befallen Venice, she has had the good fortune to become
the object of a passion to a man of splendid genius, who has
made her his own and in doing so has made her the world's.
There is no better reading at Venice therefore, as I say, than
Ruskin, for every true Venice-lover can separate the wheat
from the chaff. The narrow theological spirit, the moralism *à
tout propos*, the queer provincialities and pruderies, are mere
wild weeds in a mountain of flowers. One may doubtless be
very happy in Venice without reading at all—without criticising or analysing or thinking a strenuous thought. It is a city
in which, I suspect, there is very little strenuous thinking, and
yet it is a city in which there must be almost as much happiness as misery. The misery of Venice stands there for all the
world to see; it is part of the spectacle—a thorough-going
devotee of local colour might consistently say it is part of the
pleasure. The Venetian people have little to call their own—
little more than the bare privilege of leading their lives in the
most beautiful of towns. Their habitations are decayed; their
taxes heavy; their pockets light; their opportunities few. One
receives an impression, however, that life presents itself to
them with attractions not accounted for in this meagre train
of advantages, and that they are on better terms with it than
many people who have made a better bargain. They lie in the

sunshine; they dabble in the sea; they wear bright rags; they fall into attitudes and harmonies; they assist at an eternal *conversazione*. It is not easy to say that one would have them other than they are, and it certainly would make an immense difference should they be better fed. The number of persons in Venice who evidently never have enough to eat is painfully large; but it would be more painful if we did not equally perceive that the rich Venetian temperament may bloom upon a dog's allowance. Nature has been kind to it, and sunshine and leisure and conversation and beautiful views form the greater part of its sustenance. It takes a great deal to make a successful American, but to make a happy Venetian takes only a handful of quick sensibility. The Italian people have at once the good and the evil fortune to be conscious of few wants; so that if the civilisation of a society is measured by the number of its needs, as seems to be the common opinion to-day, it is to be feared that the children of the lagoon would make but a poor figure in a set of comparative tables. Not their misery, doubtless, but the way they elude their misery, is what pleases the sentimental tourist, who is gratified by the sight of a beautiful race that lives by the aid of its imagination. The way to enjoy Venice is to follow the example of these people and make the most of simple pleasures. Almost all the pleasures of the place are simple; this may be maintained even under the imputation of ingenious paradox. There is no simpler pleasure than looking at a fine Titian, unless it be looking at a fine Tintoret or strolling into St. Mark's—abominable the way one falls into the habit— and resting one's light-wearied eyes upon the windowless gloom; or than floating in a gondola or than hanging over a balcony or than taking one's coffee at Florian's. It is of such superficial pastimes that a Venetian day is composed, and the pleasure of the matter is in the emotions to which they minister. These are fortunately of the finest—otherwise Venice would be insufferably dull. Reading Ruskin is good; reading the old records is perhaps better; but the best thing of all is simply staying on. The only way to care for Venice as she deserves it is to give her a chance to touch you often—to linger and remain and return.

II

The danger is that you will not linger enough—a danger of which the author of these lines had known something. It is possible to dislike Venice, and to entertain the sentiment in a responsible and intelligent manner. There are travellers who think the place odious, and those who are not of this opinion often find themselves wishing that the others were only more numerous. The sentimental tourist's sole quarrel with his Venice is that he has too many competitors there. He likes to be alone; to be original; to have (to himself, at least) the air of making discoveries. The Venice of to-day is a vast museum where the little wicket that admits you is perpetually turning and creaking, and you march through the institution with a herd of fellow-gazers. There is nothing left to discover or describe, and originality of attitude is completely impossible. This is often very annoying; you can only turn your back on your impertinent playfellow and curse his want of delicacy. But this is not the fault of Venice; it is the fault of the rest of the world. The fault of Venice is that, though she is easy to admire, she is not so easy to live with as you count living in other places. After you have stayed a week and the bloom of novelty has rubbed off you wonder if you can accommodate yourself to the peculiar conditions. Your old habits become impracticable and you find yourself obliged to form new ones of an undesirable and unprofitable character. You are tired of your gondola (or you think you are) and you have seen all the principal pictures and heard the names of the palaces announced a dozen times by your gondolier, who brings them out almost as impressively as if he were an English butler bawling titles into a drawing-room. You have walked several hundred times round the Piazza and bought several bushels of photographs. You have visited the antiquity-mongers whose horrible sign-boards dishonour some of the grandest vistas in the Grand Canal; you have tried the opera and found it very bad; you have bathed at the Lido and found the water flat. You have begun to have a shipboard-feeling—to regard the Piazza as an enormous saloon and the Riva degli Schiavoni as a promenade-deck. You are obstructed and encaged; your desire for space is unsatisfied; you miss your usual exercise. You

try to take a walk and you fail, and meantime, as I say, you
have come to regard your gondola as a sort of magnified
baby's cradle. You have no desire to be rocked to sleep,
though you are sufficiently kept awake by the irritation produced, as you gaze across the shallow lagoon, by the attitude
of the perpetual gondolier, with his turned-out toes, his protruded chin, his absurdly unscientific stroke. The canals have a
horrible smell, and the everlasting Piazza, where you have
looked repeatedly at every article in every shop-window and
found them all rubbish, where the young Venetians who sell
bead bracelets and "panoramas" are perpetually thrusting
their wares at you, where the same tightly-buttoned officers
are for ever sucking the same black weeds, at the same empty
tables, in front of the same cafés—the Piazza, as I say, has
resolved itself into a magnificent tread-mill. This is the state of
mind of those shallow inquirers who find Venice all very well
for a week; and if in such a state of mind you take your departure you act with fatal rashness. The loss is your own,
moreover; it is not—with all deference to your personal attractions—that of your companions who remain behind; for
though there are some disagreeable things in Venice there is
nothing so disagreeable as the visitors. The conditions are peculiar, but your intolerance of them evaporates before it has
had time to become a prejudice. When you have called for the
bill to go, pay it and remain, and you will find on the morrow
that you are deeply attached to Venice. It is by living there
from day to day that you feel the fulness of her charm; that
you invite her exquisite influence to sink into your spirit. The
creature varies like a nervous woman, whom you know only
when you know all the aspects of her beauty. She has high
spirits or low, she is pale or red, grey or pink, cold or warm,
fresh or wan, according to the weather or the hour. She is
always interesting and almost always sad; but she has a thousand occasional graces and is always liable to happy accidents.
You become extraordinarily fond of these things; you count
upon them; they make part of your life. Tenderly fond you
become; there is something indefinable in those depths of
personal acquaintance that gradually establish themselves. The
place seems to personify itself, to become human and sentient
and conscious of your affection. You desire to embrace it, to

caress it, to possess it; and finally a soft sense of possession grows up and your visit becomes a perpetual love-affair. It is very true that if you go, as the author of these lines on a certain occasion went, about the middle of March, a certain amount of disappointment is possible. He had paid no visit for several years, and in the interval the beautiful and helpless city had suffered an increase of injury. The barbarians are in full possession and you tremble for what they may do. You are reminded from the moment of your arrival that Venice scarcely exists any more as a city at all; that she exists only as a battered peep-show and bazaar. There was a horde of savage Germans encamped in the Piazza, and they filled the Ducal Palace and the Academy with their uproar. The English and Americans came a little later. They came in good time, with a great many French, who were discreet enough to make very long repasts at the Caffè Quadri, during which they were out of the way. The months of April and May of the year 1881 were not, as a general thing, a favourable season for visiting the Ducal Palace and the Academy. The *valet-de-place* had marked them for his own and held triumphant possession of them. He celebrates his triumphs in a terrible brassy voice, which resounds all over the place, and has, whatever language he be speaking, the accent of some other idiom. During all the spring months in Venice these gentry abound in the great resorts, and they lead their helpless captives through churches and galleries in dense irresponsible groups. They infest the Piazza; they pursue you along the Riva; they hang about the bridges and the doors of the cafés. In saying just now that I was disappointed at first, I had chiefly in mind the impression that assails me to-day in the whole precinct of St. Mark's. The condition of this ancient sanctuary is surely a great scandal. The pedlars and commissioners ply their trade—often a very unclean one—at the very door of the temple; they follow you across the threshold, into the sacred dusk, and pull your sleeve, and hiss into your ear, scuffling with each other for customers. There is a great deal of dishonour about St. Mark's altogether, and if Venice, as I say, has become a great bazaar, this exquisite edifice is now the biggest booth.

III

It is treated as a booth in all ways, and if it had not somehow a great spirit of solemnity within it the traveller would soon have little warrant for regarding it as a religious affair. The restoration of the outer walls, which has lately been so much attacked and defended, is certainly a great shock. Of the necessity of the work only an expert is, I suppose, in a position to judge; but there is no doubt that, if a necessity it be, it is one that is deeply to be regretted. To no more distressing necessity have people of taste lately had to resign themselves. Wherever the hand of the restorer has been laid all semblance of beauty has vanished; which is a sad fact, considering that the external loveliness of St. Mark's has been for ages less impressive only than that of the still comparatively uninjured interior. I know not what is the measure of necessity in such a case, and it appears indeed to be a very delicate question. To-day, at any rate, that admirable harmony of faded mosaic and marble which, to the eye of the traveller emerging from the narrow streets that lead to the Piazza, filled all the further end of it with a sort of dazzling silvery presence—to-day this lovely vision is in a way to be completely reformed and indeed well-nigh abolished. The old softness and mellowness of colour—the work of the quiet centuries and of the breath of the salt sea—is giving way to large crude patches of new material which have the effect of a monstrous malady rather than of a restoration to health. They look like blotches of red and white paint and dishonourable smears of chalk on the cheeks of a noble matron. The face toward the Piazzetta is in especial the newest-looking thing conceivable—as new as a new pair of boots or as the morning's paper. We do not profess, however, to undertake a scientific quarrel with these changes; we admit that our complaint is a purely sentimental one. The march of industry in united Italy must doubtless be looked at as a whole, and one must endeavour to believe that it is through innumerable lapses of taste that this deeply interesting country is groping her way to her place among the nations. For the present, it is not to be denied, certain odd phases of the process are more visible than the result, to arrive at which it seems necessary that, as she was of old a passionate votary of the beautiful, she should to-day burn everything that she has adored. It is doubtless too soon to judge her, and there are moments when one is willing to forgive her even the restoration of St. Mark's. Inside as well there has been a considerable attempt to make the place more tidy; but the general effect, as yet, has not seriously suffered. What I chiefly remember is the straightening out of that dark and rugged old pavement—those deep undulations of primitive mosaic in which the fond spectator was thought to perceive an intended resemblance to the waves of the ocean. Whether intended or not the analogy was an image the more in a treasure-house of images; but from a considerable portion of the church it has now disappeared. Throughout the greater part indeed the pavement remains as recent generations have known it— dark, rich, cracked, uneven, spotted with porphyry and time-blackened malachite, polished by the knees of innumerable worshippers; but in other large stretches the idea imitated by the restorers is that of the ocean in a dead calm, and the model they have taken the floor of a London club-house or of a New York hotel. I think no Venetian and scarcely any Italian cares much for such differences; and when, a year ago, people in England were writing to the *Times* about the whole business and holding meetings to protest against it the dear children of the lagoon—so far as they heard or heeded the rumour—thought them partly busy-bodies and partly asses. Busy-bodies they doubtless were, but they took a good deal of disinterested trouble. It never occurs to the Venetian mind of to-day that such trouble may be worth taking; the Venetian mind vainly endeavours to conceive a state of existence in which personal questions are so insipid that people have to look for grievances in the wrongs of brick and marble. I must not, however, speak of St. Mark's as if I had the pretension of giving a description of it or as if the reader desired one. The reader has been too well served already. It is surely the best-described building in the world. Open the *Stones of Venice*, open Théophile Gautier's *Italia*, and you will see. These writers take it very seriously, and it is only because there is another way of taking it that I venture to speak of it; the way that offers itself after you have been in Venice a couple of

months, and the light is hot in the great Square, and you pass
in under the pictured porticoes with a feeling of habit and
friendliness and a desire for something cool and dark. There
are moments, after all, when the church is comparatively quiet
and empty, and when you may sit there with an easy consciousness of its beauty. From the moment, of course, that
you go into any Italian church for any purpose but to say
your prayers or look at the ladies, you rank yourself among
the trooping barbarians I just spoke of; you treat the place as
an orifice in the peep-show. Still, it is almost a spiritual function—or, at the worst, an amorous one—to feed one's eyes
on the molten colour that drops from the hollow vaults and
thickens the air with its richness. It is all so quiet and sad and
faded and yet all so brilliant and living. The strange figures in
the mosaic pictures, bending with the curve of niche and
vault, stare down through the glowing dimness; the burnished gold that stands behind them catches the light on its
little uneven cubes. St. Mark's owes nothing of its character
to the beauty of proportion or perspective; there is nothing
grandly balanced or far-arching; there are no long lines nor
triumphs of the perpendicular. The church arches indeed, but
arches like a dusky cavern. Beauty of surface, of tone, of detail, of things near enough to touch and kneel upon and lean
against—it is from this the effect proceeds. In this sort of
beauty the place is incredibly rich, and you may go there
every day and find afresh some lurking pictorial nook. It is a
treasury of bits, as the painters say; and there are usually three
or four of the fraternity with their easels set up in uncertain
equilibrium on the undulating floor. It is not easy to catch the
real complexion of St. Mark's, and these laudable attempts at
portraiture are apt to look either lurid or livid. But if you
cannot paint the old loose-looking marble slabs, the great
panels of basalt and jasper, the crucifixes of which the lonely
anguish looks deeper in the vertical light, the tabernacles
whose open doors disclose a dark Byzantine image spotted
with dull, crooked gems—if you cannot paint these things
you can at least grow fond of them. You grow fond even of
the old benches of red marble, partly worn away by the
breeches of many generations and attached to the base of
those wide pilasters of which the precious plating, delightful

in its faded brownness, with a faint grey bloom upon it, bulges and yawns a little with honourable age.

IV

Even at first, when the vexatious sense of the city of the Doges reduced to earning its living as a curiosity-shop was in its keenness, there was a great deal of entertainment to be got from lodging on Riva Schiavoni and looking out at the far-shimmering lagoon. There was entertainment indeed in simply getting into the place and observing the queer incidents of a Venetian installation. A great many persons contribute indirectly to this undertaking, and it is surprising how they spring out at you during your novitiate to remind you that they are bound up in some mysterious manner with the constitution of your little establishment. It was an interesting problem for instance to trace the subtle connection existing between the niece of the landlady and the occupancy of the fourth floor. Superficially it was none too visible, as the young lady in question was a dancer at the Fenice theatre—or when that was closed at the Rossini—and might have been supposed absorbed by her professional duties. It proved necessary, however, that she should hover about the premises in a velvet jacket and a pair of black kid gloves with one little white button; as also, that she should apply a thick coating of powder to her face, which had a charming oval and a sweet weak expression, like that of most of the Venetian maidens, who, as a general thing—it was not a peculiarity of the landlady's niece—are fond of besmearing themselves with flour. You soon recognise that it is not only the many-twinkling lagoon you behold from a habitation on the Riva; you see a little of everything Venetian. Straight across, before my windows, rose the great pink mass of San Giorgio Maggiore, which has for an ugly Palladian church a success beyond all reason. It is a success of position, of colour, of the immense detached Campanile, tipped with a tall gold angel. I know not whether it is because San Giorgio is so grandly conspicuous, with a great deal of worn, faded-looking brickwork; but for many persons the whole place has a kind of suffusion of rosiness. Asked what may be the leading colour in the

Venetian concert, we should inveterately say Pink, and yet without remembering after all that this elegant hue occurs very often. It is a faint, shimmering, airy, watery pink; the bright sea-light seems to flush with it and the pale whiteish-green of lagoon and canal to drink it in. There is indeed a great deal of very evident brickwork, which is never fresh or loud in colour, but always burnt out, as it were, always exquisitely mild.

Certain little mental pictures rise before the collector of memories at the simple mention, written or spoken, of the places he has loved. When I hear, when I see, the magical name I have written above these pages, it is not of the great Square that I think, with its strange basilica and its high arcades, nor of the wide mouth of the Grand Canal, with the stately steps and the well-poised dome of the Salute; it is not of the low lagoon, nor the sweet Piazzetta, nor the dark chambers of St. Mark's. I simply see a narrow canal in the heart of the city—a patch of green water and a surface of pink wall. The gondola moves slowly; it gives a great smooth swerve, passes under a bridge, and the gondolier's cry, carried over the quiet water, makes a kind of splash in the stillness. A girl crosses the little bridge, which has an arch like a camel's back, with an old shawl on her head, which makes her characteristic and charming; you see her against the sky as you float beneath. The pink of the old wall seems to fill the whole place; it sinks even into the opaque water. Behind the wall is a garden, out of which the long arm of a white June rose—the roses of Venice are splendid—has flung itself by way of spontaneous ornament. On the other side of this small water-way is a great shabby façade of Gothic windows and balconies—balconies on which dirty clothes are hung and under which a cavernous-looking doorway opens from a low flight of slimy water-steps. It is very hot and still, the canal has a queer smell, and the whole place is enchanting.

It is poor work, however, talking about the colour of things in Venice. The fond spectator is perpetually looking at it from his window, when he is not floating about with that delightful sense of being for the moment a part of it, which any gentleman in a gondola is free to entertain. Venetian windows and balconies are a dreadful lure, and while you rest

your elbows on these cushioned ledges the precious hours fly
away. But in truth Venice isn't in fair weather a place for concentration of mind. The effort required for sitting down to a
writing-table is heroic, and the brightest page of MS. looks
dull beside the brilliancy of your *milieu*. All nature beckons
you forth and murmurs to you sophistically that such hours
should be devoted to collecting impressions. Afterwards, in
ugly places, at unprivileged times, you can convert your impressions into prose. Fortunately for the present proser the
weather wasn't always fine; the first month was wet and
windy, and it was better to judge of the matter from an open
casement than to respond to the advances of persuasive gondoliers. Even then however there was a constant entertainment in the view. It was all cold colour, and the steel-grey
floor of the lagoon was stroked the wrong way by the wind.
Then there were charming cool intervals, when the churches,
the houses, the anchored fishing-boats, the whole gently-
curving line of the Riva, seemed to be washed with a pearly
white. Later it all turned warm—warm to the eye as well as
to other senses. After the middle of May the whole place was
in a glow. The sea took on a thousand shades, but they were
only infinite variations of blue, and those rosy walls I just
spoke of began to flush in the thick sunshine. Every patch of
colour, every yard of weather-stained stucco, every glimpse of
nestling garden or daub of sky above a *calle*, began to shine
and sparkle—began, as the painters say, to "compose." The
lagoon was streaked with odd currents, which played across it
like huge smooth finger-marks. The gondolas multiplied and
spotted it all over; every gondola and gondolier looking, at a
distance, precisely like every other.

There is something strange and fascinating in this mysterious impersonality of the gondola. It has an identity when you
are in it, but, thanks to their all being of the same size, shape
and colour, and of the same deportment and gait, it has none,
or as little as possible, as you see it pass before you. From my
windows on the Riva there was always the same silhouette—
the long, black, slender skiff, lifting its head and throwing
it back a little, moving yet seeming not to move, with
the grotesquely-graceful figure on the poop. This figure in-
clines, as may be, more to the graceful or to the grotesque—

standing in the "second position" of the dancing-master, but indulging from the waist upward in a freedom of movement which that functionary would deprecate. One may say as a general thing that there is something rather awkward in the movement even of the most graceful gondolier, and something graceful in the movement of the most awkward. In the graceful men of course the grace predominates, and nothing can be finer than the large, firm way in which, from their point of vantage, they throw themselves over their tremendous oar. It has the boldness of a plunging bird and the regularity of a pendulum. Sometimes, as you see this movement in profile, in a gondola that passes you—see, as you recline on your own low cushions, the arching body of the gondolier lifted up against the sky—it has a kind of nobleness which suggests an image on a Greek frieze. The gondolier at Venice is your very good friend—if you choose him happily—and on the quality of the personage depends a good deal that of your impressions. He is a part of your daily life, your double, your shadow, your complement. Most people, I think, either like their gondolier or hate him; and if they like him, like him very much. In this case they take an interest in him after his departure; wish him to be sure of employment, speak of him as the gem of gondoliers and tell their friends to be certain to "secure" him. There is usually no difficulty in securing him; there is nothing elusive or reluctant about a gondolier. Nothing would induce me not to believe them for the most part excellent fellows, and the sentimental tourist must always have a kindness for them. More than the rest of the population, of course, they are the children of Venice; they are associated with its idiosyncrasy, with its essence, with its silence, with its melancholy.

When I say they are associated with its silence I should immediately add that they are associated also with its sound. Among themselves they are an extraordinarily talkative company. They chatter at the *traghetti*, where they always have some sharp point under discussion; they bawl across the canals; they bespeak your commands as you approach; they defy each other from afar. If you happen to have a *traghetto* under your window, you are well aware that they are a vocal race. I should go even further than I went just now, and say that the voice of the gondolier is in fact for audibility the dominant or rather the only note of Venice. There is scarcely another heard sound, and that indeed is part of the interest of the place. There is no noise there save distinctly human noise; no rumbling, no vague uproar, nor rattle of wheels and hoofs. It is all articulate and vocal and personal. One may say indeed that Venice is emphatically the city of conversation; people talk all over the place because there is nothing to interfere with its being caught by the ear. Among the populace it is a general family party. The still water carries the voice, and good Venetians exchange confidences at a distance of half a mile. It saves a world of trouble, and they don't like trouble. Their delightful garrulous language helps them to make Venetian life a long *conversazione*. This language, with its soft elisions, its odd transpositions, its kindly contempt for consonants and other disagreeables, has in it something peculiarly human and accommodating. If your gondolier had no other merit he would have the merit that he speaks Venetian. This may rank as a merit even—some people perhaps would say especially—when you don't understand what he says. But he adds to it other graces which make him an agreeable feature in your life. The price he sets on his services is touchingly small, and he has a happy art of being obsequious without being, or at least without seeming, abject. For occasional liberalities he evinces an almost lyrical gratitude. In short he has delightfully good manners, a merit which he shares for the most part with the Venetians at large. One grows very fond of these people, and the reason of one's fondness is the frankness and sweetness of their address. That of the Italian family at large has much to recommend it; but in the Venetian manner there is something peculiarly ingratiating. One feels that the race is old, that it has a long and rich civilisation in its blood, and that if it hasn't been blessed by fortune it has at least been polished by time. It hasn't a genius for stiff morality, and indeed makes few pretensions in that direction. It scruples but scantly to represent the false as the true, and has been accused of cultivating the occasion to grasp and to overreach, and of steering a crooked course—not to your and my advantage—amid the sanctities of property. It has been accused further of loving if not too well at least too often, of being in fine as little austere

Riva Schiavoni, Venice

as possible. I am not sure it is very brave, nor struck with its being very industrious. But it has an unfailing sense of the amenities of life; the poorest Venetian is a natural man of the world. He is better company than persons of his class are apt to be among the nations of industry and virtue—where people are also sometimes perceived to lie and steal and otherwise misconduct themselves. He has a great desire to please and to be pleased.

V

In that matter at least the cold-blooded stranger begins at last to imitate him; begins to lead a life that shall be before all things easy; unless indeed he allow himself, like Mr. Ruskin, to be put out of humour by Titian and Tiepolo. The hours he spends among the pictures are his best hours in Venice, and I am ashamed to have written so much of common things when I might have been making festoons of the names of the masters. Only, when we have covered our page with such festoons what more is left to say? When one has said Carpaccio and Bellini, the Tintoret and the Veronese, one has struck a note that must be left to resound at will. Everything has been said about the mighty painters, and it is of little importance that a pilgrim the more has found them to his taste. "Went this morning to the Academy; was very much pleased with Titian's 'Assumption.'" That honest phrase has doubtless been written in many a traveller's diary, and was not indiscreet on the part of its author. But it appeals little to the general reader, and we must moreover notoriously not expose our deepest feelings. Since I have mentioned Titian's "Assumption" I must say that there are some people who have been less pleased with it than the observer we have just imagined. It is one of the possible disappointments of Venice, and you may if you like take advantage of your privilege of not caring for it. It imparts a look of great richness to the side of the beautiful room of the Academy on which it hangs; but the same room contains two or three works less known to fame which are equally capable of inspiring a passion. "The 'Annunciation' struck me as coarse and superficial": that note was once made in a simple-minded tourist's book. At Venice, strange to say, Titian is altogether a disappointment; the city of his adoption is far from containing the best of him. Madrid, Paris, London, Florence, Dresden, Munich—these are the homes of his greatness.

There are other painters who have but a single home, and the greatest of these is the Tintoret. Close beside him sit Carpaccio and Bellini, who make with him the dazzling Venetian trio. The Veronese may be seen and measured in other places; he is most splendid in Venice, but he shines in Paris and in Dresden. You may walk out of the noon-day dusk of Trafalgar Square in November, and in one of the chambers of the National Gallery see the family of Darius rustling and pleading and weeping at the feet of Alexander. Alexander is a beautiful young Venetian in crimson pantaloons, and the picture sends a glow into the cold London twilight. You may sit before it for an hour and dream you are floating to the water-gate of the Ducal Palace, where a certain old beggar who has one of the handsomest heads in the world—he has sat to a hundred painters for Doges and for personages more sacred—has a prescriptive right to pretend to pull your gondola to the steps and to hold out a greasy immemorial cap. But you must go to Venice in very fact to see the other masters, who form part of your life while you are there, who illuminate your view of the universe. It is difficult to express one's relation to them; the whole Venetian art-world is so near, so familiar, so much an extension and adjunct of the spreading actual, that it seems almost invidious to say one owes more to one of them than to the other. Nowhere, not even in Holland, where the correspondence between the real aspects and the little polished canvases is so constant and so exquisite, do art and life seem so interfused and, as it were, so consanguineous. All the splendour of light and colour, all the Venetian air and the Venetian history are on the walls and ceilings of the palaces; and all the genius of the masters, all the images and visions they have left upon canvas, seem to tremble in the sunbeams and dance upon the waves. That is the perpetual interest of the place—that you live in a certain sort of knowledge as in a rosy cloud. You don't go into the churches and galleries by way of a change from the streets; you go into them because they offer you an exquisite reproduction of the things that surround you. All Venice was both model and painter, and life was so pictorial that art couldn't help becoming so. With all diminutions life is pictorial still, and this fact gives an extraordinary freshness to one's perception of the great Venetian works. You judge of them not as a connoisseur, but as a man of the world, and you enjoy them because they are so social and so true. Perhaps of all works of art that are equally great they demand least reflection on the part of the spectator— they make least of a mystery of being enjoyed. Reflection only confirms your admiration, yet is almost ashamed to show its head. These things speak so frankly and benignantly to the sense that even when they arrive at the highest style—as in the Tintoret's "Presentation of the little Virgin at the Temple"—they are still more familiar.

But it is hard, as I say, to express all this, and it is painful as well to attempt it—painful because in the memory of vanished hours so filled with beauty the consciousness of present loss oppresses. Exquisite hours, enveloped in light and silence, to have known them once is to have always a terrible standard of enjoyment. Certain lovely mornings of May and June come back with an ineffaceable fairness. Venice isn't smothered in flowers at this season, in the manner of Florence and Rome; but the sea and sky themselves seem to blossom and rustle. The gondola waits at the wave-washed steps, and if you are wise you will take your place beside a discriminating companion. Such a companion in Venice should of course be of the sex that discriminates most finely. An intelligent woman who knows her Venice seems doubly intelligent, and it makes no woman's perceptions less keen to be aware that she can't help looking graceful as she is borne over the waves. The handsome Pasquale, with uplifted oar, awaits your command, knowing, in a general way, from observation of your habits, that your intention is to go to see a picture or two. It perhaps doesn't immensely matter what picture you choose: the whole affair is so charming. It is charming to wander through the light and shade of intricate canals, with perpetual architecture above you and perpetual fluidity beneath. It is charming to disembark at the polished steps of a little empty *campo*—a sunny shabby square with an old well in the middle, an old church on one side and tall Venetian windows

looking down. Sometimes the windows are tenantless; sometimes a lady in a faded dressing-gown leans vaguely on the
sill. There is always an old man holding out his hat for coppers; there are always three or four small boys dodging possible umbrella-pokes while they precede you, in the manner of
custodians, to the door of the church.

VI

The churches of Venice are rich in pictures, and many a
masterpiece lurks in the unaccommodating gloom of side-
chapels and sacristies. Many a noble work is perched behind
the dusty candles and muslin roses of a scantily-visited altar;
some of them indeed, hidden behind the altar, suffer in a
darkness that can never be explored. The facilities offered you
for approaching the picture in such cases are a mockery of
your irritated wish. You stand at tip-toe on a three-legged
stool, you climb a rickety ladder, you almost mount upon the
shoulders of the *custode*. You do everything but see the picture. You see just enough to be sure it's beautiful. You catch a
glimpse of a divine head, of a fig-tree against a mellow sky,
but the rest is impenetrable mystery. You renounce all hope,
for instance, of approaching the magnificent Cima da Cone-
gliano in San Giovanni in Bragora; and bethinking yourself of
the immaculate purity that shines in the spirit of this master,
you renounce it with chagrin and pain. Behind the high altar
in that church hangs a Baptism of Christ by Cima which I
believe has been more or less repainted. You make the thing
out in spots, you see it has a fulness of perfection. But you
turn away from it with a stiff neck and promise yourself consolation in the Academy and at the Madonna dell' Orto,
where two noble works by the same hand—pictures as clear
as a summer twilight—present themselves in better circumstances. It may be said as a general thing that you never see
the Tintoret. You admire him, you adore him, you think him
the greatest of painters, but in the great majority of cases your
eyes fail to deal with him. This is partly his own fault; so
many of his works have turned to blackness and are positively
rotting in their frames. At the Scuola di San Rocco, where
there are acres of him, there is scarcely anything at all ade-

quately visible save the immense "Crucifixion" in the upper story. It is true that in looking at this huge composition you look at many pictures; it has not only a multitude of figures but a wealth of episodes; and you pass from one of these to the other as if you were "doing" a gallery. Surely no single picture in the world contains more of human life; there is everything in it, including the most exquisite beauty. It is one of the greatest things of art; it is always interesting. There are works of the artist which contain touches more exquisite, revelations of beauty more radiant, but there is no other vision of so intense a reality, an execution so splendid. The interest, the impressiveness, of that whole corner of Venice, however melancholy the effect of its gorgeous and ill-lighted chambers, gives a strange importance to a visit to the Scuola. Nothing that all travellers go to see appears to suffer less from the incursions of travellers. It is one of the loneliest booths of the bazaar, and the author of these lines has always had the good fortune, which he wishes to every other traveller, of having it to himself. I think most visitors find the place rather alarming and wicked-looking. They walk about a while among the fitful figures that gleam here and there out of the great tapestry (as it were) with which the painter has hung all the walls, and then, depressed and bewildered by the portentous solemnity of these objects, by strange glimpses of unnatural scenes, by the echo of their lonely footsteps on the vast stone floors, they take a hasty departure, finding themselves again, with a sense of release from danger, a sense that the *genius loci* was a sort of mad white-washer who worked with a bad mixture, in the bright light of the *campo*, among the beggars, the orange-vendors and the passing gondolas. Solemn indeed is the place, solemn and strangely suggestive, for the simple reason that we shall scarcely find four walls elsewhere that inclose within a like area an equal quantity of genius. The air is thick with it and dense and difficult to breathe; for it was genius that was not happy, inasmuch as it lacked the art to fix itself for ever. It is not immortality that we breathe at the Scuola di San Rocco, but conscious, reluctant mortality.

Fortunately, however, we can turn to the Ducal Palace, where everything is so brilliant and splendid that the poor dusky Tintoret is lifted in spite of himself into the concert.

This deeply original building is of course the loveliest thing in Venice, and a morning's stroll there is a wonderful illumination. Cunningly select your hour—half the enjoyment of Venice is a question of dodging—and enter at about one o'clock, when the tourists have flocked off to lunch and the echoes of the charming chambers have gone to sleep among the sunbeams. There is no brighter place in Venice—by which I mean that on the whole there is none half so bright. The reflected sunshine plays up through the great windows from the glittering lagoon and shimmers and twinkles over gilded walls and ceilings. All the history of Venice, all its splendid stately past, glows around you in a strong sea-light. Every one here is magnificent, but the great Veronese is the most magnificent of all. He swims before you in a silver cloud; he thrones in an eternal morning. The deep blue sky burns behind him, streaked across with milky bars; the white colonnades sustain the richest canopies, under which the first gentlemen and ladies in the world both render homage and receive it. Their glorious garments rustle in the air of the sea and their sun-lighted faces are the very complexion of Venice. The mixture of pride and piety, of politics and religion, of art and patriotism, gives a splendid dignity to every scene. Never was a painter more nobly joyous, never did an artist take a greater delight in life, seeing it all as a kind of breezy festival and feeling it through the medium of perpetual success. He revels in the gold-framed ovals of the ceilings, multiplies himself there with the fluttering movement of an embroidered banner that tosses itself into the blue. He was the happiest of painters and produced the happiest picture in the world. "The Rape of Europa" surely deserves this title; it is impossible to look at it without aching with envy. Nowhere else in art is such a temperament revealed; never did inclination and opportunity combine to express such enjoyment. The mixture of flowers and gems and brocade, of blooming flesh and shining sea and waving groves, of youth, health, movement, desire—all this is the brightest vision that ever descended upon the soul of a painter. Happy the artist who could entertain such a vision; happy the artist who could paint it as the masterpiece I here recall is painted.

The Tintoret's visions were not so bright as that; but he

had several that were radiant enough. In the room that contains the work just cited are several smaller canvases by the greatly more complex genius of the Scuola di San Rocco, which are almost simple in their loveliness, almost happy in their simplicity. They have kept their brightness through the centuries, and they shine with their neighbours in those golden rooms. There is a piece of painting in one of them which is one of the sweetest things in Venice and which reminds one afresh of those wild flowers of execution that bloom so profusely and so unheeded in the dark corners of all of the Tintoret's work. "Pallas chasing away Mars" is, I believe, the name that is given to the picture; and it represents in fact a young woman of noble appearance administering a gentle push to a fine young man in armour, as if to tell him to keep his distance. It is of the gentleness of this push that I speak, the charming way in which she puts out her arm, with a single bracelet on it, and rests her young hand, its rosy fingers parted, on his dark breastplate. She bends her enchanting head with the effort—a head which has all the strange fairness that the Tintoret always sees in women—and the soft, living, flesh-like glow of all these members, over which the brush has scarcely paused in its course, is as pretty an example of genius as all Venice can show. But why speak of the Tintoret when I can say nothing of the great "Paradise," which unfolds its somewhat smoky splendour and the wonder of its multitudinous circles in one of the other chambers? If it were not one of the first pictures in the world it would be about the biggest, and we must confess that the spectator gets from it at first chiefly an impression of quantity. Then he sees that this quantity is really wealth; that the dim confusion of faces is a magnificent composition, and that some of the details of this composition are extremely beautiful. It is impossible however in a retrospect of Venice to specify one's happiest hours, though as one looks backward certain ineffaceable moments start here and there into vividness. How is it possible to forget one's visits to the sacristy of the Frari, however frequent they may have been, and the great work of John Bellini which forms the treasure of that apartment?

VII

Nothing in Venice is more perfect than this, and we know of no work of art more complete. The picture is in three compartments: the Virgin sits in the central division with her child; two venerable saints, standing close together, occupy each of the others. It is impossible to imagine anything more finished or more ripe. It is one of those things that sum up the genius of a painter, the experience of a life, the teaching of a school. It seems painted with molten gems, which have only been clarified by time, and it is as solemn as it is gorgeous and as simple as it is deep. Giovanni Bellini is more or less everywhere in Venice, and, wherever he is, almost certain to be first—first, I mean, in his own line: he paints little else than the Madonna and the saints; he has not Carpaccio's care for human life at large, nor the Tintoret's nor that of the Veronese. Some of his greater pictures, however, where several figures are clustered together, have a richness of sanctity that is almost profane. There is one of them on the dark side of the room at the Academy that contains Titian's "Assumption," which if we could only see it—its position is an inconceivable scandal—would evidently be one of the mightiest of so-called sacred pictures. So too is the Madonna of San Zaccaria, hung in a cold, dim, dreary place, ever so much too high, but so mild and serene, and so grandly disposed and accompanied, that the proper attitude for even the most critical amateur, as he looks at it, strikes one as the bended knee. There is another noble John Bellini, one of the very few in which there is no Virgin, at San Giovanni Crisostomo—a St. Jerome, in a red dress, sitting aloft upon the rocks and with a landscape of extraordinary purity behind him. The absence of the peculiarly erect Madonna makes it an interesting surprise among the works of the painter and gives it a somewhat less strenuous air. But it has brilliant beauty and the St. Jerome is a delightful old personage.

The same church contains another great picture for which the haunter of these places must find a shrine apart in his memory; one of the most interesting things he will have seen, if not the most brilliant. Nothing appeals more to him than

three figures of Venetian ladies which occupy the foreground
of a smallish canvas of Sebastian del Piombo, placed above
the high altar of San Giovanni Crisostomo. Sebastian was a
Venetian by birth, but few of his productions are to be seen in
his native place; few indeed are to be seen anywhere. The
picture represents the patron-saint of the church, accompanied by other saints and by the worldly votaries I have mentioned. These ladies stand together on the left, holding in
their hands little white caskets; two of them are in profile, but
the foremost turns her face to the spectator. This face and
figure are almost unique among the beautiful things of Venice, and they leave the susceptible observer with the impression of having made, or rather having missed, a strange, a
dangerous, but a most valuable, acquaintance. The lady, who
is superbly handsome, is the typical Venetian of the sixteenth
century, and she remains for the mind the perfect flower of
that society. Never was there a greater air of breeding, a
deeper expression of tranquil superiority. She walks a goddess—as if she trod without sinking the waves of the Adriatic. It is impossible to conceive a more perfect expression of
the aristocratic spirit either in its pride or in its benignity.
This magnificent creature is so strong and secure that she is
gentle, and so quiet that in comparison all minor assumptions
of calmness suggest only a vulgar alarm. But for all this there
are depths of possible disorder in her light-coloured eye.

I had meant however to say nothing about her, for it's not
right to speak of Sebastian when one hasn't found room for
Carpaccio. These visions come to one, and one can neither
hold them nor brush them aside. Memories of Carpaccio, the
magnificent, the delightful—it's not for want of such visitations, but only for want of space, that I haven't said of him
what I would. There is little enough need of it for Carpaccio's
sake, his fame being brighter to-day—thanks to the generous
lamp Mr. Ruskin has held up to it—than it has ever been. Yet
there is something ridiculous in talking of Venice without
making him almost the refrain. He and the Tintoret are the
two great realists, and it is hard to say which is the more
human, the more various. The Tintoret had the mightier temperament, but Carpaccio, who had the advantage of more
newness and more responsibility, sailed nearer to perfection.

Here and there he quite touches it, as in the enchanting picture, at the Academy, of St. Ursula asleep in her little white bed, in her high clean room, where the angel visits her at dawn; or in the noble St. Jerome in his study at S. Giorgio Schiavoni. This latter work is a pearl of sentiment, and I may add without being fantastic a ruby of colour. It unites the most masterly finish with a kind of universal largeness of feeling, and he who has it well in his memory will never hear the name of Carpaccio without a throb of almost personal affection. Such indeed is the feeling that descends upon you in that wonderful little chapel of St. George of the Slaves, where this most personal and sociable of artists has expressed all the sweetness of his imagination. The place is small and incommodious, the pictures are out of sight and ill-lighted, the custodian is rapacious, the visitors are mutually intolerable, but the shabby little chapel is a palace of art. Mr. Ruskin has written a pamphlet about it which is a real aid to enjoyment, though I can't but think the generous artist, with his keen senses and his just feeling, would have suffered to hear his eulogist declare that one of his other productions—in the Museo Civico of Palazzo Correr, a delightful portrait of two Venetian ladies with pet animals—is the "finest picture in the world." It has no need of that to be thought admirable; and what more can a painter desire?

VIII

May in Venice is better than April, but June is best of all. Then the days are hot, but not too hot, and the nights are more beautiful than the days. Then Venice is rosier than ever in the morning and more golden than ever as the day descends. She seems to expand and evaporate, to multiply all her reflections and iridescences. Then the life of her people and the strangeness of her constitution become a perpetual comedy, or at least a perpetual drama. Then the gondola is your sole habitation, and you spend days between sea and sky. You go to the Lido, though the Lido has been spoiled. When I first saw it, in 1869, it was a very natural place, and there was but a rough lane across the little island from the landing-place to the beach. There was a bathing-place in those days, and a restaurant, which was very bad, but where in the warm evenings your dinner didn't much matter as you sat letting it cool on the wooden terrace that stretched out into the sea. To-day the Lido is a part of united Italy and has been made the victim of villainous improvements. A little cockney village has sprung up on its rural bosom and a third-rate boulevard leads from Santa Elisabetta to the Adriatic. There are bitumen walks and gas-lamps, lodging-houses, shops and a *teatro diurno*. The bathing-establishment is bigger than before, and the restaurant as well; but it is a compensation perhaps that the cuisine is no better. Such as it is, however, you won't scorn occasionally to partake of it on the breezy platform under which bathers dart and splash, and which looks out to where the fishing-boats, with sails of orange and crimson, wander along the darkening horizon. The beach at the Lido is still lonely and beautiful, and you can easily walk away from the cockney village. The return to Venice in the sunset is classical and indispensable, and those who at that glowing hour have floated toward the towers that rise out of the lagoon will not easily part with the impression. But you indulge in larger excursions—you go to Burano and Torcello, to Malamocco and Chioggia. Torcello, like the Lido, has been improved; the deeply interesting little cathedral of the eighth century, which stood there on the edge of the sea, as touching in its ruin, with its grassy threshold and its primitive mosaics, as the bleached bones of a human skeleton washed ashore by the tide, has now been restored and made cheerful, and the charm of the place, its strange and suggestive desolation, has well-nigh departed.

It will still serve you as a pretext, however, for a day on the lagoon, especially as you will disembark at Burano and admire the wonderful fisher-folk, whose good looks—and bad manners, I am sorry to say—can scarcely be exaggerated. Burano is celebrated for the beauty of its women and the rapacity of its children, and it is a fact that though some of the ladies are rather bold about it every one of them shows you a handsome face. The children assail you for coppers, and in their desire to be satisfied pursue your gondola into the sea. Chioggia is a larger Burano, and you carry away from either place a half-sad, half-cynical, but altogether pictorial impression; the impression of bright-coloured hovels, of bathing in stagnant canals, of young girls with faces of a delicate shape and a susceptible expression, with splendid heads of hair and complexions smeared with powder, faded yellow shawls that hang like old Greek draperies, and little wooden shoes that click as they go up and down the steps of the convex bridges; of brown-cheeked matrons with lustrous tresses and high tempers, massive throats encased with gold beads, and eyes that meet your own with a certain traditional defiance. The men throughout the islands of Venice are almost as handsome as the women; I have never seen so many good-looking rascals. At Burano and Chioggia they sit mending their nets, or lounge at the street corners, where conversation is always high-pitched, or clamour to you to take a boat; and everywhere they decorate the scene with their splendid colour—cheeks and throats as richly brown as the sails of their fishing-smacks—their sea-faded tatters which are always a "costume," their soft Venetian jargon, and the gallantry with which they wear their hats, an article that nowhere sits so well as on a mass of dense Venetian curls. If you are happy you will find yourself, after a June day in Venice (about ten o'clock), on a balcony that overhangs the Grand Canal, with your elbows on the broad ledge, a cigarette in your teeth and a little good company beside you. The gondolas pass beneath, the watery surface gleams here and there from their lamps, some of which are coloured lanterns that move mysteriously in the darkness. There are some evenings in June when there are too many gondolas, too many lanterns, too many serenades in front of the hotels. The serenading in particular is overdone; but on such a balcony as I speak of you needn't suffer from it, for in the apartment behind you—an accessible refuge—there is more good company, there are more cigarettes. If you are wise you will step back there presently.

1882.

The Grand Canal

THE HONOUR of representing the plan and the place at
their best might perhaps appear, in the City of St. Mark,
properly to belong to the splendid square which bears the
patron's name and which is the centre of Venetian life so far
(this is pretty well all the way indeed) as Venetian life is a
matter of strolling and chaffering, of gossiping and gaping, of
circulating without a purpose, and of staring—too often with
a foolish one—through the shop-windows of dealers whose
hospitality makes their doorsteps dramatic, at the very vulgar-
est rubbish in all the modern market. If the Grand Canal,
however, is not quite technically a "street," the perverted
Piazza is perhaps even less normal; and I hasten to add that
I am glad not to find myself studying my subject under
the international arcades, or yet (I will go the length of saying) in the solemn presence of the church. For indeed in that
case I foresee I should become still more confoundingly conscious of the stumbling-block that inevitably, even with his
first few words, crops up in the path of the lover of Venice
who rashly addresses himself to expression. "Venetian life" is a
mere literary convention, though it be an indispensable figure.
The words have played an effective part in the literature of
sensibility; they constituted thirty years ago the title of Mr.
Howells's delightful volume of impressions; but in using
them to-day one owes some frank amends to one's own lucidity. Let me carefully premise therefore that so often as they
shall again drop from my pen, so often shall I beg to be
regarded as systematically superficial.

Venetian life, in the large old sense, has long since come to
an end, and the essential present character of the most melancholy of cities resides simply in its being the most beautiful of
tombs. Nowhere else has the past been laid to rest with such
tenderness, such a sadness of resignation and remembrance.
Nowhere else is the present so alien, so discontinuous, so like
a crowd in a cemetery without garlands for the graves. It has
no flowers in its hands, but, as a compensation perhaps—and
the thing is doubtless more to the point—it has money and

little red books. The everlasting shuffle of these irresponsible visitors in the Piazza is contemporary Venetian life. Everything else is only a reverberation of that. The vast mausoleum has a turnstile at the door, and a functionary in a shabby uniform lets you in, as per tariff, to see how dead it is. From this *constatation*, this cold curiosity, proceed all the industry, the prosperity, the vitality of the place. The shopkeepers and gondoliers, the beggars and the models, depend upon it for a living; they are the custodians and the ushers of the great museum—they are even themselves to a certain extent the objects of exhibition. It is in the wide vestibule of the square that the polyglot pilgrims gather most densely; Piazza San Marco is the lobby of the opera in the intervals of the performance. The present fortune of Venice, the lamentable difference, is most easily measured there, and that is why, in the effort to resist our pessimism, we must turn away both from the purchasers and from the vendors of *ricordi*. The *ricordi* that we prefer are gathered best where the gondola glides— best of all on the noble waterway that begins in its glory at the Salute and ends in its abasement at the railway station. It is, however, the cockneyfied Piazzetta (forgive me, shade of St. Theodore—has not a brand new café begun to glare there, electrically, this very year?) that introduces us most directly to the great picture by which the Grand Canal works its first spell, and to which a thousand artists, not always with a talent apiece, have paid their tribute. We pass into the Piazzetta to look down the great throat, as it were, of Venice, and the vision must console us for turning our back on St. Mark's.

We have been treated to it again and again, of course, even if we have never stirred from home; but that is only a reason the more for catching at any freshness that may be left in the world of photography. It is in Venice above all that we hear the small buzz of this vulgarising voice of the familiar; yet perhaps it is in Venice too that the picturesque fact has best mastered the pious secret of how to wait for us. Even the classic Salute waits like some great lady on the threshold of her saloon. She is more ample and serene, more seated at her door, than all the copyists have told us, with her domes and scrolls, her scolloped buttresses and statues forming a pompous crown, and her wide steps disposed on the ground like the train of a robe. This fine air of the woman of the world is carried out by the well-bred assurance with which she looks in the direction of her old-fashioned Byzantine neighbour; and the juxtaposition of two churches so distinguished and so different, each splendid in its sort, is a sufficient mark of the scale and range of Venice. However, we ourselves are looking away from St. Mark's—we must blind our eyes to that dazzle; without it indeed there are brightnesses and fascinations enough. We see them in abundance even while we look away from the shady steps of the Salute. These steps are cool in the morning, yet I don't know that I can justify my excessive fondness for them any better than I can explain a hundred of the other vague infatuations with which Venice sophisticates the spirit. Under such an influence fortunately one needn't explain—it keeps account of nothing but perceptions and affections. It is from the Salute steps perhaps, of a summer morning, that this view of the open mouth of the city is most brilliantly amusing. The whole thing composes as if composition were the chief end of human institutions. The charming architectural promontory of the Dogana stretches out the most graceful of arms, balancing in its hand the gilded globe on which revolves the delightful satirical figure of a little weathercock of a woman. This Fortune, this Navigation, or whatever she is called—she surely needs no name—catches the wind in the bit of drapery of which she has divested her rotary bronze loveliness. On the other side of the Canal twinkles and glitters the long row of the happy palaces which are mainly expensive hotels. There is a little of everything everywhere, in the bright Venetian air, but to these houses belongs especially the appearance of sitting, across the water, at the receipt of custom, of watching in their hypocritical loveliness for the stranger and the victim. I call them happy, because even their sordid uses and their vulgar signs melt somehow, with their vague sea-stained pinks and drabs, into that strange gaiety of light and colour which is made up of the reflection of superannuated things. The atmosphere plays over them like a laugh, they are of the essence of the sad old joke. They are almost as charming from other places as they are from their own balconies, and share fully in that universal privilege of Venetian objects which consists of being both the picture and the point of view.

This double character, which is particularly strong in the Grand Canal, adds a difficulty to any control of one's notes. The Grand Canal may be practically, as an impression, the cushioned balcony of a high and well-loved palace—the memory of irresistible evenings, of the sociable elbow, of endless lingering and looking; or it may evoke the restlessness of a fresh curiosity, of methodical inquiry, in a gondola piled with references. There are no references, I ought to mention, in the present remarks, which sacrifice to accident, not to completeness. A rhapsody on Venice is always in order, but I think the catalogues are finished. I should not attempt to write here the names of all the palaces, even if the number of those I find myself able to remember in the immense array were less insignificant. There are many I delight in that I don't know, or at least don't keep, apart. Then there are the bad reasons for preference that are better than the good, and all the sweet bribery of association and recollection. These things, as one stands on the Salute steps, are so many delicate fingers to pick straight out of the row a dear little featureless house which, with its pale green shutters, looks straight across at the great door and through the very keyhole, as it were, of the church, and which I needn't call by a name—a pleasant American name—that every one in Venice, these many years, has had on grateful lips. It is the very friendliest house in all the wide world, and it has, as it deserves to have, the most beautiful position. It is a real *porto di mare*, as the gondoliers say—a port within a port; it sees everything that comes and goes, and takes it all in with practised eyes. Not a tint or a hint of the immense iridescence is lost upon it, and there are days of exquisite colour on which it may fancy itself the heart of the wonderful prism. We wave to it from the Salute steps, which we must decidedly leave if we wish to get on, a grateful hand across the water, and turn into the big white church of Longhena—an empty shaft beneath a perfunctory dome—where an American family and a German party, huddled in a corner upon a pair of benches, are gazing, with a conscientiousness worthy of a better cause, at nothing in particular.

For there is nothing particular in this cold and conventional temple to gaze at save the great Tintoretto of the sacristy, to which we quickly pay our respects, and which we are glad to have for ten minutes to ourselves. The picture, though full of beauty, is not the finest of the master's; but it serves again as well as another to transport—there is no other word—those of his lovers for whom, in far-away days when Venice was an early rapture, this strange and mystifying painter was almost the supreme revelation. The plastic arts may have less to say to us than in the hungry years of youth, and the celebrated picture in general be more of a blank; but more than the others any fine Tintoret still carries us back, calling up not only the rich particular vision but the freshness of the old wonder. Many things come and go, but this great artist remains for us in Venice a part of the company of the mind. The others are there in their obvious glory, but he is the only one for whom the imagination, in our expressive modern phrase, sits up. "The Marriage in Cana," at the Salute, has all his characteristic and fascinating unexpectedness—the sacrifice of the figure of our Lord, who is reduced to the mere final point of a clever perspective, and the free, joyous presentation of all the other elements of the feast. Why, in spite of this queer one-sidedness, does the picture give us no impression of a lack of what the critics call reverence? For no other reason that I can think of than because it happens to be the work of its author, in whose very mistakes there is a singular wisdom. Mr. Ruskin has spoken with sufficient eloquence of the serious loveliness of the row of heads of the women on the right, who talk to each other as they sit at the foreshortened banquet. There could be no better example of the roving independence of the painter's vision, a real spirit of adventure for which his subject was always a cluster of accidents; not an obvious order, but a sort of peopled and agitated chapter of life, in which the figures are submissive pictorial notes. These notes are all there in their beauty and heterogeneity, and if the abundance is of a kind to make the principle of selection seem in comparison timid, yet the sense of "composition" in the spectator—if it happen to exist—reaches out to the painter in peculiar sympathy. Dull must be the spirit of the worker tormented in any field of art with that particular question who

Rialto, Venice

is not moved to recognise in the eternal problem the high fellowship of Tintoretto.

If the long reach from this point to the deplorable iron bridge which discharges the pedestrian at the Academy—or, more comprehensively, to the painted and gilded Gothic of the noble Palazzo Foscari—is too much of a curve to be seen at any one point as a whole, it represents the better the arched neck, as it were, of the undulating serpent of which the Canalazzo has the likeness. We pass a dozen historic houses, we note in our passage a hundred component "bits," with the baffled sketcher's sense, and with what would doubtless be, save for our intensely Venetian fatalism, the baffled sketcher's temper. It is the early palaces, of course, and also, to be fair, some of the late, if we could take them one by one, that give the Canal the best of its grand air. The fairest are often cheek-by-jowl with the foulest, and there are few, alas, so fair as to have been completely protected by their beauty. The ages and the generations have worked their will on them, and the wind and the weather have had much to say; but disfigured and dishonoured as they are, with the bruises of their marbles and the patience of their ruin, there is nothing like them in the world, and the long succession of their faded, conscious faces makes of the quiet water-way they overhang a *promenade historique* of which the lesson, however often we read it, gives, in the depth of its interest, an incomparable dignity to Venice. We read it in the Romanesque arches, crooked to-day in their very curves, of the early middle-age, in the exquisite individual Gothic of the splendid time, and in the cornices and columns of a decadence almost as proud. These things at present are almost equally touching in their good faith; they have each in their degree so effectually parted with their pride. They have lived on as they could and lasted as they might, and we hold them to no account of their infirmities, for even those of them whose blank eyes to-day meet criticism with most submission are far less vulgar than the uses we have mainly managed to put them to. We have botched them and patched them and covered them with sordid signs; we have restored and improved them with a merciless taste, and the best of them we have made over to the pedlars. Some of the most

striking objects in the finest vistas at present are the huge advertisements of the curiosity-shops.

The antiquity-mongers in Venice have all the courage of
their opinion, and it is easy to see how well they know they
can confound you with an unanswerable question. What is
the whole place but a curiosity-shop, and what are you here
for yourself but to pick up odds and ends? "We pick them up
for you," say these honest Jews, whose prices are marked in
dollars, "and who shall blame us if, the flowers being pretty
well plucked, we add an artificial rose or two to the composition of the bouquet?" They take care in a word that there be
plenty of relics, and their establishments are huge and active.
They administer the antidote to pedantry, and you can complain of them only if you never cross their thresholds. If you
take this step you are lost, for you have parted with the cor-
rectness of your attitude. Venice becomes frankly from such a
moment the big depressing dazzling joke in which after all
our sense of her contradictions sinks to rest—the grimace of
an over-strained philosophy. It's rather a comfort, for the
curiosity-shops are amusing. You have bad moments indeed as
you stand in their halls of humbug and, in the intervals of
haggling, hear through the high windows the soft plash of
the sea on the old water-steps, for you think with anger of the
noble homes that are laid waste in such scenes, of the delicate
lives that must have been, that might still be, led there. You
reconstruct the admirable house according to your own
needs; leaning on a back balcony, you drop your eyes into
one of the little green gardens with which, for the most part,
such establishments are exasperatingly blessed, and end by
feeling it a shame that you yourself are not in possession. (I
take for granted, of course, that as you go and come you are,
in imagination, perpetually lodging yourself and setting up
your gods; for if this innocent pastime, this borrowing of the
mind, be not your favourite sport there is a flaw in the appeal
that Venice makes to you.) There may be happy cases in
which your envy is tempered, or perhaps I should rather say
intensified, by real participation. If you have had the good
fortune to enjoy the hospitality of an old Venetian home
and to lead your life a little in the painted chambers that still
echo with one of the historic names, you have entered by the

shortest step into the inner spirit of the place. If it didn't savour of treachery to private kindness I should like to speak frankly of one of these delightful, even though alienated, structures, to refer to it as a splendid example of the old palatial type. But I can only do so in passing, with a hundred precautions, and, lifting the curtain at the edge, drop a commemorative word on the success with which, in this particularly happy instance, the cosmopolite habit, the modern sympathy, the intelligent, flexible attitude, the latest fruit of time, adjust themselves to the great gilded, relinquished shell and try to fill it out. A Venetian palace that has not too grossly suffered and that is not overwhelming by its mass makes almost any life graceful that may be led in it. With cultivated and generous contemporary ways it reveals a pre-established harmony. As you live in it day after day its beauty and its interest sink more deeply into your spirit; it has its moods and its hours and its mystic voices and its shifting expressions. If in the absence of its masters you have happened to have it to yourself for twenty-four hours you will never forget the charm of its haunted stillness, late on the summer afternoon for instance, when the call of playing children comes in behind from the campo, nor the way the old ghosts seemed to pass on tip-toe on the marble floors. It gives you practically the essence of the matter that we are considering, for beneath the high balconies Venice comes and goes, and the particular stretch you command contains all the characteristics. Everything has its turn, from the heavy barges of merchandise, pushed by long poles and the patient shoulder, to the floating pavilions of the great serenades, and you may study at your leisure the admirable Venetian arts of managing a boat and organising a spectacle. Of the beautiful free stroke with which the gondola, especially when there are two oars, is impelled, you never, in the Venetian scene, grow weary; it is always in the picture, and the large profiled action that lets the standing rowers throw themselves forward to a constant recovery has the double value of being, at the fag-end of greatness, the only energetic note. The people from the hotels are always afloat, and, at the hotel pace, the solitary gondolier (like the solitary horseman of the old-fashioned novel) is, I confess, a somewhat melancholy figure. Perched on his poop without a mate, he re-enacts perpetually, in high relief, with his toes turned out, the comedy of his odd and charming movement. He always has a little the look of an absent-minded nursery-maid pushing her small charges in a perambulator.

But why should I risk too free a comparison, where this picturesque and amiable class are concerned? I delight in their sun-burnt complexions and their childish dialect; I know them only by their merits, and I am grossly prejudiced in their favour. They are interesting and touching, and alike in their virtues and their defects human nature is simplified as with a big effective brush. Affecting above all is their dependence on the stranger, the whimsical stranger who swims out of their ken, yet whom Providence sometimes restores. The best of them at any rate are in their line great artists. On the swarming feast-days, on the strange feast-night of the Redentore, their steering is a miracle of ease. The master-hands, the celebrities and winners of prizes—you may see them on the private gondolas in spotless white, with brilliant sashes and ribbons, and often with very handsome persons—take the right of way with a pardonable insolence. They penetrate the crush of boats with an authority of their own. The crush of boats, the universal sociable bumping and squeezing, is great when, on the summer nights, the ladies shriek with alarm, the city pays the fiddlers and the illuminated barges, scattering music and song, lead a long train down the Canal. The barges used to be rowed in rhythmic strokes, but now they are towed by the steamer. The coloured lamps, the vocalists before the hotels, are not to my sense the greatest seduction of Venice; but it would be an uncandid sketch of the Canalazzo that shouldn't touch them with indulgence. Taking one nuisance with another, they are probably the prettiest in the world, and if they have in general more magic for the new arrival than for the old Venice-lover, they in any case, at their best, keep up the immemorial tradition. The Venetians have had from the beginning of time the pride of their processions and spectacles, and it's a wonder how with empty pockets they still make a clever show. The Carnival is dead, but these are the scraps of its inheritance. Vauxhall on the water is of course more Vauxhall than ever, with the good fortune of home-made music and of a mirror that reduplicates and mul-

tiplies. The feast of the Redeemer—the great popular feast of
the year—is a wonderful Venetian Vauxhall. All Venice on
this occasion takes to the boats for the night and loads them
with lamps and provisions. Wedged together in a mass it sups
and sings; every boat is a floating arbour, a private *café-
concert*. Of all Christian commemorations it is the most ingen-
uously and harmlessly pagan. Toward morning the passengers
repair to the Lido, where, as the sun rises, they plunge, still
sociably, into the sea. The night of the Redentore has been
described, but it would be interesting to have an account,
from the domestic point of view, of its usual morrow. It is
mainly an affair of the Giudecca, however, which is bridged
over from the Zattere to the great church. The pontoons are
laid together during the day—it is all done with extraordinary celerity and art—and the bridge is prolonged across the
Canalazzo (to Santa Maria Zobenigo), which is my only warrant for glancing at the occasion. We glance at it from our
palace windows; lengthening our necks a little, as we look up
toward the Salute, we see all Venice, on the July afternoon, so
serried as to move slowly, pour across the temporary footway.
It is a flock of very good children, and the bridged Canal is
their toy. All Venice on such occasions is gentle and friendly;
not even all Venice pushes any one into the water.

But from the same high windows we catch without any
stretching of the neck a still more indispensable note in the
picture, a famous pretender eating the bread of bitterness.
This repast is served in the open air, on a neat little terrace, by
attendants in livery, and there is no indiscretion in our seeing
that the pretender dines. Ever since the table d'hôte in "Candide" Venice has been the refuge of monarchs in want of
thrones—she wouldn't know herself without her *rois en exil*.
The exile is agreeable and soothing, the gondola lets them
down gently. Its movement is an anodyne, its silence a phil-
tre, and little by little it rocks all ambitions to sleep. The pro-
script has plenty of leisure to write his proclamations and
even his memoirs, and I believe he has organs in which they
are published; but the only noise he makes in the world is the
harmless splash of his oars. He comes and goes along the
Canalazzo, and he might be much worse employed. He is but
one of the interesting objects it presents, however, and I am

by no means sure that he is the most striking. He has a rival, if not in the iron bridge, which, alas, is within our range, at least—to take an immediate example—in the Montecuculi Palace. Far-descended and weary, but beautiful in its crooked old age, with its lovely proportions, its delicate round arches, its carvings and its disks of marble, is the haunted Montecuculi. Those who have a kindness for Venetian gossip like to remember that it was once for a few months the property of Robert Browning, who, however, never lived in it, and who died in the splendid Rezzonico, the residence of his son and a wonderful cosmopolite "document," which, as it presents itself, in an admirable position, but a short way further down the Canal, we can almost see, in spite of the curve, from the window at which we stand. This great seventeenth-century pile, throwing itself upon the water with a peculiar florid assurance, a certain upward toss of its cornice which gives it the air of a rearing sea-horse, decorates immensely—and within, as well as without—the wide angle that it commands.

There is a more formal greatness in the high square Gothic Foscari, just below it, one of the noblest creations of the fifteenth century, a masterpiece of symmetry and majesty. Dedicated to-day to official uses—it is the property of the State—it looks conscious of the consideration it enjoys, and is one of the few great houses within our range whose old age strikes us as robust and painless. It is visibly "kept up"; perhaps it is kept up too much; perhaps I am wrong in thinking so well of it. These doubts and fears course rapidly through my mind—I am easily their victim when it is a question of architecture—as they are apt to do to-day, in Italy, almost anywhere, in the presence of the beautiful, of the desecrated or the neglected. We feel at such moments as if the eye of Mr. Ruskin were upon us; we grow nervous and lose our confidence. This makes me inevitably, in talking of Venice, seek a pusillanimous safety in the trivial and the obvious. I am on firm ground in rejoicing in the little garden directly opposite our windows—it is another proof that they really show us everything—and in feeling that the gardens of Venice would deserve a page to themselves. They are infinitely more numerous than the arriving stranger can suppose; they nestle with a charm all their own in the complications of most back-views.

Some of them are exquisite, many are large, and even the scrappiest have an artful understanding, in the interest of colour, with the waterways that edge their foundations. On the small canals, in the hunt for amusement, they are the prettiest surprises of all. The tangle of plants and flowers crowds over the battered walls, the greenness makes an arrangement with the rosy sordid brick. Of all the reflected and liquefied things in Venice, and the number of these is countless, I think the lapping water loves them most. They are numerous on the Canalazzo, but wherever they occur they give a brush to the picture and in particular, it is easy to guess, give a sweetness to the house. Then the elements are complete—the trio of air and water and of things that grow. Venice without them would be too much a matter of the tides and the stones. Even the little trellises of the *traghetti* count charmingly as reminders, amid so much artifice, of the woodland nature of man. The vine-leaves, trained on horizontal poles, make a roof of chequered shade for the gondoliers and ferrymen, who doze there according to opportunity, or chatter or hail the approaching "fare." There is no "hum" in Venice, so that their voices travel far; they enter your windows and mingle even with your dreams. I beg the reader to believe that if I had time to go into everything, I would go into the *traghetti*, which have their manners and their morals, and which used to have their piety. This piety was always a *madonnina*, the protectress of the passage—a quaint figure of the Virgin with the red spark of a lamp at her feet. The lamps appear for the most part to have gone out, and the images doubtless have been sold for *bric-a-brac*. The ferrymen, for aught I know, are converted to Nihilism—a faith consistent happily with a good stroke of business. One of the figures has been left, however—the Madonnetta which gives its name to a *traghetto* near the Rialto. But this sweet survivor is a carven stone inserted ages ago in the corner of an old palace and doubtless difficult of removal. *Pazienza*, the day will come when so marketable a relic will also be extracted from its socket and purchased by the devouring American. I leave that expression, on second thought, standing; but I repent of it when I remember that it is a devouring American—a lady long resident in Venice and whose kindnesses all Venetians, as

well as her country-people, know, who has rekindled some of
the extinguished tapers, setting up especially the big brave
Gothic shrine, of painted and gilded wood, which, on the top
of its stout *palo*, sheds its influence on the place of passage
opposite the Salute.

If I may not go into those of the palaces this devious discourse has left behind, much less may I enter the great galleries of the Academy, which rears its blank wall, surmounted
by the lion of St. Mark, well within sight of the windows at
which we are still lingering. This wondrous temple of Venetian art—for all it promises little from without—overhangs,
in a manner, the Grand Canal, but if we were so much as to
cross its threshold we should wander beyond recall. It contains, in some of the most magnificent halls—where the ceilings have all the glory with which the imagination of Venice
alone could over-arch a room—some of the noblest pictures
in the world; and whether or not we go back to them on any
particular occasion for another look, it is always a comfort to
know that they are there, as the sense of them on the spot is a
part of the furniture of the mind—the sense of them close at
hand, behind every wall and under every cover, like the inevitable reverse of a medal, of the side exposed to the air that
reflects, intensifies, completes the scene. In other words, as it
was the inevitable destiny of Venice to be painted, and
painted with passion, so the wide world of picture becomes,
as we live there, and however much we go about our affairs,
the constant habitation of our thoughts. The truth is, we are
in it so uninterruptedly, at home and abroad, that there is
scarcely a pressure upon us to seek it in one place more than
in another. Choose your standpoint at random and trust the
picture to come to you. This is manifestly why I have not, I
find myself conscious, said more about the features of the
Canalazzo which occupy the reach between the Salute and the
position we have so obstinately taken up. It is still there before us, however, and the delightful little Palazzo Dario, intimately familiar to English and American travellers, picks itself
out in the foreshortened brightness. The Dario is covered
with the loveliest little marble plates and sculptured circles; it
is made up of exquisite pieces—as if there had been only
enough to make it small—so that it looks, in its extreme an-

tiquity, a good deal like a house of cards that hold together by a tenure it would be fatal to touch. An old Venetian house dies hard indeed, and I should add that this delicate thing, with submission in every feature, continues to resist the contact of generations of lodgers. It is let out in floors (it used to be let as a whole) and in how many eager hands—for it is in great requisition—under how many fleeting dispensations have we not known and loved it? People are always writing in advance to secure it, as they are to secure the Jenkins's gondolier, and as the gondola passes we see strange faces at the windows—though it's ten to one we recognise them—and the millionth artist coming forth with his traps at the watergate. The poor little patient Dario is one of the most flourishing booths at the fair.

The faces at the window look out at the great Sansovino—the splendid pile that is now occupied by the Prefect. I feel decidedly that I don't object as I ought to the palaces of the sixteenth and seventeenth centuries. Their pretensions impose upon me, and the imagination peoples them more freely than it can people the interiors of the prime. Was not moreover this masterpiece of Sansovino once occupied by the Venetian post-office, and thereby intimately connected with an ineffaceable first impression of the author of these remarks? He had arrived, wondering, palpitating, twenty-three years ago, after nightfall, and, the first thing on the morrow, had repaired to the post-office for his letters. They had been waiting a long time and were full of delayed interest, and he returned with them to the gondola and floated slowly down the Canal. The mixture, the rapture, the wonderful temple of the *poste restante*, the beautiful strangeness, all humanised by good news—the memory of this abides with him still, so that there always proceeds from the splendid water-front I speak of a certain secret appeal, something that seems to have been uttered first in the sonorous chambers of youth. Of course this association falls to the ground—or rather splashes into the water—if I am the victim of a confusion. *Was* the edifice in question twenty-three years ago the post-office, which has occupied since, for many a day, very much humbler quarters? I am afraid to take the proper steps for finding out, lest I should learn that during these years I have misdirected my emotion. A better reason for the sentiment, at any rate, is that such a great house has surely, in the high beauty of its tiers, a refinement of its own. They make one think of colosseums and aqueducts and bridges, and they constitute doubtless, in Venice, the most pardonable specimen of the imitative. I have even a timid kindness for the huge Pesaro, far down the Canal, whose main reproach, more even than the coarseness of its forms, is its swaggering size, its want of consideration for the general picture, which the early examples so reverently respect. The Pesaro is as far out of the frame as a modern hotel, and the Cornaro, close to it, oversteps almost equally the modesty of art. One more thing they and their kindred do, I must add, for which, unfortunately, we can patronise them less. They make even the most elaborate material civilisation of the present day seem woefully shrunken and *bourgeois*, for they simply—I allude to the biggest palaces—can't be lived in as they were intended to be. The modern tenant may take in all the magazines, but he bends not the bow of Achilles. He occupies the place, but he doesn't fill it, and he has guests from the neighbouring inns with ulsters and Baedekers. We are far at the Pesaro, by the way, from our attaching window, and we take advantage of it to go in rather a melancholy mood to the end. The long straight vista from the Foscari to the Rialto, the great middle stretch of the Canal, contains, as the phrase is, a hundred objects of interest, but it contains most the bright oddity of its general Deluge air. In all these centuries it has never got over its resemblance to a flooded city; for some reason or other it is the only part of Venice in which the houses look as if the waters had overtaken them. Everywhere else they reckon with them—have chosen them; here alone the lapping seaway seems to confess itself an accident.

There are persons who hold this long, gay, shabby, spotty perspective, in which, with its immense field of confused reflection, the houses have infinite variety, the dullest expanse in Venice. It was not dull, we imagine, for Lord Byron, who lived in the midmost of the three Mocenigo palaces, where the writing-table is still shown at which he gave the rein to his passions. For other observers it is sufficiently enlivened by so delightful a creation as the Palazzo Loredan, once a masterpiece and at present the Municipio, not to speak of a variety of other immemorial bits whose beauty still has a degree of freshness. Some of the most touching relics of early Venice are here—for it was here she precariously clustered—peeping out of a submersion more pitiless than the sea. As we approach the Rialto indeed the picture falls off and a comparative commonness suffuses it. There is a wide paved walk on either side of the Canal, on which the waterman—and who in Venice is not a waterman?—is prone to seek repose. I speak of the summer days—it is the summer Venice that is the visible Venice. The big tarry barges are drawn up at the *fondamenta*, and the bare-legged boatmen, in faded blue cotton, lie asleep on the hot stones. If there were no colour anywhere else there would be enough in their tanned personalities. Half the low doorways open into the warm interior of waterside drinking-shops, and here and there, on the quay, beneath the bush that overhangs the door, there are rickety tables and chairs. Where in Venice is there not the amusement of character and of detail? The tone in this part is very vivid, and is largely that of the brown plebeian faces looking out of the patchy miscellaneous houses—the faces of fat undressed women and of other simple folk who are not aware that they enjoy, from balconies once doubtless patrician, a view the knowing ones of the earth come thousands of miles to envy them. The effect is enhanced by the tattered clothes hung to dry in the windows, by the sun-faded rags that flutter from the polished balustrades—these are ivory-smooth with time; and the whole scene profits by the general law that renders decadence and ruin in Venice more brilliant than any prosperity. Decay is in this extraordinary place golden in tint and misery *couleur de rose*. The gondolas of the correct people are unmitigated sable, but the poor market-boats from the islands are kaleidoscopic.

The Bridge of the Rialto is a name to conjure with, but, honestly speaking, it is scarcely the gem of the composition. There are of course two ways of taking it—from the water or from the upper passage, where its small shops and booths abound in Venetian character; but it mainly counts as a feature of the Canal when seen from the gondola or even from the awful *vaporetto*. The great curve of its single arch is much

Venetian Palace

to be commended, especially when, coming from the direction of the railway-station, you see it frame with its sharp
compass-line the perfect picture, the reach of the Canal on the
other side. But the backs of the little shops make from the
water a graceless collective hump, and the inside view is the
diverting one. The big arch of the bridge—like the arches of
all the bridges—is the waterman's friend in wet weather. The
gondolas, when it rains, huddle beside the peopled barges,
and the young ladies from the hotels, vaguely fidgeting, complain of the communication of insect life. Here indeed is a
little of everything, and the jewellers of this celebrated precinct—they have their immemorial row—make almost as fine
a show as the fruiterers. It is a universal market, and a fine
place to study Venetian types. The produce of the islands is
discharged there, and the fishmongers announce their presence. All one's senses indeed are vigorously attacked; the
whole place is violently hot and bright, all odorous and noisy.
The churning of the screw of the *vaporetto* mingles with the
other sounds—not indeed that this offensive note is confined
to one part of the Canal. But just here the little piers of the
resented steamer are particularly near together, and it seems
somehow to be always kicking up the water. As we go further
down we see it stopping exactly beneath the glorious windows of the Ca' d'Oro. It has chosen its position well, and
who shall gainsay it for having put itself under the protection
of the most romantic façade in Europe? The companionship
of these objects is a symbol; it expresses supremely the present
and the future of Venice. Perfect, in its prime, was the marble
Ca' d'Oro, with the noble recesses of its *loggie*, but even then
it probably never "met a want," like the successful *vaporetto*.
If, however, we are not to go into the Museo Civico—the
old Museo Correr, which rears a staring renovated front far
down on the left, near the station, so also we must keep out
of the great vexed question of steam on the Canalazzo, just as
a while since we prudently kept out of the Accademia. These
are expensive and complicated excursions. It is obvious that if
the *vaporetti* have contributed to the ruin of the gondoliers,
already hard pressed by fate, and to that of the palaces, whose
foundations their waves undermine, and that if they have
robbed the Grand Canal of the supreme distinction of its

Palazzo Vendramin, Venice

tranquillity, so on the other hand they have placed "rapid transit," in the New York phrase, in everybody's reach, and enabled everybody—save indeed those who wouldn't for the world—to rush about Venice as furiously as people rush about New York. The suitability of this consummation needn't be pointed out.

Even we ourselves, in the irresistible contagion, are going so fast now that we have only time to note in how clever and costly a fashion the Museo Civico, the old Fondaco dei Turchi, has been reconstructed and restored. It is a glare of white marble without, and a series of showy majestic halls within, where a thousand curious mementos and relics of old Venice are gathered and classified. Of its miscellaneous treasures I fear I may perhaps frivolously prefer the series of its remarkable living Longhis, an illustration of manners more copious than the celebrated Carpaccio, the two ladies with their little animals and their long sticks. Wonderful indeed to-day are the museums of Italy, where the renovations and the *belle ordonnance* speak of funds apparently unlimited, in spite of the fact that the numerous custodians frankly look starved. What is the pecuniary source of all this civic magnificence—it is shown in a hundred other ways—and how do the Italian cities manage to acquit themselves of expenses that would be formidable to communities richer and doubtless less æsthetic? Who pays the bills for the expressive statues alone, the general exuberance of sculpture, with which every *piazzetta* of almost every village is patriotically decorated? Let us not seek an answer to the puzzling question, but observe instead that we are passing the mouth of the populous Canareggio, next widest of the water-ways, where the race of Shylock abides, and at the corner of which the big colourless church of San Geremia stands gracefully enough on guard. The Canareggio, with its wide lateral footways and humpbacked bridges, makes on the feast of St. John an admirable noisy, tawdry theatre for one of the prettiest and the most infantile of the Venetian processions.

The rest of the course is a reduced magnificence, in spite of interesting bits, of the battered pomp of the Pesaro and the Cornaro, of the recurrent memories of royalty in exile which cluster about the Palazzo Vendramin Calergi, once the residence of the Comte de Chambord and still that of his half-brother, in spite too of the big Papadopoli gardens, opposite the station, the largest private grounds in Venice, but of which Venice in general mainly gets the benefit in the usual form of irrepressible greenery climbing over walls and nodding at water. The rococo church of the Scalzi is here, all marble and malachite, all a cold, hard glitter and a costly, curly ugliness, and here too, opposite, on the top of its high steps, is San Simeone Profeta, I won't say immortalised, but unblushingly misrepresented, by the perfidious Canaletto. I shall not stay to unravel the mystery of this prosaic painter's malpractices; he falsified without fancy, and as he apparently transposed at will the objects he reproduced, one is never sure of the particular view that may have constituted his subject. It would look exactly like such and such a place if almost everything were not different. San Simeone Profeta appears to hang there upon the wall; but it is on the wrong side of the Canal and the other elements quite fail to correspond. One's confusion is the greater because one doesn't know that everything may not really have changed, even beyond all probability—though it's only in America that churches cross the street or the river—and the mixture of the recognisable and the different makes the ambiguity maddening, all the more that the painter is almost as attaching as he is bad. Thanks at any rate to the white church, domed and porticoed, on the top of its steps, the traveller emerging for the first time upon the terrace of the railway-station seems to have a Canaletto before him. He speedily discovers indeed even in the presence of this scene of the final accents of the Canalazzo—there is a charm in the old pink warehouses on the hot *fondamenta*—that he has something much better. He looks up and down at the gathered gondolas; he has his surprise after all, his little first Venetian thrill; and as the terrace of the station ushers in these things we shall say no harm of it, though it is not lovely. It is the beginning of his experience, but it is the end of the Grand Canal.

1892.

Venice: an Early Impression

THERE would be much to say about that golden chain of historic cities which stretches from Milan to Venice, in which the very names—Brescia, Verona, Mantua, Padua—are an ornament to one's phrase; but I should have to draw upon recollections now three years old and to make my short story a long one. Of Verona and Venice only have I recent impressions, and even to these I must do hasty justice. I came into Venice, just as I had done before, toward the end of a summer's day, when the shadows begin to lengthen and the light to glow, and found that the attendant sensations bore repetition remarkably well. There was the same last intolerable delay at Mestre, just before your first glimpse of the lagoon confirms the already distinct sea-smell which has added speed to the precursive flight of your imagination; then the liquid level, edged afar off by its band of undiscriminated domes and spires, soon distinguished and proclaimed, however, as excited and contentious heads multiply at the windows of the train; then your long rumble on the immense white railway-bridge, which, in spite of the invidious contrast drawn, and very properly, by Mr. Ruskin between the old and the new approach, does truly, in a manner, shine across the green lap of the lagoon like a mighty causeway of marble; then the plunge into the station, which would be exactly similar to every other plunge save for one little fact—that the keynote of the great medley of voices borne back from the exit is not "Cab, sir!" but "Barca, signore!"

I do not mean, however, to follow the traveller through every phase of his initiation, at the risk of stamping poor Venice beyond repair as the supreme bugbear of literature; though for my own part I hold that to a fine healthy romantic appetite the subject can't be too diffusely treated. Meeting in the Piazza on the evening of my arrival a young American painter who told me that he had been spending the summer just where I found him, I could have assaulted him for very envy. He was painting forsooth the interior of St. Mark's. To be a young American painter unperplexed by the mocking,

336

elusive soul of things and satisfied with their wholesome light-bathed surface and shape; keen of eye; fond of colour, of sea and sky and anything that may chance between them; of old lace and old brocade and old furniture (even when made to order); of time-mellowed harmonies on nameless canvases and happy contours in cheap old engravings; to spend one's mornings in still, productive analysis of the clustered shadows of the Basilica, one's afternoons anywhere, in church or campo, on canal or lagoon, and one's evenings in starlight gossip at Florian's, feeling the sea-breeze throb languidly between the two great pillars of the Piazzetta and over the low black domes of the church—this, I consider, is to be as happy as is consistent with the preservation of reason.

The mere use of one's eyes in Venice is happiness enough, and generous observers find it hard to keep an account of their profits in this line. Everything the attention touches holds it, keeps playing with it—thanks to some inscrutable flattery of the atmosphere. Your brown-skinned, white-shirted gondolier, twisting himself in the light, seems to you, as you lie at contemplation beneath your awning, a perpetual symbol of Venetian "effect." The light here is in fact a mighty magician and, with all respect to Titian, Veronese and Tintoret, the greatest artist of them all. You should see in places the material with which it deals—slimy brick, marble battered and be-fouled, rags, dirt, decay. Sea and sky seem to meet half-way, to blend their tones into a soft iridescence, a lustrous compound of wave and cloud and a hundred nameless local reflections, and then to fling the clear tissue against every object of vision. You may see these elements at work everywhere, but to see them in their intensity you should choose the finest day in the month and have yourself rowed far away across the lagoon to Torcello. Without making this excursion you can hardly pretend to know Venice or to sympathise with that longing for pure radiance which animated her great colourists. It is a perfect bath of light, and I couldn't get rid of a fancy that we were cleaving the upper atmosphere on some hurrying cloud-skiff. At Torcello there is nothing but the light to see—nothing at least but a sort of blooming sand-bar intersected by a single narrow creek which does duty as a canal and occupied by a meagre cluster of huts, the dwellings

apparently of market-gardeners and fishermen, and by a ruinous church of the eleventh century. It is impossible to imagine a more penetrating case of unheeded collapse. Torcello
was the mother-city of Venice, and she lies there now, a mere
mouldering vestige, like a group of weather-bleached parental
bones left impiously unburied. I stopped my gondola at the
mouth of the shallow inlet and walked along the grass beside
a hedge to the low-browed, crumbling cathedral. The charm
of certain vacant grassy spaces, in Italy, overfrowned by
masses of brickwork that are honeycombed by the suns of
centuries, is something that I hereby renounce once for all the
attempt to express; but you may be sure that whenever I mention such a spot enchantment lurks in it.

A delicious stillness covered the little campo at Torcello; I
remember none so subtly audible save that of the Roman
Campagna. There was no life but the visible tremor of the
brilliant air and the cries of half-a-dozen young children who
dogged our steps and clamoured for coppers. These children,
by the way, were the handsomest little brats in the world, and
each was furnished with a pair of eyes that could only have
signified the protest of nature against the meanness of fortune. They were very nearly as naked as savages, and their
little bellies protruded like those of infant cannibals in the
illustrations of books of travel; but as they scampered and
sprawled in the soft, thick grass, grinning like suddenly-
translated cherubs and showing their hungry little teeth, they
suggested forcibly that the best assurance of happiness in this
world is to be found in the maximum of innocence and the
minimum of wealth. One small urchin—framed, if ever a
child was, to be the joy of an aristocratic mamma—was the
most expressively beautiful creature I had ever looked upon.
He had a smile to make Correggio sigh in his grave; and yet
here he was running wild among the sea-stunted bushes, on
the lonely margin of a decaying world, in prelude to how
blank or to how dark a destiny? Verily nature is still at odds
with propriety; though indeed if they ever really pull together
I fear nature will quite lose her distinction. An infant citizen
of our own republic, straight-haired, pale-eyed and freckled,
duly darned and catechised, marching into a New England
schoolhouse, is an object often seen and soon forgotten; but I

A Balcony, Venice

think I shall always remember with infinite tender conjecture, as the years roll by, this little unlettered Eros of the Adriatic strand. Yet all youthful things at Torcello were not cheerful, for the poor lad who brought us the key of the cathedral was shaking with an ague, and his melancholy presence seemed to point the moral of forsaken nave and choir. The church, admirably primitive and curious, reminded me of the two or three oldest churches of Rome—St. Clement and St. Agnes. The interior is rich in grimly mystical mosaics of the twelfth century and the patchwork of precious fragments in the pavement not inferior to that of St. Mark's. But the terribly distinct Apostles are ranged against their dead gold backgrounds as stiffly as grenadiers presenting arms—intensely personal sentinels of a personal Deity. Their stony stare seems to wait forever vainly for some visible revival of primitive orthodoxy, and one may well wonder whether it finds much beguilement in idly-gazing troops of Western heretics—passionless even in their heresy.

I had been curious to see whether in the galleries and temples of Venice I should be disposed to transpose my old estimates—to burn what I had adored and adore what I had burned. It is a sad truth that one can stand in the Ducal Palace for the first time but once, with the deliciously ponderous sense of that particular half-hour's being an era in one's mental history; but I had the satisfaction of finding at least—a great comfort in a short stay—that none of my early memories were likely to change places and that I could take up my admirations where I had left them. I still found Carpaccio delightful, Veronese magnificent, Titian supremely beautiful and Tintoret scarce to be appraised. I repaired immediately to the little church of San Cassano, which contains the smaller of Tintoret's two great Crucifixions; and when I had looked at it awhile I drew a long breath and felt I could now face any other picture in Venice with proper self-possession. It seemed to me I had advanced to the uttermost limit of painting; that beyond this another art—inspired poetry—begins, and that Bellini, Veronese, Giorgione, and Titian, all joining hands and straining every muscle of their genius, reach forward not so far but that they leave a visible space in which Tintoret alone is master. I well remember the exaltations to which he lifted

In the Lagoon, Venice

me when first I learned to know him; but the glow of that comparatively youthful amazement is dead, and with it, I fear, that confident vivacity of phrase of which, in trying to utter my impressions, I felt less the magniloquence than the impotence. In his power there are many weak spots, mysterious lapses and fitful intermissions; but when the list of his faults is complete he still remains to me the most *interesting* of painters. His reputation rests chiefly on a more superficial sort of merit—his energy, his unsurpassed productivity, his being, as Théophile Gautier says, *le roi des fougueux*. These qualities are immense, but the great source of his impressiveness is that his indefatigable hand never drew a line that was not, as one may say, a moral line. No painter ever had such breadth and such depth; and even Titian, beside him, scarce figures as more than a great decorative artist. Mr. Ruskin, whose eloquence in dealing with the great Venetians sometimes outruns his discretion, is fond of speaking even of Veronese as a painter of deep spiritual intentions. This, it seems to me, is pushing matters too far, and the author of "The Rape of Europa" is, pictorially speaking, no greater casuist than any other genius of supreme good taste. Titian was assuredly a mighty poet, but Tintoret—well, Tintoret was almost a prophet. Before his greatest works you are conscious of a sudden evaporation of old doubts and dilemmas, and the eternal problem of the conflict between idealism and realism dies the most natural of deaths. In his genius the problem is practically solved; the alternatives are so harmoniously interfused that I defy the keenest critic to say where one begins and the other ends. The homeliest prose melts into the most ethereal poetry—the literal and the imaginative fairly confound their identity.

This, however, is vague praise. Tintoret's great merit, to my mind, was his unequalled distinctness of vision. When once he had conceived the germ of a scene it defined itself to his imagination with an intensity, an amplitude, an individuality of expression, which make one's observation of his pictures seem less an operation of the mind than a kind of supplementary experience of life. Veronese and Titian are content with a much looser specification, as their treatment of any subject that the author of the Crucifixion at San Cassano has also treated abundantly proves. There are few more suggestive contrasts than that between the absence of a total character at all commensurate with its scattered variety and brilliancy in Veronese's "Marriage of Cana," at the Louvre, and the poignant, almost startling, completeness of Tintoret's illustration of the theme at the Salute church. To compare his "Presentation of the Virgin," at the Madonna dell' Orto, with Titian's at the Academy, or his "Annunciation" with Titian's close at hand, is to measure the essential difference between observation and imagination. One has certainly not said all that there is to say for Titian when one has called him an observer. *Il y mettait du sien*, and I use the term to designate roughly the artist whose apprehension, infinitely deep and strong when applied to the single figure or to easily balanced groups, spends itself vainly on great dramatic combinations—or rather leaves them ungauged. It was the whole scene that Tintoret seemed to have beheld in a flash of inspiration intense enough to stamp it ineffaceably on his perception; and it was the whole scene, complete, peculiar, individual, unprecedented, that he committed to canvas with all the vehemence of his talent. Compare his "Last Supper," at San Giorgio—its long, diagonally placed table, its dusky spaciousness, its scattered lamp-light and halo-light, its startled, gesticulating figures, its richly realistic foreground—with the customary formal, almost mathematical rendering of the subject, in which impressiveness seems to have been sought in elimination rather than comprehension. You get from Tintoret's work the impression that he *felt*, pictorially, the great, beautiful, terrible spectacle of human life very much as Shakespeare felt it poetically—with a heart that never ceased to beat a passionate accompaniment to every stroke of his brush. Thanks to this fact his works are signally grave, and their almost universal and rapidly increasing decay doesn't relieve their gloom. Nothing indeed can well be sadder than the great collection of Tintorets at San Rocco. Incurable blackness is settling fast upon all of them, and they frown at you across the sombre splendour of their great chambers like gaunt twilight phantoms of pictures. To our children's children Tintoret, as things are going, can be hardly more than a name; and such of them as shall miss the tragic beauty, already so dimmed and stained, of the great "Bearing of the

Cross" in that temple of his spirit will live and die without knowing the largest eloquence of art. If you wish to add the last touch of solemnity to the place recall as vividly as possible while you linger at San Rocco the painter's singularly interesting portrait of himself, at the Louvre. The old man looks out of the canvas from beneath a brow as sad as a sunless twilight, with just such a stoical hopelessness as you might fancy him to wear if he stood at your side gazing at his rotting canvases. It isn't whimsical to read it as the face of a man who felt that he had given the world more than the world was likely to repay. Indeed before every picture of Tintoret you may remember this tremendous portrait with profit. On one side the power, the passion, the illusion of his art; on the other the mortal fatigue of his spirit. The world's knowledge of him is so small that the portrait throws a doubly precious light on his personality; and when we wonder vainly what manner of man he was, and what were his purpose, his faith and his method, we may find forcible assurance there that they were at any rate his life—one of the most intellectually passionate ever led.

Verona, which was my last Italian stopping-place, is in any conditions a delightfully interesting city; but the kindness of my own memory of it is deepened by a subsequent ten days' experience of Germany. I rose one morning at Verona, and went to bed at night at Botzen! The statement needs no comment, and the two places, though but fifty miles apart, are as painfully dissimilar as their names. I had prepared myself for your delectation with a copious tirade on German manners, German scenery, German art and the German stage—on the lights and shadows of Innsbrück, Munich, Nüremberg and Heidelberg; but just as I was about to put pen to paper I glanced into a little volume on these very topics lately published by that famous novelist and moralist, M. Ernest Feydeau, the fruit of a summer's observation at Homburg. This work produced a reaction; and if I chose to follow M. Feydeau's own example when he wishes to qualify his approbation I might call his treatise by any vile name known to the speech of man. But I content myself with pronouncing it superficial. I then reflect that my own opportunities for seeing and judging were extremely limited, and I suppress my tirade, lest some more enlightened critic should come and hang me with the same rope. Its sum and substance was to have been that—superficially—Germany is ugly; that Munich is a nightmare, Heidelberg a disappointment (in spite of its charming castle) and even Nüremberg not a joy for ever. But comparisons are odious, and if Munich is ugly Verona is beautiful enough. You may laugh at my logic, but will probably assent to my meaning. I carried away from Verona a precious mental picture upon which I cast an introspective glance whenever between Botzen and Strassburg the oppression of external circumstance became painful. It was a lovely August afternoon in the Roman arena—a ruin in which repair and restoration have been so watchfully and plausibly practised that it seems all of one harmonious antiquity. The vast stony oval rose high against the sky in a single clear, continuous line, broken here and there only by strolling and reclining loungers. The massive tiers inclined in solid monotony to the central circle, in which a small open-air theatre was in active operation. A small quarter of the great slope of masonry facing the stage was roped off into an auditorium, in which the narrow level space between the foot-lights and the lowest step figured as the pit. Foot-lights are a figure of speech, for the performance was going on in the broad glow of the afternoon, with a delightful and apparently by no means misplaced confidence in the good-will of the spectators. What the piece was that was deemed so superbly able to shift for itself I know not—very possibly the same drama that I remember seeing advertised during my former visit to Verona; nothing less than *La Tremenda Giustizia di Dio.* If titles are worth anything this product of the melodramatist's art might surely stand upon its own legs. Along the tiers above the little group of regular spectators was gathered a free-list of unauthorised observers, who, although beyond ear-shot, must have been enabled by the generous breadth of Italian gesture to follow the tangled thread of the piece. It was all deliciously Italian—the mixture of old life and new, the mountebank's booth (it was hardly more) grafted on the antique circus, the dominant presence of a mighty architecture, the loungers and idlers beneath the kindly sky and upon the sun-warmed stones. I never felt more keenly the difference between the background to life in very old and very new civilisations. There are other things in Verona to make it a liberal education to be born there, though that it *is* one for the contemporary Veronese I don't pretend to say. The Tombs of the Scaligers, with their soaring pinnacles, their high-poised canopies, their exquisite refinement and concentration of the Gothic idea, I can't profess, even after much worshipful gazing, to have fully comprehended and enjoyed. They seemed to me full of deep architectural meanings, such as must drop gently into the mind one by one, after infinite tranquil contemplation. But even to the hurried and preoccupied traveller the solemn little chapel-yard in the city's heart, in which they stand girdled by their great swaying curtain of linked and twisted iron, is one of the most impressive spots in Italy. Nowhere else is such a wealth of artistic achievement crowded into so narrow a space; nowhere else are the daily comings and goings of men blessed by the presence of *manlier* art. Verona is rich furthermore in beautiful churches—several with beautiful names: San Fermo, Santa Anastasia, San Zenone. This last is a structure of high antiquity and of the most impressive loveliness. The nave terminates in a double choir, that is a sub-choir or crypt into which you descend and where you wander among primitive columns whose variously grotesque capitals rise hardly higher than your head, and an upper choral plane reached by broad stairways of the bravest effect. I shall never forget the impression of majestic chastity that I received from the great nave of the building on my former visit. I then decided to my satisfaction that every church is from the devotional point of view a solecism that has not something of a similar absolute felicity of proportion; for strictly formal beauty seems best to express our conception of spiritual beauty. The nobly serious character of San Zenone is deepened by its single picture—a masterpiece of the most serious of painters, the severe and exquisite Mantegna.

1872.

Two Old Houses and
Three Young Women

THERE are times and places that come back yet again, but
that, when the brooding tourist puts out his hand to
them, meet it a little slowly, or even seem to recede a step, as
if in slight fear of some liberty he may take. Surely they
should know by this time that he is capable of taking none.
He has his own way—he makes it all right. It now becomes
just a part of the charming solicitation that it presents precisely a problem—that of *giving* the particular thing as much
as possible without at the same time giving it, as we say,
away. There are considerations, proprieties, a necessary indi-
rectness—he must use, in short, a little art. No necessity,
however, more than this, makes him warm to his work, and
thus it is that, after all, he hangs his three pictures.

I

The evening that was to give me the first of them was by
no means the first occasion of my asking myself if that inveterate "style" of which we talk so much be absolutely conditioned—in dear old Venice and elsewhere—on decrepitude.
Is it the style that has brought about the decrepitude, or the
decrepitude that has, as it were, intensified and consecrated
the style? There is an ambiguity about it all that constantly
haunts and beguiles. Dear old Venice has lost her complexion,
her figure, her reputation, her self-respect; and yet, with it all,
has so puzzlingly not lost a shred of her distinction. Perhaps
indeed the case is simpler than it seems, for the poetry of
misfortune is familiar to us all, whereas, in spite of a stroke
here and there of some happy justice that charms, we scarce
find ourselves anywhere arrested by the poetry of a run of
luck. The misfortune of Venice being, accordingly, at every
point, what we most touch, feel and see, we end by assuming
it to be of the essence of her dignity; a consequence, we become aware, by the way, sufficiently discouraging to the general application or pretension of style, and all the more that,

to make the final felicity deep, the original greatness must have been something tremendous. If it be the ruins that are noble we have known plenty that were not, and moreover there are degrees and varieties: certain monuments, solid survivals, hold up their heads and decline to ask for a grain of your pity. Well, one knows of course when to keep one's pity to oneself; yet one clings, even in the face of the colder stare, to one's prized Venetian privilege of making the sense of doom and decay a part of every impression. Cheerful work, it may be said of course; and it is doubtless only in Venice that you gain more by such a trick than you lose. What was most beautiful is gone; what was next most beautiful is, thank goodness, going—that, I think, is the monstrous description of the better part of your thought. Is it really your fault if the place makes you want so desperately to read history into everything?

You do that wherever you turn and wherever you look, and you do it, I should say, most of all at night. It comes to you there with longer knowledge, and with all deference to what flushes and shimmers, that the night is the real time. It perhaps even wouldn't take much to make you award the palm to the nights of winter. This is certainly true for the form of progression that is most characteristic, for every question of departure and arrival by gondola. The little closed cabin of this perfect vehicle, the movement, the darkness and the plash, the indistinguishable swerves and twists, all the things you don't see and all the things you do feel—each dim recognition and obscure arrest is a possible throb of your sense of being floated to your doom, even when the truth is simply and sociably that you are going out to tea. Nowhere else is anything as innocent so mysterious, nor anything as mysterious so pleasantly deterrent to protest. These are the moments when you are most daringly Venetian, most content to leave cheap trippers and other aliens the high light of the mid-lagoon and the pursuit of pink and gold. The splendid day is good enough for *them*; what is best for you is to stop at last, as you are now stopping, among clustered *pali* and softly-shifting poops and prows, at a great flight of water-steps that play their admirable part in the general effect of a great entrance. The high doors stand open from them to the paved

chamber of a basement tremendously tall and not vulgarly
lighted, from which, in turn, mounts the slow stone staircase
that draws you further on. The great point is, that if you are
worthy of this impression at all, there isn't a single item of it
of which the association isn't noble. Hold to it fast that there
is no other such dignity of arrival as arrival by water. Hold to
it that to float and slacken and gently bump, to creep out of
the low, dark *felze* and make the few guided movements and
find the strong crooked and offered arm, and then, beneath
lighted palace-windows, pass up the few damp steps on the
precautionary carpet—hold to it that these things constitute a
preparation of which the only defect is that it may sometimes
perhaps really prepare too much. It's so stately that what can
come after?—it's so good in itself that what, upstairs, as we
comparative vulgarians say, can be better? Hold to it, at any
rate, that if a lady, in especial, scrambles out of a carriage,
tumbles out of a cab, flops out of a tram-car, and hurtles,
projectile-like, out of a "lightning-elevator," she alights from
the Venetian conveyance as Cleopatra may have stepped from
her barge. Upstairs—whatever may be yet in store for her—
her entrance shall still advantageously enjoy the support most
opposed to the "momentum" acquired. The beauty of the
matter has been in the absence of all momentum—elsewhere
so scientifically applied to us, from behind, by the terrible life
of our day—and in the fact that, as the elements of slowness,
the felicities of deliberation, doubtless thus all hang together,
the last of calculable dangers is to enter a great Venetian room
with a rush.

Not the least happy note, therefore, of the picture I am
trying to frame is that there was absolutely no rushing; not
only in the sense of a scramble over marble floors, but, by
reason of something dissuasive and distributive in the very air
of the place, a suggestion, under the fine old ceilings and
among types of face and figure abounding in the unexpected,
that here were many things to consider. Perhaps the simplest
rendering of a scene into the depths of which there are good
grounds of discretion for not sinking would be just this
emphasis on the value of the unexpected for such occasions
—with due qualification, naturally, of its degree. Unexpectedness pure and simple, it is needless to say, may easily en-

danger any social gathering, and I hasten to add moreover that the figures and faces I speak of were probably not in the least unexpected to each other. The stage they occupied was a stage of variety—Venice has ever been a garden of strange social flowers. It is only as reflected in the consciousness of the visitor from afar—brooding tourist even call him, or sharp-eyed bird on the branch—that I attempt to give you the little drama; beginning with the felicity that most appealed to him, the visible, unmistakable fact that he was the only representative of his class. The whole of the rest of the business was but what he saw and felt and fancied—what he was to remember and what he was to forget. Through it all, I may say distinctly, he clung to his great Venetian clue—the explanation of everything by the historic idea. It was a high historic house, with such a quantity of recorded past twinkling in the multitudinous candles that one grasped at the idea of something waning and displaced, and might even fondly and secretly nurse the conceit that what one was having was just the very last. Wasn't it certainly, for instance, no mere illusion that there is no appreciable future left for such manners—an urbanity so comprehensive, a form so transmitted, as those of such a hostess and such a host? The future is for a different conception of the graceful altogether—so far as it's for a conception of the graceful at all. Into that computation I shall not attempt to enter; but these representative products of an antique culture, at least, and one of which the secret seems more likely than not to be lost, were not common, nor indeed was any one else—in the circle to which the picture most insisted on restricting itself.

Neither, on the other hand, was any one either very beautiful or very fresh: which was again, exactly, a precious "value" on an occasion that was to shine most, to the imagination, by the complexity of its references. Such old, old women with such old, old jewels; such ugly, ugly ones with such handsome, becoming names; such battered, fatigued gentlemen with such inscrutable decorations; such an absence of youth, for the most part, in either sex—of the pink and white, the "bud" of new worlds; such a general personal air, in fine, of being the worse for a good deal of wear in various old ones. It was not a society—that was clear—in which little girls and boys set the tune; and there was that about it all that might well have cast a shadow on the path of even the most successful little girl. Yet also—let me not be rudely inexact—it was in honour of youth and freshness that we had all been convened. The *fiançailles* of the last—unless it were the last but one—unmarried daughter of the house had just been brought to a proper climax; the contract had been signed, the betrothal rounded off—I'm not sure that the civil marriage hadn't, that day, taken place. The occasion then had in fact the most charming of heroines and the most ingenuous of heroes, a young man, the latter, all happily suffused with a fair Austrian blush. The young lady had had, besides other more or less shining recent ancestors, a very famous paternal grandmother, who had played a great part in the political history of her time and whose portrait, in the taste and dress of 1830, was conspicuous in one of the rooms. The granddaughter of this celebrity, of royal race, was strikingly like her and, by a fortunate stroke, had been habited, combed, curled in a manner exactly to reproduce the portrait. These things were charming and amusing, as indeed were several other things besides. The great Venetian beauty of our period was there, and nature had equipped the great Venetian beauty for her part with the properest sense of the suitable, or in any case with a splendid generosity—since on the ideally suitable *character* of so brave a human symbol who shall have the last word? This responsible agent was at all events the beauty in the world about whom probably, most, the absence of question (an absence never wholly propitious) would a little smugly and monotonously flourish: the one thing wanting to the interest she inspired was thus the possibility of ever discussing it. There were plenty of suggestive subjects round about, on the other hand, as to which the exchange of ideas would by no means necessarily have dropped. You profit to the full at such times by all the old voices, echoes, images—by that element of the history of Venice which represents all Europe as having at one time and another revelled or rested, asked for pleasure or for patience there; which gives you the place supremely as the refuge of endless strange secrets, broken fortunes and wounded hearts.

II

There had been, on lines of further or different speculation, a young Englishman to luncheon, and the young Englishman had proved "sympathetic"; so that when it was a question afterwards of some of the more hidden treasures, the browner depths of the old churches, the case became one for mutual guidance and gratitude—for a small afternoon tour and the wait of a pair of friends in the warm little *campi*, at locked doors for which the nearest urchin had scurried off to fetch the keeper of the key. There are few brown depths to-day into which the light of the hotels doesn't shine, and few hidden treasures about which pages enough, doubtless, haven't already been printed: my business, accordingly, let me hasten to say, is not now with the fond renewal of any discovery—at least in the order of impressions most usual. Your discovery may be, for that matter, renewed every week; the only essential is the good luck—which a fair amount of practice has taught you to count upon—of not finding, for the particular occasion, other discoverers in the field. Then, in the quiet corner, with the closed door—then in the presence of the picture and of your companion's sensible emotion—not only the original happy moment, but everything else, is renewed. Yet once again it can all come back. The old custode, shuffling about in the dimness, jerks away, to make sure of his tip, the old curtain that isn't much more modern than the wonderful work itself. He does his best to create light where light can never be; but you have your practised groping gaze, and in guiding the young eyes of your less confident associate, moreover, you feel you possess the treasure. These are the most refined pleasures that Venice has still to give, these odd happy passages of communication and response.

But the point of my reminiscence is that there were other communications that day, as there were certainly other responses. I have forgotten exactly what it was we were looking for—without much success—when we met the three Sisters. Nothing requires more care, as a long knowledge of Venice

works in, than not to lose the useful faculty of getting lost. I
had so successfully done my best to preserve it that I could at
that moment conscientiously profess an absence of any suspicion of where we might be. It proved enough that, wherever
we were, we were where the three sisters found us. This was
on a little bridge near a big campo, and a part of the charm of
the matter was the theory that it was very much out of the
way. They took us promptly in hand—they were only walking over to San Marco to match some coloured wool for the
manufacture of such belated cushions as still bloom with purple and green in the long leisures of old palaces; and that mild
errand could easily open a parenthesis. The obscure church
we had feebly imagined we were looking for proved, if I am
not mistaken, that of the sisters' parish; as to which I have but
a confused recollection of a large grey void and of admiring
for the first time a fine work of art of which I have now quite
lost the identity. This was the effect of the charming benefi-
cence of the three sisters, who presently were to give our adventure a turn in the emotion of which everything that had
preceded seemed as nothing. It actually strikes me even as a
little dim to have been told by them, as we all fared together,
that a certain low, wide house, in a small square as to which I
found myself without particular association, had been in the
far-off time the residence of George Sand. And yet this was
a fact that, though I could then only feel it must be for another day, would in a different connection have set me richly
reconstructing.

Madame Sand's famous Venetian year has been of late immensely in the air—a tub of soiled linen which the muse of
history, rolling her sleeves well up, has not even yet quite
ceased energetically and publicly to wash. The house in question must have been the house to which the wonderful lady
betook herself when, in 1834, after the dramatic exit of Alfred
de Musset, she enjoyed that remarkable period of rest and
refreshment with the so long silent, the but recently rediscov-
ered, reported, extinguished, Doctor Pagello. As an old Sandist—not exactly indeed of the *première heure*, but of the fine
high noon and golden afternoon of the great career—I had
been, though I confess too inactively, curious as to a few
points in the topography of the eminent adventure to which I

here allude; but had never got beyond the little public fact, in itself always a bit of a thrill to the Sandist, that the present Hotel Danieli had been the scene of its first remarkable stages. I am not sure indeed that the curiosity I speak of has not at last, in my breast, yielded to another form of wonderment—truly to the rather rueful question of why we have so continued to concern ourselves, and why the fond observer of the footprints of genius is likely so to continue attentive to an altercation neither in itself and in its day, nor in its preserved and attested records, at all positively edifying. The answer to such an inquiry would doubtless reward patience, but I fear we can now glance at its possibilities only long enough to say that interesting persons—so they be of a sufficiently approved and established interest—render in some degree interesting whatever happens to them, and give it an importance even when very little else (as in the case I refer to) may have operated to give it a dignity. Which is where I leave the issue of further identifications.

For the three sisters, in the kindest way in the world, had asked us if we already knew their sequestered home and whether, in case we didn't, we should be at all amused to see it. My own acquaintance with them, though not of recent origin, had hitherto lacked this enhancement, at which we both now grasped with the full instinct, indescribable enough, of what it was likely to give. But how, for that matter, either, can I find the right expression of what was to remain with us of this episode? It is the fault of the sad-eyed old witch of Venice that she so easily puts more into things that can pass under the common names that do for them elsewhere. Too much for a rough sketch was to be seen and felt in the home of the three sisters, and in the delightful and slightly pathetic deviation of their doing us so simply and freely the honours of it. What was most immediately marked was their resigned cosmopolite state, the effacement of old conventional lines by foreign contact and example; by the action, too, of causes full of a special interest, but not to be emphasised perhaps—granted indeed they be named at all—without a certain sadness of sympathy. If "style," in Venice, sits among ruins, let us always lighten our tread when we pay her a visit.

Our steps were in fact, I am happy to think, almost soft enough for a death-chamber as we stood in the big, vague *sala* of the three sisters, spectators of their simplified state and their beautiful blighted rooms, the memories, the portraits, the shrunken relics of nine Doges. If I wanted a first chapter it was here made to my hand; the painter of life and manners, as he glanced about, could only sigh—as he so frequently has to—over the vision of so much more truth than he can use. What on earth is the need to "invent," in the midst of tragedy and comedy that never cease? Why, with the subject itself, all round, so inimitable, condemn the picture to the silliness of trying not to be aware of it? The charming lonely girls, carrying so simply their great name and fallen fortunes, the despoiled *decaduta* house, the unfailing Italian grace, the space so out of scale with actual needs, the absence of books, the presence of ennui, the sense of the length of the hours and the shortness of everything else—all this was a matter not only for a second chapter and a third, but for a whole volume, a *dénoûment* and a sequel.

This time, unmistakably, it *was* the last—Wordsworth's stately "shade of that which once was great"; and it was almost as if our distinguished young friends had consented to pass away slowly in order to treat us to the vision. Ends are only ends in truth, for the painter of pictures, when they are more or less conscious and prolonged. One of the sisters had been to London, whence she had brought back the impression of having seen at the British Museum a room exclusively filled with books and documents devoted to the commemoration of her family. She must also then have encountered at the National Gallery the exquisite specimen of an early Venetian master in which one of her ancestors, then head of the State, kneels with so sweet a dignity before the Virgin and Child. She was perhaps old enough, none the less, to have seen this precious work taken down from the wall of the room in which we sat and—on terms so far too easy—carried away for ever; and not too young, at all events, to have been present, now and then, when her candid elders, enlightened too late as to what their sacrifice might really have done for them, looked at each other with the pale hush of the irreparable. We let ourselves note that these were matters to put a great deal of old, old history into sweet young Venetian faces.

III

In Italy, if we come to that, this particular appearance is far from being only in the streets, where we are apt most to observe it—in countenances caught as we pass and in the objects marked by the guide-books with their respective stellar allowances. It is behind the walls of the houses that old, old history is thick and that the multiplied stars of Baedeker might often best find their application. The feast of St. John the Baptist is the feast of the year in Florence, and it seemed to me on that night that I could have scattered about me a handful of these signs. I had the pleasure of spending a couple of hours on a signal high terrace that overlooks the Arno, as well as in the galleries that open out to it, where I met more than ever the pleasant curious question of the disparity between the old conditions and the new manners. Make our manners, we moderns, as good as we can, there is still no getting over it that they are not good enough for many of the great places. This was one of those scenes, and its greatness came out to the full into the hot Florentine evening, in which the pink and golden fires of the pyrotechnics arranged on Ponte Carraja—the occasion of our assembly—lighted up the large issue. The "good people" beneath were a huge, hot, gentle, happy family; the fireworks on the bridge, kindling river as well as sky, were delicate and charming; the terrace connected the two wings that give bravery to the front of the palace, and the close-hung pictures in the rooms, open in a long series, offered to a lover of quiet perambulation an alternative hard to resist.

Wherever he stood—on the broad loggia, in the cluster of company, among bland ejaculations and liquefied ices, or in the presence of the mixed masters that led him from wall to wall—such a seeker for the spirit of each occasion could only turn it over that in the first place this was an intenser, finer little Florence than ever, and that in the second the testimony was again wonderful to former fashions and ideas. What did they do, in the other time, the time of so much smaller a society, smaller and fewer fortunes, more taste perhaps as to some particulars, but fewer tastes, at any rate, and fewer habits and wants—what did they do with chambers so multitudinous and so vast? Put their "state" at its highest—and we know of many ways in which it must have broken down— how did they live in them without the aid of variety? How did they, in minor communities in which every one knew every one, and every one's impression and effect had been long, as we say, discounted, find representation and emulation sufficiently amusing? Much of the charm of thinking of it, however, is doubtless that we are not able to say. This leaves us with the conviction that does them most honour: the old generations built and arranged greatly for the simple reason that they liked it, and they could bore themselves—to say nothing of each other, when it came to that—better in noble conditions than in mean ones.

It was not, I must add, of the far-away Florentine age that I most thought, but of periods more recent and of which the sound and beautiful house more directly spoke. If one had always been homesick for the Arno-side of the seventeenth and eighteenth centuries, here was a chance, and a better one than ever, to taste again of the cup. Many of the pictures— there was a charming quarter of an hour when I had them to myself—were bad enough to have passed for good in those delightful years. Shades of Grand-Dukes encompassed me— Dukes of the pleasant later sort who weren't really grand. There was still the sense of having come too late—yet not too late, after all, for this glimpse and this dream. My business was to people the place—its own business had never been to save us the trouble of understanding it. And then the deepest spell of all was perhaps that just here I was supremely out of the way of the so terribly actual Florentine question. This, as all the world knows, is a battle-ground, to-day, in many journals, with all Italy practically pulling on one side and all England, America and Germany pulling on the other: I speak of course of the more or less articulate opinion. The "improvement," the rectification of Florence is in the air, and the problem of the particular ways in which, given such desperately delicate cases, these matters should be understood. The little treasure-city is, if there ever was one, a delicate case—more delicate perhaps than any other in the world save that of our taking on ourselves to persuade the Italians that they mayn't do as they like with their own. They so absolutely may that I profess I see no happy issue from the fight. It will take more tact than our combined tactful genius may at all probably muster to convince them that their own is, by an ingenious logic, much rather *ours*. It will take more subtlety still to muster for them that truly dazzling show of examples from which they may learn that what in general is "ours" shall appear to them as a rule a sacrifice to beauty and a triumph of taste. The situation, to the truly analytic mind, offers in short, to perfection, all the elements of despair; and I am afraid that if I hung back, at the Corsini palace, to woo illusions and invoke the irrelevant, it was because I could think, in the conditions, of no better way to meet the acute responsibility of the critic than just to shirk it.

1899.

Casa Alvisi

Invited to "introduce" certain pages of cordial and faithful reminiscence from another hand,* in which a frankly predominant presence seems to live again, I undertook that office with an interest inevitably somewhat sad—so passed and gone to-day is so much of the life suggested. Those who fortunately knew Mrs. Bronson will read into her notes still more of it—more of her subject, more of herself too, and of many things—than she gives, and some may well even feel tempted to do for her what she has done here for her distinguished friend. In Venice, during a long period, for many pilgrims, Mrs. Arthur Bronson, originally of New York, was, so far as society, hospitality, a charming personal welcome were concerned, almost in sole possession; she had become there, with time, quite the prime representative of those private amenities which the Anglo-Saxon abroad is apt to miss just in proportion as the place visited is publicly wonderful, and in which he therefore finds a value twice as great as at home. Mrs. Bronson really earned in this way the gratitude of mingled generations and races. She sat for twenty years at the wide mouth, as it were, of the Grand Canal, holding out her hand, with endless good-nature, patience, charity, to all decently accredited petitioners, the incessant troop of those either bewilderedly making or fondly renewing acquaintance with the dazzling city.

Casa Alvisi is directly opposite the high, broad-based florid church of S. Maria della Salute—so directly that from the balcony over the water-entrance your eye, crossing the canal, seems to find the key-hole of the great door right in a line with it; and there was something in this position that for the time made all Venice-lovers think of the genial *padrona* as thus levying in the most convenient way the toll of curiosity and sympathy. Every one passed, every one was seen to pass, and few were those not seen to stop and to return. The most generous of hostesses died a year ago at Florence; her house

*"Browning in Venice," being Recollections of the late Katharine De Kay Bronson, with a Prefatory Note by H. J. (*Cornhill Magazine*, February 1902).

knows her no more—it had ceased to do so for some time
before her death; and the long, pleased procession—the
charmed arrivals, the happy sojourns at anchor, the reluctant
departures that made Ca' Alvisi, as was currently said, a social
porto di mare—is, for remembrance and regret, already a possession of ghosts; so that, on the spot, at present, the attention ruefully averts itself from the dear little old faded but
once familiarly bright façade, overtaken at last by the comparatively vulgar uses that are doing their best to "paint out" in
Venice, right and left, by staring signs and other vulgarities,
the immemorial note of distinction. The house, in a city of
palaces, was small, but the tenant clung to her perfect, her
inclusive position—the one right place that gave her a better
command, as it were, than a better house obtained by a
harder compromise; not being fond, moreover, of spacious
halls and massive treasures, but of compact and familiar
rooms, in which her remarkable accumulation of minute and
delicate Venetian objects could show. She adored—in the
way of the Venetian, to which all her taste addressed itself—
the small, the domestic and the exquisite; so that she would
have given a Tintoretto or two, I think, without difficulty, for
a cabinet of tiny gilded glasses or a dinner-service of the right
old silver.

   The general receptacle of these multiplied treasures played
at any rate, through the years, the part of a friendly private-
box at the constant operatic show, a box at the best point of
the best tier, with the cushioned ledge of its front raking the
whole scene and with its withdrawing rooms behind for more
detached conversation; for easy—when not indeed slightly
difficult—polyglot talk, artful *bibite*, artful cigarettes too,
straight from the hand of the hostess, who could do all that
belonged to a hostess, place people in relation and keep them
so, take up and put down the topic, cause delicate tobacco
and little gilded glasses to circulate, without ever leaving her
sofa-cushions or intermitting her good-nature. She exercised
in these conditions, with never a block, as we say in London,
in the traffic, with never an admission, an acceptance of the
least social complication, her positive genius for easy interest,
easy sympathy, easy friendship. It was as if, at last, she had
taken the human race at large, quite irrespective of geography,

Ponte Pennelli, Venice

for her neighbours, with neighbourly relations as a matter of course. These things, on her part, had at all events the greater appearance of ease from their having found to their purpose—and as if the very air of Venice produced them—a cluster of forms so light and immediate, so pre-established by picturesque custom. The old bright tradition, the wonderful Venetian legend had appealed to her from the first, closing round her house and her well-plashed water-steps, where the waiting gondolas were thick, quite as if, actually, the ghost of the defunct Carnival—since I have spoken of ghosts—still played some haunting part.

Let me add, at the same time, that Mrs. Bronson's social facility, which was really her great refuge from importunity, a defence with serious thought and serious feeling quietly cherished behind it, had its discriminations as well as its inveteracies, and that the most marked of all these, perhaps, was her attachment to Robert Browning. Nothing in all her beneficent life had probably made her happier than to have found herself able to minister, each year, with the returning autumn, to his pleasure and comfort. Attached to Ca' Alvisi, on the land side, is a somewhat melancholy old section of a Giustiniani palace, which she had annexed to her own premises mainly for the purpose of placing it, in comfortable guise, at the service of her friends. She liked, as she professed, when they were the real thing, to have them under her hand; and here succeeded each other, through the years, the company of the privileged and the more closely domesticated, who liked, harmlessly, to distinguish between themselves and outsiders. Among visitors partaking of this pleasant provision Mr. Browning was of course easily first. But I must leave her own pen to show him as her best years knew him. The point was, meanwhile, that if her charity was great even for the outsider, this was by reason of the inner essence of it—her perfect tenderness for Venice, which she always recognised as a link. That was the true principle of fusion, the key to communication. She communicated in proportion—little or much, measuring it as she felt people more responsive or less so; and she expressed herself, or in other words her full affection for the place, only to those who had most of the same sentiment. The rich and interesting form in which she found it in Browning may well be imagined—together with the quite independent quantity of the genial at large that she also found; but I am not sure that his favour was not primarily based on his paid tribute of such things as "Two in a Gondola" and "A Toccata of Galuppi." He had more ineffaceably than any one recorded his initiation from of old.

She was thus, all round, supremely faithful; yet it was perhaps after all with the very small folk, those to the manner born, that she made the easiest terms. She loved, she had from the first enthusiastically adopted, the engaging Venetian people, whose virtues she found touching and their infirmities but such as appeal mainly to the sense of humour and the love of anecdote; and she befriended and admired, she studied and spoiled them. There must have been a multitude of whom it would scarce be too much to say that her long residence among them was their settled golden age. When I consider that they have lost her now I fairly wonder to what shifts they have been put and how long they may not have to wait for such another messenger of Providence. She cultivated their dialect, she renewed their boats, she piously relighted—at the top of the tide-washed *pali* of traghetto or lagoon—the neglected lamp of the tutelary Madonnetta; she took cognisance of the wives, the children, the accidents, the troubles, as to which she became, perceptibly, the most prompt, the established remedy. On lines where the amusement was happily less one-sided she put together in dialect many short comedies, dramatic proverbs, which, with one of her drawing-rooms permanently arranged as a charming diminutive theatre, she caused to be performed by the young persons of her circle—often, when the case lent itself, by the wonderful small offspring of humbler friends, children of the Venetian lower class, whose aptitude, teachability, drollery, were her constant delight. It was certainly true that an impression of Venice as humanly sweet might easily found itself on the frankness and quickness and amiability of these little people. They were at least so much to the good; for the philosophy of their patroness was as Venetian as everything else; helping her to accept experience without bitterness and to remain fresh, even in the fatigue which finally overtook her, for pleasant surprises and proved sincerities. She was herself sincere to the last for the place of her predilection; inasmuch as though she had arranged herself, in the later time—and largely for the love of "Pippa Passes"—an alternative refuge at Asolo, she absented herself from Venice with continuity only under co-ercion of illness.

At Asolo, periodically, the link with Browning was more confirmed than weakened, and there, in old Venetian terri-tory, and with the invasion of visitors comparatively checked, her preferentially small house became again a setting for the pleasure of talk and the sense of Italy. It contained again its own small treasures, all in the pleasant key of the homelier Venetian spirit. The plain beneath it stretched away like a pur-ple sea from the lower cliffs of the hills, and the white *campa-nili* of the villages, as one was perpetually saying, showed on the expanse like scattered sails of ships. The rumbling car-riage, the old-time, rattling, red-velveted carriage of provin-cial, rural Italy, delightful and quaint, did the office of the gondola; to Bassano, to Treviso, to high-walled Castelfranco, all pink and gold, the home of the great Giorgione. Here also memories cluster; but it is in Venice again that her vanished presence is most felt, for there, in the real, or certainly the finer, the more sifted Cosmopolis, it falls into its place among the others evoked, those of the past seekers of poetry and dispensers of romance. It is a fact that almost every one inter-esting, appealing, melancholy, memorable, odd, seems at one time or another, after many days and much life, to have grav-itated to Venice by a happy instinct, settling in it and treating it, cherishing it, as a sort of repository of consolations; all of which to-day, for the conscious mind, is mixed with its air and constitutes its unwritten history. The deposed, the de-feated, the disenchanted, the wounded, or even only the bored, have seemed to find there something that no other place could give. But such people came for themselves, as we seem to see them—only with the egotism of their grievances and the vanity of their hopes. Mrs. Bronson's case was beau-tifully different—she had come altogether for others.

From Chambéry to Milan

Y OUR truly sentimental tourist will never take it from any occasion that there is absolutely nothing for him, and it was at Chambéry—but four hours from Geneva—that I accepted the situation and decided there might be mysterious delights in entering Italy by a whizz through an eight-mile tunnel, even as a bullet through the bore of a gun. I found my reward in the Savoyard landscape, which greets you betimes with the smile of anticipation. If it is not so Italian as Italy it is at least more Italian than anything *but* Italy—more Italian, too, I should think, than can seem natural and proper to the swarming red-legged soldiery who so publicly proclaim it of the empire of M. Thiers. The light and the complexion of things had to my eyes not a little of that mollified depth last loved by them rather further on. It was simply perhaps that the weather was hot and the mountains drowsing in that iridescent haze that I have seen nearer home than at Chambéry. But the vegetation, assuredly, had an all but Transalpine twist and curl, and the classic wayside tangle of corn and vines left nothing to be desired in the line of careless grace. Chambéry as a town, however, constitutes no foretaste of the monumental cities. There is shabbiness and shabbiness, the fond critic of such things will tell you; and that of the ancient capital of Savoy lacks style. I found a better pastime, however, than strolling through the dark dull streets in quest of effects that were not forthcoming. The first urchin you meet will show you the way to Les Charmettes and the Maison Jean-Jacques. A very pleasant way it becomes as soon as it leaves the town—a winding, climbing by-road, bordered with such a tall and sturdy hedge as to give it the air of an English lane—if you can fancy an English lane introducing you to the haunts of a Madame de Warens.

The house that formerly sheltered this lady's singular ménage stands on a hillside above the road, which a rapid path connects with the little grass-grown terrace before it. It is a small shabby, homely dwelling, with a certain reputable solidity, however, and more of internal spaciousness than of outside promise. The place is shown by an elderly competent dame who points out the very few surviving objects which you may touch with the reflection—complacent in whatsoever degree suits you—that they have known the familiarity of Rousseau's hand. It was presumably a meagrely-appointed house, and I wondered that on such scanty features so much expression should linger. But the structure has an ancient ponderosity, and the dust of the eighteenth century seems to lie on its worm-eaten floors, to cling to the faded old *papiers à ramages* on the walls and to lodge in the crevices of the brown wooden ceilings. Madame de Warens's bed remains, with the narrow couch of Jean-Jacques as well, his little warped and cracked yellow spinet, and a battered, turnip-shaped silver timepiece, engraved with its master's name—its primitive tick as extinct as his passionate heart-beats. It cost me, I confess, a somewhat pitying acceleration of my own to see this intimately personal relic of the *genius loci*—for it had dwelt in his waistcoat-pocket, than which there is hardly a material point in space nearer to a man's consciousness—tossed so irreverently upon the table on which you deposit your fee, beside the dog's-eared visitors' record or *livre de cuisine* recently denounced by Madame George Sand. In fact the place generally, in so far as some faint ghostly presence of its famous inmates seems to linger there, is by no means exhilarating. Coppet and Ferney tell, if not of pure happiness, at least of prosperity and honour, wealth and success. But Les Charmettes is haunted by ghosts unclean and forlorn. The place tells of poverty, perversity, distress. A good deal of clever modern talent in France has been employed in touching up the episode of which it was the scene and tricking it out in idyllic love-knots. But as I stood on the charming terrace I have mentioned—a little jewel of a terrace, with grassy flags and a mossy parapet, and an admirable view of great swelling violet hills—stood there reminded how much sweeter Nature is than man, the story looked rather wan and unlovely beneath these literary decorations, and I could pay it no livelier homage than is implied in perfect pity. Hero and heroine have become too much creatures of history to take up attitudes as part of any poetry. But, not to moralise too sternly for a tourist between trains, I should add that, as an illustration, to be inserted mentally in the text of the "Confessions," a glimpse of Les Charmettes is pleasant enough. It completes the rare charm of good autobiography to behold with one's eyes the faded and battered background of the story; and Rousseau's narrative is so incomparably vivid and forcible that the sordid little house at Chambéry seems of a hardly deeper shade of reality than so many other passages of his projected truth.

If I spent an hour at Les Charmettes, fumbling thus helplessly with the past, I recognised on the morrow how strongly the Mont Cenis Tunnel smells of the time to come. As I passed along the Saint-Gothard highway a couple of months since, I perceived, half up the Swiss ascent, a group of navvies at work in a gorge beneath the road. They had laid bare a broad surface of granite and had punched in the centre of it a round black cavity, of about the dimensions, as it seemed to me, of a soup-plate. This was to attain its perfect development some eight years hence. The Mont Cenis may therefore be held to have set a fashion which will be followed till the highest Himalaya is but the ornamental apex or snow-capped gable-tip of some resounding fuliginous corridor. The tunnel differs but in length from other tunnels; you spend half an hour in it. But you whirl out into the blest peninsula, and as you look back seem to see the mighty mass shrug its shoulders over the line, the mere turn of a dreaming giant in his sleep. The tunnel is certainly not a poetic object, but there is no perfection without its beauty; and as you measure the long rugged outline of the pyramid of which it forms the base you accept it as the perfection of a short cut. Twenty-four hours from Paris to Turin is speed for the times—speed which may content us, at any rate, until expansive Berlin has succeeded in placing itself at thirty-six from Milan.

To enter Turin then of a lovely August afternoon was to find a city of arcades, of pink and yellow stucco, of innumerable cafés, of blue-legged officers, of ladies draped in the North-Italian mantilla. An old friend of Italy coming back to her finds an easy waking for dormant memories. Every object is a reminder and every reminder a thrill. Half an hour after my arrival, as I stood at my window, which overhung the great square, I found the scene, within and without, a rough epitome of every pleasure and every impression I had formerly gathered from Italy: the balcony and the Venetian-blind, the cool floor of speckled concrete, the lavish delusions of frescoed wall and ceiling, the broad divan framed for the noonday siesta, the massive mediæval Castello in mid-piazza, with its shabby rear and its pompous Palladian front, the brick campaniles beyond, the milder, yellower light, the range of colour, the suggestion of sound. Later, beneath the arcades, I found many an old acquaintance: beautiful officers, resplendent, slow-strolling, contemplative of female beauty; civil and peaceful dandies, hardly less gorgeous, with that religious faith in moustache and shirt-front which distinguishes the *belle jeunesse* of Italy; ladies with heads artfully shawled in Spanish-looking lace, but with too little art—or too much nature at least—in the region of the bodice; well-conditioned young *abbati* with neatly drawn stockings. These indeed are not objects of first-rate interest, and with such Turin is rather meagrely furnished. It has no architecture, no churches, no monuments, no romantic street-scenery. It has the great votive temple of the Superga, which stands on a high hilltop above the city, gazing across at Monte Rosa and lifting its own fine dome against the sky with no contemptible art. But when you have seen the Superga from the quay beside the Po, a skein of a few yellow threads in August, despite its frequent habit of rising high and running wild, and said to yourself that in architecture position is half the battle, you have nothing left to visit but the Museum of pictures. The Turin Gallery, which is large and well arranged, is the fortunate owner of three or four masterpieces; a couple of magnificent Vandycks and a couple of Paul Veroneses; the latter a Queen of Sheba and a Feast at the House of Levi—the usual splendid combination of brocades, grandees and marble colonnades dividing those skies *de turquoise malade* to which Théophile Gautier is fond of alluding. The Veroneses are fine, but with Venice in prospect the traveller feels at liberty to keep his best attention in reserve. If, however, he has the proper relish for Vandyck, let him linger long and fondly here; for that admiration will never be more potently stirred than by the adorable group of the three little royal highnesses, sons and the daughter of Charles I. All the purity of childhood is here, and all its soft solidity of structure, rounded tenderly beneath the spangled satin and contrasted charmingly with the pompous rigidity. Clad respectively in crimson, white and blue, these small scions stand up in their ruffs and fardingales in dimpled serenity, squaring their infantine stomachers at the spectator with an innocence, a dignity, a delightful grotesqueness, which make the picture a thing of close truth as well as of fine decorum. You might kiss their hands, but you certainly would think twice before pinching their cheeks—provocative as they are of this tribute of admiration—and would altogether lack presumption to lift them off the ground or the higher level or dais on which they stand so sturdily planted by right of birth. There is something inimitable in the paternal gallantry with which the painter has touched off the young lady. She was a princess, yet she was a baby, and he has contrived, we let ourselves fancy, to interweave an intimation that she was a creature whom, in her teens, the lucklessly smitten—even as he was prematurely—must vainly sigh for. Though the work is a masterpiece of execution its merits under this head may be emulated, at a distance; the lovely modulations of colour in the three contrasted and harmonised little satin petticoats, the solidity of the little heads, in spite of all their prettiness, the happy, unexaggerated squareness and maturity of *pose*, are, severally, points to study, to imitate, and to reproduce with profit. But the taste of such a consummate thing is its great secret as well as its great merit—a taste which seems one of the lost instincts of mankind. Go and enjoy this supreme expression of Vandyck's fine sense, and admit that never was a politer production.

Milan speaks to us of a burden of felt life of which Turin is innocent, but in its general aspect still lingers a northern reserve which makes the place rather perhaps the last of the prose capitals than the first of the poetic. The long Austrian occupation perhaps did something to Germanise its physiognomy; though indeed this is an indifferent explanation when one remembers how well, temperamentally speaking, Italy held her own in Venetia. Milan, at any rate, if not bristling with the æsthetic impulse, opens to us frankly enough the thick volume of her past. Of that volume the Cathedral is the fairest and fullest page—a structure not supremely interesting, not logical, not even, to some minds, commandingly beautiful, but grandly curious and superbly rich. I hope, for my own part, never to grow too particular to admire it. If it had no other distinction it would still have that of impressive, immeasurable achievement. As I strolled beside its vast indented base one evening, and felt it, above me, rear its grey mysteries into the starlight while the restless human tide on which I floated rose no higher than the first few layers of street-soiled marble, I was tempted to believe that beauty in great architecture is almost a secondary merit, and that the main point is mass—such mass as may make it a supreme embodiment of vigorous effort. Viewed in this way a great building is the greatest conceivable work of art. More than any other it represents difficulties mastered, resources combined, labour, courage and patience. And there are people who tell us that art has nothing to do with morality! Little enough, doubtless, when it is concerned, even ever so little, in painting the roof of Milan Cathedral within to represent carved stone-work. Of this famous roof every one has heard—how good it is, how bad, how perfect a delusion, how transparent an artifice. It is the first thing your cicerone shows you on entering the church. The occasionally accommodating art-lover may accept it philosophically, I think; for the interior, though admirably effective as a whole, has no great sublimity, nor even purity, of pitch. It is splendidly vast and dim; the altar-lamps twinkle afar through the incense-thickened air like fog-lights at sea, and the great columns rise straight to the roof, which hardly curves to meet them, with the girth and altitude of oaks of a thousand years; but there is little refinement of design—few of those felicities of proportion which the eye caresses, when it finds them, very much as the memory retains and repeats some happy line of poetry or some haunting musical phrase. Consistently brave, none the less, is the result produced, and nothing braver than a certain exhibition that I privately enjoyed of the relics of St. Charles Borromeus. This holy man lies at his eternal rest in a small but gorgeous sepulchral chapel, beneath the boundless pavement and before the high altar; and for the modest sum of five francs you may have his shrivelled mortality unveiled and gaze at it with whatever re-

serves occur to you. The Catholic Church never renounces a
chance of the sublime for fear of a chance of the ridiculous—
especially when the chance of the sublime may be the very
excellent chance of five francs. The performance in question,
of which the good San Carlo paid in the first instance the
cost, was impressive certainly, but as a monstrous matter or a
grim comedy may still be. The little sacristan, having secured
his audience, whipped on a white tunic over his frock, lighted
a couple of extra candles and proceeded to remove from
above the altar, by means of a crank, a sort of sliding shutter,
just as you may see a shop-boy do of a morning at his master's window. In this case too a large sheet of plate-glass was
uncovered, and to form an idea of the *étalage* you must imagine that a jeweller, for reasons of his own, has struck an unnatural partnership with an undertaker. The black mummified
corpse of the saint is stretched out in a glass coffin, clad in his
mouldering canonicals, mitred, crosiered and gloved, glittering with votive jewels. It is an extraordinary mixture of death
and life; the desiccated clay, the ashen rags, the hideous little
black mask and skull, and the living, glowing, twinkling
splendour of diamonds, emeralds and sapphires. The collection is really fine, and many great historic names are attached
to the different offerings. Whatever may be the better opinion
as to the future of the Church, I can't help thinking she will
make a figure in the world so long as she retains this great
fund of precious "properties," this prodigious capital decora-
tively invested and scintillating throughout Christendom at
effectively-scattered points. You see I am forced to agree after
all, in spite of the sliding shutter and the profane swagger of
the sacristan, that a certain pastoral majesty saved the situation, or at least made irony gape. Yet it was from a natural
desire to breathe a sweeter air that I immediately afterwards
undertook the interminable climb to the roof of the cathedral.
This is another world of wonders, and one which enjoys due
renown, every square inch of wall on the winding stairways
being bescribbled with a traveller's name. There is a great
glare from the far-stretching slopes of marble, a confusion
(like the masts of a navy or the spears of an army) of image-
capped pinnacles, biting the impalpable blue, and, better than
either, the goodliest view of level Lombardy sleeping in its

rich transalpine light and resembling, with its white-walled dwellings and the spires on its horizon, a vast green sea spotted with ships. After two months of Switzerland the Lombard plain is a rich rest to the eye, and the yellow, liquid, free-flowing light—as if on favoured Italy the vessels of heaven were more widely opened—had for mine a charm which made me think of a great opaque mountain as a blasphemous invasion of the atmospheric spaces.

I have mentioned the cathedral first, but the prime treasure of Milan at the present hour is the beautiful, tragical Leonardo. The cathedral is good for another thousand years, but we ask whether our children will find in the most majestic and most luckless of frescoes much more than the shadow of a shadow. Its fame has been for a century or two that, as one may say, of an illustrious invalid whom people visit to see how he lasts, with leave-taking sighs and almost death-bed or tiptoe precautions. The picture needs not another scar or stain, now, to be the saddest work of art in the world; and battered, defaced, ruined as it is, it remains one of the greatest. We may really compare its anguish of decay to the slow conscious ebb of life in a human organism. The production of the prodigy was a breath from the infinite, and the painter's conception not immeasurably less complex than the scheme, say, of his own mortal constitution. There has been much talk lately of the irony of fate, but I suspect fate was never more ironical than when she led the most scientific, the most calculating of all painters to spend fifteen long years in building his goodly house upon the sand. And yet, after all, may not the playing of that trick represent but a deeper wisdom, since if the thing enjoyed the immortal health and bloom of a first-rate Titian we should have lost one of the most pertinent lessons in the history of art? We know it as hearsay, but here is the plain proof, that there is no limit to the amount of "stuff" an artist may put into his work. Every painter ought once in his life to stand before the Cenacolo and decipher its moral. Mix with your colours and mess on your palette every particle of the very substance of your soul, and this lest perchance your "prepared surface" shall play you a trick! Then, and then only, it will fight to the last—it will resist even in death. Raphael was a happier genius; you look at his lovely

The Approach to Como

"Marriage of the Virgin" at the Brera, beautiful as some first deep smile of conscious inspiration, but to feel that he foresaw no complaint against fate, and that he knew the world he wanted to know and charmed it into never giving him away. But I have left no space to speak of the Brera, nor of that paradise of bookworms with an eye for their background—if such creatures exist—the Ambrosian Library; nor of that mighty basilica of Saint Ambrose, with its spacious atrium and its crudely solemn mosaics, in which it is surely your own fault if you don't forget Dr. Strauss and M. Renan and worship as grimly as a Christian of the ninth century.

It is part of the sordid prose of the Mont Cenis road that, unlike those fine old unimproved passes, the Simplon, the Splügen and—yet awhile longer—the Saint-Gothard, it denies you a glimpse of that paradise adorned by the four lakes even that of uncommented Scripture by the rivers of Eden. I made, however, an excursion to the Lake of Como, which, though brief, lasted long enough to suggest to me that I too was a hero of romance with leisure for a love-affair, and not a hurrying tourist with a Bradshaw in his pocket. The Lake of Como has figured largely in novels of "immoral" tendency— being commonly the spot to which inflamed young gentlemen invite the wives of other gentlemen to fly with them and ignore the restrictions of public opinion. But even the Lake of Como has been revised and improved; the fondest prejudices yield to time; it gives one somehow a sense of an aspiringly high tone. I should pay a poor compliment at least to the swarming inmates of the hotels which now alternate attractively by the water-side with villas old and new were I to read the appearances more cynically. But if it is lost to florid fiction it still presents its blue bosom to most other refined uses, and the unsophisticated tourist, the American at least, may do any amount of private romancing there. The pretty hotel at Cadenabbia offers him, for instance, in the most elegant and assured form, the so often precarious adventure of what he calls at home summer board. It is all so unreal, so fictitious, so elegant and idle, so framed to undermine a rigid sense of the chief end of man not being to float forever in an ornamental boat, beneath an awning tasselled like a circus-horse, impelled by an affable Giovanni or Antonio from one stately stretch of

lake-laved villa steps to another, that departure seems as harsh
and unnatural as the dream-dispelling note of some punctual
voice at your bedside on a dusky winter morning. Yet I wondered, for my own part, where I had seen it all before—the
pink-walled villas gleaming through their shrubberies of
orange and oleander, the mountains shimmering in the hazy
light like so many breasts of doves, the constant presence of
the melodious Italian voice. Where indeed but at the Opera
when the manager has been more than usually regardless of
expense? Here in the foreground was the palace of the nefar-
ious barytone, with its banqueting-hall opening as freely on
the stage as a railway buffet on the platform; beyond, the
delightful back scene, with its operatic gamut of colouring; in
the middle the scarlet-sashed *barcaiuoli*, grouped like a chorus,
hat in hand, awaiting the conductor's signal. It was better
even than being in a novel—this being, this fairly wallowing,
in a libretto.

The Old Saint-Gothard

LEAVES FROM A NOTE-BOOK

BERNE, *September*, 1873.—In Berne again, some eleven weeks after having left it in July. I have never been in Switzerland so late, and I came hither innocently supposing the last Cook's tourist to have paid out his last coupon and departed. But I was lucky, it seems, to discover an empty cot in an attic and a very tight place at a table d'hôte. People are all flocking out of Switzerland, as in July they were flocking in, and the main channels of egress are terribly choked. I have been here several days, watching them come and go; it is like the march-past of an army. It gives one, for an occasional change from darker thoughts, a lively impression of the numbers of people now living, and above all now moving, at extreme ease in the world. Here is little Switzerland disgorging its tens of thousands of honest folk, chiefly English, and rarely, to judge by their faces and talk, children of light in any eminent degree; for whom snow-peaks and glaciers and passes and lakes and chalets and sunsets and a *café complet*, "including honey," as the coupon says, have become prime necessities for six weeks every year. It's not so long ago that lords and nabobs monopolised these pleasures; but nowadays a month's tour in Switzerland is no more a *jeu de prince* than a Sunday excursion. To watch this huge Anglo-Saxon wave ebbing through Berne suggests, no doubt most fallaciously, that the common lot of mankind isn't after all so very hard and that the masses have reached a high standard of comfort. The view of the Oberland chain, as you see it from the garden of the hotel, really butters one's bread most handsomely; and here are I don't know how many hundred Cook's tourists a day looking at it through the smoke of their pipes. Is it really the "masses," however, that I see every day at the table d'hôte? They have rather too few h's to the dozen, but their good-nature is great. Some people complain that they "vulgarise" Switzerland; but as far as I am concerned I freely give it up to them and offer them a personal welcome and take a peculiar satisfaction in seeing them here. Switzerland is a "show country"—I am more and more struck with the bearings of that truth; and its use in the world is to reassure persons of a benevolent imagination when they begin to wish for the drudging millions a greater supply of elevating amusement. Here is amusement for a thousand years, and as elevating certainly as mountains three miles high can make it. I expect to live to see the summit of Monte Rosa heated by steam-tubes and adorned with a hotel setting three tables d'hôte a day.

I have been walking about the arcades, which used to bestow a grateful shade in July, but which seem rather dusky and chilly in these shortening autumn days. I am struck with the way the English always speak of them—with a shudder, as gloomy, as dirty, as evil-smelling, as suffocating, as freezing, as anything and everything but admirably picturesque. I take us Americans for the only people who, in travelling, judge things on the first impulse—when we do judge them at all—not from the standpoint of simple comfort. Most of us, strolling forth into these bustling basements, are, I imagine, too much amused, too much diverted from the sense of an alienable right to public ease, to be conscious of heat or cold, of thick air, or even of the universal smell of strong *charcuterie*. If the visible romantic were banished from the face of the earth I am sure the idea of it would still survive in some typical American heart. . . .

Lucerne, September.—Berne, I find, has been filling with tourists at the expense of Lucerne, which I have been having almost to myself. There are six people at the table d'hôte; the excellent dinner denotes on the part of the *chef* the easy leisure in which true artists love to work. The waiters have nothing to do but lounge about the hall and chink in their pockets the fees of the past season. The day has been lovely in itself, and pervaded, to my sense, by the gentle glow of a natural satisfaction at my finding myself again on the threshold of Italy. I am lodged *en prince*, in a room with a balcony hanging over the lake—a balcony on which I spent a long time this morning at dawn, thanking the mountain-tops, from the depths of a landscape-lover's heart, for their promise of superbly fair weather. There were a great many mountain-tops to thank, for the crags and peaks and pinnacles tumbled away through the morning mist in an endless confusion of grandeur. I have been all day in better humour with Lucerne than ever before—a forecast reflection of Italian moods. If Switzerland, as I wrote the other day, is so furiously a show-place, Lucerne is certainly one of the biggest booths at the fair. The little quay, under the trees, squeezed in between the decks of the steamboats and the doors of the hotels, is a terrible medley of Saxon dialects—a jumble of pilgrims in all the phases of devotion, equipped with book and staff, alpenstock and Baedeker. There are so many hotels and trinket-shops, so many omnibuses and steamers, so many Saint-Gothard *vetturini*, so many ragged urchins poking photographs, minerals and Lucernese English at you, that you feel as if lake and mountains themselves, in all their loveliness, were but a part of the "enterprise" of landlords and pedlars, and half expect to see the Righi and Pilatus and the fine weather figure as items on your hotel-bill between the *bougie* and the *siphon*. Nature herself assists you to this conceit; there is something so operatic and suggestive of footlights and scene-shifters in the view on which Lucerne looks out. You are one of five thousand—fifty thousand—"accommodated" spectators; you have taken your season-ticket and there is a responsible impresario somewhere behind the scenes. There is such a luxury of beauty in the prospect—such a redundancy of composition and effect—so many more peaks and pinnacles than are needed to make one heart happy or regale the vision of one quiet observer, that you finally accept the little Babel on the quay and the looming masses in the clouds as equal parts of a perfect system, and feel as if the mountains had been waiting so many ages for the hotels to come and balance the colossal group, that they show a right, after all, to have them big and numerous. The scene-shifters have been at work all day long, composing and discomposing the beautiful background of the prospect— massing the clouds and scattering the light, effacing and reviving, making play with their wonderful machinery of mist and haze. The mountains rise, one behind the other, in an enchanting gradation of distances and of melting blues and greys; you think each successive tone the loveliest and haziest possible till you see another loom dimly behind it. I couldn't enjoy even *The Swiss Times*, over my breakfast, till I had marched forth to the office of the Saint-Gothard service of coaches and demanded the banquette for to-morrow. The one place at the disposal of the office was taken, but I might possibly *m'entendre* with the conductor for his own seat—the conductor being generally visible, in the intervals of business, at the post-office. To the post-office, after breakfast, I repaired, over the fine new bridge which now spans the green Reuss and gives such a woeful air of country-cousinship to the crooked old wooden structure which did sole service when I was here four years ago. The old bridge is covered with a running hood of shingles and adorned with a series of very quaint and vivid little paintings of the "Dance of Death," quite in the Holbein manner; the new sends up a painful glare from its white limestone, and is ornamented with candelabra in a meretricious imitation of platinum. As an almost professional cherisher of the quaint I ought to have chosen to return at least by the dark and narrow way; but mark how luxury unmans us. I was already demoralised. I crossed the threshold of the timbered portal, took a few steps, and retreated. It *smelt badly*! So I marched back, counting the lamps in their fine falsity. But the other, the crooked and covered way, smelt very badly indeed; and no good American is without a fund of accumulated sensibility to the odour of stale timber.

Meanwhile I had spent an hour in the great yard of the post-office, waiting for my conductor to turn up and seeing the yellow malles-postes pushed to and fro. At last, being told my man was at my service, I was brought to speech of a huge, jovial, bearded, delightful Italian, clad in the blue coat and waistcoat, with close, round silver buttons, which are a heritage of the old postilions. No, it was not he; it was a friend of his; and finally the friend was produced, *en costume de ville*, but equally jovial, and Italian enough—a brave Lucernese, who had spent half of his life between Bellinzona and Camerlata. For ten francs this worthy man's perch behind the luggage was made mine as far as Bellinzona, and we separated with reciprocal wishes for good weather on the morrow. To-morrow is so manifestly determined to be as fine as any other 30th of September since the weather became on this planet a topic of conversation that I have had nothing to do but stroll about Lucerne, staring, loafing and vaguely intent on regarding the fact that, whatever happens, my place is paid to Milan. I loafed into the immense new Hôtel National and read the *New York Tribune* on a blue satin divan; after which I was rather surprised, on coming out, to find myself staring at a green Swiss lake and not at the Broadway omnibuses. The Hôtel National is adorned with a perfectly appointed Broadway bar—one of the "prohibited" ones seeking hospitality in foreign lands after the manner of an old-fashioned French or Italian refugee.

Milan, October.—My journey hither was such a pleasant piece of traveller's luck that I feel a delicacy for taking it to pieces to see what it was made of. Do what we will, however, there remains in all deeply agreeable impressions a charming something we can't analyse. I found it agreeable even, given the rest of my case, to turn out of bed, at Lucerne, by four o'clock, into the chilly autumn darkness. The thick-starred sky was cloudless, and there was as yet no flush of dawn; but the lake was wrapped in a ghostly white mist which crept halfway up the mountains and made them look as if they too had been lying down for the night and were casting away the vaporous tissues of their bedclothes. Into this fantastic fog the little steamer went creaking away, and I hung about the deck with the two or three travellers who had known better than to believe it would save them francs or midnight sighs—over those debts you "pay with your person"—to go and wait for the diligence at the Poste at Flüelen, or yet at the Guillaume Tell. The dawn came sailing up over the mountain-tops, flushed but unperturbed, and blew out the little stars and then the big ones, as a thrifty matron after a party blows out her candles and lamps; the mist went melting and wandering away into the duskier hollows and recesses of the mountains, and the summits defined their profiles against the cool soft light.

At Flüelen, before the landing, the big yellow coaches were actively making themselves bigger, and piling up boxes and bags on their roofs in a way to turn nervous people's thoughts to the sharp corners of the downward twists of the great road. I climbed into my own banquette, and stood eating peaches—half-a-dozen women were hawking them about under the horses' legs—with an air of security that might have been offensive to the people scrambling and protesting below between coupé and intérieur. They were all English and all had false alarms about the claim of somebody else to their place, the place for which they produced their ticket, with a declaration in three or four different tongues of the inalienable right to it given them by the expenditure of British gold. They were all serenely confuted by the stout, purple-faced, many-buttoned conductors, patted on the backs, assured that their bath-tubs had every advantage of position on the top, and stowed away according to their dues. When once one has fairly started on a journey and has but to go and go by the impetus received, it is surprising what entertainment one finds in very small things. We surrender to the gaping traveller's mood, which surely isn't the unwisest the heart knows. I don't envy people, at any rate, who have outlived or outworn the simple sweetness of feeling settled to go somewhere with bag and umbrella. If we are settled on the top of a coach, and the "somewhere" contains an element of the new and strange, the case is at its best. In this matter wise people are content to become children again. We don't turn about on our knees to look out of the omnibus-window, but we indulge in very much the same round-eyed contemplation of accessible objects. Responsibility is left at home or at the worst packed away in the valise, relegated to quite another part of the diligence with the clean shirts and the writing-case. I sucked in the gladness of gaping, for this occasion, with the somewhat acrid juice of my indifferent peaches; it made me think them very good. This was the first of a series of kindly services it rendered me. It made me agree next, as we started, that the gentleman at the booking-office at Lucerne had but played a harmless joke when he told me the regular seat in the banquette was taken. No one appeared to claim it; so the conductor and I reversed positions, and I found him quite as conversible as the usual Anglo-Saxon.

He was trolling snatches of melody and showing his great yellow teeth in a jovial grin all the way to Bellinzona—and this in face of the sombre fact that the Saint-Gothard tunnel is scraping away into the mountain, all the while, under his nose, and numbering the days of the many-buttoned brotherhood. But he hopes, for long service's sake, to be taken into the employ of the railway; *he* at least is no cherisher of quaintness and has no romantic perversity. I found the railway coming on, however, in a manner very shocking to mine. About an hour short of Andermatt they have pierced a huge black cavity in the mountain, around which has grown up a swarming, digging, hammering, smoke-compelling colony. There are great barracks, with tall chimneys, down in the gorge that bristled the other day but with natural graces, and a wonderful increase of wine-shops in the little village of Göschenen above. Along the breast of the mountain, beside the road, come wandering several miles of very handsome iron pipes, of a stupendous girth—a conduit for the water-power with which some of the machinery is worked. It lies at its mighty length among the rocks like an immense black serpent, and serves, as a mere detail, to give one the measure of the central enterprise. When at the end of our long day's journey, well down in warm Italy, we came upon the other aperture of the tunnel, I could but uncap with a grim reverence. Truly Nature is great, but she seems to me to stand in very much the shoes of my poor friend the conductor. She is being superseded at her strongest points, successively, and nothing remains but for her to take humble service with her master. If she can hear herself think amid that din of blasting and hammering she must be reckoning up the years to elapse before the cleverest of Ober-Ingénieurs decides that mountains are mere obstructive matter and has the Jungfrau melted down and the residuum carried away in balloons and dumped upon another planet.

The Devil's Bridge, with the same failing apparently as the good Homer, was decidedly nodding. The volume of water in the torrent was shrunken, and I missed the thunderous uproar and far-leaping spray that have kept up a miniature tempest in the neighbourhood on my other passages. It suddenly occurs to me that the fault is not in the good Homer's inspiration, but simply in the big black pipes above-mentioned. They dip into the rushing stream higher up, presumably, and pervert its fine frenzy to their prosaic uses. There could hardly be a more vivid reminder of the standing quarrel between use and beauty, and of the hard time poor beauty is having. I looked wistfully, as we rattled into dreary Andermatt, at the great white zigzags of the Oberalp road, which climbed away to the left. Even on one's way to Italy one may spare a throb of desire for the beautiful vision of the castled Grisons. Dear to me the memory of my day's drive last summer through that long blue avenue of mountains, to queer little mouldering Ilanz, visited before supper in the ghostly dusk. At Andermatt a sign over a little black doorway flanked by two dunghills seemed to me tolerably comical: *Minéraux, Quadrupèdes, Oiseaux, Œufs, Tableaux Antiques*. We bundled in to dinner and the American gentleman in the banquette made the acquaintance of the Irish lady in the coupé, who talked of the weather as *foine* and wore a Persian scarf twisted about her head. At the other end of the table sat an Englishman, out of the intérieur, who bore an extraordinary resemblance to the portraits of Edward VI.'s and Mary's reigns. He was a walking, a convincing Holbein. The impression was of value to a cherisher of quaintness, and he must have wondered—not knowing me for such a character—why I stared at him. It wasn't him I was staring at, but some handsome Seymour or Dudley or Digby with a ruff and a round cap and plume.

From Andermatt, through its high, cold, sunny valley, we passed into rugged little Hospenthal, and then up the last stages of the ascent. From here the road was all new to me. Among the summits of the various Alpine passes there is little to choose. You wind and double slowly into keener cold and deeper stillness; you put on your overcoat and turn up the collar; you count the nestling snow-patches and then you cease to count them; you pause, as you trudge before the lumbering coach, and listen to the last-heard cow-bell tinkling away below you in kindlier herbage. The sky was tremendously blue, and the little stunted bushes on the snow-streaked slopes were all dyed with autumnal purples and crimsons. It was a great display of colour. Purple and crimson too, though not so fine, were the faces thrust out at us from the greasy little double casements of a barrack beside the road, where the horses paused before the last pull. There was one little girl in particular, beginning to *lisser* her hair, as civilisation approached, in a manner not to be described, with her poor little blue-black hands. At the summit are the two usual

grim little stone taverns, the steel-blue tarn, the snow-white
peaks, the pause in the cold sunshine. Then we begin to rattle
down with two horses. In five minutes we are swinging along
the famous zigzags. Engineer, driver, horses—it's very handsomely done by all of them. The road curves and curls and
twists and plunges like the tail of a kite; sitting perched in the
banquette, you see it making below you and in mid-air certain
bold gyrations which bring you as near as possible, short of
the actual experience, to the philosophy of that immortal
Irishman who wished that his fall from the house-top would
only last. But the zigzags last no more than Paddy's fall, and
in due time we were all coming to our senses over *café au lait*
in the little inn at Faido. After Faido the valley, plunging
deeper, began to take thick afternoon shadows from the hills,
and at Airolo we were fairly in the twilight. But the pink and
yellow houses shimmered through the gentle gloom, and Italy
began in broken syllables to whisper that she was at hand. For
the rest of the way to Bellinzona her voice was muffled in the
grey of evening, and I was half vexed to lose the charming
sight of the changing vegetation. But only half vexed, for the
moon was climbing all the while nearer the edge of the crags
that overshadowed us, and a thin magical light came trickling
down into the winding, murmuring gorges. It was a most
enchanting business. The chestnut-trees loomed up with double their daylight stature; the vines began to swing their low
festoons like nets to trip up the fairies. At last the ruined towers of Bellinzona stood gleaming in the moonshine, and we
rattled into the great post-yard. It was eleven o'clock and I
had risen at four; moonshine apart I wasn't sorry.

All that was very well; but the drive next day from Bellinzona to Como is to my mind what gives its supreme beauty
to this great pass. One can't describe the beauty of the Italian
lakes, nor would one try if one could; the floweriest rhetoric
can recall it only as a picture on a fireboard recalls a Claude.
But it lay spread before me for a whole perfect day: in the
long gleam of the Major, from whose head the diligence
swerves away and begins to climb the bosky hills that divide it
from Lugano; in the shimmering, melting azure of the southern slopes and masses; in the luxurious tangle of nature and
the familiar amenity of man; in the lawn-like inclinations,

Monte Generoso

where the great grouped chestnuts make so cool a shadow in
so warm a light; in the rusty vineyards, the littered cornfields
and the tawdry wayside shrines. But most of all it's the deep
yellow light that enchants you and tells you where you are.
See it come filtering down through a vine-covered trellis on
the red handkerchief with which a ragged contadina has
bound her hair, and all the magic of Italy, to the eye, makes
an aureole about the poor girl's head. Look at a brown-
breasted reaper eating his chunk of black bread under a
spreading chestnut; nowhere is shadow so charming, nowhere is colour so charged, nowhere has accident such grace.
The whole drive to Lugano was one long loveliness, and the
town itself is admirably Italian. There was a great unlading
of the coach, during which I wandered under certain brown
old arcades and bought for six sous, from a young woman in
a gold necklace, a hatful of peaches and figs. When I came
back I found the young man holding open the door of the
second diligence, which had lately come up, and beckoning to
me with a despairing smile. The young man, I must note, was
the most amiable of Ticinese; though he wore no buttons he
was attached to the diligence in some amateurish capacity,
and had an eye to the mail-bags and other valuables in the
boot. I grumbled at Berne over the want of soft curves in the
Swiss temperament; but the children of the tangled Tessin are
cast in the Italian mould. My friend had as many quips and
cranks as a Neapolitan; we walked together for an hour under
the chestnuts, while the coach was plodding up from Bellinzona, and he never stopped singing till we reached a little
wine-house where he got his mouth full of bread and cheese.
I looked into his open door, à la Sterne, and saw the young
woman sitting rigid and grim, staring over his head and with
a great pile of bread and butter in her lap. He had only informed her most politely that she was to be transferred to
another diligence and must do him the favour to descend; but
she evidently knew of but one way for a respectable young
insulary of her sex to receive the politeness of a foreign adventurer guilty of an eye betraying latent pleasantry. Heaven only
knew what he was saying! I told her, and she gathered up her
parcels and emerged. A part of the day's great pleasure perhaps was my grave sense of being an instrument in the hands

of the powers toward the safe consignment of this young woman and her boxes. When once you have really bent to the helpless you are caught; there is no such steel trap, and it holds you fast. My rather grim Abigail was a neophyte in foreign travel, though doubtless cunning enough at her trade, which I inferred to be that of making up those prodigious chignons worn mainly by English ladies. Her mistress had gone on a mule over the mountains to Cadenabbia, and she herself was coming up with the wardrobe, two big boxes and a bath-tub. I had played my part, under the powers, at Bellinzona, and had interposed between the poor girl's frightened English and the dreadful Ticinese French of the functionaries in the post-yard. At the custom-house on the Italian frontier I was of peculiar service; there was a kind of fateful fascination in it. The wardrobe was voluminous; I exchanged a paternal glance with my charge as the *douanier* plunged his brown fists into it. Who was the lady at Cadenabbia? What was she to me or I to her? She wouldn't know, when she rustled down to dinner next day, that it was I who had guided the frail skiff of her public basis of vanity to port. So unseen but not unfelt do we cross each other's orbits. The skiff however may have foundered that evening in sight of land. I disengaged the young woman from among her fellow-travellers and placed her boxes on a hand-cart in the picturesque streets of Como, within a stone's-throw of that lovely striped and toned cathedral which has the façade of cameo medallions. I could only make the *facchino* swear to take her to the steamboat. He too was a jovial dog, but I hope he was polite with precautions.

1873.

Italy Revisited

I WAITED in Paris until after the elections for the new Chamber (they took place on the 14th of October); as only after one had learned that the famous attempt of Marshal MacMahon and his ministers to drive the French nation to the polls like a flock of huddling sheep, each with the white ticket of an official candidate round his neck, had not achieved the success which the energy of the process might have promised—only then it was possible to draw a long breath and deprive the republican party of such support as might have been conveyed in one's sympathetic presence. Seriously speaking too, the weather had been enchanting—there were Italian fancies to be gathered without leaving the banks of the Seine. Day after day the air was filled with golden light, and even those chalkish vistas of the Parisian *beaux quartiers* assumed the iridescent tints of autumn. Autumn-weather in Europe is often such a very sorry affair that a fair-minded American will have it on his conscience to call attention to a rainless and radiant October.

The echoes of the electoral strife kept me company for a while after starting upon that abbreviated journey to Turin which, as you leave Paris at night, in a train unprovided with encouragements to slumber, is a singular mixture of the odious and the charming. The charming indeed I think prevails; for the dark half of the journey is the least interesting. The morning light ushers you into the romantic gorges of the Jura, and after a big bowl of *café au lait* at Culoz you may compose yourself comfortably for the climax of your spectacle. The day before leaving Paris I met a French friend who had just returned from a visit to a Tuscan country-seat where he had been watching the vintage. "Italy," he said, "is more lovely than words can tell, and France, steeped in this electoral turmoil, seems no better than a bear-garden." The part of the bear-garden through which you travel as you approach the Mont-Cenis seemed to me that day very beautiful. The autumn colouring, thanks to the absence of rain, had been vivid and crisp, and the vines that swung their low garlands between the mulberries round about Chambéry looked like long festoons of coral and amber. The frontier station of Modane, on the further side of the Mont-Cenis Tunnel, is a very ill-regulated place; but even the most irritable of tourists, meeting it on his way southward, will be disposed to consider it good-naturedly. There is far too much bustling and scrambling, and the facilities afforded you for the obligatory process of ripping open your luggage before the officers of the Italian custom-house are much scantier than should be; but for myself there is something that deprecates irritation in the shabby green and grey uniforms of all the Italian officials who stand loafing about and watching the northern invaders scramble back into marching order. Wearing an administrative uniform doesn't necessarily spoil a man's temper, as in France one is sometimes led to believe; for these excellent under-paid Italians carry theirs as lightly as possible, and their answers to your inquiries don't in the least bristle with rapiers, buttons and cockades. After leaving Modane you slide straight downhill into the Italy of your desire; from which point the road edges, after the grand manner, along those great precipices that stand shoulder to shoulder, in a prodigious perpendicular file, till they finally admit you to a distant glimpse of the ancient capital of Piedmont.

Turin is no city of a name to conjure with, and I pay an extravagant tribute to subjective emotion in speaking of it as ancient. But if the place is less bravely peninsular than Florence and Rome, at least it is more in the scenic tradition than New York and Paris; and while I paced the great arcades and looked at the fourth-rate shop windows I didn't scruple to cultivate a shameless optimism. Relatively speaking, Turin touches a chord; but there is after all no reason in a large collection of shabbily-stuccoed houses, disposed in a rigidly rectangular manner, for passing a day of deep, still gaiety. The only reason, I am afraid, is the old superstition of Italy — that property in the very look of the written word, the evocation of a myriad images, that makes any lover of the arts take Italian satisfactions on easier terms than any others. The written word stands for something that eternally tricks us; we juggle

to our credulity even with such inferior apparatus as is offered
to our hand at Turin. I roamed all the morning under the tall
porticoes, thinking it sufficient joy to take note of the soft,
warm air, of that local colour of things that is at once so
broken and so harmonious, and of the comings and goings,
the physiognomy and manners, of the excellent Turinese. I
had opened the old book again; the old charm was in the
style; I was in a more delightful world. I saw nothing surpassingly beautiful or curious; but your true taster of the most
seasoned of dishes finds well-nigh the whole mixture in any
mouthful. Above all on the threshold of Italy he knows again
the solid and perfectly definable pleasure of finding himself
among the traditions of the grand style in architecture. It
must be said that we have still to go there to recover the sense
of the domiciliary mass. In northern cities there are beautiful
houses, picturesque and curious houses; sculptured gables
that hang over the street, charming bay-windows, hooded
doorways, elegant proportions, a profusion of delicate ornament; but a good specimen of an old Italian palazzo has a
nobleness that is all its own. We laugh at Italian "palaces," at
their peeling paint, their nudity, their dreariness; but they
have the great palatial quality—elevation and extent. They
make of smaller things the apparent abode of pigmies; they
round their great arches and interspace their huge windows
with a proud indifference to the cost of materials. These
grand proportions—the colossal basements, the doorways
that seem meant for cathedrals, the far away cornices—impart
by contrast a humble and *bourgeois* expression to interiors
founded on the sacrifice of the whole to the part, and in
which the air of grandeur depends largely on the help of the
upholsterer. At Turin my first feeling was really one of renewed shame for our meaner architectural manners. If the
Italians at bottom despise the rest of mankind and regard
them as barbarians, disinherited of the tradition of form, the
idea proceeds largely, no doubt, from our living in comparative mole-hills. They alone were really to build their
civilisation.

An impression which on coming back to Italy I find even
stronger than when it was first received is that of the contrast
between the fecundity of the great artistic period and the vul-

garity there of the genius of to-day. The first few hours spent on Italian soil are sufficient to renew it, and the question I allude to is, historically speaking, one of the oddest. That the people who but three hundred years ago had the best taste in the world should now have the worst; that having produced the noblest, loveliest, costliest works, they should now be given up to the manufacture of objects at once ugly and paltry; that the race of which Michael Angelo and Raphael, Leonardo and Titian were characteristic should have no other title to distinction than third-rate *genre* pictures and catch-penny statues—all this is a frequent perplexity to the observer of actual Italian life. The flower of "great" art in these latter years ceased to bloom very powerfully anywhere; but no-where does it seem so drooping and withered as in the shadow of the immortal embodiments of the old Italian ge-nius. You go into a church or a gallery and feast your fancy upon a splendid picture or an exquisite piece of sculpture, and on issuing from the door that has admitted you to the beau-tiful past are confronted with something that has the effect of a very bad joke. The aspect of your lodging—the carpets, the curtains, the upholstery in general, with their crude and vio-lent colouring and their vulgar material—the trumpery things in the shops, the extreme bad taste of the dress of the women, the cheapness and baseness of every attempt at decoration in the cafés and railway-stations, the hopeless frivolity of every-thing that pretends to be a work of art—all this modern crudity runs riot over the relics of the great period.

We can do a thing for the first time but once; it is but once for all that we can have a pleasure in its freshness. This is a law not on the whole, I think, to be regretted, for we some-times learn to know things better by not enjoying them too much. It is certain, however, at the same time, that a visitor who has worked off the immediate ferment for this inexhaust-ibly interesting country has by no means entirely drained the cup. After thinking of Italy as historical and artistic it will do him no great harm to think of her for a while as panting both for a future and for a balance at the bank; aspirations sup-posedly much at variance with the Byronic, the Ruskinian, the artistic, poetic, æsthetic manner of considering our eter-nally attaching peninsula. He may grant—I don't say it is

absolutely necessary—that its actual aspects and economics
are ugly, prosaic, provokingly out of relation to the diary and
the album; it is nevertheless true that, at the point things have
come to, modern Italy in a manner imposes herself. I hadn't
been many hours in the country before that truth assailed me;
and I may add that, the first irritation past, I found myself
able to accept it. For, if we think, nothing is more easy to
understand than an honest ire on the part of the young Italy
of to-day at being looked at by all the world as a kind of
soluble pigment. Young Italy, preoccupied with its economical and political future, must be heartily tired of being admired for its eyelashes and its pose. In one of Thackeray's
novels occurs a mention of a young artist who sent to the
Royal Academy a picture representing "A Contadino dancing
with a Trasteverina at the door of a Locanda, to the music of
a Pifferaro." It is in this attitude and with these conventional
accessories that the world has hitherto seen fit to represent
young Italy, and one doesn't wonder that if the youth has any
spirit he should at last begin to resent our insufferable æsthetic patronage. He has established a line of tram-cars in
Rome, from the Porta del Popolo to the Ponte Molle, and it is
on one of these democratic vehicles that I seem to see him
taking his triumphant course down the vista of the future. I
won't pretend to rejoice with him any more than I really do; I
won't pretend, as the sentimental tourists say about it all, as if
it were the setting of an intaglio or the border of a Roman
scarf, to "like" it. Like it or not, as we may, it is evidently
destined to be; I see a new Italy in the future which in many
important respects will equal, if not surpass, the most enterprising sections of our native land. Perhaps by that time Chicago and San Francisco will have acquired a pose, and their
sons and daughters will dance at the doors of *locande*.

However this may be, the accomplished schism between
the old order and the new is the promptest moral of a fresh
visit to this ever-suggestive part of the world. The old has
become more and more a museum, preserved and perpetuated
in the midst of the new, but without any further relation to
it—it must be admitted indeed that such a relation is considerable—than that of the stock on his shelves to the shop-
keeper, or of the Siren of the South to the showman who

stands before his booth. More than once, as we move about nowadays in the Italian cities, there seems to pass before our eyes a vision of the coming years. It represents to our satisfaction an Italy united and prosperous, but altogether scientific and commercial. The Italy indeed that we sentimentalise and romance about was an ardently mercantile country; though I suppose it loved not its ledgers less, but its frescoes and altar-pieces more. Scattered through this paradise regained of trade—this country of a thousand ports—we see a large number of beautiful buildings in which an endless series of dusky pictures are darkening, dampening, fading, failing, through the years. By the doors of the beautiful buildings are little turnstiles at which there sit a great many uniformed men to whom the visitor pays a tenpenny fee. Inside, in the vaulted and frescoed chambers, the art of Italy lies buried as in a thousand mausoleums. It is well taken care of; it is constantly copied; sometimes it is "restored"—as in the case of that beautiful boy-figure of Andrea del Sarto at Florence, which may be seen at the gallery of the Uffizi with its honourable duskiness quite peeled off and heaven knows what raw, bleeding cuticle laid bare. One evening lately, near the same Florence, in the soft twilight, I took a stroll among those encircling hills on which the massive villas are mingled with the vaporous olives. Presently I arrived where three roads met at a wayside shrine, in which, before some pious daub of an old-time Madonna, a little votive lamp glimmered through the evening air. The hour, the atmosphere, the place, the twinkling taper, the sentiment of the observer, the thought that some one had been rescued here from an assassin or from some other peril and had set up a little grateful altar in consequence, against the yellow-plastercd wall of a tangled *podere*; all this led me to approach the shrine with a reverent, an emotional step. I drew near it, but after a few steps I paused. I became aware of an incongruous odour; it seemed to me that the evening air was charged with a perfume which, although to a certain extent familiar, had not hitherto associated itself with rustic frescoes and wayside altars. I wondered, I gently sniffed, and the question so put left me no doubt. The odour was that of petroleum; the votive taper was nourished with the essence of Pennsylvania. I confess that I burst out laughing,

and a picturesque contadino, wending his homeward way in
the dusk, stared at me as if I were an iconoclast. He noticed
the petroleum only, I imagine, to snuff it fondly up; but to
me the thing served as a symbol of the Italy of the future.
There is a horse-car from the Porta del Popolo to the Ponte
Molle, and the Tuscan shrines are fed with kerosene.

II

If it's very well meanwhile to come to Turin first it's better
still to go to Genoa afterwards. Genoa is the tightest topo-
graphic tangle in the world, which even a second visit helps
you little to straighten out. In the wonderful crooked, twisting, climbing, soaring, burrowing Genoese alleys the traveller
is really up to his neck in the old Italian sketchability. The
pride of the place, I believe, is a port of great capacity, and
the bequest of the late Duke of Galliera, who left four millions of dollars for the purpose of improving and enlarging it,
will doubtless do much toward converting it into one of the
great commercial stations of Europe. But as, after leaving my
hotel the afternoon I arrived, I wandered for a long time at
hazard through the tortuous byways of the city, I said to myself, not without an accent of private triumph, that here at last
was something it would be almost impossible to modernise. I
had found my hotel, in the first place, extremely entertaining—the Croce di Malta, as it is called, established in a gigantic palace on the edge of the swarming and not over-clean
harbour. It was the biggest house I had ever entered—the
basement alone would have contained a dozen American caravansaries. I met an American gentleman in the vestibule who
(as he had indeed a perfect right to be) was annoyed by its
troublesome dimensions—one was a quarter of an hour ascending out of the basement—and desired to know if it were
a "fair sample" of the Genoese inns. It appeared an excellent
specimen of Genoese architecture generally; so far as I observed there were few houses perceptibly smaller than this Ti-
tanic tavern. I lunched in a dusky ballroom whose ceiling was
vaulted, frescoed and gilded with the fatal facility of a couple
of centuries ago, and which looked out upon another ancient
house-front, equally huge and equally battered, separated

from it only by a little wedge of dusky space—one of the principal streets, I believe, of Genoa—whence out of dim abysses the population sent up to the windows (I had to crane out very far to see it) a perpetual clattering, shuffling, chaffering sound. Issuing forth presently into this crevice of a street I found myself up to my neck in that element of the rich and strange—as to visible and reproducible "effect," I mean—for the love of which one revisits Italy. It offered itself indeed in a variety of colours, some of which were not remarkable for their freshness or purity. But their combined charm was not to be resisted, and the picture glowed with the rankly human side of southern low-life.

Genoa, as I have hinted, is the crookedest and most incoherent of cities; tossed about on the sides and crests of a dozen hills, it is seamed with gullies and ravines that bristle with those innumerable palaces for which we have heard from our earliest years that the place is celebrated. These great structures, with their mottled and faded complexions, lift their big ornamental cornices to a tremendous height in the air, where, in a certain indescribably forlorn and desolate fashion, overtopping each other, they seem to reflect the twinkle and glitter of the warm Mediterranean. Down about the basements, in the close crepuscular alleys, the people are for ever moving to and fro or standing in their cavernous doorways and their dusky, crowded shops, calling, chattering, laughing, lamenting, living their lives in the conversational Italian fashion. I had for a long time had no such vision of possible social pressure. I hadn't for a long time seen people elbowing each other so closely or swarming so thickly out of populous hives. A traveller is often moved to ask himself whether it has been worth while to leave his home—whatever his home may have been—only to encounter new forms of human suffering, only to be reminded that toil and privation, hunger and sorrow and sordid effort, are the portion of the mass of mankind. To travel is, as it were, to go to the play, to attend a spectacle; and there is something heartless in stepping forth into foreign streets to feast on "character" when character consists simply of the slightly different costume in which labour and want present themselves. These reflections were forced upon me as I strolled as through a twilight patched with colour and charged with stale smells; but after a time they ceased to bear me company. The reason of this, I think, is because—at least to foreign eyes—the sum of Italian misery is, on the whole, less than the sum of the Italian knowledge of life. That people should thank you, with a smile of striking sweetness, for the gift of twopence, is a proof, certainly, of extreme and constant destitution; but (keeping in mind the sweetness) it also attests an enviable ability not to be depressed by circumstances. I know that this may possibly be great nonsense; that half the time we are acclaiming the fine quality of the Italian smile the creature so constituted for physiognomic radiance may be in a sullen frenzy of impatience and pain. Our observation in any foreign land is extremely superficial, and our remarks are happily not addressed to the inhabitants themselves, who would be sure to exclaim upon the impudence of the fancy-picture.

The other day I visited a very picturesque old city upon a mountain-top, where, in the course of my wanderings, I arrived at an old disused gate in the ancient town-wall. The gate hadn't been absolutely forfeited; but the recent completion of a modern road down the mountain led most vehicles away to another egress. The grass-grown pavement, which wound into the plain by a hundred graceful twists and plunges, was now given up to ragged contadini and their donkeys, and to such wayfarers as were not alarmed at the disrepair into which it had fallen. I stood in the shadow of the tall old gateway admiring the scene, looking to right and left at the wonderful walls of the little town, perched on the edge of a shaggy precipice; at the circling mountains over against them; at the road dipping downward among the chestnuts and olives. There was no one within sight but a young man who slowly trudged upward with his coat slung over his shoulder and his hat upon his ear in the manner of a cavalier in an opera. Like an operatic performer too he sang as he came; the spectacle, generally, was operatic, and as his vocal flourishes reached my ear I said to myself that in Italy accident was always romantic and that such a figure had been exactly what was wanted to set off the landscape. It suggested in a high degree that knowledge of life for which I just now commended the Italians. I was turning back under the old gateway when the young man overtook me and, suspending his song, asked me if I could favour him with a match to light the hoarded remnant of a cigar. This request led, as I took my way again to the inn, to my falling into talk with him. He was a native of the ancient city, and answered freely all my inquiries as to its manners and customs and its note of public opinion. But the point of my anecdote is that he presently acknowledged himself a brooding young radical and communist, filled with hatred of the present Italian government, raging with discontent and crude political passion, professing a ridiculous hope that Italy would soon have, as France had had, her " '89," and declaring that he for his part would willingly lend a hand to chop off the heads of the king and the royal family. He was an unhappy, underfed, unemployed young man, who took a hard, grim view of everything and was operatic only quite in spite of himself. This made it very absurd of me to have looked at him simply as a graceful ornament to the prospect, an harmonious little figure in the middle distance. "Damn the prospect, damn the middle distance!" would have been all *his* philosophy. Yet but for the accident of my having gossipped with him I should have made him do service, in memory, as an example of sensuous optimism!

I am bound to say however that I believe a great deal of the sensuous optimism observable in the Genoese alleys and beneath the low, crowded arcades along the port was very real. Here every one was magnificently sunburnt, and there were plenty of those queer types, mahogany-coloured, bare-chested mariners with earrings and crimson girdles, that seem to people a southern seaport with the chorus of "Masaniello." But it is not fair to speak as if at Genoa there were nothing but low-life to be seen, for the place is the residence of some of the grandest people in the world. Nor are all the palaces ranged upon dusky alleys; the handsomest and most impressive form a splendid series on each side of a couple of very proper streets, in which there is plenty of room for a coach-and-four to approach the big doorways. Many of these doorways are open, revealing great marble staircases with couchant lions for balustrades and ceremonious courts surrounded by walls of sun-softened yellow. One of the great piles in the array is coloured a goodly red and contains in particular the grand people I just now spoke of. They live indeed on the

third floor; but here they have suites of wonderful painted
and gilded chambers, in which foreshortened frescoes also
cover the vaulted ceilings and florid mouldings emboss the
ample walls. These distinguished tenants bear the name of
Vandyck, though they are members of the noble family of
Brignole-Sale, one of whose children—the Duchess of Galliera—has lately given proof of nobleness in presenting the
gallery of the red palace to the city of Genoa.

III

On leaving Genoa I repaired to Spezia, chiefly with a view
of accomplishing a sentimental pilgrimage, which I in fact
achieved in the most agreeable conditions. The Gulf of Spezia
is now the headquarters of the Italian fleet, and there were
several big iron-plated frigates riding at anchor in front of the
town. The streets were filled with lads in blue flannel, who
were receiving instruction at a schoolship in the harbour, and
in the evening—there was a brilliant moon—the little breakwater which stretched out into the Mediterranean offered a
scene of recreation to innumerable such persons. But this fact
is from the point of view of the cherisher of quaintness of
little account, for since it has become prosperous Spezia has
grown ugly. The place is filled with long, dull stretches of
dead wall and great raw expanses of artificial land. It wears
that look of monstrous, of more than far-western newness
which distinguishes all the creations of the young Italian
State. Nor did I find any great compensation in an immense
inn of recent birth, an establishment seated on the edge of the
sea in anticipation of a *passeggiata* which is to come that way
some five years hence, the region being in the meantime of
the most primitive formation. The inn was filled with grave
English people who looked respectable and bored, and there
was of course a Church of England service in the gaudily-
frescoed parlour. Neither was it the drive to Porto Venere that
chiefly pleased me—a drive among vines and olives, over the
hills and beside the Mediterranean, to a queer little crumbling
village on a headland, as sweetly desolate and superannuated
as the name it bears. There is a ruined church near the village,
which occupies the site (according to tradition) of an ancient

temple of Venus; and if Venus ever revisits her desecrated shrines she must sometimes pause a moment in that sunny stillness and listen to the murmur of the tideless sea at the base of the narrow promontory. If Venus sometimes comes there Apollo surely does as much; for close to the temple is a gateway surmounted by an inscription in Italian and English, which admits you to a curious, and it must be confessed rather cockneyfied, cave among the rocks. It was here, says the inscription, that the great Byron, swimmer and poet, "defied the waves of the Ligurian sea." The fact is interesting, though not supremely so; for Byron was always defying something, and if a slab had been put up wherever this performance came off these commemorative tablets would be in many parts of Europe as thick as milestones.

No; the great merit of Spezia, to my eye, is that I engaged a boat there of a lovely October afternoon and had myself rowed across the gulf —it took about an hour and a half—to the little bay of Lerici, which opens out of it. This bay of Lerici is charming; the bosky grey-green hills close it in, and on either side of the entrance, perched on a bold headland, a wonderful old crumbling castle keeps ineffectual guard. The place is classic to all English travellers, for in the middle of the curving shore is the now desolate little villa in which Shelley spent the last months of his short life. He was living at Lerici when he started on that short southern cruise from which he never returned. The house he occupied is strangely shabby and as sad as you may choose to find it. It stands directly upon the beach, with scarred and battered walls and a loggia of several arches opening to a little terrace with a rugged parapet, which, when the wind blows, must be drenched with the salt spray. The place is very lonely—all overwearied with sun and breeze and brine—very close to nature, as it was Shelley's passion to be. I can fancy a great lyric poet sitting on the terrace of a warm evening and feeling very far from England in the early years of the century. In that place, and with his genius, he would as a matter of course have heard in the voice of nature a sweetness which only the lyric movement could translate. It is a place where an English-speaking pilgrim himself may very honestly think thoughts and feel moved to lyric utterance. But I must content myself with saying in halting prose that I remember few episodes of Italian travel more sympathetic, as they have it here, than that perfect autumn afternoon; the half-hour's station on the little battered terrace of the villa; the climb to the singularly felicitous old castle that hangs above Lerici; the meditative lounge, in the fading light, on the vine-decked platform that looked out toward the sunset and the darkening mountains and, far below, upon the quiet sea, beyond which the pale-faced tragic villa stared up at the brightening moon.

IV

I had never known Florence more herself, or in other words more attaching, than I found her for a week in that brilliant October. She sat in the sunshine beside her yellow river like the little treasure-city she has always seemed, without commerce, without other industry than the manufacture of mosaic paper-weights and alabaster Cupids, without actuality or energy or earnestness or any of those rugged virtues which in most cases are deemed indispensable for civic cohesion; with nothing but the little unaugmented stock of her mediæval memories, her tender-coloured mountains, her churches and palaces, pictures and statues. There were very few strangers; one's detested fellow-pilgrim was infrequent; the native population itself seemed scanty; the sound of wheels in the streets was but occasional; by eight o'clock at night, apparently, every one had gone to bed, and the musing wanderer, still wandering and still musing, had the place to himself—had the thick shadow-masses of the great palaces, and the shafts of moonlight striking the polygonal paving-stones, and the empty bridges, and the silvered yellow of the Arno, and the stillness broken only by a homeward step, a step accompanied by a snatch of song from a warm Italian voice. My room at the inn looked out on the river and was flooded all day with sunshine. There was an absurd orange-coloured paper on the walls; the Arno, of a hue not altogether different, flowed beneath; and on the other side of it rose a line of sallow houses, of extreme antiquity, crumbling and mouldering, bulging and protruding over the stream. (I seem to speak of their fronts; but what I saw was their shabby backs, which were exposed to the cheerful flicker of the river, while the fronts stood for ever in the deep damp shadow of a narrow mediæval street.) All this brightness and yellowness was a perpetual delight; it was a part of that indefinably charming colour which Florence always seems to wear as you look up and down at it from the river, and from the bridges and quays. This is a kind of grave radiance—a harmony of high tints—which I scarce know how to describe. There are yellow walls and green blinds and red roofs, there are intervals of brilliant brown and natural-looking blue; but the picture is not spotty nor gaudy, thanks to the distribution of the colours in large and comfortable masses, and to the washing-over of the scene by some happy softness of sunshine. The river-front of Florence is in short a delightful composition. Part of its charm comes of course from the generous aspect of those high-based Tuscan palaces which a renewal of acquaintance with them has again commended to me as the most dignified dwellings in the world. Nothing can be finer than that look of giving up the whole immense ground-floor to simple purposes of vestibule and staircase, of court and high-arched entrance; as if this were all but a massive pedestal for the real habitation and people weren't properly housed unless, to begin with, they should be lifted fifty feet above the pavement. The great blocks of the basement; the great intervals, horizontally and vertically, from window to window (telling of the height and breadth of the rooms within); the armorial shield hung forward at one of the angles; the wide-brimmed roof, overshadowing the narrow street; the rich old browns and yellows of the walls: these definite elements put themselves together with admirable art.

Take a Tuscan pile of this type out of its oblique situation in the town; call it no longer a palace, but a villa; set it down by a terrace on one of the hills that encircle Florence, place a row of high-waisted cypresses beside it, give it a grassy courtyard and a view of the Florentine towers and the valley of the Arno, and you will think it perhaps even more worthy of your esteem. It was a Sunday noon, and brilliantly warm, when I again arrived; and after I had looked from my windows

awhile at that quietly-basking river-front I have spoken of I
took my way across one of the bridges and then out of one of
the gates—that immensely tall Roman Gate in which the
space from the top of the arch to the cornice (except that
there is scarcely a cornice, it is all a plain massive piece of
wall) is as great, or seems to be, as that from the ground to
the former point. Then I climbed a steep and winding way—
much of it a little dull if one likes, being bounded by mottled,
mossy garden-walls—to a villa on a hill-top, where I found
various things that touched me with almost too fine a point.
Seeing them again, often, for a week, both by sunlight and
moonshine, I never quite learned not to covet them; not to
feel that not being a part of them was somehow to miss an
exquisite chance. What a tranquil, contented life it seemed,
with romantic beauty as a part of its daily texture!—the
sunny terrace, with its tangled *podere* beneath it; the bright
grey olives against the bright blue sky; the long, serene, horizontal lines of other villas, flanked by their upward cypresses,
disposed upon the neighbouring hills; the richest little city in
the world in a softly-scooped hollow at one's feet, and beyond
it the most appealing of views, the most majestic, yet the
most familiar. Within the villa was a great love of art and a
painting-room full of felicitous work, so that if human life
there confessed to quietness, the quietness was mostly but
that of the intent act. A beautiful occupation in that beautiful
position, what could possibly be better? That is what I spoke
just now of envying—a way of life that doesn't wince at such
refinements of peace and ease. When labour self-charmed presents itself in a dull or an ugly place we esteem it, we admire
it, but we scarce feel it to be the ideal of good fortune. When,
however, its votaries move as figures in an ancient, noble
landscape, and their walks and contemplations are like a turning of the leaves of history, we seem to have before us an
admirable case of virtue made easy; meaning here by virtue
contentment and concentration, a real appreciation of the
rare, the exquisite though composite, medium of life. You
needn't want a rush or a crush when the scene itself, the mere
scene, shares with you such a wealth of consciousness.

It is true indeed that I might after a certain time grow

weary of a regular afternoon stroll among the Florentine lanes; of sitting on low parapets, in intervals of flower-topped wall, and looking across at Fiesole or down the rich-hued valley of the Arno; of pausing at the open gates of villas and wondering at the height of cypresses and the depth of loggias; of walking home in the fading light and noting on a dozen westward-looking surfaces the glow of the opposite sunset. But for a week or so all this was delightful. The villas are innumerable, and if you're an aching alien half the talk is about villas. This one has a story; that one has another; they all look as if they had stories—none in truth predominantly gay. Most of them are offered to rent (many of them for sale) at prices unnaturally low; you may have a tower and a garden, a chapel and an expanse of thirty windows, for five hundred dollars a year. In imagination you hire three or four; you take possession and settle and stay. Your sense of the fineness of the finest is of something very grave and stately; your sense of the bravery of two or three of the best something quite tragic and sinister. From what does this latter impression come? You gather it as you stand there in the early dusk, with your eyes on the long, pale-brown façade, the enormous windows, the iron cages fastened to the lower ones. Part of the brooding expression of these great houses comes, even when they have not fallen into decay, from their look of having outlived their original use. Their extraordinary largeness and massiveness are a satire on their present fate. They weren't built with such a thickness of wall and depth of embrasure, such a solidity of staircase and superfluity of stone, simply to afford an economical winter residence to English and American families. I don't know whether it was the appearance of these stony old villas, which seemed so dumbly conscious of a change of manners, that threw a tinge of melancholy over the general prospect; certain it is that, having always found this note as of a myriad old sadnesses in solution in the view of Florence, it seemed to me now particularly strong. "Lovely, lovely, but it makes me 'blue,'" the sensitive stranger couldn't but murmur to himself as, in the late afternoon, he looked at the landscape from over one of the low parapets, and then, with his hands in his pockets, turned away indoors to candles and dinner.

V

Below, in the city, through all frequentation of streets and churches and museums, it was impossible not to have a good deal of the same feeling; but here the impression was more easy to analyse. It came from a sense of the perfect separateness of all the great productions of the Renaissance from the present and the future of the place, from the actual life and manners, the native ideal. I have already spoken of the way in which the vast aggregation of beautiful works of art in the Italian cities strikes the visitor nowadays—so far as present Italy is concerned—as the mere stock-in-trade of an impecunious but thrifty people. It is this spiritual solitude, this conscious disconnection of the great works of architecture and sculpture that deposits a certain weight upon the heart; when we see a great tradition broken we feel something of the pain with which we hear a stifled cry. But regret is one thing and resentment is another. Seeing one morning, in a shop-window, the series of *Mornings in Florence* published a few years since by Mr. Ruskin, I made haste to enter and purchase these amusing little books, some passages of which I remembered formerly to have read. I couldn't turn over many pages without observing that the "separateness" of the new and old which I just mentioned had produced in their author the liveliest irritation. With the more acute phases of this condition it was difficult to sympathise, for the simple reason, it seems to me, that it savours of arrogance to demand of any people, as a right of one's own, that they shall be artistic. "Be artistic yourselves!" is the very natural reply that young Italy has at hand for English critics and censors. When a people produces beautiful statues and pictures it gives us something more than is set down in the bond, and we must thank it for its generosity; and when it stops producing them or caring for them we may cease thanking, but we hardly have a right to begin and rail. The wreck of Florence, says Mr. Ruskin, "is now too ghastly and heart-breaking to any human soul that remembers the days of old;" and these desperate words are an allusion to the fact that the little square in front of the cathedral, at the foot of Giotto's Tower, with the grand Baptistery on the other side, is now the resort of a number of hackney-coaches and omnibuses. This fact is doubtless lamentable, and it would be a hundred times more agreeable to see among people who have been made the heirs of so priceless a work of art as the sublime campanile some such feeling about it as would keep it free even from the danger of defilement. A cab-stand is a very ugly and dirty thing, and Giotto's Tower should have nothing in common with such conveniences. But there is more than one way of taking such things, and the sensitive stranger who has been walking about for a week with his mind full of the sweetness and suggestiveness of a hundred Florentine places may feel at last in looking into Mr. Ruskin's little tracts that, discord for discord, there isn't much to choose between the importunity of the author's personal ill-humour and the incongruity of horse-pails and bundles of hay. And one may say this without being at all a partisan of the doctrine of the inevitableness of new desecrations. For my own part, I believe there are few things in this line that the new Italian spirit isn't capable of, and not many indeed that we aren't destined to see. Pictures and buildings won't be completely destroyed, because in that case the *forestieri*, scatterers of cash, would cease to arrive and the turn-stiles at the doors of the old palaces and convents, with the little patented slit for absorbing your half-franc, would grow quite rusty, would stiffen with disuse. But it's safe to say that the new Italy growing into an old Italy again will continue to take her elbow-room wherever she may find it.

I am almost ashamed to say what I did with Mr. Ruskin's little books. I put them into my pocket and betook myself to Santa Maria Novella. There I sat down and, after I had looked about for a while at the beautiful church, drew them forth one by one and read the greater part of them. Occupying one's self with light literature in a great religious edifice is perhaps as bad a piece of profanation as any of those rude dealings which Mr. Ruskin justly deplores; but a traveller has to make the most of odd moments, and I was waiting for a friend in whose company I was to go and look at Giotto's beautiful frescoes in the cloister of the church. My friend was a long time coming, so that I had an hour with Mr. Ruskin, whom I called just now a light *littérateur* because in these little Mornings in Florence he is for ever making his readers laugh. I remembered of course where I was, and in spite of my latent hilarity felt I had rarely got such a snubbing. I had really been enjoying the good old city of Florence, but I now learned from Mr. Ruskin that this was a scandalous waste of charity. I should have gone about with an imprecation on my lips, I should have worn a face three yards long. I had taken great pleasure in certain frescoes by Ghirlandaio in the choir of that very church; but it appeared from one of the little books that these frescoes were as naught. I had much admired Santa Croce and had thought the Duomo a very noble affair; but I had now the most positive assurance I knew nothing about them. After a while, if it was only ill-humour that was needed for doing honour to the city of the Medici, I felt that I had risen to a proper level; only now it was Mr. Ruskin himself I had lost patience with, not the stupid Brunelleschi, not the vulgar Ghirlandaio. Indeed I lost patience altogether, and asked myself by what right this informal votary of form pretended to run riot through a poor charmed *flâneur's* quiet contemplations, his attachment to the noblest of pleasures, his enjoyment of the loveliest of cities. The little books seemed invidious and insane, and it was only when I remembered that I had been under no obligation to buy them that I checked myself in repenting of having done so.

Then at last my friend arrived and we passed together out of the church and, through the first cloister beside it, into a smaller enclosure where we stood a while to look at the tomb of the Marchesa Strozzi-Ridolfi, upon which the great Giotto has painted four superb little pictures. It was easy to see the pictures were superb; but I drew forth one of my little books again, for I had observed that Mr. Ruskin spoke of them. Hereupon I recovered my tolerance; for what could be better in this case, I asked myself, than Mr. Ruskin's remarks? They are in fact excellent and charming—full of appreciation of the deep and simple beauty of the great painter's work. I read them aloud to my companion; but my companion was rather, as the phrase is, "put off" by them. One of the frescoes—it is a picture of the birth of the Virgin—contains a figure coming through a door. "Of ornament," I quote, "there is only the entirely simple outline of the vase which the servant carries;

of colour two or three masses of sober red and pure white, with brown and grey. That is all," Mr. Ruskin continues. "And if you are pleased with this you can see Florence. But if not, by all means amuse yourself there, if you find it amusing, as long as you like; you can never see it." *You can never see it.* This seemed to my friend insufferable, and I had to shuffle away the book again, so that we might look at the fresco with the unruffled geniality it deserves. We agreed afterwards, when in a more convenient place I read aloud a good many more passages from the precious tracts, that there are a great many ways of seeing Florence, as there are of seeing most beautiful and interesting things, and that it is very dry and pedantic to say that the happy vision depends upon our squaring our toes with a certain particular chalk-mark. We see Florence wherever and whenever we enjoy it, and for enjoying it we find a great many more pretexts than Mr. Ruskin seems inclined to allow. My friend and I convinced ourselves also, however, that the little books were an excellent purchase, on account of the great charm and felicity of much of their incidental criticism; to say nothing, as I hinted just now, of their being extremely amusing. Nothing in fact is more comical than the familiar asperity of the author's style and the pedagogic fashion in which he pushes and pulls his unhappy pupils about, jerking their heads toward this, rapping their knuckles for that, sending them to stand in corners and giving them Scripture texts to copy. But it is neither the felicities nor the aberrations of detail, in Mr. Ruskin's writings, that are the main affair for most readers; it is the general tone that, as I have said, puts them off or draws them on. For many persons he will never bear the test of being read in this rich old Italy, where art, so long as it really lived at all, was spontaneous, joyous, irresponsible. If the reader is in daily contact with those beautiful Florentine works which do still, in a way, force themselves into notice through the vulgarity and cruelty of modern profanation, it will seem to him that this commentator's comment is pitched in the strangest falsetto key. "One may read a hundred pages of this sort of thing," said my friend, "without ever dreaming that he is talking about *art*. You can say nothing worse about him than that." Which is

perfectly true. Art is the one corner of human life in which we
may take our ease. To justify our presence there the only thing
demanded of us is that we shall have felt the representational
impulse. In other connections our impulses are conditioned
and embarrassed; we are allowed to have only so many as are
consistent with those of our neighbours; with their convenience and well-being, with their convictions and prejudices,
their rules and regulations. Art means an escape from all this.
Wherever her shining standard floats the need for apology
and compromise is over; there it is enough simply that we
please or are pleased. There the tree is judged only by its
fruits. If these are sweet the tree is justified—and not less so
the consumer.

One may read a great many pages of Mr. Ruskin without
getting a hint of this delightful truth; a hint of the not unim-
portant fact that art after all is made for us and not we for art.
This idea that the value of a work is in the amount of illusion
it yields is conspicuous by its absence. And as for Mr.
Ruskin's world's being a place—his world of art—where we
may take life easily, woe to the luckless mortal who enters it
with any such disposition. Instead of a garden of delight, he
finds a sort of assize court in perpetual session. Instead of a
place in which human responsibilities are lightened and suspended, he finds a region governed by a kind of Draconic
legislation. His responsibilities indeed are tenfold increased;
the gulf between truth and error is for ever yawning at his
feet; the pains and penalties of this same error are advertised,
in apocalyptic terminology, upon a thousand sign-posts; and
the rash intruder soon begins to look back with infinite longing to the lost paradise of the artless. There can be no greater
want of tact in dealing with those things with which men
attempt to ornament life than to be perpetually talking about
"error." A truce to all rigidities is the law of the place; the
only thing absolute there is that some force and some charm
have worked. The grim old bearer of the scales excuses herself; she feels this not to be her province. Differences here are
not iniquity and righteousness; they are simply variations of
temperament, kinds of curiosity. We are not under theological
government.

VI

It was very charming, in the bright, warm days, to wander from one corner of Florence to another, paying one's respects again to remembered masterpieces. It was pleasant also to find that memory had played no tricks and that the rarest things of an earlier year were as rare as ever. To enumerate these felicities would take a great deal of space; for I never had been more struck with the mere quantity of brilliant Florentine work. Even giving up the Duomo and Santa Croce to Mr. Ruskin as very ill-arranged edifices, the list of the Florentine treasures is almost inexhaustible. Those long outer galleries of the Uffizi had never beguiled me more; sometimes there were not more than two or three figures standing there, Baedeker in hand, to break the charming perspective. One side of this upstairs portico, it will be remembered, is entirely composed of glass; a continuity of old-fashioned windows, draped with white curtains of rather primitive fashion, which hang there till they acquire a perceptible tone. The light, passing through them, is softly filtered and diffused; it rests mildly upon the old marbles—chiefly antique Roman busts—which stand in the narrow intervals of the casements. It is projected upon the numerous pictures that cover the opposite wall and that are not by any means, as a general thing, the gems of the great collection; it imparts a faded brightness to the old ornamental arabesques upon the painted wooden ceiling, and it makes a great soft shining upon the marble floor, in which, as you look up and down, you see the strolling tourists and the motionless copyists almost reflected. I don't know why I should find all this very pleasant, but in fact, I have seldom gone into the Uffizi without walking the length of this third-story cloister, between the (for the most part) third-rate canvases and panels and the faded cotton curtains. Why is it that in Italy we see a charm in things in regard to which in other countries we always take vulgarity for granted? If in the city of New York a great museum of the arts were to be provided, by way of decoration, with a species of verandah inclosed on one side by a series of small-paned windows draped in dirty linen, and furnished on the other with an array of pictorial feebleness, the place being surmounted by a thinly-painted wooden roof, strongly suggestive of summer heat, of winter cold, of frequent leakage, those amateurs who had had the advantage of foreign travel would be at small pains to conceal their contempt.

Contemptible or respectable, to the judicial mind, this quaint old loggia of the Uffizi admitted me into twenty chambers where I found as great a number of ancient favourites. I don't know that I had a warmer greeting for any old friend than for Andrea del Sarto, that most touching of painters who is not one of the first. But it was on the other side of the Arno that I found him in force, in those dusky drawing-rooms of the Pitti Palace to which you take your way along the tortuous tunnel that wanders through the houses of Florence and is supported by the little goldsmiths' booths on the Ponte Vecchio. In the rich insufficient light of these beautiful rooms, where, to look at the pictures, you sit in damask chairs and rest your elbows on tables of malachite, the elegant Andrea becomes deeply effective. Before long he has drawn you close. But the great pleasure, after all, was to revisit the earlier masters, in those specimens of them chiefly that bloom so unfadingly on the big plain walls of the Academy. Fra Angelico and Filippo Lippi, Botticelli and Lorenzo di Credi are the clearest, the sweetest and best of all painters; as I sat for an hour in their company, in the cold great hall of the institution I have mentioned—there are shabby rafters above and an immense expanse of brick tiles below, and many bad pictures as well as good—it seemed to me more than ever that if one really had to choose one couldn't do better than choose here. You may rest at your ease at the Academy, in this big first room—at the upper end especially, on the left—because more than many other places it savours of old Florence. More for instance, in reality, than the Bargello, though the Bargello makes great pretensions. Beautiful and masterful though the Bargello is, it smells too strongly of restoration, and, much of old Italy as still lurks in its furbished and renovated chambers, it speaks even more distinctly of the ill-mannered young kingdom that has—as "unavoidably" as you please—lifted down a hundred delicate works of sculpture from the convent-walls where their pious authors placed them. If the early Tuscan painters are exquisite I can think of no praise pure enough for the sculptors of the same period, Donatello and Luca della Robbia, Matteo Civitale and Mina da Fiesole, who, as I refreshed my memory of them, seemed to me to leave absolutely nothing to be desired in the way of straightness of inspiration and grace of invention. The Bargello is full of early Tuscan sculpture, most of the pieces of which have come from suppressed religious houses; and even if the visitor be an ardent liberal he is uncomfortably conscious of the rather brutal process by which it has been collected. One can hardly envy young Italy the number of odious things she has had to do.

The railway journey from Florence to Rome has been altered both for the better and for the worse; for the better in that it has been shortened by a couple of hours; for the worse inasmuch as when about half the distance has been traversed the train deflects to the west and leaves the beautiful old cities of Assisi, Perugia, Terni, Narni, unvisited. Of old it was possible to call at these places, in a manner, from the window of the train; even if you didn't stop, as you probably couldn't, every time you passed, the immensely interesting way in which, like a loosened belt on an aged and shrunken person, their ample walls held them easily together was something well worth noting. Now, however, for compensation, the express train to Rome stops at Orvieto, and in consequence. . . . In consequence what? What is the result of the stop of an express train at Orvieto? As I glibly wrote that sentence I suddenly paused, aware of the queer stuff I was uttering. That an express train would graze the base of the horrid purple mountain from the apex of which this dark old Catholic city uplifts the glittering front of its cathedral—that might have been foretold by a keen observer of contemporary manners. But that it would really have the grossness to hang about is a fact over which, as he records it, an inveterate, a perverse cherisher of the sense of the past order, the order still largely prevailing at the time of his first visit to Italy, may well make what is vulgarly called an ado. The train does stop at Orvieto, not very long, it is true, but long enough to let you out. The same phenomenon takes place on the following day, when, having visited the city, you get in again. I availed myself with-

out scruple of both of these occasions, having formerly neglected to drive to the place in a post-chaise. But frankly, the
railway-station being in the plain and the town on the summit
of an extraordinary hill, you have time to forget the puffing
indiscretion while you wind upwards to the city-gate. The
position of Orvieto is superb—worthy of the "middle distance" of an eighteenth-century landscape. But, as every one
knows, the splendid Cathedral is the proper attraction of the
spot, which, indeed, save for this fine monument and for its
craggy and crumbling ramparts, is a meanly arranged and, as
Italian cities go, not particularly impressive little town. I spent
a beautiful Sunday there and took in the charming church. I
gave it my best attention, though on the whole I fear I found
it inferior to its fame. A high concert of colour, however, is
the densely carved front, richly covered with radiant mosaics.
The old white marble of the sculptured portions is as softly
yellow as ancient ivory; the large exceedingly bright pictures
above them flashed and twinkled in the glorious weather.
Very striking and interesting the theological frescoes of Luca
Signorelli, though I have seen compositions of this general
order that appealed to me more. Characteristically fresh, finally, the clear-faced saints and seraphs, in robes of pink and
azure, whom Fra Angelico has painted upon the ceiling of the
great chapel, along with a noble sitting figure—more expressive of movement than most of the creations of this pictorial
peace-maker—of Christ in judgment. Yet the interest of the
cathedral of Orvieto is mainly not the visible result, but the
historical process that lies behind it; those three hundred
years of the applied devotion of a people of which an American scholar has written an admirable account.*

1877.

*Charles Eliot Norton, *Study and Travel in Italy*.

A Roman Holiday

IT IS certainly sweet to be merry at the right moment; but the right moment hardly seems to me the ten days of the Roman Carnival. It was my rather cynical suspicion perhaps that they wouldn't keep to my imagination the brilliant promise of legend; but I have been justified by the event and have been decidedly less conscious of the festal influences of the season than of the inalienable gravity of the place. There was a time when the Carnival was a serious matter—that is a heartily joyous one; but, thanks to the seven-league boots the kingdom of Italy has lately donned for the march of progress in quite other directions, the fashion of public revelry has fallen woefully out of step. The state of mind and manners under which the Carnival was kept in generous good faith I doubt if an American can exactly conceive: he can only say to himself that for a month in the year there must have been things—things considerably of humiliation—it was comfortable to forget. But now that Italy is made the Carnival is unmade; and we are not especially tempted to envy the attitude of a population who have lost their relish for play and not yet acquired to any striking extent an enthusiasm for work. The spectacle on the Corso has seemed to me, on the whole, an illustration of that great breach with the past of which Catholic Christendom felt the somewhat muffled shock in September 1870. A traveller acquainted with the fully papal Rome, coming back any time during the past winter, must have immediately noticed that something momentous had happened—something hostile to the elements of picture and colour and "style." My first warning was that ten minutes after my arrival I found myself face to face with a newspaper stand. The impossibility in the other days of having anything in the journalistic line but the *Osservatore Romano* and the *Voce della Verità* used to seem to me much connected with the extraordinary leisure of thought and stillness of mind to which the place admitted you. But now the slender piping of the Voice of Truth is stifled by the raucous note of eventide vendors of the *Capitale*, the *Libertà* and the *Fanfulla*; and Rome

413

reading unexpurgated news is another Rome indeed. For
every subscriber to the *Libertà* there may well be an antique
masker and reveller less. As striking a sign of the new régime
is the extraordinary increase of population. The Corso was
always a well-filled street, but now it's a perpetual crush. I
never cease to wonder where the new-comers are lodged, and
how such spotless flowers of fashion as the gentlemen who
stare at the carriages can bloom in the atmosphere of those
camere mobiliate of which I have had glimpses. This, however,
is their own question, and bravely enough they meet it. They
proclaimed somehow, to the first freshness of my wonder, as I
say, that by force of numbers Rome had been secularised. An
Italian dandy is a figure visually to reckon with, but these
goodly throngs of them scarce offered compensation for the
absent monsignori, treading the streets in their purple stockings and followed by the solemn servants who returned on
their behalf the bows of the meaner sort; for the mourning
gear of the cardinals' coaches that formerly glittered with scarlet and swung with the weight of the footmen clinging behind; for the certainty that you'll not, by the best of traveller's
luck, meet the Pope sitting deep in the shadow of his great
chariot with uplifted fingers like some inaccessible idol in his
shrine. You may meet the King indeed, who is as ugly, as
imposingly ugly, as some idols, though not so inaccessible.
The other day as I passed the Quirinal he drove up in a low
carriage with a single attendant; and a group of men and
women who had been waiting near the gate rushed at him
with a number of folded papers. The carriage slackened pace
and he pocketed their offerings with a business-like air—that
of a good-natured man accepting hand-bills at a street-corner.
Here was a monarch at his palace gate receiving petitions
from his subjects—being adjured to right their wrongs. The
scene ought to have thrilled me, but somehow it had no more
intensity than a woodcut in an illustrated newspaper. Homely
I should call it at most; admirably so, certainly, for there were
lately few sovereigns standing, I believe, with whom their
people enjoyed these filial hand-to-hand relations. The King
this year, however, has had as little to do with the Carnival as
the Pope, and the innkeepers and Americans have marked it
for their own.

It was advertised to begin at half-past two o'clock of a certain Saturday, and punctually at the stroke of the hour, from my room across a wide court, I heard a sudden multiplication of sounds and confusion of tongues in the Corso. I was writing to a friend for whom I cared more than for any mere romp; but as the minutes elapsed and the hubbub deepened curiosity got the better of affection, and I remembered that I was really within eye-shot of an affair the fame of which had ministered to the day-dreams of my infancy. I used to have a scrap-book with a coloured print of the starting of the bedizened wild horses, and the use of a library rich in keepsakes and annuals with a frontispiece commonly of a masked lady in a balcony, the heroine of a delightful tale further on. Agitated by these tender memories I descended into the street; but I confess I looked in vain for a masked lady who might serve as a frontispiece, in vain for any object whatever that might adorn a tale. Masked and muffled ladies there were in abundance; but their masks were of ugly wire, perfectly resembling the little covers placed upon strong cheese in German hotels, and their drapery was a shabby water-proof with the hood pulled over their chignons. They were armed with great tin scoops or funnels, with which they solemnly shovelled lime and flour out of bushel-baskets and down on the heads of the people in the street. They were packed into balconies all the way along the straight vista of the Corso, in which their calcareous shower maintained a dense, gritty, unpalatable fog. The crowd was compact in the street, and the Americans in it were tossing back confetti out of great satchels hung round their necks. It was quite the "you're another" sort of repartee, and less seasoned than I had hoped with the airy mockery tradition hangs about this festival. The scene was striking, in a word; but somehow not as I had dreamed of its being. I stood regardful, I suppose, but with a peculiarly tempting blankness of visage, for in a moment I received half a bushel of flour on my too-philosophic head. Decidedly it was an ignoble form of humour. I shook my ears like an emergent diver, and had a sudden vision of how still and sunny and solemn, how peculiarly and undisturbedly themselves, how secure from any intrusion less sympathetic than one's own, certain outlying parts of Rome must just then be. The Carnival had received its death-blow in my imagination; and it has been ever since but a thin and dusky ghost of pleasure that has flitted at intervals in and out of my consciousness.

I turned my back accordingly on the Corso and wandered away to the grass-grown quarters delightfully free even from the possibility of a fellow-countryman. And so having set myself an example I have been keeping Carnival by strolling perversely along the silent circumference of Rome. I have doubtless lost a great deal. The Princess Margaret has occupied a balcony opposite the open space which leads into Via Condotti and, I believe, like the discreet princess she is, has dealt in no missiles but bonbons, bouquets and white doves. I would have waited half an hour any day to see the Princess Margaret hold a dove on her forefinger; but I never chanced to notice any preparation for that effect. And yet do what you will you can't really elude the Carnival. As the days elapse it filters down into the manners of the common people, and before the week is over the very beggars at the church-doors seem to have gone to the expense of a domino. When you meet these specimens of dingy drollery capering about in dusky back-streets at all hours of the day and night, meet them flitting out of black doorways between the greasy groups that cluster about Roman thresholds, you feel that a love of "pranks," the more vivid the better, must from far back have been implanted in the Roman temperament with a strong hand. An unsophisticated American is wonderstruck at the number of persons, of every age and various conditions, whom it costs nothing in the nature of an ingenuous blush to walk up and down the streets in the costume of a theatrical supernumerary. Fathers of families do it at the head of an admiring progeniture; aunts and uncles and grandmothers do it; all the family does it, with varying splendour but with the same good conscience. "A pack of babies!" the doubtless too self-conscious alien pronounces it for its pains, and tries to imagine himself strutting along Broadway in a battered tin helmet and a pair of yellow tights. Our vices are certainly different; it takes those of the innocent sort to be so ridiculous. A self-consciousness lapsing so easily, in fine, strikes me as so near a relation to amenity, urbanity and general gracefulness that, for myself, I should be sorry to lay a tax on it, lest these other commodities should also cease to come to market.

I was rewarded, when I had turned away with my ears full of flour, by a glimpse of an intenser life than the dingy foolery of the Corso. I walked down by the back streets to the steps mounting to the Capitol—that long inclined plane, rather, broken at every two paces, which is the unfailing disappointment, I believe, of tourists primed for retrospective raptures. Certainly the Capitol seen from this side isn't commanding. The hill is so low, the ascent so narrow, Michael Angelo's architecture in the quadrangle at the top so meagre, the whole place somehow so much more of a mole-hill than a mountain, that for the first ten minutes of your standing there Roman history seems suddenly to have sunk through a trap-door. It emerges however on the other side, in the Forum; and here meanwhile, if you get no sense of the sublime, you get gradually a sense of exquisite composition. Nowhere in Rome is more colour, more charm, more sport for the eye. The mild incline, during the winter months, is always covered with lounging sun-seekers, and especially with those more constantly obvious members of the Roman population—beggars, soldiers, monks and tourists. The beggars and peasants lie kicking their heels along that grandest of loafing-places the great steps of the Ara Cœli. The dwarfish look of the Capitol is intensified, I think, by the neighbourhood of this huge blank staircase, mouldering away in disuse, the weeds thick in its crevices, and climbing to the rudely solemn façade of the church. The sunshine glares on this great unfinished wall only to light up its featureless despair, its expression of conscious, irremediable incompleteness. Sometimes, massing its rusty screen against the deep blue sky, with the little cross and the sculptured porch casting a clear-cut shadow on the bricks, it seems to have even more than a Roman desolation, it confusedly suggests Spain and Africa—lands with no latent *risorgimenti*, with absolutely nothing but a fatal past. The legendary wolf of Rome has lately been accommodated with a little artificial grotto, among the cacti and the palms, in the fantastic triangular garden squeezed between the steps of the church and the ascent to the Capitol, where she holds a perpetual levee and "draws" apparently as powerfully as the Pope himself. Above, in the piazzetta before the stuccoed palace which rises so jauntily on a basement of thrice its magnitude, are more loungers and knitters in the sun, seated round the massively inscribed base of the statue of Marcus Aurelius. Hawthorne has perfectly expressed the attitude of this admirable figure in saying that it extends its arm with "a command which is in itself a benediction." I doubt if any statue of king or captain in the public places of the world has more to commend it to the general heart. Irrecoverable simplicity—residing so in irrecoverable Style—has no sturdier representative. Here is an impression that the sculptors of the last three hundred years have been laboriously trying to reproduce; but contrasted with this mild old monarch their prancing horsemen suggest a succession of riding-masters taking out young ladies' schools. The admirably human character of the figure survives the rusty decomposition of the bronze and the slight "debasement" of the art; and one may call it singular that in the capital of Christendom the portrait most suggestive of a Christian conscience is that of a pagan emperor.

You recover in some degree your stifled hopes of sublimity as you pass beyond the palace and take your choice of either curving slope to descend into the Forum. Then you see that the little stuccoed edifice is but a modern excrescence on the mighty cliff of a primitive construction, whose great squares of porous tufa, as they underlie each other, seem to resolve themselves back into the colossal cohesion of unhewn rock. There are prodigious strangenesses in the union of this airy and comparatively fresh-faced superstructure and these deep-plunging, hoary foundations; and few things in Rome are more entertaining to the eye than to measure the long plumb-line which drops from the inhabited windows of the palace, with their little over-peeping balconies, their muslin curtains and their bird-cages, down to the rugged constructional work of the Republic. In the Forum proper the sublime is eclipsed again, though the late extension of the excavations gives a chance for it.

Nothing in Rome helps your fancy to a more vigorous backward flight than to lounge on a sunny day over the railing which guards the great central researches. It "says" more things to you than you can repeat to see the past, the ancient

Quirinal

world, as you stand there, bodily turned up with the spade and transformed from an immaterial, inaccessible fact of time into a matter of soils and surfaces. The pleasure is the same—in kind—as what you enjoy at Pompeii, and the pain the same. It wasn't here, however, that I found my compensation for forfeiting the spectacle on the Corso, but in a little church at the end of the narrow byway which diverges up the Palatine from just beside the Arch of Titus. This byway leads you between high walls, then takes a bend and introduces you to a long row of rusty, dusty little pictures of the stations of the cross. Beyond these stands a small church with a front so modest that you hardly recognise it till you see the leather curtain. I never see a leather curtain without lifting it; it is sure to cover a constituted *scene* of some sort—good, bad or indifferent. The scene this time was meagre—whitewash and tarnished candlesticks and mouldy muslin flowers being its principal features. I shouldn't have remained if I hadn't been struck with the attitude of the single worshipper—a young priest kneeling before one of the side-altars, who, as I entered, lifted his head and gave me a sidelong look so charged with the languor of devotion that he immediately became an object of interest. He was visiting each of the altars in turn and kissing the balustrade beneath them. He was alone in the church, and indeed in the whole region. There were no beggars even at the door; they were plying their trade on the skirts of the Carnival. In the entirely deserted place he alone knelt for religion, and as I sat respectfully by it seemed to me I could hear in the perfect silence the far-away uproar of the maskers. It was my late impression of these frivolous people, I suppose, joined with the extraordinary gravity of the young priest's face—his pious fatigue, his droning prayer and his isolation—that gave me just then and there a supreme vision of the religious passion, its privations and resignations and exhaustions and its terribly small share of amusement. He was young and strong and evidently of not too refined a fibre to enjoy the Carnival; but, planted there with his face pale with fasting and his knees stiff with praying, he seemed so stern a satire on it and on the crazy thousands who were preferring it to *his* way, that I half expected to see some heavenly portent out of a monastic legend come down and confirm his choice.

Yet I confess that though I wasn't enamoured of the Carnival myself his seemed a grim preference and this forswearing of the world a terrible game—a gaining one only if your zeal never falters; a hard fight when it does. In such an hour, to a stout young fellow like the hero of my anecdote, the smell of incense must seem horribly stale and the muslin flowers and gilt candlesticks to figure no great bribe. And it wouldn't have helped him much to think that not so very far away, just beyond the Forum, in the Corso, there was sport for the million, and for nothing. I doubt on the other hand whether my young priest had thought of this. He had made himself a temple out of the very elements of his innocence, and his prayers followed each other too fast for the tempter to slip in a whisper. And so, as I say, I found a solider fact of human nature than the love of *coriandoli*.

One of course never passes the Colosseum without paying it one's respects—without going in under one of the hundred portals and crossing the long oval and sitting down awhile, generally at the foot of the cross in the centre. I always feel, as I do so, as if I were seated in the depths of some Alpine valley. The upper portions of the side toward the Esquiline look as remote and lonely as an Alpine ridge, and you raise your eyes to their rugged sky-line, drinking in the sun and silvered by the blue air, with much the same feeling with which you would take in a grey cliff on which an eagle might lodge. This roughly mountainous quality of the great ruin is its chief interest; beauty of detail has pretty well vanished, especially since the high-growing wild-flowers have been plucked away by the new government, whose functionaries, surely, at certain points of their task, must have felt as if they shared the dreadful trade of those who gather samphire. Even if you are on your way to the Lateran you won't grudge the twenty minutes it will take you, on leaving the Colosseum, to turn away under the Arch of Constantine, whose noble battered bas-reliefs, with the chain of tragic statues—fettered, drooping barbarians—round its summit, I assume you to have profoundly admired, toward the piazzetta of the church of San Giovanni e Paolo, on the slope of Cælian. No spot in Rome can show a cluster of more charming accidents. The ancient brick apse of the church peeps down into the trees of

the little wooded walk before the neighbouring church of San
Gregorio, intensely venerable beneath its excessive modernisation; and a series of heavy brick buttresses, flying across to an
opposite wall, overarches the short, steep, paved passage
which leads into the small square. This is flanked on one side
by the long mediæval portico of the church of the two saints,
sustained by eight time-blackened columns of granite and
marble. On another rise the great scarce-windowed walls of a
Passionist convent, and on the third the portals of a grand
villa, whose tall porter, with his cockade and silver-topped
staff, standing sublime behind his grating, seems a kind of
mundane St. Peter, I suppose, to the beggars who sit at the
church door or lie in the sun along the farther slope which
leads to the gate of the convent. The place always seems to me
the perfection of an out-of-the-way corner—a place you
would think twice before telling people about, lest you should
find them there the next time you were to go. It is such a
group of objects, singly and in their happy combination, as
one must come to Rome to find at one's house door; but
what makes it peculiarly a picture is the beautiful dark red
campanile of the church, which stands embedded in the mass
of the convent. It begins, as so many things in Rome begin,
with a stout foundation of antique travertine, and rises high,
in delicately quaint mediæval brickwork—little tiers and apertures sustained on miniature columns and adorned with small
cracked slabs of green and yellow marble, inserted almost at
random. When there are three or four brown-breasted contadini sleeping in the sun before the convent doors, and a departing monk leading his shadow down over them, I think
you will not find anything in Rome more *sketchable*.

If you stop, however, to observe everything worthy of your
water-colours you will never reach St. John Lateran. My business was much less with the interior of that vast and empty,
that cold clean temple, which I have never found peculiarly
interesting, than with certain charming features of its surrounding precinct—the crooked old court beside it, which
admits you to the Baptistery and to a delightful rear-view of
the queer architectural odds and ends that may in Rome compose a florid ecclesiastical façade. There are more of these,
a stranger jumble of chance detail, of lurking recesses and

wanton projections and inexplicable windows, than I have memory or phrase for; but the gem of the collection is the oddly perched peaked turret, with its yellow travertine welded upon the rusty brickwork, which was not meant to be suspected, and the brickwork retreating beneath and leaving it in the odd position of a tower *under* which you may see the sky. As to the great front of the church overlooking the Porta San Giovanni, you are not admitted behind the scenes; the term is quite in keeping, for the architecture has a vastly theatrical air. It is extremely imposing—that of St. Peter's alone is more so; and when from far off on the Campagna you see the colossal images of the mitred saints along the top standing distinct against the sky, you forget their coarse construction and their inflated draperies. The view from the great space which stretches from the church steps to the city wall is the very prince of views. Just beside you, beyond the great alcove of mosaic, is the Scala Santa, the marble staircase which (says the legend) Christ descended under the weight of Pilate's judgment, and which all Christians must forever ascend on their knees; before you is the city gate which opens upon the Via Appia Nuova, the long gaunt file of arches of the Claudian aqueduct, their jagged ridge stretching away like the vertebral column of some monstrous mouldering skeleton, and upon the blooming brown and purple flats and dells of the Campagna and the glowing blue of the Alban Mountains, spotted with their white, high-nestling towns; while to your left is the great grassy space, lined with dwarfish mulberry-trees, which stretches across to the damp little sister-basilica of Santa Croce in Gerusalemme. During a former visit to Rome I lost my heart to this idle tract,* and wasted much time in sitting on the steps of the church and watching certain white-cowled friars who were sure to be passing there for the delight of my eyes. There are fewer friars now, and there are a great many of the king's recruits, who inhabit the ex-conventual barracks adjoining Santa Croce and are led forward to practise their goose-step on the sunny turf. Here too the poor old cardinals who are no longer to be seen on the Pincio descend from their mourning-coaches and relax their venerable knees. These

*Utterly overbuilt and gone—1909.

members alone still testify to the traditional splendour of the princes of the Church; for as they advance the lifted black petticoat reveals a flash of scarlet stockings and makes you groan at the victory of civilisation over colour.

If St. John Lateran disappoints you internally, you have an easy compensation in pacing the long lane which connects it with Santa Maria Maggiore and entering the singularly perfect nave of that most delightful of churches. The first day of my stay in Rome under the old dispensation I spent in wandering at random through the city, with accident for my *valet-de-place*. It served me to perfection and introduced me to the best things; among others to an immediate happy relation with Santa Maria Maggiore. First impressions, memorable impressions, are generally irrecoverable; they often leave one the wiser, but they rarely return in the same form. I remember, of my coming uninformed and unprepared into the place of worship and of curiosity that I have named, only that I sat for half an hour on the edge of the base of one of the marble columns of the beautiful nave and enjoyed a perfect revel of—what shall I call it?—taste, intelligence, fancy, perceptive emotion? The place proved so endlessly suggestive that perception became a throbbing confusion of images, and I departed with a sense of knowing a good deal that is not set down in Murray. I have seated myself more than once again at the base of the same column; but you live your life only once, the parts as well as the whole. The obvious charm of the church is the elegant grandeur of the nave—its perfect shapeliness and its rich simplicity, its long double row of white marble columns and its high flat roof, embossed with intricate gildings and mouldings. It opens into a choir of an extraordinary splendour of effect, which I recommend you to look out for of a fine afternoon. At such a time the glowing western light, entering the high windows of the tribune, kindles the scattered masses of colour into sombre brightness, scintillates on the great solemn mosaic of the vault, touches the porphyry columns of the superb baldachino with ruby lights, and buries its shining shafts in the deep-toned shadows that hang about frescoes and sculptures and mouldings. The deeper charm even than in such things, however, is the social or historic note or tone or atmosphere of the church—I fumble, you see, for my right expression; the sense it gives you, in common with most of the Roman churches, and more than any of them, of having been prayed in for several centuries by an endlessly curious and complex society. It takes no great attention to let it come to you that the authority of Italian Catholicism has lapsed not a little in these days; not less also perhaps than to feel that, as they stand, these deserted temples were the fruit of a society leavened through and through by ecclesiastical manners, and that they formed for ages the constant background of the human drama. They are, as one may say, the *churchiest* churches in Europe--the fullest of gathered memories, of the experience of their office. There's not a figure one has read of in old-world annals that isn't to be imagined on proper occasion kneeling before the lamp-decked Confession beneath the altar of Santa Maria Maggiore. One sees after all, however, even among the most palpable realities, very much what the play of one's imagination projects there; and I present my remarks simply as a reminder that one's constant excursions into these places are not the least interesting episodes of one's walks in Rome.

I had meant to give a simple illustration of the church-habit, so to speak, but I have given it at such a length as leaves scant space to touch on the innumerable topics brushed by the pen that begins to take Roman notes. It is by the aimless *flânerie* which leaves you free to follow capriciously every hint of entertainment that you get to know Rome. The greater part of the life about you goes on in the streets; and for an observer fresh from a country in which town scenery is at the least monotonous incident and character and picture seem to abound. I become conscious with compunction, let me hasten to add, that I have launched myself thus on the subject of Roman churches and Roman walks without so much as a preliminary allusion to St. Peter's. One is apt to proceed thither on rainy days with intentions of exercise—to put the case only at that—and to carry these out body and mind. Taken as a walk not less than as a church, St. Peter's of course reigns alone. Even for the profane "constitutional" it serves where the Boulevards, where Piccadilly and Broadway, fall short, and if it didn't offer to our use the grandest area in the world it would still offer the most diverting. Few great

works of art last longer to the curiosity, to the perpetually
transcended attention. You think you have taken the whole
thing in, but it expands, it rises sublime again, and leaves your
measure itself poor. You never let the ponderous leather curtain bang down behind you—your weak lift of a scant edge
of whose padded vastness resembles the liberty taken in fold-
ing back the parchment corner of some mighty folio page—
without feeling all former visits to have been but missed
attempts at apprehension and the actual to achieve your first
real possession. The conventional question is ever as to
whether one hasn't been "disappointed in the size," but a few
honest folk here and there, I hope, will never cease to say no.
The place struck me from the first as the hugest thing conceivable—a real exaltation of one's idea of space; so that one's
entrance, even from the great empty square which either
glares beneath the deep blue sky or makes of the cool far-cast
shadow of the immense front something that resembles a big
slate-coloured country on a map, seems not so much a going
in somewhere as a going out. The mere man of pleasure in
quest of new sensations might well not know where to better
his encounter there of the sublime shock that brings him,
within the threshold, to an immediate gasping pause. There
are days when the vast nave looks mysteriously vaster than on
others and the gorgeous baldachino a longer journey beyond
the far-spreading tessellated plain of the pavement, and when
the light has yet a quality which lets things loom their largest,
while the scattered figures—I mean the human, for there are
plenty of others—mark happily the scale of items and parts.
Then you have only to stroll and stroll and gaze and gaze; to
watch the glorious altar-canopy lift its bronze architecture, its
colossal embroidered contortions, like a temple within a temple, and feel yourself, at the bottom of the abysmal shaft of
the dome, dwindle to a crawling dot.

  Much of the constituted beauty resides in the fact that it is
all general beauty, that you are appealed to by no specific details, or that these at least, practically never importunate, are
as taken for granted as the lieutenants and captains are taken
for granted in a great standing army—among whom indeed
individual aspects may figure here the rather shifting range of
decorative dignity in which details, when observed, often

Ponte San Angelo, Rome

prove poor (though never not massive and substantially precious) and sometimes prove ridiculous. The sculptures, with the sole exception of Michael Angelo's ineffable "Pièta," which lurks obscurely in a side-chapel—this indeed to my sense the rarest artistic *combination* of the greatest things the hand of man has produced—are either bad or indifferent; and the universal incrustation of marble, though sumptuous enough, has a less brilliant effect than much later work of the same sort, that for instance of St. Paul's without the Walls. The supreme beauty is the splendidly sustained simplicity of the whole. The thing represents a prodigious imagination extraordinarily strained, yet strained, at its happiest pitch, without breaking. Its happiest pitch I say, because this is the only creation of its strenuous author in presence of which you are in presence of serenity. You may invoke the idea of ease at St. Peter's without a sense of sacrilege—which you can hardly do, if you are at all spiritually nervous, in Westminster Abbey or Notre Dame. The vast enclosed clearness has much to do with the idea. There are no shadows to speak of, no marked effects of shade; only effects of light innumerable—points at which this element seems to mass itself in airy density and scatter itself in enchanting gradations and cadences. It performs the office of gloom or of mystery in Gothic churches; hangs like a rolling mist along the gilded vault of the nave, melts into bright interfusion the mosaic scintillations of the dome, clings and clusters and lingers, animates the whole huge and otherwise empty shell. A good Catholic, I suppose, is the same Catholic anywhere, before the grandest as well as the humblest altars; but to a visitor not formally enrolled St. Peter's speaks less of aspiration than of full and convenient assurance. The soul infinitely expands there, if one will, but all on its quite human level. It marvels at the reach of our dream and the immensity of our resources. To be so impressed and put in our place, we say, is to be sufficiently "saved"; we can't be more than that in heaven itself; and what specifically celestial beauty such a show or such a substitute may lack it makes up for in certainty and tangibility. And yet if one's hours on the scene are not actually spent in praying, the spirit seeks it again as for the finer comfort, for the blessing, exactly, of its example, its protection and its exclusion. When you are weary

of the swarming democracy of your fellow-tourists, of the unremunerative aspects of human nature on Corso and Pincio,
of the oppressively frequent combination of coronets on carriage panels and stupid faces in carriages, of addled brains and
lacquered boots, of ruin and dirt and decay, of priests and
beggars and takers of advantage, of the myriad tokens of a
halting civilisation, the image of the great temple depresses
the balance of your doubts, seems to rise above even the highest tide of vulgarity and make you still believe in the heroic
will and the heroic act. It's a relief, in other words, to feel
that there's nothing but a cab-fare between your pessimism
and one of the greatest of human achievements.

This might serve as a Lenten peroration to these remarks of
mine which have strayed so woefully from their jovial text,
save that I ought fairly to confess that my last impression of
the Carnival was altogether Carnivalesque. The merry-making
of Shrove Tuesday had life and felicity; the dead letter of tradition broke out into nature and grace. I pocketed my scepticism and spent a long afternoon on the Corso. Almost every
one was a masker, but you had no need to conform; the pelting rain of confetti effectually disguised you. I can't say I
found it all very exhilarating; but here and there I noticed a
brighter episode—a capering clown inflamed with contagious
jollity, some finer humourist forming a circle every thirty
yards to crow at his indefatigable sallies. One clever performer
so especially pleased me that I should have been glad to catch
a glimpse of the natural man. You imagined for him that he
was taking a prodigious intellectual holiday and that his gaiety was in inverse ratio to his daily mood. Dressed as a needy
scholar, in an ancient evening-coat and with a rusty black hat
and gloves fantastically patched, he carried a little volume
carefully under his arm. His humours were in excellent taste,
his whole manner the perfection of genteel comedy. The
crowd seemed to relish him vastly, and he at once com-
manded a gleefully attentive audience. Many of his sallies I
lost; those I caught were excellent. His trick was often to begin by taking some one urbanely and caressingly by the chin
and complimenting him on the *intelligenza della sua fisionomia*. I kept near him as long as I could; for he struck me as
a real ironic artist, cherishing a disinterested, and yet at the

same time a motived and a moral, passion for the grotesque. I should have liked, however—if indeed I shouldn't have feared—to see him the next morning, or when he unmasked that night over his hard-earned supper in a smoky *trattoria*. As the evening went on the cloud thickened and became a motley press of shouting, pushing, scrambling, everything but squabbling, revellers. The rain of missiles ceased at dusk, but the universal deposit of chalk and flour was trampled into a cloud made lurid by flaring pyramids of the gas-lamps that replaced for the occasion the stingy Roman luminaries. Early in the evening came off the classic exhibition of the *moccoletti*, which I but half saw, like a languid reporter resigned beforehand to be cashiered for want of enterprise. From the mouth of a side-street, over a thousand heads, I caught a huge slow-moving illuminated car, from which blue-lights and rockets and Roman candles were in course of discharge, meeting all in a dim fuliginous glare far above the house-tops. It was like a glimpse of some public orgy in ancient Babylon. In the small hours of the morning, walking homeward from a private entertainment, I found Ash-Wednesday still kept at bay. The Corso, flaring with light, smelt like a circus. Every one was taking friendly liberties with every one else and using up the dregs of his festive energy in convulsive hootings and gymnastics. Here and there certain indefatigable spirits, clad all in red after the manner of devils and leaping furiously about with torches, were supposed to affright you. But they shared the universal geniality and bequeathed me no midnight fears as a pretext for keeping Lent, the *carnevale dei preti*, as I read in that profanely radical sheet the *Capitale*. Of this too I have been having glimpses. Going lately into Santa Francesca Romana, the picturesque church near the Temple of Peace, I found a feast for the eyes—a dim crimson-toned light through curtained windows, a great festoon of tapers round the altar, a bulging girdle of lamps before the sunken shrine beneath, and a dozen white-robed Dominicans scattered in the happiest composition on the pavement. It was better than the *moccoletti*.

1873.

Roman Rides

I SHALL always remember the first I took: out of the Porta del Popolo, to where the Ponte Molle, whose single arch sustains a weight of historic tradition, compels the sallow Tiber to flow between its four great-mannered ecclesiastical statues, over the crest of the hill and along the old posting-road to Florence. It was mild midwinter, the season peculiarly of colour on the Roman Campagna; and the light was full of that mellow purple glow, that tempered intensity, which haunts the after-visions of those who have known Rome like the memory of some supremely irresponsible pleasure. An hour away I pulled up and at the edge of a meadow gazed away for some time into remoter distances. Then and there, it seemed to me, I measured the deep delight of knowing the Campagna. But I saw more things in it than I can easily tell. The country rolled away around me into slopes and dells of long-drawn grace, chequered with purple and blue and blooming brown. The lights and shadows were at play on the Sabine Mountains—an alternation of tones so exquisite as to be conveyed only by some fantastic comparison to sapphire and amber. In the foreground a contadino in his cloak and peaked hat jogged solitary on his ass; and here and there in the distance, among blue undulations, some white village, some gray tower, helped deliciously to make the picture the typical "Italian landscape" of old-fashioned art. It was so bright and yet so sad, so still and yet so charged, to the super-sensuous ear, with the murmur of an extinguished life, that you could only say it was intensely and adorably strange, could only impute to the whole overarched scene an unsur-passed secret for bringing tears of appreciation to no matter how ignorant—archeologically ignorant—eyes. To ride once, in these conditions, is of course to ride again and to allot to the Campagna a generous share of the time one spends in Rome.

It is a pleasure that doubles one's horizon, and one can scarcely say whether it enlarges or limits one's impression of the city proper. It certainly makes St. Peter's seem a trifle smaller and blunts the edge of one's curiosity in the Forum. It must be the effect of the experience, at all extended, that when you think of Rome afterwards you will think still respectfully and regretfully enough of the Vatican and the Pincio, the streets and the picture-making street life; but will even more wonder, with an irrepressible contraction of the heart, when again you shall feel yourself bounding over the flower-smothered turf, or pass from one framed picture to another beside the open arches of the crumbling aqueducts. You look back at the City so often from some grassy hill-top—hugely compact within its walls, with St. Peter's over-topping all things and yet seeming small, and the vast girdle of marsh and meadow receding on all sides to the mountains and the sea—that you come to remember it at last as hardly more than a respectable parenthesis in a great sweep of gen-eralisation. Within the walls, on the other hand, you think of your intended ride as the most romantic of all your possi-bilities; of the Campagna generally as an illimitable experi-ence. One's rides certainly give Rome an inordinate scope for the reflective—by which I suppose I mean after all the æsthetic and the "esoteric"—life. To dwell in a city which, much as you grumble at it, is after all very fairly a modern city; with crowds and shops and theatres and cafés and balls and receptions and dinner-parties and all the modern confu-sion of social pleasures and pains; to have at your door the good and evil of it all; and yet to be able in half an hour to gallop away and leave it a hundred miles, a hundred years, behind, and to look at the tufted broom glowing on a lonely tower-top in the still blue air, and the pale pink asphodels trembling none the less for the stillness, and the shaggy-legged shepherds leaning on their sticks in motionless broth-erhood with the heaps of ruin, and the scrambling goats and staggering little kids treading out wild desert smells from the top of hollow-sounding mounds; and then to come back through one of the great gates and a couple of hours later find yourself in the "world," dressed, introduced, enter-tained, inquiring, talking about "Middlemarch" to a young English lady or listening to Neapolitan songs from a gentle-man in a very low-cut shirt—all this is to lead in a manner a double life and to gather from the hurrying hours more impressions than a mind of modest capacity quite knows how to dispose of.

I touched lately upon this theme with a friend who, I fancied, would understand me, and who immediately assured me that he had just spent a day that this mingled diversity of sensation made to the days one spends elsewhere what an uncommonly good novel may be to the daily paper. "There was an air of idleness about it, if you will," he said, "and it was certainly pleasant enough to have been wrong. Perhaps, being after all unused to long stretches of dissipation, this was why I had a half-feeling that I was reading an odd chapter in the history of a person very much more of a *héros de roman* than myself." Then he proceeded to relate how he had taken a long ride with a lady whom he extremely admired. "We turned off from the Tor di Quinto Road to that castellated farm-house you know of—once a Ghibelline fortress—whither Claude Lorraine used to come to paint pictures of which the surrounding landscape is still so artistically, so compositionally, suggestive. We went into the inner court, a cloister almost, with the carven capitals of its loggia columns, and looked at a handsome child swinging shyly against the half-opened door of a room whose impenetrable shadow, behind her, made her, as it were, a sketch in bituminous water-colours. We talked with the farmer, a handsome, pale, fever-tainted fellow with a well-to-do air that didn't in the least deter his affability from a turn compatible with the acceptance of small coin; and then we galloped away and away over the meadows which stretch with hardly a break to Veii. The day was strangely delicious, with a cool grey sky and just a touch of moisture in the air stirred by our rapid motion. The Campagna, in the colourless even light, was more solemn and romantic than ever; and a ragged shepherd, driving a meagre straggling flock, whom we stopped to ask our way of, was a perfect type of pastoral, weather-beaten misery. He was precisely the shepherd for the foreground of a scratchy etching. There were faint odours of spring in the air, and the grass here and there was streaked with great patches of daisies; but it was spring with a foreknowledge of autumn, a day to be enjoyed with a substrain of sadness, the foreboding of regret, a day somehow to make one feel as if one had seen and felt a great deal—quite, as I say, like a *héros de roman*. Touching such characters, it was the illustrious Pelham, I think, who, on being asked if he rode, replied that he left those violent exercises to the ladies. But under such a sky, in such an air, over acres of daisied turf, a long, long gallop is certainly a supersubtle joy. The elastic bound of your horse is the poetry of motion; and if you are so happy as to add to it not the prose of companionship riding comes almost to affect you as a spiritual exercise. My gallop, at any rate," said my friend, "threw me into a mood which gave an extraordinary zest to the rest of the day." He was to go to a dinner-party at a villa on the edge of Rome, and Madame X——, who was also going, called for him in her carriage. "It was a long drive," he went on, "through the Forum, past the Colosseum. She told me a long story about a most interesting person. Toward the end my eyes caught through the carriage window a slab of rugged sculptures. We were passing under the Arch of Constantine. In the hall pavement of the villa is a rare antique mosaic—one of the largest and most perfect; the ladies on their way to the drawing-room trail over it the flounces of Worth. We drove home late, and there's my day."

On your exit from most of the gates of Rome you have generally half-an-hour's progress through winding lanes, many of which are hardly less charming than the open meadows. On foot the walls and high hedges would vex you and spoil your walk; but in the saddle you generally overtop them, to an endless peopling of the minor vision. Yet a Roman wall in the springtime is for that matter almost as interesting as anything it conceals. Crumbling grain by grain, coloured and mottled to a hundred tones by sun and storm, with its rugged structure of brick extruding through its coarse complexion of peeling stucco, its creeping lacework of wandering ivy starred with miniature violets, and its wild fringe of stouter flowers against the sky—it is as little as possible a blank partition; it is practically a luxury of landscape. At the moment at which I write, in mid-April, all the ledges and cornices are wreathed with flaming poppies, nodding there as if they knew so well what faded greys and yellows are an offset to their scarlet. But the best point in a dilapidated enclosing surface of vineyard or villa is of course the gateway, lifting

Villa Doria

its great arch of cheap rococo scroll-work, its balls and shields and mossy dish-covers—as they always perversely figure to me—and flanked with its dusky cypresses. I never pass one without taking out my mental sketch-book and jotting it down as a vignette in the insubstantial record of my ride. They are as sad and dreary as if they led to the moated grange where Mariana waited in desperation for something to happen; and it's easy to take the usual inscription over the porch as a recommendation to those who enter to renounce all hope of anything but a glass of more or less agreeably acrid *vino romano*. For what you chiefly see over the walls and at the end of the straight short avenue of rusty cypresses are the appurtenances of a *vigna*—a couple of acres of little upright sticks blackening in the sun, and a vast sallow-faced, scantily windowed mansion, whose expression denotes little of the life of the mind beyond what goes to the driving of a hard bargain over the tasted hogsheads. If Mariana is there she certainly has no pile of old magazines to beguile her leisure. The life of the mind, if the term be in any application here not ridiculous, appears to any asker of curious questions, as he wanders about Rome, the very thinnest deposit of the past. Within the rococo gateway, which itself has a vaguely æsthetic self-consciousness, at the end of the cypress walk, you will probably see a mythological group in rusty marble—a Cupid and Psyche, a Venus and Paris, an Apollo and Daphne—the relic of an age when a Roman proprietor thought it fine to patronise the arts. But I imagine you are safe in supposing it to constitute the only allusion savouring of culture that has been made on the premises for three or four generations.

There is a franker cheerfulness—though certainly a proper amount of that forlornness which lurks about every object to which the Campagna forms a background—in the primitive little taverns where, on the homeward stretch, in the waning light, you are often glad to rein up and demand a bottle of their best. Their best and their worst are indeed the same, though with a shifting price, and plain *vino bianco* or *vino rosso* (rarely both) is the sole article of refreshment in which they deal. There is a ragged bush over the door, and within, under a dusky vault, on crooked cobble-stones, sit half-a-dozen contadini in their indigo jackets and goatskin breeches and with their elbows on the table. There is generally a rabble of infantile beggars at the door, pretty enough in their dusty rags, with their fine eyes and intense Italian smile, to make you forget your private vow of doing your individual best to make these people, whom you like so much, unlearn their old vices. Was Porta Pia bombarded three years ago that Peppino should still grow up to whine for a copper? But the Italian shells had no direct message for Peppino's stomach—and you are going to a dinner-party at a villa. So Peppino "points" an instant for the copper in the dust and grows up a Roman beggar. The whole little place represents the most primitive form of hostelry; but along any of the roads leading out of the city you may find establishments of a higher type, with Garibaldi, superbly mounted and foreshortened, painted on the wall, or a lady in a low-necked dress opening a fictive lattice with irresistible hospitality, and a yard with the classic vine-wreathed arbour casting thin shadows upon benches and tables draped and cushioned with the white dust from which the highways from the gates borrow most of their local colour. None the less, I say, you avoid the highroads, and, if you are a person of taste, don't grumble at the occasional need of following the walls of the city. City walls, to a properly constituted American, can never be an object of indifference; and it is emphatically "no end of a sensation" to pace in the shadow of this massive cincture of Rome. I have found myself, as I skirted its base, talking of trivial things, but never without a sudden reflection on the deplorable impermanence of first impressions. A twelvemonth ago the raw plank fences of a Boston suburb, inscribed with the virtues of healing drugs, bristled along my horizon: now I glance with idle eyes at a compacted antiquity in which a more learned sense may read portentous dates and signs—Servius, Aurelius, Honorius. But even to idle eyes the prodigious, the continuous thing bristles with eloquent passages. In some places, where the huge brickwork is black with time and certain strange square towers look down at you with still blue eyes, the Roman sky peering through lidless loopholes, and there is nothing but white dust in the road and solitude in the air, I might take myself for a wandering Tartar touching on the confines of the Celestial Empire. The wall of China must have very much such a gaunt robustness. The colour of the Roman ramparts is everywhere fine, and their rugged patchwork has been subdued by time and weather into a mellow harmony that the brush only asks to catch up. On the northern side of the city, behind the Vatican, St. Peter's and the Trastevere, I have seen them glowing in the late afternoon with the tones of ancient bronze and rusty gold. Here at various points they are embossed with the Papal insignia, the tiara with its flying bands and crossed keys; to the high style of which the grace that attaches to almost any lost cause—even if not quite the "tender" grace of a day that is dead—considerably adds a style. With the dome of St. Peter's resting on their cornice and the hugely clustered architecture of the Vatican rising from them as from a terrace, they seem indeed the valid bulwark of an ecclesiastical city. Vain bulwark, alas! sighs the sentimental tourist, fresh from the meagre entertainment of this latter Holy Week. But he may find monumental consolation in this neighbourhood at a source where, as I pass, I never fail to apply for it. At half-an-hour's walk beyond Porta San Pancrazio, beneath the wall of the Villa Doria, is a delightfully pompous ecclesiastical gateway of the seventeenth century, erected by Paul V. to commemorate his restoration of the aqueducts through which the stream bearing his name flows towards the fine florid portico protecting its clear-sheeted outgush on the crest of the Janiculan. It arches across the road in the most ornamental manner of the period, and one can hardly pause before it without seeming to assist at a ten minutes' revival of old Italy—without feeling as if one were in a cocked hat and sword and were coming up to Rome, in another mood than Luther's, with a letter of recommendation to the mistress of a cardinal.

The Campagna differs greatly on the two sides of the Tiber; and it is hard to say which, for the rider, has the greater charm. The half-dozen rides you may take from Porta San Giovanni possess the perfection of traditional Roman interest and lead you through a far-strewn wilderness of ruins—a scattered maze of tombs and towers and nameless fragments of antique masonry. The landscape here has two great features; close before you on one side is the long, gentle swell of the Alban Hills, deeply, fantastically blue in most weathers, and marbled with the vague white masses of their

Ponte Molle, Rome

scattered towns and villas. It would be difficult to draw the hard figure to a softer curve than that with which the heights sweep from Albano to the plain; this a perfect example of the classic beauty of line in the Italian landscape—that beauty which, when it fills the background of a picture, makes us look in the foreground for a broken column couched upon flowers and a shepherd piping to dancing nymphs. At your side, constantly, you have the broken line of the Claudian Aqueduct, carrying its broad arches far away into the plain. The meadows along which it lies are not the smoothest in the world for a gallop, but there is no pleasure greater than to wander near it. It stands knee-deep in the flower-strewn grass, and its rugged piers are hung with ivy as the columns of a church are draped for a festa. Every archway is a picture, massively framed, of the distance beyond—of the snow-tipped Sabines and lonely Soracte. As the spring advances the whole Campagna smiles and waves with flowers; but I think they are nowhere more rank and lovely than in the shifting shadow of the aqueducts, where they muffle the feet of the columns and smother the half-dozen brooks which wander in and out like silver meshes between the legs of a file of giants. They make a niche for themselves too in every crevice and tremble on the vault of the empty conduits. The ivy hereabouts in the spring-time is peculiarly brilliant and delicate; and though it cloaks and muffles these Roman fragments far less closely than the castles and abbeys of England it hangs with the light elegance of all Italian vegetation. It is partly doubtless because their mighty outlines are still unsoftened that the aqueducts are so impressive. They seem the very source of the solitude in which they stand; they look like architectural spectres and loom through the light mists of their grassy desert, as you recede along the line, with the same insubstantial vastness as if they rose out of Egyptian sands. It is a great neighbourhood of ruins, many of which, it must be confessed, you have applauded in many an album. But station a peasant with sheepskin coat and bandaged legs in the shadow of a tomb or tower best known to drawing-room art, and scatter a dozen goats on the mound above him, and the picture has a charm which has not yet been sketched away.

The other quarter of the Campagna has wider fields and

smoother turf and perhaps a greater number of delightful rides; the earth is sounder, and there are fewer pitfalls and ditches. The land for the most part lies higher and catches more wind, and the grass is here and there for great stretches as smooth and level as a carpet. You have no Alban Mountains before you, but you have in the distance the waving ridge of the nearer Apennines, and west of them, along the course of the Tiber, the long seaward level of deep-coloured fields, deepening as they recede to the blue and purple of the sea itself. Beyond them, of a very clear day, you may see the glitter of the Mediterranean. These are the occasions perhaps to remember most fondly, for they lead you to enchanting nooks, and the landscape has details of the highest refinement. Indeed when my sense reverts to the lingering impressions of so blest a time, it seems a fool's errand to have attempted to express them, and a waste of words to do more than recommend the reader to go citywards at twilight of the end of March, making for Porta Cavalleggieri, and note what he sees. At this hour the Campagna is to the last point its melancholy self, and I remember roadside "effects" of a strange and intense suggestiveness. Certain mean, mouldering villas behind grass-grown courts have an indefinably sinister look; there was one in especial of which it was impossible not to argue that a despairing creature must have once committed suicide there, behind bolted door and barred window, and that no one has since had the pluck to go in and see why he never came out. Every wayside mark of manners, of history, every stamp of the past in the country about Rome, touches my sense to a thrill, and I may thus exaggerate the appeal of very common things. This is the more likely because the appeal seems ever to rise out of heaven knows what depths of ancient trouble. To delight in the aspects of *sentient* ruin might appear a heartless pastime, and the pleasure, I confess, shows the note of perversity. The sombre and the hard are as common an influence from southern things as the soft and the bright, I think; sadness rarely fails to assault a northern observer when he misses what he takes for comfort. Beauty is no compensation for the loss, only making it more poignant. Enough beauty of climate hangs over these Roman cottages and farmhouses—beauty of light, of atmosphere and of vegetation;

but their charm for the maker-out of the stories in things is the way the golden air shows off their desolation. Man lives more with Nature in Italy than in New or than in Old England; she does more work for him and gives him more holidays than in our short-summered climes, and his home is therefore much more bare of devices for helping him to do without her, forget her and forgive her. These reflections are perhaps the source of the character you find in a moss-coated stone stairway climbing outside of a wall; in a queer inner court, befouled with rubbish and drearily bare of convenience; in an ancient quaintly carven well, worked with infinite labour from an overhanging window; in an arbour of time-twisted vines under which you may sit with your feet in the dirt and remember as a dim fable that there are races for which the type of domestic allurement is the parlour hearthrug. For reasons apparent or otherwise these things amuse me beyond expression, and I am never weary of staring into gateways, of lingering by dreary, shabby, half-barbaric farm-yards, of feasting a foolish gaze on sun-cracked plaster and unctuous indoor shadows.

I mustn't forget, however, that it's not for wayside effects that one rides away behind St. Peter's, but for the strong sense of wandering over boundless space, of seeing great classic lines of landscape, of watching them dispose themselves into pictures so full of "style" that you can think of no painter who deserves to have you admit that they suggest him— hardly knowing whether it is better pleasure to gallop far and drink deep of air and grassy distance and the whole delicious opportunity, or to walk and pause and linger, and try and grasp some ineffaceable memory of sky and colour and outline. Your pace can hardly help falling into a contemplative measure at the time, everywhere so wonderful, but in Rome so persuasively divine, when the winter begins palpably to soften and quicken. Far out on the Campagna, early in February, you feel the first vague earthly emanations, which in a few weeks come wandering into the heart of the city and throbbing through the close, dark streets. Springtime in Rome is an immensely poetic affair; but you must stand often far out in the ancient waste, between grass and sky, to measure its deep, full, steadily accelerated rhythm. The winter has

an incontestable beauty, and is pre-eminently the time of colour—the time when it is no affectation, but homely verity,
to talk about the "purple" tone of the atmosphere. As February comes and goes your purple is streaked with green and
the rich, dark bloom of the distance begins to lose its intensity. But your loss is made up by other gains; none more
precious than that inestimable gain to the ear—the disem-
bodied voice of the lark. It comes with the early flowers, the
white narcissus and the cyclamen, the half-buried violets and
the pale anemones, and makes the whole atmosphere ring like
a vault of tinkling glass. You never see the source of the
sound, and are utterly unable to localise his note, which seems
to come from everywhere at once, to be some hundred-
throated voice of the air. Sometimes you fancy you just catch
him, a mere vague spot against the blue, an intenser throb in
the universal pulsation of light. As the weeks go on the flowers multiply and the deep blues and purples of the hills, turning to azure and violet, creep higher toward the narrowing
snow-line of the Sabines. The temperature rises, the first hour
of your ride you feel the heat, but you beguile it with brushing the hawthorn-blossoms as you pass along the hedges, and
catching at the wild rose and honeysuckle; and when you get
into the meadows there is stir enough in the air to lighten the
dead weight of the sun. The Roman air, however, is not a
tonic medicine, and it seldom suffers exercise to be all exhilarating. It has always seemed to me indeed part of the charm
of the latter that your keenest consciousness is haunted with a
vague languor. Occasionally when the sirocco blows that sensation becomes strange and exquisite. Then, under the grey
sky, before the dim distances which the south-wind mostly
brings with it, you seem to ride forth into a world from
which all hope has departed and in which, in spite of the
flowers that make your horse's footfalls soundless, nothing is
left save some queer probability that your imagination is unable to measure, but from which it hardly shrinks. This quality in the Roman element may now and then "relax" you
almost to ecstasy; but a season of sirocco would be an overdose of morbid pleasure. You may at any rate best feel the
peculiar beauty of the Campagna on those mild days of winter when the mere quality and temper of the sunshine suffice

to move the landscape to joy, and you pause on the brown grass in the sunny stillness and, by listening long enough, almost fancy you hear the shrill of the midsummer cricket. It is detail and ornament that vary from month to month, from week to week even, and make your returns to the same places a constant feast of unexpectedness; but the great essential features of the prospect preserve throughout the year the same impressive serenity. Soracte, be it January or May, rises from its blue horizon like an island from the sea and with an elegance of contour which no mood of the year can deepen or diminish. You know it well; you have seen it often in the mellow backgrounds of Claude; and it has such an irresistibly classic, academic air that while you look at it you begin to take your saddle for a faded old arm-chair in a palace gallery. A month's rides in different directions will show you a dozen prime Claudes. After I had seen them all I went piously to the Doria gallery to refresh my memory of its two famous specimens and to enjoy to the utmost their delightful air of reference to something that had become a part of my personal experience. Delightful it certainly is to feel the common element in one's own sensibility and those of a genius whom that element has helped to do great things. Claude must have haunted the very places of one's personal preference and adjusted their divine undulations to his splendid scheme of romance, his view of the poetry of life. He was familiar with aspects in which there wasn't a single uncompromising line. I saw a few days ago a small finished sketch from his hand, in the possession of an American artist, which was almost startling in its clear reflection of forms unaltered by the two centuries that have dimmed and cracked the paint and canvas.

This unbroken continuity of the impressions I have tried to indicate is an excellent example of the intellectual background of all enjoyment in Rome. It effectually prevents pleasure from becoming vulgar, for your sensation rarely begins and ends with itself; it reverberates—it recalls, commemorates, resuscitates something else. At least half the merit of everything you enjoy must be that it suits you absolutely; but the larger half here is generally that it has suited some one else and that you can never flatter yourself you have discovered it. It has been addressed to some use a million miles out of your range, and has had great adventures before ever condescending to please you. It was in admission of this truth that my discriminating friend who showed me the Claudes found it impossible to designate a certain delightful region which you enter at the end of an hour's riding from Porta Cavalleggieri as anything but Arcadia. The exquisite correspondence of the term in this case altogether revived its faded bloom; here veritably the oaten pipe must have stirred the windless air and the satyrs have laughed among the brookside reeds. Three or four long grassy dells stretch away in a chain between low hills over which delicate trees are so discreetly scattered that each one is a resting place for a shepherd. The elements of the scene are simple enough, but the composition has extraordinary refinement. By one of those happy chances which keep observation in Italy always in her best humour a shepherd had thrown himself down under one of the trees in the very attitude of Melibœus. He had been washing his feet, I suppose, in the neighbouring brook, and had found it pleasant afterwards to roll his short breeches well up on his thighs. Lying thus in the shade, on his elbow, with his naked legs stretched out on the turf and his soft peaked hat over his long hair crushed back like the veritable bonnet of Arcady, he was exactly the figure of the background of this happy valley. The poor fellow, lying there in rustic weariness and ignorance, little fancied that he was a symbol of old-world meanings to new-world eyes.

Such eyes may find as great a store of picturesque meanings in the cork-woods of Monte Mario, tenderly loved of all equestrians. These are less severely pastoral than our Arcadia, and you might more properly lodge there a damosel of Ariosto than a nymph of Theocritus. Among them is strewn a lovely wilderness of flowers and shrubs, and the whole place has such a charming woodland air, that, casting about me the other day for a compliment, I declared that it reminded me of New Hampshire. My compliment had a double edge, and I had no sooner uttered it than I smiled—or sighed—to perceive in all the undiscriminated botany about me the wealth of detail, the idle elegance and grace of Italy alone, the natural stamp of the land which has the singular privilege of making one love her unsanctified beauty all but as well as those features of one's own country toward which nature's small allowance doubles that of one's own affection. For this effect of casting a spell no rides have more value than those you take in Villa Doria or Villa Borghese; or don't take, possibly, if you prefer to reserve these particular regions—the latter in especial—for your walking hours. People do ride, however, in both villas, which deserve honourable mention in this regard. Villa Doria, with its noble site, its splendid views, its great groups of stone-pines, so clustered and yet so individual, its lawns and flowers and fountains, its altogether princely disposition, is a place where one may pace, well mounted, of a brilliant day, with an agreeable sense of its being rather a more elegant pastime to balance in one's stirrups than to trudge on even the smoothest gravel. But at Villa Borghese the walkers have the best of it; for they are free of those adorable outlying corners and bosky byways which the rumble of barouches never reaches. In March the place becomes a perfect epitome of the spring. You cease to care much for the melancholy greenness of the disfeatured statues which has been your chief winter's intimation of verdure; and before you are quite conscious of the tender streaks and patches in the great quaint grassy arena round which the Propaganda students, in their long skirts, wander slowly, like dusky seraphs revolving the gossip of Paradise, you spy the brave little violets uncapping their azure brows beneath the high-stemmed pines. One's walks here would take us too far, and one's pauses detain us too long, when in the quiet parts under the wall one comes across a group of charming small school-boys in full-dress suits and white cravats, shouting over their play in clear Italian, while a grave young priest, beneath a tree, watches them over the top of his book. It sounds like nothing, but the force behind it and the frame round it, the setting, the air, the chord struck, make it a hundred wonderful things.

1873.

Roman Neighbourhoods

I MADE a note after my first stroll at Albano to the effect that I had been talking of the "picturesque" all my life, but that now for a change I beheld it. I had been looking all winter across the Campagna at the free-flowing outline of the Alban Mount, with its half-dozen towns shining on its purple side even as vague sun-spots in the shadow of a cloud, and thinking it simply an agreeable incident in the varied background of Rome. But now that during the last few days I have been treating it as a foreground, have been suffering St. Peter's to play the part of a small mountain on the horizon, with the Campagna swimming mistily through the ambiguous lights and shadows of the interval, I find the interest as great as in the best of the by-play of Rome. The walk I speak of was just out of the village, to the south, toward the neighbouring town of L'Ariccia, neighbouring these twenty years, since the Pope (the late Pope, I was on the point of calling him) threw his superb viaduct across the deep ravine which divides it from Albano. At the risk of seeming to fantasticate I confess that the Pope's having built the viaduct—in this very recent antiquity—made me linger there in a pensive posture and marvel at the march of history and at Pius the Ninth's beginning already to profit by the sentimental allowances we make to vanished powers. An ardent *nero* then would have had his own way with me and obtained a frank admission that the Pope was indeed a father to his people. Far down into the charming valley which slopes out the ancestral woods of the Chigis into the level Campagna winds the steep stone-paved road at the bottom of which, in the good old days, tourists in no great hurry saw the mules and oxen tackled to their carriage for the opposite ascent. And indeed even an impatient tourist might have been content to lounge back in his jolting chaise and look out at the mouldy foundations of the little city plunging into the verdurous flank of the gorge. Questioned, as a cherisher of quaintness, as to the best "bit" hereabouts, I should certainly name the way in which the crumbling black houses of these ponderous villages plant their

447

weary feet on the flowery edges of all the steepest chasms. Before you enter one of them you invariably find yourself lingering outside its pretentious old gateway to see it clutched and stitched to the stony hillside by this rank embroidery of the wildest and bravest things that grow. Just at this moment nothing is prettier than the contrast between their dusky ruggedness and the tender, the yellow and pink and violet fringe of that mantle. All this you may observe from the viaduct at the Ariccia; but you must wander below to feel the full force of the eloquence of our imaginary *papalino*. The pillars and arches of pale grey peperino arise in huge tiers with a magnificent spring and solidity. The older Romans built no better; and the work has a deceptive air of being one of their sturdy bequests which help one to drop another sigh over the antecedents the Italians of to-day are so eager to repudiate. Will those *they* give their descendants be as good?

At the Ariccia, in any case, I found a little square with a couple of mossy fountains, occupied on one side by a vast dusky-faced Palazzo Chigi and on the other by a goodly church with an imposing dome. The dome, within, covers the whole edifice and is adorned with some extremely elegant stucco-work of the seventeenth century. It gave a great value to this fine old decoration that preparations were going forward for a local festival and that the village carpenter was hanging certain mouldy strips of crimson damask against the piers of the vaults. The damask might have been of the seventeenth century too, and a group of peasant-women were seeing it unfurled with evident awe. I regarded it myself with interest—it seemed so the tattered remnant of a fashion that had gone out for ever. I thought again of the poor disinherited Pope, wondering whether, when such venerable frippery will no longer bear the carpenter's nails, any more will be provided. It was hard to fancy anything but shreds and patches in that musty tabernacle. Wherever you go in Italy you receive some such intimation as this of the shrunken proportions of Catholicism, and every church I have glanced into on my walks hereabouts has given me an almost pitying sense of it. One finds one's self at last—without fatuity, I hope—feeling sorry for the solitude of the remaining faithful. It's as if the churches had been made so for the world, in its social sense, and the world had so irrevocably moved away. They are in size out of all modern proportion to the local needs, and the only thing at all alive in the melancholy waste they collectively form is the smell of stale incense. There are pictures on all the altars by respectable third-rate painters; pictures which I suppose once were ordered and paid for and criticised by worshippers who united taste with piety. At Genzano, beyond the Ariccia, rises on the grey village street a pompous Renaissance temple whose imposing nave and aisles would contain the population of a capital. But where is the *taste* of the Ariccia and Genzano? Where are the choice spirits for whom Antonio Raggi modelled the garlands of his dome and a hundred clever craftsmen imitated Guido and Caravaggio? Here and there, from the pavement, as you pass, a dusky crone interlards her devotions with more profane importunities, or a grizzled peasant on rusty-jointed knees, tilted forward with his elbows on a bench, reveals the dimensions of the patch in his blue breeches. But where is the connecting link between Guido and Caravaggio and those poor souls for whom an undoubted original is only a something behind a row of candlesticks, of no very clear meaning save that you must bow to it? You find a vague memory of it at best in the useless grandeurs about you, and you seem to be looking at a structure of which the stubborn earth-scented foundations alone remain, with the carved and painted shell that bends above them, while the central substance has utterly crumbled away.

I shall seem to have adopted a more meditative pace than befits a brisk constitutional if I say that I also fell a-thinking before the shabby façade of the old Chigi Palace. But it seemed somehow in its grey forlornness to respond to the sadly superannuated expression of the opposite church; and indeed in any condition what self-respecting cherisher of quaintness can forbear to do a little romancing in the shadow of a provincial palazzo? On the face of the matter, I know, there is often no very salient peg to hang a romance on. A sort of dusky blankness invests the establishment, which has often a rather imbecile old age. But a hundred brooding secrets lurk in this inexpressive mask, and the Chigi Palace did duty for me in the suggestive twilight as the most haunted of houses. Its basement walls sloped outward like the beginning of a pyramid, and its lower windows were covered with massive iron cages. Within the doorway, across the court, I saw the pale glimmer of flowers on a terrace, and I made much, for the effect of the roof, of a great covered loggia or belvedere with a dozen window-panes missing or mended with paper. Nothing gives one a stronger impression of old manners than an ancestral palace towering in this haughty fashion over a shabby little town; you hardly stretch a point when you call it an impression of feudalism. The scene may pass for feudal to American eyes, for which a hundred windows on a façade mean nothing more exclusive than a hotel kept (at the most invidious) on the European plan. The mouldy grey houses on the steep crooked street, with their black cavernous archways pervaded by bad smells, by the braying of asses and by human intonations hardly more musical, the haggard and tattered peasantry staring at you with hungry-heavy eyes, the brutish-looking monks (there are still enough to point a moral), the soldiers, the mounted constables, the dirt, the dreariness, the misery, and the dark overgrown palace frowning over it all from barred window and guarded gateway—what more than all this do we dimly descry in a mental image of the dark ages? For all his desire to keep the peace with the vivid image of things if it be only vivid enough, the votary of this ideal may well occasionally turn over such values with the wonder of what one takes them as paying for. They pay sometimes for such sorry "facts of life." At Genzano, out of the very midst of the village squalor, rises the Palazzo Cesarini, separated from its gardens by a dirty lane. Between peasant and prince the contact is unbroken, and one would suppose Italian good-nature sorely taxed by their mutual allowances; that the prince in especial must cultivate a firm impervious shell. There are no comfortable townsfolk about him to remind him of the blessings of a happy mediocrity of fortune. When he looks out of his window he sees a battered old peasant against a sunny wall sawing off his dinner from a hunch of black bread.

I must confess, however, that "feudal" as it amused me to find the little piazza of the Ariccia, it appeared to threaten in no manner an exasperated rising. On the contrary, the afternoon being cool, many of the villagers were contentedly muffled in those ancient cloaks, lined with green baize, which, when tossed over the shoulder and surmounted with a peaked hat, form one of the few lingering remnants of "costume" in Italy; others were tossing wooden balls light-heartedly enough on the grass outside the town. The egress on this side is under a great stone archway thrown out from the palace and surmounted with the family arms. Nothing could better confirm your theory that the townsfolk are groaning serfs. The road leads away through the woods, like many of the roads hereabouts, among trees less remarkable for their size than for their picturesque contortions and posturings. The woods, at the moment at which I write, are full of the raw green light of early spring, a *jour* vastly becoming to the various complexions of the wild flowers that cover the waysides. I have never seen these untended parterres in such lovely exuberance; the sturdiest pedestrian becomes a lingering idler if he allows them to catch his eye. The pale purple cyclamen, with its hood thrown back, stands up in masses as dense as tulip-beds; and here and there in the duskier places great sheets of forget-me-not seem to exhale a faint blue mist. These are the commonest plants; there are dozens more I know no name for—a rich profusion in especial of a beautiful five-petalled flower whose white texture is pencilled with hairstrokes certain fair copyists I know of would have to hold their breath to imitate. An Italian oak has neither the girth nor the height of its English brothers, but it contrives in proportion to be perhaps even more effective. It crooks its back and twists its arms and clinches its hundred fists with the queerest extravagance, and wrinkles its bark into strange rugosities from which its first scattered sprouts of yellow green seem to break out like a morbid fungus. But the tree which has the greatest charm to northern eyes is the cold grey-green ilex, whose clear crepuscular shade drops against a Roman sun a veil impenetrable, yet not oppressive. The ilex has even less colour than the cypress, but it is much less funereal, and a landscape in which it is frequent may still be said to smile faintly, though by no means to laugh. It abounds in old Italian gardens, where the boughs are trimmed and interlocked into vaulted corridors in which, from point to point, as in the niches of some dimly frescoed hall, you see mildewed busts stare at you with a solemnity which the even grey light makes strangely intense. A humbler relative of the ilex, though it does better things than help broken-nosed emperors to look dignified, is the olive, which covers many of the neighbouring hillsides with its little smoky puffs of foliage. A stroke of composition I never weary of is that long blue stretch of the Campagna which makes a high horizon and rests on this vaporous base of olive-tops. A reporter intent upon a simile might liken it to the ocean seen above the smoke of watch-fires kindled on the strand.

To do perfect justice to the wood-walk away from the Aricia I ought to touch upon the birds that were singing vespers as I passed. But the reader would find my rhapsody as poor entertainment as the programme of a concert he had been unable to attend. I have no more learning about bird-music than would help me to guess that a dull dissyllabic refrain in the heart of the wood came from the cuckoo; and when at moments I heard a twitter of fuller tone, with a more suggestive modulation, I could only *hope* it was the nightingale. I have listened for the nightingale more than once in places so charming that his song would have seemed but the articulate expression of their beauty, and have never heard much beyond a provoking snatch or two—a prelude that came to nothing. In spite of a natural grudge, however, I generously believe him a great artist or at least a great genius—a creature who despises any prompting short of absolute inspiration. For the rich, the multitudinous melody around me seemed but the offering to my ear of the prodigal spirit of tradition. The wood was ringing with sound because it was twilight, spring and Italy. It was also because of these good things and various others besides that I relished so keenly my visit to the Capuchin convent upon which I emerged after half-an-hour in the wood. It stands above the town, on the slope of the Alban Mount, and its wild garden climbs away behind it and extends its melancholy influence. Before it is a small stiff avenue of trimmed live-oaks which conducts you to a grotesque little shrine beneath the staircase ascending to the church. Just here, if you are apt to grow timorous at twilight, you may take a very pretty fright; for as you draw near you catch behind the grating of the shrine the startling semblance of a gaunt and livid monk. A sickly lamplight plays down upon his face, and he stares at you from cavernous eyes with a dreadful air of death in life. Horror of horrors, you murmur, is this a Capuchin penance? You discover of course in a moment that it is only a Capuchin joke, that the monk is a pious dummy and his spectral visage a matter of the paint-brush. You resent his intrusion on the surrounding loveliness; and as you proceed to demand entertainment at their convent you pronounce the Capuchins very foolish fellows. This declaration, as I made it, was supported by the conduct of the simple brother who opened the door of the cloister in obedience to my knock and, on learning my errand, demurred about admitting me at so late an hour. If I would return on the morrow morning he'd be most happy. He broke into a blank grin when I assured him that this was the very hour of my desire and that the garish morning light would do no justice to the view. These were mysteries beyond his ken, and it was only his good-nature (of which he had plenty) and not his imagination that was moved. So that when, passing through the narrow cloister and out upon the grassy terrace, I saw another cowled brother standing with folded hands profiled against the sky, in admirable harmony with the scene, I questioned his knowing the uses for which he is still most precious. This, however, was surely too much to ask of him, and it was cause enough for gratitude that, though he was there before me, he was not a fellow-tourist with an opera-glass slung over his shoulder. There was support to my idea of the convent in the expiring light, for the scene was in its way unsurpassable. Directly below the terrace lay the deep-set circle of the Alban Lake, shining softly through the light mists of evening. This beautiful pool—it is hardly more—occupies the crater of a prehistoric volcano, a perfect cup, shaped and smelted by furnace-fires. The rim of the cup, rising high and densely wooded round the placid stone-blue water, has a sort of natural artificiality. The sweep and contour of the long circle are admirable; never was a lake so charmingly lodged. It is said to be of extraordinary depth; and though stone-blue water seems at first a very innocent substitute for boiling lava it has a sinister look which betrays its dangerous antecedents. The winds never reach it and its surface is never ruffled; but its deep-bosomed placidity seems to cover guilty secrets, and you fancy it in communication with the capricious and treacherous forces of nature. Its very colour is of a joyless beauty, a blue as cold and opaque as a solidified sheet of lava. Streaked and wrinkled by a mysterious motion of its own, it affects the very type of a legendary pool, and I could easily have believed that I had only to sit long enough into the evening to see the ghosts of classic nymphs and naiads cleave its sullen flood and beckon me with irresistible arms. Is it because its shores are haunted with these vague Pagan influences that two convents have risen there to purge the atmosphere? From the Capuchin terrace you look across at the grey Franciscan monastery of Palazzuola, which is not less romantic certainly than the most obstinate myth it may have exorcised. The Capuchin garden is a wild tangle of great trees and shrubs and clinging, trembling vines which in these hard days are left to take care of themselves; a weedy garden, if there ever was one, but none the less charming for that, in the deepening dusk, with its steep grassy vistas struggling away into impenetrable shadow. I braved the shadow for the sake of climbing upon certain little flat-roofed crumbling pavilions that rise from the corners of the further wall and give you a wider and lovelier view of lake and hills and sky.

I have perhaps justified to the reader the mild proposition with which I started—convinced him, that is, that Albano is worth a walk. It may be a different walk each day, moreover, and not resemble its predecessors save by its keeping in the shade. "Galleries" the roads are prettily called, and with the justice that they are vaulted and draped overhead and hung with an immense succession of pictures. As you follow the few miles from Genzano to Frascati you have perpetual views of the Campagna framed by clusters of trees; the vast iridescent expanse of which completes the charm and comfort of your verdurous dusk. I compared it just now to the sea, and with a good deal of truth, for it has the same incalculable lights and shades, the same confusion of glitter and gloom. But I have seen it at moments—chiefly in the misty twilight—when it resembled less the waste of waters than something more portentous, the land itself in fatal dissolution. I could believe the fields to be dimly surging and tossing and

melting away into quicksands, and that one's very last chance
of an impression was taking place. A view, however, which
has the merit of being really as interesting as it seems, is that
of the Lake of Nemi; which the enterprising traveller hastens
to compare with its sister sheet of Albano. Comparison in this
case is particularly odious, for in order to prefer one lake to
the other you have to discover faults where there are none.
Nemi is a smaller circle, but lies in a deeper cup, and if with
no grey Franciscan pile to guard its woody shores, at least, in
the same position, the little high-perched black town to which
it gives its name and which looks across at Genzano on the
opposite shore as Palazzuola regards Castel Gandolfo. The
walk from the Ariccia to Genzano is charming, most of all
when it reaches a certain grassy piazza from which three public avenues stretch away under a double row of stunted and
twisted elms. The Duke Cesarini has a villa at Genzano—I
mentioned it just now—whose gardens overhang the lake;
but he has also a porter in a faded rakish-looking livery who
shakes his head at your proffered franc unless you can rein-
force it with a permit countersigned at Rome. For this annoying complication of dignities he is justly to be denounced; but
I forgive him for the sake of that ancestor who in the seventeenth century planted this shady walk. Never was a prettier
approach to a town than by these low-roofed light-chequered
corridors. Their only defect is that they prepare you for a
town of rather more rustic coquetry than Genzano exhibits. It
has quite the usual allowance, the common cynicism, of accepted decay, and looks dismally as if its best families had
all fallen into penury together and lost the means of keeping
anything better than donkeys in their great dark, vaulted
basements and mending their broken window-panes with
anything better than paper. It was on the occasion of this
drear Genzano that I had a difference of opinion with a friend
who maintained that there was nothing in the same line so
pretty in Europe as a pretty New England village. The proposition seemed to a cherisher of quaintness on the face of it
inacceptable; but calmly considered it has a measure of truth.
I am not fond of chalk-white painted planks, certainly; I
vastly prefer the dusky tones of ancient stucco and peperino;
but I succumb on occasion to the charms of a vine-shaded

porch, of tulips and dahlias glowing in the shade of high-arching elms, of heavy-scented lilacs bending over a white paling to brush your cheek.

"I prefer Siena to Lowell," said my friend; "but I prefer Farmington to such a thing as this." In fact an Italian village is simply a miniature Italian city, and its various parts imply a town of fifty times the size. At Genzano are neither dahlias nor lilacs, and no odours but foul ones. Flowers and other graces are all confined to the high-walled precincts of Duke Cesarini, to which you must obtain admission twenty miles away. The houses on the other hand would generally lodge a New England cottage, porch and garden and high-arching elms included, in one of their cavernous basements. These vast grey dwellings are all of a fashion denoting more generous social needs than any they serve nowadays. They speak of better days and of a fabulous time when Italy was either not shabby or could at least "carry off" her shabbiness. For what follies are they doing penance? Through what melancholy stages have their fortunes ebbed? You ask these questions as you choose the shady side of the long blank street and watch the hot sun glare upon the dust-coloured walls and pause before the fetid gloom of open doors.

I should like to spare a word for mouldy little Nemi, perched upon a cliff high above the lake, at the opposite side; but after all, when I had climbed up into it from the waterside, passing beneath a great arch which I suppose once topped a gateway, and counted its twenty or thirty apparent inhabitants peeping at me from black doorways, and looked at the old round tower at whose base the village clusters, and declared that it was all queer, queer, desperately queer, I had said all that is worth saying about it. Nemi has a much better appreciation of its lovely position than Genzano, where your only view of the lake is from a dunghill behind one of the houses. At the foot of the round tower is an overhanging terrace, from which you may feast your eyes on the only freshness they find in these dusky human hives—the blooming seam, as one may call it, of strong wild-flowers which binds the crumbling walls to the face of the cliff. Of Rocca di Papa I must say as little. It consorted generally with the bravery of its name; but the only object I made a note of as I passed through it on my way to Monte Cavo, which rises directly above it, was a little black house with a tablet in its face setting forth that Massimo d'Azeglio had dwelt there. The story of his sojourn is not the least attaching episode in his delightful *Ricordi*. From the summit of Monte Cavo is a prodigious view, which you may enjoy with whatever good-nature is left you by the reflection that the modern Passionist convent occupying this admirable site was erected by the Cardinal of York (grandson of James II.) on the demolished ruins of an immemorial temple of Jupiter: the last foolish act of a foolish race. For me I confess this folly spoiled the convent, and the convent all but spoiled the view; for I kept thinking how fine it would have been to emerge upon the old pillars and sculptures from the lava pavement of the Via Triumphalis, which wanders grass-grown and untrodden through the woods. A convent, however, which nothing spoils is that of Palazzuola, to which I paid my respects on this same occasion. It rises on a lower spur of Monte Cavo, on the edge, as we have seen, of the Alban Lake, and though it occupies a classic site, that of early Alba Longa, it displaced nothing more precious than memories and legends so dim that the antiquarians are still quarrelling about them. It has a meagre little church and the usual sham Perugino with a couple of tinsel crowns for the Madonna and the Infant inserted into the canvas; and it has also a musty old room hung about with faded portraits and charts and queer ecclesiastical knick-knacks, which borrowed a mysterious interest from the sudden assurance of the simple Franciscan brother who accompanied me that it was the room of the Son of the King of Portugal. But my peculiar pleasure was the little thick-shaded garden which adjoins the convent and commands from its massive artificial foundations an enchanting view of the lake. Part of it is laid out in cabbages and lettuce, over which a rubicund brother, with his frock tucked up, was bending with a solicitude which he interrupted to remove his skull-cap and greet me with the unsophisticated sweet-humoured smile that every now and then in Italy does so much to make you forget the ambiguities of monachism. The rest is occupied by cypresses and other funereal umbrage, making a dank circle round an old cracked fountain black with water-moss. The parapet of the terrace is furnished with good stone seats where you may lean on your elbows to gaze away a sunny half-hour and, feeling the general charm of the scene, declare that the best mission of such a country in the world has been simply to produce, in the way of prospect and picture, these masterpieces of mildness. Mild here as a dream the whole attained effect, mild as resignation, mild as one's thoughts of another life. Such a session wasn't surely an experience of the irritable flesh; it was the deep degustation, on a summer's day, of something immortally expressed by a man of genius.

From Albano you may take your way through several ancient little cities to Frascati, a rival centre of *villeggiatura*, the road following the hillside for a long morning's walk and passing through alternations of denser and clearer shade—the dark vaulted alleys of ilex and the brilliant corridors of fresh-sprouting oak. The Campagna is beneath you continually, with the sea beyond Ostia receiving the silver arrows of the sun upon its chased and burnished shield, and mighty Rome, to the north, lying at no great length in the idle immensity around it. The highway passes below Castel Gandolfo, which stands perched on an eminence behind a couple of gateways surmounted with the Papal tiara and twisted cordon; and I have more than once chosen the roundabout road for the sake of passing beneath these pompous insignia. Castel Gandolfo is indeed an ecclesiastical village and under the peculiar protection of the Popes, whose huge summer-palace rises in the midst of it like a rural Vatican. In speaking of the road to Frascati I necessarily revert to my first impressions, gathered on the occasion of the feast of the Annunziata, which falls on the 25th of March and is celebrated by a peasants' fair. As Murray strongly recommends you to visit this spectacle, at which you are promised a brilliant exhibition of all the costumes of modern Latium, I took an early train to Frascati and measured, in company with a prodigious stream of humble pedestrians, the half-hour's interval to Grotta Ferrata, where the fair is held. The road winds along the hillside, among the silver-sprinkled olives and through a charming wood where the ivy seemed tacked upon the oaks by women's fingers and the birds were singing to the late anemones. It was covered with a very jolly crowd of vulgar pleasure-takers, and the only creatures not in a state of manifest hilarity were the pitiful little overladen, overbeaten donkeys (who surely deserve a chapter to themselves in any description of these neighbourhoods) and the horrible beggars who were thrusting their sores and stumps at you from under every tree. Every one was shouting, singing, scrambling, making light of dust and distance and filling the air with that childlike jollity which the blessed Italian temperament never goes roundabout to conceal. There is no crowd surely at once so jovial and so gentle as an Italian crowd, and I doubt if in any other country the tightly packed third-class car in which I went out from Rome would have introduced me to so much smiling and so little swearing. Grotta Ferrata is a very dirty little village, with a number of raw new houses baking on the hot hillside and nothing to charm the fond gazer but its situation and its old fortified abbey. After pushing about among the shabby little booths and declining a number of fabulous bargains in tinware, shoes and pork, I was glad to retire to a comparatively uninvaded corner of the abbey and divert myself with the view. This grey ecclesiastical stronghold is a thoroughly scenic affair, hanging over the hillside on plunging foundations which bury themselves among the dense olives. It has massive round towers at the corners and a grass-grown moat, enclosing a church and a monastery. The forecourt, within the abbatial gateway, now serves as the public square of the village and in fair-time of course witnesses the best of the fun. The best of the fun was to be found in certain great vaults and cellars of the abbey, where wine was in free flow from gigantic hogsheads. At the exit of these trickling grottos shady trellises of bamboo and gathered twigs had been improvised, and under them a grand guzzling proceeded. All of which was so in the fine old style that I was roughly reminded of the wedding-feast of Gamacho. The banquet was far less substantial of course, but it had a note as of immemorial manners that couldn't fail to suggest romantic analogies to a pilgrim from the land of no cooks. There was a feast of reason close at hand, however, and I was careful to visit the famous frescoes of Domenichino in the adjoining church. It sounds rather brutal perhaps to say that, when I came back into the clamorous little piazza, the sight of the peasants swilling down their sour wine appealed to me more than the masterpieces—Murray calls them so—of the famous Bolognese. It amounts after all to saying that I prefer Teniers to Domenichino; which I am willing to let pass for the truth. The scene under the rickety trellises was the more suggestive of Teniers that there were no costumes to make it too Italian. Murray's attractive statement on this point was, like many of his statements, much truer twenty years ago than to-day. Costume is gone or fast going; I saw among the women not a single crimson bodice and not a couple of classic head-cloths. The poorer sort, dressed in vulgar rags of no fashion and colour, and the smarter ones in calico gowns and printed shawls of the vilest modern fabric, had honoured their dusky tresses but with rich applications of grease. The men are still in jackets and breeches, and, with their slouched and pointed hats and open-breasted shirts and rattling leather leggings, may remind one sufficiently of the Italian peasant as he figured in the woodcuts familiar to our infancy. After coming out of the church I found a delightful nook—a queer little terrace before a more retired and tranquil drinking-shop—where I called for a bottle of wine to help me to guess why I "drew the line" at Domenichino.

This little terrace was a capricious excrescence at the end of the piazza, itself simply a greater terrace; and one reached it, picturesquely, by ascending a short inclined plane of grass-grown cobble-stones and passing across a little dusky kitchen through whose narrow windows the light of the mighty landscape beyond touched up old earthen pots. The terrace was oblong and so narrow that it held but a single small table, placed lengthwise; yet nothing could be pleasanter than to place one's bottle on the polished parapet. Here you seemed by the time you had emptied it to be swinging forward into immensity—hanging poised above the Campagna. A beautiful gorge with a twinkling stream wandered down the hill far below you, beyond which Marino and Castel Gandolfo peeped above the trees. In front you could count the towers of Rome and the tombs of the Appian Way. I don't know that I came to any very distinct conclusion about Domenichino; but it was perhaps because the view was perfection that he struck me as more than ever mediocrity. And yet I don't think it was one's bottle of wine, either, that made one after all maudlin about him; it was the sense of the foolishly usurped in his tenure of fame, of the derisive in his ever having been put forward. To say so indeed savours of flogging a dead horse, but it is surely an unkind stroke of fate for him that Murray assures ten thousand Britons every winter in the most emphatic manner that his Communion of St. Jerome is the "second finest picture in the world." If this were so one would certainly here in Rome, where such institutions are convenient, retire into the very nearest convent; with such a world one would have a standing quarrel. And yet this sport of destiny is an interesting case, in default of being an interesting painter, and I would take a moderate walk, in most moods, to see one of his pictures. He is so supremely good an example of effort detached from inspiration and school-merit divorced from spontaneity, that one of his fine frigid performances ought to hang in a conspicuous place in every academy of design. Few things of the sort contain more urgent lessons or point a more precious moral; and I would have the head-master in the drawing-school take each ingenuous pupil by the hand and lead him up to the Triumph of David or the Chase of Diana or the red-nosed Persian Sibyl and make him some such little speech as the following: "This great picture, my son, was hung here to show you how you must *never* paint; to give you a perfect specimen of what in its boundless generosity the providence of nature created for our fuller knowledge—an artist whose development was a negation. The great thing in art is charm, and the great thing in charm is spontaneity. Domenichino, having talent, is here and there an excellent model—he was devoted, conscientious, observant, industrious; but now that we've seen pretty well what can simply be learned do its best, these things help him little with us, because his imagination was cold. It loved nothing, it lost itself in nothing, its efforts never gave it the heartache. It went about trying this and that, concocting cold pictures after cold receipts, dealing in the second-hand, in the ready-made, and putting into its performances a little of everything but itself. When you see so many things in a composition you might suppose that among them all some charm might be born; yet they're really but the hundred mouths through which you may hear the unhappy thing murmur 'I'm dead!' It's by the simplest thing it has that a picture lives—by its temper. Look at all the great talents, Domenichino as well as at Titian; but think less of dogma than of plain nature, and I can almost promise you that yours will remain true." This is very little to what the æsthetic sage I have imagined *might* say; and we are after all unwilling to let our last verdict be an unkind one on any great bequest of human effort. The faded frescoes in the chapel at Grotta Ferrata leave us a memory the more of man's effort to dream beautifully; and they thus mingle harmoniously enough with our multifold impressions of Italy, where dreams and realities have both kept such pace and so strangely diverged. It was absurd—that was the truth—to be critical at all among the appealing old Italianisms round me and to treat the poor exploded Bolognese more harshly than, when I walked back to Frascati, I treated the charming old water-works of the Villa Aldobrandini. I confound these various products of antiquated art in a genial absolution, and should like especially to tell how fine it was to watch this prodigious fountain come tumbling down its channel of mouldy rock-work, through its magnificent vista of ilex, to the fantastic old hemicycle where a dozen tritons and naiads sit posturing to receive it. The sky above the ilexes was incredibly blue and the ilexes themselves incredibly black; and to see the young white moon peeping above the trees you could easily have fancied it was midnight. I should like furthermore to expatiate on Villa Mondragone, the most grandly impressive hereabouts, of all such domestic monuments. The great Casino in the midst is as big as the Vatican, which it strikingly resembles, and it stands perched on a terrace as vast as the parvise of St. Peter's, looking straight away over black cypress-tops into the shining vastness of the Campagna. Everything somehow seemed immense and solemn; there was nothing small but certain little nestling blue shadows on the Sabine Mountains, to which the terrace seems to carry you wonderfully near. The place has been for some time lost to private uses, since it figures fantastically in a novel of George Sand—*La Daniella*—and now, in quite another way, as a Jesuit college for boys. The afternoon was perfect, and as it waned it filled the dark alleys with a wonderful golden haze.

Into this came leaping and shouting a herd of little collegians with a couple of long-skirted Jesuits striding at their heels. We all know—I make the point for my antithesis—the monstrous practices of these people; yet as I watched the group I verily believe I declared that if I had a little son he should go to Mondragone and receive their crooked teachings for the sake of the other memories, the avenues of cypress and ilex, the view of the Campagna, the atmosphere of antiquity. But doubtless when a sense of "mere character," shameless incomparable character, has brought one to this it is time one should pause.

The After-Season in Rome

ONE MAY at the blest end of May say without injustice to anybody that the state of mind of many a *forestiero* in Rome is one of intense impatience for the moment when all other *forestieri* shall have taken themselves off. One may confess to this state of mind and be no misanthrope. The place has passed so completely for the winter months into the hands of the barbarians that that estimable character the passionate pilgrim finds it constantly harder to keep his passion clear. He has a rueful sense of impressions perverted and adulterated; the all-venerable visage disconcerts us by a vain eagerness to see itself mirrored in English, American, German eyes. It isn't simply that you are never first or never alone at the classic or historic spots where you have dreamt of persuading the shy *genius loci* into confidential utterance; it isn't simply that St. Peter's, the Vatican, the Palatine, are forever ringing with the false note of the languages without style: it is the general oppressive feeling that the city of the soul has become for the time a monstrous mixture of watering-place and curiosity-shop and that its most ardent life is that of the tourists who haggle over false intaglios and yawn through palaces and temples. But you are told of a happy time when these abuses begin to pass away, when Rome becomes Rome again and you may have her all to yourself. "You may like her more or less now," I was assured at the height of the season; "but you must wait till the month of May, when she'll give you *all* she has, to love her. Then the foreigners, or the excess of them, are gone; the galleries and ruins are empty, and the place," said my informant, who was a happy Frenchman of the Académie de France, "*renaît à elle-même.*" Indeed I was haunted all winter by an irresistible prevision of what Rome *must* be in declared spring. Certain charming places seemed to murmur: "Ah, this is nothing! Come back at the right weeks and see the sky above us almost black with its excess of blue, and the new grass already deep, but still vivid, and the white roses tumble in odorous spray and the warm radiant air distil gold for the smelting-pot that the *genius loci* then dips his brush into before making play with it, in his inimitable way, for the general effect of complexion."

A month ago I spent a week in the country, and on my return, the first time I approached the Corso, became conscious of a change. Something delightful had happened, to which at first I couldn't give a name, but which presently shone out as the fact that there were but half of many people present and that these were chiefly the natural or the naturalised. We had been docked of half our irrelevance, our motley excess, and now physically, morally, æsthetically there was elbow-room. In the afternoon I went to the Pincio, and the Pincio was almost dull. The band was playing to a dozen ladies who lay in landaus poising their lace-fringed parasols; but they had scarce more than a light-gloved dandy apiece hanging over their carriage doors. By the parapet to the great terrace that sweeps the city stood but three or four interlopers looking at the sunset and with their Baedekers only just showing in their pockets—the sunsets not being down among the tariffed articles in these precious volumes. I went so far as to hope for them that, like myself, they were, under every precaution, taking some amorous intellectual liberty with the scene.

Practically I violate thus the instinct of monopoly, since it's a shame not to publish that Rome in May is indeed exquisitely worth your patience. I have just been so gratified at finding myself in undisturbed possession for a couple of hours of the Museum of the Lateran that I can afford to be magnanimous. It's almost as if the old all-papal paradise had come back. The weather for a month has been perfect, the sky an extravagance of blue, the air lively enough, the nights cool, nippingly cool, and the whole ancient greyness lighted with an irresistible smile. Rome, which in some moods, especially to new-comers, seems a place of almost sinister gloom, has an occasional art, as one knows her better, of brushing away care by the grand gesture with which some splendid impatient mourning matron—just the Niobe of Nations, surviving, emerging and looking about her again—might pull off and cast aside an oppression of muffling crape. This admirable power still temperamentally to react and take notice lurks in all her darkness and dirt and decay—a something more careless and hopeless than our thrifty northern cheer, and yet more genial and urbane than the Parisian spirit of *blague*. The collective Roman nature is a healthy and hearty one, and you feel it abroad in the streets even when the sirocco blows and the medium of life seems to proceed more or less from the mouth of a furnace. But who shall analyse even the simplest Roman impression? It is compounded of so many things, it says so much, it involves so much, it so quickens the intelligence and so flatters the heart, that before we fairly grasp the case the imagination has marked it for her own and exposed us to a perilous likelihood of talking nonsense about it.

The smile of Rome, as I have called it, and its insidious message to those who incline to ramble irresponsibly and take things as they come, is ushered in with the first breath of spring, and then grows and grows with the advancing season till it wraps the whole place in its tenfold charm. As the process develops you can do few better things than go often to Villa Borghese and sit on the grass—on a stout bit of drapery—and watch its exquisite stages. It has a frankness and a sweetness beyond any relenting of *our* clumsy climates even when ours leave off their damnable faces and begin. Nature departs from every reserve with a confidence that leaves one at a loss where, as it were, to look—leaves one, as I say, nothing to do but to lay one's head among the anemones at the base of a high-stemmed pine and gaze up crestward and skyward along its slanting silvery column. You may watch the whole business from a dozen of these choice standpoints and have a different villa for it every day in the week. The Doria, the Ludovisi, the Medici, the Albani, the Wolkonski, the Chigi, the Mellini, the Massimo—there are more of them, with all their sights and sounds and odours and memories, than you have senses for. But I prefer none of them to the Borghese, which is free to all the world at all times and yet never crowded; for when the whirl of carriages is great in the middle regions you may find a hundred untrodden spots and silent corners, tenanted at the worst by a group of those long-skirted young Propagandists who stalk about with solemn angularity, each with a book under his arm, like silhouettes from a mediæval missal, and "compose" so extremely well with the still more processional cypresses and with stretches of golden-russet wall overtopped by ultramarine. And yet if the Borghese is good the Medici is strangely charming, and you may stand in the little belvedere which rises with such surpassing oddity out of the dusky heart of the Boschetto at the latter establishment—a miniature presentation of the wood of the Sleeping Beauty—and look across at the Ludovisi pines lifting their crooked parasols into a sky of what a painter would call the most morbid blue, and declare that the place where *they* grow is the most delightful in the world. Villa Ludovisi has been all winter the residence of the lady familiarly known in Roman society as "Rosina," Victor Emmanuel's morganatic wife, the only familiarity, it would seem, that she allows, for the grounds were rigidly closed, to the inconsolable regret of old Roman sojourners. Just as the nightingales began to sing, however, the quasi-august *padrona* departed, and the public, with certain restrictions, have been admitted to hear them. The place takes, where it lies, a princely ease, and there could be no better example of the expansive tendencies of ancient privilege than the fact that its whole vast extent is contained by the city walls. It has in this respect very much the same enviable air of having got up early that marks the great intramural demesne of Magdalen College at Oxford. The stern old ramparts of Rome form the outer enclosure of the villa, and hence a series of "striking scenic effects" which it would be unscrupulous flattery to say you can imagine. The grounds are laid out in the formal last-century manner; but nowhere do the straight black cypresses lead off the gaze into vistas of a melancholy more charged with associations—poetic, romantic, historic; nowhere are there grander smoother walls of laurel and myrtle.

I recently spent an afternoon hour at the little Protestant cemetery close to St. Paul's Gate, where the ancient and the modern world are insidiously contrasted. They make between them one of the solemn places of Rome—although indeed when funereal things are so interfused it seems ungrateful to call them sad. Here is a mixture of tears and smiles, of stones and flowers, of mourning cypresses and radiant sky, which gives us the impression of our looking back at death from the brighter side of the grave. The cemetery nestles in an angle of the city wall, and the older graves are sheltered by a mass of ancient brickwork, through whose narrow loopholes you peep at the wide purple of the Campagna. Shelley's grave is here, buried in roses—a happy grave every way for the very type and figure of the Poet. Nothing could be more impenetrably tranquil than this little corner in the bend of the protecting rampart, where a cluster of modern ashes is held tenderly in the rugged hand of the Past. The past is tremendously embodied in the hoary pyramid of Caius Cestius, which rises hard by, half within the wall and half without, cutting solidly into the solid blue of the sky and casting its pagan shadow upon the grass of English graves—that of Keats, among them—with an effect of poetic justice. It is a wonderful confusion of mortality and a grim enough admonition of our helpless promiscuity in the crucible of time. But the most touching element of all is the appeal of the pious English inscriptions among all these Roman memories; touching because of their universal expression of that trouble within trouble, misfortune in a foreign land. Something special stirs the heart through the fine Scriptural language in which everything is recorded. The echoes of massive Latinity with which the atmosphere is charged suggest nothing more majestic and monumental. I may seem unduly to refine, but the injunction to the reader in the monument to Miss Bathurst, drowned in the Tiber in 1824, "If thou art young and lovely, build not thereon, for she who lies beneath thy feet in death was the loveliest flower ever cropt in its bloom," affects us irresistibly as a case for tears on the spot. The whole elaborate inscription indeed says something over and beyond all it does say. The English have the reputation of being the most reticent people in the world, and as there is no smoke without fire I suppose they have done something to deserve it; yet who can say that one doesn't constantly meet the most startling examples of the insular faculty to "gush?" In this instance the mother of the deceased takes the public into her confidence with surprising frankness and omits no detail, seizing the opportunity to mention by the way that she had already lost her husband by a most mysterious visitation. The appeal to one's attention and the confidence in it are withal most moving. The whole record has an old-fashioned gentility that makes its frankness tragic. You seem to hear the garrulity of passionate grief.

To be choosing these positive commonplaces of the Roman tone for a theme when there are matters of modern moment going on may seem none the less to require an apology. But I make no claim to your special correspondent's faculty for getting an "inside" view of things, and I have hardly more than a pictorial impression of the Pope's illness and of the discussion of the Law of the Convents. Indeed I am afraid to speak of the Pope's illness at all, lest I should say something egregiously heartless about it, recalling too forcibly that unnatural husband who was heard to wish that his wife would "either" get well——! He had his reasons, and Roman tourists have theirs in the shape of a vague longing for something spectacular at St. Peter's. If it takes the sacrifice of somebody to produce it let somebody then be sacrificed. Meanwhile we have been having a glimpse of the spectacular side of the Religious Corporations Bill. Hearing one morning a great hubbub in the Corso I stepped forth upon my balcony. A couple of hundred men were strolling slowly down the street with their hands in their pockets, shouting in unison "Abbasso il ministero!" and huzzaing in chorus. Just beneath my window they stopped and began to murmur "Al Quirinale, al Quirinale!" The crowd surged a moment gently and then drifted to the Quirinal, where it scuffled harmlessly with half-a-dozen of the king's soldiers. It ought to have been impressive, for what was it, strictly, unless the seeds of revolution? But its carriage was too gentle and its cries too musical to send the most timorous tourist to packing his trunk. As I began with saying: in Rome, in May, everything has an amiable side, even popular uprisings.

From a Roman Note-Book

DECEMBER 28, 1872.—In Rome again for the last three days—that second visit which, when the first isn't followed by a fatal illness in Florence, the story goes that one is doomed to pay. I didn't drink of the Fountain of Trevi on the eve of departure the other time; but I feel as if I had drunk of the Tiber itself. Nevertheless as I drove from the station in the evening I wondered what I should think of it at this first glimpse hadn't I already known it. All manner of evil perhaps. Paris, as I passed along the Boulevards three evenings before to take the train, was swarming and glittering as befits a great capital. Here, in the black, narrow, crooked, empty streets, I saw nothing I would fain regard as eternal. But there were new gas-lamps round the spouting Triton in Piazza Barberini and a newspaper stall on the corner of the Condotti and the Corso—salient signs of the emancipated state. An hour later I walked up to Via Gregoriana by Piazza di Spagna. It was all silent and deserted, and the great flight of steps looked surprisingly small. Everything seemed meagre, dusky, provincial. Could Rome after all really *be* a world-city? That queer old rococo garden gateway at the top of the Gregoriana stirred a dormant memory; it awoke into a consciousness of the delicious mildness of the air, and very soon, in a little crimson drawing-room, I was reconciled and re-initiated. . . . Everything is dear (in the way of lodgings) but it hardly matters, as everything is taken and some one else paying for it. I must make up my mind to a bare perch. But it seems poorly perverse here to aspire to an "interior" or to be conscious of the economic side of life. The æsthetic is so intense that you feel you should live on the taste of it, should extract the nutritive essence of the atmosphere. For positively it's *such* an atmosphere! The weather is perfect, the sky as blue as the most exploded tradition fames it, the whole air glowing and throbbing with lovely colour. . . . The glitter of Paris is now all gaslight. And oh the monotonous miles of rain-washed asphalte!

December 30th.—I have had nothing to do with the "ceremonies." In fact I believe there have hardly been any—no midnight mass at the Sistine chapel, no silver trumpets at St. Peter's. Everything is remorselessly clipped and curtailed—the Vatican in deepest mourning. But I saw it in its superbest scarlet in '69 . . . I went yesterday with L. to the Colonna gardens—an adventure that would have reconverted me to Rome if the thing weren't already done. It's a rare old place—rising in mouldy bosky terraces and mossy stairways and winding walks from the back of the palace to the top of the Quirinal. It's the grand style of gardening, and resembles the present natural manner as a chapter of Johnsonian rhetoric resembles a piece of clever contemporary journalism. But it's a better style in horticulture than in literature; I prefer one of the long-drawn blue-green Colonna vistas, with a maimed and mossy-coated garden goddess at the end, to the finest possible quotation from a last-century classic. Perhaps the best thing there is the old orangery with its trees in fantastic terra-cotta tubs. The late afternoon light was gilding the monstrous jars and suspending golden chequers among the golden-fruited leaves. Or perhaps the best thing is the broad terrace with its mossy balustrade and its benches; also its view of the great naked Torre di Nerone (I think) which might look stupid if the rosy brickwork didn't take such a colour in the blue air. Delightful, at any rate, to stroll and talk there in the afternoon sunshine.

January 2nd, 1873.—Two or three drives with A.—one to St. Paul's without the Walls and back by a couple of old churches on the Aventine. I was freshly struck with the rare distinction of the little Protestant cemetery at the Gate, lying in the shadow of the black sepulchral Pyramid and the thick-growing black cypresses. Bathed in the clear Roman light the place is heart-breaking for what it asks you—in such a world as *this*—to renounce. If it should "make one in love with death to lie there," that's only if death should be conscious. As the case stands the weight of a tremendous past presses upon the flowery sod, and the sleeper's mortality feels the contact of all the mortality with which the brilliant air is tainted. . . . The restored Basilica is incredibly splendid. It seems a last pompous effort of formal Catholicism, and there are few more striking emblems of later Rome—the Rome foredoomed to see Victor Emmanuel in the Quirinal, the Rome of abortive councils and unheeded anathemas. It rises there, gorgeous and useless, on its miasmatic site, with an air of conscious bravado—a florid advertisement of the super-abundance of faith. Within it's magnificent, and its magnificence has no shabby spots—a rare thing in Rome. Marble and mosaic, alabaster and malachite, lapis and porphyry, incrust it from pavement to cornice and flash back their polished lights at each other with such a splendour of effect that you seem to stand at the heart of some immense prismatic crystal. One has to come to Italy to know marbles and love them. I remember the fascination of the first great show of them I met in Venice—at the Scalzi and Gesuiti. Colour has in no other form so cool and unfading a purity and lustre. Softness of tone and hardness of substance—isn't that the sum of the artist's desire? G., with his beautiful caressing, open-lipped Roman utterance, so easy to understand and, to my ear, so finely suggestive of genuine Latin, not our horrible Anglo-Saxon and Protestant kind, urged upon us the charms of a return by the Aventine and the sight of a couple of old churches. The best is Santa Sabina, a very fine old structure of the fifth century, mouldering in its dusky solitude and consuming its own antiquity. What a massive heritage Christianity and Catholicism are leaving here! What a substantial fact, in all its decay, this memorial Christian temple outliving its uses among the sunny gardens and vineyards! It has a noble nave, filled with a stale smell which (like that of the onion) brought tears to my eyes, and bordered with twenty-four fluted marble columns of Pagan origin. The crudely primitive little mosaics along the entablature are extremely curious. A Dominican monk, still young, who showed us the church, seemed a creature generated from its musty shadows and odours. His physiognomy was wonderfully *de l'emploi*, and his voice, most agreeable, had the strangest jaded humility. His lugubrious salute and sanctimonious impersonal appropriation of my departing franc would have been a master-touch on the stage. While we were still in the church a bell rang that he had to go and answer, and as he came back and approached us along the nave he made with his white gown and hood and his cadaverous face, against the dark church background, one of those pictures which, thank the Muses, have not yet been reformed out of Italy. It was the exact illustration, for insertion in a text, of heaven knows how many old romantic and conventional literary Italianisms—plays, poems, mysteries of Udolpho. We got back into the carriage and talked of profane things and went home to dinner—drifting recklessly, it seemed to me, from æsthetic luxury to social.

On the 31st we went to the musical vesper-service at the Gesù—hitherto done so splendidly before the Pope and the cardinals. The manner of it was eloquent of change— no Pope, no cardinals, and indifferent music; but a great *mise-en-scène* nevertheless. The church is gorgeous; late Renaissance, of great proportions, and full, like so many others, but in a pre-eminent degree, of seventeenth and eighteenth century Romanism. It doesn't impress the imagination, but richly feeds the curiosity, by which I mean one's sense of the curious; suggests no legends, but innumerable anecdotes à la Stendhal. There is a vast dome, filled with a florid concave fresco of tumbling foreshortened angels, and all over the ceilings and cornices a wonderful outlay of dusky gildings and mouldings. There are various Bernini saints and seraphs in stucco-sculpture, astride of the tablets and door-tops, backing against their rusty machinery of coppery *nimbi* and egg-shaped cloudlets. Marble, damask and tapers in gorgeous profusion. The high altar a great screen of twinkling chandeliers. The choir perched in a little loft high up in the right transept, like a balcony in a side-scene at the opera, and indulging in surprising roulades and flourishes. . . . Near me sat a handsome, opulent-looking nun—possibly an abbess or prioress of noble lineage. Can a holy woman of such a complexion listen to a fine operatic barytone in a sumptuous temple and receive none but ascetic impressions? What a cross-fire of influences does Catholicism provide!

January 4th.—A drive with A. out of Porta San Giovanni and along Via Appia Nuova. More and more beautiful as you get well away from the walls and the great view opens out before you—the rolling green-brown dells and flats of the Campagna, the long, disjointed arcade of the aqueducts, the deep-shadowed blue of the Alban hills, touched into pale lights by their scattered towns. We stopped at the ruined basilica of San Stefano, an affair of the fifth century, rather meaningless without a learned companion. But the perfect little sepulchral chambers of the Pancratii, disinterred beneath the church, tell their own tale—in their hardly dimmed frescoes, their beautiful sculptured coffin and great sepulchral slab. Better still the tomb of the Valerii adjoining it—a single chamber with an arched roof, covered with stucco mouldings perfectly intact, exquisite figures and arabesques as sharp and delicate as if the plasterer's scaffold had just been taken from under them. Strange enough to think of these things—so many of them as there are—surviving their immemorial eclipse in this perfect shape and coming up like long-lost divers from the sea of time.

January 16th.—A delightful walk last Sunday with F. to Monte Mario. We drove to Porta Angelica, the little gate hidden behind the right wing of Bernini's colonnade, and strolled thence up the winding road to the Villa Mellini, where one of the greasy peasants huddled under the wall in the sun admits you for half a franc into the finest old ilex-walk in Italy. It is all vaulted grey-green shade with blue Campagna stretches in the interstices. The day was perfect; the still sunshine, as we sat at the twisted base of the old trees, seemed to have the drowsy hum of midsummer—with that charm of Italian vegetation that comes to us as its confession of having scenically served, to weariness at last, for some pastoral these many centuries a classic. In a certain cheapness and thinness of substance—as compared with the English stoutness, never left athirst—it reminds me of our own, and it is relatively dry enough and pale enough to explain the contempt of many unimaginative Britons. But it has an idle abundance and wantonness, a romantic shabbiness and dishevelment. At the Villa Mellini is the famous lonely pine which "tells" so in the landscape from other points, bought off from the axe by (I believe) Sir George Beaumont, commemorated in a like connection in Wordsworth's great sonnet. He at least was not an unimaginative Briton. As you stand under it, its far-away shallow dome, supported on a single column almost white enough to be marble, seems to dwell in the dizziest depths of the blue. Its pale grey-blue boughs and its silvery stem make a wonderful harmony with the ambient air. The Villa Mellini is

full of the elder Italy of one's imagination—the Italy of Boccaccio and Ariosto. There are twenty places where the Florentine story-tellers might have sat round on the grass. Outside
the villa walls, beneath the overcrowding orange-boughs,
straggled old Italy as well—but not in Boccaccio's velvet: a
row of ragged and livid contadini, some simply stupid in their
squalor, but some downright brigands of romance, or of reality, with matted locks and terribly sullen eyes.

A couple of days later I walked for old acquaintance sake
over to San Onofrio on the Janiculan. The approach is one of
the dirtiest adventures in Rome, and though the view is fine
from the little terrace, the church and convent are of a meagre
and musty pattern. Yet here—almost like pearls in a dunghill—are hidden mementos of two of the most exquisite of
Italian minds. Torquato Tasso spent the last months of his life
here, and you may visit his room and various warped and
faded relics. The most interesting is a cast of his face taken
after death—looking, like all such casts, almost more than
mortally gallant and distinguished. But who should look all
ideally so if not he? In a little shabby, chilly corridor adjoining is a fresco of Leonardo, a Virgin and Child with the *donatorio*. It is very small, simple and faded, but it has all the
artist's magic, that mocking, illusive refinement and hint of a
vague *arrière-pensée* which mark every stroke of Leonardo's
brush. Is it the perfection of irony or the perfection of tenderness? What does he mean, what does he affirm, what does he
deny? Magic wouldn't be magic, nor the author of such
things stand so absolutely alone, if we were ready with an
explanation. As I glanced from the picture to the poor stupid
little red-faced brother at my side I wondered if the thing
mightn't pass for an elegant epigram on monasticism. Certainly, at any rate, there is more intellect in it than under all
the monkish tonsures it has seen coming and going these
three hundred years.

January 21st.—The last three or four days I have regularly
spent a couple of hours from noon baking myself in the sun
of the Pincio to get rid of a cold. The weather perfect and the
crowd (especially to-day) amazing. Such a staring, lounging,
dandified, amiable crowd! Who does the vulgar stay-at-home
work of Rome? All the grandees and half the foreigners are

there in their carriages, the *bourgeoisie* on foot staring at them and the beggars lining all the approaches. The great difference between public places in America and Europe is in the number of unoccupied people of every age and condition sitting about early and late on benches and gazing at you, from your hat to your boots, as you pass. Europe is certainly the continent of the practised stare. The ladies on the Pincio have to run the gauntlet; but they seem to do so complacently enough. The European woman is brought up to the sense of having a definite part in the way of manners or manner to play in public. To lie back in a barouche alone, balancing a parasol and seeming to ignore the extremely immediate gaze of two serried ranks of male creatures on each side of her path, save here and there to recognise one of them with an imperceptible nod, is one of her daily duties. The number of young men here who, like the cœnobites of old, lead the purely contemplative life is enormous. They muster in especial force on the Pincio, but the Corso all day is thronged with them. They are well-dressed, good-humoured, good-looking, polite; but they seem never to do a harder stroke of work than to stroll from the Piazza Colonna to the Hôtel de Rome or *vice versâ*. Some of them don't even stroll, but stand leaning by the hour against the doorways, sucking the knobs of their canes, feeling their back hair and settling their shirt-cuffs. At my café in the morning several stroll in already (at nine o'clock) in light, in "evening" gloves. But they order nothing, turn on their heels, glance at the mirrors and stroll out again. When it rains they herd under the *portes-cochères* and in the smaller cafés. . . . Yesterday Prince Humbert's little *primogenito* was on the Pincio in an open landau with his governess. He's a sturdy blond little man and the image of the King. They had stopped to listen to the music, and the crowd was planted about the carriage-wheels, staring and criticising under the child's snub little nose. It appeared bold cynical curiosity, without the slightest manifestation of "loyalty," and it gave me a singular sense of the vulgarisation of Rome under the new régime. When the Pope drove abroad it was a solemn spectacle; even if you neither kneeled nor uncovered you were irresistibly impressed. But the Pope never stopped to listen to opera tunes, and he had no little popelings, under the charge of superior nurse-maids, whom you might take liberties with. The family at the Quirinal make something of a merit, I believe, of their modest and inexpensive way of life. The merit is great; yet, representationally, what a change for the worse from an order which proclaimed stateliness a part of its essence! The divinity that doth hedge a king must be pretty well on the wane. But how many more fine old traditions will the extremely sentimental traveller miss in the Italians over whom that little jostled prince in the landau will have come into his kinghood? . . . The Pincio continues to beguile; it's a great resource. I am forever being reminded of the "æsthetic luxury," as I called it above, of living in Rome. To be able to choose of an afternoon for a lounge (respectfully speaking) between St. Peter's and the high precinct you approach by the gate just beyond Villa Medici—counting nothing else—is a proof that if in Rome you may suffer from ennui, at least your ennui has a throbbing soul in it. It is something to say for the Pincio that you don't always choose St. Peter's. Sometimes I lose patience with its parade of eternal idleness, but at others this very idleness is balm to one's conscience. Life on just these terms seems so easy, so monotonously sweet, that you feel it would be unwise, would be really unsafe, to change. The Roman air is charged with an elixir, the Roman cup seasoned with some insidious drop, of which the action is fatally, yet none the less agreeably, "lowering."

January 26th.—With S. to the Villa Medici—perhaps on the whole the most enchanting place in Rome. The part of the garden called the Boschetto has an incredible, impossible charm; an upper terrace, behind locked gates, covered with a little dusky forest of evergreen oaks. Such a dim light as of a fabled, haunted place, such a soft suffusion of tender grey-green tones, such a company of gnarled and twisted little miniature trunks—dwarfs playing with each other at being giants—and such a shower of golden sparkles drifting in from the vivid west! At the end of the wood is a steep, circular mound, up which the short trees scramble amain, with a long mossy staircase climbing up to a belvedere. This staircase, rising suddenly out of the leafy dusk to you don't see where, is delightfully fantastic. You expect to see an old woman in a crimson petticoat and with a distaff come hobbling

down and turn into a fairy and offer you three wishes. I
should name for my own first wish that one didn't have to be
a Frenchman to come and live and dream and work at the
Académie de France. Can there be for a while a happier destiny than that of a young artist conscious of talent and of no
errand but to educate, polish and perfect it, transplanted to
these sacred shades? One has fancied Plato's Academy—his
gleaming colonnades, his blooming gardens and Athenian
sky; but was it as good as this one, where Monsieur Hébert
does the Platonic? The blessing in Rome is not that this or
that or the other isolated object is so very unsurpassable; but
that the general air so contributes to interest, to impressions
that are not as any other impressions anywhere in the world.
And from this general air the Villa Medici has distilled an
essence of its own—walled it in and made it delightfully private. The great façade on the gardens is like an enormous
rococo clock-face all incrusted with images and arabesques
and tablets. What mornings and afternoons one might spend
there, brush in hand, unpreoccupied, untormented, pen-
sioned, satisfied—either persuading one's self that one would
be "doing something" in consequence or not caring if one
shouldn't be.

At a later date—middle of March.—A ride with S. W. out
of the Porta Pia to the meadows beyond the Ponte Nomen-
tana—close to the site of Phaon's villa where Nero in hiding
had himself stabbed. It all spoke as things here only speak,
touching more chords than one can *now* really know or say.
For these are predestined memories and the stuff that regrets
are made of; the mild divine efflorescence of spring, the wonderful landscape, the talk suspended for another gallop. . . .
Returning, we dismounted at the gate of the Villa Medici and
walked through the twilight of the vaguely perfumed, bird-
haunted alleys to H.'s studio, hidden in the wood like a cottage in a fairy tale. I spent there a charming half-hour in the
fading light, looking at the pictures while my companion discoursed of her errand. The studio is small and more like a
little salon; the painting refined, imaginative, somewhat morbid, full of consummate French ability. A portrait, idealised
and etherealised, but a likeness of Mme. de —— (from last
year's Salon) in white satin, quantities of lace, a coronet, dia-

monds and pearls; a striking combination of brilliant silvery
tones. A "Femme Sauvage," a naked dusky girl in a wood,
with a wonderfully clever pair of shy, passionate eyes. The
author is different enough from any of the numerous American artists. They may be producers, but he's a product as
well—a product of influences of a sort of which we have as
yet no general command. One of them is his charmed lapse of
life in that unprofessional-looking little studio, with his enchanted wood on one side and the plunging wall of Rome on
the other.

January 30th. —A drive the other day with a friend to Villa
Madama, on the side of Monte Mario; a place like a page out
of one of Browning's richest evocations of this clime and
civilisation. Wondrous in its haunting melancholy, it might
have inspired half "The Ring and the Book" at a stroke.
What a grim commentary on history such a scene—what an
irony of the past! The road up to it through the outer enclosure is almost impassable with mud and stones. At the end,
on a terrace, rises the once elegant Casino, with hardly a
whole pane of glass in its façade, reduced to its sallow stucco
and degraded ornaments. The front away from Rome has in
the basement a great loggia, now walled in from the weather,
preceded by a grassy belittered platform with an immense
sweeping view of the Campagna; the sad-looking, more than
sad-looking, evil-looking, Tiber beneath (the colour of gold,
the sentimentalists say, the colour of mustard, the realists); a
great vague stretch beyond, of various complexions and uses;
and on the horizon the ever-iridescent mountains. The place
has become the shabbiest farm-house, with muddy water in
the old *pièces d'eau* and dunghills on the old parterres. The
"feature" is the contents of the loggia: a vaulted roof and
walls decorated by Giulio Romano; exquisite stucco-work
and still brilliant frescoes; arabesques and figurini, nymphs
and fauns, animals and flowers—gracefully lavish designs of
every sort. Much of the colour—especially the blues—still
almost vivid, and all the work wonderfully ingenious, elegant
and charming. Apartments so decorated can have been meant
only for the recreation of people greater than any we know,
people for whom life was impudent ease and success. Margaret Farnese was the lady of the house, but where she trailed

her cloth of gold the chickens now scamper between your legs over rotten straw. It is all inexpressibly dreary. A stupid peasant scratching his head, a couple of critical Americans picking their steps, the walls tattered and befouled breast-high, dampness and decay striking in on your heart, and the scene overbowed by these heavenly frescoes, mouldering there in their airy artistry! It's poignant; it provokes tears; it tells so of the waste of effort. Something human seems to pant beneath the grey pall of time and to implore you to rescue it, to pity it, to stand by it somehow. But you leave it to its lingering death without compunction, almost with pleasure; for the place seems vaguely crime-haunted—paying at least the penalty of some hard immorality. The end of a Renaissance pleasure-house. Endless for the didactic observer the moral, abysmal for the story-seeker the tale.

February 12th.—Yesterday to the Villa Albani. Over-formal and (as my companion says) too much like a tea-garden; but with beautiful stairs and splendid geometrical lines of immense box-hedge, intersected with high pedestals supporting little antique busts. The light to-day magnificent; the Alban hills of an intenser broken purple than I had yet seen them—their white towns blooming upon it like vague projected lights. It was like a piece of very modern painting, and a good example of how Nature has at times a sort of mannerism which ought to make us careful how we condemn out of hand the more refined and affected artists. The collection of marbles in the Casino (Winckelmann's) admirable and to be seen again. The famous Antinous crowned with lotus a strangely beautiful and impressive thing. The "Greek manner," on the showing of something now and again encountered here, moves one to feel that even for purely romantic and imaginative effects it surpasses any since invented. If there be not imagination, even in our comparatively modern sense of the word, in the baleful beauty of that perfect young profile there is none in "Hamlet" or in "Lycidas." There is five hundred times as much as in "The Transfiguration." With this at any rate to point to it's not for sculpture not professedly to produce any emotion producible by painting. There are numbers of small and delicate fragments of bas-reliefs of exquisite grace, and a huge piece (two combatants—one, on horseback, beating down another—murder made eternal and beautiful) attributed to the Parthenon and certainly as grandly impressive as anything in the Elgin marbles. S. W. suggested again the Roman villas as a "subject." Excellent if one could find a feast of facts à la Stendhal. A lot of vague ecstatic descriptions and anecdotes wouldn't at all pay. There have been too many already. Enough facts are recorded, I suppose; one should discover them and soak in them for a twelvemonth. And yet a Roman villa, in spite of statues, ideas and atmosphere, affects me as of a scanter human and social *portée*, a shorter, thinner reverberation, than an old English country-house, round which experience seems piled so thick. But this perhaps is either hair-splitting or "racial" prejudice.

March 9th.—The Vatican is still deadly cold; a couple of hours there yesterday with R. W. E. Yet he, illustrious and enviable man, fresh from the East, had no overcoat and wanted none. Perfect bliss, I think, would be to live in Rome without thinking of overcoats. The Vatican seems very familiar, but strangely smaller than of old. I never lost the sense before of confusing vastness. *Sancta simplicitas!* All my old friends however stand there in undimmed radiance, keeping most of them their old pledges. I am perhaps more struck now with the enormous amount of padding—the number of third-rate, fourth-rate things that weary the eye desirous to approach freshly the twenty and thirty best. In spite of the padding there are dozens of treasures that one passes regretfully; but the impression of the whole place is the great thing—the feeling that through these solemn vistas flows the source of an incalculable part of our present conception of Beauty.

April 10th.—Last night, in the rain, to the Teatro Valle to see a comedy of Goldoni in Venetian dialect—"I Quattro Rustighi." I could but half follow it; enough, however, to be sure that, for all its humanity of irony, it wasn't so good as Molière. The acting was capital—broad, free and natural; the play of talk easier even than life itself; but, like all the Italian acting I have seen, it was wanting in *finesse*, that shade of the shade by which, and by which alone, one really knows art. I contrasted the affair with the evening in December last that I walked over (also in the rain) to the Odéon and saw the

"Plaideurs" and the "Malade Imaginaire." There, too, was hardly more than a handful of spectators; but what rich, ripe, fully representational and above all intellectual comedy, and what polished, educated playing! These Venetians in particular, however, have a marvellous *entrain* of their own; they seem even less than the French to recite. In some of the women—ugly, with red hands and shabby dresses—an extraordinary gift of natural utterance, of seeming to invent joyously as they go.

Later.—Last evening in H.'s box at the Apollo to hear Ernesto Rossi in "Othello." He shares supremacy with Salvini in Italian tragedy. Beautiful great theatre with boxes you can walk about in; brilliant audience. The Princess Margaret was there—I have never been to the theatre that she was not—and a number of other princesses in neighbouring boxes. G. G. came in and instructed us that they were the M., the L., the P., &c. Rossi is both very bad and very fine; bad where anything like taste and discretion is required, but "all there," and more than there, in violent passion. The last act reduced too much, however, to mere exhibitional sensibility. The interesting thing to me was to observe the Italian conception of the part—to see how crude it was, how little it expressed the hero's moral side, his depth, his dignity—anything more than his being a creature terrible in mere tantrums. The great point was his seizing Iago's head and whacking it half-a-dozen times on the floor, and then flinging him twenty yards away. It was wonderfully done, but in the doing of it and in the evident relish for it in the house there was I scarce knew what force of easy and thereby rather cheap expression.

April 27th.—A morning with L. B. at Villa Ludovisi, which we agreed that we shouldn't soon forget. The villa now belongs to the King, who has lodged his morganatic wife there. There is nothing so blissfully *right* in Rome, nothing more consummately consecrated to style. The grounds and gardens are immense, and the great rusty-red city wall stretches away behind them and makes the burden of the seven hills seem vast without making *them* seem small. There is everything—dusky avenues trimmed by the clippings of centuries, groves and dells and glades and glowing pastures and reedy fountains and great flowering meadows studded with enormous slanting pines. The day was delicious, the trees all one melody, the whole place a revelation of what Italy and hereditary pomp can do together. Nothing could be more in the grand manner than this garden view of the city ramparts, lifting their fantastic battlements above the trees and flowers. They are all tapestried with vines and made to serve as sunny fruit-walls—grim old defence as they once were; now giving nothing but a splendid buttressed privacy. The sculptures in the little Casino are few, but there are two great ones—the beautiful sitting Mars and the head of the great Juno, the latter thrust into a corner behind a shutter. These things it's almost impossible to praise; we can only mark them well and keep them clear, as we insist on silence to hear great music. . . . If I don't praise Guercino's Aurora in the greater Casino, it's for another reason; this is certainly a very muddy masterpiece. It figures on the ceiling of a small low hall; the painting is coarse and the ceiling too near. Besides, it's unfair to pass straight from the Greek mythology to the Bolognese. We were left to roam at will through the house; the custode shut us in and went to walk in the park. The apartments were all open, and I had an opportunity to reconstruct, from its *milieu* at least, the character of a morganatic queen. I saw nothing to indicate that it was not amiable; but I should have thought more highly of the lady's discrimination if she had had the Juno removed from behind her shutter. In such a house, girdled about with such a park, methinks I could be amiable—and perhaps discriminating too. The Ludovisi Casino is small, but the perfection of the life of ease might surely be led there. There are English houses enough in wondrous parks, but they expose you to too many small needs and observances—to say nothing of a red-faced butler dropping his *h*'s. You are oppressed with the detail of accommodation. Here the billiard-table is old-fashioned, perhaps a trifle crooked; but you have Guercino above your head, and Guercino, after all, is almost as good as Guido. The rooms, I noticed, all pleased by their shape, by a lovely proportion, by a mass of delicate ornamentation on the high concave ceilings. One might live over again in them some deliciously benighted life of a forgotten type—with graceful old *sale*, and immensely thick walls, and a winding stone staircase, and a view from the loggia at the top; a view of twisted parasol-pines balanced, high above a wooden horizon, against a sky of faded sapphire.

May 17th. —It was wonderful yesterday at St. John Lateran. The spring now has turned to perfect summer; there are cascades of verdure over all the walls; the early flowers are a fading memory, and the new grass knee-deep in the Villa Borghese. The winter aspect of the region about the Lateran is one of the best things in Rome; the sunshine is nowhere so golden and the lean shadows nowhere so purple as on the long grassy walk to Santa Croce. But yesterday I seemed to see nothing but green and blue. The expanse before Santa Croce was vivid green; the Campagna rolled away in great green billows, which seemed to break high about the gaunt aqueducts; and the Alban Hills, which in January and February keep shifting and melting along the whole scale of azure, were almost monotonously fresh, and had lost some of their finer modelling. But the sky was ultramarine and everything radiant with light and warmth—warmth which a soft steady breeze kept from excess. I strolled some time about the church, which has a grand air enough, though I don't seize the point of view of Miss ——, who told me the other day how vastly finer she thought it than St. Peter's. But on Miss ——'s lips this seemed a very pretty paradox. The choir and transepts have a sombre splendour, and I like the old vaulted passage with its slabs and monuments behind the choir. The charm of charms at St. John Lateran is the admirable twelfth-century cloister, which was never more charming than yesterday. The shrubs and flowers about the ancient well were blooming away in the intense light, and the twisted pillars and chiselled capitals of the perfect little colonnade seemed to enclose them like the sculptured rim of a precious vase. Standing out among the flowers you may look up and see a section of the summit of the great façade of the church. The robed and mitred apostles, bleached and rain-washed by the ages, rose into the blue air like huge snow figures. I spent at the incorporated museum a subsequent hour of fond vague attention, having it quite to myself. It is rather scantily stocked, but the great cool halls open out impressively one after the other, and the wide spaces between the statues seem to suggest at first that each is a masterpiece. I was in the loving mood of one's last days in Rome, and when I had nothing else to admire I admired the magnificent thickness of the embrasures of the doors and windows. If there were no objects of interest at all in the Lateran the palace would be worth walking through every now and then, to keep up one's idea of solid architecture. I went over to the Scala Santa, where was no one but a very shabby priest sitting like a ticket-taker at the door. But he let me pass, and I ascended one of the profane lateral stairways and treated myself to a glimpse of the Sanctum Sanctorum. Its threshold is crossed but once or twice a year, I believe, by three or four of the most exalted divines, but you may look into it freely enough through a couple of gilded lattices. It is very sombre and splendid, and conveys the impression of a very holy place. And yet somehow it suggested irreverent thoughts; it had to my fancy—perhaps on account of the lattice—an Oriental, a Mahometan note. I expected every moment to see a sultana appear in a silver veil and silken trousers and sit down on the crimson carpet.

Farewell, packing, the sharp pang of going. One would like to be able after five months in Rome to sum up, for tribute and homage, one's experience, one's gains, the whole adventure of one's sensibility. But one has really vibrated too much—the addition of so many items isn't easy. What is simply clear is the sense of an acquired passion for the place and of an incalculable number of gathered impressions. Many of these have been intense and momentous, but one has trodden on the other—there are always the big fish that swallow up the little—and one can hardly say what has become of them. They store themselves noiselessly away, I suppose, in the dim but safe places of memory and "taste," and we live in a quiet faith that they will emerge into vivid relief if life or art should demand them. As for the passion we needn't perhaps trouble ourselves about that. Fifty swallowed palmfuls of the Fountain of Trevi couldn't make us more ardently sure that we shall at any cost come back.

1873.

A Few Other
Roman Neighbourhoods

I F I FIND my old notes, in all these Roman connections,
inevitably bristle with the spirit of the postscript, so I give
way to this prompting to the extent of my scant space and
with the sense of other occasions awaiting me on which I
shall have to do no less. The impression of Rome was repeatedly to renew itself for the author of these now rather antique
and artless accents; was to overlay itself again and again with
almost heavy thicknesses of experience, the last of which is, as
I write, quite fresh to memory; and he has thus felt almost
ashamed to drop his subject (though it be one that tends so
easily to turn to the infinite) as if the law of change had in all
the years had nothing to say to his case. It's of course but of
his case alone that he speaks—wondering little what he may
make of it for the profit of others by an attempt, however
brief, to point the moral of the matter, or in other words
compare the musing *mature* visitor's "feeling about Rome"
with that of the extremely agitated, even if though extremely
inexpert, consciousness reflected in the previous pages. The
actual, the current Rome affects him as a world governed by
new conditions altogether and ruefully pleading that sorry
fact in the ear of the antique wanderer wherever he may yet
mournfully turn for some re-capture of what he misses. The
city of his first unpremeditated rapture shines to memory, on
the other hand, in the manner of a lost paradise the rustle of
whose gardens is still just audible enough in the air to make
him wonder if some sudden turn, some recovered vista,
mayn't lead him back to the thing itself. My genial, my helpful tag, at this point, would doubtless properly resolve itself,
for the reader, into a clue toward some such successful ingenuity of quest; a remark I make, I may add, even while
reflecting that the Paradise isn't apparently at all "lost" to
visitors not of my generation. It is the seekers of *that* remote
and romantic tradition who have seen it, from one period of
ten, or even of five, years to another, systematically and remorselessly built out from their view. Their helpless plaint,

their sense of the generally irrecoverable and unspeakable, is not, however, what I desire here most to express; I should like, on the contrary, with ampler opportunity, positively to enumerate the cases, the cases of contact, impression, experience, in which the cold ashes of a long-chilled passion may fairly feel themselves made to glow again. No one who has ever loved Rome as Rome could be loved in youth and before her poised basketful of the finer appeals to fond fancy was actually upset, wants to stop loving her; so that our bleeding and wounded, though perhaps not wholly moribund, loyalty attends us as a hovering admonitory, anticipatory ghost, one of those magnanimous life-companions who before complete extinction designate to the other member of the union their approved successor. So it is at any rate that I conceive the pilgrim old enough to have become aware in all these later years of what he misses to be counselled and pacified in the interest of recognitions that shall a little make up for it.

It was this wisdom I was putting into practice, no doubt, for instance, when I lately resigned myself to motoring of a splendid June day "out to" Subiaco; as a substitute for a resignation that had anciently taken, alas, but the form of my never getting there at all. Everything that day, moreover, seemed right, surely; everything on certain other days that were like it through their large indebtedness, at this, that and the other point, to the last new thing, seemed so right that they come back to me now, after a moderate interval, in the full light of that unchallenged felicity. I couldn't at all gloriously recall, for instance, as I floated to Subiaco on vast brave wings, how on the occasion of my first visit to Rome, thirty-eight years before, I had devoted certain evenings, evenings of artless "preparation" in my room at the inn, to the perusal of Alphonse Dantier's admirable *Monastères Bénédictins d'Italie*, taking piously for granted that I should get myself somehow conveyed to Monte Cassino and to Subiaco at least: such an affront to the passion of curiosity, the generally infatuated state then kindled, would any suspicion of my foredoomed, my all but interminable, privation during visits to come have seemed to me. Fortune, in the event, had never favoured my going, but I was to give myself up at last to the sense of her quite taking me by the hand, and that is how I now think of our splendid June day at Subiaco. The note of the wondrous place itself is conventional "wild" Italy raised to the highest intensity, the ideally, the sublimely conventional and wild, complete and supreme in itself, without a disparity or a flaw; which character of perfect picturesque orthodoxy seemed more particularly to begin for me, I remember, as we passed, on our way, through that indescribable and indestructible Tivoli, where the jumble of the elements of the familiarly and exploitedly, the all too notoriously fair and queer, was more violent and vociferous than ever—so the whole spectacle there seemed at once to rejoice in cockneyfication and to resist it. There at least I had old memories to renew—including that, in especial, from a few years back, of one of the longest, hottest, dustiest return-drives to Rome that the Campagna on a sirocco day was ever to have treated me to.

That was to be more than made up on this later occasion by an hour of early evening, snatched on the run back to Rome, that remains with me as one of those felicities we are wise to leave for ever just as they are, just, that is, where they fell, never attempting to renew or improve them. So happy a chance was it that ensured me at the afternoon's end a solitary stroll through the Villa d'Este, where the day's invasion, whatever it might have been, had left no traces and where I met nobody in the great rococo passages and chambers, and in the prodigious alleys and on the repeated flights of tortu-ous steps, but the haunting Genius of Style, into whose noble battered old face, as if it had come out clearer in the golden twilight and on recognition of response so deeply moved, I seemed to exhale my sympathy. This was truly, amid a con-ception and order of things all mossed over from disuse, but still without a form abandoned or a principle disowned, one of the hours that one doesn't forget. The ruined fountains seemed strangely to *wait*, in the stillness and under cover of the approaching dusk, not to begin ever again to play, also, but just only to be tenderly imagined to do so; quite as every-thing held its breath, at the mystic moment, for the drop of the cruel and garish exposure, for the Spirit of the place to steal forth and go his round. The vistas of the innumerable mighty cypresses ranged themselves, in their files and compa-nies, like beaten heroes for their captain's review; the great artificial "works" of every description, cascades, hemicycles, all graded and grassed and stone-seated as for floral games, mazes and bowers and alcoves and grottos, brave indissoluble unions of the planted and the builded symmetry, with the terraces and staircases that overhang and the arcades and cloisters that underspread, made common cause together as for one's taking up a little, in kindly lingering wonder, the "feeling" out of which they have sprung. One didn't see it, under the actual influence, one wouldn't for the world have seen it, as that they longed to be justified, during a few minutes in the twenty-four hours, of their absurdity of pomp and circumstance—but only that they asked for company, once in a way, as they were so splendidly formed to give it, and that the best company, in a changed world, at the end of time, what could they hope it to be but just the lone, the dawdling person of taste, the visitor with a flicker of fancy, not to speak of a pang of pity, to spare for them? It was in the flicker of fancy, no doubt, that as I hung about the great topmost terrace in especial, and then again took my way through the high gaunt corridors and the square and bare alcoved and recessed saloons, all overscored with such a dim waste of those painted, those delicate and capricious decorations which the loggie of the Vatican promptly borrowed from the ruins of the Palatine, or from whatever other revealed and inspiring ancientries, and which make ghostly confession here of that descent, I gave the rein to my sense of the sinister too, of that vague after-taste as of evil things that lurks so often, for a suspicious sensibility, wherever the terrible game of the life of the Renaissance was played as the Italians played it; wherever the huge tesselated chessboard seems to stretch about us, swept bare, almost always violently swept bare, of its chiselled and shifting figures, of every value and degree, but with this echoing desolation itself representing the long gasp, as it were, of overstrained time, the great after-hush that follows on things too wonderful or dreadful.

I am putting here, however, my cart before my horse, for the hour just glanced at was but a final tag to a day of much brighter curiosity, and which seemed to take its baptism, as we passed through prodigious perched and huddled, adorably scattered and animated and even crowded Tivoli, from the universal happy spray of the drumming Anio waterfalls, all set in their permanent rainbows and Sibylline temples and classic allusions and Byronic quotations; a wondrous romantic jumble of such things and quite others—heterogeneous inns and clamorous *guingettes* and factories grabbing at the torrent, to say nothing of innumerable guides and donkeys and white-tied, swallow-tailed waiters dashing out of grottos and from under cataracts, and of the air, on the part of the whole population, of standing about, in the most characteristic *contadino* manner, to pounce on you and take you somewhere, snatch you from somebody else, shout something at you, the aqueous and other uproar permitting, and then charge you for it, your innocence aiding. I'm afraid our run the rest of the way to Subiaco remains with me but as an after-sense of that exhilaration, in spite of our rising admirably higher, all the while, and plunging constantly deeper into splendid solitary gravities, supreme romantic solemnities and sublimities, of landscape. The Benedictine convent, which clings to certain more or less vertiginous ledges and slopes of a vast precipitous gorge, constitutes, with the whole perfection of its setting, the very ideal of the tradition of that *extraordinary in the romantic* handed down to us, as the most attaching and inviting spell of Italy, by all the old academic literature of travel and art of the Salvator Rosas and Claudes. This is the main tribute I may pay in a few words to an impression of which a sort of divine rightness of oddity, a pictorial felicity that was almost not of this world, but of a higher degree of distinction altogether, affected me as the leading note; yet about the whole exquisite complexity of which I can't pretend to be informing.

All the elements of the scene melted for me together; even from the pause for luncheon on a grassy wayside knoll, over heaven knows what admirable preparatory headlong slopes and ravines and iridescent distances, under spreading chestnuts and in the high air that was cool and sweet, to the final pedestrian climb of sinuous mountain-paths that the shining limestone and the strong green of shrub and herbage made as white as silver. There the miraculous home of St. Benedict awaited us in the form of a builded and pictured-over maze of chapels and shrines, cells and corridors, stupefying rock-chambers and caves, places all at an extraordinary variety of different levels and with labyrinthine intercommunications; there the spirit of the centuries sat like some invisible icy presence that only permits you to stare and wonder. I stared, I wondered, I went up and down and in and out and lost myself in the fantastic fable of the innumerable hard facts themselves; and whenever I could, above all, I peeped out of small windows and hung over chance terraces for the love of the general outer picture, the splendid fashion in which the fretted mountains of marble, as they might have been, round about, seemed to inlay themselves, for the effect of the "distinction" I speak of, with vegetations of dark emerald. There above all—or at least in what such aspects did further for the prodigy of the Convent, whatever that prodigy might do for *them*—was, to a life-long victim of Italy, almost verily as never before, the operation of the old love-philtre; there were the inexhaustible sources of interest and charm.

These mystic fountains broke out for me elsewhere, again and again, I rejoice to say—and perhaps more particularly, to be frank about it, where the ground about them was pressed with due emphasis of appeal by the firm wheels of the great winged car. I motored, under invitation and protection, repeatedly back into the sense of the other years, that sense of the "old" and comparatively idle Rome of my particular infatuated prime which I was living to see superseded, and this even when the fond vista bristled with innumerable "signs of the times," unmistakable features of the new era, that, by I scarce know what perverse law, succeeded in ministering to a happy effect. Some of these false notes proceed simply from the immense growth of every sort of facilitation—so that people are much more free than of old to come and go and do, to inquire and explore, to pervade and generally "infest"; with a consequent loss, for the fastidious individual, of his blest earlier sense, not infrequent, of having the occasion and the impression, as he used complacently to say, all to himself. We none of us had anything quite all to ourselves during an afternoon at Ostia, on a beautiful June Sunday; it was a different affair, rather, from the long, the comparatively slow and quite unpeopled drive that I was to remember having last taken early in the autumn thirty years before, and which

occupied the day—with the aid of a hamper from once supreme old Spillman, the provider for picnics to a vanished
world (since I suspect the antique ideal of "a picnic in the
Campagna," the fondest conception of a happy day, has lost
generally much of its glamour). Our idyllic afternoon, at any
rate, left no chord of sensibility that could possibly have been
in question untouched—not even that of tea on the shore at
Fiumincino, after we had spent an hour among the ruins of
Ostia and seen our car ferried across the Tiber, almost
saffron-coloured here and swirling towards its mouth, on a
boat that was little more than a big rustic raft and that yet
bravely resisted the prodigious weight. What shall I say, in
the way of the particular, of the general felicity before me, for
the sweetness of the hour to which the incident just named,
with its strange and amusing juxtapositions of the patriar-
chally primitive and the insolently supersubtle, the earliest and
the latest efforts of restless science, were almost immediately
to succeed?

We had but skirted the old gold-and-brown walls of Castel
Fusano, where the massive Chigi tower and the immemorial
stone-pines and the afternoon sky and the desolate sweetness
and concentrated rarity of the picture all kept their appointment, to fond memory, with that especial form of Roman
faith, the fine æsthetic conscience in things, that is never,
never broken. We had wound through tangled lanes and met
handsome sallow country-folk lounging at leisure, as became
the Sunday, and ever so pleasantly and garishly clothed, if not
quite consistently costumed, as just on purpose to feed our
wanton optimism; and then we had addressed ourselves with
a soft superficiality to the open, the exquisite little Ostian reliquary, an exhibition of stony vaguenesses half straightened
out. The ruins of the ancient port of Rome, the still recover-
able identity of streets and habitations and other forms of civil
life, are a not inconsiderable handful, though making of the
place at best a very small sister to Pompeii; but a soft superficiality is ever the refuge of my shy sense before any ghost of
informed reconstitution, and I plead my surrender to it with
the less shame that I believe I "enjoy" such scenes even on
such futile pretexts as much as it can be appointed them by
the invidious spirit of History to *be* enjoyed. It may be said,

of course, that enjoyment, question-begging term at best, isn't in these austere connections designated—but rather some principle of appreciation that can at least give a coherent account of itself. On that basis then—as I could, I profess, *but* revel in the looseness of my apprehension, so wide it seemed to fling the gates of vision and divination—I won't pretend to dot, as it were, too many of the i's of my incompetence. I was competent only to have been abjectly interested. On reflection, moreover, I see that no impression of over-much company invaded the picture till the point was exactly reached for its contributing thoroughly to character and amusement; across at Fiumincino, which the age of the bicycle has made, in a small way, the handy Gravesend or Coney Island of Rome, the cafés and *birrerie* were at high pressure, and the bustle all motley and friendly beside the melancholy river, where the waterside life itself had twenty quaint and vivid notes and where a few upstanding objects, ancient or modern, looked eminent and interesting against the delicate Roman sky that dropped down and down to the far-spreading marshes of malaria. Besides which "company" is ever intensely gregarious, hanging heavily together and easily outwitted; so that we had but to proceed a scant distance further and meet the tideless Mediterranean, where it tumbled in a trifle breezily on the sands, to be all to ourselves with our tea-basket, quite as in the good old fashion—only in truth with the advantage that the contemporary tea-basket is so much improved.

I jumble my memories as a tribute to the whole idyll—I give the golden light in which they come back to me for what it is worth; worth, I mean, as allowing that the possibilities of charm of the Witch of the Seven Hills, as we used to call her in magazines, haven't all been vulgarised away. It was precisely there, on such an occasion and in such a place, that this might seem signally to have happened; whereas in fact the mild suburban riot, in which the so gay but so light potations before the array of little houses of entertainment were what struck one as really making most for mildness, was brushed over with a fabled grace, was harmonious, felicitous, distinguished, quite after the fashion of some thoroughly trained chorus or phalanx of opera or ballet. Bicycles were stacked up by the hundred; the youth of Rome are ardent cyclists, with a great taste for flashing about in more or less denuded or costumed athletic and romantic bands and guilds, and on our return cityward, toward evening, along the right bank of the river, the road swarmed with the patient wheels and bent backs of these budding *cives Romani* quite to the effect of its finer interest. Such at least, I felt, could only be one's acceptance of almost any feature of a scene bathed in that extraordinarily august air that the waning Roman day is so insidiously capable of taking on when any other element of style happens at all to contribute. Weren't they present, these other elements, in the great classic lines and folds, the fine academic or historic attitudes of the darkening land itself as it hung about the old highway, varying its vague accidents, but achieving always perfect "composition"? I shamelessly add that cockneyfied impression, at all events, to what I have called my jumble; Rome, to which we all swept on together in the wondrous glowing medium, *saved* everything, spreading afar her wide wing and applying after all but her supposed grand gift of the secret of salvation. We kept on and on into the great dim rather sordidly papal streets that approach the quarter of St. Peter's; to the accompaniment, finally, of that markedly felt provocation of fond wonder which had never failed to lie in wait for me under any question of a renewed glimpse of the huge unvisited rear of the basilica. There was no renewed glimpse just then, in the gloaming; but the region I speak of had been for me, in fact, during the previous weeks, less unvisited than ever before, so that I had come to count an occasional walk round and about it as quite of the essence of the convenient small change with which the heterogeneous City may still keep paying you. These frequentations in the company of a sculptor friend had been incidental to our reaching a small artistic foundry of fine metal, an odd and interesting little establishment placed, as who should say in the case of such a mere left-over scrap of a large loose margin, nowhere: it lurked so unsuspectedly, that is, among the various queer things that Rome comprehensively refers to as "behind St. Peter's."

We had passed then, on the occasion of our several pilgrimages, in beneath the great flying, or at least straddling buttresses to the left of the mighty façade, where you enter that great idle precinct of fine dense pavement and averted and sacrificed grandeur, the reverse of the monstrous medal of the front. Here the architectural monster rears its back and shoulders on an equal scale and this whole unregarded world of colossal consistent symmetry and hidden high finish gives you the measure of the vast total treasure of items and features. The outward face of all sorts of inward majesties of utility and ornament here above all correspondingly reproduces itself; the expanses of golden travertine—the freshness of tone, the cleanness of surface, in the sunny air, being extraordinary—climb and soar and spread under the crushing weight of a scheme carried out in every ponderous particular. Never was such a show of *wasted* art, of pomp for pomp's sake, as where all the chapels bulge and all the windows, each one a separate constructional masterpiece, tower above almost grass-grown vacancy; with the full and immediate effect, of course, of reading us a lesson on the value of lawful pride. The pride is the pride of indifference as to whether a greatness so founded be gaped at in all its features or not. My friend and I were alone to gape at them most often while, for the unfailing impression of them, on our way to watch the casting of our figure, we extended our circuit of the place. To which I may add, as another example of that tentative, that appealing twitch of the garment of Roman association of which one kept renewing one's consciousness, the half-hour at the little foundry itself was all charming—with its quite shabby and belittered and ramshackle recall of the old Roman "art-life" of one's early dreams. Everything was somehow in the picture, the rickety sheds, the loose paraphernalia, the sunny, grassy yard where a goat was browsing; then the queer interior gloom of the pits, frilled with little overlooking scaffoldings and bridges, for the sinking fireward of the image that was to take on hardness; and all the pleasantness and quickness, the beguiling refinement, of the three or four light fine "hands" of whom the staff consisted and into whose type and tone one liked to read, with whatever harmless extravagance, so many signs that a lively sense of stiff processes, even in humble life, could still leave untouched the traditional rare feeling for the artistic. How delightful such an occupation in such a general setting—those of my friend, I at such moments irrepressibly moralised; and how one might after such a fashion endlessly go and come and ask nothing better; or if better, only so to the extent of another impression I was to owe to him: that of an evening meal spread, in the warm still darkness that made no candle flicker, on the wide high space of an old loggia that overhung, in one quarter, the great obelisked Square preceding one of the Gates, and in the other the Tiber and the far Trastevere and more things than I can say—above all, as it were, the whole backward past, the mild confused romance of the Rome one had loved and of which one was exactly taking leave under protection of the friendly lanterned and garlanded feast and the commanding, all-embracing roof-garden. It was indeed a reconciling, it was an altogether penetrating, last hour.

1909.

A Chain of Cities

ONE DAY in midwinter, some years since, during a journey from Rome to Florence perforce too rapid to allow much wayside sacrifice to curiosity, I waited for the train at Narni. There was time to stroll far enough from the station to have a look at the famous old bridge of Augustus, broken short off in mid-Tiber. While I stood admiring the measure of impression was made to overflow by the gratuitous grace of a white-cowled monk who came trudging up the road that wound to the gate of the town. Narni stood, in its own presented felicity, on a hill a good space away, boxed in behind its perfect grey wall, and the monk, to oblige me, crept slowly along and disappeared within the aperture. Everything was distinct in the clear air, and the view exactly as like the bit of background by an Umbrian master as it ideally should have been. The winter is bare and brown enough in southern Italy and the earth reduced to more of a mere anatomy than among ourselves, for whom the very *crânerie* of its exposed state, naked and unashamed, gives it much of the robust serenity, not of a fleshless skeleton, but of a fine nude statue. In these regions, at any rate, the tone of the air, for the eye, during the brief desolation, has often an extraordinary charm: nature still smiles as with the deputed and provisional charity of colour and light, the duty of not ceasing to cheer man's heart. Her whole behaviour, at the time, cast such a spell on the broken bridge, the little walled town and the trudging friar, that I turned away with the impatient vow and the fond vision of how I would take the journey again and pause to my heart's content at Narni, at Spoleto, at Assisi, at Perugia, at Cortona, at Arezzo. But we have generally to clip our vows a little when we come to fulfil them; and so it befell that when my blest springtime arrived I had to begin as resignedly as possible, yet with comparative meagreness, at Assisi.

I suppose enjoyment would have a simple zest which it often lacks if we always did things at the moment we want to, for it's mostly when we can't that we're thoroughly sure we *would*, and we can answer too little for moods in the future conditional. Winter at least seemed to me to have put something into these seats of antiquity that the May sun had more or less melted away—a desirable strength of tone, a depth upon depth of queerness and quaintness. Assisi had been in the January twilight, after my mere snatch at Narni, a vignette out of some brown old missal. But you'll have to be a fearless explorer now to find of a fine spring day any such cluster of curious objects as doesn't seem made to match before anything else Mr. Baedeker's polyglot estimate of its chief recommendations. This great man was at Assisi in force, and a brand-new inn for his accommodation has just been opened cheek by jowl with the church of St. Francis. I don't know that even the dire discomfort of this harbourage makes it seem less impertinent; but I confess I sought its protection, and the great view seemed hardly less beautiful from my window than from the gallery of the convent. This view embraces the whole wide reach of Umbria, which becomes as twilight deepens a purple counterfeit of the misty sea. The visitor's first errand is with the church; and it's fair furthermore to admit that when he has crossed that threshold the position and quality of his hotel cease for the time to be matters of moment. This twofold temple of St. Francis is one of the very sacred places of Italy, and it would be hard to breathe anywhere an air more heavy with holiness. Such seems especially the case if you happen thus to have come from Rome, where everything ecclesiastical is, in aspect, so very much of this world—so florid, so elegant, so full of accommodations and excrescences. The mere site here makes for authority, and they were brave builders who laid the foundation-stones. The thing rises straight from a steep mountain-side and plunges forward on its great substructure of arches even as a crowned headland may frown over the main. Before it stretches a long, a grassy piazza, at the end of which you look up a small grey street, to see it first climb a little way the rest of the hill and then pause and leave a broad green slope, crested, high in the air, with a ruined castle. When I say before it I mean before the upper church; for by way of doing something supremely handsome and impressive the sturdy architects of the thirteenth century piled temple upon temple and bequeathed a double version of their idea. One may imagine them to have intended perhaps an architectural image of the relation between heart and head. Entering the lower church at the bottom of the great flight of steps which leads from the upper door, you seem to push at least into the very heart of Catholicism.

For the first minutes after leaving the clearer gloom you catch nothing but a vista of low black columns closed by the great fantastic cage surrounding the altar, which is thus placed, by your impression, in a sort of gorgeous cavern. Gradually you distinguish details, become accustomed to the penetrating chill, and even manage to make out a few frescoes; but the general effect remains splendidly sombre and subterranean. The vaulted roof is very low and the pillars dwarfish, though immense in girth, as befits pillars supporting substantially a cathedral. The tone of the place is a triumph of mystery, the richest harmony of lurking shadows and dusky corners, all relieved by scattered images and scintillations. There was little light but what came through the windows of the choir over which the red curtains had been dropped and were beginning to glow with the downward sun. The choir was guarded by a screen behind which a dozen venerable voices droned vespers; but over the top of the screen came the heavy radiance and played among the ornaments of the high fence round the shrine, casting the shadow of the whole elaborate mass forward into the obscured nave. The darkness of vaults and side-chapels is overwrought with vague frescoes, most of them by Giotto and his school, out of which confused richness the terribly distinct little faces characteristic of these artists stare at you with a solemn formalism. Some are faded and injured, and many so ill-lighted and ill-placed that you can only glance at them with decent conjecture; the great group, however—four paintings by Giotto on the ceiling above the altar—may be examined with some success. Like everything of that grim and beautiful master they deserve examination; but with the effect ever of carrying one's appreciation in and in, as it were, rather than of carrying it out and out, off and off, as happens for us with those artists who have been helped by the process of "evolution" to grow wings. This one, "going in" for emphasis at any price, stamps hard, as who should say, on the very spot of his idea—thanks to

which fact he has a concentration that has never been surpassed. He was in other words, in proportion to his means, a
genius supremely expressive; he makes the very shade of an
intended meaning or a represented attitude so unmistakable
that his figures affect us at moments as creatures all too suddenly, too alarmingly, too menacingly met. Meagre, primitive, undeveloped, he yet is immeasurably strong; he even
suggests that if he had lived the due span of years later
Michael Angelo might have found a rival. Not that he is
given, however, to complicated postures or superhuman
flights. The something strange that troubles and haunts us in
his work springs rather from a kind of fierce familiarity.

It is part of the wealth of the lower church that it contains
an admirable primitive fresco by an artist of genius rarely encountered, Pietro Cavallini, pupil of Giotto. This represents
the Crucifixion; the three crosses rising into a sky spotted
with the winged heads of angels while a dense crowd presses
below. You will nowhere see anything more direfully lugubrious, or more approaching for direct force, though not of
course for amplitude of style, Tintoretto's great renderings of
the scene in Venice. The abject anguish of the crucified and
the straddling authority and brutality of the mounted guards
in the foreground are contrasted in a fashion worthy of a
great dramatist. But the most poignant touch is the tragic
grimaces of the little angelic heads that fall like hailstones
through the dark air. It is genuine realistic weeping, the act of
irrepressible "crying," that the painter has depicted, and the
effect is pitiful at the same time as grotesque. There are many
more frescoes besides; all the chapels on one side are lined
with them, but these are chiefly interesting in their general
impressiveness—as they people the dim recesses with startling presences, with apparitions out of scale. Before leaving
the place I lingered long near the door, for I was sure I
shouldn't soon again enjoy such a feast of scenic composition.
The opposite end glowed with subdued colour; the middle
portion was vague and thick and brown, with two or three
scattered worshippers looming through the obscurity; while,
all the way down, the polished pavement, its uneven slabs
glittering dimly in the obstructed light, was of the very essence of expensive picture. It is certainly desirable, if one takes

the lower church of Saint Francis to represent the human heart, that one should find a few bright places there. But if the general effect is of brightness terrorised and smothered, is the symbol less valid? For the contracted, prejudiced, passionate heart let it stand.

One thing at all events we can say, that we should rejoice to boast as capacious, symmetrical and well-ordered a head as the upper sanctuary. Thanks to these merits, in spite of a brave array of Giottesque work which has the advantage of being easily seen, it lacks the great character of its counterpart. The frescoes, which are admirable, represent certain leading events in the life of Saint Francis, and suddenly remind you, by one of those anomalies that are half the secret of the consummate *mise-en-scène* of Catholicism, that the apostle of beggary, the saint whose only tenement in life was the ragged robe which barely covered him, is the hero of this massive structure. Church upon church, nothing less will adequately shroud his consecrated clay. The great reality of Giotto's designs adds to the helpless wonderment with which we feel the passionate pluck of the Hero, the sense of being separated from it by an impassable gulf, the reflection on all that has come and gone to make morality at that vertiginous pitch impossible. There are no such high places of humility left to climb to. An observant friend who has lived long in Italy lately declared to me, however, that she detested the name of this moralist, deeming him chief propagator of the Italian vice most trying to the would-be lover of the people, the want of personal self-respect. There is a solidarity in the use of soap, and every cringing beggar, idler, liar and pilferer flourished for her under the shadow of the great Franciscan indifference to it. She was possibly right; at Rome, at Naples, I might have admitted she was right; but at Assisi, face to face with Giotto's vivid chronicle, we admire too much in its main subject the exquisite play of that subject's genius—we don't remit to him, and this for very envy, a single throb of his consciousness. It took in, that human, that divine embrace, everything *but* soap.

I should find it hard to give an orderly account of my next adventures or impressions at Assisi, which couldn't well be anything more than mere romantic *flânerie*. One may easily plead as the final result of a meditation at the shrine of Saint Francis a great and even an amused charity. This state of mind led me slowly up and down for a couple of hours through the steep little streets, and at last stretched itself on the grass with me in the shadow of the great ruined castle that decorates so grandly the eminence above the town. I remember edging along the sunless side of the small mouldy houses and pausing very often to look at nothing in particular. It was all very hot, very hushed, very resignedly but very persistently old. A wheeled vehicle in such a place is an event, and the *forestiero's* interrogative tread in the blank sonorous lanes has the privilege of bringing the inhabitants to their doorways. Some of the better houses, however, achieve a sombre stillness that protests against the least curiosity as to what may happen in any such century as this. You wonder, as you pass, what lingering old-world social types vegetate there, but you won't find out; albeit that in one very silent little street I had a glimpse of an open door which I have not forgotten. A long-haired peddler who must have been a Jew, and who yet carried without prejudice a burden of mass-books and rosaries, was offering his wares to a stout old priest. The priest had opened the door rather stingily and appeared half-heartedly to dismiss him. But the peddler held up something I couldn't see; the priest wavered with a timorous concession to profane curiosity and then furtively pulled the agent of sophistication, or whatever it might be, into the house. I should have liked to enter with that worthy.

I saw later some gentlemen of Assisi who also seemed bored enough to have found entertainment in his tray. They were at the door of the café on the Piazza, and were so thankful to me for asking them the way to the cathedral that, answering all in chorus, they lighted up with smiles as sympathetic as if I had done them a favour. Of that type were my mild, my delicate adventures. The Piazza has a fine old portico of an ancient Temple of Minerva—six fluted columns and a pediment, of beautiful proportions, but sadly battered and decayed. Goethe, I believe, found it much more interesting than the mighty mediæval church, and Goethe, as a cicerone, doubtless could have persuaded one that it was so; but in the humble society of Murray we shall most of us find a richer sense in the later monument. I found quaint old meanings enough in the dark yellow façade of the small cathedral as I sat on a stone bench by the oblong green stretched before it. This is a pleasing piece of Italian Gothic and, like several of its companions at Assisi, has an elegant wheel window and a number of grotesque little carvings of creatures human and bestial. If with Goethe I were to balance anything against the attractions of the double church I should choose the ruined castle on the hill above the town. I had been having glimpses of it all the afternoon at the end of steep street-vistas, and promising myself half-an-hour beside its grey walls at sunset. The sun was very late setting, and my half-hour became a long lounge in the lee of an abutment which arrested the gentle uproar of the wind. The castle is a splendid piece of ruin, perched on the summit of the mountain to whose slope Assisi clings and dropping a pair of stony arms to enclose the little town in its embrace. The city wall, in other words, straggles up the steep green hill and meets the crumbling skeleton of the fortress. On the side off from the town the mountain plunges into a deep ravine, the opposite face of which is formed by the powerful undraped shoulder of Monte Subasio, a fierce reflector of the sun. Gorge and mountain are wild enough, but their frown expires in the teeming softness of the great vale of Umbria. To lie aloft there on the grass, with silver-grey ramparts at one's back and the warm rushing wind in one's ears, and watch the beautiful plain mellow into the tones of twilight, was as exquisite a form of repose as ever fell to a tired tourist's lot.

Perugia too has an ancient stronghold, which one must speak of in earnest as that unconscious humourist the classic American traveller is supposed invariably to speak of the Colosseum: it will be a very handsome building when it's finished. Even Perugia is going the way of all Italy—straightening out her streets, preparing her ruins, laying her venerable ghosts. The castle is being completely *remis à neuf*—a Massachusetts school-house couldn't cultivate a "smarter" ideal. There are shops in the basement and fresh putty on all the windows; so that the only thing proper to a castle it has kept is its magnificent position and range, which you may enjoy from the broad platform where the Perugini assemble at eventide. Perugia is chiefly known to fame as the city of Raphael's master; but it has a still higher claim to renown and ought to figure in the gazetteer of fond memory as the little City of the infinite View. The small dusky, crooked place tries by a hundred prompt pretensions, immediate contortions, rich mantling flushes and other ingenuities, to waylay your attention and keep it at home; but your consciousness, alert and uneasy from the first moment, is all abroad even when your back is turned to the vast alternative or when fifty house-walls conceal it, and you are forever rushing up by-streets and peeping round corners in the hope of another glimpse or reach of it. As it stretches away before you in that eminent indifference to limits which is at the same time at every step an eminent homage to style, it is altogether too free and fair for compasses and terms. You can only say, and rest upon it, that you prefer it to any other visible fruit of position or claimed empire of the eye that you are anywhere likely to enjoy.

For it is such a wondrous mixture of blooming plain and gleaming river and wavily-multitudinous mountain vaguely dotted with pale grey cities, that, placed as you are, roughly speaking, in the centre of Italy, you all but span the divine peninsula from sea to sea. Up the long vista of the Tiber you look—almost to Rome; past Assisi, Spello, Foligno, Spoleto, all perched on their respective heights and shining through the violet haze. To the north, to the east, to the west, you see a hundred variations of the prospect, of which I have kept no record. Two notes only I have made: one—though who hasn't made it over and over again?—on the exquisite elegance of mountain forms in this endless play of the excrescence, it being exactly as if there were variation of sex in the upheaved mass, with the effect here mainly of contour and curve and complexion determined in the feminine sense. It further came home to me that the command of such an outlook on the world goes far, surely, to give authority and centrality and experience, those of the great seats of dominion, even to so scant a cluster of attesting objects as here. It must deepen the civic consciousness and take off the edge of ennui. It performs this kindly office, at any rate, for the traveller who may overstay his curiosity as to Perugino and the Etruscan relics. It continually solicits his wonder and praise—it reinforces the historic page. I spent a week in the place, and when it was gone I had had enough of Perugino, but hadn't had enough of the View.

I should perhaps do the reader a service by telling him just how a week at Perugia may be spent. His first care must be to ignore the very dream of haste, walking everywhere very slowly and very much at random, and to impute an esoteric sense to almost anything his eye may happen to encounter. Almost everything in fact lends itself to the historic, the romantic, the æsthetic fallacy—almost everything has an antique queerness and richness that ekes out the reduced state; that of a grim and battered old adventuress, the heroine of many shames and scandals, surviving to an extraordinary age and a considerable penury, but with ancient gifts of princes and other forms of the wages of sin to show, and the most beautiful garden of all the world to sit and doze and count her beads in and remember. He must hang a great deal about the huge Palazzo Pubblico, which indeed is very well worth any acquaintance you may scrape with it. It masses itself gloomily above the narrow street to an immense elevation, and leads up the eye along a cliff-like surface of rugged wall, mottled with old scars and new repairs, to the loggia dizzily perched on its cornice. He must repeat his visit to the Etruscan Gate, by whose immemorial composition he must indeed linger long to resolve it back into the elements originally attending it. He must uncap to the irrecoverable, the inimitable style of the statue of Pope Julius III. before the cathedral, remembering that Hawthorne fabled his Miriam, in an air of romance from which we are well-nigh as far to-day as from the building of Etruscan gates, to have given rendezvous to Kenyon at its base. Its material is a vivid green bronze, and the mantle and tiara are covered with a delicate embroidery worthy of a silversmith.

Then our leisurely friend must bestow on Perugino's frescoes in the Exchange, and on his pictures in the University, all the placid contemplation they deserve. He must go to the theatre every evening, in an orchestra-chair at twenty-two soldi, and enjoy the curious didacticism of Amore senza Stima, Severità e Debolezza, La Società Equivoca, and other

popular specimens of contemporaneous Italian comedy—unless indeed the last-named be not the edifying title applied,
for peninsular use, to "Le Demi-Monde" of the younger Dumas. I shall be very much surprised if, at the end of a week of
this varied entertainment, he hasn't learnt how to live, not
exactly in, but with, Perugia. His strolls will abound in small
accidents and mercies of vision, but of which a dozen pencil-
strokes would be a better memento than this poor word-
sketching. From the hill on which the town is planted radiate
a dozen ravines, down whose sides the houses slide and
scramble with an alarming indifference to the cohesion of
their little rugged blocks of flinty red stone. You ramble really
nowhither without emerging on some small court or terrace
that throws your view across a gulf of tangled gardens or
vineyards and over to a cluster of serried black dwellings
which have to hollow in their backs to keep their balance on
the opposite ledge. On archways and street-staircases and
dark alleys that bore through a density of massive basements,
and curve and climb and plunge as they go, all to the truest
mediæval tune, you may feast your fill. These are the local, the
architectural, the compositional commonplaces. Some of the
little streets in out-of-the-way corners are so rugged and
brown and silent that you may imagine them passages long
since hewn by the pick-axe in a deserted stone-quarry. The
battered black houses, of the colour of buried things—things
buried, that is, in accumulations of time, closer packed, even
as such are, than spadefuls of earth—resemble exposed sections of natural rock; none the less so when, beyond some
narrow gap, you catch the blue and silver of the sublime circle
of landscape.

But I oughtn't to talk of mouldy alleys, or yet of azure
distances, as if they formed the main appeal to taste in this
accomplished little city. In the Sala del Cambio, where in ancient days the money-changers rattled their embossed coin
and figured up their profits, you may enjoy one of the se-
renest æsthetic pleasures that the golden age of art anywhere
offers us. Bank parlours, I believe, are always handsomely appointed, but are even those of Messrs. Rothschild such models of mural bravery as this little counting-house of a bygone
fashion? The bravery is Perugino's own; for, invited clearly to

do his best, he left it as a lesson to the ages, covering the four low walls and the vault with scriptural and mythological figures of extraordinary beauty. They are ranged in artless attitudes round the upper half of the room—the sybils, the prophets, the philosophers, the Greek and Roman heroes—looking down with broad serene faces, with small mild eyes and sweet mouths that commit them to nothing in particular unless to being comfortably and charmingly alive, at the incongruous proceedings of a Board of Brokers. Had finance a very high tone in those days, or were genius and faith then simply as frequent as capital and enterprise are among ourselves? The great distinction of the Sala del Cambio is that it has a friendly Yes for both these questions. There was a rigid transactional probity, it seems to say; there was also a high tide of inspiration. About the artist himself many things come up for us—more than I can attempt in their order; for he was not, I think, to an attentive observer, the mere smooth and entire and devout spirit we at first are inclined to take him for. He has that about him which leads us to wonder if he may not, after all, play a proper part enough here as the patron of the money-changers. He is the delight of a million of young ladies; but who knows whether we shouldn't find in his works, might we "go into" them a little, a trifle more of manner than of conviction and of system than of deep sincerity?

This, I allow, would put no great affront on them, and one speculates thus partly but because it's a pleasure to hang about him on any pretext, and partly because his immediate effect is to make us quite inordinately embrace the pretext of his lovely soul. His portrait, painted on the wall of the Sala (you may see it also in Rome and Florence) might at any rate serve for the likeness of Mr. Worldly-Wiseman in Bunyan's allegory. He was fond of his glass, I believe, and he made his art lucrative. This tradition is not refuted by his preserved face, and after some experience—or rather after a good deal, since you can't have a *little* of Perugino, who abounds wherever old masters congregate, so that one has constantly the sense of being "in" for all there is—you may find an echo of it in the uniform type of his creatures, their monotonous grace, their prodigious invariability. He may very well have wanted to produce figures of a substantial, yet at the same time of an impeccable innocence; but we feel that he had taught himself *how* even beyond his own belief in them, and had arrived at a process that acted at last mechanically. I confess at the same time that, so interpreted, the painter affects me as hardly less interesting, and one can't but become conscious of one's style when one's style has become, as it were, so conscious of one's, or at least of its own, fortune. If he was the inventor of a remarkably calculable *facture*, a calculation that never fails is in its way a grace of the first order, and there are things in this special appearance of perfection of practice that make him the forerunner of a mighty and more modern race. More than any of the early painters who strongly charm, you may take all his measure from a single specimen. The other samples infallibly match, reproduce unerringly the one type he had mastered, but which had the good fortune to be adorably fair, to seem to have dawned on a vision unsullied by the shadows of earth. Which truth, moreover, leaves Perugino all delightful as composer and draughtsman; he has in each of these characters a sort of spacious neatness which suggests that the whole conception has been washed clean by some spiritual chemistry the last thing before reaching the canvas; after which it has been applied to that surface with a rare economy of time and means. Giotto and Fra Angelico, beside him, are full of interesting waste and irrelevant passion. In the sacristy of the charming church of San Pietro—a museum of pictures and carvings—is a row of small heads of saints formerly covering the frame of the artist's Ascension, carried off by the French. It is almost miniature work, and here at least Perugino triumphs in sincerity, in apparent candour, as well as in touch. Two of the holy men are reading their breviaries, but with an air of infantine innocence quite consistent with their holding the book upside down.

Between Perugia and Cortona lies the large weedy water of Lake Thrasymene, turned into a witching word forever by Hannibal's recorded victory over Rome. Dim as such records have become to us and remote such realities, he is yet a passionless pilgrim who doesn't, as he passes, of a heavy summer's day, feel the air and the light and the very faintness of the breeze all charged and haunted with them, all interfused as with the wasted ache of experience and with the vague historic haze. Processions of indistinguishable ghosts bore me company to Cortona itself, most sturdily ancient of Italian towns. It must have been a seat of ancient knowledge even when Hannibal and Flaminius came to the shock of battle, and have looked down afar from its grey ramparts on the contending swarm with something of the philosophic composure suitable to a survivor of Pelasgic and Etruscan revolutions. These grey ramparts are in great part still visible, and form the chief attraction of Cortona. It is perched on the very pinnacle of a mountain, and I wound and doubled interminably over the face of the great hill, while the jumbled roofs and towers of the arrogant little city still seemed nearer to the sky than to the railway-station. "Rather rough," Murray pronounces the local inn; and rough indeed it was; there was scarce a square foot of it that you would have cared to stroke with your hand. The landlord himself, however, was all smoothness and the best fellow in the world; he took me up into a rickety old loggia on the tip-top of his establishment and played showman as to half the kingdoms of the earth. I was free to decide at the same time whether my loss or my gain was the greater for my seeing Cortona through the medium of a festa. On the one hand the museum was closed (and in a certain sense the smaller and obscurer the town the more I like the museum); the churches—an interesting note of manners and morals—were impenetrably crowded, though, for that matter, so was the café, where I found neither an empty stool nor the edge of a table. I missed a sight of the famous painted Muse, the art-treasure of Cortona and supposedly the most precious, as it falls little short of being the only, sample of the Greek painted picture that has come down to us. On the other hand, I saw—but this is what I saw.

A part of the mountain-top is occupied by the church of St. Margaret, and this was St. Margaret's day. The houses pause roundabout it and leave a grassy slope, planted here and there with lean black cypresses. The contadini from near and far had congregated in force and were crowding into the church or winding up the slope. When I arrived they were all kneeling or uncovered; a bedizened procession, with banners and censers, bearing abroad, I believe, the relics of the saint, was re-entering the church. The scene made one of those pictures that Italy still brushes in for you with an incomparable hand and from an inexhaustible palette when you find her in the mood. The day was superb—the sky blazed overhead like a vault of deepest sapphire. The grave brown peasantry, with no great accent of costume, but with sundry small ones— decked, that is, in cheap fineries of scarlet and yellow—made a mass of motley colour in the high wind-stirred light. The procession halted in the pious hush, and the lovely land around and beneath us melted away, almost to either sea, in tones of azure scarcely less intense than the sky. Behind the church was an empty crumbling citadel, with half-a-dozen old women keeping the gate for coppers. Here were views and breezes and sun and shade and grassy corners to the heart's content, together with one couldn't say what huge seated mystic melancholy presence, the after-taste of everything the still open maw of time had consumed. I chose a spot that fairly combined all these advantages, a spot from which I seemed to look, as who should say, straight down the throat of the monster, no dark passage now, but with all the glorious day playing into it, and spent a good part of my stay at Cortona lying there at my length and observing the situation over the top of a volume that I must have brought in my pocket just for that especial wanton luxury of the resource provided and slighted. In the afternoon I came down and hustled awhile through the crowded little streets, and then strolled forth under the scorching sun and made the outer circuit of the wall. There I found tremendous uncemented blocks; they glared and twinkled in the powerful light, and I had to put on a blue eye-glass in order to throw into its proper perspective the vague Etruscan past, obtruded and magnified in such masses quite as with the effect of inadequately-withdrawn hands and feet in photographs.

I spent the next day at Arezzo, but I confess in very much the same uninvestigating fashion—taking in the "general impression," I dare say, at every pore, but rather systematically leaving the dust of the ages unfingered on the stored records: I should doubtless, in the poor time at my command, have fingered it to so little purpose. The seeker for the story of

things has moreover, if he be worth his salt, a hundred insidious arts; and in that case indeed—by which I mean when his
sensibility has come duly to adjust itself—the story assaults
him but from too many sides. He even feels at moments that
he must sneak along on tiptoe in order not to have too much
of it. Besides which the case all depends on the kind of use,
the range of application, his tangled consciousness, or his
intelligible genius, say, may come to recognize for it. At
Arezzo, however this might be, one was far from Rome, one
was well within genial Tuscany, and the historic, the romantic
decoction seemed to reach one's lips in less stiff doses. There
at once was the "general impression"—the exquisite sense of
the scarce expressible Tuscan quality, which makes immediately, for the whole pitch of one's perception, a grateful, a not
at all strenuous difference, attaches to almost any coherent
group of objects, to any happy aspect of the scene, for a main
note, some mild recall, through pleasant friendly colour,
through settled ample form, through something homely and
economic too at the very heart of "style," of an identity of
temperament and habit with those of the divine little Florence
that one originally knew. Adorable Italy in which, for the
constant renewal of interest, of attention, of affection, these
refinements of variety, these so harmoniously-grouped and
individually-seasoned fruits of the great garden of history,
keep presenting themselves! It seemed to fall in with the
cheerful Tuscan mildness for instance—sticking as I do to
that ineffectual expression of the Tuscan charm, of the yellow-
brown Tuscan dignity at large—that the ruined castle on the
hill (with which agreeable feature Arezzo is no less furnished
than Assisi and Cortona) had been converted into a great
blooming, and I hope all profitable, podere or market-garden.
I lounged away the half hours there under a spell as potent as
the "wildest" forecast of propriety—propriety to all the particular conditions—could have figured it. I had seen Santa
Maria della Pieve and its campanile of quaint colonnades, the
stately, dusky cathedral—grass-plotted and residenced about
almost after the fashion of an English "close"—and John of
Pisa's elaborate marble shrine; I had seen the museum and its
Etruscan vases and majolica platters. These were very well,
but the old pacified citadel somehow, through a day of soft

saturation, placed me most in relation. Beautiful hills surrounded it, cypresses cast straight shadows at its corners,
while in the middle grew a wondrous Italian tangle of wheat
and corn, vines and figs, peaches and cabbages, memories and
images, anything and everything.

   1873.

Siena Early and Late

FLORENCE being oppressively hot and delivered over to the mosquitoes, the occasion seemed to favour that visit to Siena which I had more than once planned and missed. I arrived late in the evening, by the light of a magnificent moon, and while a couple of benignantly-mumbling old crones were making up my bed at the inn strolled forth in quest of a first impression. Five minutes brought me to where I might gather it unhindered as it bloomed in the white moonshine. The great Piazza of Siena is famous, and though in this day of multiplied photographs and blunted surprises and profaned revelations none of the world's wonders can pretend, like Wordsworth's phantom of delight, really to "startle and waylay," yet as I stepped upon the waiting scene from under a dark archway I was conscious of no loss of the edge of a precious presented sensibility. The waiting scene, as I have called it, was in the shape of a shallow horse-shoe—as the untravelled reader who has turned over his travelled friends' portfolios will respectfully remember; or, better, of a bow in which the high wide face of the Palazzo Pubblico forms the cord and everything else the arc. It was void of any human presence that could figure to me the current year; so that, the moonshine assisting, I had half-an-hour's infinite vision of mediæval Italy. The Piazza being built on the side of a hill—or rather, as I believe science affirms, in the cup of a volcanic crater—the vast pavement converges downwards in slanting radiations of stone, the spokes of a great wheel, to a point directly before the Palazzo, which may mark the hub, though it is nothing more ornamental than the mouth of a drain. The great monument stands on the lower side and might seem, in spite of its goodly mass and its embattled cornice, to be rather defiantly out-countenanced by vast private constructions occupying the opposite eminence. This *might* be, without the extraordinary dignity of the architectural gesture with which the huge high-shouldered pile asserts itself.

On the firm edge of the palace, from bracketed base to grey-capped summit against the sky, there grows a tall slim tower which soars and soars till it has given notice of the city's greatness over the blue mountains that mark the horizon. It rises as slender and straight as a pennoned lance planted on the steel-shod toe of a mounted knight, and keeps all to itself in the blue air, far above the changing fashions of the market, the proud consciousness or rare arrogance once built into it. This beautiful tower, the finest thing in Siena and, in its rigid fashion, as permanently fine thus as a really handsome nose on a face of no matter what accumulated age, figures there still as a Declaration of Independence beside which such an affair as ours, thrown off at Philadelphia, appears to have scarce done more than helplessly give way to time. Our Independence has become a dependence on a thousand such dreadful things as the incorrupt declaration of Siena strikes us as looking for ever straight over the level of. As it stood silvered by the moonlight, while my greeting lasted, it seemed to speak, all as from soul to soul, very much indeed as some ancient worthy of a lower order, buttonholing one on the coveted chance and at the quiet hour, might have done, of a state of things long and vulgarly superseded, but to the pride and power, the once prodigious vitality of which who could expect any one effect to testify more incomparably, more indestructibly, quite, as it were, more immortally? The gigantic houses enclosing the rest of the Piazza took up the tale and mingled with it their burden. "We are very old and a trifle weary, but we were built strong and piled high, and we shall last for many an age. The present is cold and heedless, but we keep ourselves in heart by brooding over our store of memories and traditions. We are haunted houses in every creaking timber and aching stone." Such were the gossiping connections I established with Siena before I went to bed.

Since that night I have had a week's daylight knowledge of the surface of the subject at least, and don't know how I can better present it than simply as another and a vivider page of the lesson that the ever-hungry artist has only to *trust* old Italy for her to feed him at every single step from her hand — and if not with one sort of sweetly-stale grain from that wondrous mill of history which during so many ages ground finer than any other on earth, why then always with something else. Siena has at any rate "preserved appearances"—kept the greatest number of them, that is, unaltered for the eye—about as consistently as one can imagine the thing done. Other places perhaps may treat you to as drowsy an odour of antiquity, but few exhale it from so large an area. Lying massed within her walls on a dozen clustered hilltops, she shows you at every turn in how much greater a way she once lived; and if so much of the grand manner is extinct the receptacle of the ashes still solidly rounds itself. This heavy general stress of all her emphasis on the past is what she constantly keeps in your eyes and your ears, and if you be but a casual observer and admirer the generalised response is mainly what you give her. The casual observer, however beguiled, is mostly not very learned, not over-equipped in advance with data; he hasn't specialised, his notions are necessarily vague, the chords of his imagination, for all his good-will, are inevitably muffled and weak. But such as it is, his received, his welcome impression serves his turn so far as the life of sensibility goes, and reminds him from time to time that even the lore of German doctors is but the shadow of satisfied curiosity. I have been living at the inn, walking about the streets, sitting in the Piazza; these are the simple terms of my experience. But streets and inns in Italy are the vehicles of half one's knowledge; if one has no fancy for their lessons one may burn one's note-book. In Siena everything is Sienese. The inn has an English sign over the door—a little battered plate with a rusty representation of the lion and the unicorn; but advance hopefully into the mouldy stone alley which serves as vestibule and you will find local colour enough. The landlord, I was told, had been servant in an English family, and I was curious to see how he met the probable argument of the casual Anglo-Saxon after the latter's first twelve hours in his establishment. As he failed to appear I asked the waiter if he weren't at home. "Oh," said the latter, "he's a *piccolo grasso vecchiotto* who doesn't like to move." I'm afraid this little fat old man has simply a bad conscience. It's no small burden for one who likes the Italians—as who doesn't, under this restriction?—to have so much indifference even to rudimentary purifying processes to dispose of. What is the real philosophy

of dirty habits, and are foul surfaces merely superficial? If unclean manners have in truth the moral meaning which I suspect in them we must love Italy better than consistency. This
a number of us are prepared to do, but while we are making
the sacrifice it is as well we should be aware.

We may plead moreover for these impecunious heirs of the
past that even if it were easy to be clean in the midst of their
mouldering heritage it would be difficult to appear so. At the
risk of seeming to flaunt the silly superstition of restless renovation for the sake of renovation, which is but the challenge
of the infinitely precious principle of duration, one is still
moved to say that the prime result of one's contemplative
strolls in the dusky alleys of such a place is an ineffable sense
of disrepair. Everything is cracking, peeling, fading, crumbling, rotting. No young Sienese eyes rest upon anything
youthful; they open into a world battered and befouled with
long use. Everything has passed its meridian except the brilliant façade of the cathedral, which is being diligently re-
touched and restored, and a few private palaces whose broad
fronts seem to have been lately furbished and polished. Siena
was long ago mellowed to the pictorial tone; the operation of
time is now to deposit shabbiness upon shabbiness. But it's
for the most part a patient, sturdy, sympathetic shabbiness,
which soothes rather than irritates the nerves, and has in
many cases doubtless as long a career to run as most of our
pert and shallow freshnesses. It projects at all events a deeper
shadow into the constant twilight of the narrow streets—that
vague historic dusk, as I may call it, in which one walks and
wonders. These streets are hardly more than sinuous flagged
alleys, into which the huge black houses, between their almost
meeting cornices, suffer a meagre light to filter down over
rough-hewn stone, past windows often of graceful Gothic
form, and great pendent iron rings and twisted sockets for
torches. Scattered over their many-headed hill, they suffer the
roadway often to incline to the perpendicular, becoming so
impracticable for vehicles that the sound of wheels is only a
trifle less anomalous than it would be in Venice. But all day
long there comes up to my window an incessant shuffling of
feet and clangour of voices. The weather is very warm for the
season, all the world is out of doors, and the Tuscan tongue

(which in Siena is reputed to have a classic purity) wags in every imaginable key. It doesn't rest even at night, and I am often an uninvited guest at concerts and *conversazioni* at two o'clock in the morning. The concerts are sometimes charming. I not only don't curse my wakefulness, but go to my window to listen. Three men come carolling by, trolling and quavering with voices of delightful sweetness, or a lonely troubadour in his shirt-sleeves draws such artful love-notes from his clear, fresh tenor, that I seem for the moment to be behind the scenes at the opera, watching some Rubini or Mario go "on" and waiting for the round of applause. In the intervals a couple of friends or enemies stop—Italians always make their points in conversation by pulling up, letting you walk on a few paces, to turn and find them standing with finger on nose and engaging your interrogative eye—they pause, by a happy instinct, directly under my window, and dispute their point or tell their story or make their confidence. One scarce is sure which it may be; everything has such an explosive promptness, such a redundancy of inflection and action. But everything for that matter takes on such dramatic life as *our* lame colloquies never know—so that almost any uttered communications here become an acted play, improvised, mimicked, proportioned and rounded, carried bravely to its *dénoûment*. The speaker seems actually to establish his stage and face his foot-lights, to create by a gesture a little scenic circumscription about him; he rushes to and fro and shouts and stamps and postures, he ranges through every phase of his inspiration. I noted the other evening a striking instance of the spontaneity of the Italian gesture, in the person of a small Sienese of I hardly know what exact age—the age of inarticulate sounds and the experimental use of a spoon. It was a Sunday evening, and this little man had accompanied his parents to the café. The Caffè Greco at Siena is a most delightful institution; you get a capital *demi-tasse* for three sous, and an excellent ice for eight, and while you consume these easy luxuries you may buy from a little hunchback the local weekly periodical, the *Vita Nuova*, for three centimes (the two centimes left from your sou, if you are under the spell of this magical frugality, will do to give the waiter). My young friend was sitting on his father's knee and helping

himself to the half of a strawberry-ice with which his mamma
had presented him. He had so many misadventures with his
spoon that this lady at length confiscated it, there being nothing left of the ice but a little crimson liquid which he might
dispose of by the common instinct of childhood. But he was
no friend, it appeared, to such freedoms; he was a perfect
little gentleman and he resented its being expected of him that
he should drink down his remnant. He protested therefore,
and it was the manner of his protest that struck me. He didn't
cry audibly, though he made a very wry face. It was no stupid
squall, and yet he was too young to speak. It was a penetrating concord of inarticulately pleading, accusing sounds, accompanied by gestures of the most exquisite propriety. These
were perfectly mature; he did everything that a man of forty
would have done if he had been pouring out a flood of sonorous eloquence. He shrugged his shoulders and wrinkled his
eyebrows, tossed out his hands and folded his arms, obtruded
his chin and bobbed about his head—and at last, I am happy
to say, recovered his spoon. If I had had a solid little silver
one I would have presented it to him as a testimonial to a
perfect, though as yet unconscious, artist.

My actual tribute to him, however, has diverted me from
what I had in mind—a much weightier matter—the great
private palaces which are the massive majestic syllables, sen-
tences, periods, of the strange message the place addresses to
us. They are extraordinarily spacious and numerous, and one
wonders what part they can play in the meagre economy of
the actual city. The Siena of to-day is a mere shrunken semblance of the rabid little republic which in the thirteenth century waged triumphant war with Florence, cultivated the arts
with splendour, planned a cathedral (though it had ultimately
to curtail the design) of proportions almost unequalled, and
contained a population of two hundred thousand souls. Many
of these dusky piles still bear the names of the old mediæval
magnates the vague mild occupancy of whose descendants has
the effect of armour of proof worn over "pot" hats and tweed
jackets and trousers. Half-a-dozen of them are as high as the
Strozzi and Riccardi palaces in Florence; they couldn't well be
higher. The very essence of the romantic and the scenic is in
the way these colossal dwellings are packed together in their

steep streets, in the depths of their little enclosed, agglomer-
ated city. When we, in our day and country, raise a structure
of half the mass and dignity, we leave a great space about it in
the manner of a pause after a showy speech. But when a Sienese countess, as things are here, is doing her hair near the
window, she is a wonderfully near neighbour to the cavalier
opposite, who is being shaved by his valet. Possibly the countess doesn't object to a certain chosen publicity at her toilet;
what does an Italian gentleman assure me but that the aristocracy make very free with each other? Some of the palaces are
shown, but only when the occupants are at home, and now
they are in *villeggiatura*. Their villeggiatura lasts eight months
of the year, the waiter at the inn informs me, and they spend
little more than the carnival in the city. The gossip of an inn-
waiter ought perhaps to be beneath the dignity of even such
thin history as this; but I confess that when, as a story-seeker
always and ever, I have come in from my strolls with an irritated sense of the dumbness of stones and mortar, it has been
to listen with avidity, over my dinner, to the proffered confidences of the worthy man who stands by with a napkin. His
talk is really very fine, and he prides himself greatly on his
cultivated tone, to which he calls my attention. He has very
little good to say about the Sienese nobility. They are "proprio d'origine egoista"—whatever that may be—and there are
many who can't write their names. This may be calumny; but
I doubt whether the most blameless of them all could have
spoken more delicately of a lady of peculiar personal appearance who had been dining near me. "She's too fat," I grossly
said on her leaving the room. The waiter shook his head with
a little sniff: "E troppo materiale." This lady and her companion were the party whom, thinking I might relish a little company—I had been dining alone for a week—he gleefully
announced to me as newly arrived Americans. They were
Americans, I found, who wore, pinned to their heads in permanence, the black lace veil or mantilla, conveyed their beans
to their mouth with a knife, and spoke a strange raucous
Spanish. They were in fine compatriots from Montevideo.
The genius of old Siena, however, would make little of any
stress of such distinctions; one representative of a far-off
social platitude being about as much in order as another as

he stands before the great loggia of the Casino di Nobili, the club of the best society. The nobility, which is very numerous and very rich, is still, says the apparently competent native I began by quoting, perfectly feudal and uplifted and separate. Morally and intellectually, behind the walls of its palaces, the fourteenth century, it's thrilling to think, hasn't ceased to hang on. There is no bourgeoisie to speak of; immediately after the aristocracy come the poor people, who are very poor indeed. My friend's account of these matters made me wish more than ever, as a lover of the preserved social specimen, of type at almost any price, that one weren't, a helpless victim of the historic sense, reduced simply to staring at black stones and peeping up stately staircases; and that when one had examined the street-face of the palace, Murray in hand, one might walk up to the great drawing-room, make one's bow to the master and mistress, the old abbé and the young count, and invite them to favour one with a sketch of their social philosophy or a few first-hand family anecdotes.

The dusky labyrinth of the streets, we must in default of such initiations content ourselves with noting, is interrupted by two great candid spaces: the fan-shaped piazza, of which I just now said a word, and the smaller square in which the cathedral erects its walls of many-coloured marble. Of course since paying the great piazza my compliments by moonlight I have strolled through it often at sunnier and shadier hours. The market is held there, and wherever Italians buy and sell, wherever they count and chaffer—as indeed you hear them do right and left, at almost any moment, as you take your way among them—the pulse of life beats fast. It has been doing so on the spot just named, I suppose, for the last five hundred years, and during that time the cost of eggs and earthen pots has been gradually but inexorably increasing. The buyers nevertheless wrestle over their purchases as lustily as so many fourteenth-century burghers suddenly waking up in horror to current prices. You have but to walk aside, however, into the Palazzo Pubblico really to feel yourself a thrifty old mediævalist. The state affairs of the Republic were formerly transacted here, but it now gives shelter to modern law-courts and other prosy business. I was marched through a number of vaulted halls and chambers, which, in the intervals of the administrative sessions held in them, are peopled only by the great mouldering archaic frescoes—anything but inanimate these even in their present ruin—that cover the walls and ceiling. The chief painters of the Sienese school lent a hand in producing the works I name, and you may complete there the connoisseurship in which, possibly, you will have embarked at the Academy. I say "possibly" to be very judicial, my own observation having led me no great length. I have rather than otherwise cherished the thought that the Sienese school suffers one's eagerness peacefully to slumber—benignantly abstains in fact from whipping up a languid curiosity and a tepid faith. "A formidable rival to the Florentine," says some book—I forget which—into which I recently glanced. Not a bit of it thereupon boldly say I; the Florentines may rest on their laurels and the lounger on his lounge. The early painters of the two groups have indeed much in common; but the Florentines had the good fortune to see their efforts gathered up and applied by a few pre-eminent spirits, such as never came to the rescue of the groping Sienese. Fra Angelico and Ghirlandaio said all their feebler *confrères* dreamt of and a great deal more beside, but the inspiration of Simone Memmi and Ambrogio Lorenzetti and Sano di Pietro has a painful air of never efflorescing into a maximum. Sodoma and Beccafumi are to my taste a rather abortive maximum. But one should speak of them all gently—and I do, from my soul; for their labour, by their lights, has wrought a precious heritage of still-living colour and rich figure-peopled shadow for the echoing chambers of their old civic fortress. The faded frescoes cover the walls like quaintly-storied tapestries; in one way or another they cast their spell. If one owes a large debt of pleasure to pictorial art one comes to think tenderly and easily of its whole evolution, as of the conscious experience of a single mysterious, striving spirit, and one shrinks from saying rude things about any particular phase of it, just as one would from referring without precautions to some error or lapse in the life of a person one esteemed. You don't care to remind a grizzled veteran of his defeats, and why should we linger in Siena to talk about Beccafumi? I by no means go so far as to say, with an amateur with whom I have just been discussing the matter, that "Sodoma is a precious poor

painter and Beccafumi no painter at all"; but, opportunity being limited, I am willing to let the remark about Beccafumi
pass for true. With regard to Sodoma, I remember seeing four
years ago in the choir of the Cathedral of Pisa a certain small
dusky specimen of the painter—an Abraham and Isaac, if I
am not mistaken—which was charged with a gloomy grace.
One rarely meets him in general collections, and I had never
done so till the other day. He was not prolific, apparently; he
had however his own elegance, and his rarity is a part of it.

Here in Siena are a couple of dozen scattered frescoes and
three or four canvases; his masterpiece, among others, an harmonious Descent from the Cross. I wouldn't give a fig for the
equilibrium of the figures or the ladders; but while it lasts the
scene is all intensely solemn and graceful and sweet—too
sweet for so bitter a subject. Sodoma's women are strangely
sweet; an imaginative sense of morbid appealing attitude—as
notably in the sentimental, the pathetic, but the none the less
pleasant, "Swooning of Saint Catherine," the great Sienese
heroine, at San Domenico—seems to me the author's finest
accomplishment. His frescoes have all the same almost appealing evasion of difficulty, and a kind of mild melancholy which
I am inclined to think the sincerest part of them, for it strikes
me as practically the artist's depressed suspicion of his own
want of force. Once he determined, however, that if he
couldn't be strong he would make capital of his weakness, and
painted the Christ bound to the Column, of the Academy.
Here he got much nearer and I have no doubt mixed his
colours with his tears; but the result can't be better described
than by saying that it is, pictorially, the first of the modern
Christs. Unfortunately it hasn't been the last.

The main strength of Sienese art went possibly into the
erection of the Cathedral, and yet even here the strength is
not of the greatest strain. If, however, there are more interesting temples in Italy, there are few more richly and variously
scenic and splendid, the comparative meagreness of the architectural idea being overlaid by a marvellous wealth of ingenious detail. Opposite the church—with the dull old
archbishop's palace on one side and a dismantled residence of
the late Grand Duke of Tuscany on the other—is an ancient
hospital with a big stone bench running all along its front.

Here I have sat awhile every morning for a week, like a philosophic convalescent, watching the florid façade of the cathedral glitter against the deep blue sky. It has been lavishly
restored of late years, and the fresh white marble of the
densely clustered pinnacles and statues and beasts and flowers
flashes in the sunshine like a mosaic of jewels. There is more
of this goldsmith's work in stone than I can remember or
describe; it is piled up over three great doors with immense
margins of exquisite decorative sculpture—still in the ancient
cream-coloured marble—and beneath three sharp pediments
embossed with images relieved against red marble and tipped
with golden mosaics. It is in the highest degree fantastic and
luxuriant—it is on the whole very lovely. As a triumph of the
many-hued it prepares you for the interior, where the same
parti-coloured splendour is endlessly at play—a confident
complication of harmonies and contrasts and of the minor
structural refinements and braveries. The internal surface is
mainly wrought in alternate courses of black and white marble; but as the latter has been dimmed by the centuries to a
fine mild brown the place is all a concert of relieved and dispersed glooms. Save for Pinturicchio's brilliant frescoes in the
Sacristy there are no pictures to speak of; but the pavement is
covered with many elaborate designs in black and white mosaic after cartoons by Beccafumi. The patient skill of these
compositions makes them a rare piece of decoration; yet even
here the friend whom I lately quoted rejects this over-ripe
fruit of the Sienese school. The designs are nonsensical, he
declares, and all his admiration is for the cunning artisans
who have imitated the hatchings and shadings and hairstrokes of the pencil by the finest curves of inserted black
stone. But the true romance of handiwork at Siena is to be
seen in the wondrous stalls of the choir, under the coloured
light of the great wheel-window. Wood-carving has ever been
a cherished craft of the place, and the best masters of the art
during the fifteenth century lavished themselves on this prodigious task. It is the frost-work on one's window-panes interpreted in polished oak. It would be hard to find, doubtless, a
more moving illustration of the peculiar patience, the sacred
candour, of the great time. Into such artistry as this the
author seems to put more of his personal substance than into

any other; he has to wrestle not only with his subject, but with his material. He is richly fortunate when his subject is charming—when his devices, inventions and fantasies spring lightly to his hand; for in the material itself, after age and use have ripened and polished and darkened it to the richness of ebony and to a greater warmth there is something surpassingly delectable and venerable. Wander behind the altar at Siena when the chanting is over and the incense has faded, and look well at the stalls of the Barili.

1873.

II

I leave the impression noted in the foregoing pages to tell its own small story, but have it on my conscience to wonder, in this connection, quite candidly and publicly and by way of due penance, at the scantness of such first-fruits of my sensibility. I was to see Siena repeatedly in the years to follow, I was to know her better, and I would say that I was to do her an ampler justice didn't that remark seem to reflect a little on my earlier poor judgment. This judgment strikes me to-day as having fallen short—true as it may be that I find ever a value, or at least an interest, even in the moods and humours and lapses of any brooding, musing or fantasticating observer to whom the finer sense of things is *on the whole* not closed. If he has on a given occasion nodded or stumbled or strayed, this fact by itself speaks to me of him—speaks to me, that is, of his faculty and his idiosyncrasies, and I care nothing for the application of his faculty unless it be, first of all, in itself interesting. Which may serve as my reply to any objection here breaking out—on the ground that if a spectator's languors are evidence, of a sort, about that personage, they are scarce evidence about the case before him, at least if the case be important. I let my perhaps rather weak expression of the sense of Siena stand, at any rate—for the sake of what I myself read into it; but I should like to amplify it by other memories, and would do so eagerly if I might here enjoy the space. The difficulty for these rectifications is that if the early vision has failed of competence or of full felicity, if initiation has thus been slow, so, with renewals and extensions, so, with the larger experience, one hindrance is exchanged for another. There is quite such a possibility as having lived into a relation too much to be able to make a statement of it.

I remember on one occasion arriving very late of a summer night, after an almost unbroken run from London, and the note of that approach—I was the only person alighting at the station below the great hill of the little fortress city, under whose at once frowning and gaping gate I must have passed, in the warm darkness and the absolute stillness, very much after the felt fashion of a person of importance about to be enormously incarcerated—gives me, for preservation thus belated, the pitch, as I may call it, at various times, though always at one season, of an almost systematised æsthetic use of the place. It wasn't to be denied that the immensely better "accommodations" instituted by the multiplying, though alas more bustling, years had to be recognised as supplying a basis, comparatively prosaic if one would, to that luxury. No sooner have I written which words, however, than I find myself adding that one "wouldn't," that one doesn't—doesn't, that is, consent now to regard the then "new" hotel (pretty old indeed by this time) as anything but an aid to a free play of perception. The strong and rank old Arme d'Inghilterra, in the darker street, had passed away; but its ancient rival the Aquila Nera put forth claims to modernisation, and the Grand Hotel, the still fresher flower of modernity near the gate by which you enter from the station, takes on to my present remembrance a mellowness as of all sorts of comfort, cleanliness and kindness. The particular facts, those of the visit I began here by alluding to and those of still others, at all events, inveterately made in June or early in July, enter together into a fusion as of hot golden-brown objects seen through the practicable crevices of shutters drawn upon high, cool, darkened rooms where the scheme of the scene involved longish days of quiet work, with late afternoon emergence and contemplation waiting on the better or the worse conscience. I thus associate the compact world of the admirable hilltop, the world of a predominant golden-brown, with a general invocation of sensibility and fancy, and think of myself as going forth into the lingering light of summer evenings all attuned to intensity of the idea of compositional beauty, or in other words, freely speaking, to the question of colour, to intensity of picture. To communicate with Siena in this charming way was thus, I admit, to have no great margin for the prosecution of inquiries, but I am not sure that it wasn't, little by little, to feel the whole combination of elements better than by a more exemplary method, and this from beginning to end of the scale.

More of the elements indeed, for memory, hang about the days that were ushered in by that straight flight from the north than about any other series—if partly, doubtless, but because of my having then stayed longest. I specify it at all events for fond reminiscence as the year, the only year, at which I was present at the Palio, the earlier one, the series of furious horse-races between elected representatives of different quarters of the town taking place toward the end of June, as the second and still more characteristic exhibition of the same sort is appointed to the month of August; a spectacle that I am far from speaking of as the finest flower of my old and perhaps even a little faded cluster of impressions, but which smudges that special sojourn as with the big thumb-mark of a slightly soiled and decidedly ensanguined hand. For really, after all, the great loud gaudy romp or heated frolic, simulating ferocity if not achieving it, that is the annual pride of the town, was not intrinsically, to my view, extraordinarily impressive—in spite of its bristling with all due testimony to the passionate Italian clutch of any pretext for costume and attitude and utterance, for mumming and masquerading and raucously representing; the vast cheap vividness rather somehow refines itself, and the swarm and hubbub of the immense square melt, to the uplifted sense of a very high-placed balcony of the overhanging Chigi palace, where everything was superseded but the intenser passage, across the ages, of the great Renaissance tradition of architecture and the infinite sweetness of the waning golden day. The Palio, indubitably, was *criard*—and the more so for quite monopolising, at Siena, the note of crudity; and much of it demanded doubtless of one's patience a due respect for the long local continuity of such things; it drops into its humoured position, however, in any retrospective command of the many brave aspects of the prodigious place. Not that I am pretending here, even for rectification, to take these at all in turn; I only go on a little with my rueful glance at the marked gaps left in my original report of sympathies entertained.

I bow my head for instance to the mystery of my not having mentioned that the coolest and freshest flower of the day was ever that of one's constant renewal of a charmed homage to Pinturicchio, coolest and freshest and signally youngest and most matutinal (as distinguished from merely primitive or crepuscular) of painters, in the library or sacristy of the Cathedral. Did I *always* find time before work to spend half-an-hour of immersion, under that splendid roof, in the clearest and tenderest, the very cleanest and "straightest," as it masters our envious credulity, of all storied fresco-worlds? This wondrous apartment, a monument in itself to the ancient pride and power of the Church, and which contains an unsurpassed treasure of gloriously illuminated missals, psalters and other vast parchment folios, almost each of whose successive leaves gives the impression of rubies, sapphires and emeralds set in gold and practically embedded in the page, offers thus to view, after a fashion splendidly sustained, a pictorial record of the career of Pope Pius II., Æneas Sylvius of the Siena Piccolomini (who gave him for an immediate successor a second of their name), most profanely literary of Pontiffs and last of would-be Crusaders, whose adventures and achievements under Pinturicchio's brush smooth themselves out for us very much to the tune of the "stories" told by some fine old man of the world, at the restful end of his life, to the cluster of his grandchildren. The end of Æneas Sylvius was not restful; he died at Ancona in troublous times, preaching war, and attempting to make it, against the then terrific Turk; but over no great worldly personal legend, among those of men of arduous affairs, arches a fairer, lighter or more pacific memorial vault than the shining Libreria of Siena. I seem to remember having it and its unfrequented enclosing precinct so often all to myself that I must indeed mostly have resorted to it for a prompt benediction on the day. Like no other strong solicitation, among artistic appeals to which one may compare it up and down the whole wonderful country, is the felt neighbouring presence of the overwrought Cathedral in its little proud possessive town: you may so often feel by the week at a time that it stands there really for your own personal enjoyment, your romantic convenience, your small wanton æsthetic use. In such a light shines for me, at all events, under such an accumulation and complication of tone flushes and darkens and richly recedes for me, across the years, the treasure-house of many-coloured marbles in the untrodden, the drowsy, empty Sienese square. One could positively do, in the free exercise of any responsible fancy or luxurious taste, what one would with it.

But that proposition holds true, after all, for almost any mild pastime of the incurable student of loose meanings and stray relics and odd references and dim analogies in an Italian hill-city bronzed and seasoned by the ages. I ought perhaps, for justification of the right to talk, to have plunged into the Siena archives of which, on one occasion, a kindly custodian gave me, in rather dusty and stuffy conditions, as the incident vaguely comes back to me, a glimpse that was like a moment's stand at the mouth of a deep, dark mine. I didn't descend into the pit; I did, instead of this, a much idler and easier thing: I simply went every afternoon, my stint of work over, I like to recall, for a musing stroll upon the Lizza—the Lizza which had its own unpretentious but quite insidious art of meeting the lover of old stories half-way. The great and subtle thing, if you are not a strenuous specialist, in places of a heavily charged historic consciousness, is to profit by the sense of that consciousness—or in other words to cultivate a relation with the oracle—after the fashion that suits yourself; so that if the general after-taste of experience, experience at large, the fine distilled essence of the matter, seems to breathe, in such a case, from the very stones and to make a thick strong liquor of the very air, you may thus gather as you pass what is most to your purpose; which is more the indestructible mixture of lived things, with its concentrated lingering odour, than any interminable list of numbered chapters and verses. Chapters and verses, literally scanned, refuse coincidence, mostly, with the divisional proprieties of your own pile of manuscript—which is but another way of saying, in short, that if the Lizza is a mere fortified promontory of the great Sienese hill, serving at once as a stronghold for the present military garrison and as a planted and benched and band-standed walk and recreation-ground for the citizens, so I could never, toward close of day, either have enough of it or yet feel the vaguest saunterings there to be vain. They were vague with the qualification always of that finer massing, as one wandered off, of the bronzed and seasoned element, the huge rock pedestal, the bravery of walls and gates and towers and palaces and loudly asserted dominion; and then of that pervaded or mildly infested air in which one feels the experience of the ages, of which I just spoke, to be exquisitely in solution; and lastly of the wide, strange, sad, beautiful horizon, a rim of far mountains that always pictured, for the leaner on old rubbed and smoothed parapets at the sunset hour, a country not exactly blighted or deserted, but that had had its life, on an immense scale, and had gone, with all its memories and relics, into rather austere, in fact into almost grim and misanthropic, retirement. This was a manner and a mood, at any rate, in all the land, that favoured in the late afternoons the divinest landscape blues and purples—not to speak of its favouring still more my practical contention that the whole guarded headland in question, with the immense ramparts of golden brown and red that dropped into vineyards and orchards and cornfields and all the rustic elegance of the Tuscan *podere*, was knitting for me a chain of unforgettable hours; to the justice of which claim let these divagations testify.

It wasn't, however, that one mightn't without disloyalty to that scheme of profit seek impressions further afield—though indeed I may best say of such a matter as the long pilgrimage to the pictured convent of Monte Oliveto that it but played on the same fine chords as the overhanging, the far-gazing Lizza. What it came to was that one simply put to the friendly test, as it were, the mood and manner of the country. This remembrance is precious, but the demonstration of that sense as of a great heaving region stilled by some final shock and returning thoughtfully, in fact tragically, on itself, couldn't have been more pointed. The long-drawn rural road I refer to, stretching over hill and dale and to which I devoted the whole of the longest day of the year—I was in a small single-horse conveyance, of which I had already made appreciative use, and with a driver as disposed as myself ever to sacrifice

speed to contemplation—is doubtless familiar now with the
rush of the motor-car; the thought of whose free dealings
with the solitude of Monte Oliveto makes me a little ruefully
reconsider, I confess, the spirit in which I have elsewhere
in these pages, on behalf of the lust, the landscape lust, of
the eyes, acknowledged our general increasing debt to that
vehicle. For that we met nothing whatever, as I seem at this
distance of time to recall, while we gently trotted and trotted
through the splendid summer hours and a dry desolation that
yet somehow smiled and smiled, was part of the charm and
the intimacy of the whole impression—the impression that
culminated at last, before the great cloistered square, lonely,
bleak and stricken, in the almost aching vision, more frequent
in the Italy of to-day than anywhere in the world, of the un-
calculated waste of a myriad forms of piety, forces of labour,
beautiful fruits of genius. However, one gaped above all
things for the impression, and what one mainly asked was
that it should be strong of its kind. That was the case, I think
I couldn't but feel, at every moment of the couple of hours I
spent in the vast, cold, empty shell, out of which the Benedictine brotherhood sheltered there for ages had lately been
turned by the strong arm of a secular State. There was but
one good brother left, a very lean and tough survivor, a
dusky, elderly, friendly Abbate, of an indescribable type and a
perfect manner, of whom I think I felt immediately thereafter
that I should have liked to say much, but as to whom I must
have yielded to the fact that ingenious and vivid commemoration was even then in store for him. Literary portraiture had
marked him for its own, and in the short story of *Un Saint*,
one of the most finished of contemporary French *nouvelles*,
the art and the sympathy of Monsieur Paul Bourget preserve
his interesting image. He figures in the beautiful tale, the Abbate of the desolate cloister and of those comparatively quiet
years, as a clean, clear type of sainthood; a circumstance this
in itself to cause a fond analyst of other than "Latin" race
(model and painter in this case having their Latinism so
strongly in common) almost endlessly to meditate. Oh, the
unutterable differences in any scheme or estimate of physiognomic values, in any range of sensibility to expressional association, among observers of different, of inevitably more or

less opposed, traditional and "racial" points of view! One had heard convinced Latins—or at least I had!—speak of situations of trust and intimacy in which they couldn't have endured near them a Protestant or, as who should say for instance, an Anglo-Saxon; but I was to remember my own private attempt to measure such a change of sensibility as might have permitted the prolonged close approach of the dear dingy, half-starved, very possibly all heroic, and quite ideally urbane Abbate. The depth upon depth of things, the cloud upon cloud of associations, on one side and the other, that would have had to change first!

To which I may add nevertheless that since one ever supremely invoked intensity of impression and abundance of character, I feasted my fill of it at Monte Oliveto, and that for that matter this would have constituted my sole refreshment in the vast icy void of the blighted refectory if I hadn't bethought myself of bringing with me a scrap of food, too scantly apportioned, I recollect—very scantly indeed, since my *cocchiere* was to share with me—by my purveyor at Siena. Our tragic—even if so tenderly tragic—entertainer had nothing to give us; but the immemorial cold of the enormous monastic interior in which we smilingly fasted would doubtless not have had for me without that such a wealth of reference. I was to have "liked" the whole adventure, so I must somehow have liked that; by which remark I am recalled to the special treasure of the desecrated temple, those extraordinarily strong and brave frescoes of Luca Signorelli and Sodoma that adorn, in admirable condition, several stretches of cloister wall. These creations in a manner took care of themselves; aided by the blue of the sky above the cloister-court they glowed, they insistently lived; I remember the frigid prowl through all the rest of the bareness, including that of the big dishonoured church and that even of the Abbate's abysmally resigned testimony to his mere human and personal situation; and then, with such a force of contrast and effect of relief, the great sheltered sun flares and colour-patches of scenic composition and design where a couple of hands centuries ago turned to dust had so wrought the defiant miracle of life and beauty that the effect is of a garden blooming among ruins. Discredited somehow, since they all would, the destroyers themselves, the ancient piety, the general spirit and intention, but still bright and assured and sublime—practically, enviably immortal—the other, the still subtler, the all æsthetic good faith.

1909.

The Autumn in Florence

FLORENCE too has its "season," not less than Rome, and I have been rejoicing for the past six weeks in the fact that this comparatively crowded parenthesis hasn't yet been opened. Coming here in the first days of October I found the summer still in almost unmenaced possession, and ever since, till within a day or two, the weight of its hand has been sensible. Properly enough, as the city of flowers, Florence mingles the elements most artfully in the spring—during the divine crescendo of March and April, the weeks when six months of steady shiver have still not shaken New York and Boston free of the long Polar reach. But the very quality of the decline of the year as we at present here feel it suits peculiarly the mood in which an undiscourageable gatherer of the sense of things, or taster at least of "charm," moves through these many-memoried streets and galleries and churches. Old things, old places, old people, or at least old races, ever strike us as giving out their secrets most freely in such moist, grey, melancholy days as have formed the complexion of the past fortnight. With Christmas arrives the opera, the only opera worth speaking of—which indeed often means in Florence the only opera worth talking through; the gaiety, the gossip, the reminders in fine of the cosmopolite and watering-place character to which the city of the Medici long ago began to bend her antique temper. Meanwhile it is pleasant enough for the tasters of charm, as I say, and for the makers of invidious distinctions, that the Americans haven't all arrived, however many may be on their way, and that the weather has a monotonous overcast softness in which, apparently, aimless contemplation grows less and less ashamed. There is no crush along the Cascine, as on the sunny days of winter, and the Arno, wandering away toward the mountains in the haze, seems as shy of being looked at as a good picture in a bad light. No light, to my eyes, nevertheless, could be better than this, which reaches us, all strained and filtered and refined, exquisitely coloured and even a bit conspicuously sophisticated, through the heavy air of the past that hangs about the place forever.

I first knew Florence early enough, I am happy to say, to have heard the change for the worse, the taint of the modern order, bitterly lamented by old haunters, admirers, lovers— those qualified to present a picture of the conditions prevailing under the good old Grand-Dukes, the two last of their line in especial, that, for its blest reflection of sweetness and mildness and cheapness and ease, of every immediate boon in life to be enjoyed quite for nothing, could but draw tears from belated listeners. Some of these survivors from the golden age—just the beauty of which indeed was in the gold, of sorts, that it poured into your lap, and not in the least in its own importunity on that head—have needfully lingered on, have seen the ancient walls pulled down and the compact and belted mass of which the Piazza della Signoria was the immemorial centre expand, under the treatment of enterprising syndics, into an ungirdled organism of the type, as they viciously say, of Chicago; one of those places of which, as their grace of a circumference is nowhere, the dignity of a centre can no longer be predicated. Florence loses itself to-day in dusty boulevards and smart *beaux quartiers*, such as Napoleon III. and Baron Haussmann were to set the fashion of to a too mediæval Europe—with the effect of some precious page of antique text swallowed up in a marginal commentary that smacks of the style of the newspaper. So much for what has happened on this side of that line of demarcation which, by an odd law, makes us, with our preference for what we are pleased to call the picturesque, object to such occurrences even *as* occurrences. The real truth is that objections are too vain, and that he would be too rude a critic here, just now, who shouldn't be in the humour to take the thick with the thin and to try at least to read something of the old soul into the new forms.

There is something to be said moreover for your liking a city (once it's a question of your actively circulating) to pretend to comfort you more by its extent than by its limits; in addition to which Florence was anciently, was in her palmy days peculiarly, a daughter of change and movement and variety, of shifting moods, policies and *régimes*—just as the

Florentine character, as we have it to-day, is a character that takes all things easily for having seen so many come and go. It saw the national capital, a few years since, arrive and sit down by the Arno, and took no further thought than sufficed for the day; then it saw the odd visitor depart and whistled her cheerfully on her way to Rome. The new boulevards of the Sindaco Peruzzi come, it may be said, but they don't go; which, after all, it isn't from the æsthetic point of view strictly necessary they should. A part of the essential amiability of Florence, of her genius for making you take to your favour on easy terms everything that in any way belongs to her, is that she has already flung an element of her grace over all their undried mortar and plaster. Such modern arrangements as the Piazza d'Azeglio and the *viale* or Avenue of the Princess Margaret please not a little, I think—for what they are!—and do so even in a degree, by some fine local privilege, just because they are Florentine. The afternoon lights rest on them as if to thank them for not being worse, and their vistas are liberal where they look toward the hills. They carry you close to these admirable elevations, which hang over Florence on all sides, and if in the foreground your sense is a trifle perplexed by the white pavements dotted here and there with a policeman or a nursemaid, you have only to reach beyond and see Fiesole turn to violet, on its ample eminence, from the effect of the opposite sunset.

Facing again then to Florence proper you have local colour enough and to spare—which you enjoy the more, doubtless, from standing off to get your light and your point of view. The elder streets abutting on all this newness bore away into the heart of the city in narrow, dusky perspectives that quite refine, in certain places, by an art of their own, on the romantic appeal. There are temporal and other accidents thanks to which, as you pause to look down them and to penetrate the deepening shadows that accompany their retreat, they resemble little corridors leading out from the past, mystical like the ladder in Jacob's dream; so that when you see a single figure advance and draw nearer you are half afraid to wait till it arrives—it must be too much of the nature of a ghost, a messenger from an underworld. However this may be, a place paved with such great mosaics of slabs and lined with palaces of so massive a tradition, structures which, in their large dependence on pure proportion for interest and beauty, reproduce more than other modern styles the simple nobleness of Greek architecture, must ever have placed dignity first in the scale of invoked effect and laid up no great treasure of that ragged picturesqueness—the picturesqueness of large poverty—on which we feast our idle eyes at Rome and Naples. Except in the unfinished fronts of the churches, which, however, unfortunately, are mere ugly blankness, one finds less of the poetry of ancient over-use, or in other words less romantic southern shabbiness, than in most Italian cities. At two or three points, none the less, this sinister grace exists in perfection—just such perfection as so often proves that what is literally hideous may be constructively delightful and what is intrinsically tragic play on the finest chords of appreciation. On the north side of the Arno, between Ponte Vecchio and Ponte Santa Trinità, is a row of immemorial houses that back on the river, in whose yellow flood they bathe their sore old feet. Anything more battered and befouled, more cracked and disjointed, dirtier, drearier, poorer, it would be impossible to conceive. They look as if fifty years ago the liquid mud had risen over their chimneys and then subsided again and left them coated forever with its unsightly slime. And yet forsooth, because the river is yellow, and the light is yellow, and here and there, elsewhere, some mellow mouldering surface, some hint of colour, some accident of atmosphere, takes up the foolish tale and repeats the note—because, in short, it is Florence, it is Italy, and the fond appraiser, the infatuated alien, may have had in his eyes, at birth and afterwards, the micaceous sparkle of brown-stone fronts no more interesting than so much sand-paper, these miserable dwellings, instead of suggesting mental invocations to an enterprising board of health, simply create their own standard of felicity and shamelessly live in it. Lately, during the misty autumn nights, the moon has shone on them faintly and refined their shabbiness away into something ineffably strange and spectral. The turbid stream sweeps along without a sound, and the pale tenements hang above it like a vague miasmatic exhalation. The dimmest back-scene at the opera, when the tenor is singing his sweetest, seems hardly to belong to a world more detached from responsibility.

What it is that infuses so rich an interest into the general charm is difficult to say in a few words; yet as we wander hither and thither in quest of sacred canvas and immortal bronze and stone we still feel the genius of the place hang about. Two industrious English ladies, the Misses Horner, have lately published a couple of volumes of "Walks" by the Arno-side, and their work is a long enumeration of great artistic deeds. These things remain for the most part in sound preservation, and, as the weeks go by and you spend a constant portion of your days among them the sense of one of the happiest periods of human Taste—to put it only at that—settles upon your spirit. It was not long; it lasted, in its splendour, for less than a century; but it has stored away in the palaces and churches of Florence a heritage of beauty that these three enjoying centuries since haven't yet exhausted. This forms a clear intellectual atmosphere into which you may turn aside from the modern world and fill your lungs as with the breath of a forgotten creed. The memorials of the past here address us moreover with a friendliness, win us by we scarcely know what sociability, what equal amenity, that we scarce find matched in other great æsthetically endowed communities and periods. Venice, with her old palaces cracking under the weight of their treasures, is, in her influence, insupportably sad; Athens, with her maimed marbles and dishonoured memories, transmutes the consciousness of sensitive observers, I am told, into a chronic heartache; but in one's impression of old Florence the abiding felicity, the sense of saving sanity, of something sound and human, predominates, offering you a medium still conceivable for life. The reason of this is partly, no doubt, the "sympathetic" nature, the temperate joy, of Florentine art in general—putting the sole Dante, greatest of literary artists, aside; partly the tenderness of time, in its lapse, which, save in a few cases, has been as sparing of injury as if it knew that when it should have dimmed and corroded these charming things it would have nothing so sweet again for its tooth to feed on. If the beautiful Ghirlandaios and Lippis are fading this generation will never know it.

The large Fra Angelico in the Academy is as clear and keen as if the good old monk stood there wiping his brushes; the colours seem to *sing*, as it were, like new-fledged birds in June. Nothing is more characteristic of early Tuscan art than the high-reliefs of Luca della Robbia; yet there isn't one of them that, except for the unique mixture of freshness with its wisdom, of candour with its expertness, mightn't have been modelled yesterday.

But perhaps the best image of the absence of stale melancholy or wasted splendour, of the positive presence of what I have called temperate joy, in the Florentine impression and genius, is the bell-tower of Giotto, which rises beside the Cathedral. No beholder of it will have forgotten how straight and slender it stands there, how strangely rich in the common street, plated with coloured marble patterns, and yet so far from simple or severe in design that we easily wonder how its author, the painter of exclusively and portentously grave little pictures, should have fashioned a building which in the way of elaborate elegance, of the true play of taste, leaves a jealous modern criticism nothing to miss. Nothing can be imagined at once more lightly and more pointedly fanciful; it might have been handed over to the city, as it stands, by some Oriental genie tired of too much detail. Yet for all that suggestion it seems of no particular time — not grey and hoary like a Gothic steeple, not cracked and despoiled like a Greek temple; its marbles shining so little less freshly than when they were laid together, and the sunset lighting up its cornice with such a friendly radiance, that you come at last to regard it simply as the graceful, indestructible soul of the place made visible. The Cathedral, externally, for all its solemn hugeness, strikes the same note of would-be reasoned elegance and cheer; it has conventional grandeur, of course, but a grandeur so frank and ingenuous even in its *parti-pris*. It has seen so much, and outlived so much, and served so many sad purposes, and yet remains in aspect so full of the fine Tuscan geniality, the feeling for life, one may almost say the feeling for amusement, that inspired it. Its vast many-coloured marble walls become at any rate, with this, the friendliest note of all Florence; there is an unfailing charm in walking past them while they lift their great acres of geometrical mosaic higher in the air than you have time or other occasion to look. You greet them from the deep street as you greet the side of a mountain when you move in the gorge—not twisting back your head to keep looking at the top, but content with the minor accidents, the nestling hollows and soft cloud-shadows, the general protection of the valley.

Florence is richer in pictures than we really know till we have begun to look for them in outlying corners. Then, here and there, one comes upon lurking values and hidden gems that it quite seems one might as a good New Yorker quietly "bag" for the so aspiring Museum of that city without their being missed. The Pitti Palace is of course a collection of masterpieces; they jostle each other in their splendour, they perhaps even, in their merciless multitude, rather fatigue our admiration. The Uffizi is almost as fine a show, and together with that long serpentine artery which crosses the Arno and connects them, making you ask yourself, whichever way you take it, what goal can be grand enough to crown such a journey, they form the great central treasure-chamber of the town. But I have been neglecting them of late for love of the Academy, where there are fewer copyists and tourists, above all fewer pictorial lions, those whose roar is heard from afar and who strike us as expecting overmuch to have it their own way in the jungle. The pictures at the Academy are all, rather, doves—the whole impression is less pompously tropical. Selection still leaves one too much to say, but I noted here, on my last occasion, an enchanting Botticelli so obscurely hung, in one of the smaller rooms, that I scarce knew whether most to enjoy or to resent its relegation. Placed, in a mean black frame, where you wouldn't have looked for a masterpiece, it yet gave out to a good glass every characteristic of one. Representing as it does the walk of Tobias with the angel, there are really parts of it that an angel might have painted; but I doubt whether it is observed by half-a-dozen persons a year. That was my excuse for my wanting to know, on the spot, though doubtless all sophistically, what dishonour, could the transfer be artfully accomplished, a strong American light and a brave gilded frame would, comparatively speaking, do it. There and then it would shine with the intense authority that we claim for the fairest things—would exhale its wondrous beauty as a sovereign example. What it comes to is that this master is the most interesting of a great band—the only Florentine save Leonardo and Michael in whom the impulse was original and the invention rare. His imagination is of things strange, subtle and complicated—things it at first strikes us that we moderns have reason to know, and that it has taken us all the ages to learn; so that we permit ourselves to wonder how a "primitive" could come by them. We soon enough reflect, however, that we ourselves have come by them almost only *through* him, exquisite spirit that he was, and that when we enjoy, or at least when we encounter, in our William Morrises, in our Rossettis and Burne-Joneses, the note of the haunted or over-charged consciousness, we are but treated, with other matters, to repeated doses of diluted Botticelli. He practically set with his own hand almost all the copies to almost all our so-called pre-Raphaelites, earlier and later, near and remote.

Let us at the same time, none the less, never fail of response to the great Florentine geniality at large. Fra Angelico, Filippo Lippi, Ghirlandaio, were not "subtly" imaginative, were not even riotously so; but what other three were ever more gladly observant, more vividly and richly true? If there should some time be a weeding out of the world's possessions the best works of the early Florentines will certainly be counted among the flowers. With the ripest performances of the Venetians—by which I don't mean the over-ripe—we can but take them for the most valuable things in the history of art. Heaven forbid we should be narrowed down to a cruel choice; but if it came to a question of keeping or losing between half-a-dozen Raphaels and half-a-dozen things it would be a joy to pick out at the Academy, I fear that, for myself, the memory of the Transfiguration, or indeed of the other Roman relics of the painter, wouldn't save the Raphaels. And yet this was so far from the opinion of a patient artist whom I saw the other day copying the finest of Ghirlandaios—a beautiful Adoration of the Kings at the Hospital of the Innocenti. Here was another sample of the buried art-wealth of Florence. It hangs in an obscure chapel, far aloft, behind an altar, and though now and then a stray tourist wanders in and puzzles awhile over the vaguely-glowing forms, the picture is never really seen and enjoyed. I found an aged Frenchman of modest mien perched on a little platform beneath it, behind a great hedge of altar-candlesticks, with an admirable copy all completed. The difficulties of his task had been well-nigh insuperable, and his performance seemed to me a real feat of magic. He could scarcely move or turn, and could find room for his canvas but by rolling it together and painting a small piece at a time, so that he never enjoyed a view of his *ensemble*. The original is gorgeous with colour and bewildering with decorative detail, but not a gleam of the painter's crimson was wanting, not a curl in his gold arabesques. It seemed to me that if I had copied a Ghirlandaio in such conditions I would at least maintain for my own credit that he was the first painter in the world. "Very good of its kind," said the weary old man with a shrug of reply for my raptures; "but oh how far short of Raphael!" However that may be, if the reader chances to observe this consummate copy in the so commendable Museum devoted in Paris to such works, let him stop before it with a due reverence; it is one of the patient things of art. Seeing it wrought there, in its dusky nook, under such scant convenience, I found no bar in the painter's foreignness to a thrilled sense that the old art-life of Florence isn't yet extinct. It still at least works spells and almost miracles.

1873.

Florentine Notes

I

YESTERDAY that languid organism known as the Florentine Carnival put on a momentary semblance of vigour, and decreed a general *corso* through the town. The spectacle was not brilliant, but it suggested some natural reflections. I encountered the line of carriages in the square before Santa Croce, of which they were making the circuit. They rolled solemnly by, with their inmates frowning forth at each other in apparent wrath at not finding each other more worth while. There were no masks, no costumes, no decorations, no throwing of flowers or sweetmeats. It was as if each carriageful had privately and not very heroically resolved not to be at costs, and was rather discomfited at finding that it was getting no better entertainment than it gave. The middle of the piazza was filled with little tables, with shouting mountebanks, mostly disguised in battered bonnets and crinolines, offering chances in raffles for plucked fowls and kerosene lamps. I have never thought the huge marble statue of Dante, which overlooks the scene, a work of the last refinement; but, as it stood there on its high pedestal, chin in hand, frowning down on all this cheap foolery, it seemed to have a great moral intention. The carriages followed a prescribed course—through Via Ghibellina, Via del Proconsolo, past the Badia and the Bargello, beneath the great tessellated cliffs of the Cathedral, through Via Tornabuoni and out into ten minutes' sunshine beside the Arno. Much of all this is the gravest and stateliest part of Florence, a quarter of supreme dignity, and there was an almost ludicrous incongruity in seeing Pleasure leading her train through these dusky historic streets. It was most uncomfortably cold, and in the absence of masks many a fair nose was fantastically tipped with purple. But as the carriages crept solemnly along they seemed to keep a funeral march—to follow an antique custom, an exploded faith, to its tomb. The Carnival is dead, and these good people who had come abroad to make merry were funeral mutes and grave-diggers.

Last winter in Rome it showed but a galvanised life, yet compared with this humble exhibition it was operatic. At Rome
indeed it was too operatic. The knights on horseback there
were a bevy of circus-riders, and I'm sure half the mad revellers repaired every night to the Capitol for their twelve sous a
day.

I have just been reading over the Letters of the Président de
Brosses. A hundred years ago, in Venice, the Carnival lasted
six months; and at Rome for many weeks each year one was
free, under cover of a mask, to perpetrate the most fantastic
follies and cultivate the most remunerative vices. It's very well
to read the President's notes, which have indeed a singular
interest; but they make us ask ourselves why we should expect
the Italians to persist in manners and practices which we ourselves, if we had responsibilities in the matter, should find
intolerable. The Florentines at any rate spend no more money
nor faith on the carnivalesque. And yet this truth has a qualification; for what struck me in the whole spectacle yesterday,
and prompted these observations, was not at all the more or
less of costume of the occupants of the carriages, but the obstinate survival of the merrymaking instinct in the people at
large. There could be no better example of it than that so dim
a shadow of entertainment should keep all Florence standing
and strolling, densely packed for hours, in the cold streets.
There was nothing to see that mightn't be seen on the
Cascine any fine day in the year—nothing but a name, a
tradition, a pretext for sweet staring idleness. The faculty of
making much of common things and converting small occasions into great pleasures is, to a son of communities strenuous as ours are strenuous, the most salient characteristic of the
so-called Latin civilisations. It charms him and vexes him, according to his mood; and for the most part it represents a
moral gulf between his own temperamental and indeed spiritual sense of race, and that of Frenchmen and Italians, far
wider than the watery leagues that a steamer may annihilate.
But I think his mood is wisest when he accepts the "foreign"
easy surrender to *all* the senses as the sign of an unconscious
philosophy of life, instilled by the experience of centuries—
the philosophy of people who have lived long and much, who
have discovered no short cuts to happiness and no effective

circumvention of effort, and so have come to regard the average lot as a ponderous fact that absolutely calls for a certain amount of sitting on the lighter tray of the scales. Florence yesterday then took its holiday in a natural, placid fashion that seemed to make its own temper an affair quite independent of the splendour of the compensation decreed on a higher line to the weariness of its legs. That the *corso* was stupid or lively was the shame or the glory of the powers "above"—the fates, the gods, the *forestieri*, the town-councilmen, the rich or the stingy. Common Florence, on the narrow footways, pressed against the houses, obeyed a natural need in looking about complacently, patiently, gently, and never pushing, nor trampling, nor swearing, nor staggering. This liberal margin for festivals in Italy gives the masses a more than man-of-the-world urbanity in taking their pleasure.

Meanwhile it occurs to me that by a remote New England fireside an unsophisticated young person of either sex is reading in an old volume of travels or an old romantic tale some account of these anniversaries and appointed revels as old Catholic lands offer them to view. Across the page swims a vision of sculptured palace-fronts draped in crimson and gold and shining in a southern sun; of a motley train of maskers sweeping on in voluptuous confusion and pelting each other with nosegays and love-letters. Into the quiet room, quenching the rhythm of the Connecticut clock, floats an uproar of delighted voices, a medley of stirring foreign sounds, an echo of far-heard music of a strangely alien cadence. But the dusk is falling, and the unsophisticated young person closes the book wearily and wanders to the window. The dusk is falling on the beaten snow. Down the road is a white wooden meeting-house, looking grey among the drifts. The young person surveys the prospect awhile, and then wanders back and stares at the fire. The Carnival of Venice, of Florence, of Rome; colour and costume, romance and rapture! The young person gazes in the firelight at the flickering chiaroscuro of the future, discerns at last the glowing phantasm of opportunity, and determines with a wild heart-beat to go and see it all—twenty years hence!

II

A couple of days since, driving to Fiesole, we came back by the castle of Vincigliata. The afternoon was lovely; and, though there is as yet (February 10th) no visible revival of vegetation, the air was full of a vague vernal perfume, and the warm colours of the hills and the yellow western sunlight flooding the plain seemed to contain the promise of Nature's return to grace. It's true that above the distant pale blue gorge of Vallombrosa the mountain-line was tipped with snow; but the liberated soul of Spring was nevertheless at large. The view from Fiesole seems vaster and richer with each visit. The hollow in which Florence lies, and which from below seems deep and contracted, opens out into an immense and generous valley and leads away the eye into a hundred gradations of distance. The place itself showed, amid its chequered fields and gardens, with as many towers and spires as a chess-board half cleared. The domes and towers were washed over with a faint blue mist. The scattered columns of smoke, interfused with the sinking sunlight, hung over them like streamers and pennons of silver gauze; and the Arno, twisting and curling and glittering here and there, was a serpent cross-striped with silver.

Vincigliata is a product of the millions, the leisure and the eccentricity, I suppose people say, of an English gentleman — Mr. Temple Leader, whose name should be commemorated. You reach the castle from Fiesole by a narrow road, returning toward Florence by a romantic twist through the hills and passing nothing on its way save thin plantations of cypress and cedar. Upward of twenty years ago, I believe, this gentleman took a fancy to the crumbling shell of a mediæval fortress on a breezy hilltop overlooking the Val d'Arno and forthwith bought it and began to "restore" it. I know nothing of what the original ruin may have cost; but in the dusky courts and chambers of the present elaborate structure this impassioned archæologist must have buried a fortune. He has, however, the compensation of feeling that he has erected a monument which, if it is never to stand a feudal siege, may encounter at least some critical overhauling. It is a disinterested work of art

and really a triumph of æsthetic culture. The author has reproduced with minute accuracy a sturdy home-fortress of the
fourteenth century, and has kept throughout such rigid terms
with his model that the result is literally uninhabitable to degenerate moderns. It is simply a massive facsimile, an elegant
museum of archaic images, mainly but most amusingly counterfeit, perched on a spur of the Apennines. The place is most
politely shown. There is a charming cloister, painted with extremely clever "quaint" frescoes, celebrating the deeds of the
founders of the castle—a cloister that is everything delightful
a cloister should be except truly venerable and employable.
There is a beautiful castle court, with the embattled tower
climbing into the blue far above it, and a spacious loggia with
rugged medallions and mild-hued Luca della Robbias fastened unevenly into the walls. But the apartments are the
great success, and each of them as good a "reconstruction" as
a tale of Walter Scott; or, to speak frankly, a much better one.
They are all low-beamed and vaulted, stone-paved, decorated
in grave colours and lighted, from narrow, deeply recessed
windows, through small leaden-ringed plates of opaque glass.

The details are infinitely ingenious and elaborately grim,
and the indoor atmosphere of mediævalism most forcibly revived. No compromising fact of domiciliary darkness and cold
is spared us, no producing condition of mediæval manners
not glanced at. There are oaken benches round the room, of
about six inches in depth, and gaunt fauteuils of wrought
leather, illustrating the suppressed transitions which, as
George Eliot says, unite all contrasts—offering a visible link
between the modern conceptions of torture and of luxury.
There are fireplaces nowhere but in the kitchen, where a
couple of sentry-boxes are inserted on either side of the great
hooded chimney-piece, into which people might creep and
take their turn at being toasted and smoked. One may doubt
whether this dearth of the hearthstone could have raged on
such a scale, but it's a happy stroke in the representation of an
Italian dwelling of any period. It shows how the graceful
fiction that Italy is all "meridional" flourished for some time
before being refuted by grumbling tourists. And yet amid this
cold comfort you feel the incongruous presence of a constant
intuitive regard for beauty. The shapely spring of the vaulted

ceilings; the richly figured walls, coarse and hard in substance
as they are; the charming shapes of the great platters and flag-
ons in the deep recesses of the quaintly carved black dressers;
the wandering hand of ornament, as it were, playing here and
there for its own diversion in unlighted corners—such things
redress, to our fond credulity, with all sorts of grace, the balance of the picture.

And yet, somehow, with what dim, unillumined vision one
fancies even such inmates as those conscious of finer needs
than the mere supply of blows and beef and beer would meet
passing their heavy eyes over such slender household beguile-
ments! These crepuscular chambers at Vincigliata are a mystery and a challenge; they seem the mere propounding of an
answerless riddle. You long, as you wander through them,
turning up your coat-collar and wondering whether ghosts
can catch bronchitis, to answer it with some positive notion
of what people so encaged and situated "did," how they
looked and talked and carried themselves, how they took their
pains and pleasures, how they counted off the hours. Deadly
ennui seems to ooze out of the stones and hang in clouds in
the brown corners. No wonder men relished a fight and
panted for a fray. "Skull-smashers" were sweet, ears ringing
with pain and ribs cracking in a tussle were soothing music,
compared with the cruel quietude of the dim-windowed castle. When they came back they could only have slept a good
deal and eased their dislocated bones on those meagre oaken
ledges. Then they woke up and turned about to the table and
ate their portion of roasted sheep. They shouted at each other
across the board and flung the wooden plates at the serving-
men. They jostled and hustled and hooted and bragged; and
then, after gorging and boozing and easing their doublets,
they squared their elbows one by one on the greasy table and
buried their scarred foreheads and dreamed of a good gallop
after flying foes. And the women? They must have been
strangely simple—simpler far than any moral archæologist
can show us in a learned restoration. Of course, their simplicity had its graces and devices; but one thinks with a sigh
that, as the poor things turned away with patient looks from
the viewless windows to the same, same looming figures on
the dusky walls, they hadn't even the consolation of knowing

that just this attitude and movement, set off by their peaked coifs, their falling sleeves and heavily-twisted trains, would sow the seed of yearning envy—of sorts—on the part of later generations.

There are moods in which one feels the impulse to enter a tacit protest against too gross an appetite for pure æsthetics in this starving and sinning world. One turns half away, musingly, from certain beautiful useless things. But the healthier state of mind surely is to lay no tax on any really intelligent manifestation of the curious and exquisite. Intelligence hangs together essentially, all along the line; it only needs time to make, as we say, its connections. The massive *pastiche* of Vincigliata has no superficial use; but, even if it were less complete, less successful, less brilliant, I should feel a reflective kindness for it. So disinterested and so expensive a toy is its own justification; it belongs to the heroics of dilettantism.

III

One grows to feel the collection of pictures at the Pitti Palace splendid rather than interesting. After walking through it once or twice you catch the key in which it is pitched—you know what you are likely not to find on closer examination; none of the works of the uncompromising period, nothing from the half-groping geniuses of the early time, those whose colouring was sometimes harsh and their outlines sometimes angular. Vague to me the principle on which the pictures were originally gathered and of the æsthetic creed of the princes who chiefly selected them. A princely creed I should roughly call it—the creed of people who believed in things presenting a fine face to society; who esteemed showy results rather than curious processes, and would have hardly cared more to admit into their collection a work by one of the laborious precursors of the full efflorescence than to see a bucket and broom left standing in a state saloon. The gallery contains in literal fact some eight or ten paintings of the early Tuscan School—notably two admirable specimens of Filippo Lippi and one of the frequent circular pictures of the great Botticelli—a Madonna, chilled with tragic prescience, laying a pale cheek against that of a blighted Infant. Such a melancholy mother as this of Botticelli would have strangled her baby in its cradle to rescue it from the future. But of Botticelli there is much to say. One of the Filippo Lippis is perhaps his master-piece—a Madonna in a small rose-garden (such a "flowery close" as Mr. William Morris loves to haunt), leaning over an Infant who kicks his little human heels on the grass while half-a-dozen curly-pated angels gather about him, looking back over their shoulders with the candour of children in *tableaux vivants*, and one of them drops an armful of gathered roses one by one upon the baby. The delightful earthly inno-cence of these winged youngsters is quite inexpressible. Their heads are twisted about toward the spectator as if they were playing at leap-frog and were expecting a companion to come and take a jump. Never did "young" art, never did subjective freshness, attempt with greater success to represent those phases. But these three fine works are hung over the tops of doors in a dark back room—the bucket and broom are thrust behind a curtain. It seems to me, nevertheless, that a fine Fi-lippo Lippi is good enough company for an Allori or a Cigoli, and that that too deeply sentient Virgin of Botticelli might happily balance the flower-like irresponsibility of Raphael's "Madonna of the Chair."

Taking the Pitti collection, however, simply for what it pre-tends to be, it gives us the very flower of the sumptuous, the courtly, the grand-ducal. It is chiefly official art, as one may say, but it presents the fine side of the type—the brilliancy, the facility, the amplitude, the sovereignty of good taste. I agree on the whole with a nameless companion and with what he lately remarked about his own humour on these mat-ters; that, having been on his first acquaintance with pictures nothing if not critical, and held the lesson incomplete and the opportunity slighted if he left a gallery without a headache, he had come, as he grew older, to regard them more as the grandest of all pleasantries and less as the most strenuous of all lessons, and to remind himself that, after all, it is the priv-ilege of art to make us friendly to the human mind and not to make us suspicious of it. We do in fact as we grow older un-string the critical bow a little and strike a truce with invidious comparisons. We work off the juvenile impulse to heated par-tisanship and discover that one spontaneous producer isn't different enough from another to keep the all-knowing Fates from smiling over our loves and our aversions. We perceive a certain human solidarity in all cultivated effort, and are conscious of a growing accommodation of judgment—an easier disposition, the fruit of experience, to take the joke for what it is worth as it passes. We have in short less of a quarrel with the masters we don't delight in, and less of an impulse to pin all our faith on those in whom, in more zealous days, we fancied that we made out peculiar meanings. The meanings no longer seem quite so peculiar. Since then we have arrived at a few in the depths of our own genius that are not sensibly less striking.

And yet it must be added that all this depends vastly on one's mood—as a traveller's impressions do, generally, to a degree which those who give them to the world would do well more explicitly to declare. We have our hours of expansion and those of contraction, and yet while we follow the traveller's trade we go about gazing and judging with unadjusted confidence. We can't suspend judgment; we must take our notes, and the notes are florid or crabbed, as the case may be. A short time ago I spent a week in an ancient city on a hill-top, in the humour, for which I was not to blame, which produces crabbed notes. I knew it at the time, but couldn't help it. I went through all the motions of liberal appreciation; I uncapped in all the churches and on the massive ramparts stared all the views fairly out of countenance; but my imagination, which I suppose at bottom had very good reasons of its own and knew perfectly what it was about, refused to project into the dark old town and upon the yellow hills that sympathetic glow which forms half the substance of our genial impressions. So it is that in museums and palaces we are alternate radicals and conservatives. On some days we ask but to be somewhat sensibly affected; on others, Ruskin-haunted, to be spiritually steadied. After a long absence from the Pitti Palace I went back there the other morning and transferred myself from chair to chair in the great golden-roofed saloons—the chairs are all gilded and covered with faded silk—in the humour to be diverted at any price. I needn't mention the things that diverted me; I yawn now when I think of some of them. But an artist, for instance, to whom my kindlier judgment has made permanent concessions is that charming Andrea del Sarto. When I first knew him, in my cold youth, I used to say without mincing that I didn't like him. *Cet âge est sans pitié.* The fine sympathetic, melancholy, pleasing painter! He has a dozen faults, and if you insist pedantically on your rights the conclusive word you use about him will be the word weak. But if you are a generous soul you will utter it low—low as the mild grave tone of his own sought harmonies. He is monotonous, narrow, incomplete; he has but a dozen different figures and but two or three ways of distributing them; he seems able to utter but half his thought, and his canvases lack apparently some final return on the whole matter—some process which his impulse failed him before he could bestow. And yet in spite of these limitations his genius is both itself of the great pattern and lighted by the air of a great period. Three gifts he had largely: an instinctive, unaffected, unerring grace; a large and rich, and yet a sort of withdrawn and indifferent, sobriety; and best of all, as well as rarest of all, an indescribable property of relatedness as to the moral world. Whether he was aware of the connection or not, or in what measure, I cannot say; but he gives, so to speak, the taste of it. Before his handsome vague-browed Madonnas; the mild, robust young saints who kneel in his foregrounds and look round at you with a conscious anxiety which seems to say that, though in the picture, they are not of it, but of your own sentient life of commingled love and weariness; the stately apostles, with comely heads and harmonious draperies, who gaze up at the high-seated Virgin like early astronomers at a newly seen star—there comes to you the brush of the dark wing of an inward life. A shadow falls for the moment, and in it you feel the chill of moral suffering. Did the Lippis suffer, father or son? Did Raphael suffer? Did Titian? Did Rubens suffer? Perish the thought—it wouldn't be fair to *us* that they should have had everything. And I note in our poor second-rate Andrea an element of interest lacking to a number of stronger talents.

Interspersed with him at the Pitti hang the stronger and the weaker in splendid abundance. Raphael is there, strong in portraiture—easy, various, bountiful genius that he was—and (strong here isn't the word, but) happy beyond the com-

mon dream in his beautiful "Madonna of the Chair." The
general instinct of posterity seems to have been to treat this
lovely picture as a semi-sacred, an almost miraculous, manifestation. People stand in a worshipful silence before it, as they
would before a taper-studded shrine. If we suspend in imagination on the right of it the solid realistic, unidealised portrait
of Leo the Tenth (which hangs in another room) and transport to the left the fresco of the School of Athens from the
Vatican, and then reflect that these were three separate fancies
of a single youthful, amiable genius we recognise that such a
producing consciousness must have been a "treat." My companion already quoted has a phrase that he "doesn't care for
Raphael," but confesses, when pressed, that he was a most
remarkable young man. Titian has a dozen portraits of unequal interest. I never particularly noticed till lately—it is very
ill hung—that portentous image of the Emperor Charles the
Fifth. He was a burlier, more imposing personage than his
usual legend figures, and in his great puffed sleeves and gold
chains and full-skirted over-dress he seems to tell of a tread
that might sometimes have been inconveniently resonant. But
the *purpose* to have his way and work his will is there—the
great stomach for divine right, the old monarchical temperament. The great Titian, in portraiture, however, remains that
formidable young man in black, with the small compact head,
the delicate nose and the irascible blue eye. Who was he?
What was he? *"Ritratto virile"* is all the catalogue is able to
call the picture. "Virile!" Rather! you vulgarly exclaim. You
may weave what romance you please about it, but a romance
your dream must be. Handsome, clever, defiant, passionate,
dangerous, it was not his own fault if he hadn't adventures
and to spare. He was a gentleman and a warrior, and his adventures balanced between camp and court. I imagine him the
young orphan of a noble house, about to come into mort-
gaged estates. One wouldn't have cared to be his guardian,
bound to paternal admonitions once a month over his preco-
cious transactions with the Jews or his scandalous abduction
from her convent of such and such a noble maiden.

The Pitti Gallery contains none of Titian's golden-toned
groups; but it boasts a lovely composition by Paul Veronese,
the dealer in silver hues—a Baptism of Christ. W—— named

it to me the other day as the picture he most enjoyed, and surely painting seems here to have proposed to itself to discredit and annihilate—and even on the occasion of such a subject—everything but the loveliness of life. The picture bedims and enfeebles its neighbours. We ask ourselves whether painting as such can go further. It is simply that here at last the art stands complete. The early Tuscans, as well as Leonardo, as Raphael, as Michael, saw the great spectacle that surrounded them in beautiful sharp-edged elements and parts. The great Venetians felt its indissoluble unity and recognised that form and colour and earth and air were equal members of every possible subject; and beneath their magical touch the hard outlines melted together and the blank intervals bloomed with meaning. In this beautiful Paul Veronese of the Pitti everything is part of the charm—the atmosphere as well as the figures, the look of radiant morning in the white-streaked sky as well as the living human limbs, the cloth of Venetian purple about the loins of the Christ as well as the noble humility of his attitude. The relation to Nature of the other Italian schools differs from that of the Venetian as courtship—even ardent courtship—differs from marriage.

IV

I went the other day to the secularised Convent of San Marco, paid my franc at the profane little wicket which creaks away at the door—no less than six custodians, apparently, are needed to turn it, as if it may have a recusant conscience—passed along the bright, still cloister and paid my respects to Fra Angelico's Crucifixion, in that dusky chamber in the basement. I looked long; one can hardly do otherwise. The fresco deals with the pathetic on the grand scale, and after taking in its beauty you feel as little at liberty to go away abruptly as you would to leave church during the sermon. You may be as little of a formal Christian as Fra Angelico was much of one; you yet feel admonished by spiritual decency to let so yearning a view of the Christian story work its utmost will on you. The three crosses rise high against a strange completely crimson sky, which deepens mysteriously the tragic expression of the scene, though I remain perforce vague as to whether this lurid background be a fine intended piece of symbolism or an effective accident of time. In the first case the extravagance quite triumphs. Between the crosses, under no great rigour of composition, are scattered the most exemplary saints—kneeling, praying, weeping, pitying, worshipping. The swoon of the Madonna is depicted at the left, and this gives the holy presences, in respect to the case, the strangest historical or actual air. Everything is so real that you feel a vague impatience and almost ask yourself how it was that amid the army of his consecrated servants our Lord was permitted to suffer. On reflection you see that the painter's design, so far as coherent, has been simply to offer an immense representation of Pity, and all with such concentrated truth that his colours here seem dissolved in tears that drop and drop, however softly, through all time. Of this single yearning consciousness the figures are admirably expressive. No later painter learned to render with deeper force than Fra Angelico the one state of the spirit he could conceive—a passionate pious tenderness. Immured in his quiet convent, he apparently never received an intelligible impression of evil; and his conception of human life was a perpetual sense of sacredly loving and being loved. But how, immured in his quiet convent, away from the streets and the studios, did he become that genuine, finished, perfectly professional painter? No one is less of a mere mawkish amateur. His range was broad, from this really heroic fresco to the little trumpeting seraphs, in their opaline robes, enamelled, as it were, on the gold margins of his pictures.

I sat out the sermon and departed, I hope, with the gentle preacher's blessing. I went into the smaller refectory, near by, to refresh my memory of the beautiful Last Supper of Domenico Ghirlandaio. It would be putting things coarsely to say that I adjourned thus from a sermon to a comedy, though Ghirlandaio's theme, as contrasted with the blessed Angelico's, was the dramatic, spectacular side of human life. How keenly he observed it and how richly he rendered it, the world about him of colour and costume, of handsome heads and pictorial groupings! In his admirable school there is no painter one enjoys—*pace* Ruskin—more sociably and irresponsibly. Lippo Lippi is simpler, quainter, more frankly expressive; but we retain before him a remnant of the sympathetic discomfort provoked by the masters whose conceptions were still a trifle too large for their means. The pictorial vision in their minds seems to stretch and strain their undeveloped skill almost to a sense of pain. In Ghirlandaio the skill and the imagination are equal, and he gives us a delightful impression of enjoying his own resources. Of all the painters of his time he affects us least as positively not of ours. He enjoyed a crimson mantle spreading and tumbling in curious folds and embroidered with needlework of gold, just as he enjoyed a handsome well-rounded head, with vigorous dusky locks, profiled in courteous adoration. He enjoyed in short the various reality of things, and had the good fortune to live in an age when reality flowered into a thousand amusing graces—to speak only of those. He was not especially addicted to giving spiritual hints; and yet how hard and meagre they seem, the professed and finished realists of our own day, with the spiritual *bonhomie* or candour that makes half Ghirlandaio's richness left out! The Last Supper at San Marco is an excellent example of the natural reverence of an artist of that time with whom reverence was not, as one may say, a specialty. The main idea with him has been the variety, the material bravery and positively social charm of the scene, which finds expression, with irrepressible generosity, in the accessories of the background. Instinctively he imagines an opulent garden—imagines it with a good faith which quite tides him over the reflection that Christ and his disciples were poor men and unused to sit at meat in palaces. Great fullfruited orange-trees peep over the wall before which the table is spread, strange birds fly through the air, while a peacock perches on the edge of the partition and looks down on the sacred repast. It is striking that, without any at all intense religious purpose, the figures, in their varied naturalness, have a dignity and sweetness of attitude that admits of numberless reverential constructions. I should call all this the happy tact of a robust faith.

On the staircase leading up to the little painted cells of the Beato Angelico, however, I suddenly faltered and paused. Somehow I had grown averse to the intenser zeal of the Monk of Fiesole. I wanted no more of him that day. I wanted no more macerated friars and spear-gashed sides. Ghirlandaio's elegant way of telling his story had put me in the humour for something more largely intelligent, more profanely pleasing. I departed, walked across the square, and found it in the Academy, standing in a particular spot and looking up at a particular high-hung picture. It is difficult to speak adequately, perhaps even intelligibly, of Sandro Botticelli. An accomplished critic—Mr. Pater, in his *Studies on the History of the Renaissance*—has lately paid him the tribute of an exquisite, a supreme, curiosity. He was rarity and distinction incarnate, and of all the multitudinous masters of his group incomparably the most interesting, the one who detains and perplexes and fascinates us most. Exquisitely fine his imagination—infinitely audacious and adventurous his fancy. Alone among the painters of his time he strikes us as having invention. The glow and thrill of expanding observation—this was the feeling that sent his comrades to their easels; but Botticelli's moved him to reactions and emotions of which they knew nothing, caused his faculty to sport and wander and explore on its own account. These impulses have fruits often so ingenious and so lovely that it would be easy to talk nonsense about them. I hope it is not nonsense, however, to say that the picture to which I just alluded (the "Coronation of the Virgin," with a group of life-sized saints below and a garland of miniature angels above) is one of the supremely beautiful productions of the human mind. It is hung so high that you need a good glass to see it; to say nothing of the unprecedented delicacy of the work. The lower half is of moderate interest; but the dance of hand-clasped angels round the heavenly couple above has a beauty newly exhaled from the deepest sources of inspiration. Their perfect little hands are locked with ineffable elegance; their blowing robes are tossed into folds of which each line is a study; their charming feet have the relief of the most delicate sculpture. But, as I have already noted, of Botticelli there is much, too much to say—besides which Mr. Pater has said all. Only add thus to his inimitable grace of design that the exquisite pictorial force driving him goes a-Maying not on wanton errands of its own, but on those of some mystic superstition which trembles forever in his heart.

V

The more I look at the old Florentine domestic architecture the more I like it—that of the great examples at least; and if I ever am able to build myself a lordly pleasure-house I don't see how in conscience I can build it different from these. They are sombre and frowning, and look a trifle more as if they were meant to keep people out than to let them in; but what equally "important" type—if there be an equally important—is more expressive of domiciliary dignity and security and yet attests them with a finer æsthetic economy? They are impressively "handsome," and yet contrive to be so by the simplest means. I don't say at the smallest pecuniary cost—that's another matter. There is money buried in the thick walls and diffused through the echoing excess of space. The merchant nobles of the fifteenth century had deep and full pockets, I suppose, though the present bearers of their names are glad to let out their palaces in suites of apartments which are occupied by the commercial aristocracy of another republic. One is told of fine old mouldering chambers of which possession is to be enjoyed for a sum not worth mentioning. I am afraid that behind these so gravely harmonious fronts there is a good deal of dusky discomfort, and I speak now simply of the large serious faces themselves as you can see them from the street; see them ranged cheek to cheek in the grey historic light of Via dei Bardi, Via Maggio, Via degli Albizzi. The force of character, the familiar severity and majesty, depend on a few simple features: on the great iron-caged windows of the rough-hewn basement; on the noble stretch of space between the summit of one high, round-topped window and the bottom of that above; on the high-hung sculptured shield at the angle of the house; on the flat far-projecting roof; and, finally, on the magnificent tallness of the whole building, which so dwarfs our modern attempts at size. The finest of these Florentine palaces are, I imagine, the tallest habitations in Europe that are frankly and amply habitations—not mere shafts for machinery of the American grain-elevator pattern. Some of the creations of M. Haussmann in Paris may climb very nearly as high; but there is all the difference in the world between the impressiveness of a building which takes breath, as it were, some six or seven times, from storey to storey, and of one that erects itself to an equal height in three long-drawn pulsations. When a house is ten windows wide and the drawing-room floor is as high as a chapel it can afford but three floors. The spaciousness of some of those ancient drawing-rooms is that of a Russian steppe. The "family circle," gathered anywhere within speaking distance, must resemble a group of pilgrims encamped in the desert on a little oasis of carpet. Madame Gryzanowska, living at the top of a house in that dusky, tortuous old Borgo Pinti, initiated me the other evening most good-naturedly, lamp in hand, into the far-spreading mysteries of her apartment. Such quarters seem a translation into space of the old-fashioned idea of leisure. Leisure and "room" have been passing out of our manners together, but here and there, being of stouter structure, the latter lingers and survives.

Here and there, indeed, in this blessed Italy, reluctantly modern in spite alike of boasts and lamentations, it seems to have been preserved for curiosity's and fancy's sake, with a vague, sweet odour of the embalmer's spices about it. I went the other morning to the Corsini Palace. The proprietors obviously are great people. One of the ornaments of Rome is their great white-faced palace in the dark Trastevere and its voluminous gallery, none the less delectable for the poorness of the pictures. Here they have a palace on the Arno, with another large, handsome, respectable and mainly uninteresting collection. It contains indeed three or four fine examples of early Florentines. It was not especially for the pictures that I went, however; and certainly not for the pictures that I stayed. I was under the same spell as the inveterate companion with whom I walked the other day through the beautiful private apartments of the Pitti Palace and who said: "I suppose I care for nature, and I know there have been times when I have thought it the greatest pleasure in life to lie under a tree and gaze away at blue hills. But just now I had rather lie on that faded sea-green satin sofa and gaze down through the open door at that retreating vista of gilded, deserted, haunted chambers. In other words I prefer a good 'interior' to a good landscape. The impression has a greater intensity—the thing itself a more complex animation. I like fine old rooms that have been occupied in a fine old way. I like the musty upholstery, the antiquated knick-knacks, the view out of the tall deep-embrasured windows at garden cypresses rocking against a grey sky. If you don't know why I'm afraid I can't tell you." It seemed to me at the Palazzo Corsini that I did know why. In places that have been lived in so long and so much and in such a fine old way, as my friend said— that is under social conditions so multifold and to a comparatively starved and democratic sense so curious—the past seems to have left a sensible deposit, an aroma, an atmosphere. This ghostly presence tells you no secrets, but it prompts you to try and guess a few. What has been done and said here through so many years, what has been ventured or suffered, what has been dreamed or despaired of? Guess the riddle if you can, or if you think it worth your ingenuity. The rooms at Palazzo Corsini suggest indeed, and seem to recall, but a monotony of peace and plenty. One of them imaged such a noble perfection of a home-scene that I dawdled there until the old custodian came shuffling back to see whether possibly I was trying to conceal a Caravaggio about my person: a great crimson-draped drawing-room of the amplest and yet most charming proportions; walls hung with large dark pictures, a great concave ceiling frescoed and moulded with dusky richness, and half-a-dozen south windows looking out on the Arno, whose swift yellow tide sends up the light in a cheerful flicker. I fear that in my appreciation of the particular effect so achieved I uttered a monstrous folly—some momentary willingness to be maimed or crippled all my days if I might pass them in such a place. In fact half the pleasure of inhabiting this spacious saloon would be that of using one's legs, of strolling up and down past the windows, one by one, and making desultory journeys from station to station and corner to corner. Near by is a colossal ball-room, domed and pilastered like a Renaissance cathedral, and superabundantly decorated with marble effigies, all yellow and grey with the years.

VI

In the Carthusian Monastery outside the Roman Gate, mutilated and profaned though it is, one may still snuff up a strong if stale redolence of old Catholicism and old Italy. The road to it is ugly, being encumbered with vulgar waggons and fringed with tenements suggestive of an Irish-American suburb. Your interest begins as you come in sight of the convent perched on its little mountain and lifting against the sky, around the bell-tower of its gorgeous chapel, a coronet of clustered cells. You make your way into the lower gate, through a clamouring press of deformed beggars who thrust at you their stumps of limbs, and you climb the steep hillside through a shabby plantation which it is proper to fancy was better tended in the monkish time. The monks are not totally abolished, the government having the grace to await the natural extinction of the half-dozen old brothers who remain, and who shuffle doggedly about the cloisters, looking, with their white robes and their pale blank old faces, quite anticipatory ghosts of their future selves. A prosaic, profane old man in a coat and trousers serves you, however, as custodian. The melancholy friars have not even the privilege of doing you the honours of their dishonour. One must imagine the pathetic effect of their former silent pointings to this and that conventual treasure under stress of the feeling that such pointings were narrowly numbered. The convent is vast and irregular—it bristles with those picture-making arts and accidents which one notes as one lingers and passes, but which in Italy the overburdened memory learns to resolve into broadly general images. I rather deplore its position at the gates of a bustling city—it ought rather to be lodged in some lonely fold of the Apennines. And yet to look out from the shady porch of one of the quiet cells upon the teeming vale of the Arno and the clustered towers of Florence must have deepened the sense of monastic quietude.

The chapel, or rather the church, which is of great proportions and designed by Andrea Orcagna, the primitive painter, refines upon the consecrated type or even quite glorifies it. The massive cincture of black sculptured stalls, the dusky Gothic roof, the high-hung, deep-toned pictures and the superb pavement of verd-antique and dark red marble, polished into glassy lights, must throw the white-robed figures of the gathered friars into the highest romantic relief. All this luxury of worship has nowhere such value as in the chapels of monasteries, where we find it contrasted with the otherwise so ascetic economy of the worshippers. The paintings and gildings of their church, the gem-bright marbles and fantastic carvings, are really but the monastic tribute to sensuous delight—an imperious need for which the fond imagination of Rome has officiously opened the door. One smiles when one thinks how largely a fine starved sense for the forbidden things of earth, if it makes the most of its opportunities, may gratify this need under cover of devotion. Nothing is too base, too hard, too sordid for real humility, but nothing too elegant, too amiable, too caressing, caressed, caressable, for the exaltation of faith. The meaner the convent cell the richer the convent chapel. Out of poverty and solitude, inanition and cold, your honest friar may rise at his will into a Mahomet's Paradise of luxurious analogies.

There are further various dusky subterranean oratories where a number of bad pictures contend faintly with the friendly gloom. Two or three of these funereal vaults, however, deserve mention. In one of them, side by side, sculptured by Donatello in low relief, lie the white marble effigies of the three members of the Accaiuoli family who founded the convent in the thirteenth century. In another, on his back, on the pavement, rests a grim old bishop of the same stout race by the same honest craftsman. Terribly grim he is, and scowling as if in his stony sleep he still dreamed of his hates and his hard ambitions. Last and best, in another low chapel, with the trodden pavement for its bed, shines dimly a grand image of a later bishop—Leonardo Buonafede, who, dying in 1545, owes his monument to Francesco di San Gallo. I have seen little from this artist's hand, but it was clearly of the cunningest. His model here was a very sturdy old prelate, though I should say a very genial old man. The sculptor has respected his monumental ugliness, but has suffused it with a singular homely charm—a look of confessed physical comfort in the privilege of paradise. All these figures have an inimitable reality, and their lifelike marble seems such an incorruptible incarnation of the genius of the place that you begin to think of it as even more reckless than cruel on the part of the present public powers to have begun to pull the establishment down, morally speaking, about their ears. They are lying quiet

yet awhile; but when the last old friar dies and the convent
formally lapses, won't they rise on their stiff old legs and
hobble out to the gates and thunder forth anathemas before
which even a future and more enterprising régime may be
disposed to pause?

Out of the great central cloister open the snug little detached dwellings of the absent fathers. When I said just now
that the Certosa in Val d'Ema gives you a glimpse of old Italy
I was thinking of this great pillared quadrangle, lying half in
sun and half in shade, of its tangled garden-growth in the
centre, surrounding the ancient customary well, and of the
intense blue sky bending above it, to say nothing of the indispensable old white-robed monk who pokes about among the
lettuce and parsley. We have seen such places before; we have
visited them in that divinatory glance which strays away into
space for a moment over the top of a suggestive book. I don't
quite know whether it's more or less as one's fancy would
have it that the monkish cells are no cells at all, but very tidy
little *appartements complets*, consisting of a couple of chambers,
a sitting-room and a spacious loggia, projecting out into
space from the cliff-like wall of the monastery and sweeping
from pole to pole the loveliest view in the world. It's poor
work, however, taking notes on views, and I will let this one
pass. The little chambers are terribly cold and musty now.
Their odour and atmosphere are such as one used, as a child,
to imagine those of the school-room during Saturday and
Sunday.

VII

In the Roman streets, wherever you turn, the façade of a
church in more or less degenerate flamboyance is the principal
feature of the scene; and if, in the absence of purer motives,
you are weary of æsthetic trudging over the corrugated surface of the Seven Hills, a system of pavement in which small
cobblestones anomalously endowed with angles and edges are
alone employed, you may turn aside at your pleasure and take
a reviving sniff at the pungency of incense. In Florence, one
soon observes, the churches are relatively few and the dusky
house-fronts more rarely interrupted by specimens of that

extraordinary architecture which in Rome passes for sacred. In Florence, in other words, ecclesiasticism is less cheap a commodity and not dispensed in the same abundance at the street-corners. Heaven forbid, at the same time, that I should undervalue the Roman churches, which are for the most part treasure-houses of history, of curiosity, of promiscuous and associational interest. It is a fact, nevertheless, that, after Saint Peter's, I know but one really beautiful church by the Tiber, the enchanting basilica of Saint Mary Major. Many have structural character, some a great *allure*, but as a rule they all lack the dignity of the best of the Florentine temples. Here, the list being immeasurably shorter and the seed less scattered, the principal churches are all beautiful. And yet I went into the Annunziata the other day and sat there for half-an-hour because, forsooth, the gildings and the marbles and the frescoed dome and the great rococo shrine near the door, with its little black jewelled fetish, reminded me so poignantly of Rome. Such is the city properly styled eternal—since it is eternal, at least, as regards the consciousness of the individual. One loves it in its sophistications—though for that matter isn't it all rich and precious sophistication?—better than other places in their purity.

Coming out of the Annunziata you look past the bronze statue of the Grand Duke Ferdinand I. (whom Mr. Browning's heroine used to watch for—in the poem of "The Statue and the Bust"—from the red palace near by), and down a street vista of enchanting picturesqueness. The street is narrow and dusky and filled with misty shadows, and at its opposite end rises the vast bright-coloured side of the Cathedral. It stands up in very much the same mountainous fashion as the far-shining mass of the bigger prodigy at Milan, of which your first glimpse as you leave your hotel is generally through another such dark avenue; only that, if we talk of mountains, the white walls of Milan must be likened to snow and ice from their base, while those of the Duomo of Florence may be the image of some mighty hillside enamelled with blooming flowers. The big bleak interior here has a naked majesty which, though it may fail of its effect at first, becomes after a while extraordinarily touching. Originally disconcerting, it soon inspired me with a passion. Externally, at any rate, it is one of the loveliest works of man's hands, and an overwhelming proof into the bargain that when elegance belittles grandeur you have simply had a bungling artist.

Santa Croce within not only triumphs here, but would triumph almost anywhere. "A trifle naked if you like," said my irrepressible companion, "but that's what I call architecture, just as I don't call bronze or marble clothes (save under urgent stress of portraiture) statuary." And indeed we are far enough away from the clustering odds and ends borrowed from every art and every province without which the ritually builded thing doesn't trust its spell to work in Rome. The vastness, the lightness, the open spring of the arches at Santa Croce, the beautiful shape of the high and narrow choir, the impression made as of mass without weight and the gravity yet reigning without gloom—these are my frequent delight, and the interest grows with acquaintance. The place is the great Florentine Valhalla, the final home or memorial harbour of the native illustrious dead, but that consideration of it would take me far. It must be confessed moreover that, between his coarsely-imagined statue out in front and his horrible monument in one of the aisles, the author of *The Divine Comedy*, for instance, is just hereabouts rather an extravagant figure. "Ungrateful Florence," declaims Byron. Ungrateful indeed—would she were more so! the susceptible spirit of the great exile may be still aware enough to exclaim; in common, that is, with most of the other immortals sacrificed on so very large a scale to current Florentine "plastic" facility. In explanation of which remark, however, I must confine myself to noting that, as almost all the old monuments at Santa Croce are small, comparatively small, and interesting and exquisite, so the modern, well nigh without exception, are disproportionately vast and pompous, or in other words distressingly vague and vain. The aptitude of hand, the compositional assurance, with which such things are nevertheless turned out, constitutes an anomaly replete with suggestion for an observer of the present state of the arts on the soil and in the air that once befriended them, taking them all together, as even the soil and the air of Greece scarce availed to do. But on this head, I repeat, there would be too much to say; and I find myself checked by the same warning at the threshold of the church in

Florence really interesting beyond Santa Croce, beyond all others. Such, of course, easily, is Santa Maria Novella, where the chapels are lined and plated with wonderful figured and peopled fresco-work even as most of those in Rome with precious inanimate substances. These overscored retreats of devotion, as dusky, some of them, as eremitic caves swarming with importunate visions, have kept me divided all winter between the love of Ghirlandaio and the fear of those seeds of catarrh to which their mortal chill seems propitious till far on into the spring. So I pause here just on the praise of that delightful painter—as to the spirit of whose work the reflections I have already made are but confirmed by these examples. In the choir at Santa Maria Novella, where the incense swings and the great chants resound, between the gorgeous coloured window and the florid grand altar, he still "goes in," with all his might, for the wicked, the amusing world, the world of faces and forms and characters, of every sort of curious human and rare material thing.

VIII

I had always felt the Boboli Gardens charming enough for me to "haunt" them; and yet such is the interest of Florence in every quarter that it took another *corso* of the same cheap pattern as the last to cause me yesterday to flee the crowded streets, passing under that archway of the Pitti Palace which might almost be the gate of an Etruscan city, so that I might spend the afternoon among the mouldy statues that compose with their screens of cypress, looking down at our clustered towers and our background of pale blue hills vaguely freckled with white villas. These pleasure-grounds of the austere Pitti pile, with its inconsequent charm of being so rough-hewn and yet somehow so elegantly balanced, plead with a voice all their own the general cause of the ample enclosed, planted, cultivated private preserve—preserve of tranquillity and beauty and immunity—in the heart of a city; a cause, I allow, for that matter, easy to plead anywhere, once the pretext is found, the large, quiet distributed town-garden, with the vague hum of big grudging boundaries all about it, but with everything worse excluded, being of course the most insolently-pleasant thing in the world. In addition to which, when the garden is in the Italian manner, with flowers rather remarkably omitted, as too flimsy and easy and cheap, and without lawns that are too smart, paths that are too often swept and shrubs that are too closely trimmed, though with a fanciful formalism giving style to its shabbiness, and here and there a dusky ilex-walk, and here and there a dried-up fountain, and everywhere a piece of mildewed sculpture staring at you from a green alcove, and just in the right place, above all, a grassy amphitheatre curtained behind with black cypresses and sloping downward in mossy marble steps—when, I say, the place possesses these attractions, and you lounge there of a soft Sunday afternoon, the racier spectacle of the streets having made your fellow-loungers few and left you to the deep stillness and the shady vistas that lead you wonder where, left you to the insidious irresistible mixture of nature and art, nothing too much of either, only a supreme happy resultant, a divine *tertium quid*: under these conditions, it need scarce be said, the revelation invoked descends upon you.

The Boboli Gardens are not large—you wonder how compact little Florence finds room for them within her walls. But they are scattered, to their extreme, their all-romantic advantage and felicity, over a group of steep undulations between the rugged and terraced palace and a still-surviving stretch of city wall, where the unevenness of the ground much adds to their apparent size. You may cultivate in them the fancy of their solemn and haunted character, of something faint and dim and even, if you like, tragic, in their prescribed, their functional smile; as if they borrowed from the huge monument that overhangs them certain of its ponderous memories and regrets. This course is open to you, I mention, but it isn't enjoined, and will doubtless indeed not come up for you at all if it isn't your habit, cherished beyond any other, to spin your impressions to the last tenuity of fineness. Now that I bethink myself I must always have happened to wander here on grey and melancholy days. It remains none the less true that the place contains, thank goodness—or at least thank the grave, the infinitely-distinguished traditional *taste* of Florence—no cheerful, trivial object, neither parterres, nor pagodas, nor peacocks, nor swans. They have their famous amphitheatre already referred to, with its degrees or stone benches of a thoroughly aged and mottled complexion and its circular wall of evergreens behind, in which small cracked images and vases, things that, according to association, and with the law of the same quite indefinable, may make as much on one occasion for exquisite dignity as they may make on another for (to express it kindly) nothing at all. Something was once done in this charmed and forsaken circle—done or meant to be done; what was it, dumb statues, who saw it with your blank eyes? Opposite stands the huge flat-roofed palace, putting forward two great rectangular arms and looking, with its closed windows and its foundations of almost unreduced rock, like some ghost of a sample of a ruder Babylon. In the wide court-like space between the wings is a fine old white marble fountain that never plays. Its dusty idleness completes the general air of abandonment. Chancing on such a cluster of objects in Italy—glancing at them in a certain light and a certain mood—I get (perhaps on too easy terms, you may think) a sense of *history* that takes away my breath. Generations of Medici have stood at these closed windows, embroidered and brocaded according to their period, and held *fêtes champêtres* and floral games on the greensward, beneath the mouldering hemicycle. And the Medici were great people! But what remains of it all now is a mere tone in the air, a faint sigh in the breeze, a vague expression in things, a passive—or call it rather, perhaps, to be fair, a shyly, pathetically responsive— accessibility to the yearning guess. Call it much or call it little, the ineffaceability of this deep stain of experience, it is the interest of old places and the bribe to the brooding analyst. Time has devoured the doers and their doings, but there still hangs about some effect of their passage. We can "lay out" parks on virgin soil, and cause them to bristle with the most expensive importations, but we unfortunately can't scatter abroad again this seed of the eventual human soul of a place—that comes but in its time and takes too long to grow. There is nothing like it when it *has* come.

Tuscan Cities

THE CITIES I refer to are Leghorn, Pisa, Lucca and Pistoia, among which I have been spending the last few days. The most striking fact as to Leghorn, it must be conceded at the outset, is that, being in Tuscany, it should be so scantily Tuscan. The traveller curious in local colour must content himself with the deep blue expanse of the Mediterranean. The streets, away from the docks, are modern, genteel and rectangular; Liverpool might acknowledge them if it weren't for their clean-coloured, sun-bleached stucco. They are the offspring of the new industry which is death to the old idleness. Of interesting architecture, fruit of the old idleness or at least of the old leisure, Leghorn is singularly destitute. It has neither a church worth one's attention, nor a municipal palace, nor a museum, and it may claim the distinction, unique in Italy, of being the city of no pictures. In a shabby corner near the docks stands a statue of one of the elder Grand-Dukes of Tuscany, appealing to posterity on grounds now vague—chiefly that of having placed certain Moors under tribute. Four colossal negroes, in very bad bronze, are chained to the base of the monument, which forms with their assistance a sufficiently fantastic group; but to patronise the arts is not the line of the Livornese, and for want of the slender annuity which would keep its precinct sacred this curious memorial is buried in dockyard rubbish. I must add that on the other hand there is a very well-conditioned and, in attitude and gesture, extremely natural and familiar statue of Cavour in one of the city squares, and in another a couple of effigies of recent Grand-Dukes, represented, that is dressed, or rather undressed, in the character of heroes of Plutarch. Leghorn is a city of magnificent spaces, and it was so long a journey from the sidewalk to the pedestal of these images that I never took the time to go and read the inscriptions. And in truth, vaguely, I bore the originals a grudge, and wished to know as little about them as possible; for it seemed to me that as *patres patriæ*, in their degree, they might have decreed that the great blank, ochre-faced piazza should be a trifle less ugly.

There is a distinct amenity, however, in any experience of Italy almost anywhere, and I shall probably in the future not be above sparing a light regret to several of the hours of which the one I speak of was composed. I shall remember a large cool bourgeois villa in the garden of a noiseless suburb—a middle-aged Villa Franco (I owe it as a genial pleasant *pension* the tribute of recognition), roomy and stony, as an Italian villa should be. I shall remember that, as I sat in the garden and, looking up from my book, saw through a gap in the shrubbery the red house-tiles against the deep blue sky and the grey underside of the ilex-leaves turned up by the Mediterranean breeze, it was all still quite Tuscany, if Tuscany in the minor key.

If you should naturally desire, in such conditions, a higher intensity, you have but to proceed, by a very short journey, to Pisa—where, for that matter, you will seem to yourself to have hung about a good deal already, and from an early age. Few of us can have had a childhood so unblessed by contact with the arts as that one of its occasional diversions shan't have been a puzzled scrutiny of some alabaster model of the Leaning Tower under a glass cover in a back-parlour. Pisa and its monuments have, in other words, been industriously vulgarised, but it is astonishing how well they have survived the process. The charm of the place is in fact of a high order and but partially foreshadowed by the famous crookedness of its campanile. I felt it irresistibly and yet almost inexpressibly the other afternoon, as I made my way to the classic corner of the city through the warm drowsy air which nervous people come to inhale as a sedative. I was with an invalid companion who had had no sleep to speak of for a fortnight. "Ah! stop the carriage," she sighed, or yawned, as I could feel, deliciously, "in the shadow of this old slumbering palazzo, and let me sit here and close my eyes, and taste for an hour of oblivion." Once strolling over the grass, however, out of which the quartette of marble monuments rises, we awaked responsively enough to the present hour. Most people remember the happy remark of tasteful, old-fashioned Forsyth (who touched a hundred other points in his "Italy" scarce less happily) as to the fact that the four famous objects are "fortunate alike in their society and their solitude." It must be admitted that they are more fortunate in their society than we felt our-selves to be in ours; for the scene presented the animated ap-pearance for which, on any fine spring day, all the choicest haunts of ancient quietude in Italy are becoming yearly more remarkable. There were clamorous beggars at all the sculp-tured portals, and bait for beggars, in abundance, trailing in and out of them under convoy of loquacious ciceroni. I forget just how I apportioned the responsibility of intrusion, for it was not long before fellow-tourists and fellow-countrymen became a vague, deadened, muffled presence, that of the den-tist's last words when he is giving you ether. They suffered mystic disintegration in the dense, bright, tranquil air, so charged with its own messages. The Cathedral and its com-panions are fortunate indeed in everything—fortunate in the spacious angle of the grey old city-wall which folds about them in their sculptured elegance like a strong protecting arm; fortunate in the broad greensward which stretches from the marble base of Cathedral and cemetery to the rugged foot of the rampart; fortunate in the little vagabonds who dot the grass, plucking daisies and exchanging Italian cries; fortunate in the pale-gold tone to which time and the soft sea-damp have mellowed and darkened their marble plates; fortunate, above all, in an indescribable grace of grouping, half hazard, half design, which insures them, in one's memory of things admired, very much the same isolated corner that they occupy in the charming city.

Of the smaller cathedrals of Italy I know none I prefer to that of Pisa; none that, on a moderate scale, produces more the impression of a great church. It has without so modest a measurability, represents so clean and compact a mass, that you are startled when you cross the threshold at the apparent space it encloses. An architect of genius, for all that he works with colossal blocks and cumbrous pillars, is certainly the most cunning of conjurors. The front of the Duomo is a small pyramidal screen, covered with delicate carvings and chasings, distributed over a series of short columns upholding narrow arches. It might be a sought imitation of goldsmith's work in stone, and the area covered is apparently so small that extreme fineness has been prescribed. How it is therefore that on the inner side of this façade the wall should appear to rise to a splendid height and to support one end of a ceiling as remote in its gilded grandeur, one could almost fancy, as that of St. Peter's; how it is that the nave should stretch away in such solemn vastness, the shallow transepts emphasise the grand impression and the apse of the choir hollow itself out like a dusky cavern fretted with golden stalactites, is all matter for exposition by a keener architectural analyst than I. To sit somewhere against a pillar where the vista is large and the incidents cluster richly, and vaguely revolve these mysteries without answering them, is the best of one's usual enjoyment of a great church. It takes no deep sounding to conclude indeed that a gigantic Byzantine Christ in mosaic, on the concave roof of the choir, contributes largely to the particular impression here as of very old and choice and original and individual things. It has even more of stiff solemnity than is common to works of its school, and prompts to more wonder than ever on the nature of the human mind at a time when such unlovely shapes could satisfy its conception of holiness. Truly pathetic is the fate of these huge mosaic idols, thanks to the change that has overtaken our manner of acceptance of them. Strong the contrast between the original sublimity of their pretensions and the way in which they flatter that free sense of the grotesque which the modern imagination has smuggled even into the appreciation of religious forms. They were meant to yield scarcely to the Deity itself in grandeur, but the only part they play now is to stare helplessly at our critical, our æsthetic patronage of them. The spiritual refinement marking the hither end of a progress hadn't, however, to wait for *us* to signalise it; it found expression three centuries ago in the beautiful specimen of the painter Sodoma on the wall of the choir. This latter, a small Sacrifice of Isaac, is one of the best examples of its exquisite author, and perhaps, as chance has it, the most perfect opposition that could be found in the way of the range of taste to the effect of the great mosaic. There are many painters more powerful than Sodoma—painters who, like the author of the mosaic, attempted and compassed grandeur; but none has a more persuasive grace, none more than he was to sift and chasten a conception till it should affect one with the sweetness of a perfectly distilled perfume.

Of the patient successive efforts of painting to arrive at the supreme refinement of such a work as the Sodoma the Campo Santo hard by offers a most interesting memorial. It presents a long, blank marble wall to the relative profaneness of the Cathedral close, but within it is a perfect treasure-house of art. This quadrangular defence surrounds an open court where weeds and wild roses are tangled together and a sunny stillness seems to rest consentingly, as if Nature had been won to consciousness of the precious relics committed to her. Something in the quality of the place recalls the collegiate cloisters of Oxford, but it must be added that this is the handsomest compliment to that seat of learning. The open arches of the quadrangles of Magdalen and Christ Church are not of mellow Carrara marble, nor do they offer to sight columns, slim and elegant, that seem to frame the unglazed windows of a cathedral. To be buried in the Campo Santo of Pisa, I may however further qualify, you need only be, or to have more or less anciently been, illustrious, and there is a liberal allowance both as to the character and degree of your fame. The most obtrusive object in one of the long vistas is a most complicated monument to Madame Catalani, the singer, recently erected by her possibly too-appreciative heirs. The wide pavement is a mosaic of sepulchral slabs, and the walls, below the base of the paling frescoes, are encrusted with inscriptions and encumbered with urns and antique sarcophagi. The place is at once a cemetery and a museum, and its especial charm is its strange mixture of the active and the passive, of art and rest, of life and death. Originally its walls were one vast continuity of closely pressed frescoes; but now the great capricious scars and stains have come to outnumber the pictures, and the cemetery has grown to be a burial-place of pulverised masterpieces as well as of finished lives. The fragments of painting that remain are fortunately the best; for one is safe in believing that a host of undimmed neighbours would distract but little from the two great works of Orcagna. Most people know the "Triumph of Death" and the "Last Judgment" from descriptions and engravings; but to measure the possible good faith of imitative art one must stand there and see the painter's howling potentates dragged into hell in all the vividness of his bright hard colouring; see his feudal courtiers,

Volterra

on their palfreys, hold their noses at what they are so fast coming to; see his great Christ, in judgment, refuse forgiveness with a gesture commanding enough, really inhuman enough, to make virtue merciless forever. The charge that Michael Angelo borrowed his cursing Saviour from this great figure of Orcagna is more valid than most accusations of plagiarism; but of the two figures one at least could be spared. For direct, triumphant expressiveness these two superb frescoes have probably never been surpassed. The painter aims at no very delicate meanings, but he drives certain gross ones home so effectively that for a parallel to his process one must look to the art of the actor, the emphasising "point"-making mime. Some of his female figures are superb—they represent creatures of a formidable temperament.

There are charming women, however, on the other side of the cloister—in the beautiful frescoes of Benozzo Gozzoli. If Orcagna's work was appointed to survive the ravage of time it is a happy chance that it should be balanced by a group of performances of such a different temper. The contrast is the more striking that in subject the inspiration of both painters is strictly, even though superficially, theological. But Benozzo cares, in his theology, for nothing but the story, the scene and the drama—the chance to pile up palaces and spires in his backgrounds against pale blue skies cross-barred with pearly, fleecy clouds, and to scatter sculptured arches and shady trellises over the front, with every incident of human life going forward lightly and gracefully beneath them. Lightness and grace are the painter's great qualities, marking the hithermost limit of unconscious elegance, after which "style" and science and the wisdom of the serpent set in. His charm is natural fineness; a little more and we should have refinement—which is a very different thing. Like all *les délicats* of this world, as M. Renan calls them, Benozzo has suffered greatly. The space on the walls he originally covered with his Old Testament stories is immense; but his exquisite handiwork has peeled off by the acre, as one may almost say, and the latter compartments of the series are swallowed up in huge white scars, out of which a helpless head or hand peeps forth like those of creatures sinking into a quicksand. As for Pisa at large, although it is not exactly what one would call a mouldering city—for it has a certain well-aired cleanness and brightness, even in its supreme tranquillity—it affects the imagination very much in the same way as the Campo Santo. And, in truth, a city so ancient and deeply historic as Pisa is at every step but the burial-ground of a larger life than its present one. The wide empty streets, the goodly Tuscan palaces—which look as if about all of them there were a genteel private understanding, independent of placards, that they are to be let extremely cheap—the delicious relaxing air, the full-flowing yellow river, the lounging Pisani, smelling, metaphorically, their poppy-flowers, seemed to me all so many admonitions to resignation and oblivion. And this is what I mean by saying that the charm of Pisa (apart from its cluster of monuments) is a charm of a high order. The architecture has but a modest dignity; the lions are few; there are no fixed points for stopping and gaping. And yet the impression is profound; the charm is a moral charm. If I were ever to be incurably disappointed in life, if I had lost my health, my money, or my friends, if I were resigned forevermore to pitching my expectations in a minor key, I should go and invoke the Pisan peace. Its quietude would seem something more than a stillness—a hush. Pisa may be a dull place to live in, but it's an ideal place to wait for death.

Nothing could be more charming than the country between Pisa and Lucca—unless possibly the country between Lucca and Pistoia. If Pisa is dead Tuscany, Lucca is Tuscany still living and enjoying, desiring and intending. The town is a charming mixture of antique "character" and modern inconsequence; and not only the town, but the country—the blooming romantic country which you admire from the famous promenade on the city-wall. The wall is of superbly solid and intensely "toned" brickwork and of extraordinary breadth, and its summit, planted with goodly trees and swelling here and there into bastions and outworks and little open gardens, surrounds the city with a circular lounging-place of a splendid dignity. This well-kept, shady, ivy-grown rampart reminded me of certain mossy corners of England; but it looks away to a prospect of more than English loveliness—a broad green plain where the summer yields a double crop of grain, and a circle of bright blue mountains speckled with high-hung convents and profiled castles and nestling villas, and traversed by valleys of a deeper and duskier blue. In one of the deepest and shadiest of these recesses one of the most "sympathetic" of small watering-places is hidden away yet awhile longer from easy invasion—the Baths to which Lucca has lent its name. Lucca is pre-eminently a city of churches; ecclesiastical architecture being indeed the only one of the arts to which it seems to have given attention. There are curious bits of domestic architecture, but no great palaces, and no importunate frequency of pictures. The Cathedral, however, sums up the merits of its companions and is a singularly noble and interesting church. Its peculiar boast is a wonderful inlaid front, on which horses and hounds and hunted beasts are lavishly figured in black marble over a white ground. What I chiefly appreciated in the grey solemnity of the nave and transepts was the superb effect of certain second-story Gothic arches—those which rest on the pavement being Lombard. These arches are delicate and slender, like those of the cloister at Pisa, and they play their part in the dusky upper air with real sublimity.

At Pistoia there is of course a Cathedral, and there is nothing unexpected in its being, externally at least, highly impressive; in its having a grand campanile at its door, a gaudy baptistery, in alternate layers of black and white marble, across the way, and a stately civic palace on either side. But even had I the space to do otherwise I should prefer to speak less of the particular objects of interest in the place than of the pleasure I found it to lounge away in the empty streets the quiet hours of a warm afternoon. To say where I lingered longest would be to tell of a little square before the hospital, out of which you look up at the beautiful frieze in coloured earthenware by the brothers Della Robbia, which runs across the front of the building. It represents the seven orthodox offices of charity and, with its brilliant blues and yellows and its tender expressiveness, brightens up amazingly, to the sense and soul, this little grey corner of the mediæval city. Pistoia is still mediæval. How grass-grown it seemed, how drowsy, how full of idle vistas and melancholy nooks! If nothing was supremely wonderful, everything was delicious.

1874.

Other Tuscan Cities

I

I HAD scanted charming Pisa even as I had scanted great Siena in my original small report of it, my scarce more than stammering notes of years before; but even if there had been meagreness of mere gaping vision—which there in fact hadn't been—as well as insufficiency of public tribute, the indignity would soon have ceased to weigh on my conscience. For to this affection I was to return again still oftener than to the strong call of Siena; my eventual frequentations of Pisa, all merely impressionistic and amateurish as they might be— and I pretended, up and down the length of the land, to none other—leave me at the hither end of time with little more than a confused consciousness of exquisite *quality* on the part of the small sweet scrap of a place of ancient glory; a consciousness so pleadingly content to be general and vague that I shrink from pulling it to pieces. The Republic of Pisa fought with the Republic of Florence, through the ages, so ferociously and all but invincibly that what is so pale and languid in her to-day may well be the aspect of any civil or, still more, military creature bled and bled and bled at the "critical" time of its life. She has verily a just languor and is touchingly anæmic; the past history, or at any rate the present perfect acceptedness, of which condition hangs about her with the last grace of weakness, making her state in this particular the very secret of her irresistible appeal. I was to find the appeal, again and again, one of the sweetest, tenderest, even if not one of the fullest and richest impressions possible; and if I went back whenever I could it was very much as one doesn't indecently neglect a gentle invalid friend. The couch of the invalid friend, beautifully, appealingly resigned, has been wheeled, say, for the case, into the warm still garden, and your visit but consists of your sitting beside it with kind, discreet, testifying silences. Such is the figurative form under which the once rugged enemy of Florence, stretched at her length by the rarely troubled Arno, to-day presents herself;

577

and I find my analogy complete even to my sense of the mere mild *séance*, the inevitably tacit communion or rather blank interchange, between motionless cripple and hardly more incurable admirer.

The terms of my enjoyment of Pisa scarce departed from that ideal—slow contemplative perambulations, rather late in the day and after work done mostly in the particular decent inn-room that was repeatedly my portion; where the sunny flicker of the river played up from below to the very ceiling, which, by the same sign, anciently and curiously raftered and hanging over my table at a great height, had been colour-pencilled into ornament as fine (for all practical purposes) as the page of a missal. I add to this, for remembrance, an inveteracy of evening idleness and of reiterated ices in front of one of the quiet cafés—quiet as everything at Pisa is quiet, or will certainly but in these latest days have ceased to be; one in especial so beautifully, so mysteriously void of bustle that almost always the neighbouring presence and admirable chatter of some group of the local University students would fall upon my ear, by the half-hour at a time, not less as a privilege, frankly, than as a clear-cut image of the young Italian mind and life, by which I lost nothing. I use such terms as "admirable" and "privilege," in this last most casual of connections—which was moreover no connection at all but what my attention made it—simply as an acknowledgment of the interest that might play there through some inevitable thoughts. These were, for that matter, intensely in keeping with the ancient scene and air: they dealt with the exquisite difference between that tone and type of ingenuous adolescence—in the mere relation of charmed *audition*—and other forms of juvenility of whose mental and material accent one had elsewhere met the assault. Civilised, charmingly civilised, were my loquacious neighbours—as how hadn't they to be, one asked oneself, through the use of a medium of speech that is in itself a sovereign saturation? *There* was the beautiful congruity of the happily-caught impression; the fact of my young men's general Tuscanism of tongue, which related them so on the spot to the whole historic consensus of things. It wasn't dialect—as it of course easily might have been elsewhere, at Milan, at Turin, at Bologna, at Naples; it was the clear Italian in which all the rest of the surrounding story was told, all the rest of the result of time recorded; and it made them delightful, prattling, unconscious men of the particular little constituted and bequeathed world which everything else that was charged with old meanings and old beauty referred to—all the more that their talk was never by any chance of romping games or deeds of violence, but kept flowering, charmingly and incredibly, into eager ideas and literary opinions and philosophic discussions and, upon my honour, vital questions.

They have taken me too far, for so light a reminiscence; but I claim for the loose web of my impressions at no point a heavier texture. Which comes back to what I was a moment ago saying—that just in proportion as you "feel" the morbid charm of Pisa you press on it gently, and this somehow even under stress of whatever respectful attention. I found this last impulse, at all events, so far as I was concerned, quite contentedly spend itself in a renewed sense of the simple large pacified felicity of such an afternoon aspect as that of the Lung' Arno, taken up or down its course; whether to within sight of small Santa Maria della Spina, the tiny, the delicate, the exquisite Gothic chapel perched where the quay drops straight, or, in the other direction, toward the melting perspective of the narrow local pleasure-ground, the rather thin and careless bosky grace of which recedes, beside the stream whose very turbidity pleases, to a middle distance of hot and tangled and exuberant rural industry and a proper blue horizon of Carrara mountains. The Pisan Lung' Arno is shorter and less featured and framed than the Florentine, but it has the fine accent of a marked curve and is quite as bravely Tuscan; witness the type of river-fronting palace which, in half-a-dozen massive specimens, the last word of the anciently "handsome," are of the essence of the physiognomy of the place. In the glow of which retrospective admission I ask myself how I came, under my first flush, reflected in other pages, to fail of justice to so much proud domestic architecture—in the very teeth moreover of the fact that I was forever paying my compliments, in a wistful, wondering way, to the fine Palazzo Lanfranchi, occupied in 1822 by the migratory Byron, and whither Leigh Hunt, as commemorated in the latter's Autobiography, came out to join him in an odd journalistic scheme.

Of course, however, I need scarcely add, the centre of my daily revolution—quite thereby on the circumference—was the great Company of Four in their sequestered corner; objects of regularly recurrent pious pilgrimage, if for no other purpose than to see whether each would each time again so inimitably carry itself as one of a group of wonderfully-worked old ivories. Their charm of relation to each other and to everything else that concerns them, that of the quartette of monuments, is more or less inexpressible all round; but not the least of it, ever, is in their beautiful secret for taking at different hours and seasons, in different states of the light, the sky, the wind, the weather—in different states, even, it used verily to seem to me, of an admirer's imagination or temper or nerves—different complexional appearances, different shades and pallors, different glows and chills. I have seen them look almost viciously black, and I have seen them as clear and fair as pale gold. And these things, for the most part, off on the large grassy carpet spread for them, and with the elbow of the old city-wall, not elsewhere erect, respectfully but protectingly crooked about, to the tune of a usual unanimity save perhaps in the case of the Leaning Tower—so abnormal a member of any respectable family this structure at best that I always somehow fancied its three companions, the Cathedral, the Baptistery and the Campo Santo, capable of quiet common understandings, for the major or the minor effect, into which their odd fellow, no hint thrown out to him, was left to enter as he might. If one haunted the place one ended by yielding to the conceit that, beautifully though the others of the group may be said to behave about him, one sometimes caught them in the act of tacitly combining to ignore him—as if he had, after so long, begun to give on their nerves. Or is that absurdity but my shamefaced form of admission that, for all the wonder of him, he finally gave on mine? Frankly—I would put it at such moments—he becomes at last an optical bore or *bêtise*.

II

To Lucca I was not to return often—I was to return only once; when that compact and admirable little city, the very

model of a small *pays de Cocagne*, overflowing with everything
that makes for ease, for plenty, for beauty, for interest and
good example, renewed for me, in the highest degree, its
genial and robust appearance. The perfection of this renewal
must indeed have been, at bottom, the ground of my rather
hanging back from possible excess of acquaintance—with the
instinct that so right and rich and rounded a little impression
had better be left than endangered. I remember positively saying to myself the second time that no brown-and-gold Tuscan
city, even, could *be* as happy as Lucca looked—save always,
exactly, Lucca; so that, on the chance of any shade of human
illusion in the case, I wouldn't, as a brooding analyst, go
within fifty miles of it again. Just so, I fear I must confess, it
was this mere face-value of the place that, when I went back,
formed my sufficiency; I spent all my scant time—or the
greater part, for I took a day to drive over to the Bagni—just
gaping at its visible attitude. This may be described as that of
simply sitting there, through the centuries, at the receipt of
perfect felicity; on its splendid solid seat of russet masonry,
that is—for its great republican ramparts of long ago still lock
it tight—with its wide garden-land, its ancient appanage or
hereditary domain, teeming and blooming with everything
that is good and pleasant for man, all about, and with a ring
of graceful and noble, yet comparatively unbeneficed uplands
and mountains watching it, for very envy, across the plain, as
a circle of bigger boys, in the playground, may watch a privileged or pampered smaller one munch a particularly fine
apple. Half smothered thus in oil and wine and corn and all
the fruits of the earth, Lucca seems fairly to laugh for good-
humour, and it's as if one can't say more for her than that,
thanks to her putting forward for you a temperament somehow still richer than her heritage, you forgive her at every
turn her fortune. She smiles up at you her greeting as you dip
into her wide lap, out of which you may select almost any
rare morsel whatever. Looking back at my own choice indeed
I see it must have suffered a certain embarrassment—that of
the sense of too many things; for I scarce remember choosing
at all, any more than I recall having had to go hungry. I
turned into all the churches—taking care, however, to pause
before one of them, though before which I now irrecoverably

forget, for verification of Ruskin's so characteristically magnified rapture over the high and rather narrow and obscure hunting-frieze on its front—and in the Cathedral paid my respects at every turn to the greatest of Lucchesi, Matteo Civitale, wisest, sanest, homeliest, kindest of *quattro-cento* sculptors, to whose works the Duomo serves almost as a museum. But my nearest approach to anything so invidious as a discrimination or a preference, under the spell of so felt an equilibrium, must have been the act of engaging a carriage for the Baths.

That inconsequence once perpetrated, let me add, the impression was as right as any other—the impression of the drive through the huge general tangled and fruited *podere* of the countryside; that of the pair of jogging hours that bring the visitor to where the wideish gate of the valley of the Serchio opens. The question after this became quite other; the narrowing, though always more or less smiling gorge that draws you on and on is a different, a distinct proposition altogether, with its own individual grace of appeal and association. It is the association, exactly, that would even now, on this page, beckon me forward, or perhaps I should rather say backward—weren't more than a glance at it out of the question—to a view of that easier and not so inordinately remote past when "people spent the summer" in these perhaps slightly stuffy shades. I speak of that age, I think of it at least, as easier than ours, in spite of the fact that even as I made my pilgrimage the mark of modern change, the railway in construction, had begun to be distinct, though the automobile was still pretty far in the future. The relations and proportions of everything are of course now altered—I indeed, I confess, wince at the vision of the cloud of motor-dust that must in the fine season hang over the whole connection. That represents greater promptness of approach to the bosky depths of Ponte-a-Serraglio and the Bagni Caldi, but it throws back the other time, that of the old jogging relation, of the Tuscan grand-ducal "season" and the small cosmopolite sociability, into quite Arcadian air and the comparatively primitive scale. The "easier" Italy of our infatuated precursors there wears its glamour of facility not through any question of "the development of communications," but through the very absence of the dream of that boon, thanks to which every one (among the infatuated) lived on terms of so much closer intercourse with the general object of their passion. After we had crossed the Serchio that beautiful day we passed into the charming, the amiably tortuous, the thickly umbrageous, valley of the Lima, and then it was that I seemed fairly to remount the stream of time; figuring to myself wistfully, at the small scattered centres of entertainment—modest inns, pensions and other places of convenience clustered where the friendly torrent is bridged or the forested slopes adjust themselves— what the summer days and the summer rambles and the summer dreams must have been, in the blest place, when "people" (by which I mean the contingent of beguiled barbarians) didn't know better, as we say, than to content themselves with such a mild substitute, such a soft, sweet and essentially elegant apology, for adventure. One wanted not simply to hang about a little, but really to live back, as surely one might have done by staying on, into the so romantically strong, if mechanically weak, Italy of the associations of one's youth. It was a pang to have to revert to the present even in the form of Lucca—which says everything.

III

If undeveloped communications were to become enough for me at those retrospective moments, I might have felt myself supplied to my taste, let me go on to say, at the hour of my making, with great resolution, an attempt on high-seated and quite grandly out-of-the way Volterra: a reminiscence associated with quite a different year and, I should perhaps sooner have bethought myself, with my fond experience of Pisa—inasmuch as it was during a pause under that bland and motionless wing that I seem to have had to organise in the darkness of a summer dawn my approach to the old Etruscan stronghold. The railway then existed, but I rose in the dim small hours to take my train; moreover, so far as that might too much savour of an incongruous facility, the fault was in due course quite adequately repaired by an apparent repudiation of any awareness of such false notes on the part of the town. I may not invite the reader to penetrate with me by so much as a step the boundless backward reach of history to which the more massive of the Etruscan gates of Volterra, the Porta all' Arco, forms the solidest of thresholds; since I perforce take no step myself, and am even exceptionally condemned here to impressionism unashamed. My errand was to spend a Sunday with an Italian friend, a native in fact of the place, master of a house there in which he offered me hospitality; who, also arriving from Florence the night before, had obligingly come on with me from Pisa, and whose consciousness of a due urbanity, already rather overstrained, and still well before noon, by the accumulation of our matutinal vicissitudes and other grounds for patience, met all ruefully at the station the supreme shock of an apparently great desolate world of volcanic hills, of blank, though "engineered," undulations, as the emergence of a road testified, unmitigated by the smallest sign of a wheeled vehicle. The station, in other words, looked out at that time (and I daresay the case hasn't strikingly altered) on a mere bare huge hill-country, by some remote mighty shoulder of which the goal of our pilgrimage, so questionably "served" by the railway, was hidden from view. Served as well by a belated omnibus, a four-in-hand of lame and lamentable quality, the place, I hasten to add, eventually put forth some show of being; after a complete practical recognition of which, let me at once further mention, all the other, the positive and sublime, connections of Volterra established themselves for me without my lifting a finger.

The small shrunken, but still lordly prehistoric city is perched, when once you have rather painfully zigzagged to within sight of it, very much as an eagle's eyrie, oversweeping the land and the sea; and to that type of position, the ideal of the airy peak of vantage, with all accessories and minor features a drop, a slide and a giddiness, its individual items and elements strike you at first as instinctively conforming. This impression was doubtless after a little modified for me; there were levels, there were small stony practicable streets, there were walks and strolls, outside the gates and roundabout the cyclopean wall, to the far end of downward-tending protrusions and promontories, natural buttresses and pleasant terrene headlands, friendly suburban spots (one would call them if the word had less detestable references) where games of bowls and overtrellised wine-tables could put in their note; in spite of which however my friend's little house of hospitality, clean and charming and oh so immemorially Tuscan, was as perpendicular and ladder-like as so compact a residence could be; it kept up for me beautifully — as regards posture and air, though humanly and socially it rather cooed like a dovecote — the illusion of the vertiginously "balanced" eagle's nest. The air, in truth, all the rest of that splendid day, must have been the key to the promptly-produced intensity of one's relation to every aspect of the charming episode; the light, cool, keen air of those delightful high places, in Italy, that tonically correct the ardours of July, and which at our actual altitude could but affect me as the very breath of the grand local legend. I might have "had" the little house, our particular eagle's nest, for the summer, and even on such touching terms; and I well remember the force of the temptation to take it, if only other complications had permitted; to spend the series of weeks with that admirable *interesting* freshness in my lungs: interesting, I especially note as the strong appropriate medium in which a continuity with the irrecoverable but still effective past had been so robustly preserved. I couldn't yield, alas, to the conceived felicity, which had half-a-dozen appealing aspects; I could only, while thus feeling how the atmospheric medium itself made for a positively initiative exhilaration, enjoy my illusion till the morrow. The exhilaration therefore supplies to memory the whole light in which, for the too brief time, I went about "seeing" Volterra; so that my glance at the seated splendour reduces itself, as I have said, to the merest impressionism; nothing more was to be looked for, on the stretched surface of consciousness, from one breezy wash of the brush. I find there the clean strong image simplified to the three or four unforgettable particulars of the vast rake of the view; with the Maremma, of evil fame, more or less immediately below, but with those islands of the sea, Corsica and Elba, the names of which are sharply associational beyond any others, dressing the far horizon in the grand manner, and the Ligurian coast-line melting northward into beauty and history galore; with colossal uncemented blocks of Etruscan gates and walls plunging you — and by their very interest — into a sweet surrender of any privilege of appreciation more

crushing than your general synthetic stare; and with the rich
and perfectly arranged museum, an unsurpassed exhibition of
monumental treasure from Etruscan tombs, funereal urns
mainly, reliquaries of an infinite power to move and charm us
still, contributing to this same so resigned, but somehow at
the same time so inspired, collapse of the historic imagination
under too heavy a pressure, or abeyance of "private judgment" in too unequal a relation.

IV

I remember recovering private judgment indeed in the
course of two or three days following the excursion I have
just noted; which must have shaped themselves in some sort
of consonance with the idea that as we were hereabouts in the
very middle of dim Etruria a common self-respect prescribed
our somehow profiting by the fact. This kindled in us the
spirit of exploration, but with results of which I here attempt
no record, so utterly does the whole impression swoon away,
for present memory, into vagueness, confusion and intolerable heat. Our self-respect was of the common order, but the
blaze of the July sun was, even for Tuscany, of the uncommon; so that the project of a trudging quest for Etruscan
tombs in shadeless wastes yielded to its own temerity. There
comes back to me nevertheless at the same time, from the
mild misadventure, and quite as through this positive humility of failure, the sense of a supremely intimate revelation of
Italy in undress, so to speak (the state, it seemed, in which
one would most fondly, most ideally, enjoy her); Italy no
longer in winter starch and sobriety, with winter manners and
winter prices and winter excuses, all addressed to the *forestieri*
and the philistines; but lolling at her length, with her graces
all relaxed, and thereby only the more natural; the brilliant
performer, in short, *en famille*, the curtain down and her sal-
ary stopped for the season—thanks to which she is by so
much more the easy genius and the good creature as she is by
so much less the advertised *prima donna*. She received us nowhere more sympathetically, that is with less ceremony or
self-consciousness, I seem to recall, than at Montepulciano,
for instance—where it was indeed that the recovery of private

judgment I just referred to couldn't help taking place. What we were doing, or what we expected to do, at Montepulciano I keep no other trace of than is bound up in a present quite tender consciousness that I wouldn't for the world not have been there. I think my reason must have been largely just in the beauty of the name (for could any beauty be greater?), reinforced no doubt by the fame of the local vintage and the sense of how we should quaff it on the spot. Perhaps we quaffed it too constantly; since the romantic picture reduces itself for me but to two definite appearances; that of the more priggish discrimination so far reasserting itself as to advise me that Montepulciano was dirty, even remarkably dirty; and that of its being not much else besides but perched and brown and queer and crooked, and noble withal (which is what almost any Tuscan city more easily than not acquits herself of); all the while she may on such occasions figure, when one looks off from her to the end of dark street-vistas or catches glimpses through high arcades, some big battered, blistered, overladen, overmasted ship, swimming in a violet sea.

If I have lost the sense of what we were doing, that could at all suffer commemoration, at Montepulciano, so I sit helpless before the memory of small stewing Torrita, which we must somehow have expected to yield, under our confidence, a view of shy charms, but which didn't yield, to my recollection, even anything that could fairly be called a breakfast or a dinner. There may have been in the neighbourhood a rumour of Etruscan tombs; the neighbourhood, however, was vast, and that possibility not to be verified, in the conditions, save after due refreshment. Then it was, doubtless, that the question of refreshment so beckoned us, by a direct appeal, straight across country, from Perugia, that, casting consistency, if not to the winds, since alas there were none, but to the lifeless air, we made the sweltering best of our way (and it took, for the distance, a terrible time) to the Grand Hotel of that city. This course shines for me, in the retrospect, with a light even more shameless than that in which my rueful conscience then saw it; since we thus exchanged again, at a stroke, the tousled *bonne fille* of our vacational Tuscany for the formal and figged-out presence of Italy on her good be-

haviour. We had never seen her conform more to all the proprieties, we felt, than under this aspect of lavish hospitality to
that now apparently quite inveterate swarm of pampered *forestieri*, English and Americans in especial, who, having had Roman palaces and villas deliciously to linger in, break the
northward journey, when once they decide to take it, in the
Umbrian paradise. They were, goodness knows, within their
rights, and we profited, as any one may easily and cannily
profit at that time, by the sophistications paraded for them;
only I feel, as I pleasantly recover it all, that though we had
arrived perhaps at the most poetical of watering-places we
had lost our finer clue. (The difference from other days was
immense, all the span of evolution from the ancient malodor-
ous inn which somehow didn't matter, to that new type of
polyglot caravanserai which everywhere insists on mattering—mattering, even in places where other interests abound,
so much more than anything else.) That clue, the finer as I
say, I would fain at any rate to-day pick up for its close attachment to another Tuscan city or two—for a felt pull from
strange little San Gimignano delle belle Torre in especial; by
which I mean from the memory of a summer Sunday spent
there during a stay at Siena. But I have already super-
abounded, for mere love of my general present rubric—the
real thickness of experience having a good deal evaporated, so
that the Tiny Town of the Many Towers hangs before me, not
to say, rather, far behind me, after the manner of an object
directly meeting the wrong or diminishing lens of one's telescope.

It did everything, on the occasion of that pilgrimage, that it
was expected to do, presenting itself more or less in the guise
of some rare silvery shell, washed up by the sea of time,
cracked and battered and dishonoured, with its mutilated
marks of adjustment to the extinct type of creature it once
harboured figuring against the sky as maimed gesticulating
arms flourished in protest against fate. If the centuries, however, had pretty well cleaned out, vulgarly speaking, this
amazing little fortress-town, it wasn't that a mere aching void
was bequeathed us, I recognise as I consult a somewhat faded
impression; the whole scene and occasion come back to me as
the exhibition, on the contrary, of a stage rather crowded and

agitated, of no small quantity of sound and fury, of concussions, discussions, vociferations, hurryings to and fro, that could scarce have reached a higher pitch in the old days of the siege and the sortie. San Gimignano affected me, to a certainty, as not dead, I mean, but as inspired with that strange and slightly sinister new life that is now, in case after case, up and down the peninsula, and even in presence of the dryest and most scattered bones, producing the miracle of resurrection. The effect is often—and I find it strikingly involved in this particular reminiscence—that of the buried hero himself positively waking up to show you his bones for a fee, and almost capering about in his appeal to your attention. What has become of the soul of San Gimignano who shall say?— but, of a genial modern Sunday, it is as if the heroic skeleton, risen from the dust, were in high activity, officious for your entertainment and your detention, clattering and changing plates at the informal friendly inn, personally conducting you to a sight of the admirable Santa Fina of Ghirlandaio, as I believe is supposed, in a dim chapel of the Collegiata church; the poor young saint, on her low bed, in a state of ecstatic vision (the angelic apparition is given), accompanied by a few figures and accessories of the most beautiful and touching truth. This image is what has most vividly remained with me, of the day I thus so ineffectually recover; the precious ill-set gem or domestic treasure of Santa Fina, and then the wonderful drive, at eventide, back to Siena: the progress through the darkening land that was like a dense fragrant garden, all fire-flies and warm emanations and dimly-seen motionless festoons, extravagant vines and elegant branches intertwisted for miles, with couples and companies of young countryfolk almost as fondly united and raising their voices to the night as if superfluously to sing out at you that they were happy, and above all were Tuscan. On reflection, and to be just, I connect the slightly incongruous loudness that hung about me under the Beautiful Towers with the really too coarse competition for my favour among the young vetturini who lay in wait for my approach, and with an eye to my subsequent departure, on my quitting, at some unremembered spot, the morning train from Siena, from which point there was then still a drive. That onset was of a fine mediæval violence, but the subsiding echoes of it alone must have afterwards borne me company; mingled, at the worst, with certain reverberations of the animated rather than concentrated presence of sundry young sketchers and copyists of my own nationality, which element in the picture conveyed beyond anything else how thoroughly it was all to sit again henceforth in the eye of day. My final vision perhaps was of a sacred reliquary not so much rudely as familiarly and "humorously" torn open. The note had, with all its references, its own interest; but I never went again.

Ravenna

I WRITE these lines on a cold Swiss mountain-top, shut in by an intense white mist from any glimpse of the underworld of lovely Italy; but as I jotted down the other day in the ancient capital of Honorius and Theodoric the few notes of which they are composed, I let the original date stand for local colour's sake. Its mere look, as I transcribe it, emits a grateful glow in the midst of the Alpine rawness, and gives a depressed imagination something tangible to grasp while awaiting the return of fine weather. For Ravenna was glowing, less than a week since, as I edged along the narrow strip of shadow binding one side of the empty, white streets. After a long, chill spring the summer this year descended upon Italy with a sudden jump and an ominous hot breath. I stole away from Florence in the night, and even on top of the Apennines, under the dull starlight and in the rushing train, one could but sit and pant perspiringly.

At Bologna I found a festa, or rather two festas, a civil and a religious, going on in mutual mistrust and disparagement. The civil, that of the Statuto, was the one fully national Italian holiday as by law established—the day that signalises everywhere over the land at once its achieved and hard-won unification; the religious was a jubilee of certain local churches. The latter is observed by the Bolognese parishes in couples, and comes round for each couple but once in ten years—an arrangement by which the faithful at large insure themselves a liberal recurrence of expensive processions. It wasn't my business to distinguish the sheep from the goats, the pious from the profane, the prayers from the scoffers; it was enough that, melting together under the scorching sun, they filled the admirably solid city with a flood of spectacular life. The combination at one point was really dramatic. While a long procession of priests and young virgins in white veils, bearing tapers, marshalled itself in one of the streets, a review of the King's troops went forward outside the town. On its return a large detachment of cavalry passed across the space where the incense was burning, the pictured banners swaying and the litany being droned, and checked the advance of the little ecclesiastical troop. The long vista of the street, between the porticoes, was festooned with garlands and scarlet and tinsel; the robes and crosses and canopies of the priests, the clouds of perfumed smoke and the white veils of the maidens, were resolved by the hot bright air into a gorgeous medley of colour, across which the mounted soldiers rattled and flashed as if it had been a conquering army trampling on an embassy of propitiation. It was, to tell the truth, the first time an Italian festa had really exhibited to my eyes the genial glow and the romantic particulars promised by song and story; and I confess that those eyes found more pleasure in it than they were to find an hour later in the picturesque on canvas as one observes it in the Pinacoteca. I found myself scowling most unmercifully at Guido and Domenichino.

For Ravenna, however, I had nothing but smiles—grave, reflective, philosophic smiles, I hasten to add, such as accord with the historic dignity, not to say the mortal sunny sadness, of the place. I arrived there in the evening, before, even at drowsy Ravenna, the festa of the Statuto had altogether put itself to bed. I immediately strolled forth from the inn, and found it sitting up awhile longer on the piazza, chiefly at the café door, listening to the band of the garrison by the light of a dozen or so of feeble tapers, fastened along the front of the palace of the Government. Before long, however, it had dispersed and departed, and I was left alone with the grey illumination and with an affable citizen whose testimony as to the manners and customs of Ravenna I had aspired to obtain. I had, borrowing confidence from prompt observation, suggested deferentially that it wasn't the liveliest place in the world, and my friend admitted that it was in fact not a seat of ardent life. But had I seen the Corso? Without seeing the Corso one didn't exhaust the possibilities. The Corso of Ravenna, of a hot summer night, had an air of surprising seclusion and repose. Here and there in an upper closed window glimmered a light; my companion's footsteps and my own were the only sounds; not a creature was within sight. The suffocating air helped me to believe for a moment that I walked in the Italy of Boccaccio, hand-in-hand with the plague, through a city which had lost half its population by pestilence and the other half by flight. I turned back into my inn profoundly satisfied. This at last was the old-world dulness of a prime distillation; this at last was antiquity, history, repose.

The impression was largely confirmed and enriched on the following day; but it was obliged at an early stage of my visit to give precedence to another—the lively perception, namely, of the thinness of my saturation with Gibbon and the other sources of legend. At Ravenna the waiter at the café and the coachman who drives you to the Pine-Forest allude to Galla Placidia and Justinian as to any attractive topic of the hour; wherever you turn you encounter some fond appeal to your historic presence of mind. For myself I could only attune my spirit vaguely to so ponderous a challenge, could only feel I was breathing an air of prodigious records and relics. I conned my guide-book and looked up at the great mosaics, and then fumbled at poor Murray again for some intenser light on the court of Justinian; but I can imagine that to a visitor more intimate with the originals of the various great almond-eyed mosaic portraits in the vaults of the churches these extremely curious works of art may have a really formidable interest. I found in the place at large, by daylight, the look of a vast straggling depopulated village. The streets with hardly an exception are grass-grown, and though I walked about all day I failed to encounter a single wheeled vehicle. I remember no shop but the little establishment of an urbane photographer, whose views of the Pineta, the great legendary pine-forest just without the town, gave me an irresistible desire to seek that refuge. There was no architecture to speak of; and though there are a great many large domiciles with aristocratic names they stand cracking and baking in the sun in no very comfortable fashion. The houses have for the most part an all but rustic rudeness; they are low and featureless and shabby, as well as interspersed with high garden walls over which the long arms of tangled vines hang motionless into the stagnant streets. Here and there in all this dreariness, in some particularly silent and grassy corner, rises an old brick church with a front more or less spoiled by cheap modernisation, and a strange cylindrical campanile pierced with small arched windows and extremely suggestive of the fifth century.

These churches constitute the palpable interest of Ravenna, and their own principal interest, after thirteen centuries of well-intentioned spoliation, resides in their unequalled collection of early Christian mosaics. It is an interest simple, as who should say, almost to harshness, and leads one's attention along a straight and narrow way. There are older churches in Rome, and churches which, looked at as museums, are more variously and richly informing; but in Rome you stumble at every step on some curious pagan memorial, often beautiful enough to make your thoughts wander far from the strange stiff primitive Christian forms.

Ravenna, on the other hand, began with the Church, and all her monuments and relics are harmoniously rigid. By the middle of the first century she possessed an exemplary saint, Apollinaris, a disciple of Peter, to whom her two finest places of worship are dedicated. It was to one of these, jocosely entitled the "new," that I first directed my steps. I lingered outside awhile and looked at the great red, barrel-shaped bell-towers, so rusty, so crumbling, so archaic, and yet so resolute to ring in another century or two, and then went in to the coolness, the shining marble columns, the queer old sculptured slabs and sarcophagi and the long mosaics that scintillated, under the roof, along the wall of the nave. San Apollinare Nuovo, like most of its companions, is a magazine of early Christian odds and ends; fragments of yellow marble encrusted with quaint sculptured emblems of primitive dogma; great rough troughs, containing the bones of old bishops; episcopal chairs with the marble worn narrow by centuries of pressure from the solid episcopal person; slabs from the fronts of old pulpits, covered with carven hieroglyphics of an almost Egyptian abstruseness—lambs and stags and fishes and beasts of theological affinities even less apparent. Upon all these strange things the strange figures in the great mosaic panorama look down, with coloured cheeks and staring eyes, lifelike enough to speak to you and answer your wonderment and tell you in bad Latin of the decadence that it was in such and such a fashion they believed and worshipped. First, on each side, near the door, are houses and ships and various old landmarks of Ravenna; then begins a

long procession, on one side, of twenty-two white-robed virgins and three obsequious magi, terminating in a throne bearing the Madonna and Child, surrounded by four angels; on
the other side, of an equal number of male saints (twenty-five,
that is) holding crowns in their hands and leading to a Saviour enthroned between angels of singular expressiveness.
What it is these long slim seraphs express I cannot quite say,
but they have an odd, knowing, sidelong look out of the narrow ovals of their eyes which, though not without sweetness,
would certainly make me murmur a defensive prayer or so
were I to find myself alone in the church towards dusk. All
this work is of the latter part of the sixth century and brilliantly preserved. The gold backgrounds twinkle as if they had
been inserted yesterday, and here and there a figure is exc-
cuted almost too much in the modern manner to be interesting; for the charm of mosaic work is, to my sense, confined
altogether to the infancy of the art. The great Christ, in the
series of which I speak, is quite an elaborate picture, and yet
he retains enough of the orthodox stiffness to make him impressive in the simpler, elder sense. He is clad in a purple
robe, even as an emperor, his hair and beard are artfully
curled, his eyebrows arched, his complexion brilliant, his
whole aspect such a one as the popular mind may have attributed to Honorius or Valentinian. It is all very Byzantine, and
yet I found in it much of that interest which is inseparable, to
a facile imagination, from all early representations of our
Lord. Practically they are no more authentic than the more or
less plausible inventions of Ary Scheffer and Holman Hunt;
in spite of which they borrow a certain value, factitious perhaps but irresistible, from the mere fact that they are twelve
or thirteen centuries less distant from the original. It is something that this was the way the people in the sixth century
imagined Jesus to have looked; the image has suffered by so
many the fewer accretions. The great purple-robed monarch
on the wall of Ravenna is at least a very potent and positive
Christ, and the only objection I have to make to him is that
though in this character he must have had a full apportion-
ment of divine foreknowledge he betrays no apprehension of
Dr. Channing and M. Renan. If one's preference lies, for dis-

tinctness' sake, between the old plainness and the modern fantasy, one must admit that the plainness has here a very grand outline.

I spent the rest of the morning in charmed transition between the hot yellow streets and the cool grey interiors of the churches. The greyness everywhere was lighted up by the scintillation, on vault and entablature, of mosaics more or less archaic, but always brilliant and elaborate, and everywhere too by the same deep amaze of the fact that, while centuries had worn themselves away and empires risen and fallen, these little cubes of coloured glass had stuck in their allotted places and kept their freshness. I have no space for a list of the various shrines so distinguished, and, to tell the truth, my memory of them has already become a very generalised and undiscriminated record. The total aspect of the place, its sepulchral stillness, its absorbing perfume of evanescence and decay and mortality, confounds the distinctions and blurs the details. The Cathedral, which is vast and high, has been excessively modernised, and was being still more so by a lavish application of tinsel and cotton-velvet in preparation for the centenary feast of Saint Apollinaris, which befalls next month. Things on this occasion are to be done handsomely, and a fair Ravennese informed me that a single family had contributed three thousand francs towards a month's vesper-music. It seemed to me hereupon that I should like in the August twilight to wander into the quiet nave of San Apollinare, and look up at the great mosaics through the resonance of some fine chanting. I remember distinctly enough, however, the tall basilica of San Vitale, of octagonal shape, like an exchange or custom-house—modelled, I believe, upon Saint Sophia at Constantinople. It has a great span of height and a great solemnity, as well as a choir densely pictured over on arch and apse with mosaics of the time of Justinian. These are regular pictures, full of movement, gesture and perspective, and just enough sobered in hue by time to bring home their remoteness. In the middle of the church, under the great dome, sat an artist whom I envied, making at an effective angle a study of the choir and its broken lights, its decorated altar and its encrusted twinkling walls. The picture, when finished, will hang, I suppose, on the library wall of some person of taste;

but even if it is much better than is probable—I didn't look at it—all his taste won't tell the owner, unless he has been there, in just what a soundless, mouldering, out-of-the-way corner of old Italy it was painted. An even better place for an artist fond of dusky architectural nooks, except that here the dusk is excessive and he would hardly be able to tell his green from his red, is the extraordinary little church of the Santi Nazaro e Celso, otherwise known as the mausoleum of Galla Placidia. This is perhaps on the whole the spot in Ravenna where the impression is of most sovereign authority and most thrilling force. It consists of a narrow low-browed cave, shaped like a Latin cross, every inch of which except the floor is covered with dense symbolic mosaics. Before you and on each side, through the thick brown light, loom three enormous barbaric sarcophagi, containing the remains of potentates of the Lower Empire. It is as if history had burrowed under ground to escape from research and you had fairly run it to earth. On the right lie the ashes of the Emperor Honorius, and in the middle those of his sister, Galla Placidia, a lady who, I believe, had great adventures. On the other side rest the bones of Constantius III. The place might be a small natural grotto lined with glimmering mineral substances, and there is something quite tremendous in being shut up so closely with these three imperial ghosts. The shadow of the great Roman name broods upon the huge sepulchres and abides forever within the narrow walls.

But still other memories hang about than those of primitive bishops and degenerate emperors. Byron lived here and Dante died here, and the tomb of the one poet and the dwelling of the other are among the advertised appeals. The grave of Dante, it must be said, is anything but Dantesque, and the whole precinct is disposed with that odd vulgarity of taste which distinguishes most modern Italian tributes to greatness. The author of *The Divine Comedy* commemorated in stucco, even in a slumbering corner of Ravenna, is not "sympathetic." Fortunately of all poets he least needs a monument, as he was pre-eminently an architect in diction and built himself his temple of fame in verses more solid than Cyclopean blocks. If Dante's tomb is not Dantesque, so neither is Byron's house Byronic, being a homely, shabby, two-storied dwelling, directly on the street, with as little as possible of isolation and mystery. In Byron's time it was an inn, and it is rather a curious reflection that "Cain" and the "Vision of Judgment" should have been written at an hotel. The fact supplies a commanding precedent for self-abstraction to tourists at once sentimental and literary. I must declare indeed that my acquaintance with Ravenna considerably increased my esteem for Byron and helped to renew my faith in the sincerity of his inspiration. A man so much *de son temps* as the author of the above-named and other pieces can have spent two long years in this stagnant city only by the help of taking a great deal of disinterested pleasure in his own genius. He had indeed a notable pastime—the various churches are adorned with monuments of ancestral Guicciolis—but it is none the less obvious that Ravenna, fifty years ago, would have been an intolerably dull residence to a foreigner of distinction unequipped with intellectual resources. The hour one spends with Byron's memory then is almost compassionate. After all, one says to one's self as one turns away from the grandiloquent little slab in front of his house and looks down the deadly provincial vista of the empty, sunny street, the author of so many superb stanzas asked less from the world than he gave it. One of his diversions was to ride in the Pineta, which, beginning a couple of miles from the city, extends some twenty-five miles along the sands of the Adriatic. I drove out to it for Byron's sake, and Dante's, and Boccaccio's, all of whom have interwoven it with their fictions, and for that of a possible whiff of coolness from the sea. Between the city and the forest, in the midst of malarious rice-swamps, stands the finest of the Ravennese churches, the stately temple of San Apollinare in Classe. The Emperor Augustus constructed hereabouts a harbour for fleets, which the ages have choked up, and which survives only in the title of this ancient church. Its extreme loneliness makes it doubly impressive. They opened the great doors for me, and let a shaft of heated air go wander up the beautiful nave between the twenty-four lustrous, pearly columns of cipollino marble, and mount the wide staircase of the choir and spend itself beneath the mosaics of the vault. I passed a memorable half-hour sitting in this wave of tempered light, looking down the cool grey avenue of the nave, out of the open door, at the vivid green swamps, and listening to the melancholy stillness. I rambled for an hour in the Wood of Associations, between the tall smooth, silvery stems of the pines, and beside a creek which led me to the outer edge of the wood and a view of white sails, gleaming and gliding behind the sand-hills. It was infinitely, it was nobly "quaint," but, as the trees stand at wide intervals and bear far aloft in the blue air but a little parasol of foliage, I suppose that, of a glaring summer day, the forest itself was only the more characteristic of its clime and country for being perfectly shadelcss.

1873.

The Saint's Afternoon
and Others

BEFORE and above all was the sense that, with the narrow limits of past adventure, I had never yet had such an impression of what the summer could be in the south or the south in the summer; but I promptly found it, for the occasion, a good fortune that my terms of comparison were restricted. It was really something, at a time when the stride of the traveller had become as long as it was easy, when the seven-league boots positively hung, for frequent use, in the closet of the most sedentary, to have kept one's self so innocent of strange horizons that the Bay of Naples in June might still seem quite final. That picture struck me—a particular corner of it at least, and for many reasons—as the last word; and it is this last word that comes back to me, after a short interval, in a green, grey northern nook, and offers me again its warm, bright golden meaning before it also inevitably catches the chill. Too precious, surely, for us not to suffer it to help us as it may is the faculty of putting together again in an order the sharp minutes and hours that the wave of time has been as ready to pass over as the salt sea to wipe out the letters and words your stick has traced in the sand. Let me, at any rate, recover a sufficient number of such signs to make a sort of sense.

I

Far aloft on the great rock was pitched, as the first note, and indeed the highest, of the wondrous concert, the amazing creation of the friend who had offered me hospitality, and whom, more almost than I had ever envied any one anything, I envied the privilege of being able to reward a heated, artless pilgrim with a revelation of effects so incalculable. There was none but the loosest prefiguration as the creaking and puffing little boat, which had conveyed me only from Sorrento, drew closer beneath the prodigious island—beautiful, horrible and haunted—that does most, of all the happy elements and accidents, towards making the Bay of Naples, for the study of composition, a lesson in the grand style. There was only, above and below, through the blue of the air and sea, a great confused shining of hot cliffs and crags and buttresses, a loss, from nearness, of the splendid couchant outline and the more comprehensive mass, and an opportunity—oh, not lost, I assure you—to sit and meditate, even moralise, on the empty deck, while a happy brotherhood of American and German tourists, including, of course, many sisters, scrambled down into little waiting, rocking tubs and, after a few strokes, popped systematically into the small orifice of the Blue Grotto. There was an appreciable moment when they were all lost to view in that receptacle, the daily "psychological" moment during which it must so often befall the recalcitrant observer on the deserted deck to find himself aware of how delightful it might be if none of them should come out again. The charm, the fascination of the idea is not a little—though also not wholly—in the fact that, as the wave rises over the aperture, there is the most encouraging appearance that they perfectly may not. There it is. There is no more of them. It is a case to which nature has, by the neatest stroke and with the best taste in the world, just quietly attended.

Beautiful, horrible, haunted: that is the essence of what, about itself, Capri says to you—dip again into your Tacitus and see why; and yet, while you roast a little under the awning and in the vaster shadow, it is not because the trail of Tiberius is ineffaceable that you are most uneasy. The trail of Germanicus in Italy to-day ramifies further and bites perhaps even deeper; a proof of which is, precisely, that his eclipse in the Blue Grotto is inexorably brief, that here he is popping out again, bobbing enthusiastically back and scrambling triumphantly back. The spirit, in truth, of his effective appropriation of Capri has a broad-faced candour against which there is no standing up, supremely expressive as it is of the well-known "love that kills," of Germanicus's fatal susceptibility. If I were to let myself, however, incline to *that* aspect of the serious case of Capri I should embark on strange depths. The straightness and simplicity, the classic, synthetic directness of the German passion for Italy, make this passion probably the sentiment in the world that is in the act of supplying enjoyment in the largest, sweetest mouthfuls; and there is some-

thing unsurpassably marked in the way that on this irresistible
shore it has seated itself to ruminate and digest. It keeps the
record in its own loud accents; it breaks out in the folds of
the hills and on the crests of the crags into every manner of
symptom and warning. Huge advertisements and portents
stare across the bay; the acclivities bristle with breweries and
"restorations" and with great ugly Gothic names. I hasten, of
course, to add that some such general consciousness as this
may well oppress, under any sky, at the century's end, the
brooding tourist who makes himself a prey by staying anywhere, when the gong sounds, "behind." It is behind, in the
track and the reaction, that he least makes out the end of it
all, perceives that to visit any one's country for any one's sake
is more and more to find some one quite other in possession.
No one, least of all the brooder himself, is in his own.

II

I certainly, at any rate, felt the force of this truth when, on
scaling the general rock with the eye of apprehension, I made
out at a point much nearer its summit than its base the gleam
of a dizzily-perched white sea-gazing front which I knew for
my particular landmark and which promised so much that it
would have been welcome to keep even no more than half.
Let me instantly say that it kept still more than it promised,
and by no means least in the way of leaving far below it the
worst of the outbreak of restorations and breweries. There is
a road at present to the upper village, with which till recently
communication was all by rude steps cut in the rock and diminutive donkeys scrambling on the flints; one of those fine
flights of construction which the great road-making "Latin
races" take, wherever they prevail, without advertisement or
bombast; and even while I followed along the face of the cliff
its climbing consolidated ledge, I asked myself how I could
think so well of it without consistently thinking better still of
the temples of beer so obviously destined to enrich its terminus. The perfect answer to that was of course that the brooding tourist is never bound to be consistent. What happier law
for him than this very one, precisely, when on at last alighting, high up in the blue air, to stare and gasp and almost

Capri, the Harbour and Villa of Tiberius

disbelieve, he embraced little by little the beautiful truth particularly, on this occasion, reserved for himself, and took in the stupendous picture? For here above all had the thought and the hand come from far away—even from *ultima Thule*, and yet were in possession triumphant and acclaimed. Well, all one could say was that the way they had felt their opportunity, the divine conditions of the place, spoke of the advantage of some such intellectual perspective as a remote original standpoint alone perhaps can give. If what had finally, with infinite patience, passion, labour, taste, got itself done there, was like some supreme reward of an old dream of Italy, something perfect after long delays, was it not verily in *ultima Thule* that the vow would have been piously enough made and the germ tenderly enough nursed? For a certain art of asking of Italy all she can give, you must doubtless either be a rare *raffiné* or a rare genius, a sophisticated Norseman or just a Gabriele d'Annunzio.

All she can give appeared to me, assuredly, for that day and the following, gathered up and enrolled there: in the wondrous cluster and dispersal of chambers, corners, courts, galleries, arbours, arcades, long white ambulatories and vertiginous points of view. The greatest charm of all perhaps was that, thanks to the particular conditions, she seemed to abound, to overflow, in directions in which I had never yet enjoyed the chance to find her so free. The indispensable thing was therefore, in observation, in reflection, to press the opportunity hard, to recognise that as the abundance was splendid, so, by the same stroke, it was immensely suggestive. It dropped into one's lap, naturally, at the end of an hour or two, the little white flower of its formula: the brooding tourist, in other words, could only continue to brood till he had made out in a measure, as I may say, what was so wonderfully the matter with him. He was simply then in the presence, more than ever yet, of the possible poetry of the personal and social life of the south, and the fun would depend much—as occasions are fleeting—on his arriving in time, in the interest of that imagination which is his only field of sport, at adequate new notations of it. The sense of all this, his obscure and special fun in the general bravery, mixed, on the morrow, with the long, human hum of the bright, hot day and filled

up the golden cup with questions and answers. The feast of
St. Antony, the patron of the upper town, was the one thing
in the air, and of the private beauty of the place, there on the
narrow shelf, in the shining, shaded loggias and above the
blue gulfs, all comers were to be made free.

III

The church-feast of its saint is of course for Anacapri, as for
any self-respecting Italian town, the great day of the year, and
the smaller the small "country," in native parlance, as well as
the simpler, accordingly, the life, the less the chance for leakage, on other pretexts, of the stored wine of loyalty. This pure
fluid, it was easy to feel overnight, had not sensibly lowered
its level; so that nothing indeed, when the hour came, could
well exceed the outpouring. All up and down the Sorrentine
promontory the early summer happens to be the time of the
saints, and I had just been witness there of a week on every
day of which one might have travelled, through kicked-up
clouds and other demonstrations, to a different hot holiday.
There had been no bland evening that, somewhere or other,
in the hills or by the sea, the white dust and the red glow
didn't rise to the dim stars. Dust, perspiration, illumination,
conversation—these were the regular elements. "They're very
civilised," a friend who knows them as well as they can be
known had said to me of the people in general; "plenty of
fireworks and plenty of talk—that's all they ever want." That
they were "civilised"—on the side on which they were most
to show—was therefore to be the word of the whole business, and nothing could have, in fact, had more interest than
the meaning that for the thirty-six hours I read into it.

Seen from below and diminished by distance, Anacapri
makes scarce a sign, and the road that leads to it is not traceable over the rock; but it sits at its ease on its high, wide
table, of which it covers—and with picturesque southern culture as well—as much as it finds convenient. As much of it as
possible was squeezed all the morning, for St. Antony, into
the piazzetta before the church, and as much more into that
edifice as the robust odour mainly prevailing there allowed
room for. It was the odour that was in prime occupation, and

one could only wonder how so many men, women and children could cram themselves into so much smell. It was surely the smell, thick and resisting, that was least successfully to be elbowed. Meanwhile the good saint, before he could move into the air, had, among the tapers and the tinsel, the opera-music and the pulpit poundings, bravely to snuff it up. The shade outside was hot, and the sun was hot; but we waited as densely for him to come out, or rather to come "on," as the pit at the opera waits for the great tenor. There were people from below and people from the mainland and people from Pomerania and a brass band from Naples. There were other figures at the end of longer strings—strings that, some of them indeed, had pretty well given way and were now but little snippets trailing in the dust. Oh, the queer sense of the good old Capri of artistic legend, of which the name itself was, in the more benighted years—years of the contadina and the pifferaro—a bright evocation! Oh, the echo, on the spot, of each romantic tale. Oh, the loafing painters, so bad and so happy, the conscious models, the vague personalities! The "beautiful Capri girl" was of course not missed, though not perhaps so beautiful as in her ancient glamour, which none the less didn't at all exclude the probable presence—with *his* legendary light quite undimmed—of the English lord in disguise who will at no distant date marry her. The whole thing was there; one held it in one's hand.

The saint comes out at last, borne aloft in long procession and under a high canopy: a rejoicing, staring, smiling saint, openly delighted with the one happy hour in the year on which he may take his own walk. Frocked and tonsured, but not at all macerated, he holds in his hand a small wax puppet of an infant Jesus and shows him to all their friends, to whom he nods and bows: to whom, in the dazzle of the sun he literally seems to grin and wink, while his litter sways and his banners flap and every one gaily greets him. The ribbons and draperies flutter, and the white veils of the marching maidens, the music blares and the guns go off and the chants resound, and it is all as holy and merry and noisy as possible. The procession—down to the delightful little tinselled and bare-bodied babies, miniature St. Antonys irrespective of sex, led

The Road to Anacapri

or carried by proud papas or brown grandsires—includes so much of the population that you marvel there is such a muster to look on—like the charades given in a family in which every one wants to act. But it is all indeed in a manner one house, the little high-niched island community, and nobody therefore, even in the presence of the head of it, puts on an air of solemnity. Singular and suggestive before everything else is the absence of any approach to our notion of the posture of respect, and this among people whose manners in general struck one as so good and, in particular, as so cultivated. The office of the saint—of which the festa is but the annual re-affirmation—involves not the faintest attribute of remoteness or mystery.

While, with my friend, I waited for him, we went for coolness into the second church of the place, a considerable and bedizened structure, with the rare curiosity of a wondrous pictured pavement of majolica, the garden of Eden done in large coloured tiles or squares, with every beast, bird and river, and a brave *diminuendo*, in especial, from portal to altar, of perspective, so that the animals and objects of the foreground are big and those of the successive distances differ with much propriety. Here in the sacred shade the old women were knitting, gossiping, yawning, shuffling about; here the children were romping and "larking"; here, in a manner, were the open parlour, the nursery, the kindergarten and the conversazione of the poor. This is everywhere the case by the southern sea. I remember near Sorrento a wayside chapel that seemed the scene of every function of domestic life, including cookery and others. The odd thing is that it all appears to interfere so little with that special civilised note— the note of manners—which is so constantly touched. It is barbarous to expectorate in the temple of your faith, but that doubtless is an extreme case. Is civilisation really measured by the number of things people do respect? There would seem to be much evidence against it. The oldest societies, the societies with most traditions, are naturally not the least ironic, the least *blasées*, and the African tribes who take so many things into account that they fear to quit their huts at night are not the fine flower.

IV

Where, on the other hand, it was impossible not to feel to the full all the charming *riguardi*—to use their own good word—in which our friends *could* abound, was, that afternoon, in the extraordinary temple of art and hospitality that had been benignantly opened to me. Hither, from three o'clock to seven, all the world, from the small in particular to the smaller and the smallest, might freely flock, and here, from the first hour to the last, the huge straw-bellied flasks of purple wine were tilted for all the thirsty. They were many, the thirsty, they were three hundred, they were unending; but the draughts they drank were neither countable nor counted. This boon was dispensed in a long, pillared portico, where everything was white and light save the blue of the great bay as it played up from far below or as you took it in, between shining columns, with your elbows on the parapet. Sorrento and Vesuvius were over against you; Naples furthest off, melted, in the middle of the picture, into shimmering vagueness and innocence; and the long arm of Posilippo and the presence of the other islands, Procida, the stricken Ischia, made themselves felt to the left. The grand air of it all was in one's very nostrils and seemed to come from sources too numerous and too complex to name. It was antiquity in solution, with every brown, mild figure, every note of the old speech, every tilt of the great flask, every shadow cast by every classic fragment, adding its touch to the impression. What was the secret of the surprising amenity?—to the essence of which one got no nearer than simply by feeling afresh the old story of the deep interfusion of the present with the past. You had felt that often before, and all that could, at the most, help you now was that, more than ever yet, the present appeared to become again really classic, to sigh with strange elusive sounds of Virgil and Theocritus. Heaven only knows how little they would in truth have had to say to it, but we yield to these visions as we must, and when the imagination fairly turns in its pain almost any soft name is good enough to soothe it.

It threw such difficulties but a step back to say that the

secret of the amenity was "style"; for what in the world was
the secret of style, which you might have followed up and
down the abysmal old Italy for so many a year only to be still
vainly calling for it? Everything, at any rate, that happy afternoon, in that place of poetry, was bathed and blessed with it.
The castle of Barbarossa had been on the height behind; the
villa of black Tiberius had overhung the immensity from the
right; the white arcades and the cool chambers offered to
every step some sweet old "piece" of the past, some rounded
porphyry pillar supporting a bust, some shaft of pale alabaster
upholding a trellis, some mutilated marble image, some
bronze that had roughly resisted. Our host, if we came to
that, had the secret; but he could only express it in grand
practical ways. One of them was precisely this wonderful "afternoon tea," in which tea only—*that*, good as it is, has never
the note of style—was not to be found. The beauty and the
poetry, at all events, were clear enough, and the extraordinary
uplifted distinction; but where, in all this, it may be asked,
was the element of "horror" that I have spoken of as sensible?—what obsession that was not charming could find a
place in that splendid light, out of which the long summer
squeezes every secret and shadow? I'm afraid I'm driven to
plead that these evils were exactly in one's imagination, a predestined victim always of the cruel, the fatal historic sense. To
make so much distinction, how much history had been
needed!—so that the whole air still throbbed and ached with
it, as with an accumulation of ghosts to whom the very climate was pitiless, condemning them to blanch for ever in the
general glare and grandeur, offering them no dusky northern
nook, no place at the friendly fireside, no shelter of legend or
song.

v

My friend had, among many original relics, in one of his
white galleries—and how he understood the effect and the
"value" of whiteness!—two or three reproductions of the finest bronzes of the Naples museum, the work of a small band
of brothers whom he had found himself justified in trusting
to deal with their problem honourably and to bring forth

something as different as possible from the usual compromise
of commerce. They had brought forth, in especial, for him, a
copy of the young resting, slightly-panting Mercury which it
was a pure delight to live with, and they had come over from
Naples on St. Antony's eve, as they had done the year before,
to report themselves to their patron, to keep up good relations, to drink Capri wine and to join in the tarantella. They
arrived late, while we were at supper; they received their welcome and their billet, and I am not sure it was not the conversation and the beautiful manners of these obscure young
men that most fixed in my mind for the time the sense of the
side of life that, all around, was to come out strongest. It
would be artless, no doubt, to represent them as high types of
innocence or even of energy—at the same time that, weighing them against *some* ruder folk of our own race, we might
perhaps have made bold to place their share even of these
qualities in the scale. It was an impression indeed never infrequent in Italy, of which I might, in these days, first have felt
the force during a stay, just earlier, with a friend at Sorrento—a friend who had good-naturedly "had in," on his
wondrous terrace, after dinner, for the pleasure of the gaping
alien, the usual local quartette, violins, guitar and flute, the
musical barber, the musical tailor, sadler, joiner, humblest
sons of the people and exponents of Neapolitan song. Neapolitan song, as we know, has been blown well about the
world, and it is late in the day to arrive with a ravished ear for
it. That, however, was scarcely at all, for me, the question: the
question, on the Sorrento terrace, so high up in the cool
Capri night, was of the present outlook, in the world, for the
races with whom it has been a tradition, in intercourse, positively to please.

The personal civilisation, for intercourse, of the musical
barber and tailor, of the pleasant young craftsmen of my
other friend's company, was something that could be trusted
to make the brooding tourist brood afresh—to say more to
him in fact, all the rest of the second occasion, than everything else put together. The happy address, the charming expression, the indistinctive discretion, the complete eclipse, in
short, of vulgarity and brutality—these things easily became
among these people the supremely suggestive note, begetting

a hundred hopes and fears as to the place that, with the present general turn of affairs about the globe, is being kept for them. They are perhaps what the races politically feeble have still most to contribute—but what appears to be the happy prospect for the races politically feeble? And so the afternoon waned, among the mellow marbles and the pleasant folk—the purple wine flowed, the golden light faded, song and dance grew free and circulation slightly embarrassed. But the great impression remained and finally was exquisite. It was all purple wine, all art and song, and nobody a grain the worse. It was fireworks and conversation—the former, in the piazzetta, were to come later; it was civilisation and amenity. I took in the greater picture, but I lost nothing else; and I talked with the contadini about antique sculpture. No, nobody was a grain the worse; and I had plenty to think of. So it was I was quickened to remember that we others, we of my own country, as a race politically *not* weak, had—by what I had somewhere just heard—opened "three hundred 'saloons' " at Manilla.

VI

The "other" afternoons I here pass on to—and I may include in them, for that matter, various mornings scarce less charmingly sacred to memory—were occasions of another and a later year; a brief but all felicitous impression of Naples itself, and of the approach to it from Rome, as well as of the return to Rome by a different wonderful way, which I feel I shall be wise never to attempt to "improve on." Let me muster assurance to confess that this comparatively recent and superlatively rich reminiscence gives me for its first train of ineffable images those of a motor-run that, beginning betimes of a splendid June day, and seeing me, with my genial companions, blissfully out of Porta San Paolo, hung over us thus its benediction till the splendour had faded in the lamplit rest of the Chiaja. "We'll go by the mountains," my friend, of the winged chariot, had said, "and we'll come back, after three days, by the sea;" which handsome promise flowered into such flawless performance that I could but feel it to have closed and rounded for me, beyond any further rehandling, the long-drawn rather indeed than thick-studded chaplet of my visitations of Naples—from the first, seasoned with the highest sensibility of youth, forty years ago, to this last the other day. I find myself noting with interest—and just to be able to emphasise it is what inspires me with these remarks —that, in spite of the milder and smoother and perhaps, pictorially speaking, considerably emptier, Neapolitan face of things, things in general, of our later time, I recognised in my final impression a grateful, a beguiling serenity. The place is at the best wild and weird and sinister, and yet seemed on this occasion to be seated more at her ease in her immense natural dignity. My disposition to feel that, I hasten to add, was doubtless my own secret; my three beautiful days, at any rate, filled themselves with the splendid harmony, several of the minor notes of which ask for a place, such as it may be, just here.

Wondrously, it was a clean and cool and, as who should say, quiet and amply interspaced Naples—in tune with itself, no harsh jangle of *forestieri* vulgarising the concert. I seemed in fact, under the blaze of summer, the only stranger— though the blaze of summer itself was, for that matter, every-where but a higher pitch of light and colour and tradition, and a lower pitch of everything else; even, it struck me, of sound and fury. The appeal in short was genial, and, faring out to Pompeii of a Sunday afternoon, I enjoyed there, for the only time I can recall, the sweet chance of a late hour or two, the hour of the lengthening shadows, absolutely alone. The impression remains ineffaceable—it was to supersede half-a-dozen other mixed memories, the sense that had remained with me, from far back, of a pilgrimage always here beset with traps and shocks and vulgar importunities, achieved un-der fatal discouragements. Even Pompeii, in fine, haunt of *all* the cockneys of creation, burned itself, in the warm still even-tide, as clear as glass, or as the glow of a pale topaz, and the particular cockney who roamed without a plan and at his ease, but with his feet on Roman slabs, his hands on Roman stones, his eyes on the Roman void, his consciousness really at last of some good to him, could open himself as never before to the fond luxurious fallacy of a close communion, a direct revelation. With which there were other moments for him not less the fruit of the slow unfolding of time; the clearest of these again being those enjoyed on the terrace of a small island-villa—the island a rock and the villa a wondrous little rock-garden, unless a better term would be perhaps rock-salon, just off the extreme point of Posilippo and where, thanks to a friendliest hospitality, he was to hang ecstatic, through another sublime afternoon, on the wave of a magical wand. Here, as happened, were charming wise, original people even down to delightful amphibious American children, enamelled by the sun of the Bay as for figures of miniature Tritons and Nereids on a Renaissance plaque; and above all, on the part of the general prospect, a demonstration of the grand style of composition and effect that one was never to wish to see bettered. The way in which the Italian scene on such occasions as this seems to purify itself to the transcendent and perfect *idea* alone—idea of beauty, of dignity, of comprehensive grace, with all accidents merged, all defects disowned, all experience outlived, and to gather itself up into the mere mute eloquence of what has just incalculably *been*, remains forever the secret and the lesson of the subtlest daughter of History. All one could do, at the heart of the overarching crystal, and in presence of the relegated City, the far-trailing Mount, the grand Sorrentine headland, the islands incomparably stationed and related, was to wonder what may well become of the so many other elements of any poor human and social complexus, what might become of any successfully-working or only struggling and floundering civilisation at all, when high Natural Elegance proceeds to take such exclusive charge and recklessly assume, as it were, *all* the responsibilities.

VII

This indeed had been quite the thing I was asking myself all the wondrous way down from Rome, and was to ask myself afresh, on the return, largely within sight of the sea, as our earlier course had kept to the ineffably romantic inland valleys, the great decorated blue vistas in which the breasts of the mountains shine vaguely with strange high-lying city and castle and church and convent, even as shoulders of no diviner line might be hung about with dim old jewels. It was odd, at the end of time, long after those initiations, of comparative youth, that had then struck one as extending the very field itself of felt charm, as exhausting the possibilities of fond surrender, it was odd to have positively a new basis of enjoyment, a new gate of triumphant passage, thrust into one's consciousness and opening to one's use; just as I confess I have to brace myself a little to call by such fine names our latest, our ugliest and most monstrous aid to motion. It is true of the monster, as we have known him up to now, that one can neither quite praise him nor quite blame him without a blush—he reflects so the nature of the company he's condemned to keep. His splendid easy power addressed to noble aims make him assuredly on occasion a purely beneficent creature. I parenthesise at any rate that I know him in no other light—counting out of course the acquaintance that consists of a dismayed arrest in the road, with back flattened against wall or hedge, for the dusty, smoky, stenchy shock of his passage. To no end is his easy power more blest than to that of ministering to the ramifications, as it were, of curiosity, or to that, in other words, of achieving for us, among the kingdoms of the earth, the grander and more genial, the comprehensive and *complete* introduction. Much as was ever to be said for our old forms of pilgrimage—and I am convinced that they are far from wholly superseded—they left, they had to leave, dreadful gaps in our yearning, dreadful lapses in our knowledge, dreadful failures in our energy; there were always things off and beyond, goals of delight and dreams of desire, that dropped as a matter of course into the unattainable, and over to which our wonder-working agent now flings the firm straight bridge. Curiosity has lost, under this amazing extension, its salutary renouncements perhaps; contemplation has become one with action and satisfaction one with desire— speaking always in the spirit of the inordinate lover of an enlightened use of our eyes. That may represent, for all I know, an insolence of advantage on which there will be eventual heavy charges, as yet obscure and incalculable, to pay, and I glance at the possibility only to avoid all thought of the lesson of the long run, and to insist that I utter this dithyramb but in the immediate flush and fever of the short. For such a beat of time as our fine courteous and contemplative advance upon Naples, and for such another as our retreat northward under the same fine law of observation and homage, the bribed consciousness could only decline to question its security. The sword of Damocles suspended over that presumption, the skeleton at the banquet of extravagant ease, would have been that even at our actual inordinate rate—leaving quite apart "improvements" to come—such savings of trouble begin to use up the world; some hard grain of difficulty being always a necessary part of the composition of pleasure. The hard grain in our old comparatively pedestrian mixture, before this business of our learning not so much even to fly (which might indeed involve trouble) as to be mechanically and prodigiously flown, quite another matter, was the element of uncertainty, effort and patience; the handful of silver nails which, I admit, drove many an impression home. The seated motorist misses the silver nails, I fully acknowledge, save in so far as his æsthetic (let alone his moral) conscience may supply him with some artful subjective substitute; in which case the thing becomes a precious secret of his own.

However, I wander wild—by which I mean I look too far ahead; my intention having been only to let my sense of the merciless June beauty of Naples Bay at the sunset hour and on the island terrace associate itself with the whole inexpressible taste of our two motor-days' feast of scenery. That queer question of the exquisite grand manner as the most emphasised *all* of things—of what it may, seated so predominant in nature, insidiously, through the centuries, let generations and populations "in for," hadn't in the least waited for the special emphasis I speak of to hang about me. I must have found myself more or less consciously entertaining it by the way—since how couldn't it be of the very essence of the truth, constantly and intensely before us, that Italy is really so much the most beautiful country in the world, taking all things together, that others must stand off and be hushed while she speaks? Seen thus in great comprehensive iridescent stretches, it is the incomparable wrought *fusion*, fusion of human history and mortal passion with the elements of earth and air, of colour, composition and form, that constitute her appeal and give it the supreme heroic grace. The chariot of fire favours fusion rather than promotes analysis, and leaves much of that first June picture for me, doubtless, a great accepted blur of violet and silver. The various hours and successive aspects, the different strong passages of our reverse process, on the other hand, still figure for me even as some series of sublime landscape-frescoes—if the great Claude, say, had ever used that medium—in the immense gallery of a palace; the home-ward run by Capua, Terracina, Gaeta and its storied headland fortress, across the deep, strong, indescribable Pontine Marshes, white-cattled, strangely pastoral, sleeping in the af-ternoon glow, yet stirred by the near sea-breath. Thick some-how to the imagination as some full-bodied sweetness of syrup is thick to the palate the atmosphere of that region— thick with the sense of history and the very taste of time; as if the haunt and home (which indeed it is) of some great fair bovine aristocracy attended and guarded by halberdiers in the form of the mounted and long-lanced herdsmen, admirably congruous with the whole picture at every point, and never more so than in their manner of gaily taking up, as with bell-voices of golden bronze, the offered wayside greeting.

There had been this morning among the impressions of our first hour an unforgettable specimen of that general type— the image of one of those human figures on which our per-ception of the romantic so often pounces in Italy as on the genius of the scene personified; with this advantage, that as the scene there has, at its best, an unsurpassable distinction, so the physiognomic representative, standing for it all, and with an animation, a complexion, an expression, a fineness and fulness of humanity that appear to have gathered it in and to sum it up, becomes beautiful by the same simple process, very much, that makes the heir to a great capitalist rich. Our early start, our roundabout descent from Posilippo by shining Baiae for avoidance of the city, had been an hour of enchant-ment beyond any notation I can here recover; all lustre and azure, yet all composition and classicism, the prospect de-veloped and spread, till after extraordinary upper reaches of

radiance and horizons of pearl we came at the turn of a descent
upon a stalwart young gamekeeper, or perhaps substantial
young farmer, who, well-appointed and blooming, had un-
slung his gun and, resting on it beside a hedge, just lived for
us, in the rare felicity of his whole look, during that moment
and while, in recognition, or almost, as we felt, in homage,
we instinctively checked our speed. He pointed, as it were,
the lesson, giving the supreme right accent or final exquisite
turn to the immense magnificent phrase; which from those
moments on, and on and on, resembled doubtless nothing so
much as a page written, by a consummate verbal economist
and master of style, in the noblest of all tongues. Our splendid human plant by the wayside had flowered thus into
style—and there wasn't to be, all day, a lapse of eloquence, a
wasted word or a cadence missed.

These things are personal memories, however, with the
logic of certain insistences of that sort often difficult to seize.
Why should I have kept so sacredly uneffaced, for instance,
our small afternoon wait at tea-time or, as we made it, coffee-
time, in the little brown piazzetta of Velletri, just short of the
final push on through the flushed Castelli Romani and the
drop and home-stretch across the darkening Campagna? We
had been dropped into the very lap of the ancient civic family,
after the inveterate fashion of one's sense of such stations in
small Italian towns. There was a narrow raised terrace, with
steps, in front of the best of the two or three local cafés, and
in the soft enclosed, the warm waning light of June various
benign contemplative worthies sat at disburdened tables and,
while they smoked long black weeds, enjoyed us under those
probable workings of subtlety with which we invest so many
quite unimaginably blank (I dare say) Italian simplicities. The
charm was, as always in Italy, in the tone and the air and the
happy hazard of things, which made any positive pretension
or claimed importance a comparatively trifling question. We
slid, in the steep little place, more or less down hill; we
wished, stomachically, we had rather addressed ourselves to a
tea-basket; we suffered importunity from unchidden infants
who swarmed about our chairs and romped about our feet;
we stayed no long time, and "went to see" nothing; yet we
communicated to intensity, we lay at our ease in the bosom of

the past, we practised intimacy, in short, an intimacy so much greater than the mere accidental and ostensible: the difficulty for the right and grateful expression of which makes the old, the familiar tax on the luxury of loving Italy.

1900—1909.

OTHER TRAVELS

Contents

Swiss Notes

Thusis, August, 1872.

I HAVE often thought it, intellectually speaking, indifferent economy for the American tourist to devote many of his precious summer days to Switzerland. Switzerland represents, generally, nature in the rough, and the American traveller in search of novelty entertains a rational preference for nature in the refined state. If he have his European opportunities very much at heart, he will be apt to chafe a little on lake-side and mountain-side with a sense of the beckoning, unvisited cities of Germany, France and Italy. As to the average American tourist, however, as one actually meets him, it is hard to say whether he most neglect or abuse opportunity. It is beside the mark, at any rate, to talk to him about economy. He spends as he listeth, and if he overfees the waiters he is frugal of his hours. He has long since discovered the art of comprehensive travel, and if you think he had better not be in Switzerland—*rassurez-vous*—he will not be there long. I am, perhaps, unduly solicitous for him from a vague sense of having treated myself to an overdose of Switzerland. I relish a human flavor in my pleasures, and I fancy that it is a more equal intercourse between man and man than between man and mountain. I have found myself grumbling at moments because the large-hewn snow-peaks of the Oberland are not the marble pinnacles of a cathedral, and the liquid sapphire and emerald of Leman and Lucerne are not firm palace-floors of lapis and verd-antique. But, after all, there is a foreground in Switzerland as well as a background, and more than once, when a mountain has stared me out of countenance, I have recovered my self-respect in a sympathetic gaze at the object which here corresponds to the Yankee town-pump. Swiss village fountains are delightful; the homely village life centres about the great stone basin (roughly inscribed, generally, with an antique date), where the tinkling cattle drink, where the lettuce and the linen are washed, where dusty pedestrians, with their lips at the spout, need scarcely devote their draught to the "health" of the brawny beauties who lean, brown-armed, over the trough, and the plash of the cool, hard water is heard at either end of the village street. But I am surely not singular in my impulse thus occasionally to weigh detail against mass in Switzerland; and I apprehend that, unless you are a regular climber, or an æsthetic Buddhist, as it were, content with a purely contemplative enjoyment of natural beauty, you are obliged eventually, in self-defence, to lower, by an imaginative effort, the sky-line of your horizon. You may sit for days before the hotel at Grindelwald, looking at the superb snow-crested granite of the Wetterhorn, if you have a slowly ripening design of measuring your legs, your head, and your wind against it; and *a fortiori*, the deed being done, you may spend another week in the same position, sending up patronizing looks at those acres of ice which the foolish cockneys at your side take to be inches. But there is a limit to the satisfaction with which you can sit staring at a mountain—even the most beautiful—which you have neither ascended nor are likely to ascend; and I know of nothing to which I can better compare the effect on your nerves of what comes to seem to you, at last, its inhuman want of condescension than that of the expression of back of certain persons whom you come as near detesting as your characteristic amiability permits. I appeal on this point to all poor mountaineers. They might reply, however, that one should be either a good climber or a good idler.

If there is truth in this retort, it may help to explain an old-time kindness of mine for Geneva, to which I was introduced years ago, in my school-days, when I was as good an idler as the best. And I ought in justice to say that, with Geneva for its principal city, Switzerland may fairly pretend to possess something more than nature in the rough. An ingenious Swiss novelist has indeed written a tale expressly to prove that frank nature is wofully out of favor there, and his heroine dies of a broken heart because her spontaneity passes for impropriety. I don't know whether M. Cherbuliez's novel is as veracious as it is clever; but the susceptible stranger certainly feels that the Helvetic capital is a highly artificial compound. It makes little difference that the individuality of the place is a moral rather than an architectural one; for the streets and houses express it as clearly as if it were syllabled in their stones. The moral tone of Geneva, as I imagine it, is epigrammatically, but on the whole justly, indicated by the fact, recently related to me by a discriminating friend, that, meeting one day in the street a placard of the theatre, superscribed *Bouffes-Genevois*, he burst into irrepressible laughter. To appreciate the irony of the phrase one must have lived long enough in Geneva to suffer from the want of humor in the local atmosphere, and the absence, as well, of that æsthetic character which is begotten of a generous view of life. There is no Genevese architecture, nor museum, nor theatre, nor music, not even a worthy promenade—all prime requisites of a well-appointed foreign capital; and yet somehow Geneva manages to assert herself powerfully without them, and to leave the impression of a strongly-featured little city, which, if you do not enjoy, you may at least grudgingly respect. It was, perhaps, the absence of these frivolous attributes which caused it to be thought a proper place for the settlement of our solemn wrangle with England—though surely a community which could make a joke would have afforded worthier spectators to certain phases of the affair. But there is such a thing, after all, as drawing too sober-colored a picture of the Presbyterian mother-city, and I suddenly find myself wondering whether, if it were not the most respectable of capitals, it would not still be the prettiest; whether its main interest be not, possibly, the picturesque one—the admirable contrast of the dark, homely-featured mass of the town, relieved now, indeed, at the water's edge by a shining rim of white-walled hotels—and the incomparable vivacity of color of the blue lake and Rhone. This divinely cool-hued gush of the Rhone beneath the two elder bridges is one of the loveliest things in Switzerland, and ought itself to make the fortune of unnumbered generations of innkeepers. As you linger and watch the shining tide, you make a rather vain effort to connect it with the two great human figures in the Genevese picture—Calvin and Rousseau. It seems to have no great affinity with either genius—one of which it might have brightened and the other have cleansed. There is indeed in Rousseau a strong limpidity of style which, if we choose, we may fancy an influence from the rushing stream he must so often have tarried in his boyish breeches to peep at between the bridge-rails; but I doubt whether we can twist the Rhone into a channel for even the most diluted Calvinism. It must have seemed to the grim Doctor one of the streams of the paradise he was making it so hard to enter. For ourselves, as it hurries undarkened past the gray theological city, we may liken it to the impetus of faith shooting in deep indifference past the doctrine of election. The genius that contains the clearest strain of this anti-Calvinistic azure is decidedly that of Byron. He has versified the lake in the finest Byronic manner, and I have seen its color, of a bright day, as beautiful, as unreal, as romantic as the most classical passages of "Childe Harold." Its shores have not yet lost the echo of three other eminent names—those of Voltaire, of Gibbon, and of Madame de Staël. These great writers, however, were all such sturdy non-conductors of the modern tendency of landscape to make its way into literature, that the tourist hardly feels himself indebted to their works for a deeper relish of the lake—though, indeed, they have bequeathed him the opportunity for a charming threefold pil-grimage. About Ferney and Coppet I might say a dozen things which the want of space forbids. As for the author of that great chronicle which never is but always to be read, you may take your coffee of a morning in the little garden in which he wrote *finis* to his immortal work—and if the coffee is good enough to administer a fillip to your fancy, perhaps you may yet hear the faint reverberation among the trees of the long, long breath with which he must have laid down his pen. It is, to my taste, quite the reverse of a profanation to commemorate a classic site by a good inn; and the excellent Hôtel Gibbon at Lausanne, ministering to that larger percep-tion which is almost identical with the aftertaste of a good *cuisine*, may fairly pretend to propagate the exemplary force of a great human effort. There is a charming Hôtel Byron at Villeneuve, the eastern end of the lake, of which I have re-tained a kindlier memory than of any of my Swiss resting-places. It has about it a kind of mellow gentility which is equally rare and delightful, and which perhaps rests partly on the fact that—owing, I suppose, to the absence just there-abouts of what is technically termed a "feature"—it is gener-ally just thinly enough populated to make you wonder how it can pay, and whether the landlord is not possibly entertaining you at a sacrifice. It has none of that look of heated prosperity which has come of late years to intermingle so sordid an element with the pure grandeur of Swiss scenery.

The crowd in Switzerland demands a chapter by itself, and when I pause in the anxious struggle for bed and board to take its prodigious measure—and, in especial, to comprehend its huge main factor, the terrible German element—mountains and men seem to resolve themselves into a single monstrous mass, darkening the clear heaven of rest and leisure. Crossing lately the lovely Scheideck pass, from Grindelwald to Meyringen, I needed to remember well that this is the great thoroughfare of Swiss travel, and that I might elsewhere find some lurking fragment of landscape without figures—or with fewer—not to be dismayed by its really grotesque appearance. It is hardly an exaggeration to say that the road was black with wayfarers. They darkened the slopes like the serried pine forests, they dotted the crags and fretted the sky-line like far-browsing goats, and their great collective hum rose up to heaven like the uproar of a dozen torrents. More recently, I strolled down from Andermatt, on the St. Gotthard, to look at that masterpiece of sternly romantic landscape, the Devil's Bridge. Huge walls of black granite inclose the scene, the road spans a tremendous yellow cataract which flings an icy mist all abroad, and a savage melancholy, in fine, marks the spot for her own. But half a dozen carriages, jingling cheerily up the ascent, had done their best to dispossess her. The parapet of the bridge was adorned with as many gazers as that of the Pont-Neuf when one of its classic anglers has proclaimed a bite, and I was obliged to confess that I had missed the full force of a sensation. If the reader's sympathies are touched by my discomfiture, I may remind him that though, as a fastidious few, we laugh at Mr. Cook, the great *entrepreneur* of travel, with his coupons and his caravans of "personally-conducted" sight-seers, we have all pretty well come to belong to his party in one way or another. We complain of a hackneyed and cocknefied Europe; but wherever, in desperate quest of the untrodden, we carry our much-labelled luggage, our bad French, our demand for a sitz-bath and pale ale, we rub off the primal bloom of local color and establish a precedent for unlimited intrusion. I have even fancied that it is a

sadly ineffectual pride that prevents us from buying one of
Mr. Cook's little bundles of tickets, and saving our percent-
age, whatever it is, of money and trouble; for I am sure that
the poor bewildered and superannuated genius of the old
Grand Tour as it was taken forty years ago, wherever she may
have buried her classic head, beyond hearing of the eternal
telegraphic click bespeaking "rooms" on mountain-tops, confounds us all alike in one sweeping reprobation.

I might, perhaps, have purchased exemption from her curse
by idling the summer away in the garden of the Hôtel Byron,
or by contenting myself with such wanderings as you may
enjoy on the neighboring hill-sides. The great beauty of detail
in this region seems to me to have been insufficiently noted.
People come hither, indeed, in swarms, but they talk more of
places that are not half so lovely; and when, returning from a
walk over the slopes above Montreux, I have ventured to hint
at a few of the fine things I have seen, I have been treated as if
I were jealous, forsooth, of a projected tour to Chamouny.
These slopes climb the great hills in almost park-like stretches
of verdure, studded with generous trees, among which the
walnut abounds, and into which, as you look down, the lake
seems to fling up a blue reflection. This reflection, by contrast, turns their green leaves to yellow. Here you may wander through wood and dell, by stream and meadow—streams
that narrow as they wind ever upward, and meadows often so
steep that the mowers, as they swing their scythes over them,
remind you of insects on a wall brandishing long antennæ—
and range through every possible phase of sweet sub-Alpine
scenery. Nowhere, I imagine, can you better taste the charm,
as distinguished from the grandeur, of Swiss landscape; and
as in Switzerland the grandeur and the charm are constantly
interfused and harmonized, you have only to ramble far
enough and high enough to get a hint of real mountain sternness—to overtake the topmost edge of the woods and
emerge upon the cool, sunny places where the stillness is broken only by cattle-bells and the plash of streams, and the
snow-patches, in the darker nooks, linger till midsummer. If
this does not satisfy you, you may do a little mild mountain-
eering by climbing the Rochers de Naye or the Dent de Ja-
man—a miniature Matterhorn. But the most profitable paths,

to my taste, are certain broad-flagged, grass-grown footways, which lead you through densely fruited orchards to villages of a charming quaintness, nestling often in so close a verdure that from the road by the lake you hardly suspect them. The picturesqueness of Vaudois village life ought surely to have produced more sketchers and lyrists. The bit of country between Montreux and Vevey, though disfigured with an ugly fringe of vineyards near the lake, is a perfect nest of these fantastic hamlets. The houses are, for the most part, a delightfully irregular combination of the chalet and the rustic *maison bourgeoise*; and— with their rugged stony foundations, pierced by a dusky stable-arch and topped by a random superstructure of balconies, outer stairways, and gables, weather-browned beams and sun-cracked stucco, their steep red roofs and knob-crowned turrets, their little cobble-paved courts, animated by the great stone fountain and its eternal plash—they are at once so pleasantly grotesque and yet so sturdily well-conditioned, that their aspect seems a sort of influence from the blue glitter of the lake as it plays through the trees in a genial violation of probability. The little village of Veytaux, above Chillon, where it lurks unperceived among its foliage, is rich in this Vaudois character. The little grassy main street of the village enters and passes bodily through a house—converting it into a vast dim, creaking, homely archway—with an audacity, a frank self-abandonment to local color, which is one of the finest strokes of the sort I ever encountered. And yet three English sisters whom I used to meet thereabouts had preferred one morning to station themselves at the parapet of the road by the lake, and, spreading their sketch-books there, to expend their precious little tablets of Winsor & Newton on those too, too familiar walls and towers where Byron's Bonivard languished. Even as I passed, the railway train whizzed by beneath their noses, and the *genius loci* seemed to flee howling in the shriek of its signal. Temple Bar itself witnesses a scarcely busier coming and going than, in these days, those hoary portals of Chillon. My own imagination, on experiment, proved too poor an alchemist, and such enjoyment as I got of the castle was mainly my distant daily view of it from the garden of the Hôtel Byron—a little many-pinnacled white promontory, shining against the blue lake.

When I went, Bädeker in hand, to "do" the place, I found a huge concourse of visitors awaiting the reflux of an earlier wave. "Let us at least wait till there is no one else," I said to my companion. She smiled in compassion of my naïveté, "*There is never no one else,*" she answered. "We must treat it as a crush or leave it alone."

Any truly graceful picturesqueness here is the more carefully to be noted that the graceful in Switzerland—especially in the German cantons—is a very rare commodity, and that everything that is not rigorously a mountain or a valley is distinctly tainted with ugliness. The Swiss have, apparently, an insensibility to comeliness or purity of form—a partiality to the clumsy, coarse, and prosaic, which one might almost interpret as a calculated offset to their great treasure of natural beauty, or at least as an instinctive protest of the national genius for frugality. Monte Rosa and the Jungfrau fill their pockets; why should they give double measure when single will serve? Even so solidly picturesque a town as Berne—a town full of massive Teutonic quaintness and sturdy individuality of features—nowhere by a single happy accident of architecture even grazes the line of beauty. The place is so full of entertaining detail that the fancy warms to it, and you good-naturedly pronounce it charming. But when the sense of novelty subsides, and you notice the prosaic scoop of its arcades, the wanton angularity of its grotesque, umbrella-shaped roofs, the general plebeian stride and straddle of its architecture, you half take back your kindness, and declare that nature in Switzerland might surely afford to be a trifle less jealous of art. But wherever the German tone of things prevails, a certain rich and delectable homeliness goes with it, and I have of Berne this pleasant recollection: the vision of a long main street, looking dark, somehow, in spite of its breadth, and bordered with houses supported on deep arcades, whereof the short, thick pillars resemble queerly a succession of bandy legs, and overshaded by high-piled pagoda roofs. The dusky arcades are lined with duskier shops and bustling with traffic; the windows of the houses are open and filled with charming flowers. They are invariably adorned, furthermore, with a bright red window-cushion, which in its turn sustains a fair Bernese—a Bernese fair enough, at least, to complete the not especially delicate harmony of the turkey-red cushion and the vividly blooming plants. These deep color-spots, scattered along the gray stretch of the houses, help to make the scene a picture; yet if it remains, somehow, at once so pleasant and so plain, you may almost find the explanation in the row of ancient fountains along the middle of the street—the peculiar glory of Berne—each a great stone basin with a pillar rising from the centre and supporting a sculptured figure more or less heraldic and legendary. This richly-wrought chain of fountains is a precious civic possession, and has an admirably picturesque effect; but each of the images which presides at these sounding springs—sources of sylvan music in the ancient street—appears, when you examine it, a monster of awkwardness and ugliness.

I ought to add that I write these lines in a place so charming that it seems pure perversity to remember here anything but the perfect beauty of Switzerland. From my window I look straight through the gray-blue portals of the Via Mala. Gray-blue they are with an element of melancholy red—like the rust on an ancient sword; and they rise in magnificent rocky crags on either side of this old-time evil way, in which the waning afternoon is deepening the shadows against a splendid background of sheer gray rock, muffled here and there in clinging acres of pine-forest. The carriage-road winds into it with an air of solemnity which suggests some almost metaphysical simile—the advance of a simple, credulous reader, say, into some darksome romance. If you think me fantastic, come and feel the influence of this lovely little town of Thusis. I may well be fantastic, however, for I have fresh in my memory a journey in which the fancy finds as good an account as in any you may treat it to in Switzerland—a long two-days' drive through the western Grisons and the beautiful valley of the Vorder-Rhein. The scenery is, perhaps, less characteristically Swiss than that of many other regions, but it can hardly fail to deepen your admiration for a country which is able so liberally to overheap the measure of great impressions. It is a landscape rather of ruin-crowned cliff and crag, than of more or less virginal snow-peaks; but in its own gentler fashion it is as vast and bold and free as the Oberland. Coming down from the Oberalp, which divides this valley from that of

the St. Gotthard, we entered a wondrous vista of graduated blue distances, along which the interlapping mountain-spurs grew to seem like the pillars—if one can imagine reclining pillars—of a mighty avenue. The landscape had more than picturesque accidents; it had a great artistic intention. I had never seen in nature such a wealth of blue—deep and rich in the large foreground, and splendidly contrasted with the slopes of ripening grain, blocked out without hedge or fence in yellow parallelograms, and playing thence through shades of color which were clear even in the vague distances. Foreground and distance here have alike a strong historic tinge. The little towns which yet subsist as almost formless agglomerations of rugged stone were members of the great Gray League of resistance to the baronial brigands whose crumbling towers and keeps still make the mountain-sides romantic. These little towns, Ilanz in especial, and Dissentis, overstared by the great blank façade of its useless monastery, are hardly more than rather putrid masses of mouldy masonry; but with their desolate air of having been and ceased to be, their rugged solidity of structure, their low black archways, surmounted with stiffly hewn armorial shields, their lingering treasures in window-screen and gate of fantastically wrought-iron, they are among the things which make the sentimental tourist lean forth eagerly from his carriage with an impulse which may be called the prevision of retrospect.
1872.

Homburg Reformed

I HAVE been finding Homburg a very pleasant place, but I have been half ashamed to confess it. People assure me on all sides that its glory is sadly dimmed, and that it can be rightly enjoyed only to the music of roulette and of clinking napoleons. It is known by this time, I suppose, even in those virtuously disinterested communities where these lines may circulate, that the day of roulette in these regions is over, and that in the matter of rouge-et-noir united Germany has taken a new departure. The last unhallowed gains at the green tables were pocketed last summer, and the last hard losses, doubtless, as imperturbably endured as if good-natured chance had still a career to run. Chance, I believe, at Homburg was not amazingly good-natured, and kept her choicest favors for the bank; but now that the reign of virtue has begun, I have no doubt there are plenty of irregular characters who think that she was much the more amiable creature of the two. What provision has been made for this adventurous multitude I am at loss to conceive, and how life strikes people now for whom, any time these twenty years, it has been concentrated in the shifting victory of red or black. Some of them have taken to better courses, I suppose; some of them, doubtless, to worse; but I have a notion that many of them have begun to wear away the dull remainder of existence in a kind of melancholy, ghostly hovering round the deserted Kursaals. I have seen many of these blighted survivors sitting about under the trees in the Kurgarten, with the old habit of imperturbability still in their blank, fixed faces—neat, elderly gentlemen, elderly ladies not especially venerable, whose natural attitude seems to be to sit with their elbows on the table and their eyes on the game. They have all, of course, a pack of cards in their pockets, and their only consolation must be to play "patience" forevermore. When I remember, indeed, that I am in legendary Germany, I find it easy to believe that in these mild summer nights, when the stupid people who get up at six o'clock to drink the waters are safely in bed, they

assemble in some far-away corner of the park and make a
green table of the moonlit grass. Twice a week the old
gaming-rooms at the Kursaal are thrown open, the chandeliers are lighted, and people go and stare at the painting and
gilding. There is an immense deal of it, all in the elaborate
rococo style in which French decorators of late years have
become so proficient, and which makes an apartment look
half like a throne-room and half like a café; but when you
have walked about and looked at the undressed nymphs on
the ceilings and the listless crowd in the great mirrors, you
have nothing to do but to walk out again. The clever sump-
tuosity of the rooms makes virtue look rather foolish and
dingy, and classes the famous M. Blanc, in the regard of
pleasure-loving people, with the late Emperor of the French
and other potentates more sinned against than sinning—martyred benefactors to that large portion of the human race who
would fain consider the whole world as a watering-place. It is
certainly hard to see what thrifty use the old gaming-rooms
can be put to; they must stand there always in their gorgeous emptiness, like the painted tomb-chambers of Eastern
monarchs.

There was certainly fair entertainment in watching the
play—and in playing, according to circumstances; but even in
the old days I think I should have got my chief pleasure at the
Kursaal in a spectacle which has survived the fall of M. Blanc.
As you pass in the front door, you look straight across the
breadth of the building through another great door which
opens on the gardens. The Kursaal stands on an elevation,
and the ground plunges away behind it with a great stretch,
which spreads itself in a charming park. Beyond the park it
rises again into the gentle slopes of the Taunus mountains,
and makes a high wooded horizon. This picture of the green
hollow and the blue ridge greets you as you come in, framed
by the opposite doorway, and I have sometimes wondered
whether in the gaming days an occasional novice with a tender conscience, on his way to the tables, may not have seemed
to see in it the pleading face of that mild economist, mother
Nature herself. It is, doubtless, thinking too fancifully of the
human mind to believe that a youth with a napoleon to stake,
and the consciousness of no more rigid maternal presence

than this, should especially heed the suggestion that it would be better far to take a walk in the woods. The truth is, I imagine, that nature has no absolute voice, and that she speaks to us very much according to our moods. The view from the terrace at the Kursaal has often had confusion pronounced upon it by players with empty pockets, and has been sentimentally enjoyed by players with a run of luck. We have the advantage now, at least, of finding it always the same, and always extremely pretty. Homburg, indeed, is altogether a very pretty place, and its prettiness is of that pleasing sort which steals gradually on the attention. It is one of nature's own watering-places, and has no need, like so many of the audacious sisterhood, to bully you by force of fashion into thinking it tolerable.

Your half-hour's run from Frankfort across a great sunny expanse of cornfields and crab-apple trees is indeed not particularly charming; but the sight of the town as you approach it, with its deep-red roofs rising out of thick shade at the base of its blue hills, is a pledge of salubrious repose. Homburg stands on a gentle spur of the highest of these hills, and one of its prettiest features is your seeing the line of level plain across the foot of its long sloping main street, and the line of wooded mountain across the top. The main street, which is almost all of Homburg proper, has the look of busy idleness which belongs to watering-places. There are people strolling along and looking into the shop-windows, who seem to be on the point of buying something for the sake of something to do. The shops deal chiefly in the lighter luxuries, and the young ladies who wait in them wear a great many ribbons and a great deal of hair. All the houses take lodgers, and every second one is an hotel, and every now and then you hear them chanting defiance at each other to the sound of the dinner-bell. In the middle of the street is the long red stuccoed façade of the Kursaal—the beating heart of the Homburg world, as one might have called it formerly. This heart beats much slower now, but whatever social entertainment you may still find at Homburg you must look for there. People assemble there in very goodly crowds, if only to talk about the dreadful dulness, and to commiserate each other for not having been in the place before. The Kursaal is kept up by a

tax, promptly levied on all arriving strangers, and it seems to
be prosperously enough maintained. It gives you a reading-
room where you may go and practise indifference as you see
a sturdy Briton settling down heavily over your coveted
"Times," just as you might of old when you saw the croupier
raking in your stakes; music by a very fair band twice a day; a
theatre, a café, a restaurant and a table-d'hôte, and a garden
illuminated every three or four evenings in the Vauxhall manner. People differ very much as to the satisfaction they take
in sitting about under flaring gas-lamps and watching other
people march up and down and pass and repass them by the
hour. The pastime, pushed to extremes, tends, to my own
thinking, to breed misanthropy—or an extra relish at least for
a good book in one's own room and the path through the
woods where one is least likely to meet any one. But if you
use the Kursaal sparingly, and reserve it for an hour or two in
the evening, it is certainly amusing enough.

I should be very sorry to underestimate the entertainment
to be found in observing the comings and goings of a multi-
farious European crowd, or the number of suggestions and
conclusions which, with a desultory logic of its own, the process contributes to one's philosophy of life. Every one who
prefers to sit in a chair and look rather than walk up and
down and be looked at, may be assumed to possess this intellectual treasure. The observations of the "cultivated American" bear chiefly, I think, upon the great topic of national
idiosyncrasies. He is apt to have a keener sense of them than
Europeans; it matters more to his imagination that his neighbor be English, French, or German. He often seems to me to
be a creature wandering aloof, but half naturalized himself.
His neighbors are outlined, defined, imprisoned, if you will,
by their respective national moulds, pleasing or otherwise;
but his own type has not hardened yet into the old-world
bronze. Superficially, no people carry more signs and tokens
of what they are than Americans. I recognize them, as they
advance, by the whole length of the promenade. The signs,
however, are all of the negative kind, and seem to assure you,
first of all, that the individual belongs to a country in which
the social atmosphere, like the material, is extremely thin.
American women, for the most part, in compliance with an

instinct certainly not ungraceful, fill out the ideal mould with wonderful Paris dresses; but their dresses do little toward completing them, characterizing them, shelving and labelling them socially. The usual English lady, marching definitely about under the burden of the national costume, has indescribably more the air of what one may call a social factor—the air of social responsibility, of having a part to play and a battle to fight. Sometimes, when the battle has been hard, the lady's face is very grim and unlovely, and I prefer the listless, rustling personality of my countrywomen; at others, when the cause has been graceful and the victory easy, she has a robust amenity which is one of the most agreeable things in the world. But these are metaphysical depths, though in strictness they ought not to be out of the way as one sits among German pipes and beer. The smokers and drinkers are the solid element at the Kursaal—the dominant tone is the German tone. It comes home very forcibly to the sense of our observant American, and it pervades, naturally enough, all his impressions of Homburg. People have come to feel strongly within the last four years that they must take the German tone into account, and they will find nothing here to lighten the task. If you have not been used to it, if you don't particularly relish it, you doubtless deserve some sympathy; but I advise you not to shirk it, to face it frankly as a superior critic should, and to call if necessary for a pipe and beer also, and build yourself into good-humor with it. It is very agreeable, in an unfamiliar country, to collect travellers' evidence in regard to local manners and national character. You are sure to have some vague impressions to be confirmed, some ingenious theory to be illustrated, some favourite prejudice in any case to be revised and improved. Even if your opportunities for observation are of the commonest kind, you find them serving your purpose. The smallest things become significant and eloquent and demand a place in your note-book. I have learned no especial German secrets, I have penetrated into the bosom of no German families; but somehow I have received—I constantly receive—a weighty impression of Germany. It keeps me company as I walk in the woods and fields, and sits beside me—not precisely as a black care, but with an influence, as it were, which reminds one of the after-taste of those articles of diet which you eat because they are good for you and not because you like them—when at last, of an evening, I have found the end of a bench on the promenade behind the Kursaal. One's impression of Germany may or may not be agreeable, but there is very little doubt that it is what one may call highly nutritive. In detail, it would take long to say what it consists of. I think that, in general, in such matters attentive observation confirms the common fame, and that you are very likely to find a people on your travels what you found them described to be under the mysterious wood-cut in some Peter Parley task-book or play-book of your childhood. The French are a light, pleasure-loving people; ten years of the Boulevard brings no essential amendment to the phrase. The Germans are heavy and fair-haired, deep drinkers and strong thinkers; a fortnight at Homburg doesn't reverse the formula. The only thing to be said is that, as you grow older, French lightness and German weightiness become more complex ideas. A few weeks ago I left Italy in that really demoralized condition into which Italy throws those confiding spirits who give her unlimited leave to please them. Beauty, I had come to believe, was an exclusively Italian possession, the human face was not worth looking at unless redeemed by an Italian smile, nor the human voice worth listening to unless attuned to Italian vowels. A landscape was no landscape without vines festooned to fig-trees swaying in a hot wind—a mountain a hideous excrescence unless melting off into a Tuscan haze. But now that I have absolutely exchanged vines and figs for corn and cabbages, and violet Apennines for the homely plain of Frankfort, and liquids for gutturals, and the Italian smile for the German grin, I am much better contented than I could have ventured to expect. I have shifted my standard of beauty, but it still commands a glimpse of the divine idea.

There is something here, too, which pleases, suggests and satisfies. Sitting of an evening in the Kurgarten, within earshot of the music, you have an almost inspiring feeling that you never have in Italy—a feeling that the substantial influences about you are an element of the mysterious future. They are of that varied order which seems to indicate the large needs of large natures. From its pavilion among the trees ring out the notes of the loud orchestra, playing Mozart, Beethoven, and Weber—such music as no other people has composed, as no other people can play it. Round about in close groups sit the sturdy, prosperous natives, with their capacious heads, their stout necks, their deep voices, their cigars, their beer, their intelligent applause, their talk on all things—largely enjoying, and yet strongly intending. Far away in the mild starlight stretch the dusky woods whose gentle murmur, we may suppose, unfolds here and there to a fanciful German ear some prophetic legend of a still larger success and a still richer Fatherland. The success of the Fatherland one sees reflected more or less vividly in all true German faces, and the relation between the face and the success seems demonstrated by a logic so unerring as to make envy vain. It is not the German success I envy, but the powerful German temperament and the comprehensive German brain. With these advantages one needn't be restless; one can afford to give a good deal of time to sitting out under the trees over pipes and beer and discussion tinged with metaphysics. But success of course is most forcibly embodied in the soldiers and officers who now form so large a proportion of every German group. You see them at all times lounging soberly about the gardens; you look at them (I do, at least) with a great deal of impartial deference, and you find in them something which seems a sort of pre-established negation of an adversary's chances. Compared with the shabby little unripe conscripts of France and Italy, they are indeed a solid, brilliant phalanx. They are generally of excellent stature, and they have faces in which the look of education has not spoiled the look of good-natured simplicity. They are all equipped in brandnew uniforms, and in these warm days they stroll about in spotless white trousers. Many of them wear their fine fair beards, and they all look like perfect soldiers and excellent fellows. It doesn't do, of course, for an officer to seem too much a good fellow, and the young captains and adjutants who ornament the Kurgarten of an evening seldom err in this direction. But they are business-like warriors to a man, and in their dark blue uniforms and crimson facings, with their swords depending from their unbelted waists through a hole in their plain surtouts, they seem to suggest that war is somehow a better economy than peace.

But with all this, I am giving you Hamlet with Hamlet himself omitted. Though the gaming is stopped, the wells have not dried up, and people still drink them, and find them very good. They are indeed a very palatable dose, and "medical advice" at Homburg flatters one's egotism so unblushingly as rather to try the faith of people addicted to the old-fashioned confusion between the beneficial and the disagreeable. You have indeed to get up at half past six o'clock—but of a fine summer morning this is no great hardship—and you are rewarded on your arrival at the spring by triumphant strains of music. There is an orchestra perched hard by, which plays operatic selections while you pace the shady walks and wait for your second glass. All the Homburg world is there; it is the fashionable hour; and at first I paid the antique prejudice just mentioned the tribute of thinking it was all too frivolous to be salutary. There are half a dozen springs, scattered through the charming wooded park, where you may find innumerable shady strolls and rustic benches in bosky nooks, where it is pleasant to lounge with a good light book. In the afternoon I drink at a spring with whose luxurious prettiness I still find it hard to associate a doctor's prescription. It reminds me of a back-scene at the theatre, and I feel as if I were drinking some fictitious draught prepared by the property-man; or rather, being a little white temple rising on slim columns among still green shades, it reminds me of some spot in the antique world where the goddess Hygeia was worshipped by thirsty pilgrims; and I am disappointed to find that the respectable young woman who dips my glass is not a ministering nymph in a tunic and sandals. Beyond this valley of healing waters lie the great woods of fir and birch and beech and oak which cover the soft slopes of the Taunus. They are full of pleasant paths and of the frequent benches which testify to the German love of sitting in the open air. I don't know why it is—because, perhaps, we have all read so many Teutonic legends and ballads—but it seems natural in Germany to be in a wood. One need have no very rare culture, indeed, to find a vague old-friendliness in every feature of the landscape. The villages with their peaked roofs, covered with red scalloped shingles, and the brown beams making figures on the plastered cottage walls, the grape-vine on the wall, the swallows in the eaves, the Hausfrau, sickle in hand, with her yellow hair in a top-knot and her short blue skirt showing her black stockings—what is it all but a background to one of Richter's charming woodcuts? I never see a flock of geese on the roadside, and a little tow-pated maiden driving them with a forked switch, without thinking of Grimm's household tales. I look around for the old crone who is to come and inform her she is a king's daughter. I see nothing but the white Kaiserliche Deutsche sign-post, telling one that this is such and such a district of the Landwehr. But with such easy magic as this I am perhaps right in not especially regretting that the late enchantress of the Kursaal should have been handed over to the police.

Darmstadt

S PENDING the summer just past at Homburg, I have been conscious of a sort of gentle chronic irritation of a natural sympathy with the whole race of suppressed, diminished and mutilated sovereigns. This was fostered by my frequent visits to the great dispeopled Schloss, about whose huge and awkward bulk the red roofs of the little town, as seen from a distance, cluster with an air of feudal allegiance, and which stands there as a respectable makeweight to the hardly scantier mass of the florid, fresh-colored Kursaal. It was formerly the appointed residence of the Landgrafs of the very diminutive state of Hesse-Homburg, the compact circumference of which these modest potentates might have the satisfaction of viewing, any fine morning, without a telescope, from their dressing-room windows. It is something of course to be monarch of a realm which slopes away with the slope of the globe into climates which it requires an effort to believe in and are part of the regular stock of geography; but perhaps we are apt to underestimate the peculiar complacency of a sovereign to whose possessions the blue horizon makes a liberal margin, and shows him his cherished inheritance visibly safe and sound, unclipped, unmenaced, shining like a jewel on its velvet cushion. This modest pleasure the Landgrafs of Hesse-Homburg must have enjoyed in perfection; the chronicle of their state-progresses should be put upon the same shelf as Xavier de Maistre's "Voyage autour de ma Chambre." Though small, however, this rounded particle of sovereignty was still visible to the naked eye of diplomacy, and Herr von Bismarck, in 1866, swallowed it as smoothly as a gentleman following a tonic régime disposes of his homœopathic pellet. It had been merged shortly before in the neighboring empire of Hesse-Darmstadt, but promptly after Sadowa it was "ceded" to Prussia. Whoever is the loser, it has not been a certain lounging American on hot afternoons. The gates of the Schloss are now wide open, and the great garden is public property, and much resorted to by old gentlemen who dust off the benches with bandannas before sitting down, and by sheepish soldiers with affectionate sweethearts. Picturesquely, the palace is all it should be—very huge, very bare, very ugly, with great clean courts, in which round-barrelled Mecklenburg coach-horses must often have stood waiting for their lord and master to rise from table. The gateways are adorned with hideous sculptures of about 1650, representing wigged warriors on corpulent chargers, cork-screw pilasters, and scroll-work like the "flourishes" of a country writing-master—the whole glazed over with brilliant red paint. In the middle of the larger court stands an immense isolated round tower, painted white, and seen from all the country about. The gardens have very few flowers, and the sound of the rake nowadays is seldom heard on the gravel; but there are plenty of fine trees—some really stupendous poplars, untrimmed and spreading abroad like oaks, chestnuts which would make a figure in Italy, beeches which would be called "rather good" in England; plenty of nooks and bowers and densely woven arcades, triumphs of old-fashioned gardenry; and a large dull-bosomed pond into which the unadorned castle-walls peep from above the trees. Such as it is, it is a place a small prince had rather keep than lose; and as I sat under the beeches—remembering that I was in the fatherland of ghost-stories—I used to fancy the warm twilight was pervaded by a thin spectral influence from this slender stream of empire, and that I could hear vague supernatural *Achs!* of regret among the bushes, and see the glimmer of broad-faced phantoms at the windows. One very hot Sunday the Emperor came, passed up the main street under several yards of red and white calico, and spent a couple of days at the Schloss. I don't know whether he saw any reproachful ghosts there, but he found, I believe, a rather scanty flesh-and-blood welcome in the town. The burgomasters measured off the proper number of festoons, and the innkeepers hung out their flags, but the townsfolk, who know their new master chiefly as the grim old wizard who has dried up the golden stream which used to flow so bounteously at the Kursaal, took an outing indeed, like good Germans, and stared sturdily at the show, but paid nothing for it in the way of hurrahs. The Emperor, meanwhile, rattled up and down the street in his light barouche, wearing under his white eyebrows and mustache the physiognomy of a personage quite competent to dispense with the approbation of ghosts and shopkeepers. "Homburg may have ceased to be Hessian, but evidently it is not yet Prussian," I said to a friend; and he hereupon reminded me that I was within a short distance of a more eloquent memento of the energy of Bismarck, and that I had better come over and take a look at the blighted Duchy of Darmstadt. I have followed his advice, and have been strolling about in quest of impressions. It is for the reader to say whether my impressions were worth a journey of an hour and a half.

I confess, to begin with, that they form no very terrible tale—that I saw none of the "prominent citizens" confined in chains, and no particular symptoms of the ravages of a brutal soldiery. Indeed, as you walk into the town through the grand, dull, silent street which leads from the railway station, you seem to perceive that the *genius loci* has never been frighted, like Othello's Cyprus, from its propriety. You behold this comfortable spirit embodied in heroic bronze on the top of a huge red sandstone column, in the shape of the Grand-Duke Louis the First, who, though a very small potentate, surveys posterity from a most prodigious altitude. He was a father to his people, and some fifty years ago he created the *beaux quartiers* of Darmstadt, out of the midst of which his effigy rises, looking down upon the Trafalgar Square, the Place de la Concorde, of the locality. Behind him the fine, dull street pursues its course and pauses in front of the florid façade of the Schloss. This entrance into Darmstadt responds exactly to the fanciful tourist's preconceptions, and as soon as I looked up the melancholy vista, my imagination fell to rubbing its hands and to whispering that this indeed was the ghost of a little German court-city—a mouldering Modena or Ferrara of the North. I have never known a little court-city, having, by ill-luck, come into the world a day too late; but I like to think of them, to visit them in these blank early years of their long historic sleep, and to try and guess what they must be dreaming of. They seem to murmur, as they snore everlastingly, of a very snug little social system—of gossiping whist-parties in wainscoted grand-ducal parlors, of susceptible Aulic Councillors and æsthetic canonesses, of emblazoned commanders-in-chief of five hundred warriors in periwigs, of blond young hussars, all gold-lace and billet-doux, of a miniature world of precedents, jealousies, intrigues, ceremonies, superstitions—an oppressively dull world, doubtless, to your fanciful tourist if he had been condemned to spend a month in it. But Darmstadt, obviously, was not dull to its own sense in the days before Bismarck, and doubtless the pith of its complaint of this terrible man is that he has made it so. All around Duke Louis's huge red pedestal rises a series of sober-faced palaces for the transaction of the affairs of this little empire. Before each of them is a striped red-and-white sentry-box, with a soldier in a spiked helmet mounting guard. These public offices all look highly respectable, but they have an air of sepulchral stillness. Here and there, doubtless, in their echoing chambers, is to be heard the scratching of the bureaucratic quill; but I imagine that neither the home nor the foreign affairs of Hesse-Darmstadt require nowadays an army of functionaries, and that if some grizzled old clerk were to give you an account of his avocations, they would bear a family likeness to those of Charles Lamb at the India House. There are half a dozen droshkies drawn up at the base of the monument, with the drivers sitting in the sun and wondering sleepily whether any one of the three persons in sight, up and down the street, will be likely to want a carriage. They wake up as I approach and look at me very hard; but they are phlegmatic German coachmen, and they neither hail me with persuasive cries nor project their vehicles forcibly upon me, as would certainly be the case at Modena or Ferrara. But I pass along and ascend the street, and find something that is really very Ferrarese. The grand-ducal Schloss rises in an immense mass out of a great crooked square, which has a very pretty likeness to an Italian piazza. Some of the houses have Gothic gables, and these have thrifty shop-fronts and a general air of paint and varnish; but there is shabbiness enough, and sun, and space, and bad smells, and old women under colored umbrellas selling cabbages and plums, and several persons loafing in a professional manner, and, in the midst of it all, the great moated palace, with soldiers hanging over the parapets of the little bridges, and the inner courts used as a public thoroughfare. On one side, behind the shabby Gothic gables, is

huddled that elderly Darmstadt to which Duke Louis affixed
the modern mask of which his own effigy is the most eminent
feature. A mask of some sort old Darmstadt most certainly
needs, and it were well if it might have been one of those
glass covers which in Germany are deposited over too savory
dishes. The little crooked, gabled streets presume quite too
audaciously on uncleanness being an element of the picturesque. The gutters stroll along with their hands in their pockets, as it were, and pause in great pools before crossings and
dark archways to embrace their tributary streams, till the
odorous murmur of their confluence quite smothers the voice
of legend. There is dirtiness and dirtiness. Sometimes, picturesquely, it is very much to the point; but the American traveller in Germany will generally prefer not to enjoy local color
in this particular form, for it invariably reminds him of the
most sordid, the most squalid prose he knows—the corner-
groceries and the region of the docks in the city of New York.

The Schloss, however, is characteristic without abatement,
and it seems to me a great pity there should not be some such
monumental edifice in the middle of every town, to personify
the municipal soul, as it were, to itself. If it can be beautiful,
so much the better; but the Schloss at Darmstadt is ugly
enough, and yet—to the eye—it amply serves its purpose.
The two façades toward the square date from the middle of
the last century, and are characteristically dreary and solemn,
but they hide a great rambling structure of a quainter time:
irregular courts, archways boring away into darkness, a queer
great yellow bell-tower dating from the sixteenth century, a
pile of multitudinous windows, roofs and chimneys. Seen
from the adjacent park, all this masses itself up into the semblance of a fantastic citadel. One rarely finds a citadel with a
handsomer moat. The moat at Darmstadt yawns down out of
the market-place into a deep verdurous gulf, with sloping
banks of turf, on which tame shrubs are planted—mingled
with the wild ones lodged in the stout foundations. It forms,
indeed, below the level of the street, a charming little belt of
grass and flowers. The Schloss possesses, moreover, as it
properly should, a gallery of pictures, to which I proceeded to
seek admission. I reflected, on my way, that it is of the first
importance, picturesquely speaking, that the big building

which, as I just intimated, should resume to its own sense the civic individuality of every substantial town, should always have a company of soldiers lounging under its portal and grouped about the guard-room. A green moat, a great archway, a guard-room opening out of its shadow, a couple of pacing sentinels, a group of loafing musketeers, a glimpse on one side of a sunny market-place, on the other of a dusky court—combine the objects as you may, they make a picture; they seem for the moment, as you pass, and pause, and glance, to transport you into legend. Of course the straddling men-at-arms who helped to render me this service were wearers of the spiked helmet. The Grand-Duke of Hesse-Darmstadt still occupies the Schloss, and enjoys a nominal authority. I believe that he holds it, for special reasons, on rather easy terms, but I do not envy the emotions of the grand-ducal breast when he sees a row of these peculiarly uncompromising little headpieces bristling and twinkling under his windows. It can hardly be balm to his resentment to know that they sometimes conceal the flaxen pates of his own hereditary Hessians. The spiked helmets, of course, salute rigorously when this very limited monarch passes in and out; but I sometimes think it fortunate, under these circumstances, that the average German countenance has not a turn for ironical expression. The Duke, indeed, in susceptible moods, might take an airing in his own palace without driving abroad at all. There is apparently no end to its corridors and staircases, and I found it a long journey to the picture-gallery. I spent half an hour, to begin with, in the library, waiting till the custodian was at liberty to attend to me. The half-hour, however, was not lost, as I was entertained by a very polite librarian, with a green shade over his eyes, and as I filled my lungs, moreover, with what I was in the humour to call the atmosphere of German science. It was a very warm day, but the windows were tight-closed, in the manner of the country, and had been closed, presumably, since the days of Louis the First. The air was as dry as iron filings; it smelt of old bindings, of the insides of old books; it tasted of dust and snuff. Here and there a Herr Professor, walled in with circumjacent authorities, was burying his nose in a folio; the gray light seemed to add a coating of dust to the tiers of long brown shelves. I came away with a headache, and that exalted esteem for the German brain, as a mere working organ, which invariably ensues upon my observation of the physical conditions of German life. I don't know that I received any very distinct impression from the picture-gallery beyond that of there being such and such a number of acres more of mouldering brush-work in the world. It was a good deal like the library, terribly close, and lined for room after room (it is a long series) with tiers of dusky brown canvases, on which the light of the unwashed windows seemed to turn sallow and joyless. There are a great many fine names on the frames, but they rarely correspond to anything very fine within them, though, indeed, there are several specimens of the early German school which are quite welcome (to my mind) to their assumed "originality." Early or late, German art rarely seems to me a happy adventure. Two or three of the rooms were filled with large examples of the modern German landscape school, before which I lingered, but not for the pleasure of it. I was reflecting that the burden of French philosophy just now is the dogma that the Germans are a race of *faux bonshommes*; that their transcendental æsthetics are a mere kicking up of dust to cover their picking and stealing; and that their frank-souled naïveté is no better than a sharper's "alias." I do not pretend to weigh the charge in a general sense, but I certainly think that a good French patriot, in my place, would have cried out that he had caught the hypocrites in the act. These blooming views of Switzerland and Italy seemed to me the most dishonest things in the world, and I was puzzled to understand how so very innocent an affair as a landscape in oils could be made such a vehicle of offence. These were extremely clever; the art of shuffling away trouble has rarely been brought to greater perfection. It is evidently an elaborate system; there is a school; the pictures were all from different hands, and the precious recipe had been passed round the circle.

But why should I talk of bad pictures, since I brought away from Darmstadt the memory of one of the best in the world? It forms the sole art-treasure of the place, and I duly went in quest of it; but I kept it in reserve, as one keeps the best things, and meanwhile I strolled in the Herrengarten. The fondness of Germans for a garden, wherever a garden can be conceived, is one of their most amiable characteristics, and I should be curious to know how large a section of the total soil of the fatherland is laid out in rusty lawns and gravel-paths, and adorned with beechen groves and bowers. The garden-hours of one's life, as I may say, are not the least agreeable, and there are more garden-hours in German lives than in most others. But I shall not describe my garden-hours at Darmstadt. Part of them was spent in walking around the theatre, which stands close beside the Schloss, with its face upon the square and its back among the lawns and bowers. The theatre, in the little court-city of my regrets, is quite an affair of state, and the manager second only in importance to the prime-minister or the commander-in-chief. Or rather the Grand-Duke is manager himself, and the leading actress, as a matter of course, his morganatic wife. The present Grand-Duke of Hesse-Darmstadt, I believe, is a zealous patron of the drama, and maintains a troupe of comedians, who doubtless do much to temper the dulness of his capital. The present theatre is simply a picturesque ruin, having been lately burned down, for all the world like an American opera-house. But the actors have found a provisional refuge, and I have just been presented with the programme of the opening night of the winter season. I saw the rest of Darmstadt as I took my way to the palace of Prince Karl. It was a very quiet pilgrim-age, and I perhaps met three people in the long, dull, proper street through which it led me. One of them was a sentinel with a spiked helmet marching before the snug little palace of the Prince Louis—the gentleman who awhile ago married the Princess Alice of England. Another was a school-boy in spectacles, nursing a green bag full of Greek roots, I suppose, of whom I asked my way; and the third was the sturdy little musketeer who was trying to impart a *reflet* of authority to the neat little white house occupied by the Prince Karl. But this frowning soldier is no proper symbol of the kindly cus-tom of the house. I was admitted unconditionally, ushered into the little drawing-room, and allowed half an hour's un-disturbed contemplation of the beautiful Holbein—the fa-mous picture of the Meyer family. The reader interested in such matters may remember the discussion carried on two years since, at the time of the general exhibition of the younger Holbein's works in Dresden, as to the respective merits—and I believe the presumptive priority in date—of this Darmstadt picture and the presentation of the same theme which adorns the Dresden Gallery. I forget how the question was settled—whether, indeed, it was settled at all, and I have never seen the Dresden picture; but it seems to me that if I were to choose a Holbein, this one would content me. It represents a sort of plain-lovely Virgin holding her child, crowned with a kind of gorgeous episcopal crown, and worshipped by six kneeling figures—the worthy Goodman Meyer, his wife and their progeniture. It is a wonderfully solid work, and so full of wholesome human substance that I should think its owner could go about his daily doings the better—eat and drink and sleep and perform the various functions of life more largely and smoothly—for having it constantly before his eyes. I was not disappointed, and I may now confess that my errand at Darmstadt had been much more to see the "Holbeinische Gemälde" than to examine the trail of the serpent—the footprints of Bismarck.

The Splügen

I.

I AM puzzled to say just when and where my journey began; but I think I may date it from my discovery that the heat was penetrating into the interior of Milan Cathedral. Then the case seemed serious. The Italian summer was maturing, with inexorable consistency. Florence had become intolerable; the arcades of Bologna were a defence against the sun, but not against the deadly heaviness of the air; Ravenna was plunged in its summer siesta—the sultry sleep from which it never wakes; and Milan lay basking on the Lombard plain, distributing reflected heat from every glittering pinnacle of its famous church. It seemed, for a conscientious traveller, the lowest depth of demoralization to sit all day in an American rocking-chair in the court of a hotel, watching the comings and goings of English families, under the conduct of those English papas who, in sunny climes, as a tribute to an un-wonted and possibly perilous sensation, wear their hats sheeted with white draperies so voluminous that they look as if they had chosen this method of carrying the family linen to the wash. But it was too hot to wander and explore; too many scorching pavements intervened between the Corso and the Brera. So I adjourned daily for a couple of hours to the cathedral, and found what I supposed to be an immitigable coolness in its gorgeous, dusky vastness. The Church has al-ways been, spiritually, a refuge from the world, and its virtue in this respect was here magnificently symbolized. The world without was glaring, suffocating, insupportable; the cathedral within was all shadow and comfort and delight. It was, I sup-pose, because it was so comfortable to sit there uncovered in the cool air and breathe at one's ease that I was shortly won to the opinion that Milan Cathedral is, after all, a very noble piece of Gothic architecture. Noble within I had never exactly found it, and had indulged the innocent paradox of saying that there were a dozen scantier churches that had more real grandeur. But now it seemed to me to have grandeur enough, in all conscience, and I found an endless interest in its rich picturesqueness. It is not, like St. Peter's, and even more like the beautiful cathedral of Florence, what one may call an intellectual church; it does little toward leading one's musings away into the realm of ideas; but its splendid solidity of form, its mysterious accumulations of shadow, the purple radiance of its painted windows, and the dark magnificence of the whole precinct of the high altar and choir, make it peculiarly gratifying to the sensuous side of one's imagination. I was struck more than ever with the extraordinary breadth of the church from transept to transept. That of St. Peter's may be as great, but the immense colored windows of Milan seem to lengthen the reach of these great wings. Sitting at the base of one of the stupendous columns—as massive as they need be to sustain the great city of statues, as one may call it, on the roof—you may look for hours at a great spectacle, a spectacle which in truth reminds you very much of a huge piece of scenic mechanism. There are so many odds and ends of adornment tacked about on the pillars and dangling from the roof, so many ropes and wires playing their parts in the complex machinery and swinging from vaults and arches, so many pendent lamps and tinselled draperies catching the light here and there as they traverse the dusky upper air, that you may almost fancy that you are behind the curtain on the stage, before the various loose ends of the scenic architecture have been shuffled out of sight. I do not exactly know how to speak of an immense gilded crucifix which from time immemorial has hung high above the great altar, at a short distance beneath the roof. The melancholy fashion in which it caught the afternoon light made it glitter picturesquely against the deepening shadows of the choir, and yet seemed to bring out with tragic force its moral significance. The crucifix in Catholic churches is repeated with what seems to me trivial frequency. It would be better, surely, in the interest of reverence, to present it sparingly and only on the most impressive occasions. But something in the position of this great high-hung cross of Milan makes it peculiarly commanding, and helps it to say effectually that, in spite of the color and splendor, the perfumes and draperies, the place is dedicated to a religion founded in poverty and obscurity. I found a good deal of interest of another sort in looking at the extremely handsome Milanese women who come to the Cathedral to their devotions. If the place has a theatrical air, they certainly might serve as the characters of a romantic comedy. When I call them extremely handsome I may possibly let some of them off on easy terms, for they wear on their heads those black lace Spanish mantillas which, if they make a beautiful woman irresistibly charming, supply even the plainest with a very fair imitation of good looks. But, indeed, as a rule, the ladies of Milan are extraordinarily fair, especially to an eye accustomed to the stunted stature and meagre contours of the Tuscans; and, after much respectful observation of them in the streets, the churches, and that long glass gallery (the Palais Royal of Milan), which offers to an attentive spectator a ré-sumé of the local physiognomy, I found myself ready to de-clare that of all the feminine types I had had the felicity to contemplate, this one is, as the Italians say, the most sympa-thetic. It would take too long to tell in what the sympathy consists, and in these matters a word to the wise is sufficient. The most grateful memory one can carry away from a country one is fond of is an agreeable impression of its women, and I am free to confess that these lovely Lombards gave an edge to my relish for Italy of which in other places I had been at best but fitfully conscious. South of the Apennines, and especially at Rome and Naples, one enters the circle of Oriental tradi-tion as regards female deportment. Zuleikas and Gulnares are very captivating in Byron and Moore; but in real life even those modified imitations of them which hang in dishabille over Roman balconies or sit in toilets hardly less "advanta-geous," as the French say, in Florentine barouches, have a regrettable absence of what is called style. The lovely peni-tents of Milan, with their dusky veils and their long fans, who came rustling so far over the vast cathedral pavement to say their prayers, had style in abundance, and a style altogether their own.

My impressions at the first stage of my journey, at which they passed beyond a mood of fervid meditation on the tem-perature, were of sterner things than picturesque dévotes and painted windows. I lay on a grassy hillside, five thousand feet in the air, inhaling the Alpine atmosphere and gazing away at

the Alpine view. There can be no better place for this delicious pastime than that beautiful series of turf-covered ridges
which rise out of the chestnut woods of the Lake of Lugano
and bear the charming name of Monte Generoso. Here, on a
grassy plateau, within an hour's walk of the highest of these
carpeted pinnacles, stands an excellent mountain inn, looking
down over the dim blue plain of Lombardy and just catching
on the hazy horizon the flash of the marble walls of Milan
Cathedral. The place is called the Italian Righi, which is an
indifferent compliment, unless one particularly emphasizes
the adjective. It is lovelier far, to my sense, than its Swiss
rival; and when I just now spoke of its sternness I simply
meant that everything is relative, and that an Alp, even with
an Italian exposure, has a different sort of charm from a pretty
woman. But Alpine grandeur, as you look at it from Monte
Generoso, is suffused with a wonderful softness and sweetness, and the Italian atmosphere tones down the view, as it
takes the edge from any importunate freshness in the breeze.
Views and breezes at Monte Generoso are the sum of one's
entertainment, and all are admirable in their kind. You behold
almost every mountain of notable importance in Switzerland
(exclusive of the Mont Blanc range), and see it melting away
in such enchanting confusions of aerial blue that you take it at
first for some fantastic formation of mist and cloud. Betimes
in the morning, before the clouds gather, Monte Rosa is
queen of the prospect—rising white and serene above her
blue zone of warm haze, like some Venus of divine stature
emerging from the sunny sea. Monte Generoso is an ideal
place for taking a holiday that has been well earned, and that
finds you tired and languid enough to appreciate an unlimited
opportunity to lie on shady slopes and listen to cow-bells and
watch the bees thumping into the cups of flowers, which look
tall as you see them against the sky. Shade is scarce, as on all
mountain-tops; but there are grassy hollows and screens of
rock, and the shadows grow with the afternoon, and, as you
lounge there, too contented to rise, creep across the nestling
valleys, in which white villages have been glittering, and cover
the long slopes. Even in the sun you may be fairly comfortable, with the assistance of your umbrella and of the agreeable
lightness of the air. I noted this during an afternoon which I

spent lying at my length, with a book, on the grassy apex of the mountain. It is rather a dizzy perch. You must mind your steps, and if you are subject to the baleful fascination of precipices you will lie down for your nerves' sake. Everything around me was so vast and silent and sublime that it took all meaning from the clever prose with which I had provided myself; so that I closed the volume and gave myself up to the perusal of the fine wrinkles on the azure brow of the Lake of Lugano, ever so far beneath me. It is hard to break the spell of silence and sublimity on such a spot by picking yourself up and jolting back to the hotel. You have been lifted deliciously out of the world, and the hotel seems the first stage of a melancholy return to it. This, indeed, is the mood that soon begins to govern your general attitude at Monte Generoso, among the breezes, the wild-flowers, and the cattle-bells. At first you feel exiled and cabined and confined. You are in ill-humor with the dimensions of your room, with the bad smells on the staircase, with the infrequency of the post and the frequency of the Church of England service in the parlor, where you have left the second volume of your Tauchnitz novel. But at the end of two or three days you find a charm in the very simplification of your life, and wish devoutly that the post came but half as often. You desire to know as little as possible about the horrible things that are taking place in the world, four thousand feet below you, and to steep yourself indefinitely in your bath of idleness and sunny coolness and piny smells. If you come away, as I did, after a short stay, it will probably be in self-defence. If you have work to do, it is, of course, bad policy to lapse into languid scepticism as to the existence of the powers to whom you are accountable for it.

II.

Once the charm broken, it seemed simpler and more sternly practical to leave Italy altogether, and to this end I found myself sailing in profound regretfulness along the Lake of Como. It was not for the first time, and I don't know that I made any very novel observations. The hotel at Cadennabbia looked more than ever like an artful palace at the back of the stage at the opera, and the boatmen and porters, in their

crimson sashes, like robust choristers before the foot-lights.
Bellagio, opposite, propounded with its usual force the query
as to why a tourist in the full possession of his reason should
remain there an hour, when it costs him but a franc or two to
be rowed across to Cadennabbia. Apparently the race of irra-
tional tourists is large; for the pretty villas at Bellagio are, one
and all, being turned into inns. The afternoon waned and the
violet lights on the mountains slowly cooled down into grays;
the passengers, group by group, descended into the picturesque old hooded scows which row out from the villages to
meet the little steamer; the evening came on, warm as the
day; and at last I disembarked at Colico and waited for the
lading of the Splügen diligence. Colico is a very raw little
village, and I could have fancied myself for half an hour in
some lakeside settlement of our Western world. I sat on a pile
of logs by the roadside, opposite to a tavern with an unattractive bar, amid a circle of contemplative village loafers. The
road was deep in dust, there was no gendarme within sight,
and every one seemed about equally commissioned to "heave"
the trunks and put in the horses. It was a good human, genial
last impression of ancient Italy.

I shall not undertake to describe the journey across the
Splügen Pass, as I enjoyed it in the banquette of the coach.
With this portion of my route I was also already acquainted—intimately and in detail, as a pedestrian learns to
be. My attention, indeed, during no small part of the time,
was absorbed in wonderment at my ever having found it
sport to do so laboriously what I was now doing so luxuri-
ously. For my position ceased to be luxurious only when the
fantastic crags above the close, dusky valleys had enticed the
innocent young moon to peep below their sinister battlements and we began to climb, with a long, steady pull, into
keener air. Then it became uncomfortably cold, and the temperature was not more tolerable that I sat self-convicted of a
want of imagination for having declined, at fervid Colico, to
equip myself with various incongruous draperies. But in the
middle of June the nights are short, and while still in the very
small hours and well below the top of the Pass I was treated
to the spectacle of an Alpine morning twilight. It was prodigiously fine; but the poor coffee at the village of Splügen

seemed to me finer still, in virtue of being tolerably hot. By the time we entered the Via Mala, however, the sun had climbed high, and I was able to do easy justice to the grandeur of things. They are certainly very grand indeed in the Via Mala, and there could not be a finer specimen of the regular "romantic scenery" of song and story. The crags tower above your head and the gorge plunges beneath your feet as wildly and strangely as if the genius of Doré had given them the finishing strokes. At moments you have the perfect extravagance of the sublime; the top of the ravine becomes a rugged vault, streaked crookedly with a little thread of blue, and the bottom a kind of longitudinal caldron, in which, through a deep, black fissure, you discover a terrific boiling of waters. All this grandeur gathers itself up at last on each side of a mighty portal of forest-crowned cliffs and forms a frame for the picture of a long green valley, at the entrance of which lies charming Thusis, upon soft slopes, among orchards and cornfields. You rattle out into the hard light, the cold coloring, the angular mountain forms of veritable Switzerland.

The terminus of the Splügen road is the curious little town of Chur, the ancient capital of the Grisons, which is perhaps known to the general English reader chiefly as the place in which Thackeray found the text of the first of his Roundabout Papers—"On a Lazy, Idle Boy." This young *désœuvré* was hanging over the railing of the bridge, reading a tattered volume, which Thackeray fondly conceives to be the "Three Musketeers"—starting from this facile postulate to deliver a charming puff of the novelist's trade. I did not see the boy; but I saw the bridge and the admirable little mountain river which it spans, and which washes the base of the excellent Steinbock inn and forms a magnificent moat to the ancient circumference of the city. At the end of the bridge is an old tower and archway, under which you pass into a labyrinth of clean little quiet streets, lined with houses whose doorways are capped with an armorial shield with an ancient date, and darkened by the overhanging tops of the gloomy pine-clad hills. These lead you to another gray tower and another straddling tunnel, through which you emerge into the Hof—the old ecclesiastical precinct of Chur. Here, on a little scrubbed and soundless square, flanked on one side by an old yellow episcopal palace, adorned with those rococo mouldings in white stucco which flourished late in the seventeenth century, rises one of the most venerable churches in Europe. The cathedral of Chur, however, has nothing in its favor but its thirteen centuries of duration and its little museum in the sacristy of queer ecclesiastical bric-a-brac. It is neither spacious nor elegant in an architectural way, and there is something almost pitiful in its awkward attempts at internal bedizenment. You seem to see an old woman of ninety pomaded and painted and overladen with false jewelry. The adornments at Chur are both very florid and very frugal; and, if there is pity in the matter, it should be for the story they tell of the immemorial impecuniosity of the toiling and trudging Swiss people. The old prince-bishops of Chur were persons of much consequence, and the province of the Grisons one of the largest and most powerful in Switzerland; but the cathedral chapter evidently never had the funds for doing things handsomely. Late in the sixteenth century, indeed, it treated itself to a goodly work of art in the shape of a large altar-piece in carved wood, painted and gilded with extraordinary verisimilitude, representing the Nativity and the Magi; but the church has the air of never having fairly recovered from the effect of this sumptuous purchase. It yields, however, a substantial interest in the way of glory; for, although the work belongs to a rather charmless department of art, it has remarkable merit. The figures are almost uncomfortably lifelike, and one of the kings, with a knowing black eye and a singularly clever short beard, is, I am sure, quite capable of speaking (and saying something very disagreeable) to a person of a fanciful turn of mind who should happen to be alone in the church at twilight. I suppose the church has a fund of potential wealth in its rich collection of archaic brasses and parchments. Here is a multitude of strange crosses and croziers and candlesticks and reliquaries, dating from the infancy of Christian art, and which seem somehow more intensely old and more penetrated with the melancholy of history for having played their part for so many centuries amid the remoteness and stillness of the steep pine forests which hang across the windows as a dark outer curtain. The great treasure is a series of documents of the early Carlovingian kings—grants of dominion to old bishops strong enough to ask and get; and the gem of this collection is a crumpled shred of parchment, covered with characters slowly and painfully formed, yet shapely and stately in their general aspect, which is neither more nor less than a portion of a deed of Charlemagne himself. He is such a shadowy and legendary monarch that this venerable tattler reminded me of the stories told by "spiritualists," in which the apparition, on retiring, deposits on the table a flower or a ribbon, a photograph or a visiting-card.

The last of the picturesque memories of my journey is that of a morning spent at Basel among the works of the great Hans Holbein. With the exception of a glance at the spacious red sandstone cathedral (cold, naked, and Lutheran within), and another at the broad yellow Rhine which sweeps beneath the windows of the hotel, this is the only æsthetic diversion to be found at Basel, the most prosaic and prosperous of all the Swiss cities. It is probably the only place in Switzerland which is wholly without pretensions to "scenery"; but no other place, on the other hand, has an art-treasure of the value of the collection of Holbeins. The great portraitist lived for many years at Basel, and the city fell heir in one way and another to a number of his drawings and to several of his pictures. I found it a different sort of art from any that has ever flourished in the lovely land I had left, but a very admirable art in its own way—firm, compact, and comfortable, sure alike of its end and of its means. The Museum of Basel contains many other specimens of the early German school, and to an observer freshly arrived from Italy they have a puzzling and an almost painful interest. Every artist of talent has somewhere lurking in his soul, I suppose, a guiding conception, an ideal of formal beauty, and even Martin Schongauer must have dimly discriminated in his scheme of things portrayable between a greater and a less degree of hideousness. This ruthless caricaturist of humanity, it is to be presumed, has bequeathed to us his most favorable view of things, and he leaves us wondering from what monstrous human types he can have drawn his inspiration.

The heart grows heavy as one reflects what art might have come to if it had developed exclusively in northern hands. The Italian painters of the great schools certainly often enough fall short of beauty—miss it, overlook it, wander erringly to one side of it; but its name, at least, is always on their lips and its image always at their hearts. The early Germans do not seem to have suspected that such a thing existed, and the painter's mission, in their eyes, is simply to appropriate, ready-made, the infinite variations of grotesqueness which they regard as the necessary environment of the human lot. Even Holbein, superb genius as he was, is never directly and essentially beautiful. Beauty, to his sense, is verity, dignity, opulence, goodliness of costume and circumstance; and the thoroughly handsome look of many of his figures resides simply in the picturesque assemblage of these qualities. Admirably handsome some of them are; not the least so the fascinating little drawings in pen and ink and sepia, familiar now half the world over by Messrs. Braun's photographs. Holbein had, at least, an ideal of beauty of execution, of manipulation, of touch. Anything firmer, finer, more suggestive of the fascination of what is vulgarly called "niggling" with brush and pencil it would be difficult to conceive. The finest example of this among the drawings is the artist's delightful portrait of himself. He ought to have believed in handsome forms, for he was himself a very handsome fellow. Among the paintings all the portraits are admirable, and two have an extraordinary interest. One is the famous profile of Erasmus, with his eyes dropped on a book, and that long, thin, delicate nose, which curves largely over the volume, as if it also were a kind of sympathetic absorbent of science. The other is a portrait of a mysterious young man, in a voluminous black cap, pulled forward over his brow, a searching dark eye, and a nose at once prominent and delicate, like that of Erasmus. Beside him is a tablet with a Latin inscription, and behind him a deep blue sky. The sky is crossed diagonally by the twig of a tree and bordered by a range of snow mountains. The painting is superb, and I call the subject mysterious because he was evidently no ordinary fellow, and the artist tells us of him but half that we would like to know. It was an untimely moment, I may say, in conclusion, for quarrelling with the German genius, for on turning my back upon Martin Schongauer, I went rattling across the Rhine.

1874

In Holland

The Hague, August 8, 1874.

IT WOULD amount to positive impudence, I suppose, to introduce these few impressions of Dutch scenery by an overt allusion to the beauties of the Rhine. And yet it was by the Rhine, a few day since, that I entered Holland; and it was along an arm of the Rhine, subdued to the likeness of a homely Dutch canal, that I wandered this afternoon in drowsy Leyden. As many as thirty years ago, I believe, it was good taste to make an apology for a serious mention, of the descriptive sort, of the vineyards of Bingen or the cloister of Nonnenwerth; and if the theme had been rubbed threadbare then, it can hardly be considered presentable now. But thus much I may boldly affirm, that if my corrupt modern consciousness had not assured me that these were terribly faded charms, I should not have guessed it from the testimony of my eyes. After platitudes, as well as after battles, nature has a way—all her own—of renewing herself; and in a decent attitude, at the bow of the boat, with my face to nature and my back to man, I ventured to greet the castled crags as frankly as if I were making a voyage of discovery. The time seems to me to have come round again when one ought really to say a good word for them. I insist upon the merits of no particular member of the crumbling fraternity; there are many worthy men whose pockets it might be awkward to examine; and the Rhenish dungeons, from a more familiar standpoint than the deck of the steamer, may prove to be half buried in beer-bottles and lemon-peel. But they still pass their romantic watchword from echo to echo, and they "compose" as bravely between the river and the sky as if fifty years of sketching and sonneteering had done nothing to tame them. The fine thing about the Rhine is that it has that which, when applied to architecture and painting, is called style. It is in the grand manner—on the liberal scale; that is, it is on the liberal scale while it lasts. There is less of it, in quantity, than I had been remembering these fifteen years. The classic sites come and go within an easy four hours; and if you embark at Mayence you

leave the last and most perfect of the castled crags—the
Drachenfels—behind you just as your organism, physical and
mental, is being thoroughly attuned to the supreme felicity of
river navigation. It was a grayish day as I passed, and the
Drachenfels looked as if it had been stolen from a background
of Claude to do service in the Rhenish foreground. It has the
ideal, romantic outline.

It stands there, however, like some last ringing word in an
interrupted phrase. The vast white river sweeps along into
Holland on a level with its banks, finally to die in a slush of
marshes and a mesh of canals, within sound of the surge of
the North Sea. I left it to its destiny, and gathered my first
impressions of Holland from the window of the train. The
most pertinent thing one may say of these first impressions is
that they are exactly, to the letter, what one expects them to
be. If you come this way, as I did, chiefly with an eye to
Dutch pictures, your first acquisition, is a sense, no longer an
amiable inference, but a direct perception, of the undiluted
accuracy of Dutch painters. You have seen it all before; it is
vexatiously familiar; it was hardly worth while to have come!
At Amsterdam, at Leyden, at The Hague, and in the country
between them, this is half your state of mind. When you are
looking at the originals, you seem to be looking at the copies;
and when you are looking at the copies, you seem to be looking at the originals. Is it a canal-side in Haarlem, or is it a Van
der Heyden? Is it a priceless Hobbema, or is it a meagre pastoral vista, stretching away from the railway-track? The maid-
servants in the streets seem to have stepped out of the frame
of a Gerard Dow, and appear equally adapted for stepping
back again. You have to rub your eyes to ascertain their normal situation. And so you wander about, with art and nature
playing so assiduously into each other's hands that your experience of Holland becomes something singularly compact and
complete in itself—striking no chords that lead elsewhere,
and asking no outside help to unfold itself. This is what we
mean when we say, as we do at every turn, that Holland is so
curious. Italy is not curious, as a general thing, nor is England,
in its leading features. They are simply both eminent specimens of a sort of beauty which pervades in a greater or less
degree all our conceptions of the beautiful. We admire them

because they stand, as it were, in the high-road of admiration, and whether we pass them at a run or at a walk our pace is part of the regular æsthetic business of life. But to enjoy the Low Countries, we have to put on a very particular pair of spectacles and bend our nose well over our task, and, beyond our consciousness that our gains are real gains, remain decidedly at loss how to classify them. This is the charming thing in Holland—the way one feels one's observation lowered to a relish of the harmonies of the minor key; persuaded to respect small things and take note of small differences; so that really a week's sojourn here, if properly used, ought to make one at the worst a more reasonable, and at the best a more kindly, person. The beauty which is no beauty; the ugliness which is not ugliness; the poetry which is prose, and the prose which is poetry; the landscape which seems to be all sky until you have taken particular pains to discover it, and turns out to be half water when you *have* discovered it; the virtues, when they are graceful (like cleanliness) exaggerated to a vice, and when they are sordid (like the getting and keeping of money) refined to a dignity; the mild gray light which produced in Rembrandt the very genius of chiaroscuro; the stretch of whole provinces on the principles of a billiard-table, which produced a school of consummate landscapists; the extraordinary reversal of custom, in which man seems, with a few windmills and ditches, to do what he will, and Providence, holding the North Sea in the hollow of his hand, what it can—all these elements of the general spectacle in this entertaining country at least give one's regular habits of thought the stimulus of a little confusion, and make one feel that one is dealing with an original genius.

The curious fortunately excludes neither the impressive nor the agreeable; and Amsterdam, where I took my first Dutch walk, is a stately city, even though its street-vistas do look as if they were pictured on a tea-caddy or a hand-screen. They have for the most part a broad, sluggish canal in the middle, on either side of which a row of perfectly salubrious, but extremely attenuated trees grow out of a highly cultivated soil of compact yellow bricks. Cultivated I call it by a proper license, for it is periodically raked by the broom and the scrubbing-brush, and religiously manured with soapsuds. You

lose no time, of course, in drawing the inevitable parallel between Amsterdam and Venice, and it is well worth drawing,
as an illustration of the uses to which the same materials may
be put by different minds. Sky and sea in both cases, with
architecture between; winding sea-channels washing the feet
of goodly houses erected with the profits of trade. And yet
the Dutch city is a complete reversal of the Italian, and its
founders might have carefully studied Venetian effects with
the set purpose of producing exactly the opposite ones. It
produces them in the moral line even more vividly than in the
material. It is not that one place is all warm color and the
other all cold; one all shimmer and softness and mellow interfusion of every possible phase of ruin, and the other rigidity,
angularity, opacity, prosperity, in their very essence; it is
more than anything that they tell of such different lives and of
such a different view of life. The outward expression on one
side is perfect poetry, and on the other is perfect prose; and
the marvel is the way in which thrifty Amsterdam imparts the
prosaic turn to things which in Venice seem the perfect essence of poetry. Take, for instance, the silence and quiet of the
canals; it has in the two places a difference of quality which it
is almost impossible to express. In the one it is the stillness of
order, and in the other of vacancy—the sleep of idleness and
the sleep of rest; the quiet that comes of letting everything go
by the board, and the quiet that comes of doing things betimes and being able to sit with folded hands and say they are
well done. In one of George Eliot's novels there is a portrait
of a thrifty farmer's wife who rose so early in the morning to
do her work that by ten o'clock it was all over, and she was at
her wit's end to know what to do with her day. This good
woman seems to me an excellent image of the genius of Amsterdam as it is reflected in the house-fronts—I penetrated no
deeper. It is impossible to imagine anything more expressive
of the numerous ideas represented by the French epithet *bourgeois* than these straight façades of clean black brick, capped
with a rococo gable of stone painted white and armed like the
forehead of the unicorn with a little horizontal horn—a
bracket and pulley for hauling storable goods into the attic.
The famous Dutch cleanliness seems to me quite on a level
with its reputation, and asserts itself in the most ingenious

and ludicrous ways. A rosy serving-maid, redolent of soap-suds from her white cap to her white sabots, stands squirting water from a queer little engine of polished copper over the majestic front of a genteel mansion whose complexion is not a visible shade less immaculate than her own. The performance suggests a dozen questions, and you can only answer them all with a laugh. What is she doing, and why is she doing it? Does she imagine the house has a speck or two which it is of consequence to remove, or is the squirt applied merely for purposes of light refreshment—of endearment, as it were? Where could the speck or two possibly have come from, un-less produced by spontaneous generation? There are no specks in the road, which is a neat *parquet* of scoured and polished brick; nor on the trees, whose trunks are to all ap-pearance carefully sponged every morning. The speck exists evidently only as a sort of mathematical point, capable of ex-tension, in the good woman's Batavian brain, and the opera-tion with her copper kettle is, as the metaphysicians would say, purely subjective. It is a necessity, not as regards the house, but as regards her own temperament. Of a dozen harmlessly factitious necessities of the same sort, the canal-sides at Amsterdam offer lively evidence. Nothing could be more thoroughly in keeping with the *bourgeois* spirit than the way in which you everywhere find this brilliant cleanliness and ceremonious thrift playing the part, not of a convenience, but of a restriction; not of a means, but of an end. The win-dows are of those huge plates of glass which offer a delectably uninterrupted field for friction; but they are masked internally by thick white blinds, invariably drawn, and the only use of their transparency to any mortal is to enable the passer-by to examine the texture of the stuff. The front doors are hedged in with little square padlocked barriers, to guard the door-steps from the pollution of footprints, and the visitor must pocket his pride and apply at a humbler portal with the baker and the milkman. In such houses must dwell people whose nerves are proof against the irritation of minute precau-tions—people who cover their books with white paper and find occasion for a week's conversation in a mysterious drop of candle-grease on a tablecloth. The traveller with an eye for details will find some eloquence in the fact that, though the canals at Amsterdam and Leyden offer continually this charming pretext of trees by a water-side, there is not in their whole length a single bench for a contemplative lounge. The traveller in question though, shrewd fellow, will not be prevented by the absence of benches from taking in the scene, as he looks up and down and sees the wide green barges come floating through the respectable stillness, and the quaint old scroll-work of the gables peep out through the meagre density of the trees.

At The Hague, evidently, people take life in a lighter, more irresponsible fashion. There are two or three benches by the canals and an air of mitigated devotion to compound interest. There are wide, tranquil squares, planted in the middle with shady walks and bordered with fine old abodes of moneyed leisure, where you may boldly ring at the front door. The Hague is in fact a very charming little city, and I should be at a loss to say how much I find it to my taste. It is the model of a minor capital; small enough for convenience and compact sociability, and yet large enough to exhibit certain metropolitan airs and graces. It is one of the cities which please indefinably on a short acquaintance and prompt one's fretful fancy to say that just *this*, at last, is the place where we could come and lead the (from the worldly point of view) ideal life. It hits the happy medium between the bustling and the stagnant; it is Dutch enough for all sorts of comfortable virtues, and, where these intermit, it is English and French, and, in its diplomatic character, cosmopolitan. There must be very pleasant things done here, and I hope, for symmetry's sake, there are pleasant people to do them worthily. I imagine there are. But I do wrong to consume valuable space in these fruitless speculations when I have not yet said a word on the topic on which I had it chiefly at heart to touch. A week in Holland is necessarily a week in the company of Rembrandt and Paul Potter, Ruysdael and Gerard Dow. These admirable artists have had my best attention, but I do not know that they have given me any new impressions, or indeed that, in the literal meaning of the word, they have given me any impressions at all. I looked for a long time, only this morning, at the hand of Madame van Mieris in the little picture in the Museum here, by her husband, representing him and his wife playing with a tiny spaniel. He is pulling the dog's ear and she is pressing the animal against her bosom with an arm bare to the elbow. It seemed to me that it was worth the journey to Holland simply to see this appreciative husband's version of his wife's hand, and that if I had seen nothing else I should have been repaid; but beyond producing this eminently practical reflection, the picture was not suggestive. I find in my guide-book, on the margin of the page which dilates upon the great Van der Helst at Amsterdam (the Banquet of the Civic Guard), the inscription in pencil—*superb, superb, superb!* But this simply connotes enjoyment and not criticism. Let me however have the satisfaction of repeating, in ink for the printer, that the picture *is* superb. To the great treasure (after Rembrandt's Lesson of Anatomy) of the Museum here—Paul Potter's famous Bull—one would willingly pay some more elaborate compliment; not because it is a stronger work (on the contrary), but because it is the work of a lad of twenty-two. The subject is the most prosaic conceivable, and the treatment is perfectly in keeping; but if one considers the magnificent success of the enterprise from the painter's own point of view, there is certainly real poetry in the fact of his youth. It is hardly less true of Rembrandt than of his various smaller comrades (unusual as the judgment may seem), that he is not an intellectually suggestive painter. There are no ideas in Ostade and Terburg, in Metzu and Ruysdael (who, by the way, gives me the largest sum of tranquil pleasure of any painter of the school); but you bear them no grudge, for they give you no reason to expect them. It is one of the regular traditions, however, that Rembrandt does, and I can only say that in this case tradition has distinctly missed her way. It is the more singular that he should not, inasmuch as (I should go so far as to say) he was really not, strictly speaking, a painter. He was perfectly arbitrary, and he kept on terms with observation only so long as it suited him. This may be verified by reference to any of the most delusively picturesque of his works. They are magnificent; but compare them, for simple verity, with the little Adrian van Ostade in the Van der Hoop collection, and compare them, for thought, with any fine Tintoretto.

In Belgium

BELGIUM, in most itineraries, is visited conjointly with Holland. This is all very well so long as Belgium is visited first; and my advice to travellers who relish a method in their emotions is in this region to reverse the plan which is generally most judicious, and proceed in all confidence from south to north. Passing from the Low Countries into Flanders, you come back into the common world again— into a picturesque phase of it, certainly, and a country rich in architectural and artistic treasures. But you miss that something, individual and exquisite, which forms the charm of Holland, and of which, during the last forty-eight hours of my stay there (it seems a part of the delicacy of all things that one calculates one's stay in the little Dutch garden by hours), my impression became singularly deep. It has become deeper still in retrospect, as such things do, and there are moments when I feel as if in coming away I had wantonly turned my back upon the abode of tranquil happiness. I keep seeing a green canal with a screen of thin-stemmed trees on one side of it, and a foot-path, not at all sinuous, on the other. Beside the foot-path is a red-brick wall, superstitiously clean, and if you follow it a little while you come to a large iron gate flanked with high posts, with balls on top. Although the climate is damp, the ancient iron-work of the gate has not a particle of rust, and its hinges, as you turn it, are in perfect working order. Beyond it is a garden planted with tulips of a hundred kinds, and in the middle of the garden is a pond. Over the pond is stretched, from edge to edge, a sort of trellis of tense cord, which at first excites your surprise. In a moment, however, you perceive the propriety of the pond's being carefully guarded, for its contents are singularly precious. They consist of an immense number of gigantic water-lilies, sitting motionless among their emerald pads, and of a brilliancy and softness which make you fancy they are modelled in wax; of a thousand little gold-fishes, of so deep a crimson that they look as if they were taken out every morning and neatly varnished over with a fine brush; and, lastly, of a majestic swan, of the purest porcelain. About the swan there is no doubt; he is of the finest Dutch delf—a substance which at a certain distance looks as well as flossy feathers, and has the advantage that a creature composed of it cannot circulate to the detriment of varnished fishes and waxen lilies. I do not know how this pond looks on paper, but in nature, if one may call it nature, it was delicious. There was a skyful of rolling gray clouds, with two or three little patches of blue, and over the tulip-beds there played a little cool breeze, with its edge just blurred by dampness. Under the trees was just one bench, but it was strictly sufficient.

I must not linger on Dutch benches, however, with all the art-wealth of Flanders awaiting me. I have by no means in fact examined it all, and have had to pay the tourist's usual tribute to reluctant omission. In such cases, if you are travel-ling *con amore*, the things omitted assume to the mind's eye a kind of mocking perfection, and the dozen successes of your journey seem a small compensation for this fatal failure. There is a certain little hôtel de ville at Louvain and a cathedral at Tournay which make a delicious figure in the excellent hand-book of M. Du Pays; but I hasten to declare that I have not seen them, and am well aware that my observations are by so much the less valuable. I first made acquaintance with Bel-gium, however, through the cathedral of Antwerp, and this is a first-rate introduction. I went into it of a Sunday morning during mass, and immediately perceived that I was in a stur-dily Catholic country. The immense edifice was crowded with worshippers, and their manner was much more *receuilli*, as the phrase is, than that of the faithful in Italian churches. This too in spite of the fact that the great Rubenses were unveiled in honor of the day, so that all the world might behold them gratis. To be *receuilli* in the presence of a Rubens seems to me to indicate the real devotional temperament. The crowd, the Rubenses, the atmosphere, and the presence of some hundred or so of dear fellow-tourists was rather hostile to tranquil ap-preciation, so that at first I saw little in the cathedral of Ant-werp to justify its great reputation. But I came back in the late afternoon, at that time which a wise man will always choose for visiting (finally at least) a great church—the half-hour before it closes. The Rubenses, those monstrous flowers of art, had folded their gorgeous petals; but this I did not regret, as I had been in the interval to the Museum, where there are a dozen more, and I had drifted to a conclusion. The church was empty, or filled only with the faded light and its own immense solemnity. It is very magnificent; not duskily nor mysteriously so, but with a vast, simple harmony which, like all great things, grows and grows as you observe it. Its length is extraordinary, and it has the peculiarity, unique in my observation, of possessing no less than six aisles, besides the nave. Its height is in harmony with these splendid proportions, and it gave me altogether (I do not know the literal measurements) an almost unequalled impression of vastness. Externally, its great tower, of the most florid and flamboyant, the most embroidered and perforated Gothic, is one of the few worthy rivals of the peerless steeple of Strasburg.

The Antwerp Museum is very handsomely appointed, and has an air of opulence very striking after the small and dusky treasure-houses of thrifty Holland. But there is logic in both cases. You bend your nose over a Gerard Dow and use a magnifying glass; whereas, the least that can be done by the protectors of Rubens's glory is to give you a room in which you can stand twenty yards from the canvas. I may say directly that even at twenty yards Rubens gave me less pleasure than I had hoped. I say hoped rather than expected, for I was already sufficiently familiar with him to have felt the tendency of my impressions, and yet I had fancied that in the atmosphere in which he wrought, in the city of which he is the most distinguished son, they might be diverted into the channel of sympathy. But they followed their own course, and I can express them only by saying that the painter does not please me. If Rubens does not *please* you, what is left?—for I find myself utterly unable to perceive in him a trace of that intellectual impressiveness claimed by some of his admirers. I read awhile since a charming book in which an acute French critic, M. Emile Montégut, records his impressions of Belgium and Holland, and this work was partly responsible for my supposition that I should find more in the author of the "Descent from the Cross" collectively, at Antwerp, than I had found in him, individually, at London, Paris, and Florence.

M. Montégut, I say, is acute, and the number of things his acuteness finds in Rubens it would take up all my space to recount. According to him, Rubens was not only one of the greatest of mere painters, but he was the greatest genius who ever *thought*, brush in hand. The answer to this seems simple: Rubens, to my sense, absolutely did *not* think. He not only did not think greatly, but he did not think at all. M. Montégut declares that he was a great dramatist superadded to a great painter, and calls upon the people of Antwerp to erect to him in the marketplace a colossal monument (the one already standing there will do, it seems to me) and inscribe upon the pedestal his title to the glory of having carried his art beyond its traditional limits and produced effects generally achieved only by the highest dramatic poetry. If the great painter of rosy brawn had had half his commentator's *finesse*, he would have been richly endowed. M. Montégut finds, among other things, unutterable meanings in the countenance of the Abyssinian king who is looking askance at the Virgin in the "Adoration" of the Antwerp Museum. I remembered them so well that, in leaving the cathedral, I hurried to commune with this masterpiece of expressiveness. I recommend him to the reader who may next pass that way. Let him tell me, from an unbiassed mind, how many supplementary emotions he finds reflected in the broad concupiscence of the monarch's black visage. I was disappointed; dramatists of the first order are rare, and here was one the less. If Rubens is anywhere dramatic, in the finer sense of the term, it is in his masterpiece, the "Descent from the Cross," of the cathedral; of all his pictures, this one comes the nearest to being impressive. It is superbly painted, and on the whole very noble; but it is only a happier specimen of the artist's habitual manner—painting by improvisation, not by reflection. Besides the Rubenses at Antwerp, I have seen several others. Those at Brussels, unfortunately, with most of their companions of the Flemish school, have been now some two years invisible. They are being restored; but one is curious to see the effect of two years' refreshment upon the native robustness of most Rubenses. I need not speak of these various productions in detail; some are better, some are worse, all are powerful, and all, on the whole, are irritating. They all tell the same story—

that the artist had in a magnificent degree the painter's temperament, without having in anything like a proportionate degree the painter's mind. When one, therefore, says that he was perfectly superficial, one indicates a more fatal fault than in applying the same term to many a more delicate genius. What makes Rubens irritating is the fact that he always *might* have been more interesting. Half the conditions are there— vigor, facility, color, the prodigious impulse of genius. Nature has given them all, and he holds the other half in his own hands. But just when the others should appear and give the picture that stamp which draws from us, over and above our relish of the natural gift, a certain fine sympathy with the direction it takes, Rubens uncloses his careless grasp, and drops them utterly out of sight. He never approaches something really fine but to miss it; he never attempts a really interesting effect but to vulgarize it. Our deepest interest, as to an artist, depends on the way he deliberates and chooses. Everything up to that point may be superb, but we care for him with a certain affection only when we feel him responsibly selecting among a number of possibilities. This sensible intellectual pulsation often gives a charm to the works of painters to whom nature has been anything but liberal, and the great limitation of Rubens is that in him one never perceives it. He takes what comes, and if it happens to be really pictorial, he has a singular faculty of suggesting that there is no merit in his having taken it. He never waits to choose; he never pauses to deliberate; and one may say, vulgarly, he throws away his oranges when he has given them but a single squeeze. The foolish fellow does not know how sweet they are! One ends, in a manner, by disliking his real gifts. A little less facility, we call out, a shade or so less color, a figure or so the fewer tossed in, a bosom or two less glowingly touched; only something once in a while to arrest us with the thought that it has arrested *you*!

Almost as noteworthy as anything else in the Antwerp Museum is the title of a picture by Titian, of average Titianesque merit. It is worth transcribing for its bizarre conflict of suggestions. "John, Bastard of Sforza, Lord of Pesaro, husband, by her first marriage, of Lucretia Borgia, and then Bishop of Paphos and Admiral of the Pontifical Galleys, is presented to

St. Peter by the Pope Alexander VI." Add to this that St. Peter is seated upon a fragment of antique sculpture, surrounded by a frieze representing a pagan sacrifice! Even that harshly sincere genius, Quentin Matsys, who shines hard by in a brilliantly pure piece of coloring, can hardly persuade us that we are in simple Flanders, and not in complex Italy.

It often happens in travelling that places turn out to be less curious than we had supposed, but it is a comparatively rare fortune to find them more so. And yet this was my luck with Brussels, a city of which my imagination had made so light that it hung by a hair whether I should go there or not. It is generally spoken of by its admirers as a miniature Paris, and I always viewed it with that contempt with which a properly regulated mind regards those shabby, pirated editions of the successful French books of the day which are put forth in Belgium. These ill-conditioned little volumes are miniature Victor Hugos and Michelets. But Brussels should ask to be delivered from its friends. It is not a miniature anything, but a very solid and extensive old city, with a physiognomy and character quite its own. It is very much less elegant than the Paris of the last twenty years; but it is decidedly more picturesque. Paris has nothing to compare for quaintness of interest with the Brussels Hôtel de Ville, and the queer old carved and many-windowed houses which surround the square. The Hôtel de Ville is magnificent, and its beautiful Gothic belfry gives, in quite another line, an equal companion in one's memory to the soaring campanile of the palace of the Signoria at Florence. Few cities have a cathedral in so impressive a position as St. Gudule—on a steep hill-top, with a long flight of steps at the base of its towers; and few cities, either, have so charming a public garden as the Parc. There is something peculiarly picturesque in that high-in-the-air look of the Parc as you glance from end to end of its long alleys, and see the sky beneath the arch of the immense trees meeting the bend of the path. All this part of Brussels, and the wide, windy Place Royale, handsome as the handsome was understood fifty years ago, has an extreme brightness and gaiety of aspect which is yet quite distinct from the made-to-order brilliancy of the finest parts of renovated Paris. The Brussels Museum of pictures is admirably arranged; but, unfortunately, as I have said, only half of it is now accessible. This, however, contains some gems of the Dutch school—among them a picture by Steen, representing a lad coming into a room to present a fish to a ruddy virago who sits leering at him. The young man, for reasons best known to himself, is sticking out his tongue, and these reasons, according to M. Montégut, are so numerous and recondite that I should like the downright old caricaturist himself to have heard a few of them. I wonder where *his* tongue would have gone.

Ghent I found to be an enormous, empty city, with an old Flemish gable-end peeping here and there from its rows of dull white houses, and various tall and battered old church-towers looking down over deserted, sunny squares. In the middle of all this, in the stately church of St. Bavon, is the great local treasure, the "Adoration of the Lamb," by the brothers Van Eyck. This is not only one of the pictures of Ghent, but one of the pictures of the world. It represents a large daisied meadow shut in with a great flowering tangle of hedges, out of which emerge various saints of either sex, carrying crowns and palms. In front are two other groups of apostles and prophets, all kneeling and worshipping. In the centre is an altar, surmounted with the fleecy symbol of the Word, and surrounded with a ring of adoring angels. Behind is a high horizon of blue mountains, and the silhouettes of three separate fantastic cities, all apparently composed of church-towers. The picture is too perfect for praise; the coloring seems not only not to have lost, but actually to have been intensified and purified, by time. One may say the same of the precious Memlings at Bruges—and this is all I can say of that drowsy little city of grassy streets and colossal belfries and sluggish canals and mediæval memories.

Chartres

THE SPRING, in Paris, since it has fairly begun, has been enchanting. The sun and the moon have been blazing in emulation, and the difference between the blue sky of day and of night has been as slight as possible. There are no clouds in the sky, but there are little thin green clouds, little puffs of raw, tender verdure, entangled among the branches of the trees. All the world is in the streets; the chairs and tables which have stood empty all winter before the doors of the cafés are at a premium; the theatres have become intolerably close; the puppet-shows in the Champs Elysées are the only form of dramatic entertainment which seems consistent with the season. By way of doing honour, at a small cost, to this ethereal mildness, I went out the other day to the ancient town of Chartres, where I spent several hours, which I cannot consent to pass over as if nothing had happened. It is the experience of the writer of these lines, who likes nothing so much as moving about to see the world, that if one has been for a longer time than usual resident and stationary, there is a kind of overgrown entertainment in taking the train, even for a suburban goal; and that if one takes it on a charming April day, when there is a sense, almost an odour, of change in the air, the innocent pleasure is as nearly as possible complete. My accessibility to emotions of this kind amounts to an infirmity, and the effect of it was to send me down to Chartres in a shamelessly optimistic state of mind. I was so prepared to be entertained and pleased with everything that it is only a mercy that the cathedral happens really to be a fine building. If it had not been, I should still have admired it inordinately, at the risk of falling into heaven knows what æsthetic heresy. But I am almost ashamed to say how soon my entertainment began. It began, I think, with my hailing a little open carriage on the Boulevard and causing myself to be driven to the Gare de l'Ouest—far away across the river, up the Rue Bonaparte, of art-student memories, and along the big, straight Rue de Rennes to the Boulevard Montparnasse. Of course, at this rate, by the time I reached Chartres—the journey is of a

couple of hours—I had almost drained the cup of pleasure.
But it was replenished at the station, at the buffet, from the
pungent bottle of wine I drank with my breakfast. Here, by
the way, is another excellent excuse for being delighted with
any day's excursion in France—that wherever you are, you
may breakfast to your taste. There may, indeed, if the station
is very small, be no buffet; but if there is a buffet, you may be
sure that civilisation—in the persons of a sympathetic young
woman in a well-made black dress, and a rapid, zealous, grateful waiter—presides at it. It was quite the least, as the French
say, that after my breakfast I should have thought the cathedral, as I saw it from the top of the steep hill on which the
town stands, rising high above the clustered houses and seeming to make of their red-roofed agglomeration a mere pedestal for its immense beauty, promised remarkably well. You see
it so as you emerge from the station, and then, as you climb
slowly into town, you lose sight of it. You perceive Chartres
to be a rather shabby little *ville de province*, with a few sunny,
empty open *places*, and crooked shady streets, in which two or
three times you lose your way, until at last, after more than
once catching a glimpse, high above some slit between the
houses, of the clear gray towers shining against the blue sky,
you push forward again, risk another short cut, turn another
interposing corner, and stand before the goal of your pilgrimage.

I spent a long time looking at this monument. I revolved
around it, like a moth around a candle; I went away and I
came back; I chose twenty different standpoints; I observed it
during the different hours of the day, and saw it in the moonlight as well as the sunshine. I gained, in a word, a certain
sense of familiarity with it; and yet I despair of giving any
coherent account of it. Like most French cathedrals, it rises
straight out of the street, and is destitute of that setting of
turf and trees and deaneries and canonries which contribute
so largely to the impressiveness of the great English churches.
Thirty years ago a row of old houses was glued to its base and
made their back walls of its sculptured sides. These have been
plucked away, and, relatively speaking, the church is fairly isolated. But the little square that surrounds it is deplorably narrow, and you flatten your back against the opposite houses in

the vain attempt to stand off and survey the towers. The proper way to look at them would be to go up in a balloon and hang poised, face to face with them, in the blue air. There is, however, perhaps an advantage in being forced to stand so directly under them, for this position gives you an over-whelming impression of their height. I have seen, I suppose, churches as beautiful as this one, but I do not remember ever to have been so fascinated by superpositions and vertical effects. The endless upward reach of the great west front, the clear, silvery tone of its surface, the way three or four magnificent features are made to occupy its serene expanse, its simplicity, majesty, and dignity—these things crowd upon one's sense with a force that makes the act of vision seem for the moment almost all of life. The impressions produced by architecture lend themselves as little to interpretation by another medium as those produced by music. Certainly there is an inexpressible harmony in the façade of Chartres.

The doors are rather low, as those of the English cathedrals are apt to be, but (standing three together) are set in a deep framework of sculpture—rows of arching grooves, filled with admirable little images, standing with their heels on each other's heads. The church, as it now exists, except the northern tower, dates from the middle of the thirteenth century, and these closely-packed figures are full of the grotesqueness of the period. Above the triple portals is a vast round-topped window, in three divisions, of the grandest dimensions and the stateliest effect. Above this window is a circular aperture, of huge circumference, with a double row of sculptured spokes radiating from its centre and looking on its lofty field of stone as expansive and symbolic as if it were the wheel of Time itself. Higher still is a little gallery with a delicate balustrade, supported on a beautiful cornice and stretching across the front from tower to tower; and above this is a range of niched statues of kings—fifteen, I believe, in number. Above the statues is a gable, with an image of the Virgin and Child on its front, and another of Christ on its apex. In the relation of all these parts there is such a high felicity that while on the one side the eye rests on a great many large blanks there is no approach on the other to poverty. The little gallery that I have spoken of, beneath the statues of the kings, had for me a peculiar charm. Useless, at its tremendous altitude, for other purposes, it seemed intended for the little images to step down and walk about upon. When the great façade begins to glow in the late afternoon light, you can imagine them strolling up and down their long balcony in couples, pausing with their elbows on the balustrade, resting their stony chins in their hands, and looking out, with their little blank eyes, on the great view of the old French monarchy they once ruled, and which now has passed away. The two great towers of the cathedral are among the noblest of their kind. They rise in solid simplicity to a height as great as the eye often troubles itself to travel, and then suddenly they begin to execute a magnificent series of feats in architectural gymnastics. This is especially true of the northern spire, which is a late creation, dating from the sixteenth century. The other is relatively quiet; but its companion is a sort of tapering bouquet of sculptured stone. Statues and buttresses, gargoyles, arabesques and crockets pile themselves in successive stages, until the eye loses the sense of everything but a sort of architectural lacework. The pride of Chartres, after its front, is the two portals of its transepts—great dusky porches, in three divisions, covered with more images than I have time to talk about. Wherever you look, along the sides of the church, a time-worn image is niched or perched. The face of each flying buttress is garnished with one, with the features quite melted away.

The inside of the cathedral corresponds in vastness and grandeur to the outside—it is the perfection of gothic in its prime. But I looked at it rapidly, the place was so intolerably cold. It seemed to answer one's query of what becomes of the winter when the spring chases it away. The winter hereabouts has sought an asylum in Chartres cathedral, where it has found plenty of room and may reside in a state of excellent preservation until it can safely venture abroad again. I supposed I had been in cold churches before, but the delusion had been an injustice to the temperature of Chartres. The nave was full of the little padded chairs of the local bourgeoisie, whose faith, I hope for their comfort, is of the good old red-hot complexion. In a higher temperature I should have done more justice to the magnificent old glass of the windows—which glowed through the icy dusk like the purple and orange of a winter sunset—and to the immense sculptured external casing of the choir. This latter is an extraordinary piece of work. It is a high gothic screen, shutting in the choir, and covered with elaborate bas-reliefs of the sixteenth and seventeenth centuries, representing scenes from the life of Christ and of the Virgin. Some of the figures are admirable, and the effect of the whole great semicircular wall, chiselled like a silver bowl, is superb. There is also a crypt of high antiquity and, I believe, great interest, to be seen; but my teeth chattered a respectful negative to the sacristan who offered to guide me to it. It was so agreeable to stand in the warm outer air again, that I spent the rest of the day in it.

Although, besides its cathedral, Chartres has no very rare architectural treasures, the place is pictorial, in a shabby, third-rate, poverty-stricken degree, and my observations were not unremunerative. There is a little church of Saint-Aignan, of the sixteenth century, with an elegant, decayed façade, and a small tower beside it, lower than its own roof, to which it is joined, in unequal twinship, by a single long buttress. Standing there with its crumbling Renaissance doorway, in a kind of grass-grown alcove, it reminded me of certain monuments that the tourist encounters in small Italian towns. Most of the streets of Chartres are crooked lanes, winding over the face of the steep hill, the summit of the hill being occupied by half a dozen little open squares, which seem like reservoirs of the dulness and stillness that flow through the place. In the midst of one of them rises an old dirty brick obelisk, commemorating the glories of the young General Marceau, of the first Republic—"Soldier at 16, general at 23, he died at 27." Such memorials, when one comes upon them unexpectedly, produce in the mind a series of circular waves of feeling, like a splash in a quiet pond. Chartres gives us an impression of extreme antiquity, but it is an antiquity that has gone down in the world. I saw very few of those stately little hôtels, with pilastered fronts, which look so well in the silent streets of provincial towns. The houses are mostly low, small, and of sordid aspect, and though many of them have overhanging upper stories, and steep, battered gables, they are rather wanting in character. I was struck, as an American always is in small French and English towns, with the immense number of shops, and their brilliant appearance, which seems so out of proportion to any visible body of consumers. At Chartres the shopkeepers must all feed upon each other, for, whoever buys, the whole population sells. This population appeared to consist mainly of several hundred brown old peasant women, in the seventies and eighties, with their faces cross-hatched with wrinkles and their quaint white coifs drawn tightly over their weather-blasted eye-brows. Labour-stricken grandams, all the world over, are the opposite of lovely, for the toil that wrestles for its daily bread, morsel by morsel, is not beautifying; but I thought I had never seen the possibilities of female ugliness so variously embodied as in the crones of Chartres. Some of them were leading small children by the hand—little red-cheeked girls, in the close black caps and black pinafores of humble French infancy—a costume which makes French children always look like orphans. Others were guiding along the flinty lanes the steps of small donkeys, some of them fastened into little carts, some with well-laden backs. These were the only quadrupeds I perceived at Chartres. Neither horse nor carriage did I behold, save at the station the omnibuses of the rival inns—the "Grand Monarque" and the "Duc de Chartres"—which glare at each other across the Grande Place. A friend of mine told me that a few years ago, passing through Chartres, he went by night to call upon a gentleman who lived there. During his visit it came on to rain violently, and when the hour for his departure arrived the rain had made the streets impassable. There was no vehicle to be had, and my friend was resigning himself to a soaking. "You can be taken of course in the sedan-chair," said his host with dignity. The sedan-chair was produced, a couple of serving-men grasped the handles, my friend stepped into it, and went swinging back—through the last century—to the "Grand Monarque." This little anecdote, I imagine, still paints Chartres socially.

Before dinner I took a walk on the planted promenade which encircles the town—the Tour-de-ville it is called—much of which is extremely picturesque. Chartres has lost her walls as a whole, but here and there they survive, and play a desultory part in holding the town together. In one place the rampart is really magnificent—smooth, strong and lofty, curtained with ivy, and supporting on its summit an old convent and its garden. Only one of the city-gates remains—a narrow arch of the fourteenth century, flanked by two admirable round towers, and preceded by a fosse. If you stoop a little, as you stand outside, the arch of this hoary old gate makes a capital setting for the picture of the interior of the town, and, on the inner hill-top, against the sky, the large gray mass of the cathedral. The ditch is full, and to right and to left it flows along the base of the mouldering wall, through which the shabby backs of houses extrude, and which is garnished with little wooden galleries, lavatories of the town's soiled linen. These little galleries are filled with washerwomen, who crane over and dip their many-coloured rags into the yellow stream. The old patched and interrupted wall, the ditch with its weedy edges, the spots of colour, the white-capped laundresses in their little wooden cages—one lingers to look at it all.

1876

Rouen

I T IS quite in the nature of things that a Parisian correspondence should have flagged during the last few weeks; for
even the most brilliant of capitals, when the summer has fairly
begun to be summer, affords few topics to the chronicler. To
a chronicle of small beer such a correspondence almost literally finds itself reduced. The correspondent consumes a
goodly number of those magnified thimblefuls of this fluid,
known in Paris as "bocks," and from the shadiest corner of the
coolest café he can discover watches the softened bitumen
grow more largely interspaced. There is little to do or to see,
and therefore little to write about. There is in fact only one
thing to do, namely, to get out of Paris. The lively imagination of the correspondent anticipates his departure and takes
flight to one of the innumerable watering-places whose
charms at this season are set forth in large yellow and pink
placards on all the empty walls. They order this matter, like so
many others, much better in France. Here you have not, as in
America, to hunt up the "summer retreat" about which you
desire information in a dense alphabetical list in the columns
of a newspaper; you are familiar with its merits for weeks
before you start—you have seen them half a dozen times a
day emblazoned on the line of your customary walk, over the
hand and seal of the company that runs, as we should say in
America, the Casino. If you are detained in Paris, however,
after luckier mortals have departed—your reflections upon
the fate of the luckless mortals who do not depart at all are
quite another question, demanding another chapter—it does
not perhaps make you much happier to peruse these lyrical
advertisements, which seem to flutter with the breezes of
Houlgate and Etretat. You must take your consolation where
you can find it, and it must be added that of all great cities
Paris is the most tolerable in hot weather. It is true that the
asphalt liquifies, and it is true that the brilliant limestone of
which the city is built reflects the sun with uncomfortable
fierceness. It is also true that of a summer evening you pay a
penalty for living in the best-lighted capital in the world. The

inordinate amount of gas in the streets makes the atmosphere hot and thick, so that even under the dim constellations you feel of a July night as if you were in a big music-hall. If you look down at such a time upon the central portions of Paris from a high window in a remoter quarter, you see them wrapped in a lurid haze, of the devil's own brewing. But, on the other hand, there are a hundred facilities for remaining out of doors. You are not obliged to sit on a "stoop" or on a curb-stone, as in New-York. The Boulevards are a long chain of cafés, each one with its little promontory of chairs and tables projecting into the sea of asphalt. These promontories are doubtless not exactly islands of the blessed, peopled though some of them may be with sirens addicted to beer, but they may help you to pass a hot evening. Then you may dine in the Champs Elysées, at a table spread under the trees, beside an ivied wall, and almost believe you are in the country. This illusion, imperfect as it is, is a luxury, and must be paid for accordingly; the dinner is not so good as at a restaurant on the Boulevard, and is considerably dearer, and there is after all not much difference in sitting with one's feet in dusty gravel or on a sanded floor. But the whole situation is more idyllic. I indulged in a cheap idyl the other day by taking the penny steamer down the Seine to Auteuil (a very short sail), and dining at what is called in Parisian parlance a *guingette* on the bank of the stream. It was a very humble style of entertainment, but the most ambitious pursuit of pleasure can do no more than succeed, and this was a success. The Seine at Auteuil is wide, and is spanned by a stately viaduct of two tiers of arches, which stands up against the sky in a picturesque and monumental manner. Your table is spread under a trellis which scratches your head—spread chiefly with fried fish—and an old man who looks like a political exile comes and stands before it and sings a doleful ditty on the respect due to white hairs. You testify by the bestowal of copper coin the esteem with which his own inspire you, and he is speedily replaced by a lad with one arm, who treats you to something livelier:

> "A la bonne heure; parlez-moi de ça!"

You eventually return to Paris on the top of a tram-car. It is a very different affair to go out and dine at the Bois de Boulogne, at the charming restaurant which is near the cascade and the Longchamp race-course. Here are no ballad-singers, but stately trees majestically grouped and making long evening shadows on a lawn, and irreproachable tables, and carriages rolling up behind high-stepping horses and depositing all sorts of ladies. The drive back through the wood at night is most charming, and the coolness of the air extreme, however hot you may still be certain to find the city.

The best thing, therefore, is not to go back. I write these lines at an inn at Havre, before a window which frames the picture of the seaward path of the transatlantic steamers. One of the great black ships is at this moment painted on the canvas, very near, and beginning its outward journey. I watch it to the right-hand ledge of the window, which is as far as so poor a sailor need be expected to follow it. The hotel at Havre is called, for mysterious reasons, "Frascati"—reasons which I give up the attempt to fathom, so undiscoverable are its points of analogy with the lovely village of the same name which nestles among the olives of the Roman hills. The locality has its charms, however. It is very agreeable, for instance, at the end of a hot journey, to sit down to dinner in a great open cage, hung over the Atlantic, and, while the sea-breeze cools your wine, watch the swiftly-moving ships pass before you like the figures on the field of a magic lantern. It is pleasant also to open your eyes in the early dawn, before the light is intense, and without moving your head on the pillow, enjoy the same clear vision of the ocean highway. In the vague dusk, with their rapid gliding, the passing vessels look like the ghosts of wrecked ships. Most seaports are picturesque, and Havre is not the least so; but my enjoyment has been not of my goal, but of my journey.

My head is full of the twenty-four hours I have just passed at Rouen, and of the charming sail down the Seine to Honfleur. Rouen is a city of very ancient renown, and yet I confess I was not prepared to find a little town of so much expression. The traveller who treads the Rouen streets at the present day sees but the shadow of their former characteristics; for the besom of M. Haussmann has swept through the city, and a train of "embellishments" has followed in its track. The streets have been widened and straightened, and the old houses—gems of mediæval domestic architecture—which formed the peculiar treasure of the place, have been more than decimated. A great deal remains, however, and American eyes are quick to make discoveries. The cathedral, the churches, the Palais de Justice, are alone a splendid group of monuments, and a stroll through the streets reveals a collection of brown and sculptured façades, of quaintly-timbered gables, of curious turrets and casements, of doorways which still may be called rich. Every now and then a considerable stretch of duskiness and crookedness delights the sentimental tourist who is to pass but a couple of nights at Rouen, and who does not care if his favourite adjective happen to imply another element which also is spelled with a *p*. It is nothing to him that the picturesque is pestiferous. It is everything to him that the great front of the cathedral is magnificently battered, heavy, impressive. It has been defaced immensely, and is now hardly more than a collection of empty niches. I do not mean, of course, that the wanton tourist rejoices in the absence of the statues which once filled them, but up to the present moment, at least, he is not sorry that the façade has not been restored. It consists of a sort of screen, pierced in the centre with a huge wheel-window, crowned with a pyramid of chiselled needles and spires, flanked with two turrets capped with tall empty canopies, and covered, generally, with sculptures—friezes, statues, excrescences. On each side of it rises a great tower; one a rugged mass of early Norman work, with little ornament save its hatcheted closed arches, and its great naked base, as huge and white as the bottom of a chalk-cliff; the other a specimen of sixteenth century gothic, extremely flamboyant and confounding to the eye. The sides of the cathedral are as yet more or less imbedded in certain black and dwarfish old houses, but if you pass around them by a long détour, you arrive at two superb lateral porches. The so-called Portail des Libraires, in especial, on the northern side, is a magnificent affair, sculptured from summit to base (it is now restored), and preceded by a long forecourt, in which the guild of booksellers used to hold its musty traffic. From here you see the immense central tower, perched above the junction of the transepts and the nave, and crowned with a gigantic iron spire, lately erected to replace one which was destroyed by lightning in the early part of the century. This gaunt pyramid has the drawback, to American eyes, of resembling too much the tall fire-towers which are seen in transatlantic cities, and its dimensions are such that, viewed from a distance, it fairly makes little Rouen look top-heavy. Behind the choir, within, is a beautiful lady-chapel, and in this chapel are two enchanting works of art. The larger and more striking of these is the tomb of the two Cardinals d'Amboise, uncle and nephew—the elder, if I mistake not, minister of Louis XII. It consists of a shallow, oblong recess in the wall, lined with gilded and fretted marble, and corniced with delicate little statues. Within the recess the figures of the two cardinals are kneeling, with folded hands and ruggedly earnest faces, their long robes spread out behind them with magnificent amplitude. They are full of life, dignity, and piety; they look like portraits of Holbein transferred into marble. The base of the monument is composed of a series of admirable little images representing the cardinal and other virtues, and the effect of the whole work is wonderfully grave and rich. The discreet traveller will never miss an opportunity to come into a great church at eventide—the hour when his fellow-travellers, less discreet, are lingering over the table d'hôte, when the painted windows glow with a deeper splendour, when the long wand of the beadle, slowly tapping the pavement, or the shuffle of the old sacristan, has a ghostly resonance along the empty nave, and three or four work-weary women, before a dusky chapel, are mumbling for the remission of unimaginable sins. At this hour, at Rouen, the tomb of the Duke of Brézé, husband of Diana of Poitiers, placed opposite to the monument I have just described, seemed to me the most beautiful thing in the world. It is presumably the work of the delightful Jean Goujon, and it bears the stamp of his graceful and inventive talent. The deceased is lying on his back, almost naked, with a part of his shroud bound in a knot about his head—a realistic but not a repulsive image of death. At his head kneels the amiable Diana, in sober garments, all decency and devotion; at his feet stands the Virgin, a charming young woman with a charming child. Above, on another tier, the subject of the monument is represented in the fulness of life, dressed as for a tournament, bestriding a high-stepping war-horse, riding forth like a Roland or a Galahad. The architecture of the tomb is exceedingly graceful and the subordinate figures admirable, but the image of the dead Duke is altogether a masterpiece. The other evening, in the solemn stillness and the fading light of the great cathedral, it seemed irresistibly human and touching. The spectator felt a sort of impulse to smooth out the shroud and straighten the helpless hands.

The second church of Rouen, Saint-Ouen, the beautiful and harmonious, has no monuments of this value, but it offers within a higher interest than the Cathedral. Without, it looks like an English abbey, scraped and restored, disencumbered of huddling neighbours and surrounded on three sides by a beautiful garden. Seen to this excellent advantage it is one of the noblest of churches; but within, it is one of the most fascinating. My taste in architecture greatly resembles my opinions in fruit; the particular melon or pear or peach that I am eating appears to me to place either peaches, pears, or melons, beyond all other succulent things. In the same way, in a fine building the present impression is the one that convinces me most. This is deplorable levity; yet I risk the affirmation *à propos* of Saint-Ouen. I can imagine no happier combination of lightness and majesty. Its proportions bring tears to the eyes. I have left myself space only to recommend the sail down the Seine from Rouen to the mouth of the stream; but I recommend it in the highest terms. The heat was extreme and the little steamer most primitive, but the river is as entertaining as one could wish. It makes an infinite number of bends and corners and angles, rounded off by a charming vegetation. Abrupt and rocky hills go with it all the way—hills with cornfields lying in their hollows and deep woods crowning their tops. Out of the woodland peep old manors, and beneath, between the hills and the stream, are high-thatched farmsteads, lying deep in their meadows and orchards, cottages pallisaded with hollyhocks, gray old Norman churches and villas flanked with big horse-chestnuts. It is a land of peace and plenty, and remarkable to Anglo-Saxon eyes for the English-looking details of its scenery. I noticed a hundred places where one might have been in Kent as well as in Normandy. In fact it is almost better than Kent, for Kent has no Seine. At the last the river becomes unmistakably an arm of the sea, and as a river, therefore, less interesting. But crooked little Honfleur, with its miniature port, clinging to the side of a cliff as luxuriant as one of the headlands of the Mediterranean, gratifies in a high degree the tourist with a propensity for sketching.

1876

Etretat

THE COAST of Normandy and Picardy, from Trouville to Boulogne, is a chain of *stations balnéaires*, each with its particular claim to patronage. The grounds of the claim are in some cases not especially obvious; but they are generally found to reside in the fact that if one's spirits, on arriving, are low, so also are the prices. There are the places that are dear and brilliant, like Trouville and Dieppe, and places that are cheap and dreary, like Fécamp and Cabourg. Then there are the places that are both cheap and pleasant. This delightful combination of qualities may be found at the modest *plage* from which I write these lines. At Etretat you may enjoy some of the finest cliff-scenery it has been my fortune to behold, and you may breakfast and dine at the principal hotel for the sum of five and a half francs a day. You may engage a room in the town over the butcher's, the baker's, the cobbler's, at a rate that will depend upon your talent for driving a bargain, but that in no case will be exorbitant. Add to this that there are no other opportunities at Etretat to spend money. You wear old clothes, you walk about in canvas shoes, you deck your head with a fisherman's cap (when made of white flannel these articles may be extolled for their coolness, convenience, and picturesqueness), you lie on the pebbly strand most of the day, watching the cliffs, the waves, and the bathers; in the evening you converse with your acquaintance on the terrace of the Casino, and you keep monkish hours. Though Etretat enjoys great and deserved popularity, I see no symptoms of the decline of these simple fashions—no menace of the invasion of luxury. A little more luxury, indeed, might be imported without doing any harm; though after all we soon learn that it is an idle enough prejudice that has hitherto prevented us from keeping our soap in a sugar-dish and regarding a small rock, placed against a door, as an efficient substitute for a key. From a Parisian point of view, Etretat is certainly primitive, but it would be affectation on the part of an American to pretend that he was not agreeably surprised to find a "summer resort," in which he had been warned that

he would have to rough it, so elaborately appointed and organised. Etretat may be primitive, but Etretat is French, and
therefore Etretat is "administered."

Like most of the French watering-places, the place has a
limited past. Twenty years ago it was but a cluster of fishing-
huts. A group of artists and literary people were its first colo-
nists, and Alphonse Karr became the mouthpiece of their
enthusiasm. In vulgar phrase, he wrote up Etretat, and he
lives in legend, at the present hour, as the *genius loci*. The
main street is named after him; the gable of the chief inn—
the classic Hôtel Blanquet—is adorned with a coloured me-
dallion representing his cropped head and long beard; the
shops are stocked with his photographs and with pictures of
his villa. Like the magician who has evoked the spirit, he has
made his bow and retired; but the artistic fraternity, his disciples, still haunt the place, and it enjoys also the favour of
theatrical people, three or four of whom, having retired upon
their laurels, possess villas here. From my open window, as I
write these lines, I look out beyond a little cluster of clean
housetops at the long green flank of the down, as it slopes to
the village from the summit of the cliff. To the right is the top
of an old storm-twisted grove of oaks, in the heart of which
stands a brown old farmhouse; then comes the sharp, even
outline of the down, with its side spotted with little flat
bushes and wrinkled with winding paths, along which here
and there I see a bright figure moving; on the left, above the
edge of the cliff, stands a bleak little chapel, dedicated to our
Lady of the fishing-folk. Just here a provoking chimney starts
up and cuts off my view of the downward plunge of the cliff,
showing me, with a bar of blue ocean beyond, but a glimpse
of its white cheek—its fantastic profile is to the left. But there
is not far to go to see without impediments. Three minutes'
walk along the Rue Alphonse Karr, where every house is a
shop, and every shop has lodgers above it, who scramble bed-
ward by a ladder and trap-door, brings you to the little pebbly bay where the cliffs are perpendicular and the foreign life
of Etretat goes forward. At one end are the small fishing-
smacks, with their green sides and their black sails, resting
crookedly upon the stones; at the other is the Casino, and the
two or three tiers of bathing-houses on the slope of the beach

in front of it. This beach may be said to be Etretat. It is so
steep and stony as to make circulation impossible; one's only
course is to plant a camp-chair among the stones or to look
for a soft spot in the pebbles, and to abide in the position so
chosen. And yet it is the spot in Etretat most sacred to tranquil pleasure.

The French do not treat their beaches as we do ours—as
places for a glance, a dip, or a trot, places animated simply
during the balneary hours, and wrapped in natural desolation
for the rest of the twenty-four. They love them, they adore
them, they take possession of them, they live upon them. The
people here sit upon the beach from morning to night; whole
families come early and establish themselves, with umbrellas
and rugs, books and work. The ladies get sunburnt and don't
mind it; the gentlemen smoke interminably; the children roll
over on the pointed pebbles and stare at the sun like young
eagles. (The children's lot I rather commiserate; they have no
wooden spades and pails; they have no sand to delve and
grub in; they can dig no trenches and canals, nor see the
creeping tide flood them.) The great occupation and amusement is the bathing, which has many entertaining features (I
allude to it as a spectacle), especially for strangers who keep
an eye upon national idiosyncrasies. The French take their
bathing very seriously; supplemented by opéra-bouffe in the
evening at the Casino, it is their most preferred form of communion with nature. The spectators and the bathers commin-
gle in graceful promiscuity; it is the freedom of the golden
age. The whole beach becomes a large family party, in which
the sweetest familiarities prevail. There is more or less costume, but the minimum rather than the maximum is found
the more comfortable. Bathers come out of their dressing-
houses wrapped in short white sheets, which they deposit on
the stones, taking an air-bath for some minutes before entering the water. Like everything in France, the bathing is excellently managed, and you feel the firm hand of a paternal and
overlooking government the moment you issue from your
hut. The Government will on no consideration consent to
your being rash. There are six or eight worthy old sons of
Neptune on the beach—perfect amphibious creatures—who,
if you are a new-comer, immediately accost you and demand

pledges that you know how to swim. If you do not, they give you much excellent advice, and keep an eye on you while you are in the water. They are moreover obliged to render you any service you may demand—to pour buckets of water over your head, to fetch your bathing-sheet and your slippers, to carry your wife and children into the sea, to dip them, cheer them, sustain them, to teach them how to swim and how to dive, to hover about, in short, like ministering and trickling angels. At a short distance from the shore are two boats, freighted with sundry other marine divinities, who remain there perpetually, taking it as a personal offence if you venture out too far.

The French themselves have every pretext for venturing, being in general excellent swimmers. Every one swims, and swims indefatigably—men, women, and children. I have been especially struck with the prowess of the ladies, who take the neatest possible headers from the two long plunging-boards which are rigged in the water upon high wheels. As you recline upon the beach you may observe Mademoiselle X. issue from her cabin—Mademoiselle X., the actress of the Palais Royal Theatre, whom you have seen and applauded behind the footlights. She wears a bathing-dress in which, as regards the trousers, even what I have called the minimum has been appreciably scanted; but she trips down, surveying her liberated limbs. *"C'est convenable, j'espère, hein?"* says Mademoiselle, and trots up the spring-board which projects over the waves with one end uppermost, like a great see-saw. She balances a moment, and then gives a great aerial dive, executing on the way the most graceful of somersaults. This performance the star of the Palais Royal repeats during the ensuing hour, at intervals of five minutes, and leaves you, as you lie tossing little stones into the water, to consider the curious and delicate question why a lady may go so far as to put herself into a single scant clinging garment and take a straight leap, head downward, before three hundred spectators, without violation of propriety—and why impropriety should begin only when she turns over in the air in such a way that for five seconds her head is upwards. The logic of the matter is mysterious; white and black are divided by a hair. But the fact remains that virtue is on one side of the hair and vice on the other. There are some days here so still and radiant, however, that it seems as if vice itself, steeped in such an air and such a sea, might be diluted into innocence. The sea is as blue as melted sapphires, and the rugged white faces of the bordering cliffs make a silver frame for the picture. Every one is idle, amused, good-natured; the bathers take to the water as easily as mermen and mermaids. The bathing-men in the two *bateaux de surveillance* have in their charge a freight of rosy children, more or less chubbily naked, and they have nailed a gay streamer and a rude nosegay to their low mastheads. The swimmers dip and rise, circling round the boats and playing with the children. Every now and then they grasp the sides of the boats and cling to them in a dozen harmonious attitudes, making one fancy that Eugène Delacroix's great picture of Dante and Virgil on the Styx, with the damned trying to scramble into Charon's bark, has been repainted as a scene on one of the streams of Paradise. The swimmers are not the damned, but the blessed, and the demonstrative French babies are the cherubs.

The Casino at Etretat is a modest but respectable establishment, with a sufficiently capacious terrace, directly upon the beach, a café, a billiard-room, a ballroom—which may also be used as a theatre, a reading-room, and a *salon de conversation*. It is in very good taste, without any attempt at gilding or mirrors; the ballroom, in fact, is quite a masterpiece, with its charm of effect produced simply by unpainted woods and happy proportions. Three evenings in the week a blond young man in a white necktie plays waltzes on a grand piano; but the effect is not that of an American "hop," owing to the young ladies of France not being permitted to dance in public places. They may only sit wistfully beside their mammas. Imagine a "hop" at which sweet seventeen is condemned to immobility. The burden of the gaiety is sustained by three or four rosy English maidens and as many of their American sisters. On the other evenings a weak little operatic troupe gives light specimens of the lyric drama, the privilege of enjoying which is covered by your subscription to the Casino. The French hurry in joyously (four times a week in July and August!) at the sound of the bell, but I can give no report of the performances. Sometimes I look through the lighted windows and see, on the diminutive stage, a short-skirted young woman with one hand on her heart and the other persuasively extended. Through the hot unpleasant air comes a little ghost of a roulade. I turn away and walk on the terrace and listen to the ocean vocalising to the stars.

But there are (by daylight) other walks at Etretat than the terrace, and no account of the place is complete without some commemoration of the admirable cliffs. They are the finest I have seen; their fantastic needles and buttresses, at either end of the little bay, give to careless Etretat an extreme distinction. In spite of there being no sands, a persistent admirer of nature will walk a long distance upon the tiresome sea-margin of pebbles for the sake of being under them and visiting some of their quiet caves and embrowned recesses, varnished by the ocean into splendid tones. Seen in this way from directly below, they look stupendous; they hold up their heads with attitudes quite Alpine. They are marvellously white and straight and smooth; they have the tint and something of the surface of time-yellowed marble, and here and there, at their summits, they break into quaint little pinnacles and turrets. But to be on the top of them is even better; here you may walk over miles of grassy, breezy down, with the woods, contorted and sea-stunted, of old farmsteads on your land-side (the farmhouses here have all a charming way of being buried in a wood, like the castle of the Sleeping Beauty), coming every little while upon a weather-blackened old shepherd and his flock (their conversation—the shepherds'—is delightful), or on some little seaward-plunging valley, holding in its green hollow a diminutive agricultural village, curtained round from the sea-winds by a dense stockade of trees. So you may go southward or northward, without impediment, to Havre or to Dieppe.

1876

From Normandy to the Pyrenees

T HE OTHER DAY, before the first fire of winter, when the deepening dusk had compelled me to close my book and wheel my chair closer, I indulged in a retrospect. The objects of it were not far distant, and yet they were already interfused with the mellow tints of the past. In the crackling flame the last remnant of the summer appeared to shrink up and vanish. But the flicker of its destruction made a sort of fantastic imagery, and in the midst of the winter fire the summer sunshine seemed to glow. It lit up a series of visible memories.

I.

One of the first was that of a perfect day on the coast of Normandy—a warm, still Sunday in the early part of August. From my pillow, on waking, I could look at a strip of blue sea and a great cube of white cliff. I observed that the sea had never been so brilliant, and that the cliff was shining as if it had been painted in the night. I rose and came forth with the sense that it was the finest day of summer, and that one ought to do something uncommon by way of keeping it. At Etretat it was uncommon to take a walk; the custom of the country is to lie all day upon the pebbly strand, watching, as we should say in America, one's fellow-boarders. Your leisurely stroll, in a scanty sheet, from your bathing-cabin into the water, and your trickling progress from the water back into your cabin, form, as a general thing, the sum total of your pedestrianism. For the rest you remain horizontal, contemplating the horizon. To mark the day with a white stone, therefore, it was quite sufficient to stretch my legs. So I climbed the huge grassy cliff which shuts in the little bay on the right (as you lie on the beach, head upward), and gained the bleak white chapel of Notre Dame de la Garde, which a lady told me she was sure was the original of Matthew Arnold's "little gray church on the windy shore." This is very likely; but the little church to-day was not gray, neither was the shore windy.

I had occasion, by the time I reached the summit, to wish it had been. Deep, silent sunshine filled the air, and the long grass of the downs stood up in the light without a tremor. The downs at Etretat are magnificent, and the way they stretched off toward Dieppe, with their shining levels and their faintly-shaded dells, was in itself an irresistible invitation. On the land-side they have been somewhat narrowed by cultivation; the woods, and farms, and grain-fields here and there creep close enough to the edge of the cliff almost to see the shifting of the tides at its base. But cultivation in Normandy is itself picturesque, and the pedestrian rarely need resent its encroachments. Neither walls nor hedges nor fences are anywhere visible; the whole land lies open to the breezes and to his curious footsteps. This universal absence of barriers gives an air of vastness to the landscape, so that really, in a little French province, you have more of the feeling of being in a big country than on our own huge continent, which bristles so incongruously with defensive palings and dykes. Norman farmhouses, too, with their mossy roofs and their visible beams making all kinds of triangles upon the ancient plaster of their walls, are very delightful things. Hereabouts they have always a dark little wood close beside them; often a *chênaie*, as the term is—a fantastic little grove of tempest-tossed oaks. The trees look as if, some night, when the sea-blasts were howling their loudest and their boughs were tossing most wildly, the tumult had suddenly been stilled and they had stopped short, each in the attitude into which the storm was twisting it. The only thing the storm can do with them now is to blow them straight. The long, indented coast-line had never seemed to me so charming. It stretched away into the light haze of the horizon, with such lovely violet spots in its caves and hollows, and such soft white gleams on its short headlands—such exquisite gradations of distance and such capricious interruptions of perspective—that one could only say that the land was really trying to smile as intensely as the sea. The smile of the sea was a positive simper. Such a glittering and twinkling, such a softness and blueness, such tiny little pin-points of foam, and such delicate little wrinkles of waves—all this made the ocean look like a flattered portrait.

The day I speak of was a Sunday, and there were to be races at Fécamp, ten miles away. The agreeable thing was, of course, to walk to Fécamp over the grassy downs. I walked and walked, over the levels and the dells, having land and ocean quite to myself. Here and there I met a shepherd lying flat on his stomach in the sun, while his sheep, in extreme dishabille (shearing-time being recent), went huddling in front of me as I approached. Far below, on the blue ocean, like a fly on a table of lapis, crawled a little steamer, carrying people from Etretat to the races. I seemed to go much faster, yet the steamer got to Fécamp before me. But I stopped to gossip with a shepherd on a grassy hillside, and to admire certain little villages which are niched in small, transverse, seaward-sloping valleys. The shepherd told me that he had been farm-servant to the same master for five-and-thirty years—ever since the age of ten; and that for thirty-five summers he had fed his flock upon those downs. I don't know whether his sheep were tired of their diet, but he professed himself very tired of his life. I remarked that in fine weather it must be charming, and he observed, with humility, that to thirty-five summers there went a certain number of rainy days.

The walk to Fécamp would be quite satisfactory if it were not for the *fonds*. The *fonds* are the transverse valleys just mentioned—the channels, for the most part, of small watercourses which discharge themselves into the sea. The downs subside, precipitately, to the level of the beach, and then slowly lift their grassy shoulders on the other side of the gully. As the cliffs are of immense height, these indentations are profound, and drain off a little of the exhilaration of the too elastic pedestrian. The first *fond* strikes him as delightfully picturesque, and he is down the long slope on one side and up the gigantic hump on the other before he has time to feel hot. But the second is greeted with that tempered *empressement* with which you bow in the street to an acquaintance whom you have met half an hour before; the third is a stale repetition; the fourth is decidedly one too many, and the fifth is sensibly exasperating. The *fonds*, in a word, are very tiresome. It was, if I remember rightly, in the bottom of the last and widest of the series that I discovered the little town of Yport. Every little fishing-village on the Norman coast has, within the last ten years, set up in business as a watering-place; and, though one might fancy that nature had condemned Yport to modest obscurity, it is plain she has no idea of being out of the fashion. But she is a miniature imitation of her rivals. She has a meagre little wood behind her and an evil-smelling beach, on which bathing is possible only at the highest tide. At the scorching midday hour at which I inspected her she seemed absolutely empty, and the ocean, beyond acres of slippery seaweed, looked very far away. She has everything that a properly appointed *station de bains* should have, but everything is on a Lilliputian scale. The whole place looked like a huge Nüremburg toy. There is a diminutive hotel, in which, properly, the head-waiter should be a pigmy and the chambermaid a sprite, and beside it there is a Casino on the smallest possible scale. Everything about the Casino is so consistently microscopic, that it seems a matter of course that the newspapers in the reading-room should be printed in the very finest type. Of course there is a reading-room, and a dancing-room, and a café, and a billiard-room, with a bagatelle-board instead of a table, and a little terrace on which you may walk up and down with very short steps. I hope the prices are as tiny as everything else, and I suspect, indeed, that Yport honestly claims, not that she is attractive, but that she is cheap.

I toiled up the perpendicular cliff again, and took my way over the grass, for another hour, to Fécamp, where I found the peculiarities of Yport directly reversed. The place is a huge, straggling village, seated along a wide, shallow bay, and adorned, of course, with the classic Casino and the row of hotels. But all this is on a very brave scale, though it is not manifest that the bravery at Fécamp has won a victory; and, indeed, the local attractions did not strike me as irresistible. A pebbly beach of immense length, fenced off from the town by a grassy embankment; a Casino of a bald and unsociable aspect; a principal inn, with an interminable brown façade, suggestive somehow of an asylum or an almshouse—such are the most striking features of this particular watering-place. There are magnificent cliffs on each side of the bay, but, as the French say, without impropriety, it is the devil to get to them. There was no one in the hotel, in the Casino, or on the beach; the whole town being in the act of climbing the farther cliff, to reach the downs on which the races were to be held. The green hillside was black with trudging spectators and the long sky-line was fretted with them. When I say there was no one at the inn, I forget the gentleman at the door, who informed me positively that he would give me no breakfast; he seemed to have stayed at home from the races expressly to give himself this pleasure. But I went farther and fared better, obtaining a meal of homely succulence in an unfashionable tavern, in a back street, where the wine was sound, the cutlets were tender, and the serving-maid was rosy. Then I walked along—for a mile, it seemed—through a dreary, gray *grand'-rue*, where the sunshine was hot, the odours were portentous, and the doorsteps garnished with aged fishwives, retired from business, whose plaited linen coifs gave a value, as the painters say, to the brown umber of their cheeks. I inspected the harbour and its goodly basin— with nothing in it—and certain pink and blue houses which surround it, and then, joining the last stragglers, I clambered up the side of the cliff to the downs.

The races had already begun, and the ring of spectators was dense. I picked out some of the smallest people, looked over their heads, and saw several young farmers, in parti-coloured jackets and very red in the face, bouncing up and down on handsome cart-horses. Satiated at last with this diversion, I turned away and wandered down the hill again; and after strolling through the streets of Fécamp, and gathering not a little of the wayside entertainment that a seaport and fishing-town always yields, I repaired to the Abbey-church, a monument of some importance, and almost as great an object of pride in the town as the Casino. The Abbey of Fécamp was once a very rich and powerful establishment, but nothing remains of it now save its church and its *trappistine*. The church, which is for the most part early gothic, is very stately and interesting, and the *trappistine*, a distilled liquor of the Chartreuse family, is much prized by people who take a little glass after their coffee. By the time I had done with the Abbey the townsfolk had slid *en masse* down the cliff again, the yellow afternoon had come, and the holiday-takers, before the wine-shops, made long and lively shadows. I hired a sort of two-wheeled gig, without a hood, and drove back to Etretat in the rosy stage of evening. The gig dandled me up and down in a fashion of which I had been unconscious since I left off baby-clothes; but the drive, through the charming Norman country, over roads which lay among the peaceful meadows like paths across a park, was altogether delightful. The sunset gave a deeper mellowness to the standing crops, and in the grassiest corner of the wayside villages the young men and maidens were dancing like the figures in vignette-illustrations of classic poets.

II.

It was another picked day—you see how freely I pick them—when I went to breakfast at Saint-Jouin, chez la belle Ernestine. The beautiful Ernestine is as hospitable as she is fair, and to contemplate her charms you have only to order breakfast. They shine forth the more brilliantly in proportion as your order is liberal, and Ernestine is beautiful according as your bill is large. In this case she comes and smiles, really very handsomely, round your table, and you feel some hesitation in accusing so well-favoured a person of extortion. She keeps an inn at the end of a lane which diverges from the high road between Etretat and Havre, and it is an indispensable feature of your "station" at the former place that you choose some fine morning and seek her hospitality. She has been a celebrity these twenty years, and is no longer a simple maiden in her flower; but twenty years, if they have diminished her early bloom, have richly augmented her *musée*. This is a collection of all the verses and sketches, the autographs, photographs, monographs, trinkets, presented to the amiable hostess by admiring tourists. It covers the walls of her sitting-room and fills half a dozen big albums which you look at while breakfast is being prepared, just as if you were awaiting dinner in genteel society. Most Frenchmen of the day whom one has heard of appear to have called at Saint-Jouin, and to have left their *homages*. Each of them has turned a compliment with pen or pencil, and you may see in a glass case on the parlour wall what Alexandre Dumas *fils* thought of the landlady's nose, and how several painters measured her ankles.

Of course you must make this excursion in good company, and I affirm that I was in the very best. The company prefers, equally of course, to have its breakfast in the orchard in front of the house; which, if the repast is good, will make it seem better still, and if it is poor, will carry off its poorness. Clever innkeepers should always make their victims (in tolerable weather) eat in the garden. I forget whether Ernestine's breakfast was intrinsically good or bad, but I distinctly remember enjoying it, and making everything welcome. Everything, that is, save the party at the other table—the Paris actresses and the American gentlemen. The combination of these two classes of persons, individually so delightful, results in certain phenomena which seem less in harmony with apple-boughs and summer breezes than with the gas-lamps and thick perfumes of a *cabinet particulier*; and yet it was characteristic of this odd mixture of things that Mademoiselle Ernestine, coming to chat with her customers, should bear a beautiful infant on her arm, and smile with artless pride on being assured of its filial resemblance to herself. She looked handsomer than ever as she caressed this startling attribute of presumptive spinsterhood.

Saint-Jouin is close to the sea and to the finest cliffs in the world. One of my companions, who had laden the carriage with the implements of a painter, went off into a sunny meadow to take the portrait of a windmill, and I, choosing the better portion, wandered through a little green valley with the other. Ten minutes brought us to the edge of the cliffs, which at this point of the coast are simply sublime. I had supposed the white sea-walls of Etretat the finest thing possible in this way, but the huge red porphyritic-looking masses of Saint-Jouin have an even grander character. I have rarely seen a landscape more "plastic." They are strange, fantastic, out of keeping with the country, and for some rather arbitrary reason suggested to me a Spanish or even an African prospect. Certain sun-scorched precipices in Spanish sierras must have very much the same warmth of tone and desolation of attitude. The great distinction of the cliffs of Saint-Jouin is their extraordinary doubleness. Falling to an immense depth, they encounter a certain outward ledge, or terrace, where they pause and play a dozen fantastic tricks, such as piling up rocks into the likeness of needles and watch-towers; then they plunge again, and in another splendid sweep descend to the beach. There was something very impressive in the way their evil brows, looking as if they were stained with blood and rust, were bent upon the indifferent—the sleeping—sea.

III.

In a month of beautiful weather at Etretat, every day was not an excursion, but every day seemed indeed a picked day. For that matter, as I lay on the beach watching the procession of the easygoing hours, I took a good many mental excursions. The one, perhaps, on which I oftenest embarked, was a comparison between French manners, French habits, French types, and those of my native land. These comparisons are not invidious; I do not conclude against one party and in favour of the other; as the French say, *je constate* simply. The French people about me were "spending the summer," just as I had so often seen my fellow-countrymen spend it, and it seemed to me, as it had seemed to me at home, that this operation places men and women under a sort of monstrous magnifying-glass. The human figure has a higher relief in the country than in town, and I know of no place where psychological studies prosper so much as at the seaside. I shall not pretend to relate my observations in the order in which they occurred to me (or indeed to relate them in full at all); but I may say that one of the foremost was to this effect—that the summer-question, for every one, had been more easily settled than it usually is in America. The solution of the problem of where to go had not been a thin-petalled rose, plucked from among particularly sharp-pointed thorns. People presented themselves with a calmness and freshness very different from the haggardness of aspect which announces that the American citizen and his family have "secured accommodations." This impression, with me, rests perhaps on the fact that most Frenchwomen turned of thirty—the average wives and mothers—are so comfortably endowed with flesh. I have never seen such richness of contour as among the mature *baigneuses* of Etretat. The lean and desiccated person into whom a dozen years of matrimony so often converts the blooming American

girl is not emulated in France. A majestic plumpness flourished all around me—the plumpness of triple chins and
deeply dimpled hands. I mused upon it, and I discovered that
it was the result of the best breakfasts and dinners in the
world. It was the corpulence of ladies who are thoroughly
well fed, and who never walk a step that they can spare. The
assiduity with which the women of America measure the
length of our democratic pavements is doubtless a factor in
their frequent absence of redundancy of outline. As a "regular
boarder" at the Hôtel Blanquet—pronounced by Anglo-
Saxon visitors Blanket—I found myself initiated into the
mysteries of the French dietary system. I assent to the common tradition that the French are a temperate people, so long
as it is understood in this sense—that they eat no more than
they want to. But their wants are very comprehensive. Their
capacity strikes me as enormous, and we ourselves, if we are
less regulated, are certainly much more slender consumers.

The American breakfast has, I believe, long been a subject
of irony to the foreign observer; but the American breakfast is
an ascetic meal compared with the French *déjeûner-à-la-
fourchette*. The latter, indeed, is simply a dinner without soup;
it differs neither generically nor specifically from the evening-
repast. If it excludes soup, it includes eggs, prepared in a hundred forms; and if it proscribes champagne, it admits beer in
foaming pitchers, so that the balance is fairly preserved. I
think that an American will often suffer vicariously from the
reflection that a French family which sits down at half-past
eleven to fish and entrées and roasts, to asparagus and beans,
to salad and dessert, and cheese and coffee, proposes to do
exactly the same thing at half-past six. But we may be sure at
any rate that the dinner will be as good as the breakfast, and
that the breakfast has nothing to fear from prospective comparison with the dinner; and we may further reflect that in a
country where the pleasures of the table are thoroughly organised, it is natural that they should be prolonged and reiterated. Nothing is more noticeable among the French than
their superior intelligence in dietary matters; every one seems
naturally a judge, a dilettante. They have analysed tastes and
savours to a finer point than we; they are aware of differences
and relations of which we take no heed. Observe a French-

man of any age and of any condition (I have been quite as much struck with it in the very young men as in the old), as he orders his breakfast or his dinner at a Parisian restaurant, and you will perceive that the operation is much more solemn than it is apt to be in New York or in London. Monsieur has, in a word, a certain ideal for a particular repast, and it will make a difference in his happiness whether the kidneys, for instance, of a certain style, are chopped to the ultimate or only to the penultimate smallness. His directions and admonitions to the waiter are therefore minute and exquisite, and eloquently accentuated by the pressure of thumb and fore-finger; and it must be added that the imagination of the waiter is usually quite worthy of the refined communion opened to it.

This subtler sense of quality is observable even among those classes in which in other countries it is generally fore-stalled by a depressing consciousness on the subject of quan-tity. Observe your concierge and his wife at their mid-day meal, as you pass up and down stairs. They are not satisfying nature upon green tea and potatoes; they are seated before a repast which has been reasoned out, which, on its modest scale, is served in courses, and has a beginning, a middle, an end. I will not say that the French sense of comfort is con-fined to the philosophy of nutrition, but it is certainly here that it is most highly evolved. French people must have a good dinner and a good bed; but they are willing that the bed should be stationed and the dinner be eaten in the most insuf-ferable corners. Your porter and his wife dine with a certain distinction, and sleep soft in their lodge; but their lodge is in all probability a fetid black hole, five feet square, in which, in England or in America, people of their talents would never consent to live. The French are willing to abide in the dark, to huddle together, to forego privacy, to let bad smells grow great among them. They have an accursed passion for co-quettish furniture; for cold, brittle chairs, for tables with scal-loped edges, for ottomans without backs, for fireplaces muffled in plush and fringe. A French bedroom is a bitter mockery—a ghastly attempt to serve two masters which suc-ceeds in being agreeable to neither. It is a thing of traps and delusions, constructed on the assumption that it is inelegant

to be known to wash or to sleep, and yet pervaded with suggestions of uncleanness compared with which the matutinal
"tub," well *en évidence*, is a delightful symbol of purity. This
comes of course from that supreme French quality, the source
of half the charm of the French mind as well as of all its
dryness, the genius for economy. It is wasting a room to let it
be a bedroom alone; so it must be tricked out ingeniously as a
sitting-room, and ends by being (in many cases) insufferable
both by night and by day. But allowing all weight to these
latter reflections, it is still very possible that the French have
the better part. If you are well fed, you can perhaps afford to
be ill lodged; whereas enjoyment of the most commodious
apartments is incompatible with inanition and dyspepsia.

If I had not cut short my mild retrospect by these possibly
milder generalisations, I should have touched lightly upon
some of the social phenomena of which the little beach at
Etretat was the scene. I should have narrated that the French,
at the seaside, are not "sociable" as Americans affect to be in a
similar situation, and I should subjoin that at Etretat it was
very well on the whole that they should not have been. The
immeasurably greater simplicity of composition of American
society makes sociability with us a comparatively untaxed virtue; but anything like an equal exercise of it in France would
be attended with alarming drawbacks. Sociability (in the
American sense of the word) in any aristocratic country
would indeed be very much like an attempt to establish visiting relations between birds and fishes. At Etretat no making
of acquaintance was to be perceived; people went about in
compact, cohesive groups, of natural formation, governed
doubtless, internally, by humane regulations, but presenting
to the world an impenetrable defensive front. The groups
usually formed a solid phalanx around two or three young
girls, compressed into the centre, the preservation of whose
innocence was their chief solicitude. These groups were
doubtless wisely constituted, for with half a dozen *cocottes*, in
scarlet petticoats, scattered over the sunny, harmless-looking
beach, what were mammas and duennas to do? I used to pity
the young ladies at first, for this perpetual application of the
leading-string; but a little reflection showed me that the
French have ordered this as well as they have ordered every-

thing else. The case is not nearly so hard as it would be with us, for there is this immense difference between the lot of the *jeune fille* and her American sister, that the former may as a general thing be said to be certain to marry. "Alas, to marry badly," the Anglo-Saxon objector may reply. But the objection is precipitate; for if French marriages are almost always arranged, it must be added that they are in the majority of cases arranged successfully. Therefore, if a *jeune fille* is for three or four years tied with a very short rope and compelled to browse exclusively upon the meagre herbage which sprouts in the maternal shadow, she has at least the comfort of reflecting that, according to the native phrase, *on s'occupe de la marier*—that measures are being carefully taken to promote her to a condition of unbounded liberty. Whatever, to her imagination, marriage may fail to mean, it at least means freedom and consideration. It does not mean, as it so often means in America, being socially shelved—and it is not too much to say, in certain circles, degraded; it means being socially launched and consecrated. It means becoming that exalted personage, a *mère de famille*. To be a *mère de famille* is to occupy not simply (as is mostly the case with us) a sentimental, but really an official position. The consideration, the authority, the domestic pomp and circumstance allotted to a French mamma are in striking contrast with the amiable tolerance which in our own social order is so often the most liberal measure that the female parent may venture to expect at her children's hands, and which, on the part of the young lady of eighteen who represents the family in society, is not unfrequently tempered by a conscientious severity. All this is worth waiting for, especially if you have not to wait very long. Mademoiselle is married certainly, and married early, and she is sufficiently well informed to know, and to be sustained by the knowledge, that the sentimental expansion which may not take place at present will have an open field after her marriage. That it should precede her marriage seems to her as unnatural as that she should put on her shoes before her stockings. And besides all this, to browse in the maternal shadow is not considered in the least a hardship. A young French girl who is *bien-élevée*—an expression which means so much—will be sure to consider her mother's company the most delightful in the world, and to think that the herbage which sprouts about this lady's petticoats is peculiarly tender and succulent. It may be fanciful, but it often seems to me that the tone with which such a young girl says *Ma mère* has a peculiar intensity of meaning. I am at least not wrong in affirming that in the accent with which the mamma—especially if she be of the well-rounded order alluded to above—speaks of *Ma fille* there is a kind of sacerdotal dignity.

IV.

After this came two or three pictures of quite another complexion—pictures of which a long green valley, almost in the centre of France, makes the general setting. The valley itself, indeed, forms one delightful picture, although the country which surrounds it is by no means one of the regions that place themselves on exhibition. It is the old territory of the Gâtinais, which has much history, but no renown of beauty. It is very quiet, deliciously rural, immitigably French; the typical, average, "pleasant" France of history, literature, and art—of art, of landscape-art, perhaps, especially. Wherever I look I seem to see one of the familiar pictures on a dealer's wall—a Lambinet, a Troyon, a Daubigny, a Diaz. The Lambinets perhaps are in the majority; the mood of the landscape usually expresses itself in silvery lights and vivid greens. The history of this part of France is the history of the monarchy, and its language is, I won't say absolutely the classic tongue, but a nearer approach to it than any local patois. The peasants deliver themselves with rather a drawl, but their French is as consecutive as that of Ollendorf.

Each side of the long valley is a continuous ridge, which offers it a high, wooded horizon, and through the middle of it there flows a charming stream, wandering, winding and doubling, smothered here and there in rushes, and spreading into lily-coated reaches, beneath the clear shadow of tall, straight, light-leaved trees. On each side of the stream the meadows stretch away flat, clean, magnificent, lozenged across with rows of lateral foliage, under which a cow-maiden sits on the grass, hooting now and then, nasally, to the large-uddered browsers in front of her. There are no hedges nor

palings nor walls; it is all a single estate. Occasionally in the
meadows there rises a cluster of red-roofed hovels—each a
diminutive village. At other points, at about half an hour's
walk apart, are three charming old houses. The châteaux are
extremely different, but, both as pictures and as dwellings,
each has its points. They are very intimate with each other, so
that these points may be amicably discussed. The points in
one case, however, are remarkably strong. The little old *castel*
I mention stands directly in the attenuated river, on an island
just great enough to hold it, and the garden-flowers grow
upon the farther bank. This, of course, is a most delightful
affair. But I found something very agreeable in the aspect of
one of the others, when I made it the goal of certain of those
walks before breakfast, which of cool mornings, in the late
summer, do not fall into the category of ascetic pleasures. (In
France, indeed, if one did not do a great many things before
breakfast, the work of life would be but meagrely performed.)

The dwelling in question stands on the top of the long
ridge which encloses the comfortable valley to the south, being by its position quite in the midst of its appurtenant acres.
It is not particularly "kept up," but its quiet rustiness and
untrimmedness only help it to be familiar. A grassy plateau
approaches it from the edge of the hill, bordered on one side
by a short avenue of horse-chestnuts, and on the other by a
dusky wood. Beyond the chestnuts are the steep-roofed,
yellow-walled farm-buildings, and under cover of the wood a
stretch of beaten turf, where, on Sundays and holidays, the
farm-servants play at bowls. Directly before the house is a
little square garden, enclosed by a low parapet, which is interrupted by a high gateway of mossy pillars and iron arabesques, the whole of it muffled in creeping plants. The
house, with its yellow walls and russet roof, is ample and substantial; it is a very proper *gentilhommière*. In a corner of the
garden, at the angle of the parapet, rises that classic emblem
of rural gentility, the *pigeonnier*, the old stone dovecot. It is a
great round tower, as broad of base as a lighthouse, with its
roof shaped like an extinguisher, and a big hole in its upper
portion, in and out of which a dove is always fluttering.

You see all this from the windows of the drawing-room. Be
sure that the drawing-room is panelled in white and gray,

with old rococo mouldings over the doorways and mantel-piece. The open gateway of the garden, with its tangled creepers, makes a frame for the picture that lies beyond the grassy esplanade where the thistles have been suffered to grow round a disused stone well, placed in odd remoteness from the house (if, indeed, it be not a relic of an earlier habitation): a picture of a wide green country, rising beyond the unseen valley and stretching away to a far horizon in deep blue lines of wood. Behind, through other windows, you look out on the gardens proper. There are places that take one's fancy by some accident of expression, some mystery of accident. This one is high and breezy, both genial and reserved, plain yet picturesque, extremely cheerful and a little melancholy. It has what in the arts is called "style," and so I have attempted to commemorate it.

Going to call on the peasants was as charming an affair as a chapter in one of George Sand's rural tales. I went one Sunday morning with my hostess, who knew them well and enjoyed their most garrulous confidence. I don't mean that they told her all their secrets, but they told her a good many; if the French peasant is a simpleton, he is a very shrewd simpleton. At any rate, of a Sunday morning in August, when he is stopping at home from work and has put on his best jacket and trousers, and is loafing at the door of his neighbour's cabin, he is a very charming person. The peasantry in the region I speak of had admirably good manners. The curé gave me a low account of their morals, by which he meant, on the whole, I suspect, that they were moderate church-goers. But they have the instinct of civility and a talent for conversation; they know how to play the host and the entertainer. By "he," just now, I meant she quite as much; it is rare that, in speaking superlatively of the French, in any connection, one does not think of the women even more than of the men. They constantly strike the foreigner as a stronger expression of the qualities of the race. On the occasion I speak of the first room in the very humble cabins I successively visited—in some cases, evidently, it was the only room—had been set into irreproachable order for the day. It had usually a fine brownness of tone, generated by the high chimney-place, with its swinging pots, the important bed, in its dusky niche, with its

flowered curtains, the big-bellied earthenware in the cup-
board, the long-legged clock in the corner, the thick, quiet
light of the small, deeply-set window, the mixture, on all
things, of smoke-stain and the polish of horny hands. Into the
midst of this "la Rabillon" or "la mère Léger" brings forward
her chairs and begs us to be seated, and, seating herself, with
crossed hands, smiles expressively and answers abundantly
every inquiry about her cow, her husband, her bees, her eggs,
her baby. The men linger half outside and half in, with their
shoulders against dressers and door-posts; every one smiles
with that simple, clear-eyed smile of the gratified peasant;
they talk much more like George Sand's Berrichons than
might be supposed. And if they receive us without gross awkwardness, they speed us on our way with proportionate urbanity. I go to six or eight little hovels, all of them dirty
outside and clean within; I am entertained everywhere with
the bonhomie, the quaintness, the good faces and good manners of their occupants, and I finish my tour with an esteem
for my new acquaintance which is not diminished by learning
that several of them have thirty or forty thousand francs carefully put away.

And yet, as I say, M. le Curé thinks they are in a bad way,
and he knows something about them. M. le Curé, too, is not
a dealer in scandal; there is something delightfully quaint in
the way in which he deprecates an un-Christian construction
of his words. There is more than one curé in the valley whose
charms I celebrate; but the worthy priest of whom I speak is
the pearl of the local priesthood. He has been accused, I believe, of pretensions to *illuminisme*; but even in his most illuminated moments it can never occur to him that he has been
chronicled in an American magazine, and therefore it is not
indiscreet to say that he is the curé, not of Gy, but of the
village nearest to Gy. I write this sentence half for the pleasure of putting down that briefest of village-names and seeing
how it looks in print. But it may be elongated at will, and yet
be only improved. If you wish to be very specific, you may
call it Gy-les-Nonnains—Gy of the Little Nuns. I went with
my hostess, another morning, to call upon M. le Curé, who
himself opened his garden door to us (there was a crooked
little black cross perched upon it), and, lifting his rusty *calotte*,

stood there a moment in the sunshine, smiling a greeting more benignant than his words.

A rural *presbytère* is not a very sumptuous dwelling, and M. le Curé's little drawing-room reminded me of a Yankee parlour (*minus* the subscription-books from Hartford on the centre-table) in some out-of-the-way corner of New England. But he took us into his very diminutive garden, and showed us an ornament that would not have flourished in the shadow of a Yankee parlour—a rude stone image of the Virgin, which he had become possessed of I know not how, and for which he was building a sort of niche in the wall. The work was going on slowly, for he must take the labour as he could get it; but he appealed to his visitors, with a smile of indulgent irony, for an assurance that his little structure would not make too bad a figure. One of them told him that she would send him some white flowers to set out round the statue; whereupon he clasped his hands together over his snuff-box and expressed cheerful views of the world we live in. A couple of days afterward he came to breakfast, and of course arrived early, in his new cassock and band. I found him in the billiard-room, walking up and down alone and reading his breviary. The combination of the locality, the personage and the occupation, made me smile; and I smiled again when, after breakfast, I found him strolling about the garden, puffing a cigarette. Of course he had an excellent appetite; but there is something rather cruel in those alternations of diet to which the French parish priest is subjected. At home he lives like a peasant—a fact which, in itself, is not particularly cruel, inasmuch as he has usually—or in many cases—been brought up to that life. But his fellow-peasants don't breakfast at the château and gaze down the savoury vistas opened by cutlets à la Soubise. They have not the acute pain of relapsing into the stale atmosphere of bread and beans. Of course it is by no means every day, or every week even, that M. le Curé breakfasts at the château; but there must nevertheless be a certain uncomfortable crookedness in his position. He lives like a labourer, yet he is treated like a gentleman. The latter character must seem to him sometimes to have rather a point of irony. But to the ideal curé, of course, all characters are equal; he thinks neither too ill of his bad breakfasts nor too well of his

good ones. I won't say that the excellent man I speak of is the
ideal curé, but I suspect he is an approach to it; he has a grain
of the epicurean to an ounce of stoicism. In the garden-path,
beside the moat, while he puffed his cigarette, he told me
how he had held up his head to the Prussians; for, hard as it
seemed to believe it, that pastoral valley had been occupied by
ravaging Teutons. According to this recital, he had spoken his
mind civilly, but very distinctly, to the group of officers who
had made themselves at home in his dwelling—had informed
them that it grieved him profoundly that he was obliged to
meet them standing there in his *soutane*, and not out in the
fields with a musket in his hands and a dozen congenial spirits
at his side. The scene must have been dramatic. The first of
the officers got up from table and asked for the privilege of
shaking his hand. "M. le Curé," he said, "j'estime hautement
votre caractère."

Six miles away—or nearer, by a charming shaded walk
along a canal—was an ancient town with a legend—a legend
which, as a child, I read in my lesson-book at school, marvel-
ling at the woodcut above it, in which a ferocious dog was
tearing a strange man to pieces, while the king and his courtiers sat by as if they were at the circus. I allude to it chiefly in
order to mention the name of one of its promenades, which is
the stateliest, beyond all comparison, in the world; the name,
I mean, not the street. The latter is called the Promenade des
Belles Manières. Could anything be finer than that? With
what a sweep gentlemen must once have taken off their hats
there; how ladies must once have curtsied, regardless of gutters, and how people must have turned out their toes as they
walked!

v.

My next impressions were gathered on the margin of a
southern sea—if the Bay of Biscay indeed deserve so sympathetic a name. We generally have a mental image beforehand
of a place on which we may intend to project ourself, and I
supposed I had a tolerably vivid prevision of Biarritz. I don't
know why, but I had a singular sense of having been there;
the name always seemed to me expressive. I saw the way it lay

along its gleaming beach; I had taken in imagination long walks toward Spain over the low cliffs, with the blue sea always to my right and the blue Pyrenees always before me. My only fear was that my mental picture had not been brilliant enough; but this could easily be touched up on the spot. In truth, however, on the spot I was exclusively occupied in toning it down. Biarritz seemed to be decidedly below its reputation; I am at a loss to see how its reputation was made. There is a partial explanation that is obvious enough. There is a low, square, bare brick mansion seated on the sands, under shelter of a cliff; it is one of the first objects to attract the attention of an arriving stranger. It is not picturesque, it is not romantic, and even in the days of its prosperity it never can have been impressive. It is called the Villa Eugénie, and it explains in a great measure, as I say, the Biarritz which the arriving stranger, with some dismay, perceives about him. It has the aspect of one of the "cottages" of Newport during the winter season, but is surrounded by a vegetation much less dense than the prodigies of arborescence now so frequent at Newport. It was what the newspapers call the "favourite resort" of the ex-Empress of the French, who might have been seen at her imperial avocations with a good glass, at any time, from the Casino. The Casino, I hasten to add, has quite the air of an establishment frequented by gentlemen who look at ladies' windows with telescopes. There are Casinos and Casinos, and that of Biarritz is, in the summary French phrase, "impossible." Except for its view, it is moreover very unattractive. Perched on the top of a cliff which has just space enough to hold its immense brick foundations, it has no garden, no promenade, no shade, no place of out-of-door reunion—the most indispensable feature of a Casino. It turns its back to the Pyrenees and to Spain, and looks out prettily enough over a blue ocean to an arm of the low French coast.

Biarritz, for the rest, scrambles over two or three steep hills, directly above the sea, in a promiscuous, many-coloured, noisy fashion. It is a watering-place pure and simple; every house has an expensive little shop in the basement and a still more expensive set of rooms to let above stairs. The houses are blue and pink and green; they stick to the hillsides as they can, and being near Spain, you try to fancy they look Spanish.

You succeed, perhaps, even a little, and are rewarded for your zeal by finding, when you cross the border a few days afterward, that the houses at San Sebastian look strikingly French. Biarritz is bright, crowded, irregular, filled with many sounds, and not without a certain second-rate pictorial quality; but it struck me as common and cockneyfied, and my vision travelled back to modest little Etretat, by its northern sea, as to a very much more downy couch. The south-western coast of France has little of the exquisite charm of the Mediterranean shore. It has of course a southern expression which in itself is always delightful. You see a brilliant, yellow sun, with a pink-faced, red-tiled house staring up at it. You can see here and there a trellis and an orange-tree, a peasant-woman in a gold necklace, driving a donkey, a lame beggar adorned with ear-rings, a glimpse of blue sea between white garden-walls. But the superabundant detail of the French Riviera is wanting; the softness, luxuriousness, enchantment.

The most pictorial thing at Biarritz is the Basque population, which overflows from the adjacent Spanish provinces and swarms in the crooked streets. It lounges all day in the public places, sprawls upon the curbstones, clings to the face of the cliffs, and vociferates continually a shrill, strange tongue, which has no discoverable affinity with any other. The Basques look like hardier and thriftier Neapolitan lazzaroni; if the superficial resemblance is striking, the difference is very much in their favour. Although those specimens which I observed at Biarritz appeared to enjoy an excess of leisure, they had nothing of a shiftless or beggarly air, and seemed as little disposed to ask favours as to confer them. The roads leading into Spain were dotted with them, and here they were coming and going as if on important business—the business of the abominable Don Carlos himself. They struck me as a very handsome race. The men are invariably clean-shaven; smooth chins seem a positively religious observance. They wear little round maroon-coloured caps, like those of sailor-boys, dark stuff shirts, and curious white shoes, made of strips of rope laid together—an article of toilet which makes them look like honorary members of base-ball clubs. They sling their jackets cavalier-fashion, over one shoulder, hold their heads very high, swing their arms very bravely, step out very lightly, and, when you meet them in the country at eventide, charging down a hillside in companies of half a dozen, make altogether a most impressive appearance. With their smooth chins and childish caps, they may be taken, in the distance, for a lot of very naughty little boys; for they have always a cigarette in their teeth.

The best thing at Biarritz is your opportunity for driving over into Spain. Coming speedily to a consciousness of this fact, I found a charm in sitting in a landau and rolling away to San Sebastian behind a coachman in a high glazed hat with long streamers, a jacket of scarlet and silver and a pair of yellow breeches and jack-boots. If it has been the desire of one's heart and the dream of one's life to visit the land of Cervantes, even grazing it so lightly as by a day's excursion from Biarritz is a matter to encourage visions. Everything helping—the admirable scenery, the charming day, the operatic coachman, the smooth-rolling carriage—I am afraid I became more visionary than it is decent to tell of. You move toward the magnificent undulations of the Pyrenees, as if you were going to plunge straight into them; but in reality you travel beneath them and beside them, pass between their expiring spurs and the sea. It is on proceeding beyond San Sebastian that you seriously attack them. But they are already extremely vivid—none the less so that in this region they abound in suggestions of the recent Carlist war. Their far-away peaks and ridges are crowned with lonely Spanish watch-towers, and their lower slopes are dotted with demolished dwellings. It was hereabouts that the fighting was most constant. But the healing powers of nature are as remarkable as the destructive powers of man, and the rich September landscape appeared already to have forgotten the injuries of yesterday. Everything seemed to me a small foretaste of Spain; I discovered an unreasonable amount of local colour. I discovered it at Saint-Jean-de-Luz, the last French town, in a great brown church, filled with galleries and boxes, like a play-house—the altar and choir, indeed, looked very much like a proscenium; at Bohébie, on the Bidassoa, the small yellow stream which divides France from Spain, and which at this point offers to view the celebrated Isle of Pheasants, a little bushy strip of earth adorned with a decayed commemorative monument, on

which, in the seventeenth century, the affairs of Louis XIV.
and the Iberian monarch were discussed in ornamental con-
ference; at Fuentarabia (glorious name), a mouldering relic of
Spanish stateliness; at Hendaye, at Irun, at Renteria, and
finally at San Sebastian. At all of these wayside towns the
houses show marks of Alphonsist bullets (the region was
strongly Carlist); but to be riddled and battered seems to
carry out the meaning of the pompous old escutcheons carven
above the doorways, some of them covering almost half the
house. It struck me, in fact, that the narrower and shabbier
was the poor little dusky dwelling, the grander and more
elaborate was this noble advertisement. But it represented
knightly prowess, and pitiless time had taken up the challenge. I found it a luxury to ramble through the narrow single
street of Irun and Renteria, between the strange-coloured
houses, the striped awnings, the universal balconies and the
heraldic doorways.

   San Sebastian is a lively watering-place, and is set down in
the guide-books as the Biarritz or the Brighton of Spain. It
has of course a new quarter in the provincial-elegant style
(fresh stucco cafés, barber-shops, and apartments to let), looking out upon a planted promenade and a charming bay,
locked in fortified heights, with a narrow portal to the ocean.
I walked about for two or three hours and devoted most of
my attention to the old quarter, the town proper, which has a
great frowning gate upon the harbour, through which you
look along a vista of gaudy house-fronts, balconies, awnings,
surmounted by a narrow strip of sky. Here the local colour
was richer, the manners more naïf. Here too was a church
with a flamboyant Jesuit façade and an interior redolent of
Spanish Catholicism. There was a life-sized effigy of the Virgin perched upon a table beside the great altar (she appeared
to have been walking abroad in a procession), which I looked
at with extreme interest. She seemed to me a heroine, a solid
Spanish person, as perfect a reality as Don Quixote or Saint
Theresa. She was dressed in an extraordinary splendour of
laces, brocades and jewels, her coiffure and complexion were
of the finest, and she evidently would answer to her name if
you should speak to her. Mustering up the stateliest title I
could think of, I addressed her as Doña Maria of the Holy

Office; whereupon she looked round the great dusky, perfumed church, to see whether we were alone, and then she
dropped her fringed eyelids and held out her hand to be
kissed. She was the sentiment of Spanish catholicism; gloomy,
yet bedizened, emotional as a woman and mechanical as a
doll. After a moment I grew afraid of her, and went slinking
away. After this I didn't really recover my spirits until I had
the satisfaction of hearing myself addressed as "Caballero." I
was hailed with this epithet by a ragged infant, with sickly
eyes and a cigarette in his lips, who invited me to cast a copper into the sea, that he might dive for it; and even with these
limitations, the sensation seemed worth the cost of my excursion. It appeared kinder, to my gratitude, to make the infant
dive upon the pavement.

A few days later I went back to San Sebastian, to be present
at a bull-fight; but I suppose my right to descant upon this
entertainment should be measured less by the gratification it
afforded me than by the question whether there is room in
literature for another chapter on this subject. I incline to think
there is not; the national pastime of Spain is the best-
described thing in the world. Besides, there are other reasons
for not describing it. It is extremely disgusting, and one
should not describe disgusting things—except (according to
the new school) in novels, where they have not really occurred, and are invented on purpose. Description apart, one
has taken a certain sort of pleasure in the bull-fight, and yet
how is one to state gracefully that one has taken pleasure in a
disgusting thing? It is a hard case. If you record your pleasure, you seem to exaggerate it and to calumniate your delicacy; and if you record nothing but your displeasure, you feel
as if you were wanting in suppleness. Thus much I can say, at
any rate, that as there had been no bull-fights in that part of
the country during the Carlist war, the native dilettanti (and
every man, woman, and child of them comes under this denomination) returned to their precious pastime with peculiar
zest. The spectacle, therefore, had an unusual splendour. Under these circumstances it is highly effective. The weather was
beautiful; the near mountains peeped over the top of the vast
open arena, as if they too were curious; weary of disembow-
elled horses and posturing *espadas*, the spectator (in the boxes)

might turn away and look through an unglazed window at the empty town and the cloud-shadowed sea. But few of the native spectators availed themselves of this privilege. Beside me sat a blooming matron, in a white lace mantilla, with three very juvenile daughters; and if these ladies sometimes yawned they never shuddered. For myself, I confess that if I sometimes shuddered I never yawned. A long list of bulls was sacrificed, each of whom had pretensions to originality. The *banderillos*, in their silk stockings and embroidered satin costumes, skipped about with a great deal of attitude; the *espada* folded his arms within six inches of the bull's nose and stared him out of countenance; yet I thought the bull, in any case, a finer fellow than any of his tormentors, and I thought his tormentors finer fellows than the spectators. In truth, we were all, for the time, rather sorry fellows together. A bull-fight will, to a certain extent, bear looking at, but it will not bear thinking of. There was a more innocent effect in what I saw afterward, when we all came away, in the late afternoon, as the shadows were at their longest: the bright-coloured southern crowd, spreading itself over the grass, and the women, with mantillas and fans, and the Andalusian gait, strolling up and down before the mountains and the sea.

1876

Occasional Paris

IT IS HARD to say exactly what is the profit of comparing one race with another, and weighing in opposed groups the manners and customs of neighbouring countries; but it is certain that as we move about the world we constantly indulge in this exercise. This is especially the case if we happen to be infected with the baleful spirit of the cosmopolite—that uncomfortable consequence of seeing many lands and feeling at home in none. To be a cosmopolite is not, I think, an ideal; the ideal should be to be a concentrated patriot. Being a cosmopolite is an accident, but one must make the best of it. If you have lived about, as the phrase is, you have lost that sense of the absoluteness and the sanctity of the habits of your fellow-patriots which once made you so happy in the midst of them. You have seen that there are a great many *patriæ* in the world, and that each of these is filled with excellent people for whom the local idiosyncrasies are the only thing that is not rather barbarous. There comes a time when one set of customs, wherever it may be found, grows to seem to you about as provincial as another; and then I suppose it may be said of you that you have become a cosmopolite. You have formed the habit of comparing, of looking for points of difference and of resemblance, for present and absent advantages, for the virtues that go with certain defects, and the defects that go with certain virtues. If this is poor work compared with the active practice, in the sphere to which a discriminating Providence has assigned you, of the duties of a tax-payer, an elector, a juryman or a diner-out, there is nevertheless something to be said for it. It is good to think well of mankind, and this, on the whole, a cosmopolite does. If you limit your generalisations to the sphere I mentioned just now, there is a danger that your occasional fits of pessimism may be too sweeping. When you are out of humour the whole country suffers, because at such moments one is never discriminating, and it costs you very little bad logic to lump your fellow-citizens together. But if you are living about, as I say, certain differences impose themselves. The worst you can say of the human race is, for instance, that the Germans are a detestable people. They do not represent the human race for you, as in your native town your fellow-citizens do, and your unflattering judgment has a flattering reverse. If the Germans are detestable, you are mentally saying, there are those admirable French, or those charming Americans, or those interesting English. (Of course it is simply by accident that I couple the German name here with the unfavourable adjective. The epithets may be transposed at will.) Nothing can well be more different from anything else than the English from the French, so that, if you are acquainted with both nations, it may be said that on any special point your agreeable impression of the one implies a censorious attitude toward the other, and *vice versâ*. This has rather a shocking sound; it makes the cosmopolite appear invidious and narrow-minded. But I hasten to add that there seems no real reason why even the most delicate conscience should take alarm. The consequence of the cosmopolite spirit is to initiate you into the merits of all peoples; to convince you that national virtues are numerous, though they may be very different, and to make downright preference really very hard. I have, for instance, every disposition to think better of the English race than of any other except my own. There are things which make it natural I should; there are inducements, provocations, temptations, almost bribes. There have been moments when I have almost burned my ships behind me, and declared that, as it simplified matters greatly to pin one's faith to a chosen people, I would henceforth cease to trouble my head about the lights and shades of the foreign character. I am convinced that if I had taken this reckless engagement, I should greatly have regretted it. You may find a room very comfortable to sit in with the window open, and not like it at all when the window has been shut. If one were to give up the privilege of comparing the English with other people, one would very soon, in a moment of reaction, make once for all (and most unjustly) such a comparison as would leave the English nowhere. Compare then, I say, as often as the occasion presents itself. The result as regards any particular people, and as regards the human race at large, may be pronounced agreeable, and the process is both instructive and entertaining.

So the author of these observations finds it on returning to Paris after living for upwards of a year in London. He finds himself comparing, and the results of comparison are several disjointed reflections, of which it may be profitable to make a note. Certainly Paris is a very old story, and London is a still older one; and there is no great reason why a journey across the channel and back should quicken one's perspicacity to an unprecedented degree. I therefore will not pretend to have been looking at Paris with new eyes, or to have gathered on the banks of the Seine a harvest of extraordinary impressions. I will only pretend that a good many old impressions have recovered their freshness, and that there is a sort of renovated entertainment in looking at the most brilliant city in the world with eyes attuned to a different pitch. Never, in fact, have those qualities of brightness and gaiety that are half the stock-in-trade of the city by the Seine seemed to me more uncontestable. The autumn is but half over, and Paris is, in common parlance, empty. The private houses are closed, the lions have returned to the jungle, the Champs Elysées are not at all "mondains." But I have never seen Paris more Parisian, in the pleasantest sense of the word; better humoured, more open-windowed, more naturally entertaining. A radiant September helps the case; but doubtless the matter is, as I hinted above, in a large degree "subjective." For when one comes to the point there is nothing very particular just now for Paris to rub her hands about. The Exhibition of 1878 is looming up as large as a mighty mass of buildings on the Trocadéro can make it. These buildings are very magnificent and fantastical; they hang over the Seine, in their sudden immensity and glittering newness, like a palace in a fairy-tale. But the trouble is that most people appear to regard the Exhibition as in fact a fairy-tale. They speak of the wonderful structures on the Champ de Mars and the Trocadéro as a predestined monument to the folly of a group of gentlemen destitute of a sense of the opportune. The moment certainly does not seem very well chosen for inviting the world to come to Paris to amuse itself. The world is too much occupied with graver cares — with reciprocal cannonading and chopping, with cutting of throats and burning of homes, with murder of infants and mutilation of mothers, with warding off famine and civil war, with lamenting the failure of its resources, the dulness of trade, the emptiness of its pockets. Rome is burning altogether too fast for even its most irresponsible spirits to find any great satisfaction in fiddling. But even if there is (as there very well may be) a certain scepticism at headquarters as to the accomplishment of this graceful design, there is no apparent hesitation, and everything is going forward as rapidly as if mankind were breathless with expectation. That familiar figure, the Parisian *ouvrier*, with his white, chalky blouse, his attenuated person, his clever face, is more familiar than ever, and I suppose, finding plenty of work to his hand, is for the time in a comparatively rational state of mind. He swarms in thousands, not only in the region of the Exhibition, but along the great thoroughfare—the Avenue de l'Opéra—which has just been opened in the interior of Paris.

This is an extremely Parisian creation, and as it is really a great convenience—it will save a great many steps and twists and turns—I suppose it should be spoken of with gratitude and admiration. But I confess that to my sense it belongs primarily to that order of benefits which during the twenty years of the Empire gradually deprived the streets of Paris of ninetenths of their ancient individuality. The deadly monotony of the Paris that M. Haussmann called into being—its huge, blank, pompous, featureless sameness—sometimes comes over the wandering stranger with a force that leads him to devote the author of these miles of architectural commonplace to execration. The new street is quite on the imperial system; it must make the late Napoleon III. smile with beatific satisfaction as he looks down upon it from the Bonapartist corner of Paradise. It stretches straight away from the pompous façade of the Opera to the doors of the Théâtre Français, and it must be admitted that there is something fine in the vista that is closed at one end by the great sculptured and gilded mass of the former building. But it smells of the modern asphalt; it is lined with great white houses that are adorned with machine-made arabesques, and each of which is so exact a copy of all the rest that even the little white porcelain number on a blue ground, which looks exactly like all the other numbers, hardly constitutes an identity. Presently there will be a long succession of milliners' and chocolate-makers' shops in the basement of this homogeneous row, and the pretty bonnets and bonbonnières in the shining windows will have their ribbons knotted with a *chic* that you must come to Paris to see. Then there will be little glazed sentry-boxes at regular intervals along the curbstone, in which churlish old women will sit selling half a dozen copies of each of the newspapers; and over the hardened bitumen the young Parisian of our day will constantly circulate, looking rather pallid and wearing very large shirt-cuffs. And the new avenue will be a great success, for it will place in symmetrical communication two of the most important establishments in France—the temple of French music and the temple of French comedy.

I said just now that no two things could well be more unlike than England and France; and though the remark is not original, I uttered it with the spontaneity that it must have on the lips of a traveller who, having left either country, has just disembarked in the other. It is of course by this time a very trite observation, but it will continue to be made so long as Boulogne remains the same lively antithesis of Folkestone. An American, conscious of the family-likeness diffused over his own huge continent, never quite unlearns his surprise at finding that so little of either of these two almost contiguous towns has rubbed off upon the other. He is surprised at certain English people feeling so far away from France, and at all French people feeling so far away from England. I travelled from Boulogne the other day in the same railway-carriage with a couple of amiable and ingenuous young Britons, who had come over to spend ten days in Paris. It was their first landing in France; they had never yet quitted their native island; and in the course of a little conversation that I had with them I was struck with the scantiness of their information in regard to French manners and customs. They were very intelligent lads; they were apparently fresh from a university; but in respect to the interesting country they were about to enter, their minds were almost a blank. If the conductor, appearing at the carriage door to ask for our tickets, had had the leg of a frog sticking out of his pocket, I think their only very definite preconception would have been confirmed. I parted with them at the Paris station, and I have no doubt that they very soon began to make precious discoveries; and I have alluded

to them not in the least to throw ridicule upon their "insular-
ity"—which indeed, being accompanied with great modesty,
I thought a very pretty spectacle—but because having become, since my last visit to France, a little insular myself, I
was more conscious of the emotions that attend on an arrival.

The brightness always seems to begin while you are still out
in the channel, when you fairly begin to see the French coast.
You pass into a region of intenser light—a zone of clearness
and colour. These properties brighten and deepen as you approach the land, and when you fairly stand upon that good
Boulognese quay, among the blue and red douaniers and
soldiers, the small ugly men in cerulean blouses, the charming
fishwives, with their folded kerchiefs and their crisp cap-frills,
their short striped petticoats, their tightly-drawn stockings,
and their little clicking sabots—when you look about you at
the smokeless air, at the pink and yellow houses, at the white-
fronted café, close at hand, with its bright blue letters, its
mirrors and marble-topped tables, its white-aproned, alert,
undignified waiter, grasping a huge coffee-pot by a long han-
dle—when you perceive all these things you feel the addi-
tional savour that foreignness gives to the picturesque; or feel
rather, I should say, that simple foreignness may itself make
the picturesque; for certainly the elements in the picture I
have just sketched are not especially exquisite. No matter; you
are amused, and your amusement continues—being sensibly
stimulated by a visit to the buffet at the railway-station, which
is better than the refreshment-room at Folkestone. It is a pleasure to have people offering you soup again, of their own
movement; it is a pleasure to find a little pint of Bordeaux
standing naturally before your plate; it is a pleasure to have a
napkin; it is a pleasure, above all, to take up one of the good
long sticks of French bread—as bread is called the staff of
life, the French bake it literally in the shape of staves—and
break off a loose, crisp, crusty morsel.

There are impressions, certainly, that imperil your good-
humour. No honest Anglo-Saxon can like a French railway-
station; and I was on the point of adding that no honest
Anglo-Saxon can like a French railway-official. But I will not
go so far as that; for after all I cannot remember any great
harm that such a functionary has ever done me—except in

locking me up as a malefactor. It is necessary to say, however, that the honest Anglo-Saxon, in a French railway-station, is in a state of chronic irritation—an irritation arising from his sense of the injurious effect upon the genial French nature of the possession of an administrative uniform. I believe that the consciousness of brass buttons on his coat and stripes on his trousers has spoiled many a modest and amiable Frenchman, and the sight of these aggressive insignia always stirs within me a moral protest. I repeat that my aversion to them is partly theoretic, for I have found, as a general thing, that an inquiry civilly made extracts a civil answer from even the most official-looking personage. But I have also found that such a personage's measure of the civility due to him is inordinately large; if he places himself in any degree at your service, it is apparently from the sense that true greatness can afford to unbend. You are constantly reminded that you must not presume. In England these intimations never proceed from one's "inferiors." In France the "administration" is the first thing that touches you; in a little while you get used to it, but you feel somehow that, in the process, you have lost the flower of your self-respect. Of course you are under some obligation to it. It has taken you off the steamer at Folkestone; made you tell your name to a gentleman with a sword, stationed at the farther end of the plank—not a drawn sword, it is true, but still, at the best, a very nasty weapon; marshalled you into the railway-station; assigned you to a carriage—I was going to say to a seat; transported you to Paris, marshalled you again out of the train, and under a sort of military surveillance, into an enclosure containing a number of human sheep-pens, in one of which it has imprisoned you for some half-hour. I am always on the point, in these places, of asking one of my gaolers if I may not be allowed to walk about on parole. The administration at any rate has finally taken you out of your pen, and, through the medium of a functionary who "inscribes" you in a little book, transferred you to a cab selected by a logic of its own. In doing all this it has certainly done a great deal for you; but somehow its good offices have made you feel sombre and resentful. The other day, on arriving from London, while I was waiting for my luggage, I saw several of the porters who convey travellers' impedimenta to the cab come up and deliver over the coin they had just received for this service to a functionary posted *ad hoc* in a corner, and armed with a little book in which he noted down these remittances. The *pour-boires* are apparently thrown into a common fund and divided among the guild of porters. The system is doubtless an excellent one, excellently carried out; but the sight of the poor round-shouldered man of burdens dropping his coin into the hand of the official arithmetician was to my fancy but another reminder that the individual, as an individual, loses by all that the administration assumes.

After living a while in England you observe the individual in Paris with quickened attention; and I think it must be said that at first he makes an indifferent figure. You are struck with the race being physically and personally a poorer one than that great family of largely-modelled, fresh-coloured people you have left upon the other side of the channel. I remember that in going to England a year ago and disembarking of a dismal, sleety Sunday evening at Folkestone, the first thing that struck me was the good looks of the railway porters— their broad shoulders, their big brown beards, their well-cut features. In like manner, landing lately at Boulogne of a brilliant Sunday morning, it was impossible not to think the little men in numbered caps who were gesticulating and chattering in one's path, rather ugly fellows. In arriving from other countries one is struck with a certain want of dignity in the French face. I do not know, however, whether this is anything worse than the fact that the French face is expressive; for it may be said that, in a certain sense, to express anything is to compromise with one's dignity, which likes to be understood without taking trouble. As regards the lower classes, at any rate, the impression I speak of always passes away; you perceive that the good looks of the French working-people are to be found in their look of intelligence. These people, in Paris, strike me afresh as the cleverest, the most perceptive, and, intellectually speaking, the most human of their kind. The Paris *ouvrier*, with his democratic blouse, his expressive, demonstrative, agreeable eye, his meagre limbs, his irregular, pointed features, his sallow complexion, his face at once fatigued and animated, his light, nervous organisation, is a figure that I always encounter again with pleasure. In some cases he looks depraved and perverted, but at his worst he looks refined; he is full of vivacity of perception, of something that one can appeal to.

It takes some courage to say this, perhaps, after reading *L'Assommoir*; but in M. Emile Zola's extraordinary novel one must make the part, as the French say, of the horrible uncleanness of the author's imagination. *L'Assommoir*, I have been told, has had great success in the lower walks of Parisian life; and if this fact is not creditable to the delicacy of M. Zola's humble readers, it proves a good deal in favour of their intelligence. With all its grossness the book in question is essentially a literary performance; you must be tolerably clever to appreciate it. It is highly appreciated, I believe, by the young ladies who live in the region of the Latin Quarter— those young ladies who thirty years ago were called grisettes, and now are called I don't know what. They know long passages by heart; they repeat them with infinite gusto. "Ce louchon d'Augustine"—the horrible little girl with a squint, who is always playing nasty tricks and dodging slaps and projectiles in Gervaise's shop, is their particular favourite; and it must be admitted that "ce louchon d'Augustine" is, as regards reality, a wonderful creation.

If Parisians, both small and great, have more of the intellectual stamp than the people one sees in London, it is striking, on the other hand, that the people of the better sort in Paris look very much less "respectable." I did not know till I came back to Paris how used I had grown to the English *cachet*; but I immediately found myself missing it. You miss it in the men much more than in the women; for the well-to-do Frenchwoman of the lower orders, as one sees her in public, in the streets and in shops, is always a delightfully comfortable and creditable person. I must confess to the highest admiration for her, an admiration that increases with acquaintance. She, at least, is essentially respectable; the neatness, compactness, and sobriety of her dress, the decision of her movement and accent suggest the civic and domestic virtues—order, thrift, frugality, the moral necessity of making a good appearance. It is, I think, an old story that to the stranger in France the women seem greatly superior to the men. Their superiority, in fact, appears to be conceded; for wherever you turn you meet them in the forefront of action. You meet them, indeed, too often; you pronounce them at times obtrusive. It is annoying when you go to order your boots or your shirts, to have to make known your desires to even the most neat-waisted female attendant; for the limitations to the feminine intellect are, though few in number, distinct, and women are not able to understand certain masculine needs. Mr. Worth makes ladies' dresses; but I am sure there will never be a fashionable tailoress. There are, however, points at which, from the commercial point of view, feminine assistance is invaluable. For insisting upon the merits of an article that has failed to satisfy you, talking you over, and making you take it; for defending a disputed bill, for paying the necessary compliments or supplying the necessary impertinence—for all these things the neat-waisted sex has peculiar and precious faculties. In the commercial class in Paris the man always appeals to the woman; the woman always steps forward. The woman always proposes the conditions of a bargain. Go about and look for furnished rooms, you always encounter a concierge and his wife. When you ask the price of the rooms, the woman takes the words out of her husband's mouth, if indeed he have not first turned to her with a questioning look. She takes you in hand; she proposes conditions; she thinks of things he would not have thought of.

What I meant just now by my allusion to the absence of the "respectable" in the appearance of the Parisian population was that the men do not look like gentlemen, as so many Englishmen do. The average Frenchman that one encounters in public is of so different a type from the average Englishman that you can easily believe that to the end of time the two will not understand each other. The Frenchman has always, comparatively speaking, a Bohemian, empirical look; the expression of his face, its colouring, its movement, have not been toned down to the neutral complexion of that breeding for which in English speech we reserve the epithet of "good." He is at once more artificial and more natural; the former where the Englishman is positive, the latter where the Englishman is negative. He takes off his hat with a flourish to a friend, but the Englishman never bows. He ties a knot in the end of a napkin and thrusts it into his shirt-collar, so that, as he sits at breakfast, the napkin may serve the office of a pinafore. Such an operation as that seems to the Englishman as *naïf* as the flourishing of one's hat is pretentious.

I sometimes go to breakfast at a café on the Boulevard, which I formerly used to frequent with considerable regularity. Coming back there the other day, I found exactly the same group of habitués at their little tables, and I mentally exclaimed as I looked at them over my newspaper, upon their unlikeness to the gentlemen who confront you in the same attitude at a London club. Who are they? what are they? On these points I have no information; but the stranger's imagination does not seem to see a majestic social order massing itself behind them as it usually does in London. He goes so far as to suspect that what is behind them is not adapted for exhibition; whereas your Englishmen, whatever may be the defects of their personal character, or the irregularities of their conduct, are pressed upon from the rear by an immense body of private proprieties and comforts, of domestic conventions and theological observances. But it is agreeable all the same to come back to a café of which you have formerly been an habitué. Adolphe or Edouard, in his long white apron and his large patent-leather slippers, has a perfect recollection of "les habitudes de Monsieur." He remembers the table you preferred, the wine you drank, the newspaper you read. He greets you with the friendliest of smiles, and remarks that it is a long time since he has had the pleasure of seeing Monsieur. There is something in this simple remark very touching to a heart that has suffered from that incorruptible dumbness of the British domestic. But in Paris such a heart finds consolation at every step; it is reminded of that most classic quality of the French nature—its sociability; a sociability which operates here as it never does in England, from below upward. Your waiter utters a greeting because, after all, something human within him prompts him; his instinct bids him say something, and his taste recommends that it be agreeable. The obvious reflection is that a waiter must not say too much, even for the sake of being human. But in France the people always like to make the little extra remark, to throw in something above the simply necessary. I stop before a little man who is selling newspapers at a street-corner, and ask him for the *Journal des Débats*. His answer deserves to be literally given: "Je ne l'ai plus, Monsieur; mais je pourrai vous donner quelquechose à peu près dans le même genre—la *République Française*." Even a person of his humble condition must have had a lurking sense of the comicality of offering anything as an equivalent for the "genre" of the venerable, classic, academic *Débats*. But my friend could not bear to give me a naked, monosyllabic refusal.

There are two things that the returning observer is likely to do with as little delay as possible. One is to dine at some *cabaret* of which he retains a friendly memory; another is to betake himself to the Théâtre Français. It is early in the season; there are no new pieces; but I have taken great pleasure in seeing some of the old ones. I lost no time in going to see Mademoiselle Sarah Bernhardt in *Andromaque*. *Andromaque* is not a novelty, but Mademoiselle Sarah Bernhardt has a perennial freshness. The play has been revived, to enable her to represent not the great part, the injured and passionate Hermione, but that of the doleful, funereal widow of Hector. This part is a poor one; it is narrow and monotonous, and offers few brilliant opportunities. But the actress knows how to make opportunities, and she has here a very sufficient one for crossing her thin white arms over her nebulous black robes, and sighing forth in silver accents her dolorous rhymes. Her rendering of the part is one more proof of her singular intelligence—of the fineness of her artistic nature. As there is not a great deal to be done with it in the way of declamation, she has made the most of its plastic side. She understands the art of motion and attitude as no one else does, and her extraordinary personal grace never fails her. Her Andromaque has postures of the most poetic picturesqueness—something that suggests the broken stem and drooping head of a flower that had been rudely plucked. She bends over her classic confidant like the figure of Bereavement on a bas-relief, and she has a marvellous manner of lifting and throwing back her delicate arms, locking them together, and passing them behind her hanging head.

The *Demi-Monde* of M. Dumas *fils* is not a novelty either; but I quite agree with M. Francisque Sarcey that it is on the whole, in form, the first comedy of our day. I have seen it several times, but I never see it without being forcibly struck with its merits. For the drama of our time it must always remain the model. The interest of the story, the quiet art with which it is unfolded, the naturalness and soberness of the means that are used, and by which great effects are produced, the brilliancy and richness of the dialogue—all these things make it a singularly perfect and interesting work. Of course it is admirably well played at the Théâtre Français. Madame d'Ange was originally a part of too great amplitude for Mademoiselle Croizette; but she is gradually filling it out and taking possession of it; she begins to give a sense of the "calme infernal," which George Sand somewhere mentions as the leading attribute of the character. As for Delaunay, he does nothing better, more vividly and gallantly, than Olivier de Jalin. When I say gallantry I say it with qualification; for what a very queer fellow is this same M. de Jalin! In seeing the *Demi-Monde* again I was more than ever struck with the oddity of its morality and with the way that the ideal of fine conduct differs in different nations. The *Demi-Monde* is the history of the eager, the almost heroic, effort of a clever and superior woman, who has been guilty of what the French call "faults," to pass from the irregular and equivocal circle to which these faults have consigned her into what is distinctively termed "good society." The only way in which the passage can be effected is by her marrying an honourable man; and to induce an honourable man to marry her, she must suppress the more discreditable facts of her career. Taking her for an honest woman, Raymond de Nanjac falls in love with her, and honestly proposes to make her his wife. But Raymond de Nanjac has contracted an intimate friendship with Olivier de Jalin, and the action of the play is more especially De Jalin's attempt—a successful one—to rescue his friend from the ignominy of a union with Suzanne d'Ange. Jalin knows a great deal about her, for the simple reason that he has been her lover. Their relations have been most harmonious, but from the moment that Suzanne sets her cap at Nanjac, Olivier declares war. Suzanne struggles hard to keep possession of her suitor, who is very much in love with her, and Olivier spares no pains to detach him. It is the means that Olivier uses that excite the wonderment of the Anglo-Saxon spectator. He takes the ground that in such a cause all means are fair, and when, at the climax of the play, he tells a thumping lie in order to make Madame d'Ange compromise herself, expose herself, he is pronounced by the author "le plus honnête homme que je connaisse." Madame d'Ange, as I have said, is a superior woman; the interest of the play is in her being a superior woman. Olivier has been her lover; he himself is one of the reasons why she may not marry Nanjac; he has given her a push along the downward path. But it is curious how little this is held by the author to disqualify him from fighting the battle in which she is so much the weaker combatant. An English-speaking audience is more "moral" than a French, more easily scandalised; and yet it is a singular fact that if the *Demi-Monde* were represented before an English-speaking audience, its sympathies would certainly not go with M. de Jalin. It would pronounce him rather a coward. Is it because such an audience, although it has not nearly such a pretty collection of pedestals to place under the feet of the charming sex, has, after all, in default of this degree of gallantry, a tenderness more fundamental? Madame d'Ange has stained herself, and it is doubtless not at all proper that such ladies should be led to the altar by honourable young men. The point is not that the English-speaking audience would be disposed to condone Madame d'Ange's irregularities, but that it would remain perfectly cold before the spectacle of her ex-lover's masterly campaign against her, and quite fail to think it positively admirable, or to regard the fib by which he finally clinches his victory as a proof of exceptional honesty. The ideal of our own audience would be expressed in some such words as, "I say, that's not fair game. Can't you let the poor woman alone?"

1877

Rheims and Laon:
A Little Tour

IT WAS a very little tour, but the charm of the three or four
old towns and monuments that it embraced, the beauty of
the brilliant October, the pleasure of reminding one's self
how much of the interest, strength and dignity of France is to
be found outside of that huge pretentious caravansary called
Paris (a reminder often needed), these things deserve to be
noted. I went down to Rheims to see the famous cathedral,
and to reach Rheims I travelled through the early morning
hours along the charming valley of the Marne. The Marne is a
pretty little green river, the vegetation upon whose banks,
otherwise unadorned, had begun to blush with the early
frosts in a manner that suggested the autumnal tints of American scenery. The trees and bushes were scarlet and orange;
the light was splendid and a trifle harsh; I could have fancied
myself immersed in an American "fall," if at intervals some
gray old large-towered church had not lifted a sculptured
front above a railway-station, to dispel the fond illusion. One
of these church-fronts (I saw it only from the train) is particularly impressive; the little cathedral of Meaux, of which the
great Bossuet was bishop, and along whose frigid nave he set
his eloquence rolling with an impetus which it has not wholly
lost to this day. It was entertaining, moreover, to enter the
country of champagne; for Rheims is in the ancient province
whose later fame is syllabled the world over in popping corks.
A land of vineyards is not usually accounted sketchable; but
the country about Epernay seemed to me to have a charm of
its own. It stretched away in soft undulations that were
pricked all over with little stakes muffled in leaves. The effect
at a distance was that of vast surfaces, long, subdued billows,
of pincushion; and yet it was very pretty. The deep blue sky
was over the scene; the undulations were half in sun and half
in shade; and here and there, among their myriad bristles,
were groups of vintagers, who, though they are in reality,
doubtless, a prosaic and mercenary body of labourers, yet assumed, to a fancy that glanced at them in the cursory manner

permitted by the passage of the train, the appearance of joyous and disinterested votaries of Bacchus. The blouses of the
men, the white caps of the women, were gleaming in the sunshine; they moved about crookedly among the tiny vine-
poles. I thought them full of a charming suggestiveness. Of all
the delightful gifts of France to the world, this was one of the
most agreeable—the keen, living liquid in which the finest
flower of sociability is usually dipped. It came from these
sunny places; this little maze of curling-sticks supplied the
world with half the world's gaiety. I call it little only in relation to the immense number of bottles with gilded necks in
which this gaiety is annually stored up. The acreage of the
champagne seemed to me, in fact, large; the bristling slopes
went rolling away to new horizons in a manner that was positively reassuring. Making the handsomest allowance for the
wine manufactured from baser elements, it was apparent that
this big corner of a province represents a very large number of
bottles.

As you draw near to Rheims the vineyards become sparser,
and finally disappear, a fact not to be regretted, for there is
something incongruous in the juxtaposition of champagne
and gothic architecture. It may be said, too, that for the
proper appreciation of a structure like the cathedral of
Rheims you have need of all your head. As, after my arrival, I
sat in my window at the inn, gazing up at the great façade, I
found something dizzying in the mere climbing and soaring
of one's astonished vision; and later, when I came to wander
about in the upper regions of the church, and to peep down
through the rugged lacework of the towers at the little streets
and the small spots of public places, I found myself musing
upon the beauty of soberness. My window at the Lion d'Or
was like a proscenium-box at the play; to admire the cathedral
at my leisure I had only to perch myself in the casement with
a good opera-glass. I sat there for a long time watching the
great architectural drama. A drama I may call it, for no
church-front that I have seen is more animated, more richly
figured. The density of the sculptures, the immense scale of
the images, detract, perhaps, at first, in a certain sense, from
the impressiveness of the cathedral of Rheims; the absence of
large surfaces, of ascending lines, deceives you as to the eleva-

tion of the front, and the dimensions of some of the upper statues bring them unduly near the eye. But little by little you perceive that this great figured and storied screen has a mass proportionate to its detail, and that it is the grandest part of a structure which, as a whole, is one of the noblest works of man's hands. Most people remember to have seen some print or some photograph of this heavily-charged façade of Rheims, which is usually put forward as the great example of the union of the purity and the possible richness of gothic. I must first have seen some such print in my earliest years, for I have always thought of Rheims as the typical gothic cathedral. I had vague associations with it; it seemed to me that I had already stood there in the little overwhelmed *place*. One's literary associations with Rheims are indeed very vivid and impressive; they begin with the picture of the steel-clad Maid passing under the deeply-sculptured portal, with a banner in her hand which she has no need to lower, and while she stands amid the incense and the chants, the glitter of arms and the glow of coloured lights, asking leave of the young king whom she has crowned to turn away and tend her flocks. And after that there is the sense of all the kings of France having travelled down to Rheims in their splendour to be consecrated; the great groups on the front of the church must have looked down on groups almost as stately—groups full of colour and movement—assembled in the square. (The square of Rheims, it must be confessed, is rather shabby. It is singular that the august ceremony of the *sacre* should not have left its mark upon the disposition of the houses, should not have kept them at a respectful distance. Louis XIV., smoothing his plumage before he entered the church, can hardly have had space to swing the train of his coronation-robe.) But when in driving into the town I reached the small precinct, such as it is, and saw the cathedral lift its spireless towers above the long rows of its carven saints, the huge wheel of its window, the three great caverns of its portals, with the high acute pediments above each arch, and the sides abutting outward like the beginning of a pyramid; when I looked at all this I felt that I had carried it in my mind from my earliest years, and that the stately vision had been implanted there by some forgotten glimpse of an old-fashioned water-colour sketch, in which the sky was washed in with expressive splashes, the remoter parts of the church tinted with a fascinating blueness, and the foundations represented as encumbered with little gabled and cross-timbered houses, inhabited by women in red petticoats and curious caps.

I shall not attempt any regular enumeration of the great details of the façade of Rheims; I cannot profess even to have fully apprehended them. They are a glorious company, and here and there, on its high-hung pedestal, one of the figures detaches itself with peculiar effectiveness. Over the central portal sits the Virgin Mary, meekly submitting her head to the ponderous crown which her Son prepares to place upon it; the attitude and movement of Christ are full of a kind of splendid politeness. The three great doorways are in themselves a museum of imagery, disposed in each case in five close tiers, the statues in each of the tiers packed perpendicularly against their comrades. The effect of these great hollowed and chiselled recesses is extremely striking; they are a proper vestibule to the dusky richness of the interior. The cathedral of Rheims, more fortunate than many of its companions, appears not to have suffered from the iconoclasts of the Revolution; I noticed no absent heads nor broken noses. It is very true that these members may have had adventures to which they do not, as it were, allude. But, like many of its companions, it is so pressed upon by neighbouring houses that it is not easy to get a general view of the sides and the rear. You may walk round it, and note your walk as a long one; you may observe that the choir of the church travels back almost into another quarter of the city; you may see the far-spreading mass lose itself for a while in parasitic obstructions, and then emerge again with all its buttresses flying; but you miss that wide margin of space and light which should enable it to present itself as a consistent picture. Pictures have their frames, and poems have their margins; a great work of art, such as a gothic cathedral, should at least have elbow-room. You may, however, stroll beneath the walls of Rheims, along a narrow, dark street, and look up at the mighty structure and see its higher parts foreshortened into all kinds of delusive proportions. There is a grand entertainment in the view of the church which you obtain from the farthermost point to which you may recede from it in the rear, keeping it still within sight. I have never seen a cathedral so magnificently buttressed. The buttresses of Rheims are all double; they have a tremendous spring, and are supported upon pedestals surmounted by immense crocketed canopies containing statues of wide-winged angels. A great balustrade of gothic arches connects these canopies one with another, and along this balustrade are perched strange figures of sitting beasts, unicorns and mermaids, griffins and monstrous owls. Huge, terrible gargoyles hang far over into the street, and doubtless some of them have a detail which I afterwards noticed at Laon. The gargoyle represents a grotesque beast—a creature partaking at once of the shape of a bird, a fish, and a quadruped. At Laon, on either side of the main entrance, a long-bellied monster cranes forth into the air with the head of a hippopotamus; and under its belly crouches a little man, hardly less grotesque, making up a rueful grimace and playing some ineffectual trick upon his terrible companion. One of these little figures has plunged a sword, up to the hilt, into the belly of the monster above him, so that when he draws it forth there will be a leak in the great stone gutter; another has suspended himself to a rope that is knotted round the neck of the gargoyle, and is trying in the same manner to interrupt its functions by pulling the cord as tight as possible. There was sure to be a spirit of life in an architectural conception that could range from the combination of clustering towers and opposing fronts to this infinitely minute play of humour.

There is no great play of humour in the interior of Rheims, but there is a great deal of beauty and solemnity. This interior is a spectacle that excites the sensibility, as our forefathers used to say; but it is not an easy matter to describe. It is no description of it to say that it is four hundred and sixty-six feet in length, and that the roof is one hundred and twenty-four feet above the pavement; nor is there any very vivid portraiture in the statement that if there is no coloured glass in the lower windows, there is, *per contra*, a great deal of the most gorgeous and most ancient in the upper ones. The long sweep of the nave, from the threshold to the point where the coloured light-shafts of the choir lose themselves in the gray distance, is a triumph of perpendicular perspective. The white light in the lower part of Rheims really contributes to the picturesqueness of the interior. It makes the gloom above look richer still, and throws that part of the roof which rests upon the gigantic piers of the transepts into mysterious remoteness. I wandered about for a long time; I sat first in one place and then in another; I attached myself to that most fascinating part of every great church, the angle at which the nave and transept divide. It was the better to observe this interesting point, I think, that I passed into the side gate of the choir—the gate that stood ajar in the tall gilded railing. I sat down on a stool near the threshold; I leaned back against the side of one of the stalls; the church was empty, and I lost myself in the large perfection of the place. I lost myself, but the beadle found me; he stood before me, and with a silent, imperious gesture, motioned me to depart. I risked an argumentative glance, whereupon he signified his displeasure, repeated his gesture, and pointed to an old gentleman with a red cape, who had come into the choir softly, without my seeing him, and had seated himself in one of the stalls. This old gentleman seemed plunged in pious thoughts; I was not, after all, very near him, and he did not look as if I disturbed him. A canon is at any time, I imagine, a more merciful man than a beadle. But of course I obeyed the beadle, and eliminated myself from this peculiarly sacred precinct. I found another chair, and I fell to admiring the cathedral again. But this time I think it was with a difference—a difference which may serve as an excuse for the triviality of my anecdote. Sundry other old gentlemen in red capes emerged from the sacristy and went into the choir; presently, when there were half a dozen, they began to chant, and I perceived that the impending vespers had been the reason of my expulsion. This was highly proper, and I forgave the beadle; but I was not so happy as before, for my thoughts had passed out of the architectural channel into—what shall I say?—into the political. Here they found nothing so sweet to feed upon. It was the 5th of October; ten days later the elections for the new Chamber were to take place—the Chamber which was to replace the Assembly dissolved on the 16th of May by Marshal Mac-Mahon, on a charge of "latent" radicalism. Stranger though one was, it was impossible not to be much interested in the triumph of the republican cause; it was impossible not to sympathise with this supreme effort of a brilliant and generous people to learn the lesson of national self-control and self-government. It was impossible by the same token, not to have noted and detested the alacrity with which the Catholic party had rallied to the reactionary cause, and the unction with which the clergy had converted itself into the go-betweens of Bonapartism. The clergy was giving daily evidence of its devotion to arbitrary rule and to every iniquity that shelters itself behind the mask of "authority." These had been frequent and irritating reflections; they lurked in the folds of one's morning paper. They came back to me in the midst of that tranquil grandeur of Rheims, as I listened to the droning of the old gentlemen in the red capes. Some of the canons, it was painful to observe, had not been punctual; they came hurrying out of the sacristy after the service had begun. They looked like amiable and venerable men; their chanting and droning, as it spread itself under the great arches, was not disagreeable to listen to; I could certainly bear them no grudge. But their presence there was distracting and vexatious; it had spoiled my enjoyment of their church, in which I doubtless had no business. It had set me thinking of the activity and vivacity of the great organisation to which they belonged, and of all the odious things it would have done before the 15th of October. To what base uses do we come at last! It was this same organisation that had erected the magnificent structure around and above me, and which had then seemed an image of generosity and benignant power. Such an edifice might at times make one feel tenderly sentimental toward the Catholic church—make one remember how many of the great achievements of the past we owe to her. To lapse gently into this state of mind seems indeed always, while one strolls about a great cathedral, a proper recognition of its hospitality; but now I had lapsed gently out of it, and it was one of the exasperating elements of the situation that I felt, in a manner, called upon to decide how far such a lapse was unbecoming. I found myself even extending the question a little, and picturing to myself that conflict which must often occur at such a moment as the present—which is actually going on, doubtless, in many thousands of minds—between the actively, practically liberal instinct and what one may call the historic, æsthetic sense, the sense upon which old cathedrals lay a certain palpable obligation. How far should a lover of old cathedrals let his hands be tied by the sanctity of their traditions? How far should he let his imagination bribe him, as it were, from action? This of course is a question for each man to answer for himself; but as I sat listening to the drowsy old canons of Rheims, I was visited, I scarcely know why, by a kind of revelation of the anti-catholic passion, as it must burn to-day in the breasts of certain radicals. I felt that such persons must be intent upon war to the death; how that must seem the most sacred of all duties. Can anything, in the line of action, for a votary of the radical creed, be more sacred? I asked myself; and can any instruments be too trenchant? I raised my eyes again to the dusky splendour of the upper aisles and measured their enchanting perspective, and it was with a sense of doing them full justice that I gave my fictive liberal my good wishes.

This little operation restored my equanimity, so that I climbed several hundred steps and wandered lightly over the roof of the cathedral. Climbing into cathedral-towers and gaping at the size of the statues that look small from the street has always seemed to me a rather brutal pastime; it is not the proper way to treat a beautiful building; it is like holding one's nose so close to a picture that one sees only the grain of the canvas. But when once I had emerged into the upper wilderness of Rheims the discourse of a very urbane and appreciative old bell-ringer, whom I found lurking behind some gigantic excrescence, gave an æsthetic complexion to what would otherwise have been a rather vulgar feat of gymnastics. It was very well to see what a great cathedral is made of, and in these high places of the immensity of Rheims I found the matter very impressively illustrated. I wandered for half an hour over endless expanses of roof, along the edge of sculptured abysses, through hugely-timbered attics and chambers that were in themselves as high as churches. I stood knee-high to strange images, of unsuspected proportions, and I followed the topmost staircase of one of the towers, which curls upward like the groove of a corkscrew, and gives you at the summit a hint of how a sailor feels at the masthead. The ascent was worth making to learn the fulness of beauty of the church, the solidity and perfection, the mightiness of arch and buttress, the latent ingenuity of detail. At the angles of the balustrade which ornaments the roof of the choir are perched a series of huge sitting eagles, which from below, as you look up at them, produce a great effect. They are immense, grim-looking birds, and the sculptor has given to each of them a pair of very neatly carved human legs, terminating in talons. Why did he give them human legs? Why did he indulge in this ridiculous conceit? I am unable to say, but the conceit afforded me pleasure. It seemed to tell of an imagination always at play, fond of the unexpected and delighting in its labour.

Apart from its cathedral Rheims is not an interesting city. It has a prosperous, modern, mercantile air. The streets look as if at one time M. Haussmann, in person, may have taken a good deal of exercise in them; they prove, however, that a French provincial town may be a wonderfully fresh, clean, comfortable-looking place. Very different is the aspect of the ancient city of Laon, to which you may, by the assistance of the railway, transfer yourself from Rheims in a little more than an hour. Laon is full of history, and the place, as you approach it, reminds you of a quaint woodcut in the text of an ancient folio. Out of the midst of a smiling plain rises a goodly mountain, and on the top of the mountain is perched the old feudal *commune*, from the centre of which springs, with infinite majesty, the many-towered cathedral. At Laon you are in the midst of old France; it is one of the most interesting chapters of the past. Ever since reading in the pages of M. Thierry the story of the fierce struggle for municipal independence waged by this ardent little city against its feudal and ecclesiastical lords, I had had the conviction that Laon was worthy of a visit. All the more so that her two hundred years of civic fermentation had been vainly spent, and that in the early part of the fourteenth century she had been disfranchised without appeal. M. Thierry's readers will remember the really thrilling interest of the story which he has selected as the most complete and typical among those of which the records of the mediæval communities are full; the complications and fluctuations of the action, its brilliant epi-

sodes, its sombre, tragic *dénoûment*. I did not visit Laon with
the *Lettres sur l'Histoire de France* in my pocket, nor had I any
other historic texts for reference; but a vague notion of the
vigorous manner in which for a couple of centuries the stubborn little town had attested its individuality supplied my observations with an harmonious background. Nothing can well
be more picturesque than the position of this interesting city.
The tourist who has learned his trade can tell a "good" place
at a glance. The moment Laon became visible from the window of the train I perceived that Laon was good. And then I
had the word for it of an extremely intelligent young officer
of artillery, who shared my railway-carriage in coming from
Rheims, and who spoke with an authority borrowed from
three years of garrison-life on that windy hill-top. He affirmed
that the only recreation it afforded was a walk round the ramparts which encircle the town; people went down the hill as
little as possible—it was such a dreadful bore to come up
again. But he declared, nevertheless, that, as an intelligent
traveller, I should be enchanted with the place; that the cathedral was magnificent, the view of the surrounding country a
perpetual entertainment, and the little town full of originality.
After I had spent a day there I thought of this pleasant young
officer and his familiar walk upon the city-wall; he gave a
point to my inevitable reflections upon the degree to which at
the present hour, in France, the front of the stage is occupied
by the army. Inevitable reflections, I say, because the net result of any little tour that one may make just now is a vivid
sense of red trousers and cropped heads. Wherever you go
you come upon a military quarter, you stumble upon a group
of young citizens in uniform. It is always a pretty spectacle;
they enliven the scene; they touch it here and there with an
effusion of colour. But this is not the whole of the matter,
and when you have admitted that it is pictorial to be always
sous les armes, you fall to wondering whether it is not very
expensive. A million of defenders take up a good deal of
room, even for defenders. It must be very uncomfortable to
be always defending. How do the young men bear it; how
does France bear it; how long will she be able to keep it up?
Every young Frenchman, on reaching maturity, has to give
up five years of his life to this bristling Minotaur of military

service. It is hard for a nation of shameless civilians to understand how life is arranged among people who come into the world with this heavy mortgage upon the freshest years of their strength; it seems like drinking the wine of life from a vessel with a great leak in the bottom. Is such a *régime* inspiring, or is it demoralising? Is the effect of it to quicken the sentiment of patriotism, the sense of the dangers to which one's country is exposed and of what one owes to the common cause, or to take the edge from all ambition that is not purely military, to force young men to say that there is no use trying, that nothing is worth beginning, and that a young fellow condemned to pay such a tax as that has a right to refund himself in any way that is open to him? Reminded as one is at every step of the immensity of the military burden of France, the most interesting point seems to me not its economical but its moral bearing. Its effect upon the finances of the country may be accurately computed; its effect upon the character of the young generation is more of a mystery. As the analytic tourist wanders of an autumn afternoon upon the planted rampart of an ancient town and meets young soldiers strolling in couples or leaning against the parapet and looking off at the quiet country, he is apt to take the more genial view of the dreadful trade of arms. He is disposed to say that it teaches its votaries something that is worth knowing and yet is not learned in several other trades—the hardware, say, or the dry-goods business. Five years is a good deal to ask of a young life as a sacrifice; but the sacrifice is in some ways a gain. Certainly, apart from the question of material defence, it may be said that no European nation, at present, can afford, morally, not to pass her young men, the hope of the country, through the military mill. It does for them something indispensable; it toughens, hardens, solidifies them; gives them an ideal of honour, of some other possibility in life than making a fortune. A country in which the other trades I spoke of have it all their own way appears, in comparison, less educated.

So I mused, as I strolled in the afternoon along the charming old city-wall at Laon; and if my meditations seem pretentious or fallacious, I must say in justice that I had been a good while coming to them. I had done a great many things first. I had climbed up the long straight staircase which has been dropped like a scaling-ladder from one of the town-gates to the bottom of the hill. Laon still has her gates as she still has her wall, and one of these, the old Porte d'Ardon, is a really precious relic of mediæval architecture. I had repaired to the sign of the *Hure*—a portrait of this inhospitable beast is swung from the front of the inn—and bespoken a lodging; I had spent a long time in the cathedral, in it and before it, beside it, behind it; I had walked all over the town, from the citadel, at one end of the lofty plateau on which it stands, to the artillery-barracks and the charming old church of St. Martin at the other. The cathedral of Laon has not the elaborate grandeur of that of Rheims; but it is a very noble and beautiful church. Nothing can be finer than its position; it would set off any church to stand on such a hill-crest. Laon has also a façade of many sculptures, which, however, has suffered greater violence than that of Rheims, and is now being carefully and delicately restored. Whole figures and bas-reliefs have lately been replaced by exact imitations in that fresh white French stone which looks at first like a superior sort of plaster. They were far gone, and I suppose the restorer's hand was imperiously called for. I do not know that it has been too freely used. But half the charm of Laon is the magnificent colouring of brownish, weather-battered gray which it owes to the great exposure of its position, and it will be many a year before the chalky scars and patches will be wrought into dusky harmony with the rest of the edifice. Fortunately, however, they promise not to be very numerous; the principal restorations have taken place inside. I know not what all this labour costs; but I was interested in learning from the old bell-ringer at Rheims that the sum voted by the Chamber for furbishing up his own church was two millions of francs, to be expended during ten years. That is what it is to have "national monuments" to keep up. One is apt to think of the fourteenth century as a rather ill-appointed and comfortless period; but the fact that at the present time the mere repair of one of its buildings costs forty thousand dollars a year would indicate that the original builders had a great deal of money to spend. The cathedral of Laon was intended to be a wonderful cluster of towers, but only two of these ornaments— the couple above the west front—have been carried to a great altitude; the pedestals of the rest, however, detach themselves with much vigour, and contribute to the complicated and somewhat fantastic look which the church wears at a distance, and which makes its great effectiveness. The finished towers are admirably light and graceful; with the sky shining through their large interstices they suggest an imitation of timber in masonry. They have one very quaint feature. From their topmost portions, at each angle, certain carven heads of oxen peep forward with a startling naturalness—a tribute to the patient, powerful beasts who dragged the material of the building up the long zig-zags of the mountain. We perhaps treat our dumb creatures better to-day than was done five hundred years ago; but I doubt whether a modern architect, in settling his accounts, would have "remembered," as they say, the oxen.

The whole precinct of the cathedral of Laon is picturesque. There is a charming Palais de Justice beside it, separated from it by a pleasant, homely garden, in which, as you walk about, you have an excellent view of the towering back and sides of the great church. The Palais de Justice, which is an ancient building, has a fine old gothic arcade, and on the other side, directly upon the city-wall, a picturesque, irregular rear, with a row of painted windows, through which, from the *salle d'audience*, the judge on the bench and the prisoner in the dock may enjoy a prospect, admonitory, inspiring, or depressing, as the case may be, of the expanded country. This great sea-like plain that lies beneath the town on all sides constitutes, for Laon, a striking resemblance to those Italian cities —Siena, Volterra, Perugia—which the traveller remembers so fondly as a dark silhouette lifted high against a glowing sunset. There is something Italian, too, in the mingling of rock and rampart in the old foundations of the town, and in the generous verdure in which these are muffled. At one end of the hill-top the plateau becomes a narrow ridge; the slope makes a deep indentation, which contributes to the effect of a thoroughly Italian picture. A line of crooked little red-roofed houses stands on the edge of this indentation, with their feet in the tangled verdure that blooms in it; and above them rises a large, florid, deserted-looking church, which you may be sure has a little empty, grass-grown, out-of-the-way *place* before it. Almost opposite, on another spur of the hill, the gray walls of a suppressed convent peep from among the trees. I might have been at Perugia.

There came in the evening to the inn of the Hure a very worthy man who had vehicles to hire. The Hure was decidedly a provincial hostelry, and I compared it mentally with certain English establishments of a like degree, of which I had lately had observation. In England I should have had a waiter in an old evening-suit and a white cravat, who would have treated me to cold meat and bread and cheese. There would have been a musty little inn-parlour and probably a very good fire in the grate, and the festally-attired waiter would have been my sole entertainer. At Laon I was in perpetual intercourse with the landlord and his wife, and a large body of easy-going, confidential domestics. Our intercourse was carried on in an old darksome stone kitchen, with shining copper vessels hanging all over the walls, in which I was free to wander about and take down my key in one place and rummage out my candlestick in another, while the domestics sat at table eating *pot-au-feu*. The landlord cooked the dinner; he wore a white cap and apron; he brought in the first dish at the table d'hôte. Of course there was a table d'hôte, with several lamps and a long array of little dessert-dishes, for the benefit of two commercial travellers, who tucked their napkins into their necks, and the writer of these lines. Every country has its manners. In England the benefits—whatever they are—represented by the evening dress of the waiter would have been most apparent; in France one was more sensible of the blessings of which the white cap and apron of the host were a symbol. In England, certainly, one is treated more as a gentleman. It is too often forgotten, however, that even a gentleman partakes of nourishment. But I am forgetting my dispenser of vehicles, concerning whom, however, and whose large red cheeks and crimson cravat, I have left myself room to say no more than that they were witnesses of a bargain that I should be driven early on the morrow morning, in an "Américaine," to the Château de Coucy. The Américaine proved to be a vehicle of which I should not have been eager to claim the credit for my native land; but with the aid of a ragged but resolute little horse, and a driver so susceptible as

regards his beast's appearance that, referring to the exclama-
tion of dismay with which I had greeted it, he turned to me at
the end of each successive kilometre with a rancorous "Now,
do you say he can't go?"—with these accessories, I say, it
conveyed me more than twenty miles. It was entertaining to
wind down the hillside from Laon in the early morning of a
splendid autumn day; to dip into the glistening plain, all void
of hedges and fences, and sprinkled with light and dew; to
jog along the straight white roads, between the tall, thin poplars; to rattle through the half-waked villages and past the
orchards heavy with sour-looking crimson apples. The Château de Coucy is a well-known monument; it is one of the
most considerable ruins in France, and it is in some respects
the most extraordinary. As you come from Laon a turn in the
road suddenly, at last, reveals it to you. It is still at a distance;
you will not reach it for half an hour; but its huge white
donjon stands up like some gigantic lighthouse at sea. Coucy
is altogether on a grand scale, but this colossal, shining cylinder is a wonder of bigness. As M. Viollet-le-Duc says, it
seems to have been built by giants for a race of giants. The
very quaint little town of Coucy-le-Château nestles at the foot
of this strange, half-substantial, half-spectral structure; it was,
together with a goodly part of the neighbouring country, the
feudal appanage of those terrible lords who erected the
present indestructible edifice, and whose "boastful motto" (I
quote from Murray) was

> "Roi je ne suis,
>   Prince ni comte aussi;
> Je suis le Sire de Coucy."

Coucy is a sleepy little borough, still girdled with its ancient
wall, entered by its old gateways, and supported on the verdurous flanks of a hill-top. I interviewed the host of the
Golden Apple in his kitchen; I breakfasted—*ma foi, fort bien*,
as they would say in the indigenous tongue—in his parlour;
and then I visited the château, which is at five minutes' walk.
This very interesting ruin is the property of the state, and the
state is represented by a very civil and intelligent woman, who
divests the trade of custodian of almost all its grossness. Any
feudal ruin is a charming affair, and Coucy has much of the

sweet melancholy of its class. There are four great towers, connected by a massive curtain and enclosing the tremendous donjon of which I just now spoke. All this is very crumbling and silvery; the enclosure is a tangle of wild verdure, and the pigeons perch upon the inaccessible battlements exactly where the sketcher would wish them. But the place lacked, to my sense, the peculiar softness and venerableness, the ivied mellowness, of a great English ruin. At Coucy there is no ivy to speak of; the climate has not caressed and embroidered the rugged masses of stone. This is what I meant by speaking of the famous donjon as spectral; the term is an odd one to apply to an edifice whose walls are thirty-four feet thick. Its vast, pale surface has not a speck nor a stain, not a clinging weed nor a creeping plant. It looks like a tower of ivory.

I took my way from Coucy to the ancient town of Soissons, where I found another cathedral, from which, I think, I extracted all the entertainment it could legitimately yield. There is little other to be had at Soissons, in spite of the suggestiveness of its name, which is redolent of history and local colour. The truth is, I suppose, that Soissons looks so new, precisely because she is so old. She is in her second youth; she has renewed herself. The old city was worn out; it could no longer serve; it has been succeeded by another. The new one is a quiet, rather aristocratic-looking little *ville de province*—a collection of well-conditioned, sober-faced abodes of gentility, with high-walled gardens behind them and very carefully closed portes-cochère in front. Occasionally a porte-cochère opens; an elderly lady in black emerges and paces discreetly away. An old gentleman has come to the door with her. He is comfortably corpulent; he wears gold spectacles and embroidered slippers. He looks up and down the dull street, and sees nothing at all; then he retires, closing the porte-cochère very softly and firmly. But he has stood there long enough to give an observant stranger the impression of a cautious provincial bourgeoisie that has a solid fortune well invested, and that marries its daughters only *à bon escient*. This latter ceremony, however, whenever it occurs, probably takes place in the cathedral, and though resting on a prosaic foundation must borrow a certain grace from that charming building. The cathedral of Soissons has a statueless front and only a single tower; but it is full of a certain natural elegance.

1877

Very Modern Rome

ARRIVING in Rome in the evening, just in time for dinner, the traveller, after dining, has, before going to bed, an hour or two of ancient darkness upon his hands. His natural course is to pass out of the door of his inn and stroll at hazard along the street. If he find himself for the first time in Rome the occasion will be momentous, but I am afraid it will not seem to him brilliant. In all probability, after a contemplative walk of a quarter of an hour, he will retrace his steps, and, before seeking his pillow, write it down in his diary that Rome is an ugly, shabby, third-rate provincial town, with no side-walks, very few gaslamps and cafés that look like dens of thieves. If, however, he has already some acquaintance with the Eternal City, so that as he steps out into the warm, slightly stagnant air of its streets, a hundred associations with its little cobble-stones and big dark places suddenly revive and keep him company, he will probably feel the impulse to go and look, so far as the evening allows him, at one or two of the objects of interest. It has been the practice of the writer of these lines, returning to Rome two or three times, to bend his steps, in the quiet darkness, to the most Roman quarter of all—to go and scowl for ten minutes at the dimly-descried pillars and posts in the Forum. The idea is in no sense a brilliant one, being both obvious and unremunerative; but the satisfaction lies exactly in the melancholy meagreness of the vision. The Roman Forum, of a moonless night, takes on a singularly ill-appointed look; it dwindles and contracts; the lonely columns, dear to antiquarians and poets, lose themselves in the dusk; the elevation of the Capitol grows less; the arch of Septimius Severus forfeits even the moderate impressiveness which it exerts by day; the heaps of ruin seem formless and awkward; the whole place, in a word, looks prosaic. But presently the observer whose mind has learned in some degree to lend itself to Roman impressions feels that there is a certain eloquence in this small dull corner being the Roman Forum. The thought that so much greatness should have come only to *that* grows vivid, and the rather vulgar lone-

liness of the place seems a more touching sign of fallen fortunes and the revenge of history than a more heroic desolation. When even picturesqueness intermits, then fallen empires are fallen indeed. But I must not talk too much about
the intermission of picturesqueness; for in the Roman sunshine all this neighborhood, which has lately been much more
disinterred, acquires a very different value and looks really like
a place which an antique ghost (if ghosts availed themselves
of the daylight) would not be ashamed to recognize. I was
going to say, moreover, that this supposititious stroll of the
Roman pilgrim *redux* would probably introduce him to one
of the most effective pieces of detail in the whole Roman
spectacle. Turning out of my inn the other night into the
Corso and following this famous thoroughfare, I arrived at
the Piazza Colonna. This great square has become, since the
Italian occupation, the general lounging place, and looks, every
day in the week, as if it were the scene of some exceptionally good-humored civic agitation. That numerous train of
professional loungers which appears to have followed the
present government to Rome—not that there were no
loungers before; only, in the papal days the city was virtually
under the custom of the curfew, and the streets, once night
had fallen, were not more animated than the prisons of the
Inquisition—converts the Piazza Colonna into a sort of public *conversazione*, to which the proximity of the Post-Office,
whose long open *loggia*, with its line of bustling windows,
occupies one side of the great space, contributes a further sociability. Round about are shops and cafés; close at hand are
kiosks for the sale of newspapers, in competition with which a
hundred sonorous urchins dispense the little Italian journals;
in the midst the capitally-equipped Roman cabs are perpetually cleaving the crowd. In the centre of all this rises the rugged memorial which has always been known as the Antonine
column and which bears upon its base an inscription placed
there by Sixtus V, attesting that the monument had been
erected by Marcus Aurelius to the memory of his illustrious
father. This inscription is an error, though it looks extremely
picturesque, in its rigid Latinity, under the flaring gaslamps
that surround it. The column was set up by the Senate in
honor of Marcus Aurelius himself—so at least I read in the

pages of a well-thumbed Murray—and is of the same fashion as the more admired pillar that bears the name of Trajan and stands in a great dusky, lonely *piazza*, on the other side of the Corso. Both of these antiquated monuments are covered with sculptures illustrating the brave deeds of the Romans, but those of the earlier are much the more artistic. The so-called Antonine column, however, may serve a sentimental traveller's purpose and point the moral of my present recital. Lifting its imperial record in the midst of all the oblivious modernness that surrounds it, with the great cast-iron candelabra at the angles of its railings glaring upward at its circular frieze, with the newsboys shouting telegraphic intelligence and the knots of commercial travellers discussing the wool-market, in its shadow, it is a striking, an almost touching, memento of the impermanence of even the strongest things of this world. All the strength, all the solid Roman life that was built up into that rugged cylinder has become simply a mute appeal to the imaginative charity of a tourist. The circumstances I have mentioned make the contrast particularly vivid, and if the passing traveller have a turn for versification he will find here the subject of a sonnet ready made to his hand.

The traveller who remembers an earlier day, coming back to Rome at the present hour, is certain to hear among his friends a great deal of talk about "the changes." To these changes the foreign-aesthetic mind in general is not friendly, although there are minor variations in the plaintive accent with which allusion is made to them. Some people think that, after all, the intellectual satisfaction of seeing Rome in Italian hands—the postponement of this event acting upon the mind, to their sense, as a good-sized pebble in one's shoe acts upon the physical consciousness—may be held to outbalance the awkwardness of a few tons of rock-work in the Pincian garden, or even the futility of the queer little clock, worked by a thread of water from a fountain, which now ornaments this classic resort. (This aquatic time-piece, by the way, as I am informed, is due to the ingenuity of a quiet young priest with a turn for mechanics and no sympathy whatever with the Italian invasion.) But there are other members of the contemplative colony whose sense of injury is both acute and constant, and for whom the retirement of the monks and cardinals, the removal of the wild shrubs from the crevices of the Colosseum and the Baths of Caracalla, the application of a coat of red paint to the halls of the Capitol, and two or three other revolutionary measures of equal moment, are so many chapters in a terrific impeachment of the House of Savoy. Shortly before coming to Rome I read over the introductory pages in Mr. Augustus J. C. Hare's pleasant volumes upon "Days near Rome"; and I was really depressed by their lurid picture of despoilment and defilement. I was on the point of giving up my visit, for it seemed as if the only result of it would be a more vivid comprehension of Dante's oft-quoted words about the pain of remembering happy days in the midst of misery. And indeed, when, arming myself with courage, I alighted from the train at the railway-station, my first feeling was a sense of paying the penalty of extreme temerity. When I had squeezed through the crowd at the wicket and emerged into the Roman sunshine and the presence of a couple of dozen emissaries from the hotels, each of whom attempted to push me into a big blue omnibus, lined with red plush, I felt that those portentous words "the changes" were suddenly taking on a meaning. The region of the railway station is in fact as ugly, as vulgar, as effectually drained of local color, as the most enterprising of syndics can desire. Of old, it was as mouldering a corner of Rome as any other, and it must be added that, thanks to the petty restrictions by which it was the taste of the papal administration to inform the arriving traveller that he had entered the circle of petticoat government, it was also the most uncomfortable. But it was picturesque, and the tourist had the satisfaction of hearing the Roman note struck on the very threshold. At present he is immediately confronted (in the shape of the new Via Nazionale) with a third-rate imitation of the Boulevard Haussmann; and it is not until he shakes off this incongruous impression that the desired and remembered charm begins to operate. The writer of these lines must confess that for himself this new impression was rather an incubus. Whenever it was about to efface itself some impertinent bit of novelty gave it a reviving touch. I went to the Pincian and—I don't know why—the Pincian was an exasperation. There was the familiar view of the city, and of St. Peter's on one side, and the contrasted prospect of the pine-studded meadows of the Villa Borghese on the other; but the place seemed dusky and cock-neyfied, and the mere fact that there were half a dozen little palings in places where I remembered none, and that some of those busts of ancient sages that are stationed about in the shrubbery had had the name of the original inscribed upon them by that inexpensive operation known as "stencilling"—these harmless circumstances were a tonic to my irritation. I beat a precipitate retreat and took refuge in the gardens of the Villa Medici, close at hand—that charming old castle of indolence, the property of the French government, to which half a dozen happy young art-students are annually despatched from Paris. Here I found comfort, for the Villa Medici, so far as I could make out, was utterly untouched by the reforming hand. The Italian government, I believe, has expressed a disposition to buy the place, but the proposal has found a cold welcome, and so long as the old French porter who has stood there for so many years still turns the garden gate on its heavy hinges, I suppose this most exquisite corner of Rome will keep its spell unbroken. It is always deliciously Roman. The great decorated garden-face of the villa, with its bas-reliefs and its statuettes, its pompous wings and belvederes, its little round niches filled with antique busts, surveys the tall box-hedges, the mouldy, mossy statues, the little crepuscular groves of ilex, as serenely and superbly as of yore. I lost no time, of course, in repairing to the boschetto; for one can never believe, in absence, that the boschetto is literally as picturesque as one's memory of it, and it seems a kind of wholesome duty to go and learn what abatements are necessary. I found on this occasion that none whatever were required; the boschetto was still the most improbable little piece of actuality in Europe. The western light, as usual, was playing into the clear, deep, tangled shade of the live-oaks, and filling the pure, soft dusk with a desultory glow. There was the same faint, sweet odor of damp and mould; the same disfeatured and discoloured busts, perched on their mossy pedestals, appeared to be listening to the stillness. At the end, that quaint old mound, with its high, steep steps, uplifted its little belvedere over the tree-tops, looking more than ever like a piece of furniture in a fairy-tale; as if it had been erected by an unhappy young prince and his companions to help themselves to look out for a way of egress from the enchanted wood.

In spite, however, of the pretty picture I carried away from the Villa Medici, I found myself a couple of days afterwards rather querulously expressing my sense of the "changes" to a lady who might be supposed to have seen them come on. She had lived in Rome for twenty years and she remembered the good old times. Somewhat to my surprise, she checked my plaintive strain and declared that she had already heard too many vague charges. If I found Rome so changed, would I be so good as to enumerate the particular alterations that had occurred during the preceding five years? She brought me, as the phrase is, to book. It is certain that my list of mutilations was a short one, though at the head of it figured the Colosseum, upon whose ghastly perversion from its former grandeur, whose cruel forfeiture of the ancient heritage which bloomed so prettily in its myriad crevices, whose barren excavations and pool of ditch-water and multiplication of wooden fences, I discoursed with not a little eloquence. My friend gave up the Colosseum as a lost cause; but with this exception, she affirmed, she saw no changes worth heaving sighs about. I answered that for twenty years she had spent her life in a certain rococo, frescoed parlor in an ancient Roman palace, and that, for better or worse, she had very little idea of what was going on in the vulgar world at the bottom of her great winding staircase of porous yellow travertine. Nevertheless, I date from this moment a certain relaxation in my sense of pleasures missed—a certain quickening of my relish of the actual physiognomy of Rome.

It was the next day, I think, that I went to see a friend who is a painter, and waited awhile in my friend's lodging until we might ascend together to the studio, which is at the top of the same house. The lodging is upon a second floor, and after you have rung at the door upon which the occupant's visiting card is nailed, the usual Roman incident occurs of another door being opened behind you and giving egress to the head of an inquiring maid-servant. If the maid-servant is pleased with your appearance she generally utters some genial interjection, closes the second door and presently reappears at the first. If she is not favourably impressed, she holds out her head through the aperture she has just created and invites you to give an account of your errand. In this case I was happily conscious that my friend's domestic wished me well, as the Italians say; and indeed she opened her mouth so wide to bid me good-morning that, from mere sympathy, the back-door also continued to move upon its hinges. What I saw within it led me to waive the privilege of being admitted at the more honorable portal and I immediately crossed the threshold upon which the demonstrative *serva* stood smiling. It introduced me to one of those picturesque accidents in which Roman life abounds and which are half the reason of one's kindness for it. Though we were upon the second floor there was a little open-air enclosure, half-garden, half-court, in the middle of the place, upon which opened, on one side, the kitchen and a couple of chambers, and upon the other the little dining room. Anywhere but in Italy it would have been a very unexpected little corner; but here it may be said that, in the way of domiciliary disposition, improbabilities and anomalies are the only things to be counted upon. There were some creepers on a rough white wall, there was a splendid patch of blue sky overhead and a big bar of sunshine tumbling down crookedly out of it. There were some plants in tubs; there were mossy flags under foot; in a corner there was a quaint old well, with a great tangle of bucket-ropes, boring down through the lower apartments. In short, it was a very amusing little nook and I understood perfectly how a wanderer from the north, looking about for a Roman lodging, should have elected this one for local color's sake. Leaning against the well was a brilliant peasant-woman, nursing a baby; at her side was a lad of ten or eleven years of age, in short-clothes, a sheepskin jacket and a peaked hat, drawing up a bucket. I call the woman brilliant, because she had on a great white head-cloth, a coral necklace, a crimson boddice, and a blue petticoat; and, more particularly, because her eyes, her hair, her complexion, were distinguished for what painters call tone. What the painters thought was a great matter for the poor woman, for she was an artists' model. The boy beside her followed the same avocation and she doubtless proposes to fashion the innocent babe at her breast to a similar destiny. Unfortunately, models, like poets, are born, not made; and unless a kind providence has equipped the infantine aspirant with a few appreciable "points," he will learn to no great purpose the art of posturing. These good people had learned the way to my friend's studio and sometimes, in the little upstairs garden I have spoken of, they made themselves useful in small household offices. The boy drew up the water; the mother laid down her poor little tightly-swaddled baby as if it had been a parcel from the grocer's, and washed the kitchen pots. She was a very handsome woman, with that grave, simple rather sternly maternal type of good looks which is frequent among the women of her class; the lad looked, and smiled, as Hawthorne's Donatello might have done while he was in roundabouts. My friend presently came out, and we stood in the warm air and chatted with these simple folk and admired their romantic rags and amused ourselves with their artless conversation. Hanging about in their bright-colored tatters, in the soft, yellow morning light, in this queer little in-door garden, they seemed an expression of that careless, irresponsible, consentingly passive element in Roman life which, to many a wanderer of another race, has presented itself almost as a revelation, and which, at the least, has for every lingering traveller an irresistible charm. The effect, perhaps, was disproportionate to the cause; but then and there I felt myself in as good a humor with Rome as I needed to be. The ancient charm began to work again and after that the commonest impressions seemed to contribute to it. Wandering about the Roman streets, I found it at moments as substantial as it had ever been; and as much as ever it was interesting to ask one's self whence it came, what it was composed of, why it was so magical. Why is it in fact that, suddenly, in a dirty Roman alley, one is subject to stop, for very pleasure, and stare at the first object encountered—to falter and to grow faint, like Porphyro in Keats's poem? The traveller who has not occasionally been visited by these fitful exaltations can hardly pretend to know much of the Eternal City. And yet such a traveller would have it in his power to argue very effectively against his comparatively hysterical comrade. "What is there in Rome, after all, to make a fuss about?" he might ask. "There are very few respects in which it is not one of the ugliest and shabbiest cities in Europe. It has no fine

architecture—unless, perhaps, the Farnese Palace. St. Peter's
is highly impressive; but St. Peter's, outside, is literally hideous. All the churches are hideous; they never have any
beauty, even by accident. The whole place is third-rate and
provincial. The Corso, as the main street of a capital, is simply
grotesque. Everything looks battered and slimy. The Tiber is
a most repulsive stream, and it has so insufficient a number of
bridges that in one place one has to cross it in a dirty old
flat-bottomed barge, hauled over by a rope. Except some
dozen things at the Vatican, there are no pictures; the private
galleries are not worth speaking of." One day while I was
driving with a friend I amused myself in giving experimental
utterance to a few observations of the complexion of the foregoing. We were in a little open cab; above us rose the usual
cheaply-painted Roman housefronts; beside us half a dozen
patient pedestrians flattened themselves against the spattered
walls, to allow the vehicle to roll by. My companion glanced
at these things and at the green baize lining of the cabman's
cloak, who was perched in front of us; he looked up at a dull,
pale sky and inhaled for a moment the mild, delicately-damp
air. "The charm of Rome," he then said; "the charm of Rome
is—well, it's the *mixture!*"

It is a vague sense of this mixture that makes the place interesting as no other place is, even to persons who feel themselves to be destitute of the proper intellectual apparatus for
analysing it. The charm of Rome, even the historic charm,
appeals by no means only to the select few; most Americans
who have watched there, during a season or two, the annual
coming and going of their compatriots, will have seen it take
possession of people of very meagre culture, people upon
whom fair science has smiled as briefly as possible. I remember encountering amateur antiquarians of this simple order
who were fairly transported by it. It seemed to them a lesson
in history made easy. George Eliot has in "Middlemarch" a
fine sentence about Rome being still supremely interesting to
those cultivated minds that are able to perceive "the suppressed transitions that unite all contrasts." There could be no
better characterization of the interest of Rome than such as
may be extracted from these last words; but I think a glimpse
of these "suppressed transitions" visits the Roman day-dreams

even of observers a thousand times less accomplished than the author of "Middlemarch." I have seen stout ladies from New York groping toward them through the cross-lights projected from the jewellers' windows of the Via Condotti. I have seen dessicated men of business from Western "centres" sit on the Pincian hill as if they were making them out a little—with their wrinkled eyes half closed, their heads inclined to one side, their hats pushed off their foreheads and their toothpicks slowly revolving. The other day, on my arrival in Rome, I went to spend the night at an inn, where I succumbed to the inevitable pressure brought to bear upon the "new-'lighted" stranger with regard to dining at the table d'hôte. Near me at table sat an American gentleman whom I supposed from his accent to be from the state of New Jersey; and opposite were placed three persons—also compatriots—with whom this gentleman had established the privilege of conversation. These three persons were a father, a mother and a daughter; they were very serious; they drank no wine; they only listened to the gentleman from New Jersey. They sat with their eyes fixed upon him with a kind of solemn fascination. He talked to them about Heliogabalus—about nothing but Heliogabalus; the Oriental splendor of his court, the scandalous effeminacy of his habits, the degenerate character of his rule. His auditory asked no questions and made no comments; when occasionally he paused they took a drink of water and then sat silent, looking at him and waiting for more. He always gave them more; I left him at the end of dinner eating little cakes and still talking about Heliogabalus. This little incident seemed to me very impressive and decidedly creditable to us poor Americans, who are commonly accused of lacking the historic sense. There were other people at table—English people and Germans; but I heard them make no learned allusions. The persons mentioned in my anecdote had a sentiment about George Eliot's suppressed transitions; the gentleman who talked about Heliogabalus had analysed what my friend in the cab called the mixture.

For yourself, whom I must assume to be quite up to George Eliot's standard, you analyse it constantly as you wander about. You think of the early antiquity and of the later, of the long period commemorated in the many—the too many,

volumes, of Gibbon and Merivale, of the dusky mediaeval in-
terregnum, of the brilliant, blooming Renascence, of the hey-
day of the Jesuits, of the cocked-hat civilization of the 17th and
18th centuries, of the proscriptions and revolutions of the 19th,
of the wonderful present phase of the drama; and this jumble
of the sternest antiquity and the most frivolous modernness,
of pagan and Christian pontiffs, of soldiers and priests, of the
extreme of profanity and the greatest pomp of ecclesiasticism,
of the brutality of destruction and the ecstasy of creation, the
superimposition of the later clerical arts and manners upon
the rugged heritage of the previous time, and of the fine fresh
Italian rule of today upon the whole promiscuous deposit—
this huge historic compound has a potent and inexhaustible
savor. And it may certainly be said that from the historic
point of view it is a foolish inconsistency to make one's self
unhappy over the entrance of the Italians. The interest of
Rome has never been the interest of monotony; it has always
been the interest of variety—of the procession of events. The
only monotonous element in the matter has been the spiritual
dominion of the Papacy, which has not been interrupted by
anything that has lately occurred and which is free to stretch
away into the ages as serenely as it lists. The Italian occupation is properly, therefore, only a picturesqueness the more—
another great stage in the procession of events—another of
those transformations which constitute the specialty, as it
were, of Rome.

I intimated just now that you may think of these things as
you drive about in an open cab; but they crowd upon you
even more vividly, perhaps, if you perambulate the Campagna
in that most delightful of all conveyances, the saddle. Riding
in the Roman Campagna has always been an exquisite entertainment and though there are people who will tell you that it
is no longer what it used to be, every lover of Rome who has
once enjoyed it will be willing to risk the disappointment. He
will find the pleasure as great as ever. A few places which
were formerly accessible are now forbidden ground; but,
roughly speaking, your choice of rides is still inexhaustible.
And all the old elements of pleasure are there—the golden
atmosphere, the violet mountains, the flower-strewn grass,
the lonely arches crowned with wild weeds and crumbling in

the sunshine. I had carried with me an ineffaceable recollection of the multitude of flowers that muffle your horse's footfall when you bound over the level meadows in the early springtime. But in the middle of November (the time of which I write,) the faded fields were absolutely rosy with little pink autumnal daisies. And all the rest of it—one could only note it, as one passed, with a sort of aesthetic piety; the shepherds and their flocks, posturing and "composing," in amiable diffusion, for your entertainment; the glowing dusk on one's homeward ride; the cool yellow wine handed you in the saddle, in the dusty yard of a suburban *osteria*, where half a dozen peasants in leather leggings are sitting under a scraggy trellis; the old false gateways, in villa walls, admitting you to nothing, and mouldering there, with their flower-tipped pediments and their cross-barred windows, in unappreciated elegance. If I might say more of all this I should speak of a certain day at Castel Fusano—the ancient estate of the Chigi family, which lies close to the obliterated site of Ostia, the seaport of republican Rome, and of how four happy mortals who had brought a luncheon with them from the Piazza di Spagna laid out the delicate feast upon the grass, at the base of a great umbrella-pine, partook of it under circumstances which made it seem the very poetry of picknicking, and then, in the tenderest good humor with the place, with each other, with everything, strolled along to the white beach of the Mediterranean, over a solid, superb old Roman pavement, hidden from the vulgar present in a forest of ilex.

H. James jr.

3 Bolton St. Piccadilly   London.

1878

The American Volunteer
Motor-Ambulance Corps in France

S IR,

Several of us Americans in London are so interested in the excellent work of this body, lately organised by Mr. Richard Norton and now in active operation at the rear of a considerable part of the longest line of battle known to history, that I have undertaken to express to you our common conviction that our countrymen at home will share our interest and respond to such particulars as we are by this time able to give. The idea of the admirable enterprise was suggested to Mr. Norton when, early in the course of the War, he saw at the American Hospital at Neuilly scores of cases of French and British wounded whose lives were lost, or who would have incurred lifelong disability and suffering, through the long delay of their removal from the field of battle. To help energetically to remedy this dire fact struck him at once as possible, and his application of energy was so immediate and effective that in just three weeks after his return to London to take the work in hand he had been joined by a number of his countrymen and of others possessed of cars, who had offered them as ambulances already fitted or easily convertible, and had not less promptly offered themselves as capable chauffeurs. To this promptly gathered equipment, the recruiting of which no red tape had hampered and no postponement to committee-meetings had delayed, were at once added certain other Cars of purchase—these made possible by funds rapidly received from many known and unknown friends in America. The fleet so collected amounted to some fifteen Cars. To the service of the British Red Cross and that of the St. John Ambulance it then addressed itself, gratefully welcomed, and enjoying from that moment the valuable association of Colonel A. J. Barry, of the British Army, who was already employed in part on behalf of the Red Cross. I have within a few days had the opportunity to learn from this zealous and accomplished coadjutor, as well as from Mr. Norton himself, some of the particulars of their comprehensive activity, they each having been able to dash over to London for a visit of the briefest duration. It has thus been brought home to me how much the success of the good work depends on American generosity both in the personal and the pecuniary way—exercised, that is, by the contribution of Cars, to which personal service, that of their contributors, attaches itself, and of course by such gifts of money as shall make the Corps more and more worthy of its function and of the American name.

Its function is primarily that of gathering in the wounded, and those disabled by illness (though the question is almost always of the former), from the *postes de secours* and the field hospitals, the various nearest points to the Front, bestrewn with patient victims, to which a motor-car can workably penetrate, and conveying them to the base hospitals, and when necessary the railway stations, from which they may be further directed upon places of care, centres of those possibilities of recovery which the splendid recent extension of surgical and medical science causes more and more to preponderate. The great and blessed fact is that conditions of recovery are largely secured by the promptitude and celerity that motor-transport offers, as compared with railway services at the mercy of constant interruption and arrest, in the case of bad and already neglected wounds, those aggravated by exposure and delay, the long lying on the poisonous field before the blest regimental *brancardiers* or stretcher-bearers, waiting for the shelter of night, but full also of their own strain of pluck, can come and remove them. Carried mostly by rude arts, a mercy much hindered at the best, to the shelter, often hastily improvised, at which first aid becomes possible for them, they are there, as immediately and tenderly as possible, stowed in our waiting or arriving Cars, each of which receives as large a number as may be consistent with the particular suffering state of the stricken individual. Some of these are able to sit, at whatever cost from the inevitable shake over rough country roads; for others the lying posture only is thinkable, and the ideal Car is the one which may humanely accommodate three men outstretched and four or five seated. Three outstretched is sometimes a tight fit, but when this is impossible the gain in poor *blessés assis* is the greater—wedged together though broken shoulder or smashed arm may have to be with a like shrinking and shuddering neighbour. The moral of these rigours is of course that the more numerous the rescuing vehicles the less inevitable the sore crowding. I find it difficult to express to you the sense of practical human pity, as well as the image of general helpful energy, applied in innumerable chance ways, that we get from the report of what the Corps has done, and holds itself in readiness to do, thanks to the admirable spirit of devotion without stint, of really passionate work, animating its individual members. These have been found beneficently and inexhaustibly active, it is interesting to be able to note, in proportion as they possess the general *educated* intelligence, the cultivated tradition of tact, and I may perhaps be allowed to confess that, for myself, I find a positive added beauty in the fact that the unpaid chauffeur, the wise amateur driver and ready lifter, helper, healer, and, so far as may be, consoler, is apt to be an University man and acquainted with other pursuits. One gets the sense that the labour, with its multiplied incidents and opportunities, is just unlimitedly inspiring to the keen spirit or the sympathetic soul, the recruit with energies and resources on hand that plead with him for the beauty of the vivid and palpable social result.

Not the least of the good offices open to our helpers are the odds and ends of aid determined by wayside encounters in a ravaged country, where distracted women and children flee from threatened or invaded villages, to be taken up, to be given the invaluable lift, if possible, in all the incoherence of their alarm and misery; sometimes with the elder men mixed in the tragic procession, tragi-comic even, very nearly, when the domestic or household objects they have snatched up in their headlong exodus, and are solemnly encumbered with, bear the oddest misproportion to the gravity of the case. They are hurried in, if the Car be happily free, and carried on to comparative safety, but with the admirable cleverness and courage of the Frenchwoman of whatever class essentially in evidence in whatever contact; never more so, for instance, than when a rude field hospital has had of a sudden to be knocked together in the poor schoolhouse of a village, and the mangled and lacerated brought into it on stretchers, or on any rough handcart or trundled barrow that has been impressed into the service, have found the *villageoises*, bereft of their men, full of the bravest instinctive alertness, not wincing at sights of horror fit to try even trained sensibilities, handling shattered remnants of humanity with an art as extemporised as the refuge itself, and having each precarious charge ready for the expert transfer by the time the Car has hurried up. Emphasised enough by the ceaseless thunder of the Front the quality of the French and the British resistance and the pitch of their spirit; but one feels what is meant none the less when one hears the variety of heroism and the brightness of devotion in the women over all the region of battle described from observation as unsurpassable. Do we take too much for granted in imagining that this offered intimacy of appreciation of such finest aspects of the admirable, immortal France, and of a relation with them almost as illuminating to ourselves as beneficent to them, may itself rank as something of an appeal where the seeds of response to her magnificent struggle in the eye of our free longings and liberal impulses already exist?

I should mention that a particular great Army Corps, on the arrival of our first Cars on the scene, appealed to them for all the service they could render, and that to this Corps they have been as yet uninterruptedly attached, on the condition of a reserve of freedom to respond at once to any British invitation to a transfer of activity. Such an assurance had already been given the Commissioner for the British Red Cross, on the part of Mr. Norton and Colonel Barry, with their arrival at Boulogne, where that body cordially welcomed them, and whence in fact, on its request, a four-stretcher Car, with its American owner and another of our Volunteers in charge, proceeded to work for a fortnight, night and day, along the firing line on the Belgian frontier. Otherwise we have continuously enjoyed, in large, defined limits, up to the present writing, an association with one of the most tremendously engaged French Armies. The length of its line alone, were I to state it here in kilometres, would give some measure of the prodigious fighting stretch across what is practically the whole breadth of France, and it is in relation to a fraction of the former Front that we have worked. Very quickly, I may mention, we found one of our liveliest opportunities, Mr.

Norton and Colonel Barry proceeding together to ascertain what had become of one of the field hospitals known to have served in a small assaulted town a few days before, when, during a bombardment, Colonel Barry had saved many lives. Just as our Volunteers arrived a fresh bombardment began, and though assured by the fleeing inhabitants, including the mayor of the place, who was perhaps a trifle over-responsibly in advance of them, that there were no wounded left behind—as in fact proved to be the case—we nevertheless pushed on for full assurance. There were then no wounded to bring out, but it was our first happy chance of bearing away all the hopeless and helpless women and children we could carry. This was a less complicated matter, however, than that of one of Colonel Barry's particular reminiscences, an occasion when the Germans were advancing on a small place that it was clear they would take, and when pressing news came to him of 400 wounded in it, who were to be got out if humanly possible. They were got out and motored away—though it took the rescuing party thus three days, in the face of their difficulties and dangers, to effect the blest clearance. It may be imagined how precious in such conditions the power of the chauffeur-driven vehicle becomes, though indeed I believe the more special moral of this transaction, as given, was in the happy fact that the squad had blessedly been able to bring and keep with it four doctors, whose immediate service on the spot and during transport was the means of saving very many lives. The moral of that in turn would seem to be that the very ideal for the general case is the not so quite inconceivable volunteer who should be an ardent and gallant and not otherwise too much preoccupied young doctor with the possession of a Car and the ability to drive it, above all the ability to offer it, as his crowning attribute. Perhaps I sketch in such terms a slightly fantastic figure, but there is so much of strenuous suggestion, which withal manages at the same time to be romantic, in the information before me, that it simply multiplies, for the hopeful mind, the possibilities and felicities of equipped good-will. An association of the grimmest reality clings at the same time, I am obliged to add, to the record of success I have just cited—the very last word of which seems to have been that in one of the houses of the little distracted town were two French Sisters of Mercy who were in charge of an old bedridden lady and whom, with the object of their care, every effort was made in vain to remove. They absolutely declined all such interference with the fate God had appointed them to meet as nuns—if it was His will to make them martyrs. The curtain drops upon what became of them, but they too illustrate in their way the range of the Frenchwoman's power to face the situation.

Still another form of high usefulness comes to our Corps, I should finally mention, in its opportunities for tracing the whereabouts and recovering the identity of the dead, the English dead, named in those grim lists, supplied to them by the military authorities, which their intercourse with the people in a given area where fighting has occurred enables them often blessedly to clear up. Their pervasiveness, their ubiquity, keeps them in touch with the people, witnesses of what happens on the battle-swept area when, after the storm has moved on, certain of the lifeless sweepings are gathered up. Old villagers, searched out and questioned, testify and give a clue through which the whereabouts of the committal to thin earth of the last mortality of this, that or the other of the obscurely fallen comes as a kind of irony of relief to those waiting in suspense. This uncertainty had attached itself for weeks to the fate in particular of many of the men concerned in the already so historic retreat of the Allies from Mons— ground still considerably in the hands of the Germans, but also gradually accessible and where, as quickly as it becomes so, Colonel Barry pushes out into it in search of information. Sternly touching are such notes of general indication, information from the Curé, the village carpenter, the grave-digger of the place, a man called so-and-so and a gentleman called something else, as to the burial of 45 dead English in the public cemetery of such and such a small locality, as to the interment somewhere else of "an Englishman believed to be an officer," as to a hundred English surprised in a certain church and killed all but 40, and buried, as is not always their fortune for their kindred, without removal of their discs of identification. Among such like data we move when not among those of a more immediate violence, and all to be in their way scarce less considerately handled. Mixed with such gleanings one

comes upon other matters of testimony of which one hopes
equal note is made—testimony as to ferocities perpetrated
upon the civil population which I may not here specify. Every
form of assistance and enquiry takes place of course in conditions of some danger, thanks to the risk of stray bullets and
shells, not infrequently met when Cars operate, as they neither avoid doing nor wastefully seek to do, in proximity to
the lines. The Germans, moreover, are noted as taking the
view that the insignia of the Red Cross, with the implication
of the precarious freight it covers, are in all circumstances a
good mark for their shots; a view characteristic of their bellig-
erent system at large, but not more deterrent for the ministers
of the adversary in this connection than in any other, when
the admirable end is in question.

I have doubtless said enough, however, in illustration of
the interest attaching to all this service, a service in which not
one of the forces of social energy and devotion, not one of the
true social qualities, sympathy, ingenuity, tact and taste, fail
to come into play. Such an exercise of them, as all the incidental possibilities are taken advantage of, represents for us all,
who are happily not engaged in the huge destructive work,
the play not simply of a reparatory or consolatory, but a positively productive and creative virtue in which there is a peculiar honour. We Americans are as little neutrals as possible
where any aptitude for any action, of whatever kind, that affirms life and freshly and inventively exemplifies it, instead of
overwhelming and undermining it, is concerned. Great is the
chance in fact for exhibiting this as our entirely elastic, our
supremely characteristic, social aptitude. We cannot do so
cheaply indeed, any more than the opposite course is found,
under whatever fatuity of presumption, inexpensive and
ready-made. What I therefore invite all those whom this notice may reach to understand, as for that matter they easily
will, is that the expenses of our enlightened enterprise have to
be continuously met, and that if it has confidence in such support it may go on in all the alert pride and pity that need be
desired. I am assured that the only criticism the members of
the Corps make of it is that they wish more of their friends
would come and support it either personally or financially—
or, best of all, of course, both. At the moment I write I learn

this invocation to have been met to the extent of Mr. Norton's having within two or three days annexed five fresh Cars, with their owners to work them—and all, as I hear it put with elation, "excellent University men." As an extremely helpful factor on the part of Volunteers is some facility in French and the good-will to stay on for whatever reasonable length of time, I assume the excellence of these gentlemen to include those signal merits. Most members of the Staff of 34 in all (as the number till lately at least has stood) have been glad to pay their own living expenses; but it is taken for granted that in cases where individuals are unable to meet that outlay indefinitely the subscribers to the Fund will not grudge its undertaking to find any valuable man in food and lodging. Such charges amount at the outside to 1 dollar 75 per day. The expenses of petrol and tyres are paid by the French Government or the British Red Cross, so that the contributor of the Car is at costs only for the maintenance of his chauffeur, if he brings one, or for necessary repairs. Mr. Eliot Norton, of 2, Rector Street, New York, is our recipient of donations on your side of the sea, Mr. George F. Read, Hon. Treas., care of Messrs. Brown Shipley & Co., 123, Pall Mall, S.W., kindly performs this office in London, and I am faithfully yours,

HENRY JAMES.

LONDON, *November 25th*, 1914.

France*

I THINK that if there is a general ground in the world, on which an appeal might be made, in a civilised circle, with a sense of its being uttered only to meet at once and beyond the need of insistence a certain supreme recognition and response, the idea of what France and the French mean to the educated spirit of man would be the nameable thing. It would be the cause uniting us most quickly in an act of glad intelligence, uniting us with the least need of any wondering why. We should understand and answer together just by the magic of the mention, the touch of the two or three words, and this in proportion to our feeling ourselves social and communicating creatures—to the point in fact of a sort of shame at any imputation of our not liberally understanding, of our waiting in any degree to be nudged or hustled. The case of France, as one may hold it, where the perceptive social mind is concerned and set in motion, is thus only to be called exquisite—so far as we don't seem so to qualify things *down*. We certainly all feel, in the beautiful connection, in two general ways; one of these being that the spring pressed with such happy effect lifts the sense by its mere vibration into the lightest and brightest air in which, taking our world all round, it is given to our finer interest about things to breathe and move; and the other being that just having our intelligence, our experience at its freest and bravest, taken for granted, is a compliment to us, as not purely instinctive persons, which we should miss, if it were not paid, rather to the degree of finding the omission an insult.

Such, I say, is our easy relation to the sound of a voice raised, even however allusively and casually, on behalf of that great national and social presence which has always most appositely, most sensibly, most obsessively, as I surely may put it, and above all most dazzlingly, neighboured and admonished us here: after such a fashion as really to have made the felt breath of its life, across an interval constantly narrowing, a part of our education as distinguished from our luck. Our

*Remarks at the Meeting of the Committee held on June 9, 1915.

luck in all our past has been enormous, the greatest luck on
the whole, assuredly, that any race has ever had; but it has
never been a conscious reaction or a gathered fruition, as one
may say; it has just been a singular felicity of position and of
temperament, and this felicity has made us observe and perceive and reflect much less than it has made us directly act and
profit and enjoy: enjoy of course by attending tremendously
to all the business involved in our position. So far as we have
had reactions, therefore, they have not sprung, when they
have been at all intensified, from the extraordinary good fortune of our state. Unless indeed I may put it that what they
have very considerably sprung from has been exactly a part of
our general prodigy—the good fortune itself of our being
neighboured by a native genius so different from our own, so
suggestive of wondrous and attaching comparisons, as to
keep us chronically aware of the difference and the contrast
and yet all the while help us to see into them and through
them.

We were not, to all appearance, appointed by fate for the
most perceptive and penetrative offices conceivable; so that to
have over against us and within range a proposition, as we
nowadays say, that could only grow more and more vivid,
more and more engaging and inspiring, in the measure of our
growth of criticism and curiosity, or, in other words, of the
capacity just to pay attention, pay attention otherwise than by
either sticking very fast at home or inquiring of the Antipodes, the Antipodes almost exclusively—what has that practically been for us but one of the very choicest phases of our
luck aforesaid, one of the most appraisable of our felicities?
the very one, doubtless, that our dissimilarity of temperament
and taste would have most contradictiously and most correc-
tively prescribed from the moment we were not to be left
simply to stew in our juice! If the advantage I so characterise
was to be in its own way thoroughly affirmative, there was yet
nothing about it to do real or injurious violence to that abysmal good nature which sometimes strikes me as our most effective contribution to human history. The vision of France,
at any rate, so close and so clear at propitious hours, was to
grow happily illustrational for us as nothing else in any like
relation to us could possibly have become. Other families

have a way, on good opportunity, of interesting us more than our own, and here was this immense acquaintance extraordinarily mattering for us and at the same time not irritating us by a single claim of cousinship or a single liberty taken on any such score. Any liberties taken were much rather liberties, I think, of ours—always abounding as we did in quite free, and perhaps slightly rough, and on the whole rather superficial, movement beyond our island circle and toward whatever lay in our path. France lay very much in our path, our path to almost everything that could beckon us forth from our base—and there were very few things in the world or places on the globe that didn't so beckon us; according to which she helped us along on our expansive course a good deal more, doubtless, than either she or we always knew.

All of which, you see, is but a manner of making my point that her name means more than anything in the world to us but just our own. Only at present it means ever so much more, almost unspeakably more, than it has ever done in the past, and I can't help inviting you to feel with me, for a very few moments, what the real force of this association to which we now throb consists of, and why it so moves us. We enjoy generous emotions *because* they are generous, because generosity is a noble passion and a glow, because we spring with it for the time above our common pedestrian pace—and this just in proportion as all questions and doubts about it drop to the ground. But great reasons never spoil a great sympathy, and to see an inspiring object in a strong light never made any such a shade less inspiring. So, therefore, in these days when our great neighbour and Ally is before us in a beauty that is tragic, tragic because menaced and overdarkened, the closest possible appreciation of what it is that is thereby in peril for ourselves and for the world makes the image shine with its highest brightness at the same time that the cloud upon it is made more black. When I sound the depth of my own affection so fondly excited, I take the like measure for all of us and feel the glad recognition I meet in thus putting it to you, for our full illumination, that what happens to France happens to all that part of ourselves which we are most proud, and most finely advised, to enlarge and cultivate and consecrate.

Our heroic friend sums up for us, in other words, and has

always summed up, the life of the mind and the life of the senses alike, taken together, in the most irrepressible freedom of either—and, after that fashion, positively lives *for* us, carries on experience for us; does it under our tacit and our at present utterly ungrudging view of her being formed and endowed and constantly prompted, toward such doing, on all sorts of sides that are simply so many reasons for our standing off, standing off in a sort of awed intellectual hush or social suspense, and watching and admiring and thanking her. She is sole and single in this, that she takes charge of those of the interests of man which most dispose him to fraternise with himself, to pervade all his possibilities and to taste all his faculties, and in consequence to find and to make the earth a friendlier, an easier, and especially a more various sojourn; and the great thing is the amiability and the authority, intimately combined, with which she has induced us all to trust her on this ground. There are matters as to which every set of people has of course most to trust itself, most to feel its own genius and its own stoutness—as we are here and all round about us knowing and abiding by that now as we have never done. But I verily think there has never been anything in the world—since the most golden aspect of antiquity at least—like the way in which France has been trusted to gather the rarest and fairest and sweetest fruits of our so tremendously and so mercilessly turned-up garden of life. She has gardened where the soil of humanity has been most grateful and the aspect, so to call it, most toward the sun, and there, at the high and yet mild and fortunate centre, she has grown the precious, intimate, the nourishing, finishing things that she has inexhaustibly scattered abroad. And if we have all so taken them from her, so expected them from her as our right, to the point that she would have seemed positively to fail of a passed pledge to help us to happiness if she had disappointed us, this has been because of her treating us to the impression of genius as no nation since the Greeks has treated the watching world, and because of our feeling that genius at that intensity is infallible.

What it has all amounted to, as I say, is that we have never known otherwise an agent so beautifully organised, organised from within, for a mission, and that such an organisation at free play has made us really want never to lift a finger to break the charm. We catch at every turn of our present long-drawn crisis indeed that portentous name: it's displayed to us on a measureless scale that our Enemy is organised, organised possibly to the effect of binding us with a spell if anything *could* keep us passive. The term has been in a manner, by that association, compromised and vulgarised: I say vulgarised because any history of organisation from without and for intended aggression and self-imposition, however elaborate the thing may be, shows for merely mechanical and bristling compared with the condition of being naturally and functionally endowed and appointed. This last is the only fair account of the complete and perfect case that France has shown us and that civilisation has depended on for half its assurances. Well, now, we have before us this boundless extension of the case, that, as we have always known what it was to see the wonderful character I speak of range through its variety and keep shining with another and still another light, so in these days we assist at what we may verily call the supreme evidence of its incomparable gift for vivid exhibition. It takes our great Ally, and her only, to be as vivid for concentration, for reflection, for intelligent, inspired contraction of life toward an end all but smothered in sacrifice, as she has ever been for the most splendidly wasteful diffusion and communication; and to give us a view of her nature and her mind in which, laying down almost every advantage, every art and every appeal that we have generally known her by, she takes on energies, forms of collective sincerity, silent eloquence and selected example that are fresh revelations—and so, bleeding at every pore, while at no time in all her history so completely erect, makes us feel her perhaps as never before our incalculable, immortal France.

Chronology

1843   Born April 15 at 21 Washington Place, New York City, the second child (after William, born January 11, 1842, N.Y.C.) of Henry James of Albany and Mary Robertson Walsh of New York. Father lives on inheritance of $10,000 a year, his share of litigated $3,000,000 fortune of his Albany father, William James, an Irish immigrant who came to the U.S. immediately after the Revolution.

1843–45   Accompanied by mother's sister, Catharine Walsh, and servants, the James parents take infant children to England and later to France. Reside at Windsor, where father has nervous collapse ("vastation") and experiences spiritual illumination. He becomes a Swedenborgian (May 1844), devoting his time to lecturing and religious-philosophical writings. James later claimed his earliest memory was a glimpse, during his second year, of the Place Vendôme in Paris with its Napoleonic column.

1845–47   Family returns to New York. Garth Wilkinson James (Wilky) born July 21, 1845. Family moves to Albany at 50 N. Pearl St., a few doors from grandmother Catharine Barber James. Robertson James (Bob or Rob) born August 29, 1846.

1847–55   Family moves to a large house at 58 W. 14th St., New York. Alice James born August 7, 1848. Relatives and father's friends and acquaintances—Horace Greeley, George Ripley, Charles Anderson Dana, William Cullen Bryant, Bronson Alcott, and Ralph Waldo Emerson ("I knew he was great, greater than any of our friends")—are frequent visitors. Thackeray calls during his lecture tour on the English humorists. Summers at New Brighton on Staten Island and Fort Hamilton on Long Island's south shore. On steamboat to Fort Hamilton August 1850, hears Washington Irving tell his father of Margaret Fuller's drowning in shipwreck off Fire Island. Frequently visits Barnum's American Museum on free days. Taken to art shows and theaters; writes and draws stage scenes. Described by father as "a devourer of libraries." Taught in assorted private schools and by tutors in lower Broadway and Greenwich Village. But father claims in 1848 that American schooling fails to provide "sensuous education" for his children and plans to take them to Europe.

1855–58   Family (with Aunt Kate) sails for Liverpool, June 27. James is intermittently sick with malarial fever as they travel to Paris, Lyon, and Geneva. After Swiss summer, leaves for London where Robert Thomson (later Robert Louis Stevenson's tutor) is engaged. Early summer 1856, family moves to Paris. Another tutor engaged and children attend experimental Fourierist school. Acquires fluency in French. Family goes to Boulogne-sur-mer in summer, where James contracts typhoid. Spends late October in Paris, but American crash of 1857 returns family to Boulogne where they can live more cheaply. Attends public school (fellow classmate is Coquelin, the future French actor).

1858–59   Family returns to America and settles in Newport, Rhode Island. Goes boating, fishing, and riding. Attends the Reverend W. C. Leverett's Berkeley Institute, and forms friendship with classmate Thomas Sergeant Perry. Takes long walks and sketches with the painter John La Farge.

1859–60   Father, still dissatisfied with American education, returns family to Geneva in October. James attends a pre-engineering school, Institution Rochette, because parents, with "a flattering misconception of my aptitudes," feel he might benefit from less reading and more mathematics. After a few months withdraws from all classes except French, German, and Latin, and joins William as a special student at the Academy (later the University of Geneva) where he attends lectures on literary subjects. Studies German in Bonn during summer 1860.

1860–62   Family returns to Newport in September where William studies with William Morris Hunt, and James sits in on his classes. La Farge introduces him to works of Balzac, Merimée, Musset, and Browning. Wilky and Bob attend Frank Sanborn's experimental school in Concord with children of Hawthorne and Emerson and John Brown's daughter. Early in 1861, orphaned Temple cousins come to live in Newport. Develops close friendship with cousin

Mary (Minnie) Temple. Goes on a week's walking tour in July in New Hampshire with Perry. William abandons art in autumn 1861 and enters Lawrence Scientific School at Harvard. James suffers back injury in a stable fire while serving as a volunteer fireman. Reads Hawthorne ("an American could be an artist, one of the finest").

1862–63   Enters Harvard Law School (Dane Hall). Wilky enlists in the Massachusetts 44th Regiment, and later in Colonel Robert Gould Shaw's 54th, one of the first black regiments. Summer 1863, Bob joins the Massachusetts 55th, another black regiment, under Colonel Hollowell. James withdraws from law studies to try writing. Sends unsigned stories to magazines. Wilky is badly wounded and brought home to Newport in August.

1864   Family moves from Newport to 13 Ashburton Place, Boston. First tale, "A Tragedy of Error" (unsigned), published in *Continental Monthly* (Feb. 1864). Stays in Northampton, Massachusetts, early August–November. Begins writing book reviews for *North American Review* and forms friendship with its editor, Charles Eliot Norton, and his family, including his sister Grace (with whom he maintains a long-lasting correspondence). Wilky returns to his regiment.

1865   First signed tale, "The Story of a Year," published in *Atlantic Monthly* (March 1865). Begins to write reviews for the newly founded *Nation* and publishes anonymously in it during next fifteen years. William sails on a scientific expedition with Louis Agassiz to the Amazon. During summer James vacations in the White Mountains with Minnie Temple and her family; joined by Oliver Wendell Holmes Jr. and John Chipman Gray, both recently demobilized. Father subsidizes plantation for Wilky and Bob in Florida with black hired workers. (The idealistic but impractical venture fails in 1870.)

1866–68   Continues to publish reviews and tales in Boston and New York journals. William returns from Brazil and resumes medical education. James has recurrence of back ailment and spends summer in Swampscott, Massachusetts. Begins friendship with William Dean Howells. Family moves to 20 Quincy St., Cambridge. William, suffering from nervous ailments, goes to Germany in spring 1867. "Poor Richard," James's longest story to date, published in *Atlantic Monthly* (June–Aug. 1867). William begins intermittent criticism of Henry's story-telling and style (which will continue throughout their careers). Momentary meeting with Charles Dickens at Norton's house. Vacations in Jefferson, New Hampshire, summer 1868. William returns from Europe.

1869–70   Sails in February for European tour. Visits English towns and cathedrals. Through Nortons meets Leslie Stephen, William Morris, Dante Gabriel Rossetti, Edward Burne-Jones, John Ruskin, Charles Darwin, and George Eliot (the "one marvel" of his stay in London). Goes to Paris in May, then travels in Switzerland in summer and hikes into Italy in autumn, where he stays in Milan, Venice (Sept.), Florence, and Rome (Oct. 30–Dec. 28). Returns to England to drink the waters at Malvern health spa in Worcestershire because of digestive troubles. Stays in Paris en route and has first experience of Comédie Française. Learns that his beloved cousin, Minnie Temple, has died of tuberculosis.

1870–72   Returns to Cambridge in May. Travels to Rhode Island, Vermont, and New York to write travel sketches for *The Nation*. Spends a few days with Emerson in Concord. Meets Bret Harte at Howells' home April 1871. *Watch and Ward*, his first novel, published in *Atlantic Monthly* (Aug.–Dec. 1871). Serves as occasional art reviewer for the *Atlantic* January–March 1872.

1872–74   Accompanies Aunt Kate and sister Alice on tour of England, France, Switzerland, Italy, Austria, and Germany from May through October. Writes travel sketches for *The Nation*. Spends autumn in Paris, becoming friends with James Russell Lowell. Escorts Emerson through the Louvre. (Later, on Emerson's return from Egypt, will show him the Vatican.) Goes to Florence in December and from there to Rome, where he becomes friends with actress Fanny Kemble, her daughter Sarah Butler Wister, and William Wetmore Story and his family. In Italy sees old family friend Francis Boott and his daughter Elizabeth (Lizzie), expatriates who have lived for many years in Florentine villa on Bellosguardo. Takes up horseback riding on the Campagna. Encounters Matthew Arnold in April 1873 at Story's. Moves from Rome hotel to rooms of his own. Continues writing and now earns enough to support himself. Leaves Rome in June, spends summer in Bad Homburg. In October goes to Florence, where William joins him. They also visit Rome, William returning to America in March. In Baden-Baden June–August and returns to America September 4, with *Roderick Hudson* all but finished.

1875   *Roderick Hudson* serialized in *Atlantic Monthly* from January (published by Osgood at the end of the year). First book, *A Passionate Pilgrim and Other Tales*, published January 31. Tries living and writing in New York, in rooms at 111 E. 25th Street. Earns $200 a month from novel installments and continued reviewing, but finds New York too expensive. *Transatlantic Sketches*, published in April, sells almost 1,000 copies in three months. In Cambridge in July decides to return to Europe; arranges with John Hay, assistant to the publisher, to write Paris letters for the *New York Tribune*.

1875–76   Arriving in Paris in November, he takes rooms at 29 Rue de Luxembourg (since renamed Cambon). Becomes friend of Ivan Turgenev and is introduced by him to Gustave Flaubert's Sunday parties. Meets Edmond de Goncourt, Émile Zola, G. Charpentier (the publisher), Catulle Mendès, Alphonse Daudet, Guy de Maupassant, Ernest Renan, Gustave Doré. Makes friends with Charles Sanders Peirce, who is in Paris. Reviews (unfavorably) the early Impressionists at the Durand-Ruel gallery. By midsummer has received $400 for *Tribune* pieces, but editor asks for more Parisian gossip and James resigns. Travels in France during July, visiting Normandy and the Midi, and in September crosses to San Sebastian, Spain, to see a bullfight ("I thought the bull, in any case, a finer fellow than any of his tormentors"). Moves to London in December, taking rooms at 3 Bolton Street, Piccadilly, where he will live for the next decade.

1877   *The American* published. Meets Robert Browning and George du Maurier. Leaves London in midsummer for visit to Paris and then goes to Italy. In Rome rides again in Campagna and hears of an episode that inspires "Daisy

Miller." Back in England, spends Christmas at Stratford
with Fanny Kemble.

1878   Publishes first book in England, *French Poets and Novelists*
(Macmillan). Appearance of "Daisy Miller" in *Cornhill
Magazine*, edited by Leslie Stephen, is international success, but by publishing it abroad loses American copyright
and story is pirated in U.S. *Cornhill* also prints "An International Episode." *The Europeans* is serialized in *Atlantic*.
Now a celebrity, he dines out often, visits country houses,
gains weight, takes long walks, fences, and does weight-
lifting to reduce. Elected to Reform Club. Meets Tennyson, George Meredith, and James McNeill Whistler. William marries Alice Howe Gibbens.

1879   Immersed in London society (". . . dined out during the
past winter 107 times!"). Meets Edmund Gosse and
Robert Louis Stevenson, who will later become his close
friends. Sees much of Henry Adams and his wife, Marian
(Clover), in London and later in Paris. Takes rooms in
Paris, September–December. *Confidence* is serialized in
Scribner's and published by Chatto & Windus. *Hawthorne*
appears in Macmillan's "English Men of Letters" series.

1880–81 Stays in Florence March–May to work on *The Portrait of
a Lady*. Meets Constance Fenimore Woolson, American
novelist and grandniece of James Fenimore Cooper. Returns to Bolton Street in June, where William visits him.
Washington Square serialized in *Cornhill Magazine* and
published in U.S. by Harper & Brothers (Dec. 1880). *The
Portrait of a Lady* serialized in *Macmillan's Magazine* (Oct.
1880–Nov. 1881) and *Atlantic Monthly*; published by Macmillan and Houghton, Mifflin (Nov. 1881). Publication
both in United States and in England yields him the then-
large income of $500 a month, though book sales are dis-
appointing. Leaves London in February for Paris, the
south of France, the Italian Riviera, and Venice, and returns home in July. Sister Alice comes to London with
her friend Katharine Loring. James goes to Scotland in
September.

1881–83 In November revisits America after absence of six years.
Lionized in New York. Returns to Quincy Street for
Christmas and sees ailing brother Wilky for the first time

in ten years. In January visits Washington and the Henry Adamses and meets President Chester A. Arthur. Summoned to Cambridge by mother's death January 29 ("the sweetest, gentlest, most beneficent human being I have ever known"). All four brothers are together for the first time in fifteen years at her funeral. Alice and father move from Cambridge to Boston. Prepares a stage version of "Daisy Miller" and returns to England in May. William, now a Harvard professor, comes to Europe in September. Proposed by Leslie Stephen, James becomes member, without the usual red tape, of the Atheneum Club. Travels in France in October to write *A Little Tour in France* (published 1884) and has last visit with Turgenev, who is dying. Returns to England in December and learns of father's illness. Sails for America but Henry James Sr. dies December 18, 1882, before his arrival. Made executor of father's will. Visits brothers Wilky and Bob in Milwaukee in January. Quarrels with William over division of property—James wants to restore Wilky's share. Macmillan publishes a collected pocket edition of James's novels and tales in fourteen volumes. *Siege of London* and *Portraits of Places* published. Returns to Bolton Street in September. Wilky dies in November. Constance Fenimore Woolson comes to London for the winter.

1884–86   Goes to Paris in February and visits Daudet, Zola, and Goncourt. Again impressed with their intense concern with "art, form, manner" but calls them "mandarins." Misses Turgenev, who had died a few months before. Meets John Singer Sargent and persuades him to settle in London. Returns to Bolton Street. Sargent introduces him to young Paul Bourget. During country visits encounters many British political and social figures, including W. E. Gladstone, John Bright, and Charles Dilke. Alice, suffering from nervous ailment, arrives in England for visit in November but is too ill to travel and settles near her brother. *Tales of Three Cities* ("The Impressions of a Cousin," "Lady Barbarina," "A New England Winter") and "The Art of Fiction" published 1884. Alice goes to Bournemouth in late January. James joins her in May and becomes an intimate of Robert Louis Stevenson, who resides nearby. Spends August at Dover and is visited by Paul Bourget. Stays in Paris for the next two months. Moves into a flat at 34 De Vere Gardens in Kensington early in March 1886. Alice takes rooms in London. *The Bostonians* serialized in *Century* (Feb. 1885–Feb. 1886; published 1886), *The Princess Casamassima* serialized in *Atlantic Monthly* (Sept. 1885–Oct. 1886; published 1886).

1886–87   Leaves for Italy in December for extended stay, mainly in Florence and Venice. Sees much of Constance Fenimore Woolson and stays in her villa. Writes "The Aspern Papers" and other tales. Returns to De Vere Gardens in July and begins work on *The Tragic Muse*. Pays several country visits. Dines out less often ("I know it all—all that one sees by 'going out'—today, as if I had made it. But if I had, I would have made it better!").

1888   *The Reverberator*, *The Aspern Papers*, *Louisa Pallant*, *The Modern Warning*, and *Partial Portraits* published. Elizabeth Boott Duveneck dies. Robert Louis Stevenson leaves for the South Seas. Engages fencing teacher to combat "symptoms of a portentous corpulence." Goes abroad in October to Geneva (where he visits Woolson), Genoa, Monte Carlo, and Paris.

1889–90   Catharine Walsh (Aunt Kate) dies March 1889. William comes to England to visit Alice in August. James goes to Dover in September and then to Paris for five weeks. Writes account of Robert Browning's funeral in Westminster Abbey. Dramatizes *The American* for the Compton Comedy Company. Meets and becomes close friends with American journalist William Morton Fullerton and young American publisher Wolcott Balestier. Goes to Italy for the summer, staying in Venice and Florence, and takes a brief walking tour in Tuscany with W. W. Baldwin, an American physician practicing in Florence. Miss Woolson moves to Cheltenham, England, to be near James. *Atlantic Monthly* rejects his story "The Pupil," but it appears in England. Writes series of drawing-room comedies for theater. Meets Rudyard Kipling. *The Tragic Muse* serialized in *Atlantic Monthly* (Jan. 1889–May 1890; published 1890). *A London Life* (including "The Patagonia," "The Liar," "Mrs. Temperly") published 1889.

1891   *The American* produced at Southport is a success during road tour. After residence in Leamington, Alice returns to London, cared for by Katharine Loring. Doctors discover she has breast cancer. James circulates comedies (*Mrs. Vibert*, later called *Tenants*, and *Mrs. Jasper*, later named *Disengaged*) among theater managers who are cool to his work. Unimpressed at first by Ibsen, writes an appreciative review after seeing a performance of *Hedda Gabler* with Elizabeth Robins, a young Kentucky actress; persuades her to take the part of Mme. de Cintré in the London production of *The American*. Recuperates from flu in Ireland. James Russell Lowell dies. *The American* opens in London, September 26, and runs for seventy nights. Wolcott Balestier dies, and James attends his funeral in Dresden in December.

1892   Alice James dies March 6. James travels to Siena to be near the Paul Bourgets, and Venice, June–July, to visit the Daniel Curtises, then to Lausanne to meet William and his family, who have come abroad for sabbatical. Attends funeral of Tennyson at Westminster Abbey. Augustin Daly agrees to produce *Mrs. Jasper*. *The American* continues to be performed on the road by the Compton Company. *The Lesson of the Master* (with a collection of stories including "The Marriages," "The Pupil," "Brooksmith," "The Solution," and "Sir Edmund Orme") published.

1893   Fanny Kemble dies in January. Continues to write unproduced plays. In March goes to Paris for two months. Sends Edward Compton first act and scenario for *Guy Domville*. Meets William and family in Lucerne and stays a month, returning to London in June. Spends July completing *Guy Domville* in Ramsgate. George Alexander, actor-manager, agrees to produce the play. Daly stages first reading of *Mrs. Jasper*, and James withdraws it, calling the rehearsal a mockery. *The Real Thing and Other Tales* (including "The Wheel of Time," "Lord Beaupré," "The Visit") published.

1894   Constance Fenimore Woolson dies in Venice, January. Shocked and upset, James prepares to attend funeral in Rome but changes his mind on learning she is a suicide. Goes to Venice in April to help her family settle her affairs. Receives one of four copies, privately printed by Miss Loring, of Alice's diary. Finds it impressive but is concerned that so much gossip he told Alice in private has been included (later burns his copy). Robert Louis Stevenson dies in the South Pacific. *Guy Domville* goes into rehearsal. *Theatricals: Two Comedies* and *Theatricals: Second Series* published.

1895   *Guy Domville* opens January 5 at St. James's Theatre. At play's end James is greeted by a fifteen-minute roar of boos, catcalls, and applause. Horrified and depressed, abandons the theater. Play earns him $1,300 after five-week run. Feels he can salvage something useful from playwriting for his fiction ("a key that, working in the same *general* way fits the complicated chambers of *both* the dramatic and the narrative lock"). Writes scenario for *The Spoils of Poynton*. Visits Lord Wolseley and Lord Houghton in Ireland. In the summer goes to Torquay in Devonshire and stays until November while electricity is being installed in De Vere Gardens flat. Friendship with W. E. Norris, who resides at Torquay. Writes a one-act play ("Mrs. Gracedew") at request of Ellen Terry. *Terminations* (containing "The Death of the Lion," "The Coxon Fund," "The Middle Years," "The Altar of the Dead") published.

1896–97 Finishes *The Spoils of Poynton* (serialized in *Atlantic Monthly* April–Oct. 1896 as *The Old Things*; published 1897). *Embarrassments* ("The Figure in the Carpet," "Glasses," "The Next Time," "The Way It Came") published. Takes a house on Point Hill, Playden, opposite the old town of Rye, Sussex, August–September. Ford Madox Hueffer (later Ford Madox Ford) visits him. Converts play *The Other House* into novel and works on *What Maisie Knew* (published Sept. 1897). George du Maurier dies early in October. Because of increasing pain in wrist, hires stenographer William MacAlpine in February and then purchases a typewriter; soon begins direct dictation to MacAlpine at the machine. Invites Joseph Conrad to lunch at De Vere Gardens and begins their friendship. Goes to Bournemouth in July. Serves on jury in London before going to Dunwich, Suffolk, to spend time with Temple-Emmet cousins. In late September 1897 signs a twenty-one-year lease for Lamb House in Rye for £70 a year ($350). Takes on extra work to pay for setting up his house—the life of William Wetmore Story ($1,250 advance) and will furnish an "American Letter" for new magazine *Literature* (precursor of *Times Literary Supplement*) for $200 a month. Howells visits.

1898   "The Turn of the Screw" (serialized in *Collier's* Jan.–April; published with "Covering End" under the title *The Two Magics*) proves his most popular work since "Daisy Miller." Sleeps in Lamb House for first time June 28. Soon after is visited by William's son, Henry James Jr. (Harry), followed by a stream of visitors: future Justice Oliver Wendell Holmes, Mrs. J. T. Fields, Sarah Orne Jewett, the Paul Bourgets, the Edward Warrens, the Daniel Curtises, the Edmund Gosses, and Howard Sturgis. His witty friend Jonathan Sturges, a young, crippled New Yorker, stays for two months during autumn. *In the Cage* published. Meets neighbors Stephen Crane and H. G. Wells.

1899   Finishes *The Awkward Age* and plans trip to the Continent. Fire in Lamb House delays departure. To Paris in March and then visits the Paul Bourgets at Hyères. Stays with the Curtises in their Venice palazzo, where he meets and becomes friends with Jessie Allen. In Rome meets young American-Norwegian sculptor Hendrik C. Andersen; buys one of his busts. Returns to England in July and Andersen comes for three days in August. William, his wife, Alice, and daughter, Peggy, arrive at Lamb House in October. First meeting of brothers in six years. William now has confirmed heart condition. James B. Pinker becomes literary agent and for first time James's professional relations are systematically organized; he reviews copyrights, finds new publishers, and obtains better prices for work ("the germ of a new career"). Purchases Lamb House for $10,000 with an easy mortgage.

1900   Unhappy at whiteness of beard which he has worn since the Civil War, he shaves it off. Alternates between Rye and London. Works on *The Sacred Fount*. Works on and then sets aside *The Sense of the Past* (never finished). Begins *The Ambassadors*. *The Soft Side*, a collection of twelve tales, published. Niece Peggy comes to Lamb House for Christmas.

1901   Obtains permanent room at the Reform Club for London visits and spends eight weeks in town. Sees funeral of Queen Victoria. Decides to employ a typist, Mary Weld, to replace the more expensive overqualified shorthand stenographer, MacAlpine. Completes *The Ambassadors* and begins *The Wings of the Dove*. *The Sacred Fount* published.

Has meeting with George Gissing. William James, much improved, returns home after two years in Europe. Young Cambridge admirer Percy Lubbock visits. Discharges his alcoholic servants of sixteen years (the Smiths). Mrs. Paddington is new housekeeper.

1902   In London for the winter but gout and stomach disorder force him home earlier. Finishes *The Wings of the Dove* (published in August). William James Jr. (Billy) visits in October and becomes a favorite nephew. Writes "The Beast in the Jungle" and "The Birthplace."

1903   *The Ambassadors, The Better Sort* (a collection of twelve tales), and *William Wetmore Story and His Friends* published. After another spell in town, returns to Lamb House in May and begins work on *The Golden Bowl*. Meets and establishes close friendship with Dudley Jocelyn Persse, a nephew of Lady Gregory. First meeting with Edith Wharton in December.

1904–05 Completes *The Golden Bowl* (published Nov. 1904). Rents Lamb House for six months, and sails in August for America after twenty-year absence. Sees new Manhattan skyline from New Jersey on arrival and stays with Colonel George Harvey, president of Harper's, in Jersey shore house with Mark Twain as fellow guest. Goes to William's country house at Chocorua in the White Mountains, New Hampshire. Re-explores Cambridge, Boston, Salem, Newport, and Concord, where he visits brother Bob. In October stays with Edith Wharton in the Berkshires and motors with her through Massachusetts and New York. Later visits New York, Philadelphia (where he delivers lecture "The Lesson of Balzac"), and then Washington, D.C., as a guest in Henry Adams' house. Meets (and is critical of) President Theodore Roosevelt. Returns to Philadelphia to lecture at Bryn Mawr. Travels to Richmond, Charleston, Jacksonville, Palm Beach, and St. Augustine. Then lectures in St. Louis, Chicago, South Bend, Indianapolis, Los Angeles (with a short vacation at Coronado Beach near San Diego), San Francisco, Portland, and Seattle. Returns to explore New York City ("the terrible town"), May–June. Lectures on "The Question of Our Speech" at Bryn Mawr commencement. Elected to newly founded American Academy of Arts and Letters

(William declines). Returns to England in July; lectures had more than covered expenses of his trip. Begins revision of novels for the New York Edition.

1906–08   Writes "The Jolly Corner" and *The American Scene* (published 1907). Writes eighteen prefaces for the New York Edition (twenty-four volumes published 1907–09). Visits Paris and Edith Wharton in spring 1907 and motors with her in Midi. Travels to Italy for the last time, visiting Hendrik Andersen in Rome, and goes on to Florence and Venice. Engages Theodora Bosanquet as his typist in autumn. Again visits Edith Wharton in Paris, spring 1908. William comes to England to give a series of lectures at Oxford and receives an honorary Doctor of Science degree. James goes to Edinburgh in March to see a tryout by the Forbes-Robertsons of his play *The High Bid*, a rewrite in three acts of the one-act play originally written for Ellen Terry (revised earlier as the story "Covering End"). Play gets only five special matinees in London. Shocked by slim royalties from sales of the New York Edition.

1909   Growing acquaintance with young writers and artists of Bloomsbury, including Virginia and Vanessa Stephen and others. Meets and befriends young Hugh Walpole in February. Goes to Cambridge in June as guest of admiring dons and undergraduates and meets John Maynard Keynes. Feels unwell and sees doctors about what he believes may be heart trouble. They reassure him. Late in year burns forty years of his letters and papers at Rye. Suffers severe attacks of gout. *Italian Hours* published.

1910   Very ill in January ("food-loathing") and spends much time in bed. Nephew Harry comes to be with him in February. In March is examined by Sir William Osler, who finds nothing physically wrong. James begins to realize that he has had "a sort of nervous breakdown." William, in spite of now severe heart trouble, and his wife, Alice, come to England to give him support. Brothers and Alice go to Bad Nauheim for cure, then travel to Zurich, Lucerne, and Geneva, where they learn Robertson (Bob) James has died in America of heart attack. James's health begins to improve but William is failing. Sails with William and Alice for America in August. William dies at Chocorua soon after arrival, and James remains with the family for the winter. *The Finer Grain* and *The Outcry* published.

1911   Honorary degree from Harvard in spring. Visits with Howells and Grace Norton. Sails for England July 30. On return to Lamb House, decides he will be too lonely there and starts search for a London flat. Theodora Bosanquet obtains two work rooms adjoining her flat in Chelsea and he begins autobiography, *A Small Boy and Others*. Continues to reside at the Reform Club.

1912   Delivers "The Novel in *The Ring and the Book*," on the 100th anniversary of Browning's birth, to the Royal Society of Literature. Honorary Doctor of Letters from Oxford University June 26. Spends summer at Lamb House. Sees much of Edith Wharton ("the Firebird"), who spends summer in England. (She secretly arranges to have Scribner's put $8,000 into James's account.) Takes 21 Carlyle Mansions, in Cheyne Walk, Chelsea, as London quarters. Writes a long admiring letter for William Dean Howells' seventy-fifth birthday. Meets André Gide. Contracts bad case of shingles and is ill four months, much of the time not able to leave bed.

1913   Moves into Cheyne Walk flat. Two hundred and seventy friends and admirers subscribe for seventieth birthday portrait by Sargent and present also a silver-gilt Charles II porringer and dish ("golden bowl"). Sargent turns over his payment to young sculptor Derwent Wood, who does a bust of James. Autobiography *A Small Boy and Others* published. Goes with niece Peggy to Lamb House for the summer.

1914   *Notes of a Son and Brother* published. Works on "The Ivory Tower." Returns to Lamb House in July. Niece Peggy joins him. Horrified by the war ("this crash of our civilisation," "a nightmare from which there is no waking"). In London in September participates in Belgian Relief, visits wounded in St. Bartholomew's and other hospitals; feels less "finished and useless and doddering" and recalls Walt Whitman and his Civil War hospital visits. Accepts chairmanship of American Volunteer Motor Ambulance Corps in France. *Notes on Novelists* (essays on Balzac, Flaubert, Zola) published.

1915–16 Continues work with the wounded and war relief. Has occasional lunches with Prime Minister Asquith and family, and meets Winston Churchill and other war leaders. Discovers that he is considered an alien and has to report to police before going to coastal Rye. Decides to become a British national and asks Asquith to be one of his sponsors. Receives Certificate of Naturalization on July 26. H. G. Wells satirizes him in *Boon* ("leviathan retrieving pebbles") and James, in the correspondence that follows, writes: "Art *makes* life, makes interest, makes importance." Burns more papers and photographs at Lamb House in autumn. Has a stroke December 2 in his flat, followed by another two days later. Develops pneumonia and during delirium gives his last confused dictation (dealing with the Napoleonic legend) to Theodora Bosanquet, who types it on the familiar typewriter. Mrs. William James arrives December 13 to care for him. On New Year's Day, George V confers the Order of Merit. Dies February 28. Funeral services held at the Chelsea Old Church. The body is cremated and the ashes are buried in Cambridge Cemetery family plot.

Note on the Texts

Throughout his life Henry James wrote about the places he visited. This volume prints, in the last versions revised by him, all of his travel writings about the Continent. Most of these writings appeared first in periodical form; many of them were later revised for book publication, and some appeared in more than one book version.

A Little Tour in France first appeared in the *Atlantic Monthly* (under the title *En Provence*) in the July–November 1883, February, and April–May 1884 numbers. James had used "A Little Tour in France" as the title of an unrelated 1878 article in the *Atlantic* but when he prepared that article for inclusion in *Portraits and Places* late in 1883 he retitled it "Rheims and Laon: A Little Tour" and could thus use the earlier title for his book. James extensively revised the serial version before the book was published in Boston by James R. Osgood and Company, September 1884 (the title page is dated 1885). In 1900, in preparation for publication of an illustrated edition of *A Little Tour in France*, James added a new preface, rewrote the "Introductory" and again made numerous revisions in wording and punctuation. The American edition was published by Houghton, Mifflin and Company in Boston and the English edition by William Heinemann in London, both in late October 1900. Because the English edition follows more closely James's own preferences for British spelling and light punctuation, this volume prints the text of the Heinemann edition.

Italian Hours, published on October 28, 1909, by William Heinemann in London and on November 28, 1909, by Houghton Mifflin Company in Boston, contains two essays not published elsewhere, and twenty previously published essays, eighteen of which had also appeared in earlier books. James carefully and often extensively revised and, in a few instances, expanded these essays from their earlier published versions in order to create a more consistent whole. The first essay, "Venice" (originally published in *Century Magazine*, Nov. 1882), had appeared in *Portraits of Places* (Boston, 1883).

"The Grand Canal" (originally in *Scribner's Magazine*, Nov.
1892) had appeared in *Great Streets of the World* (New York
and London, 1892). "Venice: An Early Impression" (originally
in *The Nation*, March 6, 1873, under the title "A European
Summer. VII. From Venice to Strassburg") had appeared as
"From Venice to Strasburg" in *Transatlantic Sketches* (Boston,
1875) and, in slightly revised form, in *Foreign Parts* (Leipzig,
1883). "Two Old Houses and Three Young Women" (*The Independent*, Sept. 7, 1899) and "Casa Alvisi" (*Cornhill Magazine*,
as part of "Browning in Venice. Being Recollections by the
Late Mrs. Katharine De Kay Bronson, with a Prefatory Note
by Henry James" and as a separate essay in *The Critic* under
the title "The Late Mrs. Arthur Bronson," both published in
Feb. 1902) had not been previously published in book form.
The next two essays had appeared in *Transatlantic Sketches*
(Boston, 1875) and in slightly revised form in *Foreign Parts*
(Leipzig, 1883): "From Chambéry to Milan" (originally in *The
Nation*, Nov. 21, 1872, with a general heading "A European
Summer. VI.") and "The Old Saint-Gothard" (published in
The Galaxy, April 1874, as "An Autumn Journey" and in
Transatlantic Sketches as "The St. Gothard"). "Italy Revisited"
(originally in the *Atlantic Monthly*, April–May 1878, in two
parts: "Italy Revisited" and "Recent Florence") had appeared
in *Portraits of Places* (Boston, 1883). The next five essays had
appeared in *Transatlantic Sketches* and (with the exception of
"The After-Season in Rome") in slightly revised form in *Foreign Parts* (Leipzig, 1883) after being published in periodicals:
"A Roman Holiday," *Atlantic Monthly*, July 1873; "Roman
Rides," *Atlantic Monthly*, August 1873; "Roman Neighbourhoods," *Atlantic Monthly*, December 1873; "The After-Season
in Rome," *The Nation*, June 12, 1873 (with the title "The After-
Season at Rome"); "From a Roman Note-Book," *The Galaxy*,
November 1873. "A Few Other Roman Neighbourhoods" is
one of the two essays previously unpublished. The next five
essays had also appeared in *Transatlantic Sketches* and in
slightly revised form in *Foreign Parts* after being published in
periodicals: "A Chain of Cities," *Atlantic Monthly*, February
1874 (as "A Chain of Italian Cities"); "Siena Early and Late,"
Part I, in *Atlantic Monthly*, June 1874 (as "Siena"; Part II
was written for *Italian Hours* in 1909); "The Autumn in

Florence," *The Nation*, January 1, 1874; "Florentine Notes," which had appeared in *The Independent*, April 23–July 9, 1874, in eight parts—Part I, April 30, Part II, April 23, Part III, May 21, Part IV (titled "Old Italian Art"), June 11, Part V (titled "Florentine Architecture"), June 18, Part VI (titled "An Italian Convent"), July 2, Part VII (titled "The Churches of Florence"), July 9, Part VIII (titled "A Florentine Garden"), May 14; and "Tuscan Cities," *The Nation*, May 21, 1874. "Other Tuscan Cities" is the second previously unpublished essay. "Ravenna" (originally published in *The Nation*, July 9, 1874) had appeared in *Transatlantic Sketches* and *Foreign Parts*. "The Saint's Afternoon and Others" was first published as "The Saint's Afternoon" in *The May Book*, compiled by Eliza Davis Aria "in the aid of Charing Cross Hospital" and published in London by Macmillan and Company, May 1901. Parts VI and VII appeared for the first time in *Italian Hours*. Because the English edition is more faithful to James's preference for British spelling and light use of commas, the text and illustrations (with the exception of the colored plates) printed in this volume are those of the Heinemann edition. The *errata* listed, correcting "fact," to "fact" (336.25) and "continue," to "continue" (354.8), have been inserted into the text of the present volume.

"Other Travels" includes fifteen essays, the first six of which appeared in James's first book of travel writings, *Transatlantic Sketches*, published by James R. Osgood and Company in 1875. James further revised five of the essays for inclusion in *Foreign Parts*, published by Bernhard Tauchnitz in Leipzig in 1883 ("The Splügen" was omitted from that collection). All six of the essays had first appeared in periodical form: "Swiss Notes," *The Nation*, September 19, 1872; "Homburg Reformed," *The Nation*, August 28, 1873; "Darmstadt," *The Nation*, October 9, 1873 (titled "An Ex-Grand-Ducal Capital"); "The Splügen," *The Independent*, August 20 and 27, 1874 (titled "A Northward Journey"); "In Holland," *The Nation*, August 27, 1874; and "In Belgium," *The Nation*, September 5, 1874. The next six essays were revised by James to appear in *Portraits of Places*, published in London by Macmillan and Company in 1883 (the American edition, published in Boston by James R. Osgood and Company in 1884, used the Macmillan plates). All six of these essays had appeared earlier in periodical form: "Chartres," *New-York Tribune*, April 9, 1876 (titled "Chartres Portrayed"); "Rouen," *New-York Tribune*, July 22, 1876 (titled "Summer in France"); "Etretat," *New-York Tribune*, August 4, 1876 (titled "A French Watering Place"); "From Normandy to the Pyrenees," *The Galaxy*, January 1877; "Occasional Paris," *The Galaxy*, January 1878 (titled "Paris Revisited"); and "Rheims and Laon: A Little Tour," *Atlantic Monthly*, January 1878 (titled "A Little Tour in France"). The text of "Very Modern Rome" printed here is a clear text of that printed in *The Harvard Library Bulletin*, volume 8, no. 2, Spring 1954, edited by Richard C. Harrier, from a holograph manuscript he had located in the Harvard College Library. The text of "The American Volunteer Motor-Ambulance Corps in France: A Letter to the Editor of an American Journal" printed here is from the version published in London by Macmillan and Company, December 15, 1914 (an abbreviated version titled "Famous Novelist Describes Deeds of U.S. Motor Corps," was published in the *New York World*, Jan. 4, 1915). The text of "France" printed here is from *The Book of France in Aid of the French Parliamentary Committee's Fund for the Relief of the Invaded Departments*, edited by Winifred Stephens, and published by Macmillan and Company in London on July 14, 1915.

This volume presents the texts of the printings chosen for inclusion here, but it does not attempt to reproduce features of their typographic design, such as the display capitalization of chapter openings. The illustrations to the captions "Toulouse: St Sernin (the Transept)" and "Arles: St. Trophimus," on pages 155 and 213, transposed in the Heinemann edition of *A Little Tour in France*, are placed correctly in this volume. The texts are reproduced without change except for the correction of typographical errors. Spelling, punctuation, and capitalization often are expressive features and they are not altered, even when inconsistent or irregular. The following is a list of typographical errors corrected, cited by page and line number: 25.34, Henry II.; 183.24, to having; 212.3, liked; 226.40, picked at; 237.12, good-humouor; 242.5, in shallow; 292.7, injury,; 337.40, huts; 377.6, five; 466.1, that our; 487.32, *Benedictins*; 498.16, that from; 500.12, spring; 546.26, depth;

556.17–18, Botticeili's; 575.26, Tuscany Lucca; 649.12–13, Hessen-Darmstadt; 661.15, this in; 754.15, even of; 757.12, occured; 759.28, substantial,; 761.9, slowing; 763.21–22, base a; 772.31–32, oppositely.

Glossary of Foreign Words and Phrases

(Translations of longer passages will be found in the Notes.)

abbasso il ministero]   down with the government

abbati]   priests

à bon escient]   upon deliberation, knowingly

air noble]   noble aspect

à la mort ne pensai-je mye]   never did I think of death

amant de]   lover of

amoureux-fou de la Cité]   passionate lover of the Citadel

à plat ventre]   flat on his stomach

archevêché]   archbishop's palace

arriére-pensée]   mental reservation

à tout propos]   at every turn

auberge]   inn, tavern

baigneuses]   women bathers

barca, signore]   boat, sir

barcaiuoli]   boatmen

bateaux de surveillance]   lifeguard boats

beaux quartiers]   wealthy neighborhoods

béguine]   Flemish nun; highly devout woman

bel air]   fine appearance

belle des belles]   beauty of beauties

belle jeunesse]   handsome young people

belle ordonnance]   fine arrangement

bêtise]   silliness

bibite]   drinks

797

bien-élevée] properly brought-up

bien vus] accepted, tolerated

birrerie] beer halls

blague] banter, exaggerated tales, kidding

blessés assis] wounded men who can sit up

bocage] woodland

bonne pensée] timely thought

bon temps] the good old days

Bouffes-Genevois] Comic Operas of Geneva

bougie] candle

cabinet particulier] private dining room, frequently provided, in Parisian establishments, with a sofa

café complet] a breakfast of coffee and rolls

cailloux] cobblestones

calle] a narrow lane or alley

calorifère] radiator or slow-combustion stove

camere mobiliate] furnished rooms

campagna] countryside, open country outside the city

campanile] tower, bell-tower

campo] square, piazza, field, space, ground, camp

campo santo] burial ground

caractère méridional] southern character

carnevale dei preti] priests' carnival

carriole] light cart

casa regia] royal house

caserne] barracks

ce louchon d'Augustine] that squint-eyed Augustine

Cenacolo] Last Supper

c'est bien paisible] it's very peaceful

c'est bien plaisant]　it's very agreeable

c'est du vin de ma mère]　it's homemade

c'est l'heure de la lecture]　it's reading time

cet âge est sans pitié]　that age is pitiless

chambre à coucher du roi]　king's bedroom

champ de manœuvre]　drill ground

chanoine-gardien]　canon-caretaker

château d'eau]　water tower

chaussée]　embankment

chemin de ronde]　rampart walk

citoyennes]　citizens

cives Romani]　Roman citizens

cocchiere]　coachman

Cogito ergo Sum]　I think, therefore I am

commis-voyageur]　traveling salesman

comptoir]　counter

consommation]　food, drink, refreshments; the bill

constatation]　evidencing of the facts

contadino]　peasant

conversazione]　a kind of genial social event characteristic of Italian gentility

coriandoli]　confetti; candies used as confetti during Carnival

corps de logis]　main portion

côteau]　hillside

couleur de rose]　rose-color, i.e., made to seem attractive

crânerie]　swagger

criard]　loud

culotte]　knee-breeches

custode]　caretaker

dame de comptoir]　woman at the counter, in charge of the cash

dans cette galère]　in such surroundings

dans le fond]　at the bottom

dans les habitudes Nîmoises]　a custom in Nîmes

decaduta]　impoverished

dejeûner-à-la-fourchette]　a fork lunch

de l'emploi]　appropriate to the occasion

délicieuse chapelle]　charming chapel

dès]　as early as

désœuvré]　idler

de son temps]　of his own time

de turquoise malade]　of sickly turquoise

disponibles]　available

dotation]　gift or endowment

douanier]　customs officer

doux pays]　sweet land

duomo]　cathedral

empressement]　eagerness

en bonnet]　in a matronly condition

en costume de ville]　in street clothes

enceinte]　enclosure

enfant du miracle]　miraculous child

entresols]　mezzanine floors

espadas]　matadors

établissement des bains]　bathing facilities

étalage]　display, as in a shop window

e troppo materiale]　and too material (as opposed to spiritual)

facchino]   porter

facture]   treatment

faux bonshommes]   shifty customers

felze]   gondola cabin

fiançailles]   engagement, betrothal

fille à marier]   marriageable daughter

fioriture]   flourishes

flânerie]   strolling

flâneur]   idle stroller

fondamenta]   stone foundations supporting Venice's structures and forming walks along the canals

forestieri]   foreigners

fortune infortune fort une]   good luck and bad luck are all the same

gare]   terminus, depot, railroad station

gentilhommière]   country seat

glacière]   ice-house

grand genre]   air of importance

grande salle]   great hall

gras-double]   thick stew (literally double-fat)

grisettes]   high spirited, or merry, working girls

guingette]   café

haute société]   upper classes, high society

héros de roman]   hero of fiction

hôtel]   mansion

hôtel de ville]   town hall

hure]   head (of a wild boar)

il mettait du sien]   he put something of his own into it

il monte; il monte toujours]   it's rising; it keeps rising *il s'y fait un commerce terrible*]   a staggering amount of business is done here

immortelles]   dried flowers that retain their shape and color

Indicateur des Chemins de Fer]   Railroad Guide

Indiens Galibis]   Caribbean Indians

intelligenza della sua fisionomia]   intelligence of his countenance

jardin français]   French-style garden

je constate]   I bear witness to what is the case

jeu de prince]   princely exploit

jeune fille]   girl

jeunesse]   youth

Kurgarten]   a public garden at a watering place

Kursaals]   a public hall for visitors at a watering place

langue d'oc]   Provençal

le plus honnête homme que je connaisse]   the most honest man I know

le plus vaste du midi]   the largest in the south

le roi des fougueux]   king of the high-spirited

les délicats]   refined spirits

lisser]   smooth

livre de cuisine]   household accounts

locanda]   inn

ma foi, fort bien]   and very well, too

magnifique construction ornée de statues]   magnificent building embellished with statues

maigre]   fasting (made *maigre*: abstained from meat)

mail]   mall

maison bourgeoise]   private house

maistre de l'oeuvre de maçonnerie]   master of masonry-works

malles-postes] mail coaches

manège] riding-ring

marronier] chestnut tree

mégère] shrew

mêler les genres] mix styles

m'entendre] reach an agreement

mère de famille] mother of a family

moccoletti] tapers, lanterns

morne] gloomy, grim

netteté] clarity

noyades] drownings

on s'occupe de la marier] we are taking care of getting her married

osteria] inn

ouvrier] workmen

palo] stake

papalino] a papal advocate

papiers à ramages] flowered wallpaper

parti-pris] bias

passeggiata] an evening walk in which the young people of traditional Italian communities participate

patache] rattletrap conveyance

patres patriæ] fathers of their country

pays de Cocagne] Land of Cockaigne, an imaginary utopia

petite noblesse de province] provincial minor nobility

petit verre] glass of wine

piccolo grasso vecciotto] fat little old man

pièces d'eau] artifical lakes

pifferaro] piper

place]   public square

place d'armes]   parade ground

place de foire]   fair-ground

place forte]   fortress, stronghold

plage]   beach

platanes]   plane trees

podere]   farm

portée]   bearing

porte haute et large]   wide and lofty doorway

postes de secours]   first-aid posts

potagers]   kitchen gardens

pour-boires]   tips

primogenito]   firstborn son

proprio d'origine egoista]   of a very selfish nature

Puits de Moïse]   Moses' Well

quelconque]   ordinary

raffiné]   refined, cultivated person

raffinnée]   woman of discernment

rassurez-vous]   be reassured

receuilli]   meditative

reflet]   reflection

remis à neuf]   made to look as good as new

renaît à elle-même]   returns to herself

repoussoir]   foregrounding contrast

ricordi]   souvenirs, mementos

riguardi]   considerations

ritratto virile]   portrait of a man

sage] virtuous

sale petit ville] dirty little town

salle à manger] dining room

salle d'attente] waiting room

salle des gardes] guard room

salle des pas perdus] antechamber of a court of justice

salon de lecture] reading room

sancta simplicitas] blessed simplicity

sent bien son dix-huitième siècle] redolent of the 18th century

serrurier mécanicien] locksmith and mechanic

sindaco] mayor

siphon] seltzer water

souvenir de premières amours] memento to first love

station de bains] bathing resort

stations balnéaires] seaside resorts

tant bien que mal, faute de ressources] as well as could be
    expected, lacking funds

tartines] slices of buttered bread

teatro diurno] matinee theater

tilleuls] linden trees

toilette étudiée] garments and embellishments regarded as
    particularly effective

Tourangeau] a native of Tours

tourelles] turrets

tout cela fonctionne] everything works

traghetti] ferries

Trasteverina] woman of Trastevere

trattoria] restaurant

triste compère] melancholy companion, crony, confederate

trottoir] sidewalk

ultima Thule] remotest Thule, i.e., farthest possible limit

valet-de-place] a guide who seeks employment from travelers

vaporetto] steam boat, steam ferry

velarium] awning over an amphitheater

véritable bijou artistique] a veritable artistic jewel

vetturini] cabmen

vieilles auberges de France] old inns of France

villageoises] village women

ville-basse] lower town

ville de province] country town

villeggiatura] vacation; country residence

Notes

In the notes below, the reference numbers denote page and line of the present volume (the line count includes titles or chapter headings and captions). Footnotes in the text were in the original texts. References to Baedeker and Murray are to the standard guides used by travelers in this period. Foreign words and phrases are translated in the Glossary on pages 797–806. No note is made for material included in standard desk-reference books such as *Webster's Ninth New Collegiate*, *Webster's Biographical*, and *Webster's Geographical* dictionaries. Quotations from Shakespeare are keyed to *The Riverside Shakespeare*, ed. G. Blakemore Evans (Boston: Houghton Mifflin, 1974). For further background than is provided in the notes, see *Henry James Letters*, ed. Leon Edel (Cambridge: The Belknap Press of Harvard University Press, Vol. I—1843–1875 [1974]; Vol. II—1875–1883 [1975]; Vol. III—1883–1895 [1980]; Vol. IV—1895–1916 [1984]).

A LITTLE TOUR IN FRANCE

18.4–5   between . . . Theatre]   Comfortable neighborhoods on the Right Bank catering to tourists.

20.13–14   "son climat . . . courtes."]   "Its warm and variable weather, its brief and abundant showers."

21.34   Rue Royale]   Later Rue Nationale.

22.2–4   Gambetta . . . balloon]   On September 1, 1870, Napoleon III and 83,000 of his soldiers surrendered to the Germans at Sedan. When news of the defeat reached Paris the imperial regime collapsed and on September 4 a republican Government of National Defense was proclaimed, with Gambetta as its minister of the interior. After the Germans completed their encirclement of Paris on September 20, the new government decided to send Gambetta to join its delegation at Tours and help organize resistance in the provinces. Gambetta left Paris by balloon on October 7 and reached Tours by October 9, where he assumed the post of minister of war. Despite his success in raising new armies, Gambetta was unable to break the siege of Paris or to prevent further German victories in the northern provinces, and on December 10 the delegation moved to Bordeaux. Following further defeats, Jules Favre, foreign minister of the Government of National Defense, negotiated an armistice with Bismarck without informing Gambetta, who still believed that continued fighting could gain France better peace terms. After attempting to change the armistice terms agreed to on January 28, 1871, Gambetta resigned his government posts on February 6.

22.28–29   house . . . light.]   The house in which Balzac was born was destroyed by bombing in 1940.

24.34   *Cogito ergo Sum.*]   "I think, therefore I am" (*Le Discours de la Méthode* [1637], IV), the most famous of Descartes' philosophical propositions.

25.33–34   Duke . . . Henry III.]   Henry de Lorraine, 3rd duke of Guise (1550–88), revived the Holy League of Catholic nobles in 1584 after Henry of Navarre, a Protestant, became heir presumptive to Henry III of France. Determined to secure a Catholic succession, the League forced Henry III to wage war against the Huguenots, and in August 1588 forced the appointment of the duke of Guise as lieutenant general of France. Fearing his growing power, Henry III had the duke assassinated in December 1588.

27.9   Saint Gatianus]   Gatian, who came from Rome to Gaul in the 3rd century, is venerated as the first bishop of Tours.

34.26   Mrs. Pattison's . . . France"]   English historian of French art and art critic, born Emilia Francis Strong (1840–1904), *The Renaissance of Art in France* (1879). Her first husband, 1861–84, was Mark Pattison, her second, from 1885, Sir Charles Dilke.

47.21   Duke of Guise]   See note 25.33–34. In a carefully planned ambush, the duke was summoned from a council meeting to the king's chamber, where he struggled fiercely even after being stabbed repeatedly by members of the royal bodyguard. The following day his brother Louis, cardinal of Lorraine, was also murdered; their bodies were burned and the ashes were thrown into the river Loire.

47.37   *fille à marier*]   Marriageable daughter (of Gaston d'Orléans). Louise d'Orléans, duchesse de Montpensier (1627–93), known as La Grande Mademoiselle, had wished to marry a reigning prince until she fell in love with the comte de Lauzun, an adventurer from Gascon, around 1669. Louis XIV gave his consent to their marriage, then withdrew it and had Lauzun imprisoned. Ten years later Louise managed to secure Lauzun's release and they entered into a liaison that greatly enriched him (they may have secretly married), but separated when she became disillusioned.

54.3   *fleur-de-lis*]   Emblem of the kings of France.

54.21   *enfant du miracle*]   Henri Dieudonné d'Artois, comte de Chambord, (1820–83), grandson of Charles X of France and the Legitimist claimant to the throne, was born seven months after the assassination of his father, Charles, duc de Berry, in 1820.

56.17–21   de Saxe . . . agreeable]   Maurice, comte de Saxe, (1696–1750), marshal general of France, caught a chill and died of a "putrid fever" at

Chambord in November 1750. It was widely rumored that he had been killed in a duel over a woman; others attributed his death to prolonged sexual overindulgence. Saxe was notorious for his many liaisons, and had fathered several children out of wedlock, including the grandmother of writer George Sand.

57.17   Henry V]   The comte de Chambord, who, if crowned, would have been the fifth Henry to become king of France.

60.21–61.1   Comte de Paris]   Louis-Philippe Albert d'Orléans, comte de Paris, (1838–94), the Orleanist pretender, grandson of Louis-Philippe, who had overthrown the Bourbon Charles X in 1830, and a rival of the comte de Chambord, the Legitimist claimant (see note 54.21).

61.9   Tauchnitz]   "Collection of British and American Authors" published in cheap editions by Tauchnitz (Leipzig, Germany) beginning in 1841, and generally sold on the Continent to English-speaking travelers.

64.12   conspiracy of La Renaudie]   Godfrey de Barry, sieur de la Renaudie, led an attempt by persecuted Huguenots and disaffected nobles to seize the young and feeble Francis II (1544–60; king from 1559) at Amboise and overthrow François de Lorraine, 2nd duc de Guise, and his brother Charles, cardinal of Lorraine, who had ruled France since the death of Henry II in 1559. The conspiracy was uncovered and de la Renaudie was killed in a skirmish with Guise loyalists on March 19, 1560. As many as 1200 persons were eventually executed on suspicion of involvement in the plot.

78.34   Abbé Chevalier]   Casimir Chevalier (1825–93).

80.9   Duchesse de Langeais]   Notably, in *La Duchesse de Langeais* (1833–34) and *Le Père Goriot* (1834).

81.3–5   Cinq-Mars . . . de Vigny's novel]   Henri Coiffier de Ruzé, marquis de Cinq-Mars (1620–42), conspired with Philip IV of Spain to overthrow Cardinal Richelieu. The plot was discovered and Cinq-Mars was beheaded. Alfred de Vigny (1797–1863) wrote about the conspiracy in *Cinq-Mars, ou Une Conjuration sous Louis XIII* (1826).

82.31   Blésois]   Region around Blois.

88.22–23   collegial church]   Church of St. Ours.

91.23   Balzac's "illustre Gaudissart;"]   Gaudissart is an archetypical commercial traveler, jolly, astute, and vulgar, in a number of *Comédie Humaine* stories including *L'Illustre Gaudissart* (1834), one of the "Scènes de la vie de province."

92.31   *dans cette galère*]   "In such surroundings," a usage derived from a line in Molière's play *Les Fourberies de Scapin* (1671) in which a father, hearing that his son has been kidnapped in a Turkish vessel, asks why he was *in that galley* in the first place.

98.24—25   history . . . Clément] *Jacques Coeur et Charles VII* (1853; 2nd edition, 1866).

103.1   "Biographie Universelle"] *Biographie Universelle ancienne et moderne* (52 vols., 1811—28; 29 supplementary vols., 1834—54; continually revised and augmented) contains articles by distinguished scholars, historians, and critics. It was founded by the brothers Louis and Joseph Michaud and was also known as the *Biographie Michaud*.

104.13   *tutoyer*] Address in the second-person singular (the intimate form).

109.8—15   "Celui . . . sommeille."] "He who now reposes here deserves pity rather than envy, and suffered death a thousand times before losing his life. Passer-by, be silent here, take care lest he waken, for this is the very first night that poor Scarron has been able to sleep."

115.34   Vendeans] Thousands of peasants in the Vendée region of western France rebelled in 1793 against attempts by the revolutionary regime in Paris to introduce military conscription. Harsh reprisals and guerilla fighting continued in the region until early 1795.

121.17   Duchess of Berry] Caroline Fernande Louise, duchesse de Berry (1798—1870), daughter of Francis I of the Two Sicilies. After the death of Charles, duc de Berry, she married Ettore Lucchessi-Palli (1806—64), a Sicilian count.

121.34—35   Henry IV . . . Louis XIV] The Edict of Nantes, signed in April 1598, granted freedom of conscience, full civil rights, and limited freedom of worship to French Huguenots. It was revoked in October 1685.

130.5—6   Guiton . . . oath] Guiton was threatening death to the first person who would suggest surrender of the garrison.

140.5—9   Black . . . Poitiers,] Poitiers was occupied by the English, 1356—69, after Edward (1330—76), known as the Black Prince, son of Edward III of the house of Plantagenet, defeated John the Good September 19, 1356, near Poitiers.

142.24   *Figaro*] A popular and politically conservative daily newspaper.

144.7—8   "Il . . . *douanier*] "A staggering amount of business is done here." A *douanier* is a customs officer.

144.25   Pontet-Canet.] A red Bordeaux wine.

152.5   Clémence Isaure] According to tradition, the Floral Games were instituted in 1323 by seven troubadours of Toulouse who formed themselves into a "college" and invited other troubadours to a poetry competition; the prize was a violet made of gold; later a silver marigold and a silver eglatine were also awarded. In the late 15th century Dame Clémence Isaure revived the festival and the college and endowed it with its present property.

154.7   Saint Saturninus]   First bishop (3rd century?) of Toulouse, believed to have been martyred by pagans for refusing to make sacrifices to their gods.

156.19   Saint Thomas Aquinas]   The body of Thomas Aquinas (c. 1225–74, canonized 1323), at Saint Sernin from 1368, was translated to the Jacobins' church at Toulouse in 1974.

163.19   Mexico with Bazaine.]   Achille-François Bazaine (1811–88), French marshal, was commander in chief of the French expedition in Mexico, 1863–67.

166.19   pamphlet by Viollet-le-Duc]   *Le Cité de Carcassone* (1858).

167.2–3   Albigensian . . . besieged,]   Much of the Languedoc region was devastated by the crusade waged from 1208 to 1244 against the Albigenses, members of a dualistic Cathar sect that had spread through the region in the 12th century.

168.37   Lowell Institute]   Adult educational center founded in Boston by John Lowell (1795–1836) to provide free lectures on a variety of subjects.

173.19–174.2   "C'est . . . par an."]   "You can't imagine, sir, how much money there is in these parts. There are people who make half a million francs a year out of their wine."

181.3–6   "Cette, . . . bay."]   "A Southern Night," lines 9–12.

182.22   Pembroke . . . Essay]   Locke dedicated his *Essay concerning Human Understanding* (1690) to Thomas Herbert (1656–1733), eighth earl of Pembroke, "in token of gratitude for kind offices done in evil times." Lord Pembroke had interceded with James II when Locke was accused in 1685 of having been involved in the duke of Monmouth's unsuccessful rebellion.

183.36–37   Bolognese school]   Among the Bolognese painters chiefly identified with the school, which incorporated the most important characteristics of individual great masters, were Ludovico Carracci (1555–1619) and his cousins Annibale (1560–1609) and Agostino (1557–1602), founders of the Accademia degli Incamminati in Bologna, and its students, Guido Reni (1575–1642) and Francesco Albani (1578–1660). Domenichino (1581–1641), another student, was a leader of the Baroque eclectic school.

185.1   Gerard Dow]   Dutch genre and portrait painter (1613–75) whose depictions of domestic life were widely imitated. His name is also spelled Dou and Douw.

185.28   dragonnades . . . desert]   In early 1685 the regime of Louis XIV began quartering troops, including notoriously ill-disciplined dragoons, in

Huguenot homes throughout the kingdom (the practice had first been used in Poitou in 1681). The soldiers were encouraged to treat the Huguenots with extreme brutality, and thousands were forced to convert in order to have the troops removed. The dragonnades were part of a campaign of persecution which culminated in the revocation of the Edict of Nantes (see note 121.34−35) on October 18, 1685, and which virtually destroyed the Reformed Church of France as an organized body. The "pastors of the desert" were ministers of the "Church of the Desert," as the Reformed Church was known in the period between 1715, when the still-outlawed church began to rebuild itself, and 1787, when a new edict of toleration was issued.

186.37   Camisards]   Inspired by a series of apocalyptic prophecies, the persecuted Huguenots of the Cévennes and Bas-Languedoc rebelled in 1702, killing Catholic priests and waging guerilla warfare against the army of Louis XIV. The insurrection was finally supressed in 1705 after hundreds of Huguenot villages were burned and their inhabitants massacred; a later rebellion in 1709−10 was also defeated. The name "Camisard" was derived from the white shirts (*camisa* is Provençal for "shirt") worn by the rebels, probably as a means of identification while fighting at night.

193.37−38   "C'est . . . paisible,"]   "It's very agreeable here, very peaceful."

194.12−13   interview . . . Charles V.]   After negotiating a ten-year truce through the offices of Pope Paul III, Francis I, king of France, and Charles V, the Holy Roman emperor, met at Aigues-Mortes in July 1538 and professed friendship for each other despite their long-standing rivalry in European politics. War between France and the Hapsburg dominions resumed in 1542.

198.20   *nymphæum*]   A shrine to the nymphs.

202.38   Maison Carrée.]   A Corinthian-style Greek temple restored in 1789 and converted to a museum in 1823; literally, "square house."

204.8   "Contes du Lundi."]   *Monday Tales* (1873), short stories.

208.16−18   Duke François . . . beheaded.]   François de Montmorency, comte de Boutteville, was beheaded on June 22, 1627, for fighting a duel (his 22nd) in violation of an edict issued in 1626 at the instigation of Cardinal Richelieu. Determined to suppress dueling, which had become increasingly widespread since the accession of Louis XIII in 1610, Richelieu rigorously enforced the edict, and refused to make an exception in the case of Montmorency despite his high rank in the nobility.

209.10   famous fair,]   Founded by Raymond VI, count of Toulouse, in 1217.

212.22   Dogberry]   Local constable in Shakespeare's *Much Ado About Nothing*.

225.32   Alpilles, . . . spoken]   For example, in *Lettres de mon moulin* (1866). Daudet often vacationed near Arles.

233.1–2   Troppmann . . . *Pantin*] Jean-Baptiste Troppman was guillo-tined on January 19, 1870, after having been convicted of poisoning textile manufacturer Jean Kinck, secretly burying his body in Alsace, and then luring Kinck's pregnant wife, Hortense, and their six children, aged two to sixteen, to Paris, where he killed them with knives and a pick-axe. Troppman buried the bodies in a field near the Pantin Gate northeast of the city, where they were discovered in September 1869. He allegedly committed the murders as part of a scheme to rob the Kinck family of its savings.

244.28–29   "For . . . fulfilled."] Cf. "Morality" (1852), stanza 1.

245.34   *Rime*] Petrarch's Italian lyrics *Rime Sparse*, which includes the series of poems in praise of Laura.

248.30   *amant de Laure*] Petrarch, Laura's lover.

254.7   "Presenting . . . line."] Milton, *Il Penseroso* (1631), line 99.

258.8   *Intransigeant . . . Rappel*] Radical papers (*Rappel* means *Call*).

259.19   *amant d'Elvire*] Alphonse Lamartine (1790–1860). Elvire is a character based on Mme. Julie Charles (d. 1817) in *Meditation Poetique* poems (1820), and in later works, notably *Nouvelles Méditations* (1823), a composite of Mme. Charles, Lamartine's wife, Anna Eliza Birch (married 1820), and an Italian girl called Graziella.

266.22–23   "La plus . . . qu'elle a;"] "The most beautiful girl in the world can give no more than what she has."

266.28–29   "Nous . . . mauvais,"] "We are in Bresse, and the butter isn't bad."

270.7   Adieu . . . faites!] Baskets farewell; the grape-harvest is done!

270.11–12   Emile Montégut . . . travel] Author, translator of George Eliot and Emerson, distinguished literary critic for *Revue des Deux Mondes* and other reviews; his "record of travel" is *Souvenirs de Bourgogne* (1874).

274.10–11   Président . . . Italy] Charles (known as the Président) de Brosses (1709–77), born in Dijon, writer, scholar, and a magistrate of the parliament of Burgundy, *Lettres familières écrites d'Italie en 1739 et 1740*.

274.15   Puits de Moïse] Moses' Well.

ITALIAN HOURS

288.7–8   only one . . . will be)] In 1881, just before this essay first ap-peared, Ruskin published the second and final volume of a "Traveller's Edi-tion" of *The Stones of Venice* (the first volume appeared in 1879).

289.31   Florian's] The celebrated café with a large area of outdoor seating was established on the south side of the Piazza San Marco in 1720.

290.31   Piazza]   Piazza San Marco, the main square of Venice.

290.37   Riva degli Schiavoni]   A public walk along St. Mark's Canal, adjoining the Palazzo Ducale (Palace of the Doges).

292.13   Academy]   Accademia di Belle Arti.

294.37   Théophile Gautier's *Italia*]   *Voyage en Italie* (1852). In 1872, James had called Gautier (1811–72) "the apostle of visual observation—the poet of the look of things."

304.13   the Tintoret's]   Venetian painter Jacopo Robusti (c. 1518–94) was called Tintoretto after his father's profession (*tintore* means "dyer").

308.37   Frari]   Church of Santa Maria Gloriosa dei Frari (founded 1250; rebuilt 1330–1417).

311.16–17   Ruskin . . . pamphlet]   *The Shrine of the Slaves, Being a Guide to the Principal Pictures by Victor Carpaccio in Venice.*

312.7   Santa Elisabetta]   The first bathing establishment on the Lido.

315.22   St. Theodore]   Patron saint of the ancient republic of Venice; a statue of him is in the Piazzetta.

315.37–316.21   Salute . . . Dogana]   The 17th-century church of Santa Maria della Salute and the 17th-century customhouse, the Dogana da Mar, stand across the Grand Canal from San Marco.

317.21–22   a dear . . . house]   Casa Alvisi (see pages 359–64 in this volume).

317.35–36   church of Longhena]   Baldassare Longhena (1598–1682) was the architect of Santa Maria della Salute.

318.26   Ruskin has spoken]   In *Stones of Venice* (1851–53), "Venetian Index."

320.3–4   deplorable iron bridge]   The Ponte di Ferro, or Ponte dell' Accademia, constructed in 1854; it was demolished and rebuilt in wood in 1932.

320.9   Canalazzo]   Popular name for the Grand Canal.

322.2   private kindness]   James had been the guest of Daniel and Ariana Curtis at the Palazzo Barbaro.

323.15–16   feast-night of the Redentore,]   In thanksgiving for the end of the plague of 1576, the Venetian senate built on the island of Giudecca the large church dedicated to the Redeemer; the *Festa della Redentore* is still held on the third Sunday in July.

323.37   the Carnival]   The Carnival, which lasted from the second Saturday before Ash Wednesday to Shrove Tuesday, gradually declined after the unification of Italy in 1870, as the new national government attempted to reduce the influence of the Church.

323.38   Vauxhall] Pleasure gardens laid out in the 17th century near the Thames in London. In the 19th century Vauxhall Gardens was modernized and nightly fireworks displays, music, dining facilities, and other entertainments were introduced; it closed in 1859.

324.29–30   table . . . "Candide"] In chapter 26 of Voltaire's novel (1759), Candide dines with strangers who turn out to be wandering monarchs in exile, celebrating Carnival in Venice.

325.10   his son] Robert (called Penini or Pen) Wiedemann Barrett Browning (1849–1913).

326.39–40   lady long resident] Katharine De Kay Bronson (see pages 359–68 in this volume).

328.15   the great Sansovino] Palazzo Corner della Ca' Grande, built 1532 by the architect and sculptor Jacopo Sansovino.

330.12   *fondamenta*] Stone foundations supporting the city's structures and forming walks along the canals.

335.1   Comte de Chambord] See note 54.21.

336.20–21   contrast . . . Ruskin] In *Stones of Venice*, Vol. I, "The Vestibule."

340.4–6   cathedral . . . choir.] Cathedral of Santa Maria, founded in the 7th century and rebuilt 867 and 1008. A flourishing city in the Middle Ages, Torcello was devastated by sickness, and in the 19th century the island was almost uninhabited.

342.10   *le roi des fougueux*.] "King of the high-spirited" (in *Voyage en Italie*).

344.25   Botzen!] Bozen, an Austrian city (it would be annexed to Italy, as Bolzano, in 1919).

344.32–34   volume . . . Feydeau] *L'Allemagne en 1871* (1872).

345.29   *La Tremenda Giustizia di Dio.*] *The Fearful Judgment of God.*

346.4   the Scaligers,] The Scaligeri (or della Scala) family, rulers of Verona 1260–1387.

346.32   San Zenone . . . picture] San Zeno Maggiore, 10th–13th century Romanesque church, with Andrea Mantegna's picture (1450) of the Madonna enthroned with angels and saints.

352.37   three Sisters] Bianca, Maria, and Moceniga Mocenigo.

353.28–36   Sand's . . . Pagello.] The affair between George Sand (1804–76) and Pietro Pagello (1807–98), whom she had summoned to treat her lover Alfred de Musset (1810–57) when he became seriously ill in Venice in 1833, was the subject of current publications, including Arvède Barine's *Alfred de Musset* (1893), Paul Mariéton's *Histoire d'Amour: Les Amants de Venise, George Sand et Musset* (1895), and "Letters of George Sand to Alfred de Musset" in *Revue de Paris*, November 1, 1896.

355.20–21   Wordsworth's . . . great"] From "On the Extinction of the Venetian Republic" (1807): "Men are we, and must grieve when even the Shade / Of that which once was great is passed away."

364.3   "Pippa Passes"] Browning's poetic drama in four parts (1846) is set in Asolo, which he visited in 1838.

365.27   Les Charmettes . . . Jean-Jacques.] The estate of Louise-Eléanore de Warens (1700–62), who in 1733 became the lover of Jean-Jacques Rousseau (1712–78); he lived there 1738–40.

366.25   Coppet and Ferney] Small towns on Lake Geneva. The house at Coppet that Mme. de Staël's father bought in 1784 became a center of culture when she made it her home while exiled from France, especially in 1794–97 and 1810–14. Voltaire's last home, 1760–78, was at his estate in Ferney (now Ferney-Voltaire), in French territory near the Swiss border.

367.11   Mont Cenis Tunnel] In the Alps, from Modane, France, to near Bardonnecchia, Italy, built 1857–70.

369.34–35   long Austrian occupation] The city was under Austrian rule, with two brief wartime interruptions, from 1706–96 and from 1814–59.

372.10–35   Leonardo . . . Cenacolo] The "Cenacolo" ("Last Supper," c. 1495–97), in the refectory of the monastery of Santa Maria delle Grazia, showed signs of damage as early as 1517 and by 1566, according to Giorgio Vasari in his *Vite*, was "merely a mass of blots." Damage has been attributed to humidity and also to the paint, purportedly devised by Leonardo to allow him to modify the painting over an extended period.

374.7   Ambrosian Library] Founded around 1609, one of the earliest public libraries.

374.10   Dr. Strauss and M. Renan] David Strauss (1808–74), German theologian and philosopher, increasingly skeptical about the historical validity of many Christian beliefs; Ernest Renan (1823–92), French philologist, critic, and historian of increasingly skeptical temper with regard to Christian beliefs.

374.20   Bradshaw] *Bradshaw's Monthly Railway Guide*, a series begun in 1839 by English engraver and printer George Bradshaw (1801–53).

376.6   Cook's . . . coupon]   Thomas Cook's British travel firm provided members of tours with booklets of coupons with which to pay for transportation, hotels, and meals.

378.16   Righi and Pilatus]   Adjacent Alpine peaks.

382.31   Homer . . . nodding]   Cf. Horace, *Ars Poetica*, 359: "If Homer, usually good, nods for a moment, I think it shame; and yet it may well be that over a work of great length one should grow drowsy now and then."

383.9–10   *Minéraux, . . . Antiques.*]   Minerals, Quadrupeds, Birds, Eggs, Antique Pictures.

384.34   fireboard]   Wooden panels used to close up fireplaces during the warm months.

386.24   Tessin]   The German name for the Ticino canton and river.

386.30   à la Sterne]   Cf. Laurence Sterne's *A Sentimental Journey through France and Italy* (1768), based on his own travels.

387.4   Abigail]   A usage derived from Abigail, the "waiting gentle-woman" in Beaumont and Fletcher's *The Scornful Lady* (1610), and the biblical Abigail ("thine handmaid," 1 Samuel 25).

388.3–6   elections . . . MacMahon]   After the republican majority in the chamber of deputies adopted an anticlerical resolution, Marshal MacMahon, the conservative president of the republic, sent a letter to the republican premier Jules Simon on May 16, 1877, informing him that he no longer enjoyed the confidence of the president. Simon and his ministry resigned, and MacMahon asked the conservative duc de Broglie to form a new ministry supported by the various monarchical and clerical factions. When the republican majority voted a resolution of no confidence in the Broglie ministry, MacMahon exercised his constitutional prerogative and obtained a dissolution of the chamber on June 25, 1877. In the ensuing election campaign the conservatives sought to influence the outcome by their administrative control of the electoral process, while the republicans, led by Léon Gambetta, portrayed the events of May 16 as an attempted coup d'état against the republic. The republicans won a majority in the elections of October 16, 1877, and after the new chamber refused to vote appropriations unless a ministry supported by the majority was formed, MacMahon accepted on December 13 a new government led by republican Jules Dufaure, ending the constitutional crisis.

392.12–16   Thackeray's . . . Pifferaro."]   *The Newcomes* (1855). A *contadino* is a peasant, a *Trasteverina*, a woman of Trastevere, a *locanda*, an inn, and a *pifferaro*, a piper.

397.28   "Masaniello."]   English name for Daniel Auber's 1828 opera "La Muette de Portici" (The Mute Girl of Portici), based on the 1647 Neapolitan uprising led by fisherman Tommaso Aniello (1620–47), called Masaniello, against the nobility who ruled the city under the Spanish viceroyship. The opera appealed to revolutionary sentiments.

404.38 Giotto's Tower] The Campanile was designed by Giotto (c. 1266–1337) toward the end of his life.

413.25 September 1870.] After the Kingdom of Italy was established in 1861, papal rule in Rome and the surrounding coastal plain was preserved by French intervention. The French garrison was evacuated after the early German victories in the Franco-Prussian War, and Italian forces captured Rome on September 20, 1870. The city was annexed to Italy after a plebiscite in October. See also note 323.37.

413.32–33 *Osservatore . . . Verità*] *Osservatore Romano*, daily newspaper of the Vatican, and *Voce della Verità*, conservative Catholic paper.

414.23 the King] Victor Emmanuel II (reigned 1861–78), first king of the united Italy.

416.9 Princess Margaret] Margherita di Savoia (1851–1925), cousin and wife of Crown Prince Umberto (reigned as Umberto I 1878–1900), who was to become the first queen of the united Italy (Victor Emmanuel II having made a morganatic marriage).

418.1–4 piazzetta . . . Marcus Aurelius.] The statue was moved to the Piazza del Campidoglio from the Lateran in 1538; the base is believed to be by Michelangelo. In the Middle Ages, the statue was thought to be that of Constantine, the first Christian emperor, a confusion that rescued it from the destruction meted out to other figures of Roman emperors.

418.5–7 Hawthorne . . . benediction."] In *The Marble Faun* (1860).

421.31 dreadful . . . samphire.] Cf. *King Lear* IV.vi.15: "Half way down / Hangs one that gathers sampire, dreadful trade!" Rock samphire, a plant used for pickling, grows on sea cliffs.

428.9 St. Paul's . . . Walls.] San Paolo fuori le Mura (St. Paul's outside the city walls), founded 386, was almost completely destroyed by fire in 1823; the restored church, built mostly according to the plan of the original and sumptuously decorated, was consecrated in 1854.

430.28–29 *carnevale dei preti*] Priests' carnival, a term of derision applied by the anticlerical *Capitale*.

431.3 Ponte Molle,] Or Milvian Bridge (built in 109 B.C. and later reconstructed), just north of Rome, scene of Constantine's defeat of Maxentius in

312 when, according to tradition, a flaming cross and the words *in hoc signo vinces* (by this sign you shall conquer) appeared in the sky.

432.37   talking about "Middlemarch"] George Eliot's novel (1871–72; book 1872).

434.2   Pelham] In *Pelham: or the adventures of a gentleman* (1828), Bulwer Lytton's second novel.

434.20   Worth] Dressmaking house in Paris, founded in 1858 by Charles Worth.

436.6–7   moated . . . Mariana] Cf. Shakespeare's Mariana in *Measure for Measure* III.i.264–65: "there, at the moated grange, resides this dejected Mariana," which inspired Tennyson's poem "Mariana" (1830): "My life is dreary . . . I would that I were dead."

437.6   Porta Pia bombarded] The city gate was breached by Italian troops on September 20, 1870; see note 413.25.

445.16–17   attitude of Melibœus.] In Virgil's *Eclogue* I, Tityrus invites Melibœus once more to stretch out and loll on the green grass.

446.22–23   Propaganda students] From the nearby Collegio di Propaganda Fide (College for the Propagation of the Faith).

447.17–18   Pope . . . viaduct] Pius IX (1792–1878; pope from 1846). The viaduct was destroyed in World War II.

447.24   *nero*] "Black": a traditional term used for papal supporters.

448.20   church . . . dome.] Santa Maria dell' Assunzione by Bernini (1664); restored 1771.

458.30   fair.] *Fiera di carne suina* (Pork Fair).

459.24   church . . . monastery.] Of the Greek order of the Basilians, founded by St. Nilus in 1004 and fortified in 1484.

459.33   wedding-feast of Gamacho.] In Cervante's *Don Quixote*, a lavish banquet held on the occasion of Gamacho's wedding, though his bride had been abducted.

464.29–30   Frenchman . . . France] Ernest Hébert (1817–1908), French painter and director of the Académie de France in Rome, 1867–73.

467.8   the most morbid blue] A literal translation of the Italian *azzurro morbide*, "soft blue."

467.11–12   "Rosina," . . . wife] Rosa Vercellana Guerrieri (1833–85) and Victor Emmanuel II married in 1869; his first wife was Maria Adelaide (1822–55) of Austria.

469.8   Pope's] Pius IX (1792–1878).

469.9   Law . . . Convents]   The religious orders bill passed June 19, 1873, abolished the corporate status of religious orders in Rome and the former Papal States. It placed hospitals and schools previously run by orders under civil administration and suppressed hundreds of convents and monasteries; the proceeds from their sale were used to provide pensions for nuns and monks and to establish municipal charities.

469.23   "Al Quirinale,]   "To the Quirinal!" The Palazzo del Quirinale was the official residence of Victor Emmanuel II.

471.5   scarlet in '69]   James had been in Rome when the First Vatican Council convened on December 8, 1869.

471.5–26   with L. . . . with A.]   The initials used by James are not always those of the people mentioned. For example, L. is Sarah Butler Wister, daughter of Sarah Kemble, A. is Mary Tweedy, and G., at 472.16, Mary Tweedy's coachman.

471.33–34   "make . . . there,"]   Shelley had written of Keats' grave in the old part of the Protestant cemetery: "It might make one in love with death, to think that I should be buried in so sweet a place."

473.5   mysteries of Udolpho.]   The title of a gothic novel (1794) by Ann Radcliffe.

474.3   Pancratii]   A Roman burial society common in the 3rd and 4th centuries; the tomb is believed to date from the 2nd century.

474.32–35   pine . . . sonnet.]   The deed of Sir George Beaumont (1753–1827), British painter, collector, and patron of Wordsworth, was commemorated in "The Pine of Monte Mario at Rome" (1837).

475.21–22   Virgin . . . *donatorio*.]   Portrait of donor kneeling at the feet of the Virgin.

478.3–4   Frenchman . . . France.]   The Académie de France, located at the Villa Medici since 1803, was established by Louis XIV in 1666 to enable French artists to study at Rome; the Grand Prix de Rome scholarships entitle winners to residence there.

478.9   Monsieur Hébert]   See note 464.29–30.

478.25–26   Phaon's . . . stabbed.]   According to some accounts, Nero had himself killed by a slave on the estate of his freeman Phaon to escape the senatorial decree for his execution.

479.15   "The Ring and the Book"]   Browning's poem in 12 books (1869) narrates the complex story of a 17th-century Italian murder.

479.39–40   Margaret Farnese]   "Madama" Margareta, duchess of Parma, and regent of the Netherlands, also known as Margaret of Austria (1522–86), was the daughter of Charles V and his mistress Joanna van der Gheenst. Margaret's second husband was Ottavio Farnese.

480.27   (Winckelmann's)] Johann Winckelmann (1717–86), German archaeologist who advised Cardinal Alessandro Albani on his collection of antique sculpture at the Villa Albani.

480.28   Antinous] "Relief of Antinous," from the Villa of Hadrian. Antinoüs (c. A.D. 110–130), celebrated for his beauty, was Hadrian's favorite.

480.35   "Lycidas."] Elegy (1637) by Milton on the accidental death by drowning of Edward King (1612–37).

480.36   "Transfiguration."] Raphael's final work (c. 1520).

481.3   Elgin marbles] In the British Museum: Phidias's Parthenon frieze, a caryatid, and a column from the Erechtheum, brought from Athens to England in 1806 by Thomas Bruce, earl of Elgin.

481.15   R. W. E.] Ralph Waldo Emerson.

481.40–482.1   Odéon . . . Imaginaire."] Théâtre de l'Odéon in Paris; Les Plaideurs (1668; The Litigants) is Racine's only comedy and Le Malade Imaginaire (1673; The Imaginary Invalid) is by Molière.

485.9–10   profane lateral stairways] The side steps especially constructed to allow free descent to those believers who had devoutly ascended the Scala Santa on their knees.

494.32   sculptor friend] Hendrik Andersen (1872–1940), a Norwegian sculptor whom James had met in Rome in 1899.

502.37   Goethe . . . it] Cf. *Italienische Reise* (1816–17; *Italian Journey*).

504.2   Raphael's master] Pietro di Cristoforo Vannucci (c. 1450–1523), known as Perugino.

505.29–32   Miriam . . . Kenyon] Characters in *The Marble Faun* (1860).

505.39–506.3   Amore . . . Demi-Monde"] The translated titles of these sentimental dramas are *Love without Respect*, *Severity and Weakness*, and *Ambiguous Society*. *Le Demi-Monde* (1855) had brought the French phrase for the society of women of "easy virtue" into general use.

507.32–33   Worldly-Wiseman . . . allegory.] Worldly-Wiseman of the town of Carnal-Policy in *The Pilgrim's Progress from this World to that which is to come*, Part I (1678–9). Perugino was said to have received 350 ducats from merchants' gold to create his series of frescoes in the old Court of Exchange.

513.14−15   Wordsworth's . . . waylay,"]   "She was a Phantom of delight" (1807).

524.9   stalls of the Barili.]   Intricate 16th-century woodcarving by the brothers Antonio and Giovanni de Neri Barili.

528.21   Lizza]   A public park northwest of the city, once the site of a fortress built by Charles V.

530.31   Paul Bourget]   French novelist and critic (1852−1935), whose early works about Italy impressed James deeply.

535.3   national capital,]   Florence was capital of the united Kingdom of Italy from 1865 to 1870.

535.7   Sindaco Peruzzi]   Ubaldino Peruzzi, mayor (sindaco) of Florence in 1879.

535.36   ladder in Jacob's dream;]   Genesis 21:12.

537.7−8   Misses Horner . . . "Walks"]   Susan and Joanna Horner, *Walks in Florence* (1873).

540.3   Michael]   Michelangelo.

541.18   Museum]   The École Nationale des Beaux-Arts, on the Rue Bonaparte.

543.7−8   Président de Brosses.]   See note 274.10−11.

545.25   Mr. Temple Leader]   John Temple-Leader began restoring the 14th-century castle in 1855.

546.28   George Eliot says,]   In *Middlemarch, A Study of Provincial Life.*

549.4−5   "flowery close"]   Cf. "A Garden by the Sea": "I know a garden-close / Set thick with lily and red rose . . . "

551.4   *Cet . . . pitié.*]   "That age is pitiless," from LaFontaine's fable "Les Deux Pigeons."

551.5   a dozen faults,]   An allusion to Browning's poem "Andrea del Sarto, Called ' The Faultless Painter' " (first so called by Vasari).

552.40   W——]   William James.

558.9   Madame Gryzanowska]   English-born wife (née Wright) of Dr. E. Gryzanowski, a professor of medicine, neighbor in Florence of James's friend Francis Boott.

563.14   the Annunziata]   Church of Santissima Annunziata de' Servi.

563.16−17   shrine . . . fetish,]   Originally designed by Michelozzo, the *Cappella della Vergine Annunziata* (c. 1448−52) was put under a canopy at a later date and lavishly decorated by the Medici with jewels, gold, and silver.

The shrine encloses Pietro Cavallini's "miraculous" picture of the Virgin, which is behind a silver screen (the work is called "miraculous" because, according to various accounts, Mary or an angel assisted the artist).

563.26   red palace]   Palazzo Riccardi-Manelli (erected 1565).

564.23   "Ungrateful Florence,"]   *Childe Harold's Pilgrimage* IV, 57, 505.

569.37–39   Forsyth . . . objects]   Joseph Forsyth (1763–1815), *Remarks on Antiquities, Arts, and Letters, during an Excursion into Italy, 1802–03* (1813); the famous objects are the cathedral, baptistry, leaning tower, and *campo santo.*

572.21   Madame Catalani]   Angelica Catalani (1780–1849), Italian soprano, theater manager, and founder of a singing school in Florence.

579.39–40   odd journalistic scheme.]   Shelley had conceived of founding a liberal literary magazine, but when he drowned in a boating accident in 1822, Hunt and Byron brought it out. Called *The Liberal* (four issues, 1822–24), it included works by Shelley, Hunt, Byron, James Hogg, William Hazlitt, and others.

581.1   *pays de Cocagne*]   An imaginary utopia, the land of Cockaigne. The term derives from medieval legend.

582.1–3   Ruskin's . . . hunting-frieze]   In *The Stones of Venice*, Vol. I, "Appendix."

585.33–35   Maremma, . . . Elba,]   The region of Maremma in Tuscany became the term for any unhealthy marshy country, e.g., "the malarial exhalations of a maremma" (*Oxford English Dictionary*); in Dante's *Purgatorio,* V, 133, Pia laments obscurely: "Maremma unmade me." Napoléon Bonaparte was born in Corsica in 1769 and exiled to Elba in 1814–15.

591.20   Statuto]   The Festa dello Statuto (Feast of the Constitution).

592.39–40   Boccaccio . . . plague,]   Boccaccio was in Florence at the outbreak of the Black Death in 1348, and in his *Decameron* (1349–51) a group of young people flee the stricken city to a villa in Fiesole, where they amuse one another with stories; the pine forest of Ravenna figures in one of them.

595.28   Ary Scheffer]   A French artist of Dutch origin, Scheffer (1795–1858) painted religious subjects in a romantic-classical style.

600.28   creation of the friend]   The Villa San Michele, an eclectic construction built by James's host, the Swedish doctor Axel Munthe, beginning in 1876.

604.4   *ultima Thule.*]   The classical name for the northernmost habitable regions, hence the farthest possible limit.

605.1–2   feast of St. Antony]   June 13.

605.9   "country,"]   Literal translation of *paese*, the Italian word for village as well as for native land or country.

609.20   stricken Ischia,]   A severe earthquake, July 28, 1883, destroyed the town of Casamicciola on the island of Ischia, killing more than 1,700 people.

611.19–20   a friend at Sorrento]   The novelist Francis Marion Crawford (1854–1909) with whom James stayed in June 1899.

612.19   Manilla]   The United States had gained possession of the Philippines in 1898 after the Spanish-American War. In May 1901, when this part of James's essay was first published, over 50,000 American troops were engaged in suppressing an insurrection by Filipinos seeking independence.

612.35   winged chariot]   The automobile in which James's friend Filippo de Filippi and his American wife, Caroline, drove him in his second visit to Naples, 1907.

617.35–36   shining Baiae]   Cf. Horace, *Epistles* I, 84: "nothing in the world outshines the lovely bay of Baiae."

OTHER TRAVELS

626.35   M. Cherbuliez's novel]   Probably *Paula Méré*. Victor Cherbuliez (1829–99) was a popular French novelist of Swiss origin.

627.5   *Bouffes-Genevois*]   Comic Operas of Geneva.

628.19   Ferney and Coppet]   See note 366.25.

628.21–23   great chronicle . . . *finis*]   In 1783 Gibbon went to Lausanne to share the home of a friend, and there completed *History of the Decline and Fall of the Roman Empire* (vols. I–III, 1755–81; IV–VI, 1788).

629.32–33   Mr. Cook . . . coupons]   See note 376.6.

631.32   Byron's Bonivard]   *The Prisoner of Chillon* (1816) describes the imprisonment of the Swiss patriot François de Bonivard (c. 1494–1570), who led a Genevese revolt in 1528.

631.34   Temple Bar]   Gateway adjoining the Temple Inns of Court between Fleet Street and the Strand, built by Christopher Wren in 1670, that marked the western boundary of the City of London. It was removed in 1878.

640.11   Peter Parley]   Boston author and publisher Samuel Griswald Goodrich (1793–1860) and his staff, beginning in 1827, wrote a popular series of more than 100 books for the instruction of children under the pseudonym "Peter Parley"; Hawthorne was among those who used the name.

644.27   Xavier . . . Chambre."]   Xavier de Maistre (1763–1852), French novelist whose best known work, *A Journey round my Room* (1794), is an exact and humorous description of a period of temporary imprisonment in his quarters in Turin, during his service with the Piedmontese army.

644.33   Sadowa] A village in Bohemia, near Königgrätz (now Hradec Kralové, Czech Republic), where the Prussians defeated the Austrians on July 3, 1866, in the decisive battle of the Seven Weeks' War. Hesse-Darmstadt, one of the German states that had allied itself with Austria, ceded Hesse-Homburg to Prussia in September 1866 and in 1867 joined the Prussian-dominated North German Confederation. In 1871 Hesse-Darmstadt became part of the newly united German Empire.

645.28   Emperor] William I, emperor of Germany 1871–88.

646.18   frighted . . . propriety.] Cf. *Othello* II.iii.175–76.

646.20–21   Grand-Duke Louis the First] Landgrave Louis X (1750–1830), made Grand Duke Louis I in 1806, built the new town of Darmstadt. Although much of the city was destroyed by a British air raid in September 1944, many historic buildings still survive, including the ducal castle, which was damaged, and the Landesmuseum. The statue of Louis X still stands in the Luisenplatz.

647.20   Charles Lamb . . . House.] While employed as a clerk in the accountant's office of the East India House in London from 1792 to 1825, Lamb (1775–1834) produced nearly all of his literary works, wrote for the *Reflector* and *Examiner*, and was a regular contributor to the *London Magazine* in which the first *Essays of Elia* series appeared.

649.12–13   Grand-Duke of Hesse-Darmstadt] Louis III (1806–77, grand duke from 1848).

652.20   trail . . . serpent] "Some flow'rets of Eden ye still inherit, / But the trail of the serpent is over them all." (Thomas Moore, *Lalla Rookh*, Pt. II).

655.26–27   Zuleikas . . . Moore.] Zuleika is the heroine of Byron's "Turkish tale" *The Bride of Abydos* (1813), and Gulnare, the chief harem slave in his *The Corsair* (1814). Moore's more well-known Oriental tale was *Lallah Rookh* (1817), verse stories framed by a prose romance.

657.20–21   Tauchnitz novel.] See note 61.9.

659.26–27   "Three Musketeers"] Novel (1844) by Alexandre Dumas *père*.

666.27   George Eliot's . . . wife] Mrs. Rachel Poyser in *Adam Bede* (1859).

685.38   "A la . . . ça!"] "Not so fast; what do you say to this!"

694.25   "*C'est . . . hein?*"] "I trust I'm proper enough for you, what?"

697.33–34   Arnold's . . . windy shore."] "The Forsaken Merman."

700.12   Nüremberg toy.]   The manufacture of toys was one of the chief industries of Nuremberg, Germany.

714.5–6   Prussians; . . . occupied] In   the   Franco-Prussian   War (1870–71).

714.15–16   "M. le . . . caractère."]   "Monsieur Curé, I have the highest respect for your character."

716.32   abominable Don Carlos]   During the second Carlist war in Spain (1872–76), guerrillas supporting the reactionary Don Carlos (1848–1909), fourth Carlist claimant to the Spanish throne, were accused of committing widespread atrocities, while Don Carlos himself was criticized for being an indecisive and incompetent leader. In March 1876 the Carlist revolt collapsed and Don Carlos fled from Spain into France with several thousand supporters.

718.1–2   Louis . . . Iberian monarch]   Louis XIV of France (reigned 1643–1715) and Philip IV (reigned 1621–65) concluded the Treaty of the Pyrenees on the island in 1659.

718.6   Alphonsist]   Supporters of Alphonso XII, king of Spain 1874–85.

732.15   *Andromaque.*]   Tragedy (1667) by Racine.

732.39   Francisque Sarcey]   One of the foremost dramatic critics of the 19th century, Sarcey (1827–99) was a columnist for *Le Temps* for more than thirty years.

733.10–13   Croizette . . . Delaunay] Sophie   Alexandrine   Croizette (1847–1901) was with the Théâtre-Français (later Comèdie-Français) from 1873 to 1882, and Louis Arsène Delaunay (1826–1903) was one of its principals from 1848 to 1886.

740.36–39   elections . . . MacMahon]   See note 388.3–6.

749.27–29   "Roi . . . Coucy."]   "King I am not / Nor Prince nor Count either; / I am the Lord of Coucy."

755.11   Dante's . . . words]   "Nessun maggior dolore / Che ricordarsi del tempo felice / Nella miseria" (*Inferno*, V, 121–23; "No greater sorrow than to remember happy times in misery").

756.10–11   castle of indolence]   In James Thomson's poem of that title (1748), the wizard Indolence entices weary pilgrims to luxuriate in his castle.

756.11–12   French . . . art students]   See note 478.3–4.

756.26   boschetto]   The upper garden of the villa.

759.12   Hawthorne's Donatello]   In *The Marble Faun*.

759.33   Keats's poem?]   "The Eve of St. Agnes" (1820).

762.1   Merivale]   Charles Merivale (1808–93), English author of *History of Rome under the Empire* (7 vols., 1850–64).

764.1–2   *The American . . . France*]   Subtitled on the cover: "A Letter to the Editor of an American Journal."

764.5–6   Richard Norton]   A son of Charles Eliot Norton.

769.25   retreat . . . Mons]   Germany declared war on France on August 3, 1914, and on August 4 invaded Belgium, whose neutrality Britain had guaranteed by treaty. After declaring war on Germany on August 4, Britain sent an expeditionary force of approximately 75,000 men to the Continent. On August 23 the British Expeditionary Force, positioned on the left flank of the French armies, fought its first battle with the advancing German army in the coal-mining region around Mons, Belgium. The B.E.F. repulsed several attacks by the numerically superior Germans, but was forced to withdraw on August 24 in order to protect its exposed flanks and then to continue retreating as all of the Allied armies across northern France west of Verdun fell back before the German offensive. The retreat ended on September 5, by which time the B.E.F., now southeast of Paris, had lost 15,000 men in thirteen days while marching over 200 miles. On September 6 the Allies launched a general counteroffensive and the B.E.F. began advancing north toward the Marne River. The Allied success in the first battle of the Marne caused the Germans to halt their offensive on September 9 and to retreat northward to the Aisne River, where they soon dug into defensive positions.

771.18–19   Eliot Norton]   A son of Charles Eliot Norton.

Index

CATALOGING INFORMATION

James, Henry, 1843–1916.
  Collected travel writings: The Continent.
  Edited by Richard Howard.

  (The Library of America ; 65)
  Contents: A little tour in France—Italian hours—Other travels.
  1. Europe—Description and travel—1800–1918. 2. James, Henry,
1843–1916—Journeys—Europe. 3. France—Description and travel—
1800–1918. 4. Italy—Description and travel—1861–1900. I. Title. A little
tour in France. II. Title. Italian hours. III. Series.
D919.J295   1993   818'.403—dc20   93–9193
ISBN 0–940450–77–1 (alk. paper)

This book is set in 10 point Linotron Galliard,
a face designed for photocomposition by Matthew Carter
and based on the sixteenth-century face Granjon. The paper
is acid-free Ecusta Nyalite and meets the requirements for perma-
nence of the American National Standards Institute. The binding
material is Brillianta, a 100% woven rayon cloth made by
Van Heek-Scholco Textielfabrieken, Holland. The com-
position is by Haddon Craftsmen, Inc., and The
Clarinda Company. Printing and binding
by R. R. Donnelley & Sons Company.
Designed by Bruce Campbell.

THE LIBRARY OF AMERICA SERIES

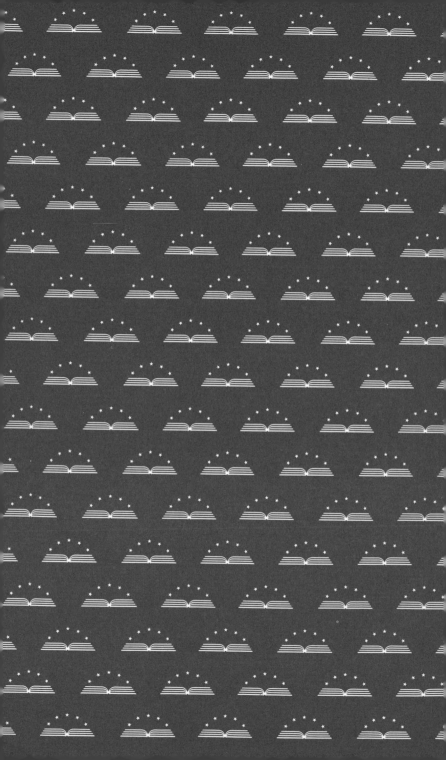